Career Interventions and Techniques

A Complete Guide for Human Service Professionals

Molly H. Duggan

Old Dominion University

Jill C. Jurgens

Old Dominion University

PEARSON

Boston • New York • San Francisco
Mexico City • Montreal • Toronto • London • Madrid • Munich • Paris
Hong Kong • Singapore • Tokyo • Cape Town • Sydney

Executive Editor: *Virginia Lanigan*
Series Editorial Assistant: *Matthew Buchholz*
Senior Marketing Manager: *Kris Ellis-Levy*
Editorial Production Service: *Barbara Gracia*
Composition Buyer: *Linda Cox*
Manufacturing Buyer: *Linda Morris*
Electronic Composition: *Omegatype Typography, Inc.*
Cover Administrator: *Kristina Mose-Libon*

For related titles and support materials, visit our online catalog at www.ablongman.com

Between the time website information is gathered and then published, it is not unusual for some sites to have closed. Also the transcription of URLs can result in typographical errors. The publisher would appreciate notification where these errors occur so that they may be corrected in subsequent editions.

Library of Congress Cataloging-in-Publication Data

Duggan, Molly H.
    Career interventions and techniques: A complete guide for human service professionals / Molly H. Duggan, Jill C. Jurgens.
        p.   cm.
    Includes bibliographical references and index.
    ISBN 0-205-45238-8
    1. Career development—United States—Handbooks, manuals, etc.
    2. People with social disabilities—Services for—United States—Handbooks, manuals, etc.
    3. Human services personnel—United States—Handbooks, manuals, etc.
    4. Social workers—United States—Handbooks, manuals, etc.
    5. Counselors—United States—Handbooks, manuals, etc.
    I. Jurgens, Jill C. II. Title.
    HF5382.5.U5D837 2006
    361.0023'73—dc22   2006046592

Printed in the United State of America

10 9 8 7 6 5 4 3 2   10 09 08 07 06

To Billie Ann—a mentor, a friend, and a role model
To John for his love, sacrifices, and support throughout this process

Dedicated to the memory of my dear friend Sherry
whose life continues to inspire me
and to Chip who said I could and should

Contents

Preface

The world of work is changing daily as new careers emerge while others vanish. As careers appear and disappear, human service professionals are left with the complex task of addressing the barriers to career success and self-sufficiency that are faced by an increasingly diverse group of clients. This task is coupled with high rates of unemployment faced by certain groups of adults and youths. Workforce demands for increased technology skills and automation, literacy, and social skills require new career development interventions and techniques. In addition to these challenges, human service agencies face a greater demand for accountability and flexibility while struggling with a decrease in funding, that require new programs to address these challenges whenever possible.

Goals

Our goal is to present a comprehensive guide to career development for aspiring human service professionals as well as those already providing career development services in a variety of settings. We propose that all human service professionals can benefit from increasing their knowledge of career development interventions and strategies, because career-related issues and concerns are common themes in the lives of our clients, despite the setting. In particular, the purpose of this book is to help students as well as seasoned professionals:

- Understand the complex challenges facing today's workers
- Increase awareness of the many career-related assessments available for use by entry-level human service professionals
- Create career development programs based on the models provided, including an evaluation model for accountability
- Recognize the career development needs of a variety of populations who are frequently served by entry-level professionals
- Choose interventions and assessments appropriate to the client
- Understand the intricacies of job search, interviews, and resume writing

Audience

This book is intended for people who plan to enter the human service profession as well as those who have been in the field for several years. Career development services, however, need not be independent of other services offered. In fact, career development services are more successful when they are integrated with other services being offered. Therefore, this book is designed for people working in shelter settings and transitional homes as well as for employment counselors, community college counselors, agency professionals, and anyone offering career development services.

Organization

This book is divided into three parts. Part I: Career Development and the World of Work addresses the life-long challenge of career development, provides an overview of the history of career counseling, and explores the major theories of career development.

This section also examines assessments appropriate for use by entry-level human service workers and explores the traditional "big books" of career counseling and corresponding web resources. Part I ends by examining ways to initiate an employment campaign and exploring career counseling program design, implementation, and evaluation.

Part II: Career Development and Diverse Populations explores in depth career development with the diverse populations—single parents and displaced homemakers, welfare-to-work clients, the working poor, victims of domestic violence, displaced or dislocated workers, the homeless, older workers, corrections and probation clients, clients with physical and/or mental disabilities, veterans, and the newly immigrated workers—that are typically handled by the entry-level human services professional as well as the seasoned professional. Each chapter in Part II provides a case study, a description of the population, barriers to career success, interventions, population appropriate career-related assessments, a career development program model, services specific to the population, key terms, and web resources.

Part III: Special Topics explores topics pertinent to both entry-level and seasoned human service professionals: ethical issues in providing career development services, career development and workplace issues of the 21st century such as maintaining balance, diversity, workplace safety, supervision, and technology.

Supplemental Materials

We have designed several supplemental materials to help both instructors and students who use this book. Instructors will have access to an ***Instructor's Manual*** that contains chapter overviews, key terms, web links, discussion topics to encourage student participation, classroom activities and projects, and a test bank. The ***Companion Website*** provides student learning objectives for each chapter, practice test questions, flashcards, a glossary of terms that appear in bold face in the text, and various web-based resources, including links to online assessments and reports.

Acknowledgements

This book not only reflects our experience in human services in a variety of settings but also a wealth of suggestions made by colleagues and friends. We want to thank our reviewers for their valuable guidance during the development of our manuscript: Warren R. Brader, Sr, University of Wisconsin—Milwaukee; Susan Claxton, Floyd College; Georgianna Glose; Sandra D. Haynes, The Metropolitan State College of Denver; and Maria Peterson, University of Tennessee—Knoxville. We also want to thank our friends and colleagues who shared their wisdom along the way: Jonathan Appel, Tiffin University; Carlos Cardoza, Virginia Troops to Teachers; Melissa Clas, Old Dominion University; Ted Daywalt, VetJobs; Katherine Feltham, Old Dominion University; Elizabeth Nelson, Old Dominion University; Ed Neukrug, Old Dominion University; Alan Schwitzer, Old Dominion University; and Lisa Schwitzer, Fleet and Family Services.

M. H. Duggan
J. C. Jurgens

Career Development and the World of Work

Welcome to "Part 1: Career Development and the World of Work!" We will begin this journey with one of our basic tenets—*All* human service professionals can benefit from career development knowledge, skills, and interventions because career-related issues and concerns are common themes in the lives of their clients, regardless of the setting.

With that principle in mind, we will begin by building a solid foundation for providing career interventions to specific populations in the human services field. First, we will lead you through a maze of career-development challenges, history, and theories. Next, we will guide you through a surplus of information on assessments, occupational resources, employment-campaign skills, and specifics on the design, implementation, and evaluation of career development programs. As you will soon discover, this repertoire of career knowledge, skills, and interventions will be indispensable in your helping career.

In all helping fields, practitioners must master a specialized vocabulary related to their specific discipline. Human service professionals who assist their clients with career-development concerns have their own specialized vocabulary. Throughout this text, we introduce a number of career-related terms. When you see a term in **bold**, be sure to review its definition in the Glossary.

Now, let your journey through career development begin.

1

Career Development: A Lifelong Challenge

The Need for Vocational and Career Guidance

Work conjures up a plethora of images. For some people, work fulfills the basic needs that enable them to support themselves and/or their families. Work allows others to fulfill altruistic needs such as giving back to society or serving humankind. Whatever the image of work one holds, one thing is certain—work is vital for world survival. Occupational projections, population factors, sociological and economic forces, technology, and diversity all impact the workforce. These factors, coupled with an abundance of human factors, can make the field of **career development** an enigma to many in the helping professions. This mystery might leave some human service professionals fearing the prospect of providing career services. Others might avoid the process altogether. Understanding the impact of work on their clients' well-being can serve helpers by motivating them to gain the skills and knowledge necessary to meet the career-development needs of their clients. With the proper education, information, and skill training, much of the helper's anxiety can be alleviated.

With any building, a solid foundation is vital to the survival of the structure. Human service professionals similarly must build a basic knowledge of the world of work, including the history and evolution of **career counseling**, prior to providing **career interventions** to clients. This chapter will serve as the foundation on which the subsequent **career** skills and interventions will rest.

The World of Work: Today and Tomorrow

Consider the entire world of work—past, present, and future in the United States. Prior to the 1900s, the majority of the labor force worked in goods-producing industries, including construction, mining, manufacturing, and farming. Today, service-producing industries dominate the labor force. The service industries educate children, serve food, provide medical treatment and counseling services, and fill and ship merchandise orders. And what is in store for the future world of work? The use of technology in the workplace certainly holds some valuable clues. For example, technology has opened the door to globalization at a level unmatched in previous decades. Rapid changes in the U.S. population, economy, and society also hold clues to the future state of the U.S. labor force.

In order to assist clients in making informed career decisions, helping professionals must have knowledge about projections for future occupational opportunities and the factors that affect these projections. The relative accuracy of occupational projections has been an area of debate for years. Forecasting occupational trends is an extremely difficult task. Some may compare it to using a crystal ball to see the future. Others view projections more methodically. Many factors influence these projections, and like a cake recipe where deviations in the ingredients will change the final product, deviations in the factors on which occupational projections are made will change the projections for the future labor force. Because many factors come into play, the "perfect recipe" for predicting these trends has yet to be discovered. Many factors impact the final results, and some of them are fundamental to the projection of occupational trends. Population factors, diversity of the workforce, sociological and economic forces, and technology are the most important considerations when making occupational projections. These factors and forces collectively impact the demand for goods and services, which in turn creates our current and projected labor force. Although projections will never be 100 percent error free, they are accurate enough for helping professionals to use them in working with their clients. Because of the time lag between the preparation for an **occupation** and a person's entry into that occupation, helping professionals must be future-oriented with respect to occupational demands in order to better prepare their clients for the world of work. We will now address the impact of population factors, diversity, sociological and economic forces, and technology on occupational projections.

Population Factors

Population trends have a tremendous impact on occupational opportunities. Goods and services are influenced by fluctuations in the population that produce corresponding changes in the size and demographic composition of the workforce (U.S. Department of Labor, 2005). According to the U.S. Department of Labor (2005), the U.S. population is projected to increase by 23.9 million people over the 2004–2014 period. This expected increase will grow at a slower rate than that of the 1984–1994 and the 1994–2004 periods. The impact of population growth on various occupations will differ, which can be explained partially by the age distribution of the future population.

> The population of youth, aged 16 to 24, is projected to increase by 2.9 percent over the 2004–2014 period. With the aging of the baby boomers, the group aged 55 to 64 is projected to increase by 36 percent or by 10.4 million individuals. This increase is greater than with any other group. The birth dearth following the baby boom generation will result in a decrease in the group aged 35 to 44 (U.S. Department of Labor, 2005).

Diversity in the Workplace

Immigrants and minorities will comprise a greater share of the U.S. population in 2012. In fact, the number of Hispanics is projected to continue growing at a faster rate than those of all other ethnic groups. Given the increased diversity within the workforce, human service professionals must address the impact of social and economic barriers, economic hardship, immigration, and racial discrimination on the career development of their clients when considering career development interventions (Leung, 1995). Human service professionals must be multiculturally competent and sensitive to their clients' values and worldviews. In addition helpers must be aware of their own cultural assumptions and how these assumptions may impact their helping relationships.

Sociological Forces

The social-class levels of individuals have a critical impact on the occupational choices that they consider, make, and implement. Consider the example of a young adolescent male raised in one of the poorest areas of Eastern Kentucky in the Appalachian Mountains. This young man has never ventured out of his community, nor has any member of his immediate or extended family left the region. Poverty, substandard education, and unemployment are key aspects of his social status. Resources appear minimal, however, a strong kinship bond is perhaps one of the resources that may assist him in overcoming some of the existing sociological barriers. How might this client view his career development options? Sociological factors interplay directly and/or indirectly in every individual's life. Helping professionals must understand that individuals who are raised in poverty-stricken environments often hold lower-class expectancies for achieving their occupational preferences (Herr & Cramer, 1996).

Research supports the concept that family socioeconomic status is comprehensively related to career choice. Social-class distinctions are associated with differences in occupational information, work experiences, and occupational stereotypes. These differences impact vocational interests (Herr, Cramer, & Niles, 2004). According to Friesen (1986), the higher the family's socioeconomic status, the more likely parents are to have the resources for financing educational opportunities that lead to higher-status occupations. Therefore, you can surmise that the social-class level of a client's family is a critical component of the client's career development and can serve either to expand or limit career choices.

Economic Forces

The United States participates in a global economy in which the economic well-being of the United States influences the economy of other countries and vice versa. Competition among industries, businesses, and workers exists both within the United States and abroad. Two major implications of increased global economy will effect the workforce in the United States. First, the number of **jobs** and job security for unskilled workers will decrease because many of the tasks unskilled workers do can be performed for less money in underdeveloped countries. Second, the global economy will result in an increased emphasis on efficiency and productivity that will require a better-educated workforce because the jobs likely to be created are in the technology and information sectors (Isaacson & Brown, 2000).

Technological Factors

The Industrial Revolution ushered in an age of automation and technology that continues to permeate the workforce. Computers, software, and robots have replaced humans in many roles in the labor force. Machines are now used for repetitive, monotonous tasks that workers previously performed. Individuals are now designing, building, operating, and selling machines whose creation brought to an end tens of thousands of jobs. The result of technological changes has been more opportunity for upgraded occupations that require more skills and training. Helping professionals must be aware of trends in technology, including occupations that can be easily automated in the future (Lock, 2000).

In addition, helping professionals must stress to their clients the fact that computer skills are no longer on the "wish list" of abilities that employers seek in candidates. Rather, computer skills are often an expectation that many employers assume candidates possess when they apply for open positions. This critical reality can certainly impact the career development and career opportunities for many clients. Take for example, a recently laid off 58-year-old male who worked 40 years as an automotive-line assembler where his primary duty was to perform the same one or two steps in the assembly operation. He has never owned nor needed a computer. He now finds himself out of work and lacking the basic computer skills that many employers, including factory employers, now expect and require of their employees. Retraining and upgrading his technological and computer skills may make him more marketable in the current workplace.

Industry and Occupational Projections

To see what these factors and forces mean for the U.S. workforce, take a look at the industry projections made by the U.S. Department of Labor (2005). First, service-producing industries are projected to continue growing and to account for approximately 18.7 million of the 18.9 million newly generated jobs over the 2004–2014 period. Specifically, the following projections have been made for service-producing occupations through the year 2014:

• *Education and Health Services.* Education and health services fields are expected to add more jobs than any other industry. Approximately 3 out of every 10 new jobs in the United States will be either in health care and social services or in private educational sectors.

• *Professional and Business Services.* Professional and business services will continue to grow. Employment in administrative and support and in waste management and remediation services is projected to grow by 27.8 percent. The fastest-growing industry in this sector is expected to be in employment services, which is projected to grow by 45.5 percent, adding almost two-thirds of all new jobs in this group. Employment in professional, scientific, and technical services is expected to increase by 28.4 percent, adding approximately 1.9 million new jobs. Jobs in computer-systems design and related services are projected to grow by 39.5 percent, adding over one-fourth of all new jobs in professional, scientific, and technical services. Management of enterprises and companies is expected to grow by 10.6 percent, adding over 182,000 new jobs.

- *Information.* Jobs in the information sector are expected to grow by 11.6 percent, adding 364,000 new jobs. This sector includes some of the fastest growing computer-related industries such as software publishing, which is expected to grow by 67.6 percent; Internet publishing and broadcasting, which are projected to grow by 43.5 percent; and Internet-service providers, web-search portals, and data-processing services, which are expected to grow by 27.8 percent.

- *Leisure and Hospitality.* Employment in **leisure** and hospitality is expected to grow by 17.7 percent. Arts, entertainment, and recreation are projected to increase by 25 percent, adding approximately 460,000 new jobs. The majority of these opportunities will come from the amusement, gambling, and recreation industries. Food services and accommodation industries are expected to increase by 16.5 percent, adding 1.8 million new jobs. Growth in this sector will be concentrated in food services and drinking establishments, which reflect population growth, dual-income families, and dining sophistication.

- *Trade, Transportation, and Utilities.* Employment in trade, transportation, and utilities is expected to grow by 10.3 percent. Transportation and warehousing is projected to grow by 11.9 percent, adding 506,000 jobs. This industry will expand as many manufacturers concentrate on core competencies and contract out their product transportation and storage roles. Retail trade is projected to increase by 11.0 percent, adding 16.7 million new jobs. Increases in personal income, population, and leisure time will add to occupational growth in this sector. Wholesale trade is expected to increase by 11.0 percent, adding 1.7 million jobs. Although employment in electric power generation and transmission, and in natural gas distribution is expected to decrease because of improved technology, employment in water, sewage, and other utility systems is expected to increase by 21 percent.

- *Financial Activities.* Employment in financial activities is expected to increase by 10.5 percent. Rental, leasing, and real estate are projected to grow by 16.9 percent, adding 353,000 new positions. Growth rates in this sector are largely due to population growth and the subsequent demand for housing. Insurance and finance industries are expected to increase by 8.3 percent, adding 496,000 jobs. Jobs in financial-investment industries are projected to grow by 15.8 percent. These increases can be attributed to the number of baby boomers in their peak savings years, the increase of tax-favorable retirement plans, and the globalization of the securities markets.

- *Government.* Government jobs, including those in public education and hospitals, are projected to grow by 10.0 percent, adding 2.2 million jobs. The shift of responsibilities from the federal government to state and local governments will fuel growth in state and local educational sectors. Because the federal government is contracting many government jobs to private companies, federal government employment, including the U.S. Postal Service, is expected to grow by only 1.6 percent.

Since the 1980s, employment in the goods-producing industries has been somewhat sluggish. Overall this sector is expected to decline 0.4 percent over the 2004–2014 period. As you will see, projected growth among the various industries varies significantly. Following are the U.S. Department of Labor's 2005 occupational projections for specific industries within the goods-producing sector through the year 2014.

- *Construction.* Demand for new housing and an increase in road, bridge, and tunnel construction will result in an increase of 11.4 percent, adding 8 million jobs in the construction industry.

- *Manufacturing.* Overall employment in the manufacturing industry will decline by 5.4 percent, losing 777,000 jobs. However, because of the aging population and the increase in life expectancies, pharmaceutical and medical manufacturing is projected to grow by 26.1 percent, adding 76,000 jobs. Automation and international competition will negatively affect employment in many of the other manufacturing industries. For example, apparel manufacturing and textile mills will lose 119,000 and 170,000 jobs, respectively.

- *Agriculture, Forestry, Fishing, and Hunting.* Employment in this industry is projected to decrease by 5.2 percent due to advances in technology. However, farm-labor contractors and farm-management services are expected to grow by 18.2 percent, adding 19,000 jobs.

- *Mining.* Because of technology gains, growing international competition, restricted access to Federal lands, and strict environmental regulations, 8.8 percent or 46,000 mining jobs will be lost. Jobs in coal mining and metal ore mining are projected to decrease by 23.3 percent and 29.3 percent, respectively. Employment in oil and gas extraction industries is also expected to decline by 13.1 percent.

As you can see from the industry projections through the year 2014, service-providing industries are expected to continue expanding, thereby creating a demand for a number of occupations. However, the job growth rate varies depending on the occupational group. Following are the U.S. Department of Labor's (2005) occupational projections for various occupations through the year 2014.

- *Professional and Related Occupations.* This group will grow faster and add more jobs than any other major occupational group. The projection for this group is an increase of 21.2 percent, adding 6 million jobs. The majority of jobs will cover computer and mathematical occupations, health-care practitioners and technical occupations, and education, training, and library occupations.

- *Service Occupations.* Jobs in service occupations are projected to increase by 19 percent, adding 5.3 million jobs. Most jobs are expected to be food preparation and serving-related occupations. However, health-care support occupations are expected to have the fastest growth rate of 33.3 percent, adding 1.2 million new jobs.

- *Management, Business, and Financial Occupations.* Jobs in this group are expected to increase by 14.4 percent, adding 2.2 million jobs. Among managers, computer information systems managers and preschool and childcare center/program educational administrators will grow the fastest by 25.9 percent and 27.9 percent, respectively. General and operations managers will add 308,000 new jobs, the most new jobs in this group. Ranch and farm jobs are expected to decline, losing approximately 155,000 jobs. Among business and financial jobs, the most jobs added will be accountants, auditors, and management analysts at around 386,000 jobs combined.

- *Construction and Extraction Occupations.* Individuals in this group construct new residential and commercial buildings, work in mines and quarries, and in oil and gas fields. Employment is expected to grow by 12 percent, adding 931,000 new jobs. Three-fourths of the new jobs will be in the construction trades and many extraction occupations will decline reflecting the overall employment losses in the mining, oil, and gas extraction fields.

- *Installation, Maintenance, and Repair Occupations.* Workers in this group install, maintain, and repair new and old equipment. Occupations in this field will increase by 11.4 percent, adding 657,000 new jobs. The fastest-growing rates will be among security and fire alarm system installers, which are expected to grow by 21.7 percent.

- *Transportation and Material Moving Occupations.* Workers in this area transport materials and people by land, air, and sea. Jobs in this group are expected to increase by 11.1 percent, adding 1.1 million new jobs. Motor vehicle operators will add the majority of jobs, approximately 629,000. The only group projected to decline is rail transportation occupations, which are expected to drop by 1.1 percent.

- *Sales and Related Occupations.* Employees in this field transfer goods and services among consumers and businesses. Occupations in this area are expected to grow by 9.6 percent, adding 1.5 million jobs. The majority of jobs in this group will be among retail salespersons and cashiers, which will add 849,000 jobs combined.

- *Office and Administrative Support Occupations.* Workers in this group perform the day-to-day activities of the office, including preparing and filing documents, dispersing information, and dealing with the public. Jobs are expected to grow by 5.8 percent, adding 1.4 million new jobs. The most new jobs will come from customer service representatives, 471,000 jobs, and the fastest-growing occupations will be desktop publishers, which are projected to increase by 23.2 percent.

- *Farming, Fishing, and Forestry Occupations.* Individuals in this group farm, fish, breed and raise livestock, catch animals, and cultivate plants in the forest. Occupations are projected to decline by 1.3 percent, losing 13,000 jobs. The majority of new jobs will come from agricultural workers. Jobs for fishing and hunting workers are expected to decline by 16.6 percent.

• *Production Occupations.* Employees in this group assemble goods and operate plants mainly in the manufacturing industry. Production occupations are projected to decline by less than 1.0 percent losing 79,000 jobs. The textile, apparel, and furnishings occupations will account for the majority of job losses in this group.

Both employment growth and replacement needs provide job opportunities. Sixty percent of all job openings will be the result of replacement needs due to workers retiring, returning to school, quitting, or dying. Even occupations projected to experience little or no growth or even to decline may still provide a number of new jobs (U.S. Department of Labor, 2005).

In addition to understanding occupational projections, human service professionals working with career-development issues and concerns must also have a conceptual knowledge of the corresponding terminology often used in career work. In sections that follow you will find some of the most popular terms (in bold) in the career development field.

Understanding the world of work, including the impact of population factors, diversity, sociological and economic forces, and technology on occupational projections, along with the knowledge of career development terminology are areas of expertise essential to career development helping professionals. However, in order to fully appreciate career development, helping professionals must have a clear understanding of its evolution. The following section will provide an historical overview of the career-guidance movement.

The Evolution of Career Guidance: An Historical Perspective

The Industrial Revolution

The Industrial Revolution was, perhaps, the most significant event to impact the history of career counseling. Prior to the industrial revolution, the handicraft economy, where most manufacturing took place in homes, was prevalent. Merchants would deliver raw materials to homes and collect finished products. With the dawn of the Industrial Revolution, machines and industry took over the labor force. The revolution began in England in the 18th century and spread to other parts of the world, including the United States. With the introduction of power-driven machinery and the creation of factories, the revolution greatly increased the amount of goods produced. Although some historians view the Industrial Revolution as a constructive period of history because of raised standards of living, others have a negative view of this era. Rapid industrialization often lead to overcrowded cities, unsanitary housing, and deplorable working conditions (Industrial Revolution, n.d.). Children, some as young as 10 years old, worked up to 14 hours a day in textile mills and mines. The frenzied and hostile working conditions led to labor unrest and violence (Zytowski,

2001). This charged atmosphere motivated a number of extraordinary scientists to direct their attention to the study of human behavior and individual differences. Thus, the career-guidance movement was born.

George A. Merrill and Early Career Development Programs

George A. Merrill, sometimes referred to as the forerunner of vocational guidance, was instrumental in the development of vocational education (Brewer, 1918). Merrill was hired as the Director of the California School of Mechanical Arts in 1894. In 1900 he also became the head of Wilmerding School of Industrial Arts, and in 1912 he became the head of The Lux School. Heading all three schools, Merrill had a goal of creating the "educated craftsman." To this end, he developed a curriculum that combined general intellectual preparation with technical and vocational instruction (Lick-Wilmerding History, 2003). Although these programs were undeniably groundbreaking, they lacked a logical, straight-forward conceptualization of career guidance.

Frank Parsons: Choosing a Vocation

Early in the 1900s, Frank Parsons created a rational and orderly plan for career guidance that has endured over time (Zunker, 2002). Frank Parsons, who was trained as a civil engineer, settled in Boston in 1885 after returning from a hiatus in the southwest. In 1895 Parsons ran for mayor of Boston. He taught political economy at Kansas State University from 1897 until his resignation from the university in 1899. The disparity between the status of the rich and the poor increased during this time. Reform efforts developed in the cities as the new middle class became increasingly restless for political change. State and federal legislatures passed acts regulating businesses. The first child labor laws were passed in Boston in 1836. Prohibition became a concern and assaults on the use of opium and cocaine escalated. In 1889 Jane Addams stimulated the development of the social work profession by organizing the first settlement house in Chicago. Labor groups marched in support of the 8-hour workday. Between 1886 and 1908, Parsons witnessed the founding of the American Federation of Labor, the National American Suffrage Association, the Teamsters Union in Boston, and the Socialist Party (Zykowski, 2001).

Around 1906 Parsons gave a lecture to the Economic Club of Boston entitled, "The Ideal City." In his lecture he stressed the need to assist youth in their vocational decision-making. His lecture was well received, and as a result, he was asked to present a similar lecture to a graduating class at a local night school. Following the presentation, some graduates requested personal interviews with Parsons. From this beginning, Parsons was asked to formulate a plan for systematic, vocational guidance. This request led to the creation of the Vocational Bureau where Parson's served as director and vocational counselor (Zykowski, 2001). The Vocational Bureau was an immediate success; Parsons stated that 80 men and women were seen during the first five months of its existence (Brewer, 1942. p. 52).

At the same time as the inception of the Vocational Bureau, Parsons was developing a training program for counselors. The purpose of the training program was to train young men to become vocational counselors and to manage vocation bureaus in association with schools, colleges and universities, YMCAs, businesses, associations, and public systems throughout the country. Parsons was scheduled to be dean of the new training program, but he died prior to its implementation. Ralph Albertson, an associate counselor at the Vocational Bureau, took over the class (Zykowski, 2001).

One of Parsons' most important contributions was his conceptual framework for helping individuals choose careers. His three-part process consists of:

1. A clear understanding of yourself, aptitudes, abilities, interests, resources, limitations, and other qualities
2. A knowledge of the requirements and conditions of success, advantages and disadvantages, compensations, opportunities, and prospects in different lines of work
3. True reasoning on the relations of these two groups of facts (Parsons, 1909, p. 5)

The commitment to social change by Frank Parsons and other initiators of the career-guidance movement continues in numerous areas of vocational psychology today. Individual career counseling, guidance work in schools, career interventions with special populations, and vocational research all have roots in the work of these founders of vocational guidance (O'Brien, 2001). In many respects the vocational guidance movement coincided with the measurement movement.

The Measurement Movement

The first psychological laboratory was founded in 1879 at the University of Leipzig, Germany through the dedication and efforts of Wilhiem Wundt. Wundt, along with two other German psychologists, Emil Kraepelin and Hermann Ebbinghaus, began constructing measuring devices. These psychologists were among the pioneers of the measurement movement (Ross & Stanley, 1954). In fact, Wundt's standardization of measurement procedures became a model for the development of standardized tests (Zunker, 2002).

James M. Cattrell who studied at Wundt's laboratory and was interested in human abilities subsequently influenced the measurement movement. He took a practical, test-oriented approach to the study of mental processes and studied reaction times as well as the affect of drugs on simple mental processes. He became one of the first American psychologists to stress quantification, ranking, and ratings. Although his work with "mental tests" and reaction times were important to the field, his tests proved unreliable and later Alfred Binet developed more acceptable tests (Parrott, n.d.).

Alfred Binet and other members of the Free Society for the Psychological Study of the Child wished to study children in a scientific manner. Binet, along with other members of the society, was appointed to the Commission for the Retarded. Binet made it his work to identify the differences that separated the normal child from the abnormal child and to measure these disparities.

A young medical student by the name of Theodore Simon applied for the position of research assistant for Binet. The two worked collaboratively in developing the intelligence test that shares their names, the Binet-Simon scale (Imhoff, n.d.). In 1916, L. M. Termen of Stanford University directed the revision of the scales, which were then published as the Stanford-Binet (Zunker, 2002).

The measurement movement received a huge push at the beginning of World War I when the U.S. Army needed to classify almost 1.5 million people and provide them with subsequent training (Zunker, 2002). Because of this need, Robert M. Yerkes chaired the committee that created the first group-administered intelligence tests. These tests, known as the Army Alpha and Beta Tests, became available to counselors of the general public following the war (McGuire, 1994; Zunker, 2002).

Special aptitude tests, interest inventories, and achievement tests were developed during the next two decades. These **assessments** were instrumental in linking the measurement movement to the guidance movement and providing much-needed standardized support materials for the career-guidance field (Zunker, 2002). In addition, these early tests were instrumental in the development of the trait and factor theory.

Edmund G. Williamson: Directive Counseling

Following World War II, much of the research on assessment took place at the University of Minnesota (Sharf, 20002). Edmund G. Williamson, who was the dean of students at the University of Minnesota between 1941 and 1969, used a directive approach to counseling. He believed that the counselor should share his or her wisdom with the client in assisting the client in decision-making. His techniques included information sharing and direct suggestions. He wrote extensively on the trait and factor approach to career counseling (Williamson, 1939, 1965).

Carl R. Rogers: Nondirective Counseling

Unlike Williamson's directive approach, Carl Rogers took a nondirective approach to counseling. He stressed the importance of the counselor reflecting the client's feelings as opposed to providing the client with information and advice. Carl Rogers laid the foundation for the formation of the counseling relationship. His essential counseling conditions—genuineness, unconditional positive regard, and empathic understanding—are the pillars of the nondirective, person-centered counseling approach (Rogers, 1951, 1961, 1989). The client–counselor relationship was to be one of mutual respect. The goal of the relationship was the client gaining a better understanding of his or herself and taking the necessary steps to control his or her destiny. In addition, the nondirective approach focused less attention on testing.

Through the impact of the Industrial Revolution, the influence of the pioneers of early career development programs, the effect of the measurement movement, and the conception of the directive and nondirective approaches to counseling, the foundation for today's career guidance field was established. We will now look at the contemporary state of career guidance.

Career Guidance Today

For the first 50 years of the career-guidance movement, vocational guidance emphasized the prediction of occupational choice or success based on the scores of clients' tests. The primary concern of counselors was to match clients' attributes, which were based on test results, to the occupational requirements of available positions. Therefore, vocational guidance was primarily confined to one aspect of the client's life—entry or reentry into the labor market (Herr et al., 2004). In the 1950s, the work of Donald Super, Carl Rogers, and other theorists challenged the way vocational guidance was conceived. Specifically, Super focused on the psychological nature of vocational choice and Rogers worked on nondirective counseling techniques. Their work had a tremendous impact on a subsequent shift in terminology. What was formerly referred to as *vocational guidance* is now called *career guidance and counseling.*

Career Education

One of the newer concepts to materialize in the innovative age of career guidance was that of **career education.** In early 1970, Sidney P. Marland, the U.S. Commissioner of Education, proposed a plan that integrated career education into the curriculum beginning in kindergarten and remaining through adulthood (Zunker, 2002). The premise behind career education was to use educational and work experiences systematically to help students and adults learn about themselves, work, and the skills necessary to plan and prepare for work and other life options (Herr et al., 2004). Career education can take on many different forms including: infusing career-related information into the curriculum, providing occupational and educational information, offering courses in career preparation and decision-making, taking field trips to industries and businesses, having guest speakers talk about their careers, setting up laboratories that simulate career experiences, and promoting work-based learning such as practica and internships (Hoyt, 1977; Isaacson & Brown, 2000). Largely because of the lobbying efforts of the National Occupational Information Coordinating Agency, career education is often referred to as **career development programs.** The latter term signifies the integration of career education with **career guidance programs** (Barnes, 2005).

Professionalism

The recognized leader in developing standards for both career counseling and the evaluation of **career information** materials is the National Career Development Association (NCDA). The association has a rich history dating back to 1913 when it was called the National Vocational Guidance Association. In 1985, the name was changed. The National Career Development Association is active in developing standards and professional guidelines for consumers of career services, providers of career services, publishers and developers, policy makers, and others. The NCDA works collaboratively with its parent organization, the American Counseling Association

(ACA), promotes global sharing of workforce policy and practices, and supports and reports on career development research (National Career Development Association, 2003b).

In 1984, NCDA developed procedures for credentialing career counselors. At this time, state registries have taken the place of national career certification. However NCDA has made great progress in defining professional and career-counseling specialties through their career-counseling competencies, code of ethics, and state licensing and registry requirements. Special NCDA membership designations include Fellow, Master Career Counselor, and Master Career Development Professional. In addition NCDA has worked vigorously in developing standards for two new designations—the Career Development Facilitator (CDF) and the Global Career Development Facilitator (GCDF).

Several professional groups recognized the fact that many individuals provide career assistance but are not professional counselors. The Career Development Facilitator (CDF) certification was developed to provide standards, training guidelines, and credentialing for these career providers. The title of CDF designates individuals who work in a variety of career-development settings. Some of the roles include career-group facilitator, job-search trainer, career coach, intake interviewer, occupational and labor market information resource person, career-development case manager, human resource career-development coordinator, employment/placement specialist, and workforce-development staff person (National Career Development Association, 2003a).

Global Career Development Facilitator (GCDF) certification is provided through the Center for Credentialing and Education, Inc. (CCE) (n.d.), a subsidiary of the National Board for Certified Counselors (NBCC). GCDF certification requires a combination of education and work experience. The National Career Development Association (NCDA), the National Employment Counseling Association (NECA), and the National Association of Workforce Development Professionals (NAWDP) have endorsed the credentialing requirements (National Career Development Association, 2003a).

The history of NCDA in providing direction and standards for the career guidance and counseling fields extends to the world of technology. Technology has made a greater impact on the career development field than on any other counseling specialization.

Technology: Appropriate Use

The Internet provides human service professionals and their clients with a vast array of career and occupational information, job postings, assessment tools, discussion forums, chat rooms, and bulletin boards. Over a billion web pages are in existence and the number rises daily. Technology can offer the helpers limitless ways to assist their clients. Caution must be taken, however, because no guarantee is given that the information and assessments obtained from websites are accurate, up to date, or suitable for clients. In addition, the possibility exists of being "scammed" by imposters who charge fees for their less-than-good services (Herr et al., 2004). Because of the enormous impact the Internet has on the delivery of career services, the human service professional should learn as much as possible about the uses and misuses of the Internet in order to offer competent, ethical career assistance.

According to the NCDA guidelines, the Internet can be used for the purpose of providing career counseling and/or career planning services to clients in four ways:

1. To deliver information about occupations, including their descriptions, employment outlook, skills requirements, estimated salary, etc. through text, still images, graphics, and/or video. In this event, the standards for information development and presentation are the same as those for print materials and audiovisual materials as stated in NCDA's documents on these matters.

2. To provide online searches of occupational databases for the purpose of identifying feasible occupational alternatives. In this event, the standards developed by NCDA and the Association of Computer-Based Systems for Career Information (ACSCI) apply.

3. To deliver interactive career counseling and career-planning services. This use assumes that clients, either as individuals or as part of a group, have intentionally placed themselves in direct communication with a professional career counselor. Standards for use of the Internet for these purposes are addressed in this document.

4. To provide searches through large databases of job openings for the purpose of identifying those that the user may pursue. Guidelines for this application are included in this document.

At times human service professionals will find themselves responsible for developing and/or maintaining a website for the agency or organization that employs the helping professional. The following standards were developed by NCDA to assist helping professionals in developing and maintaining professional career-related websites.

1. *Qualifications of Developer or Provider.* Websites and other services designed to assist clients with career planning should be developed with content input from professional career counselors. The service should clearly state the qualifications and credentials of the developers not only in the content area of professional career counseling, but also in the development of interactive online services.

2. *Access and Understanding of Environment.* The counselor has an obligation to be aware of free, public access points to the Internet within the member's community, so that a lack of financial resources does not create a significant barrier to clients accessing counseling services or information, assessment or instructional resources over the Internet. The counselor has an obligation to be as aware as possible of local conditions, cultures, and events that may impact the client.

3. *Content of Career Counseling and Planning Services on the Internet.* The content of a website or other service offering career information or planning services should be reviewed for the appropriateness of content offered in this medium. Some kinds of content have been extensively tested for online delivery due to the long existence of computer-based career information and guidance systems. This includes searching of databases by relevant search variables; display of occupational information; development of a resume; assessment of interests, abilities, and work-related values and linkage of these to occupational titles; instruction about occupational classification systems; relationship of school majors to occupational choices; and the completion of forms such as a financial-needs-assessment questionnaire or a job application. When a website offers a service, which has not previously been extensively tested (such as computer-based career guidance and information systems), this service should be carefully scrutinized to determine whether it lends itself to the Internet. The website should clearly state the kinds of client concerns that the counselor judges to be inappropriate for counseling over the Internet, or beyond the skills of the counselor.

4. *Appropriateness of Client for Receipt of Services via the Internet.* The counselor has an ethical and professional responsibility to assure that the client who is requesting service can profit from it in this mode. Appropriate screening includes the following:

    a. A clear statement by clients of their career planning or career counseling needs.

    b. An analysis by the counselor of whether meeting those needs via Internet exchange is appropriate *and* of whether this particular client can benefit from counseling services provided in this mode. A judgment about the latter should be made by means of a telephone or videophone teleconference designed to specify the client's expectations, how the client has sought to meet these through other modes, and whether or not the client appears to be able to process information through an Internet medium.

5. *Appropriate Support to the Client.* The counselor who is providing services to a client via the Internet has ethical responsibility for the following:

    a. Periodic monitoring of the client's progress via telephone or videophone teleconference.

    b. Identification by the counselor of a qualified career counselor in the client's geographic area should referral become necessary. If this is not possible, the web counselor using traditional referral sources to identify an appropriate practitioner should assist the client in the selection of a counselor.

    c. Appropriate discussion with the client about referral to face-to-face service should the counselor determine that little or no progress is being made toward the client's goals.

6. *Clarity of Contract with the Client.* The counselor should define several items in writing to the client in a document that can be downloaded from the Internet or faxed to the client. This document should include at least the following items:

    a. The counselor's credentials in the field.

    b. The agreed-upon goals of the career counseling or career planning Internet interchange.

    c. The agreed-upon cost of the services and how this will be billed.

d. Where and how clients can report any counselor behavior which they consider to be unethical.

e. Statement about the degree of security of the Internet and confidentiality of data transmitted on the Internet and about any special conditions related to the client's personal information (such as potential transmission of client records to a supervisor for quality-control purposes, or the collection of data for research purposes).

f. A statement of the nature of client information electronically stored by the counselor, including the length of time that data will be maintained before being destroyed.

g. A statement about the need for privacy when the client is communicating with the counselor, e.g., that client communication with the counselor is not limited by having others observe or hear interactions between the counselor and client.

h. If the service includes career, educational, or employment information, the counselor is responsible for making the client aware of the typical circumstances where individuals need counseling support in order to effectively use the information.

7. *Inclusion of Linkages to Other Websites.* If a career information or counseling website includes links to other websites, the professional who creates this linkage is responsible for assuring that the services to which his or hers are linked also meet these guidelines.

8. *Use of Assessment.* If the career planning or career counseling service is to include online inventories or tests and their interpretation, the following conditions should apply:

a. The assessments must have been tested in computer delivery mode to assure that their psychometric properties are the same in this mode of delivery as in print form; or the client must be informed that they have not yet been tested in this same mode of delivery.

b. The counselor must abide by the same ethical guidelines as if he or she were administering and interpreting these same inventories or tests in face-to-face mode and/or in print form.

c. Every effort must be exerted to protect the confidentiality of the user's results.

d. If there is any evidence that the client does not understand the results, as evidenced by e-mail or telephone interchanges, the counselor must refer the client to a qualified career counselor in his or her geographic area.

e. The assessments must have been validated for self-help use if no counseling support is provided, or that appropriate counseling intervention is provided before and after completion of the assessment resource if the resource has not been validated for self-help use.

This statement was developed by the National Career Development Association, 10820 East 45th Street, Suite 210, Tulsa, OK 74146, tel: (918) 663-7060, fax: (918) 663-7058, toll-free: (866) 367-6232.

Summary

Prior to providing career guidance and interventions to clients, human service professionals must first possess knowledge of the impact that population factors, sociological and economic forces, technology, and diversity have on the world of work. The population of the United States is projected to increase by 24 million by 2012, and immigrants and minorities will comprise a greater proportion of the population. The socioeconomic status of the family will continue to dictate the amount of resources available to finance educational opportunities. The global economy will push many workers to seek higher levels of education in order to remain competitive. Advances in technology will require individuals to update their skills in order to keep up with current and future technological developments. Many factors and forces have an impact on occupational projections. Specifically, service-producing industries are expected to account for approximately 20.8 million of the 21.6 million newly generated jobs through 2012 (U.S. Department of Labor, 2005).

Helping professionals must also be well versed in vocational terminology and knowledgeable about historical developments in the career-guidance movement. The impact of the Industrial Revolution lead George A. Merrill to initiate some of the first vocational education programs. Other hallmarks of the career-guidance movement included the work of Frank Parsons, one of the founders of vocational guidance, and the contributions of German psychologists, Wilhiem Wundt, Emil Kraepelin, and Hermann Ebbinghaus, who were leaders in measurement design and implementation. Finally, the development of directive and nondirective approaches to counseling has provided helping professionals with skills for which to delivery career services.

These historical markers provide a framework for understanding and appreciating changes that have impacted the career guidance movement. Today, focus is placed on career development as a *process* that spans the lifetime, not as a one-time event that takes place when an individual enters or reenters the workforce.

Finally, there is no better test for the importance of career development than the current emphasis placed on professionalism in the field. The National Career Development Association is the recognized leader in developing standards for both career counseling and the evaluation of career information materials. Helping professionals should use these standards as a guide when delivering any type of career planning services.

Key Terms

Assessments
Career
Career counseling
Career development
Career development programs
Career education

Career guidance programs
Career information
Career intervention
Job
Leisure
Occupation

Web Resources

Note that website URLs may change over time.

American Counseling Association
http://www.counseling.org

Association of Computer-Based Systems for Career Information
http://www.acsci.org

Center for Credentialing and Education, Inc.
http://www.cce-global.org

National Association of Workforce Development Professionals
http://www.nawdp.org

National Career Development Association
http://ncda.org

National Employment Counseling Association
http://www.employmentcounseling.org/neca.html

2

Theories of Career Development

Prior to implementing any career development intervention, human service professionals must first have a keen understanding of career development theories. These theories present conceptual frameworks that assist helping professionals understand career concerns that materialize during their clients' lifetimes. According to Lock (2000), "Theory attempts to give us guidelines for action and bring order out of chaos" (p. 12).

The theories we have chosen to include in this chapter are merely a sampling of some of the major career development theories that have impacted the field as well as a few up-and-coming theories. In other words, this chapter is merely a theory appetizer, not a full-course meal. It is our intent to "whet your appetite," and to leave you a bit "hungry." Hopefully this hunger will motivate you to go beyond the scope of this chapter to obtain more comprehensive information on theories of career development.

We have organized this chapter by theory types that are categorized into six broad headings: (1) trait and type theories, (2) developmental theories, (3) career decision-making theories, (4) social learning theories, (5) emerging theories, and (6) theoretical integration.

Trait and Type Theories

The early work of Frank Parsons was pivotal in the later development of what we now call **trait and type theory,** also known as **trait and factor theory.** As you may recall from Chapter 1, Frank Parsons developed a three-step conceptual framework for helping individuals choose careers. The three steps included a clear understanding of self, knowledge of different lines of work, and an understanding of the relationship between these two groups (Parsons, 1909). Trait and type theories have incorporated these very principles. The first term, **trait,** refers to individual characteristics that can be measured through testing and assessment. The second term, **type or factor,** refers to work characteristics required for successful performance in a particular job. When these two fundamental components are combined, the result is a theory that assesses and matches the characteristics of a person with the characteristics of a job.

John Holland: Theory of Vocational Choice

According to John Holland (1997) personality develops as a result of the interaction of innate characteristics, activities to which the person is exposed, and the competencies and interests that develop from these activities. In his theory, Holland identified six distinct personality types, which rarely occur in their pure form. In other words, an individual's personality type is never just one type but rather a combination of the six types in varying degrees in order of prominence.

Six Personality Types.   Holland's six personality types are realistic, investigative, artistic, social, enterprising, and conventional. Following are descriptions of each type.

Realistic.   People with this personality type are reliable, straightforward, and generally conservative in their political opinions. These individuals prefer activities where they can use their hands, machines, tools, and objects to build and repair things. They favor working with material things as opposed to working with ideas or people. They prefer working outdoors to working at a desk in an office setting. They are practical, physically strong, stable, rugged, and materialistic. People in realistic occupations include carpenters, cooks, electricians, farmers, fish and wildlife managers, foresters, mechanical engineers, and paramedics.

Investigative.   People with this personality type are curious, precise, analytical, and reserved. They prefer activities that require analytical thinking, which allows them to investigate, research, and study ideas in mathematics and in the physical, biological, and social sciences. People in investigative occupations include chemical engineers, computer programmers, design engineers, draftspersons, pharmacists, physicists, surgeons, and veterinarians.

Artistic.   Artistic types are unconventional, impulsive, introspective, flexible, creative, original, open, and independent. They value activities that involve self-expression, imagination, and artistic creativity. People in artistic occupations include actors, architects, writers, artists, interior designers, musicians, photographers, and poets.

Social.   The social personality is kind, generous, helpful, trustful, nurturing, sociable, and warm. People with this personality prefer working cooperatively with others and are typified by their need for social interaction. People in social occupations include counselors, elementary school teachers, nurses, occupational therapists, personnel managers, police officers, political scientists, and social workers.

Enterprising.   Enterprising types are extroverted, persuasive, self-confident, enthusiastic, and ambitious. They prefer activities where they can lead, control, and persuade others in order to achieve a professional or personal goal. People in enterprising occupations include business executives, financial planners, insurance agents, lawyers, marketing managers, project directors, realtors, and salespeople.

Conventional.   Conventional types are sociable, neat, rigid, careful, orderly, efficient, dependable, and conservative. They like clerical and computational tasks and prefer following as opposed to leading. People in conventional occupations include accountants, bank tellers, bookkeepers, editorial assistants, file clerks, mortgage processors, payroll clerks, and website editors.

Six Work Environments.   Not only did Holland assign personality types to people, he also proposed six different work environments and labeled them like the personality types. Work environments are atmospheres that are created by people who dominate a certain setting. Work environments also have degrees of all six environment types; two or three types dominate the pattern. According to Holland (1997), job satisfaction is likely to result when personality patterns are matched with comparable work environments. Following are brief descriptions of Holland's six work environments.

Realistic.   In realistic environments work calls for the manipulation of tools, objects, machines, and animals. Realistic settings include machine shops, farms, filling stations, military settings, and construction sites.

Investigative.   People in investigative work environments work with ideas rather than with people. The work calls for research and exploration of biological, cultural, or physical knowledge. Investigative environments include research laboratories, hospitals, universities, and libraries.

Artistic.   Work in artistic environments is creative, artistic, and interpretive and usually requires intense involvement for prolonged periods of time. Artistic environments include concert halls, dance studios, libraries, art studios, theatres, museums, and galleries.

Social.   People working in social environments interpret and transform human behavior through frequent and extended personal relationships. Social environments include counseling offices, schools and colleges, health-care agencies, churches, recreational centers, and nonprofit agencies.

Enterprising.   People in enterprising environments use verbal skills to manage and persuade other people in order to reach organizational or personal goals. Enterprising environments include various businesses, restaurants, insurance agencies, real estate offices, advertising agencies, stock brokerage firms, and car lots.

Conventional.   People in conventional environments perform systematic, detailed, routine, and repetitive processing of verbal and mathematical information. Conventional settings include business offices, banks, accounting firms, post offices, and file rooms.

Holland's Theoretical Constructs.   To help better understand the relationship among the various personality types and work environments, Holland (1997) proposed three important constructs: consistency, congruency, and differentiation.

Consistency.   The consistency construct refers to the similarity or dissimilarity among personality types and work environments. Certain types have more in common with one another than with other types. To illustrate this construct, Holland used a hexagonal diagram with each type purposefully placed on it to show relatedness. For example, types placed next to each other show the most consistent patterns. Those placed opposite each other show the least consistent patterns. As shown in Figure 2.1, investigative and artistic types are next to each other on the hexagon and therefore have more traits in common than do the investigative and enterprising types that are located across from one another on the hexagon.

Congruency.   The construct of congruency is perhaps Holland's most important construct. Congruency refers to the relationship between the personality type and the work environment. The more similar a personality type is to a work environment, the more congruent the relationship. For example, an artistic personality would likely prefer an artistic work environment. An artistic personality in a conventional work environment might find the relationship incongruent.

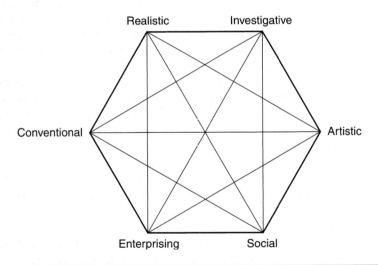

FIGURE 2.1 *Holland's Hexagonal Model.* The model is used to show consistent or inconsistent interactions among personality types and environments.

Differentiation.   The final construct, differentiation, refers to how clearly a personality type or a work environment belongs to one or more types. For instance, one individual may overwhelmingly resemble a single Holland type, while another individual may have interests and capabilities across all six types. Differentiation can be determined using the scores individuals receive on inventories that measure the six types. One determines the levels of differentiation by subtracting the lowest score of any type from the highest score. A high score signifies differentiation, and a low score indicates an undifferentiated profile. A well-differentiated person is likely to have less difficulty making career decisions than an undifferentiated person who may seek career guidance for assistance in decision-making.

Both personalities and environments vary in terms of differentiation. Some environments allow for more flexibility in movement to various environments than do others. For example, a sales representative working for a cosmetic company in a department store (enterprising) will have opportunities to sell products (enterprising), demonstrate makeup techniques (artistic), present workshops and training seminars (social), and take inventory (conventional). As you can see, this work environment is undifferentiated. On the other hand, an individual hired to harvest potatoes on a farm is likely to have only the opportunity to do realistic work.

John Holland's theory has been popular with human service professionals for a number of reasons. The theory is well researched and helpers find it relatively easy to apply. A number of reliable and uncomplicated inventories are available for use in identifying an individual's type (e.g., Self-Directed Search and the Vocational Preference Inventory.) (See Chapters 3 for additional Holland assessments.) The hexagonal model provides a valuable illustration of the links among the various types. The constructs of consistency and congruency provide vital information on the relationships among the six personality types and the corresponding work environments. And, finally, helpers find the concept of differentiation useful in explaining the meaning of scores derived from inventories that measure Holland types.

Holland's theory provides a practical way to conceptualize client concerns. However, as with any theory, it will not work with all clients. It is the responsibility of the human service professional to determine its applicability on a case-by-case basis.

Myers-Briggs® Type Theory

As opposed to the other theories described in this chapter, the Myers-Briggs® Type Theory was not intended to be a career development theory*. It was originally designed as a personality theory. Its applicability to career guidance rests on the assumption that the overlap between career development and personality is substantial. Therefore, some measures of personality may help to predict or stimulate career choice. According to Myers and McCaulley (1985), important motivators for career choice are work that uses an individual's preferred functions and attitude and work that is inherently appealing and satisfying.

MBTI, Myers-Briggs, Myers-Briggs Type Indicator and *Introduction to Type* are trademarks or registered trademarks of the Myers-Briggs Type Indicator Trust in the United States and other countries.

The **Myers-Briggs® Type Theory,** developed by the mother and daughter team of Katharine Briggs and Isabel Myers, rests on the analytical psychology of Carl Gustav Jung. Jung viewed personality as complex and consisting of interacting systems. He distinguished two orientations of personality–Extraversion and Introversion. An Extraverted personality directs energy and attention toward the external, objective world; an Introverted personality directs energy and attention toward the inner, subjective world (Jung, 1933). Jung also described four primary psychological functions: Thinking, Feeling, Sensing, and Intuiting. These functions combined with the Extraverted–Introverted orientations are the basis for the Myers-Briggs Type Indicator® (MBTI), which purports to measure the way individuals prefer to use perception and judgment.

The MBTI® measures 8 personality preferences, resulting in 16 types that are reflected in various combinations of the 4 dichotomies: Extraversion(E)–Introversion(I); Sensing(S)–Intuition(N); Thinking(T)–Feeling(F); and Judging(J)–Perceiving(P). Scores on each of the four dichotomies result in a four-letter type. Preferences making up the four-letter type are determined by responses to items on the inventory. No one preference is superior over its opposite. All types are valuable. No type is healthier, more valuable, or more desirable. Scores merely indicate the consistency with which an individual chooses one function over the other. Less-dominant preferences are not totally excluded in the personality. Individuals are simply more comfortable with one preference over another in most situations. We will now present the 8 personality preferences and the resulting 4 dichotomies.

Extraversion–Introversion (EI) Dichotomy.   Unlike the common meanings of Extraversion and Introversion, Jung and Myers used these terms to describe how one sees the world. In common usage, *Extraversion* refers to being louder and outgoing, whereas *Introversion* refers to being quieter and shy. In regards to the Myers-Briggs® Type Theory, *Extraverted* persons direct their energy and attention to the outer world of people and objects. Extraverts like to take action and prefer talking and interacting with people or things. *Introverts,* on the other hand, focus their energy on the inner world of concepts and ideas. They prefer working out problems or thinking for a while before acting on an experience.

Sensing–Intuition (SN) Dichotomy.   This dichotomy describes how one perceives, specifically in regards to how one takes in information. *Sensing* types take in information via their senses, by observing, primarily through vision, hearing, and touch. They are practical, concrete, and focused on the present. In contrast, *Intuitive* types take in information indirectly by going beyond their senses by way of insight, imagination, and unconscious processes. Intuitive individuals are often creative, abstract, and focused on the future.

Thinking–Feeling (TF) Dichotomy.   The Thinking–Feeling dichotomy explains how individuals judge the events and ideas that they have perceived. In other words, this dichotomy describes how individuals make judgments and decisions from the information they have acquired. *Thinking* individuals make decisions objectively and logically by weighing pros and cons and analyzing the data. Thinking types decide with their heads. Conversely, *Feeling* individuals make choices subjectively based on value judgments that they apply to observations or ideas. In other words, feeling types decide with their hearts. It is important to note that *feelings* used in this context refers to the process of making judgments, not to *emotions*. That is to say, any type can be *Feeling*.

Judgment–Perception (JP) Dichotomy.   When using the MBTI® instrument, it is important to understand not only how individuals perceive and judge, but also which process is the most important and results in actions. Judging as defined by Jung and Myers does not mean *judgmental*. Individuals with a preference for *Judging* use Thinking and Feeling to organize, control, and plan their lives. They prefer to make decisions based on relatively few facts. They have a sense of order in their lives and prefer structure. When faced with decision-making, they are likely to make concrete plans for implementing decisions so that they can close out other options. Individuals with a preference for *Perceiving*, on the other hand, use Sensing and Intuition to weigh many facts before reaching a judgment. They continually take in information and are open minded, adaptable, and flexible. Because they are constantly adapting and taking in information, they often have difficulty making decisions.

The four preferences in the MBTI® assessment code points to 1 of 16 different types. Table 2.1 describes preferences often associated with each type.

The MBTI® tool is used in career settings in a number of different ways. First, the four-letter codes can be useful in relating Myers-Briggs® types to occupational choice. Specifically, the MBTI® can provide information on occupational choices that are frequently made by people of each type. It can also provide insight on individuals' preferences for work situations. For example, Judging individuals may prefer work that is structured where they can plan their day and follow their plan. Conversely, Perceiving types may prefer work that is flexible and unstructured with no set plan. The MBTI® profiles can also assist clients in developing their resumes. Specifically, clients can focus on the strengths of their psychological type when formatting their resumes (Peterson, 1998). Focusing on these positive attributes can also help clients answer interview questions.

This brief overview of the Myers-Briggs® Type Theory is insufficient in providing human service professionals with the necessary knowledge and skills to use the MBTI® assessment. In order to use the MBTI® tool, the helping professional must possess a four-year college degree and have *EITHER* passed a college course in educational or psychological tests and measurements *OR* successfully completed a recognized qualifying program (Myers & Briggs Foundation, Inc., 2002).

Developmental Theories

Developmental theories, as compared to trait and type theories, are concerned with career issues over the entire life span. They emphasize the impact that biological, sociological, psychological, and cultural factors have on career choice and on life transitions.

TABLE 2.1   *Characteristics Frequently Associated with Each Myers-Briggs Type*

Sensing Types		Intuitive Types	
ISTJ	**ISFJ**	**INFJ**	**INTJ**
Quiet, serious, earn success by thoroughness and dependability. Practical, matter-of-fact, realistic, and responsible. Decide logically what should be done and work toward it steadily, regardless of distractions. Take pleasure in making everything orderly and organized—their work, their home, their life. Value traditions and loyalty.	Quiet, friendly, responsible, and conscientious. Committed and steady in meeting their obligations. Thorough, painstaking, and accurate. Loyal, considerate, notice and remember specifics about people who are important to them, concerned with how others feel. Strive to create an orderly and harmonious environment at work and at home.	Seek meaning and connection in ideas, relationships, and material possessions. Want to understand what motivates people and are insightful about others. Conscientious and committed to their firm values. Develop a clear vision about how best to serve the common good. Organized and decisive in implementing their vision.	Have original minds and great drive for implementing their ideas and achieving their goals. Quickly see patterns in external events and develop long-range explanatory perspectives. When committed, organize a job and carry it through. Skeptical and independent, have high standards of competence and performance—for themselves and others.
ISTP	**ISFP**	**INFP**	**INTP**
Tolerant and flexible, quiet observers until a problem appears, then act quickly to find workable solutions. Analyze what makes things work and readily get through large amounts of data to isolate the core of practical problems. Interested in cause and effect, organize facts using logical principles, value efficiency.	Quiet, friendly, sensitive, and kind. Enjoy the present moment, what's going on around them. Like to have their own space and to work within their own time frame. Loyal and committed to their values and to people who are important to them. Dislike disagreements and conflicts, do not force their opinions or values on others.	Idealistic, loyal to their values and to people who are important to them. Want an external life that is congruent with their values. Curious, quick to see possibilities, can be catalysts for implementing ideas. Seek to understand people and to help them fulfill their potential. Adaptable, flexible, and accepting unless a value is threatened.	Seek to develop logical explanations for everything that interests them. Theoretical and abstract, interested more in ideas than in social interaction. Quiet, contained, flexible, and adaptable. Have unusual ability to focus in depth to solve problems in their area of interest. Skeptical, sometimes critical, always analytical.

Introverts

TABLE 2.1 Continued

Sensing Types		Intuitive Types	
ESTP	**ESFP**	**ENFP**	**ENTP**
Flexible and tolerant, they take a pragmatic approach focused on immediate results. Theories and conceptual explanations bore them—they want to act energetically to solve the problem. Focus on the here-and-now, spontaneous, enjoy each moment that they can be active with others. Enjoy material comforts and style. Learn best by doing.	Outgoing, friendly, and accepting. Exuberant lovers of life, people, and material comforts. Enjoy working with others to make things happen. Bring common sense and a realistic approach to their work, and make work fun. Flexible and spontaneous, adapt readily to new people and environments. Learn best by trying a new skill with other people.	Warmly enthusiastic and imaginative. See life as full of possibilities. Make connections between events and information very quickly, and confidently proceed based on the patterns they see. Want a lot of affirmation from others, and readily give appreciation and support. Spontaneous and flexible, often rely on their ability to improvise and their verbal fluency.	Quick, ingenious, stimulating, alert, and outspoken. Resourceful in solving new and challenging problems. Adept at generating conceptual possibilities and then analyzing them strategically. Good at reading other people. Bored by routine, will seldom do the same thing the same way, apt to turn to one new interest after another.
ESTJ	**ESFJ**	**ENFJ**	**ISTJ**
Practical, realistic, matter-of-fact. Decisive, quickly move to implement decisions. Organize projects and people to get things done, focus on getting results in the most efficient way possible. Take care of routine details. Have a clear set of logical standards, systematically follow them and want other to also. Forceful in implementing their plans.	Warmhearted, conscientious, and cooperative. Want harmony in their environment, work with determination to establish it. Like to work with others to complete tasks accurately and on time. Loyal, follow through even in small matters. Notice what others need in their day-by-day lives and try to provide it. Want to be appreciated for who they are and for what they contribute.	Warm, empathetic, responsive, and responsible. Highly attuned to the emotions, needs, and motivations of others. Find potential in everyone, want to help others fulfill their potential. May act as catalysts for individual and group growth. Loyal, responsive to praise and criticism. Sociable, facilitate others in a group, and provide inspiring leadership.	Frank, decisive, assume leadership readily. Quickly see illogical and inefficient procedures and policies, develop and implement comprehensive systems to solve organizational problems. Enjoy long-term planning and goal setting. Usually well informed, well read, enjoy expanding their knowledge and passing it on to others. Forceful in presenting their ideas.

(left margin label: Extraverts)

They view career development as a continuing process as opposed to the trait and type theories, which deal with career issues at one point in time. Because developmental theories cover extended periods of time, they tend to be more complex. We have chosen two theories to present in this section. The first theory is that of Eli Ginzberg, Sol Ginsburg, Sidney Axelrad, and John Herma. We have selected their theory because of the pivotal role it has played in the developmental movement—the first developmental theory to appear in the career realm. The second theory we will present is that of Donald Super and his colleagues. Super's Life-Span Theory is perhaps the most extensive and comprehensive of all career development theories. It is our intention to provide a succinct overview of these developmental theories in order to better prepare human service professionals to respond to a wide variety of career-related issues over the life span.

Ginzberg and Associates: Career Development Theory

The team of Ginzberg, Ginsburg, Axelrad, and Herma (1951) consisted of an economist, a psychiatrist, a sociologist, and a psychologist. Their early work included an intensive study of the career-choice process in which they interviewed students (primarily upper-middle-class white adolescents) and extensively reviewed existing literature. From their research, they identified four sets of factors that interact with one another thereby impacting career choice. These factors are (1) individual values, (2) emotional factors, (3) the amount and kind of education, and (4) the effect of reality through environmental pressures. Ginzberg and his colleagues also differentiated three stages or periods in the career selection process, the fantasy stage, the tentative stage, and the realistic stage. The tentative and realistic stages also include several subphases.

The first stage, the *fantasy stage*, occurs in childhood before age 11. During this period children are involved in play and imagination when thinking about future careers.

Following the fantasy stage is the *tentative stage* that takes place during early adolescence from ages 11–17. This stage includes four subphases: the development of interests, capacities, and values, along with a transitional period. During the *interest* subphase, adolescents ages 11 and 12 base their choices on likes and dislikes. In the *capacity* subphase that covers the ages of 13 and 14, individuals assess their own capacities in relation to their career aspirations. The *value* subphase takes place when adolescents are 15 and 16. At this point adolescents are able to incorporate their goals and values into their career decisions. The *transition* period is the final subphase in the tentative stage. This period usually occurs at age 17, during the last year of high school. At this time, individuals become aware of the reality and significance of decisions that must be made, for example, whether or not to go to college. Here their focus is on the availability, demands, and benefits of certain careers, and their decisions are based on the understanding that adolescents have of themselves as a result of the information gleaned from previous subphases.

The final period, the *realistic stage* occurs from age 17 to the early 20s. It is divided into three subphases: exploration, crystallization, and specification. During the *exploration* subphase, individuals tend to be ambivalent and indecisive, but they are able to narrow their career choices to two or three. In the *crystallization* subphase individuals becoming committed to a specific career field. If a change in direction occurs during this stage, it is referred to as *pseudo-crystallization*. During the *specification* subphase, individuals select a job or the necessary training and education for a specific career.

The original research of Ginzberg and his associates proposed that the developmental process of career decision-making was irreversible, that is, individuals could not return psychologically or chronologically to previous stages (Ginzberg et al., 1951). Ginzberg reevaluated his theory in 1972 and again in 1984. In his more contemporary writings, he modified the theory and subsequently viewed the decision-making process as more open and not necessarily irreversible. He also contended that the decision-making process did not necessarily end at young adulthood but was likely to occur throughout an individual's working life (Ginzberg, 1972, 1984). The importance of the work of Ginzberg and his colleagues on the conceptualization of career choice as a developmental process cannot be overstated. These early hypotheses became the catalyst for the significant work of Donald Super.

Donald Super: Life-Span Theory

Donald Super's writings on career development are so impressive and comprehensive that it poses a major challenge to try to capture his work in a few pages of text. This section is provided solely as on overview of his theory and should not be viewed as an all-inclusive documentary of his life's work. We will attempt to highlight the main constructs of his significant work.

As with the theory of Ginzberg and his associates, the Life-Span Theory of Donald Super is caulk full of developmental tasks and stages. But in addition to his developmental tasks and stages, Super proposed some basic assumptions, including the role that psychological and socioeconomic factors play in the development of self, the impact of the self-concept on vocational development, and the notion of individual and life roles.

Super (1990) asserted that psychological characteristics such as the development of needs, values, interests, intelligence, aptitudes, and special aptitudes, lead to the development of the personality and to the accomplishments of the person. He also stated that individuals interact with social-economic forces that influence job structure and employment practices. These forces include the community, school, family, peer groups, economy, society, and the labor market. Both psychological and social-economic forces merge in the development of the self. As people learn more about themselves and their environment, they progress through a series of developmental stages in which they develop their self-concepts.

One of the most important contributions of Super's theory is his idea of how self-concept is applied in the career development process. Specifically, Super (1953) described vocational development as the process of developing and implementing a self-concept. According to Super (1984, 1990), the self-concept consists of individuals' view of self and their view of the situation or condition in which they exist. Vocational self-concept, although only a segment of the total self-concept, is the motivating force that establishes the career pattern individuals follow throughout their life.

Super's vocational development consists of a series of stages, substages, and developmental tasks. Intertwined within these stages are a variety of roles individuals take on at various ages in a number of theaters. First we will address his stages of vocational development—growth, exploration, establishment, maintenance, and disengagement.

Growth.   During this stage, children between the ages 4 and 13 form the attitudes and behaviors that shape their self-concept and their basic understanding of the world of work. Their progression through this stage includes movement through the substages of *fantasy, interest,* and *capacity.* First they use their inherent sense of curiosity to partake in occupational fantasies and to explore their environment. Through this curiosity, they begin to acquire information about work and about their own interests and capacities. During this substage, they begin to understand the importance of planning and to explore various occupational and educational prospects.

Exploration.   During this stage, adolescents ages 14 to 24 take all the information they have acquired throughout the growth stage and turn their attention to future planning. Three substages—tentative, transition, trial—take place during this period. The first of the substages, the *tentative* substage, involves the integration of needs, interests, abilities, and values into occupational choices. As individuals enter the job market or seek additional education or training, they move into the *transition* substage characterized by realistic thinking about opportunities. The *trial* substage is the final substage in the exploration period. It is marked by individuals trying on a work role, not necessarily the one they will hold for the rest of their life, but the one they believe holds potential.

The exploration stage is also marked by two tasks—crystallizing and specifying occupational preferences. *Crystallizing* requires individuals to clarify the type of work they might value. *Specifying* is the ability to choose an occupation from the various occupations being considered.

Establishment.   The establishment stage generally occurs between the ages of 25 to 45. This stage involves the developmental tasks of stabilizing, consolidating, and advancing. The period of *stabilization* occurs immediately upon a person entering an occupation and involves the evaluation of the occupation to determine whether or not the occupation provides adequate expression of the self-concept.

Following stabilization, consolidation takes place. During *consolidation,* individuals focus their energy on developing a positive reputation in the occupation, thereby leading to *advancement,* the final phase.

Maintenance.   During this stage, adults ages 45 to 65 are concerned with continuing in their chosen occupation and holding on to gains they have made. The developmental tasks in this stage include holding, updating, and innovating. Often workers are faced with having to *update* their skills in order to remain or advance in their occupation. *Holding* involves the updating of skills and the subsequent use of these new skills in *innovative* ways within the current occupation. Stagnation, or becoming "stuck," occurs when workers decide to stay in their current occupation but choose not to update their skills.

Disengagement. Toward the end of the maintenance stage at about age 65, individuals begin to lose interest in their work activities. Their focus turns to retirement planning. Deceleration, retirement planning, and retirement living become important tasks during this stage.

A core component of Super's theory is the function that roles play in the lives of individuals. Super (1980, 1990) proposed nine major roles, which materialize in chronological order. These roles include: (1) child, (2) student, (3) leisurite, (4) citizen, (5) worker, (6) spouse, (7) homemaker, (8) parent, and (9) pensioner. According to Super (1980) careers are the constellation of the interaction among the various roles. These roles are played out in the following theaters: (1) home, (2) community, (3), school, and (4) the workplace. Although most roles are played out in only one theater, some roles may pour over into other theaters.

Super's developmental theory illustrates how movement through vocational developmental stages impacts the self-concept. His concept of life roles helps to clarify the importance of each role and its subsequent theater within the various developmental stages. His theory can assist human service professionals in understanding career development concerns of individuals of all ages.

Career Decision-Making Theories

When discussing career decision-making theories, it is helpful to first understand two broad categories of decision-making models: descriptive and prescriptive. **Descriptive theories** describe or explain how career decisions are actually made. **Prescriptive theories,** on the other hand, emphasize how career decisions ought to be made (Jepsen & Dilley, 1974; Wright, 1984). In order to allow you to better differentiate between these two types of decision-making theories, we will present one of each. First we will focus on the early work of David Tiedeman and Robert O'Hara. Their model is a useful example of a *descriptive* approach. Next, we will address the prescriptive theory of Gary Peterson, James Sampson, Robert Reardon, and Janet Lenz, referred to as the cognitive information processing (CIP) approach.

Tiedeman and O'Hara: Theory of Career Decision-Making

The work of David Tiedeman and Robert O'Hara was influenced by a number of theorists, most notably Erik Erikson's (1980) ego development research and Donald Super's (1957) developmental approach to career choice. These theorists, along with a few others, are reflected in Tiedeman and O'Hara's (1963) unique two-stage model of career decision-making. Their first stage describes what happens as a person formulates a career choice, and their second stage illustrates what ensues when a person attempts to implement the choice. We will begin with stage one, anticipating a choice.

Stage One: Anticipating a Choice.   The first stage, anticipating a choice, has four phases: exploration, crystallization, choice, and specification. *Exploration* involves random and acquisitive activity where individuals try out different behaviors, visualize and fantasize about different situations and career goals, and follow various paths to choices in either systematic or unsystematic ways. During *crystallization*, various patterns emerge in the form of alternatives along with the subsequent advantages and disadvantages of each alternative. These new developments lead to more clarification and definition. The next phase, *choice*, can occur with crystallization. Individuals may be confident or unsure about their choice, depending on the complexity of the choice. Following the choice comes specification. *Specification* or clarification occurs when people reassess their choice and clarify its options. Once specification takes place, individuals move into the second stage, adjusting to a choice.

Stage Two: Adjusting to a Choice.   Stage two, adjusting to a choice, includes three phases: induction, reformation, and integration. During *induction*, individuals implement their choice. Following induction, reformation takes place. *Reformation* occurs as the individual is introduced into a new group. The subsequent reception the person receives from the other group members is also a component of this phase. The final phase, *integration*, takes place as one becomes comfortable and familiar with the new group. As the newness of the transition wears off, satisfaction may be found when both the individual and the group accept each other.

   Tiedeman and O'Hara's process illustrates a reciprocal relationship between the individual's self-concept and environmental expectations. For example, interaction with others is an integral component of the adjusting-to-a-choice stage. Specifically, as people implement choices, they need to deal with others in order to carry out their decision.

Information System for Vocational Decisions (ISVD).   One of Tiedeman's more significant contributions to career development services was the creation of a computerized guidance system. Tiedeman (1970), along with some of his colleagues, developed the Information System for Vocational Decisions (ISVD) that embed a decision-making theory in a computer-based, career planning system. The purpose for the ISVD was to enable users to learn the decision-making theory through repetition and gaming, eventually incorporating the theory into their thinking. As one of the earliest developers of such a system, Tiedeman's contributions to the field should not be underestimated.

   Next, we will describe a *prescriptive* theory of career decision-making—the cognitive information processing (CIP) approach that illustrates an ideal way in which to make career decisions.

Cognitive Information Processing and the Pyramid Model

In the early 1980s a group of professors from Florida State University began to study how thought processes impact career decision-making. The team consisted of Gary Peterson, James Sampson, Robert Reardon, and Janet Lenz (1996). Their theory, the cognitive information processing (CIP) approach uses a pyramid to illustrate the essential areas of cognition involved in career decision-making.

The base in the **pyramid model** contains the knowledge domains of self-knowledge and occupational knowledge. This level is called the *cornerstone of career planning* (Reardon, Lenz, Sampson, & Peterson, 2000). The next level of the pyramid is the *decision-making skills* domain. This dimension is labeled the CASVE cycle (communication, analysis, synthesis, valuing, and execution) and includes information processing skills that are related to career problem solving and decision-making. The communication process begins when the individual receives input from within him/herself or from the environment. The person becomes aware of a problem and realizes that he or she needs to act on the information or make a decision. During the *analysis* phase, the individual examines the self-knowledge and occupational knowledge and then focuses and reflects on the causes of the problem. After the information is analyzed, courses of action are pursued. This process, called *synthesis,* involves two phases: elaboration and crystallization. Elaboration consists of identifying and brainstorming career problems. Crystallization involves identifying solutions to the career problems based on one's abilities, interests, and/or values. Following synthesis, the individual begins the *valuing* process where he or she evaluates possible actions or career directions and prioritizes each of the alternatives based on his or her value system. Following the valuing process, the individual identifies the best possible alternative.

The final domain, located at the top of the pyramid, is the *executive* processing domain that involves metacognitions where the individual becomes aware of how he or she thinks and acts. Peterson, et al. (1996) describes three key ways of thinking about decision-making: self-talk, self-awareness, and monitoring and control. *Self-talk* describes the positive and negative internal messages people give themselves about career decisions and other issues. *Self-awareness,* an essential element of effective problem solving, occurs when the individual becomes aware of what he or she is doing and why. At this time negative self-talk can be identified and altered. *Monitoring and control* explains the process of monitoring as the way one goes through the CASVE process while controlling how much time is given to each of the various stages and phases. The executive phase allows for the development of a step-by-step action plan that can be implemented, allowing the individual to achieve his or her career goal.

According to Sampson, Lenz, Reardon, and Peterson (1999), the pyramid model can provide a useful framework for helping professionals who deliver career services. Specifically, human service professionals can use each domain of the pyramid as a guide for delivering interventions. For example, the self-knowledge domain is addressed through the administration of various inventories. The occupational knowledge domain is attended to through informational interviewing. Decision-making skills are taught by using the CASVE model. Finally, the executive processing domain serves as a model for challenging the individual's destructive and unhealthy cognitions.

John Krumboltz: Social Learning Theory

Let us now shift our attention to theories based in learning. Social learning approaches are based on psychological research into the human learning process. We will present the Social Learning Theory of John Krumboltz because of its emphasis on the importance of behavior and cognitions on career decision-making.

Determinants of Career Choice

John Krumboltz believes that an individual's career development and career decisions are based on learned behaviors. Specifically, he believes that the key determinants of career choice and career development are genetic endowment, environmental conditions and events, learning experiences, and knowledge of task approach skills (Krumboltz, 1996).

Genetic Endowment.   Genetic endowment refers to the inherited or innate aspects of the person such as physical appearance, sex, eye color, skin color, hair color, and other characteristics. It also refers to the unique talents that result from the interaction of genetic factors and exposure to selected environmental events. Examples include athletic, musical, and artistic abilities.

Environmental Conditions.   Environmental conditions and events refer to factors that affect individuals but are generally outside their control. Examples include social, cultural, economic, and political forces. For example, according to Niles and Harris-Bowlsbey (2005), when women and men enter the workforce, sex-role stereotyping can limit women's opportunities for promotions. Specifically, women may be excluded from social networks often used by men to advance in their occupations.

Learning Experiences.   Learning experiences encompass both instrumental and associative learning experiences. *Instrumental learning experiences* consists of three components: antecedents, behaviors, and consequences. *Antecedents* refer to the type of condition, including genetic endowments, special abilities, environmental conditions, and problems and tasks. Individuals respond to the antecedent with either clear or subtle *behaviors*. These behaviors then lead to *consequences*, which can also be either obvious or understated.

To illustrate instrumental learning experiences, we will look at the case of Mario. Two months before Mario graduated from a human service program at a local college, he heard "through the grapevine" that an area agency would be expanding their services in a few months and would be hiring two, new helping professionals to assist with a new substance-abuse program. Mario had always been a good listener, empathic, and a competent communicator (genetic endowment, special abilities); however, he lacked knowledge and experience in working with the substance-abuse population. Realizing that he would not likely be granted an interview because of his inexperience and skill deficits, Mario decided to volunteer at his college, assisting with their substance-abuse prevention campaign (covert and overt action). Following his work on the campaign, Mario received a special recognition award from the program coordinator. As a result of this honor, Mario believed that he possessed the necessary skills and experience to be a component provider at the area social service agency (covert reactions to consequences). He then updated his resume and called the agency to setup an informational interview. The agency was so impressed with Mario's outstanding communication skills and with his initiative in seeking related experience that they offered him a position working in their new substance-abuse program (delayed consequence of the behavior).

Associative learning takes place when an individual pairs a previously neutral situation with one that is either positive or negative. Associative learning experiences are of two types, observation and classical conditioning. *Observation* takes place by observing others, for example watching a veterinarian work with a family pet. *Classical conditioning* occurs when one generalizes an event to an entire category of experiences. As an example of classical conditioning, a person went to the dentist for a routine cleaning and instead had an emergency root canal when the dentist discovered a cracked tooth. The person began to dread all subsequent routine dental appointments.

Task-Approach Skills. The final determinant of career choice and career development according to Krumboltz is the concept of task-approach skills. *Task-approach* skills describe how one approaches a particular task in regards to career decision-making. Skill components include goal setting, values, interests, clarifying skills, generating alternatives, and gathering occupational information. These skills greatly influence outcomes and are in fact outcomes themselves.

These four determinants shape the thoughts and beliefs people hold about themselves. However, the ways in which each individual develops beliefs and acts upon them differs from person to person. In general, there are four ways in which these factors impact career decision-making: (1) through self-observation generalizations about abilities, interests, and values, (2) through worldview generalizations, (3) through task-approach skills used in career choice, and (4) through the ensuing actions one takes.

Behavioral Techniques

Human service professionals can apply social learning theory in their interventions through a number of behavioral and cognitive techniques. Some behavioral techniques include reinforcement, role-playing, the use of role models, and using simulation.

Reinforcement. Positive reinforcement is used to increase the occurrence of a response. Helping professionals can provide clients with positive reinforcement of a career decision-making activity by showing appreciation and approval. This reinforcement can be very valuable to clients who value the expertise of the human service professional.

Role-Playing. Helpers may also use role-playing in which the professional plays the role of the client and the client plays the role of another person. This technique can be especially useful for practicing interviewing skills. Videotaped, mock interviews can be very valuable because they can provide a tangible means of evaluating the client's interviewing skills.

Role Models. Role models are valuable associative learning experiences for clients. Human service professionals can provide role models for their clients and also serve as positive role models. Role models can also assist with networking by discussing their occupations and recommending colleagues or others in the industry to meet with clients to discuss various career paths and options.

Simulation.   Clients can simulate a particular occupation by doing some of the occupational tasks that are involved in a specific job. Simulation can take place in high schools through specific courses, in vocational technical schools, and also through volunteer or part-time jobs.

Cognitive Techniques

Helping professionals can use a number of cognitive techniques to help their clients understand and change inaccurate thoughts and generalizations regarding career issues. A sampling of these strategies includes goal clarification, countering troublesome beliefs, and cognitive rehearsal.

Goal Clarification.   Krumboltz (1996) stresses the importance of goal clarification in career planning. Specifically he feels that goals must be clear and identifiable in order for individuals to learn essential skills and apply them to an array of career issues. Helpers can assist clients in breaking down goals into mini, short-term, intermediate, and long-term goals.

Counter Troublesome Beliefs.   Sometimes clients make inaccurate generalizations that may hinder their career development. Helping professionals can assist clients in countering troublesome beliefs through reframing. Consider this case: A father is having difficulty at work because of a recent custody battle he is having with his former spouse. The anger he is feeling towards "the system" is resulting in poor performance and productivity at his workplace. His supervisor has referred him to counseling. The client states to his counselor, "The family court system is gender biased. Father's never get custody of their children." The counselor can take this generalization and *reframe* it based on current research and respond, "Yes, although many mothers do obtain custody of their children, research shows that one out of six fathers is now gaining custody of their children. In fact, the single-father household is the fastest growing population in the United States." Countering troublesome beliefs can help clients to get "unstuck" and move forward in their career exploration.

Cognitive Rehearsal.   Once inaccurate generalizations are addressed, helpers can further assist their clients by practicing or rehearsing positive statements in order to dispute and replace more negative statements clients may have about themselves. Mental rehearsal of positive statements can be quite beneficial.

Planned Happenstance

In addition to the aforementioned dimensions of social learning theory, planned happenstance has played an ever-important role in the social learning theory of Krumboltz. Krumboltz (1996) believes that helping professionals should follow up with their clients as clients implement their job search or career transition. According to Krumboltz, at times clients will have to deal with new, unanticipated problems and concerns that may come about while following through on their plan of action. These unplanned or unforeseen events can include unpredictable educational conditions, social factors, and occupational conditions, to name a few. Mitchell, Levin, and Krumboltz (1999) recognize the important role these unintended events have in people's lives and feel that people need to take advantage of them. Capitalizing on these events is called *planned happenstance*. Helping professionals can assist their clients in identifying and incorporating these chance events into their lives. Planned happenstance theory is very upbeat and optimistic. It provides clients with opportunities to explore a number of different options. According to Mitchell and associates (1999), five skills are beneficial in working through chance career opportunities: curiosity, persistence, flexibility, optimism, and risk taking.

One of the major strengths of social learning theory is that it addresses specific ways in which environmental and individual variables influence career development. In addition, it offers a variety of behavioral and cognitive techniques that human service professionals may find helpful when working with clients' career concerns.

Emerging Theories

Recent attention has been placed on fresh, innovative theories of career development that depart from the theories previously mentioned. Three emerging theories will be presented here. We will first address the constructivist approach to career development. Next, we will direct our attention to a spiritual approach to work. Finally, we will look at a holistic model of career development.

Constructivist Theories

Constructivist approaches focus on subjective experiences and people's ability to construct their own reality. In other words, constructivists believe that people actively partake in the construction of what they observe. Constructivist approaches are based on early work of George Kelly (1955) and have since been adapted for use in career counseling. Constructivist career counseling is a broad, all encompassing form of life planning. R. Vance Peavy (n.d., 1992, 1994) has offered the following constructivist career counseling considerations:

Receptive Inquiry.   The counselor encourages inquiry into the client's life–world within a framework where the client feels simultaneously secure and challenged. Techniques include the use of artwork and objects to construct meaning-generating inquiries, symbolic transformations, autobiographical writing, and guided visualization.

Pattern Recognition.   The counselor and client work to recognize patterns of influence, especially significant relationships that are influential in shaping the client's thinking and acting.

Primacy of Life Experience.   The helping professional and client work directly with the client's life experience (i.e., perceptions and personal meanings that have been discovered through various self-revealing activities, including journaling, artwork, narratives, etc.). The constructivist helping professional is not concerned with initiating change but rather with influencing the direction of the client's evolving self.

Mindfulness.   Mindfulness is a valuable goal for the client and helping professional. The critical components of mindfulness include: (1) formation of new categories of constructs to aid in the interpretation of experiences, (2) expansion of receptivity to new internal and external information, and (3) recognition of more than one point of view on any part of one's life-world, including career. One of the key components of mindfulness is critical reflection (Peavy, 1994).

Creating Meaning Through Activity.   Work experience, **job shadowing,** volunteer work, and other such types of activities can provide the basis for personal meaning. The value of these activities is enhanced through *reflection-on-activity* and *discussion and dialogue* with the helping professional that influence both the evolving self and career decision-making.

Constructivist approaches to career counseling are helpful with clients who have considerable self-efficacy and who have aspirations to create broad, comprehensive, long-term plans (Amundson, Harris-Bowlsbey, & Niles, 2005). Its focus on clients' perceptions of reality sets this method apart from other theories of career development that tend to concentrate on objective means of assisting clients with career decision-making.

Spiritual Perspective of Career Choice

Spiritual approaches to career development emphasize the influence that people's spirit can have on their life, career choices, and the type of person they will become. Work is seen as a place in which one's spirit can be nourished and one can develop oneself (Sharf, 2002). Helpers should be aware that spiritual approaches to career development may or may not include a religious viewpoint. We will devote this section to Anna Miller-Tiedeman's (1988) Lifecareer® approach to career choice.

The Lifecareer® method views life as a process whereby a person can free up energy, gain a sense of balance and harmony, and focus on cooperating with approaching forces rather than worrying about finding a career. This perspective views living life as the "big career" and makes for a less stressful existence, which can boost the immune system (Miller-Tiedeman, n.d.). According to Miller-Tiedeman (n.d.) key concepts of Lifecareer® include the following:

- Career is viewed as life as opposed to a job.
- Each person is viewed as his or her own theorist who has the ability to ask his or her own questions and derive personally acceptable answers as opposed to depending on answers from those perceived as authority.
- The emphasis is on self-conceiving as opposed to self-concept theory.
- Individuals must cooperate with life as opposed to trying to control life.
- The whole of the person organizes the parts.

- The emphasis is on making a life and making a living as opposed to getting a job.
- One must respect decisions that do not work out as well as those that do.
- An individual's personal experiences guide choice.
- The career is lived in the moment and becomes the path that one leaves behind.

Miller-Tiedeman has written extensively on her concept of life as a process. The model and counseling approach is called *new careering* and is based on the principle of flow and uses as its foundation a wide range of theories including quantum physics, Bohm's notion of wholeness, and Self-Organizing Systems Theory (Miller-Tiedeman, 1999).

Human service professionals who choose to integrate the New-Careering model into their career work use a different approach compared with professionals who use traditional theoretical approaches. For example, New-Careering methods emphasize listening "with considerable pauses" as opposed to focusing on "quick solutions." In addition, New Careering does not emphasize the administration of a number of inventories and assessments, nor does it focus on the helper offering advice and opinions. The goal of this approach is to support and encourage experience-based learning (Miller-Tiedeman, 2002).

Duane Brown: Values-Based, Holistic Model of Career and Life-Role Choices and Satisfaction

Duane Brown's (2002) values-based model of career choice uses values as the foundation based partially on the premise that work values are essential elements in the career development process (Fouad, 1995; Super & Sverko, 1995). Brown defines values based on Rokeach's (1973) concept that values are cognitive structures with behavioral and affective dimensions. People experience values as principles that determine how the individual should function. Values that allow people to meet their needs in socially acceptable ways are shaped by individuals' cultural context. Therefore, Brown (2002) states that cultural and work values are the most important variables in occupational choice, satisfaction, and success.

In the original draft of his theory, Brown (1996) aimed only at those holding traditional Eurocentric values such as individualism, future-time orientation, activity orientation, and domination of nature. His more recent writings identify cultural values as important variables in career development and choice (Brown, 2002; Isaacson & Brown, 2000). In addition he believes that other factors, such as socioeconomic status (SES), family or group influence, history of discrimination, gender, and the mental health of the decision maker, to name a few, interact with values to influence occupational choice and the outcomes of the choice. Following are abbreviated versions of eight propositions that serve as the basis of his updated model (Brown, 2002):

1. For people with individualistic values, highly prioritized work values are the most important determinants of career choice. Some of the factors that limit occupational options for this group are low-socioeconomic status (SES), minority status, mental health concerns, gender, physical disabilities, and low scholastic aptitude. When options under consideration require varied skills and abilities, self-efficacy will hinder the career decision-making process for this population.

2. For people with collectivistic values, the career decision-making process will be heavily influenced by the wishes of the group or family. Gender will play a significant role in the decision-making process because of stereotyped perceptions of occupations by decision makers. Perceptions regarding discrimination and perceptions regarding available resources may limit the career decision-making process of individuals in this group.

3. Cultural values regarding activity (doing, being, being-in-becoming) will not limit the career decision-making process, when taken individually.

4. Men and women and people from differing cultural backgrounds will enter occupations at various rates.

5. Choosing a career is a process that involves a series of *estimates* including estimates regarding a person's ability and values, estimates regarding the skills and abilities required for success in a position, and estimates regarding the work values that the occupations being considered will satisfy.

6. Job-related skills and aptitudes, SES, participation in the work role, and the experience of discrimination will be related to one's occupational success.

7. Job tenure will be partially impacted by the match between the cultural and work values of the worker, supervisors, and coworkers.

8. Job satisfaction for people with *individualistic* social values, in order of importance, will be the similarity between the values reinforced on the job and individuals' work values, conflicts between career role and other life roles, and approval of work roles by significant others. Job satisfaction for individuals with *collectivistic* social values, in order of importance, will be the approval of work roles by significant others, conflicts between the career role and other life roles, and the similarity between the values reinforced on the job and individuals' work values.

Brown's theory fills a gap in the literature on vocational theories. Specifically, it helps to explain the vocational behavior of individuals based on their cultural-value systems. Human service professionals may find it helpful to use Brown's theory in conjunction with other theories.

Theoretical Integration

Human service professionals sometimes will benefit from combining various theories when providing career interventions to their clients. Theoretical integration, or the combining of theories, can be especially effective when providing group interventions. Some theories may not easily integrate with other theories. For example, constructivist approaches and social cognitive theories are not good matches for trait and factor, life-span, and career decision-making theories. However, a number of theories can be combined effectively. According to Sharf (2002), life-span, trait and factor, and career decision-making theories work well together. To better illustrate this notion, we will provide an example of a career decision-making program developed by Jill Jurgens to assist undecided college students with their career decision-making skills and to increase retention rates among the undecided student population. Although the program was developed for college students, it has been revised and used with a number of human service populations.

The Career Navigator Series was developed by Jurgens (2000, 2002) at the University of Cincinnati's Career Development Center (CDC). It is a comprehensive, six-stage intervention that combines both group and individual components. The program effectively integrates a number of theories based on guidelines outlined by Sharf (1997, 2002). Specifically, Sharf (2002) states that the theories most useful to college-age students and adults include those of Super, Holland, Myers-Briggs, Krumboltz, and Tiedeman and Miller-Tiedeman, with the DISCOVER program a career guidance and information system created by Act, Inc. used as a helpful adjunct to counseling. Based on Sharf's guidelines, these theories were integrated into the program.

The Career Navigator Series consists of six stages delivered to groups of 25 people. The program involves a number of group and individual interventions that extend over a five-week time span.

Stage 1 lasts approximately one hour and consists of a group information session that provides participants with an overview of the program and evaluates individuals on their readiness and commitment to participate in the series. During this stage, students are administered the Career Decision Scale (CDS) (Osipow, Carney, Winer, Yanico, & Koschier, 1976) and the Myers-Briggs Type Indicator (MBTI®). The results of the CDS and MBTI® are used in future stages.

Stage 2 consists of a two-hour decision-making workshop during which time students participate in a number of experiential activities aimed at informing and enlightening them on career decision-making theories and skills. Components of the workshop include a group cohesion exercise; information sharing on Holland's hexagon and the organization of occupations; knowledge regarding Krumboltz's social learning theory and Tiedeman and Miller-Tiedeman's career decision-making approach; a values exercise based on Super's theory; an interest activity based on Holland's theory; a tour of the Career Resource Library; and an introduction to the DISCOVER (1994) computerized guidance system.

Stage 3 is an individual intervention that allows participants to utilize the DISCOVER computerized guidance system for two hours. During this time, students complete a series of assessments regarding their interests, values, abilities, and experiences. Once the inventories are completed, participants use the system to find occupations to explore based on their assessment results. The final component of this stage allows students to get detailed information on occupations they choose to explore. Students receive hard copies of their computer activity, which they bring with them during Stage 4.

Stage 4 involves an individual, career counseling session. During this one-hour appointment, students meet with a career counselor and explore the results of the CDS, MBTI®, and the DISCOVER printout. The CDS assists the counselor in focusing the session on areas that appear to present the client with the most concerns. The MBTI® helps students determine possible fits between their personalities and the jobs they are considering. Next, the counselor and student review the DISCOVER printout and investigate similarities and differences between the MBTI® and the DISCOVER results. Afterwards, they discuss the next steps for planning and implementation based on career decision-making models. This portion of the session is individualized to meet the unique needs of each participant.

Stage 5 is a professional forum. This popular event provides participants with an opportunity to learn about possible careers by interacting with a variety of professionals in a roundtable format. Professionals are recruited from different settings with care taken to ensure that Holland's six personality/work environment categories are represented equally. During the forum, professionals rotate from table to table every 15 minutes, discussing their careers and fielding questions posed by the students. This format allows each and every student the opportunity to interact with all the professionals during the two-hour event.

Stage 6, the final stage, is a follow-up, individual career counseling session. During this last phase, students meet with their career counselor for a one-hour session to plan the next steps and/or to finalize their career decisions. Job-shadowing experiences, internships, informational interviews, and other helpful means of clarifying career choices are discussed.

The Career Navigator Series has been an effective intervention in increasing career certainty, decreasing career indecision, and increasing student retention in college (Jurgens, 2000, 2002). Human service professionals can easily adapt the program to meet the needs of their particular population. This program is a cost-effective way of reaching large numbers of clients within a limited time frame. Additionally, the group environment can help alleviate distress felt by participants who may believe their career concerns are isolated and unique to them.

Theoretical integration can be customized to meet the needs of an agency or organization. Even the most basic, cost-effective integration of theories may offer some relief to clients struggling with career-related issues (Jurgens, 2002).

Summary

Theories provide a conceptual framework that human service professionals can use with clients to guide interventions. Of the various theories of career development, we chose to present theories based on five broad categories—trait and type theories, developmental theories, career decision-making theories, social learning theories, and emerging theories. When selecting a theory, human service professionals must consider their own view and style of helping, have confidence in the theory, match the theory with the needs of the client, and select a theory that is somewhat manageable and easy to draw upon in the helping setting (Sharf, 2002). Many human service professionals likely will choose to be "technically eclectic." This choice allows them to remain theoretically grounded in one theory but able to choose interventions and techniques from various theories to match the needs of their clients. This approach allows helping professionals to be flexible and adaptable thereby enabling them to effectively meet the needs of their diverse client population.

Key Terms

Descriptive theories
Developmental theories
Job shadowing
Myers-Briggs® Type Theory
Prescriptive theories

Pyramid model
Trait
Trait and factor theory
Trait and type theory
Type or factor

Web Resources

Note that website URLs may change over time.

CPP, Inc. (formerly Consulting Psychologists Press)
http://www.cpp.com

Myers & Briggs Foundation
http://www.myersbriggs.org/index.cfm

New Careering Institute, Inc.
http://www.life-is-career.com/index.html

Self-Directed Search by Dr. John L. Holland
http://www.self-directed-search.com

3

Gathering Client Information

Career-Related Assessments

Choosing a career path, one of the most important decisions a person can make, involves the exploration of values, interests, skills, education, personality, financial needs, and aptitudes. The world of work changes daily with new careers appearing while others vanish. As careers appear and disappear, the human service professional's task of helping others navigate through the multiple career choices becomes increasingly complex. Human service professionals are responsible for knowing which assessments they are ethically allowed to administer, which assessments are appropriate for use in what circumstances, how to administer the assessments, and how to interpret them. But why bother administering assessments? People know what they want to do for a living, right? Wrong.

In an ideal world people are exposed to a variety of career paths or **occupations** beginning at birth. They know exactly what interests them, what types of education or skills are necessary to enter their career choice or **avocation,** and how to develop a plan to achieve their goal.

While this path may be true for a select few, many people have absolutely no idea what career path to pursue and even less idea of what education and training are necessary for a specific career. Individuals often base career choice on the career fields in which relatives or friends may be employed or even on happenstance, taking the first job they can find. Again, this approach may work for a few people, but many people quickly become dissatisfied with their jobs without knowing why. A clash between the dissatisfied individual and the workplace—a clash among values, interests, skills, education requirements, personalities, financial needs, and/or aptitudes is likely happening. To avoid these clashes, human service workers need to understand the art of using assessments to help their clients become more successful in the world of work.

People can avoid clashes in the workplace by doing a better job in choosing a career. Many of the clients with whom human service professionals work are unaware of the basis of these clashes, but they know that they are not happy with their jobs, are unable to find jobs that interest them or meet their needs, or are unable to perform their jobs well. Without the knowledge of what to change and how to change it, people may continue to make the same unhappy mistakes, wondering why they cannot seem to get ahead and dreading having to go to work everyday. By using career-related **inventories** and **assessments** human service professionals can help clients ameliorate these clashes while empowering them to make better decisions about the world of work, their careers, and how their personal attributes fit into their careers.

The purpose of this chapter is to provide an overview of several career-related inventories and assessments that can be administered by entry-level human service professionals. These assessments include the traditional paper-and-pencil inventories, online inventories, and **card sorts.** Some assessments work best in an individual setting, others in group or classroom settings. This overview includes a description of each instrument, along with the instrument's purpose, intended population, and required reading levels. In Part II of this book we will detail how the professional can select and combine the various types of inventories into a battery of assessments for use with specific populations.

Career-Related Assessments and Inventories

This chapter presents five different types of assessments/**tests** and inventories that are used in career development: ability tests, interest inventories, personality tests, values inventories, and career-development inventories. Each type will be explained in further detail as the chapter progresses. The professional qualifications required to administer assessments and inventories vary.

Qualification Levels

In accordance with the Standards for Educational and Psychological Testing (American Educational Research Association, 1999), many assessments are sold only to professionals who are appropriately trained to administer, score, and interpret such tests and inventories. Eligibility to purchase materials is based on education, training, and experience. Following are the standards' qualification levels used to purchase, administer, and interpret assessments:

Qualifications Level: A.   No special qualifications are required. Assessments with this qualifications level have no educational requirements for administration.

Qualifications Level: B.   To administer assessments with this qualification level, human service professionals need a bachelor's degree in counseling, psychology, social work, or a closely related field from an accredited 4-year college or university *plus* satisfactory completion of coursework in test interpretation, psychometrics and measurement theory, educational statistics, or a closely related area; *or* license or certification from an agency that requires appropriate training and experience in the ethical and competent use of psychological tests.

Qualifications Level: C.   To administer assessments with this qualifications level, the human service professional needs to meet all qualifications for Qualification Level

B *plus* an advanced professional degree (i.e., master's or doctoral degree) that provides appropriate training in the administration and interpretation of psychological tests; *or* license or certification from an agency that requires appropriate training and experience in the ethical and competent use of psychological tests.

New purchasers may need to establish their qualifications level with a company before they are allowed to purchase the tests and inventories. Human service professionals need to contact that company for additional information. We have provided qualification levels for the assessments and inventories mentioned in this chapter when they are available. The majority of the assessments included here are available for use by human service professionals meeting the requirements for a Level A Qualification.

Ability Tests

Ability tests measure how able an individual is to learn or succeed at a particular task and often include several different sections that measuring a separate ability. They can also predict how someone is likely to perform in a training program or on a job and often identify someone's strongest areas along with those that need improvement.

Ability Explorer (AE).   The Ability Explorer (Harrington & Harrington, 1996) explores 14 work-related abilities used in job performance to provide an overall score of performance self-ratings. Based on the Guide for Occupational Exploration (GOE) literature, this assessment includes ability areas not often measured by traditional aptitude batteries (artistic, clerical, interpersonal, language, leadership, manual, musical/dramatic, numerical/mathematical, organizational, persuasive, scientific, social, spatial, and technical/mechanical) and can be group-administered and self-scored. This assessment is designed for use with middle-school students through adults who are reading on a fifth-grade level. Qualifications Level: A.

Career Key.   The Career Key (Jones & Jones, 2000) is an internet-based career assessment that provides informational links to job descriptions as part of the actual assessment. The inventory contains five checklists including job appeal, interests, skills, how individuals see themselves, and values. After the computer calculates the scores, individuals see a list of occupations that fit their scores along with web links to information from the *Occupational Outlook Handbook* (U.S. Department of Labor, n. d.). This assessment is designed for use with middle-school aged individuals through adults. Qualifications Level: Not specified.

Motivated Skills Card Sort.   This card sort developed by Knowdell (2002a) contains 48 skill cards that are sorted twice into eight categories to help pinpoint the functional-transferable skills that are central to clients' career satisfaction and success. This assessment helps clients identify their motivation to use these skills and to identify the skills that they feel would be useful to develop or improve along with the ones that they need to emphasize. The card sort includes a worksheet package that takes clients through a series of activities designed to help them apply what they have learned to develop a career direction. These activities are self-directed, but easily lend themselves to supervision by a human service professional for additional discussion and **career exploration.** Qualifications Level: A.

O*NET Ability Profiler. One part of the O*NET Career Exploration Tools, the Ability Profiler (O*NET Consortium, 2003) uses a paper-and-pencil or **objective test** to help individuals identify their strengths and the areas in which they might want to receive additional training. It also identifies occupations that fit their strengths. This assessment measures nine job-related abilities (verbal ability, arithmetic reasoning, computation, spatial ability, form perception, clerical perception, motor coordination, finger dexterity, and manual dexterity) that can be linked to over 900 occupations in O*NET On-line (O*NET Consortium, 2003). An administrator's training manual that provides guidelines for workshop preparation and assessment administration is available on-line through the O*NET Resource Center. Qualifications Level: A.

WorkKeys. Developed by ACT, Inc. (1993), WorkKeys is a **criterion-referenced** test that assesses workplace skill levels in ten areas: reading for information, applied math, business writing, writing, locating information, teamwork, observation, listening, applied technology, and readiness. Each area's assessment is available in one or more formats, ranging from pencil-and-paper to computer-based to audiovisual. Several are available in Spanish. WorkKeys also provides a job analysis to determine the level of skills required for competency in a specific job, instructional support to teach and enhance these skills, and a research and reporting system that links assessments with job profiles. Employers use WorkKeys to identify and develop workers for a variety of skilled jobs. Computer and online training modules tied in with the WorkKeys are available through many two- and four-year colleges, One-Stop Career Centers, Workforce Investment Act (WIA) centers, and school-to-work consortiums. In order to determine readiness to take these assessments, a person must complete the WorkKeys Readiness Assessment (ACT, 2002), which establishes whether or not an individual possesses the necessary skills to complete additional assessments. Human service professionals need a WorkKeys Proficiency Certificate issued by ACT to administer the assessments.

Interest Inventories

Interest inventories have no right or wrong answers, but they help to identify the interests of a person as the interests pertain to the world of work. These inventories assist in identifying training, education, or careers that contain job duties that might interest an individual.

Career Exploration Inventory 2 (CEI 2). In a 12-panel foldout, the Career Exploration Inventory 2 (Liptak, 2002b) allows unemployed youths and adults on a seventh-grade reading level an opportunity to explore and plan their work, leisure activities, and education or learning. Users consider their past, present, and future activities with regard to 120 activity statements. Completion of the assessment results in a graph that divides the responses into 15 clusters. The CEI then folds out to show scores on the assessment and related occupations from the *Occupational Outlook Handbook* (OOH), typical leisure activities, related education and training, and related GOE interest areas and workgroups. This assessment is available in three formats:

pencil-and paper in English, pencil-and-paper in Spanish, and online. Human service workers can also purchase a workshop manual with a script and reproducible overhead/handout masters. Qualifications Level: A.

CareerExplorer CD-ROM.   The CareerExplorer CD-ROM (JIST Works, 2004) combines information from the Occupational Outlook Handbook (OOH) and the Guide for Occupational Exploration (GOE) and presents it as an interest inventory that takes the user directly to job information. The inventory includes 250 occupations divided into interest groups. Users answer the same sequence of questions for each group. Screens gradually take the user into more depth and eventually rank potential jobs on a scale of 0 to 4, displaying the 20 best matches. Designed for use with high-school students through adults, CareerExplorer requires Windows 95 or newer. It is available as a CD-ROM, in a lab pack of 10 CD-ROMS. It requires a CD-ROM site license. Qualifications Level: A.

Guide for Occupational Exploration Interest Inventory (GOEII).   Organized around GOE, the GOEII (Farr, 2002) matches the interests of a person to 250 OOH and to over 800 O*NET job titles. Rather than rating items, this inventory asks which of the 14 GOE interest areas has the most appeal to the individual. Available in a pencil-and-paper format, the GOEII is used with high-school students through adults who read on at least an eighth-grade level. Qualifications Level: A.

Leisure to Occupations Connection Search (LOCS).   This inventory (McDaniels & Mullins, 1999) has individuals rate their levels of activity and skills in 100 leisure activities. It then provides lists of related occupations for each activity to help connect individuals to the jobs on which they want more information. This inventory is used with displaced homemakers, youth, welfare-to-work clients, and retired/older workers who read on at least a sixth-grade level. Qualifications Level: A.

Occupational Interests Card Sort.   The Occupational Interests Card Sort (Knowdell, 2002b) contains 110 occupational cards that help individuals quickly identify and rank their occupational interests. Users are able to clarify their high-appeal jobs and careers along with their degree of readiness and the skills and education needed. Used in an individual or a group setting, these cards provide several activities to help users clarify their career interests. Qualifications Level: A.

O*NET Career Interests Inventory.   The O*NET Career Interests Inventory (JIST Works, 2002a) is a shorter version of the U.S. Department of Labor's O*NET Interest Profiler (O*NET Consortium, n.d.). In order to explore the most closely related occupations, this paper-and-pencil inventory asks individuals to indicate whether they like or dislike 180 activities. It is designed to help them identify their work-related interests, what they consider important on the job, and their abilities. The scores identify career areas that match their interests while leading them to specific jobs for exploration. This inventory is used with high-school students through adults who read on at least a ninth-grade level. Qualifications Level: A.

O*NET Interests Profiler. The O*NET Interest Profiler (O*NET Consortium, n.d.), is part of the O*NET Career Exploration Tools. This tool is available in both a paper-and-pencil and a computerized format. It is designed to help individuals discover types of work related to their interests according to Holland's (1985a) hexagonal structure. Designed to be self-administered and self-interpreted, it links directly to over 900 jobs in O*NET On-Line (O*NET Consortium, n.d.). Qualifications Level: A.

Retirement Activities Card Sort. The Retirement Activities Card Sort Kit (Knowdell, 1998b) provides 48 cards containing common pastimes and their descriptions to aid people in the transition from formal employment to a meaningful retirement lifestyle. Used to determine current frequency as well as preferred activity patterns, these cards are a resource for organizational preplanning retirement programs. Qualifications Level: Not specified.

Self-Directed Search (SDS) Form E, Form E Audiotape, Form R, CP. All of the SDS inventories are based on Holland's (1985a) theory that both people and environments fall into six basic types: realistic, investigative, artistic, social, enterprising, and conventional. The inventories have been recently updated to include technology-related jobs. The SDS Form E (Holland, 1996a) contains 198 items to assess career interests among individuals with low-reading levels. The assessment booklet is written at a sixth-grade reading level, and the directions are at a fourth-grade level, and it is printed in larger type for easier reading. This inventory has been revised to more closely reflect the interests of individuals at lower-reading levels. The SDS Form E is also available in Spanish for Spanish-speaking individuals or those with limited reading skills in English and in an English Canadian format that lists jobs with their matching National Occupational Code (NOC) and required level of training. The SDS Form E Audiotape (Holland, 1996b) provides the same items as Form E, but it is designed for those with limited reading skills or those who might benefit from an audio presentation of the administration booklet. A seven-second delay in the audio following each item allows time for the individual to mark each response in the Form E administration booklet. The SDS Form R (Holland, 1994) is the standard version that assesses career interests in high school students, college students, and adults. This version is also available in a computer-based format as well as in an online format. The SDS Form CP (Holland, 1990) assesses long-term career planning for those on a career-development track. It focuses on the needs of individuals who aim for greater levels of professional responsibility. All forms of SDS are designed for individual or group administration. Qualifications Level: A.

Transition-to-Work Inventory. A new inventory written by Liptak (2004), the Transition-to-Work Inventory matches people's interests to job options by assessing their level of interest in 84 leisure activities. The inventory leads to information on many job titles, related employment and training, and self-employment options. The Transition-to-Work Inventory can be used in paper-and-pencil format or online. It can be used with students in school-to-work programs, clients in welfare-to-work programs, ex-offenders in incarceration-to-work programs, people returning to the workforce, clients in rehabilitation-to-work programs, and people with little or no work experience. Qualifications Level: A.

Voc-Tech Quick Screener.   The VTQS (JIST Works, 2002c) is a self-assessment inventory designed for use with those who do not feel that postsecondary education is right for them. The Screener helps individuals match their interests and goals with jobs for which they can train in a short period of time. Qualifications Level: A.

Wide Range Interest & Occupation Test (WRIOT2).   The WRIOT2 (Glutting & Wilkinson, 2003) contains 238 full-color pictures of occupations, along with Holland-type scales and occupational scales. Individuals decide whether they like, dislike, or are undetermined about each pictured occupation. Reponses are then either keyed into the computer or recorded on a response sheet. This inventory can be administered individually or in groups. This assessment is useful when working with nonreaders, non-English speakers, people with learning disabilities, individuals who are mentally challenged, and individuals who are deaf. Qualifications Level: Not specified.

Personality Inventories

Personality inventories identify an individual's personal style in dealing with people, tasks, and events. Understanding one's personality can help a person make decisions regarding training and education, along with specific careers.

Keirsey Temperament Sorter II.   The Keirsey Temperament Sorter II (Keirsey, 1998) provides 70 forced-choice (a or b) statements with no right or wrong answers. It presents an indication of personality and is based on the assumptions that people are fundamentally different and one instinct is no more important than another. The Sorter is available online through the Keirsey Temperament Sorter II website and in print (Keirsey, 1998). The online version generates two reports: the Classic Temperament Report and the Career Temperament Report. Both versions provide scores leading to 1 of 16 possible Myers-Briggs profiles. Qualifications Level: Not specified.

Vocational Preference Inventory (VPI).   The VPI (Holland, 1985b) contains 160 occupations representing the six types of Holland's theory of personality as well as five additional dimensions. The test-taker records occupational preferences in an all-in-one test booklet/answer sheet that the human service professional then scores. This inventory is used with adults and older adolescents in an individualized setting. Qualifications Level: B.

Values Inventories

Values inventories allow individuals to identify what they value in a job (i.e., responsibility, organization, honesty, support, working conditions). Once those values have been identified, the inventories lead individuals to possible jobs of interest based on the similarity between their values and the values of a specific job.

Career Values Card Sort.   The Career Values Card Sort (Knowdell, 1998a) helps users prioritize their values in five minutes. These cards include 41 values of work satisfaction (i.e., time freedom, job tranquility, creative expression, work under pressure, power, technical competence) that are sorted into 5 categories. Users are able to define factors that affect their career satisfaction, define the intensity of their feelings about these factors, and determine areas of value conflict and congruence. This card sort may be used either in individual or group settings. Qualifications Level: Not specified.

***O*NET Career Values Inventory.**   The O*NET Career Values Inventory (JIST Works, 2002b), based on O*NET Work Importance Locator and Profiler (O*NET Consortium, n. d.), uses 20 cards containing work-value statements that are sorted by the degree of importance of the value. The resulting six major work-value scores identify career groups that include these values, pinpointing specific jobs to explore. This assessment is used with high-school students through adults who are reading on a ninth-grade level. Qualifications Level: A.

***O*NET Work Importance Locator and Profiler.**   Another component of the O*NET Career Exploration Tools, the O*NET Work Importance Locator and Profiler (O*NET Consortium, n. d.) measures six work values (achievement, independence, recognition, relationships, support, and working conditions) and is self-administered and self-interpreted. Results from this assessment link directly to over 900 occupations through O*NET Online. Qualifications Level: A.

***Values-Driven Work Card Sort.**   The Values-Driven Work Card Sort (Career Action Center, n. d.) contains 70 color-coded cards that are sorted into four categories according to the importance of that value in a working situation. The user then records the top 10 values on a worksheet and completes several activities designed to clarify values, focus on organizational values, and explore work-group values. This card sort is also available in an online version. It is designed for use with college students, job seekers, company employees, people changing careers, reentry clients, and those nearing retirement. Qualifications Level: Not specified.

***Work Orientation and Values Survey (WOVS).**   This survey (Brady, 2002) identifies key work values by having individuals rate 32 statements as they related to importance in the individuals' jobs. The score is divided into eight work-values categories: earnings and benefits, working conditions, time orientation, task orientation, mission orientation, coworker relations, supervisor relations, and managing others. The WOVS provides suggestions for incorporating high-scoring values into career plans and balancing value conflicts. This assessment is used with high-school students and adults who are unhappy in their jobs or seeking a more satisfying work environment. Qualifications Level: A.

Career Development Inventories

Career development inventories measure characteristics that could interfere with an individual's personal growth. Such aspects include, but are not limited to, faulty beliefs that interfere with decision-making, levels of dysfunctional thinking, anxiety, and **career maturity**.

Barriers to Employment Success Inventory (BESI).   This inventory (Liptak, 2002a) identifies key barriers to getting and succeeding on a job. Categories of barriers include personal, physical and psychological, career planning, job-seeking skills, and education and training. This assessment also identifies for immediate intervention or referrals those with low self-esteem and substance abuse while human service professionals identify their clients' problems and develop action plans to overcome those barriers. Self-scored and self-interpreted, it may be used in group or individual settings with adults, teens, job seekers, those planning careers, displaced workers, and workers who quit shortly after being hired. It is written on an eighth-grade reading level and is available in paper-and-pencil format and online. Qualifications Level: A.

Career Attitudes and Strategies Inventory (CASI).   This inventory (Holland & Gottfredson, 1994) contains 130 items that survey nine aspects of career or work adaptation: job satisfaction, interpersonal abuse, work involvement, family commitment, skill development, risk-taking style, dominant style, geographical barriers, and career worries. Self-administered and self-scored, this assessment assesses the likelihood of job stability and clarifies situations that may lead to career problems in an adult population. Qualifications Level: A.

Career Beliefs Inventory (CBI).   The CBI (Krumboltz, 1991) helps clients identify faulty beliefs that interfere with career decision-making. This inventory provides 96 items for rating on a 5-point scale. The results are then reported using 25 scales, each representing a theme important to decision-making. Interpretive information provides suggestions for helping individuals overcome their barriers, along with information on how to strengthen individuals' values that are not barriers. The CBI is designed for use with eighth-grade students through adults, including those who are planning a future career, making a career transition, planning a recovery from being laid-off, reacting to job burnout, or planning retirement. Qualifications Level: A.

Career Decision Scale (CDS).   The CDS (Osipow, Carney, Winer, Yanico, & Koschier, 1987) measures career indecision and identifies career decision-making difficulties. Individuals respond to 18 items using a 4-point scale; the last item is an open-ended question that allows individuals to add any information they feel would be helpful. The responses result in a Certainty Scale Score and an Indecision Scale Score. The CDS can be used as a pretest and posttest for program evaluation purposes. It is designed for use with high-school and college students. Qualifications Level: B.

Career Thoughts Inventory (CTI).   The CTI (Sampson, Peterson, Lenz, & Saunders, 1996) contains 48 items on a 4-point scale yielding a total score that indicates negative thinking in career problem solving and decision-making. Using three construct scales, this instrument measures decision-making confusion, commitment anxiety, and external conflict. The accompanying workbook helps individuals to understand the nature of their negative thoughts in an effort to help them challenge and alter specific thoughts. This assessment is designed for use with high-school students, college students, and adults. Qualifications Level: B.

Career Transitions Inventory (CTI).   The CTI (Heppner, 1991, 1998) contains 40 items on a 6-point scale that assess the psychological barriers as well as resources of adults in career transition. Factors assessed include career motivation or readiness, confidence, perceived support, internal/external control, and independence/interdependence. Qualifications Level: Not specified.

Job Search Attitude Inventory (JSAI).   The JSAI (Liptak, 2002c) assesses how motivated a person is likely to be in finding a job, determines who is most likely to benefit from services, and who needs additional services or referrals. It is useful as both a pretest and posttest to measure the effectiveness of career development programs, and it fosters self-directed attitudes and behaviors. Individuals using this inventory agree or disagree with 32 statements that are then self-scored and graphed into 4 categories: (1) luck versus planning, (2) involved versus uninvolved, (3) self-directed versus other-directed, and (4) active versus passive. The JSAI is useful with convicted offenders, welfare-to-work clients, and youth who read on at least a seventh-grade level. It can be administered in either paper-and-pencil format or in an online version. Qualifications Level: A.

My Vocational Situation (MVS).   The MVS (Holland, Daiger, & Power, 1980) is a two-page questionnaire that diagnoses difficulties in vocational decision-making. It helps determine whether a lack of vocational identity, a lack of information or training, and emotional or personal barriers are causing a problem in career decision-making. Qualifications Level: A.

Overcoming Barriers Card Sort Game Kit.   The Overcoming Barriers Card Sort Kit (Harney & Angel, 1999) contains over 140 barrier cards that are sorted into 6 areas of employer needs. This kit is designed to help hard-to-serve job seekers identify potential barriers to promotion and keeping a job while they learn to think like the employer in an effort to overcome these barriers. Clients chronicle their card-sort results in a journal, creating their own plan to overcome these barriers (E. E. Harney, personal communication, June 24, 2004). Qualifications Level: Not specified.

Reading-Free Vocational Interest Inventory: 2 (R-FVCII: 2).   The R-FVCII: 2 (Becker, 2000) uses pictures of individuals engaged in different occupations to measure the likes or dislikes of students and adults with mental retardation or individuals who are learning disabled, disadvantaged, or enrolled in alternative or vocational/career training programs. The interest categories include contemporary occupational tasks of jobs at the unskilled, semiskilled, and skilled levels. The R-FVCII: 2 can be used in individual or group settings. Qualifications Level: B.

Salient Beliefs Review: Connecting Spirit to Work (SBR).   The SBR (Bloch, 2003) helps individuals to identify beliefs important to work satisfaction by rating 28 statements. Their responses allow them to compare their beliefs to their behaviors and to the policies and practices of the organizations where they work or have worked. Employers may use SBR to identify problem behaviors, increase workplace satisfaction, and reduce stress and burnout. It is used with adults with part-time or full-time work experience in an organization, with those who are self-employed, and those with volunteer or limited work experience. Qualifications Level: A.

Vocational Exploration and Insight Kit (VEIK).   The VEIK (Holland et al., 1980) includes an eight-page Action Plan Workbook that contains a variety of activities to complete over several sessions. One activity is the Vocational Card Sort where 84 cards are sorted into 3 categories. Additional activities are based on the responses in the card sort. This kit is designed for use with highly motivated students or adults who seek additional career guidance beyond that provided by SDS, Form R. The VEIK is used with people who have a difficult time making decisions or completing paper-and-pencil inventories, because it helps them clarify the number of occupations for further consideration while helping them explore the relationships between past experiences and present vocational goals. Qualification Level: A.

Miscellaneous Tools

Some tools do not fit under such headings as ability tests, interest inventories, personality tests, values inventories, and career development inventories. Several other tools that can be used in career development work follow.

Elevations® Manual Card Sort System.   The Elevations® System (Scully, 2003) contains four card sorts and a workbook, designed for use in a wide variety of settings. Written on a seventh-grade reading level, this system can be used in both individual and group career sessions and contains values, personality, career interest, skills, career research, and action planning components. An online version is also available for use in career centers and One-Stop Career Centers. Qualification Level: A.

Career Genograms.   Career Genograms are created in the same way as other **genograms,** with the addition of each person's career. By creating a career genogram, a type of **projective test,** an individual is able to explore possible barriers and family career messages while creating a bond with the human service professional. This type of assessment can be completed on a piece of newsprint or on a chalkboard while allowing individuals to consider a variety of work-related topics. Such topics include, but are not limited to, the impact of work on various family members; career aspirations of family members for themselves and for the individual; family-work choice/behavior patterns; work-related values; imbalances in learning, work, and playing; vocational patterns; and overt/covert messages about work and education (Gysbers, Heppner, & Johnson, 2003). Qualifications Level: Not specified.

Individual Employment Plan (IEP).   The IEP (Ludden & Maitlen, 2002) is a six-step plan used for **intake** and documentation of the participant's progress. It is not intended as a diagnostic tool. In Step 1, the human service helper records participant information, including personal information and work history. In Step 2, the human service helper documents assessment information for the participant, including the results from all assessments used. After listing assessment results, the helper provides assessment outcomes and a list of recommended services, including justification for the services and the steps the participant will take to achieve self-sufficiency. Steps 3 and 4 use the 84-question employability assessment that rates each item as an asset or a liability. The questions are divided into seven categories: (1) personal issues and considerations, (2) health and physical considerations, (3) work orientations, (4) career and life planning skills, (5) job-seeking skills, (6) job adaptation skills, and (7) education and training. In Step 5, the helper and participant develop a detailed training and services plan. In Step 6, the helper summarizes the participant's progress in four separate meetings. The ISP is designed for use with Workforce Investment Act program participants, welfare-to-work clients, rehabilitation clients, and company outplacement. Qualifications Level: A.

Vocational Decision-Making Interview (VDMI). The VDMI (Czerlinsky & Chandler, 1999) is a structured personal interview to evaluate the client's vocational decision-making skills and job readiness. This interview uses three scales (decision-making readiness, employment readiness, and self-appraisal) to help identify areas that need attention. Interviewers are strongly advised to use the *Vocational Decision-Making Interview Administration Manual* (Chandler & Czerlinsky, 1999) when administering and interpreting the VDMI. This interview is used with clients with low-reading skills, learning disabilities, sight limitations or blindness, mental retardation, chronic mental illness, brain injuries, and sensory disabilities. Qualifications Level: Not specified.

Combining Assessment Results: Now What Do I Do?

A client comes in for career assistance and the human service professional has a wealth of materials from which to choose in selecting the battery of assessments for the client. Now what? How do they choose? How many different assessments and inventories do they administer? When do they do this?

We do not want to imply that human service professionals need to give every client every assessment, nor do we want to imply that clients' issues should be compartmentalized into interests, barriers, and so on. Instead, human service professionals need to view clients in a more holistic manner, seeing how all of the parts fit together to create an accurate picture of each client and his or her needs. Zunker and Osborn (2000) suggest a five-step approach when doing career work with clients. In step 1, the human service professional needs to analyze the clients' needs. What interests the clients? Why? How committed are they to a specific job field? What activities do the clients enjoy? What do the clients need to go further in the employment arena? Gathering this information will help the human service professional choose which assessments/inventories to administer. Step 2 is that of establishing a reason for clients to complete any assessments or inventories. Unless clients understand why the testing is being done, they may be less likely to complete a test or even to accept its results. In step 3 the human service professional determines the instrument that will be most useful. Several factors will go into making this choice—reading level, background, and basic conversations with the client. Choosing the instrument that will most benefit the client should be the main consideration.

After the instrument has been chosen and completed, it is time for the professional helper to use the actual results. In step 4, the human service professional needs to review the results prior to the client's arrival and be ready to explore those results with the client. During this exploration, the client may agree to other assessments or inventories, so steps 3 and 4 may be repeated as necessary. In step 5, the client makes a decision. Armed with the knowledge provided by the assessments and/or inventories combined with discussions with the human service professional, the client now decides where to go next in his or her journey.

Gysbers, Heppner, and Johnson (2003) suggest ten criteria to follow when choosing an instrument: **reliability,** cost, time for administration, client response to the instrument, training needed for scoring, scoring difficulty, norms, training needed for interpretations, and usefulness of the instrument to the client. Examining an instrument's **validity** allows the human service professional to determine how well the instrument measures what it claims to measure—when an instrument indicates an individual has certain interests or values, for example, how accurate is that indication? Human service professionals also need to compare the populations on which the instrument is normed (**norm-referenced** tests/assessments) to their clients to determine how valid the instrument will be with these clients. How accurate are the instrument's results over time? If an instrument indicates that an individual has interests in one area one week and in a complete different area the following week, the reliability of the assessment may be a concern. Whether or not the instrument is a **standardized assessment** is an important consideration. Instrument cost, the time needed for administration, the ease of scoring and reporting results, along with the need for additional training for assessment interpretation also affect instrument choice.

Each population chapter in Part II contains a section on how to use assessments with specific clients along with case studies demonstrating their use.

Ethical and Professional Issues

Several ethical issues need to be addressed with regards to testing: informed consent, the use of human subjects, and the proper interpretation and use of test data (AERA, 1999). *Informed consent* involves clients' right to know the purpose and nature of all aspects of their involvement with the human service professional. Clients have the right to know the general purposes of the research in which they are involved as well as how any tests or assessments they are taking are going to be used. Except in special cases, clients also have the right to refuse to take part in any testing and research. Ethical standards and legislation guiding the use of *human subjects* puts restraints on research that might cause physical or psychological harm. Ethical guidelines often limit the amount of deception allowed in the use of research. Federal legislation requires that all organizations that conduct research supported by federal funds have a human subjects committee or institutional review board. *Proper interpretation and use of test data* requires that human service professionals carefully read the results of test reports and consult with experts in the field in order to understand how such data can best serve their clients. Human service professionals also need to understand that testing, also referred to as assessment, is only one small aspect of a broader analysis of the individual. Whenever important decisions are being made, the human service professional should undertake a careful assessment that is reliable, valid, and cross-culturally fair.

When human service professionals use tests and assessments inappropriately (i.e., requiring a series of tests that are unnecessary, using an assessment that does not meet the needs of the client), clients may not receive the assistance they truly need and deserve. To be useful, tests/assessments best serve the client when the test results are used to *enhance* career development. Reliance on assessment results alone or administering assessments that do not match the needs of the client can push clients into careers they neither fit nor want. Healy (1990) suggests that rather than relying entirely upon assessment results, career development practitioners need to collaborate with their clients, listening carefully to client self-assessment while encouraging clients to further develop their self-assessment skills. Human service professionals must use assessments judiciously and only with client consent and after full disclosure of the testing procedures, testing purpose, and any associated costs.

Human service professionals also need to take care when purchasing assessments, being sure to purchase only from credible resources. Counterfeit assessments may have names similar to the original assessment, making identification of the desired assessment difficult. Some assessments may have been validated in one format but not in another format, possibly reducing the usefulness of the assessment results. While the assessment sources given in this chapter are not the only reputable assessment sources available, they are appropriate sources worthy of consideration for assessment choice.

Summary

Choosing a career path is one of the most important decisions people make over their lifetime. Due to the constant changes in careers, the task for human service professionals of helping others navigate through the multiple career choices is becoming increasingly complex. As such, human service professionals need to understand the art of using assessments to help their clients become more successful in the world of work by avoiding clashes among values, interests, skills, education requirements, personalities, financial needs, and/or attitudes. Human service professionals are responsible for knowing which assessments they are ethically allowed to administer, which assessments are appropriate for use in what circumstances, how to administer the assessments, and how to interpret them. This chapter presents five different types of tests and inventories that are used in career development: ability tests, interest inventories, personality tests, values inventories, and career development inventories. Ability tests measure how able an individual is to learn or succeed at a particular task. They can be used to predict how well someone is likely to perform in a training program or on a job, and they often identify a person's strongest areas along with those that need improving. Interest inventories help to identify an individual's interests as they pertain to the world of work by identifying training, education, or careers that contain job duties that might interest the individual. Personality inventories identify an individual's personal style in dealing with people, tasks, and events, assisting the client in making decisions regarding training and education, along with specific careers. Values inventories allow individuals to identify what they value in a job (i.e., responsibility, organization, honesty, support, working conditions), thus leading to possible jobs of interest based on the similarity between the individual's values and the values of that job. Career development inventories measure those characteristics that could interfere with an individual's personal growth. Such characteristics include, but are not limited to, faulty beliefs that interfere with decision-making, levels of dysfunctional thinking, anxiety, and career maturity. Still other nonassessment tools can be used in the career development process with clients. Human service professionals should take care not to administer too many assessments and/or inventories. In addition, they must match those tools according to the needs of the clients, following ethical standards and legislative guidelines. More information on the tools' appropriateness for use with each population is detailed in Part II.

Key Terms

Assessments
Avocation
Battery of assessments
Card sort
Career exploration
Career maturity
Criterion-referenced
Genogram
Intake

Inventory
Norm-referenced
Objective test/Assessment
Occupation
Projective test/Assessment
Reliability
Standardized assessment
Test
Validity

Web Resources

Note that website URLs may change over time.

Career-Related Assessments
Assessments can be purchased through the following websites.

ACT
http://www.act/org

WorkKeys
http://www.act.org/workkeys

Career Action Center
http://www.careeraction.org
• Values-Driven Work Card Sort

Career Key
http://www.careerkey.org

CareerTrainer
http://www.careertrainer.com
• Career Values Card Sort
• Motivated Skills Card Sort

• Occupational Interests Card Sort
• Retirement Activities Card Sort Kit

CPP
http://www.cpp.com
• Career Beliefs Inventory (CBI)
• My Vocational Situation (MVS)

JIST Works
http://www.jist.com
• Barriers to Employment Success Inventory (BESI)
• Career Exploration Inventory: A Guide for Exploring Work (CEI)
• CareerExplorer CD-ROM
• Guide for Occupational Exploration Interest Inventory (GOEII)
• Individual Employment Plan (IEP)
• Job Search Attitude Inventory (JSAI)

- Leisure to Occupations Connection Search (LOCS)
- O*NET Career Interests Inventory
- O*NET Career Values Inventory
- Salient Beliefs Review (SBR)
- Transition-to-Work Inventory
- Vocational Decision-Making Interview (VDMI)
- Voc-Tech Quick Screener (VTQS)
- Work Orientation and Values Survey (WOVS)

Keirsey Temperament Web Site
http://keirsey.com/pumII.html
- Please Understand Me II (Keirsey Temperament Sorter)

O*NET Career Exploration Tools
http://online.onetcenter.org
- O*NET Ability Profiler
- O*NET Interest Profiler
- O*NET Work Importance Locator and Profiler

Prodigy Press
http://www.prodigypress.com
- Values-Driven Work Card Sort

Psychological Assessment Resources, Inc.
http://www.parinc.com
- Career Attitudes and Strategies Inventory (CASI)
- Career Decision Scale (CDS)
- Career Thoughts Inventory (CTI)
- My Vocational Situation (MVS)

- Reading-Free Vocational Interest Inventory: 2 (R-FVII: 2)
- Self-Directed Search (SDS) Form CP
- Self-Directed Search (SDS) Form E
- Self-Directed Search (SDS) Form E Audiotape
- Self-Directed Search (SDS) Form R
- Vocational Preference Inventory

Wide Range
http://www.widerange.com
- Wide Range Interest & Occupation Test (WRIOT2)

Worknet Training Center
http://www.worknettraining.com
- Overcoming Barriers Card Sort Game Kit

Other Web Resources

Association for Computer-Based Systems for Career Information
http://www.acsi.org

Ethical Standards for Internet On-line Counseling
http://www.counseling/org

Guidelines for the Use of the Internet for the Provision of Career Information and Planning Services
http://www.ncda.org/about/polnet.html

National Career Development Association
http://www.ncada.org

4

Career Information Sources and Resources

When assisting clients with career development concerns, human service professionals are often charged with providing quality career information and resources to their clients. Occupational information is plentiful, and the variety of resources available is great. Helping professionals must not only be aware of occupational trends, for example, but they must also know where to acquire occupational information and know how to assess the quality of the information. Good career decisions require good career information. In other words, a career decision is only as good as the quality of information provided. In this chapter we will focus on some of the most popular sources and resources of career information, including print and online resources, computer-assisted career guidance systems, informational interviews, job shadowing experiences, and One-Stop Career Centers. Finally, we address tips and guidelines for evaluating the quality of occupational information. Our focus on print and online resources, gives particular attention to some of the leading publications of occupational information.

Print and Online Resources

Occupational information is compiled, published, and distributed by a number of organizations and companies. We have chosen to provide some of the most popular sources of print and online occupational information by grouping them into logical categories: government sources, commercial publishers, private publishers, professional societies/trade associations/labor unions, educational institutions, organizations for specific groups, and magazine articles. First, we will cover one of the main sources of occupational information, the United States government.

U.S. Government Sources

The United States Government is one of the premier sources of occupational information and publishes many materials critical to human service professionals who provide career interventions to their clients. Some of the main departments that publish important occupational information include the Department of Labor, the Department of Commerce, the Department of Defense, the Department of the Interior, and the Office of Personnel Management. First we will focus on three of the major resources published through the Department of Labor, and then we will provide an overview of additional sources of occupational information provided by some of the other governmental departments.

The U.S. Department of Labor publishes numerous resources that provide important occupational information to human service professionals and to their clients. In addition to salary surveys and a number of online job banks, the agency authors the **O*NET® system,** a database that replaced the Dictionary of Occupational Titles (DOT), and the **Occupational Outlook Handbook (OOH).** It also provides information found in the **Guide for Occupational Exploration (GOE).**

O*NET®.   The O*NET® system is a comprehensive system developed for the U.S. Department of Labor by the National O*NET® Consortium (n.d.). The system contains the O*NET® database, O*NET® On-Line, and O*NET® Career Exploration Tools. O*NET® overrides information published by its predecessor, the Dictionary of Occupational Titles (DOT) and is available both online and through a number of private and public sector publications.

O*NET® Database.   The O*NET® database provides current information and skill requirements on approximately 1000 occupations. The database is updated twice a year. Descriptors are given for tasks, knowledge, skills, abilities, work activities, work context, job zone, interests, work values, work needs, related occupations, and wages and employment. Occupational titles and codes are based on the Standard Occupational Classification System (SOC) that allows the occupational information contained in the O*NET® database to be linked to additional labor information. The SOC classifies workers at four levels: major group, minor group, broad occupation, and detailed occupation. Each occupation is designated with a six-digit code with a hyphen placed between the second and third digit for reader clarity. The first two digits of the code represent the major group. The third digit represents the minor group. Digits four and five represent the broad occupation. The sixth digit represents the detailed occupation. In addition to these six digits, O*NET® adds a two-digit extension that begins with "01" and is sequentially numbered, to differentiate unique O*NET® occupations within the SOC system.

O*NET® OnLine.   O*NET® OnLine provides public access to O*NET® information through a web-based viewer. It has a built-in screen reader capability, allowing readers to adjust the font size of text. In addition it links directly to wage and occupational outlook information via America's Career InfoNet.

The O*NET® Career Exploration Tools.   Individuals using the O*NET® Career Exploration Tools will find a variety of assessments to assist them in identifying interests and abilities that will allow them to explore occupations matching their attributes. The

Career Exploration Tools include the O*NET® Interest Profiler, the O*NET® Work Importance Locator and Work Importance Profiler, and the O*NET® Ability Profiler. Assessments are available either in print or online. You can refer to Chapter 3 of this text for detailed information on a number of assessment instruments.

Occupational Outlook Handbook (OOH).   The *Occupational Outlook Handbook* (OOH) is a publication of the U.S. Bureau of Labor Statistics (2004a) that is revised every two years. It is available either online or in a print version. The handbook provides information on over 250 broad types of occupations that are grouped into 11 different clusters of related occupations. The 11 clusters include: management, professional and related occupations, service, sales, administrative support, farming and related occupations, construction, installation and related occupations, production, transportation, and job opportunities in the armed forces. For each occupation, the OOH provides information in a standard format, for the following categories:

- *Nature of the Work.* This section describes the duties and tasks of the workers, tools and/or equipment used in the work, and information regarding the degree and type of supervision found in the occupation.

- *Working Conditions.* This section includes the typical hours worked; the environment of the workplace; any physical activities required, including the possibility of injury; special equipment used; and travel requirements, if any.

- *Employment.* This section identifies the number of jobs reported in an occupation along with the major industries where the jobs are found. If significant, the number or percentage of self-employed workers in the field is reported.

- *Training, Other Qualifications, and Advancement.* Major sources of education and training are described in this section including the amount of education and training needed and preferred by employers as well as advancement prospects.

- *Job Outlook.* Included in this section are job projections, including factors that will likely result in employment growth or decline. The projections are given for a ten-year time span. Projected changes in employment for each occupation are described using the following phrases: grow much faster than average, grow faster than average, grow about as fast as average, grow more slowly than average, little or no growth, and decline.

- *Earnings.* This section identifies the typical earnings and usual means of compensation (i.e., annual salary, hourly wages, commission, bonuses, etc.).

- *Related Occupations.* Similar occupations with related tasks, duties, skills, education, and training are listed in this section.

- *Sources of Additional Information.* Contact information including addresses, phone numbers, and Internet addresses for organizations, associations, and agencies that can provide further information are listed.

A supplemental publication to the OOH, is the *Occupational Outlook Quarterly* (OOQ) (U.S. Bureau of Labor Statistics, 2004b). The OOQ, available in print and online, provides the latest projections on occupations covered in the OOH along with a variety of job-related articles.

Guide for Occupational Exploration (GOE).   The GOE was first written and published by the U.S. Department of Labor and is now published by JIST Works (Farr, Ludden, & Shatkin, 2001). The GOE is in its third edition and reflects the first major revision of this publication in over twenty years. In Part 1 of the GOE, nearly 1000 occupations are categorized into 14 interest areas and 83 work groups. These occupations represent 95 percent of the job market. Part 2 contains job descriptions, including information on compensation, projected growth rate, education and/or training needed, values, skills, and working conditions. Part 3 includes crosswalks to careers that provide cross-references to jobs that best match users work values, activities, school courses, skills, and other identifiers. The current edition of the GOE is based on information found in the O*NET® system.

Additional career information can be found through the Department of Commerce, the Department of Defense, and the Office of Personnel Management. The Department of Commerce supplies information regarding business and commerce. One of its most important publications is the *Standard Occupational Classification Manual.* This manual provides a unified classification system that is used by a variety of state and federal agencies. The Department of Defense publishes numerous brochures, documents, and handbooks related to career opportunities in the armed forces. The Office of Personnel Management provides information regarding jobs and careers in the federal government. This list of government sources is by no means all inclusive. Almost every branch of the government can provide helpful and useful occupational information, many at no cost.

Commercial Publishers

Hundreds of career publications are available through commercial publishers. The range of resources available includes: comprehensive career encyclopedias; series of career books; books on majors; materials and programs for individual or group career interventions arranged by age groups and/or grade levels; resources for special populations; and information on career instruments and assessments. A sampling of these publications include:

- *Opportunities in* . . . series, which contains over 100 books for grades 9 through adults, is published by VGM.
- *Career Opportunities in* . . . series, which contains 16 volumes, is published by Impact Publications.
- *Careers for You* . . . series, which contains over 40 titles, each with catchy and appealing titles, is published by VGM.
- *Encyclopedia of Careers and Vocational Guidance*, a four-volume set for grades 9 and up, is published by Ferguson.

Private Companies

Human service professionals can obtain occupational information from a wide variety of private companies and industries. This information is available in a range of formats including brochures, books, pamphlets, videos, DVDs, CD-ROMs, and company websites. Because some of the information is published to benefit the business or industry (i.e., as a recruitment tool), the information may be highly biased and subjective and offer only a glamorized view of the occupation or company. For this reason, helping professionals should use care in evaluating this type of occupational information.

Professional Societies, Trade Associations, and Labor Unions

Many professional societies, trade associations, and labor unions publish material geared towards the unique interests and needs of their members. These publications can provide valuable career information, but they must also be viewed critically because of their possible biases. Of the literally thousands of professional societies, a mere sampling of the titles include the National Organization for Human Services, the American Counseling Association, American Advertising Federation, National Academic Advising Association, National Association of Broadcasters, National Environmental Health Association, and The Nature Conservatory. Many of these associations publish professional journals that report on research studies as well as best practices. The information can be invaluable to helping professionals.

Trade associations are also abundant. The Federation of International Trade Associations is a valuable directory to over 7000 international trade associations. Other helpful resources include the World Trade Centers Association and the Directory of Associations.

Although declining in numbers over the past few decades, labor unions remain a vital source of occupational information. Some of the most recognized labor unions include the United Mine Workers, the United Steel Workers of America, and the American Federation of Teachers. The federation of America's unions, the AFL–CIO, provides leadership and guidance to over 13,000,000 union workers in 60 member unions in America. This organization publishes a number of resources with union information including their online publication, *America@work.*

Educational Institutions

Universities, colleges, vocational schools, colleges of technology, and other educational institutions regularly publish information about their programs of study. Some of the information available through these sources includes admission requirements, courses and programs offered, certificates and degrees awarded, cost, financial aid possibilities, size of the institution, location, modes of delivery of programs (i.e., on-site, distance learning), and graduation and placement rates. Interested individuals can obtain information by contacting directly specific educational institutions or by searching the countless directories of educational institutions available on the World Wide Web.

Organizations for Specific Groups

Helping professionals can obtain information on career planning, education, training, and/or job opportunities for specific groups from various organizations that serve particular populations. Examples include the National Organization on Disability, the State Vocational Rehabilitation Agency, the National Council on the Aging, the National Federation of the Blind, the Department of Labor's Veteran's Employment and Training Service, Job Accommodation Network, and the Department of Labor's Women's Bureau. Another valuable resource is the U.S. Equal Employment Opportunity Commission (EEOC) that provides information on laws and regulations regarding workplace discrimination and offers a variety of training seminars and outreach services. All of the aforementioned organizations have websites.

Magazine Articles

Popular magazines are yet another source of printed information. The writing style of many of the feature articles makes this medium popular with many clients. Articles relevant to career options are often human-interest stories that use vivid and colorful language to describe a personal story. Some magazines have regular columns regarding the world of work, which are often written by experts in the field. Some periodicals that may offer occupational information include: *Black Collegian, Popular Mechanics, Psychology Today, Southern Living, Sports Illustrated, Fortune, Fitness, Time, Computer Graphics World, and Cooks Illustrated.*

Computer-Assisted Career Guidance Systems

Human service professionals can use **computer-assisted career guidance (CACG) systems** to help their clients with career-related concerns by increasing self-awareness, providing occupational and educational information, and assisting with career decision-making skills. The CACGs vary in both content and process, and human service professionals need to educate themselves on the various systems available in order to determine the best match for their clients' needs. In the following sections, we provide information on five such systems: Career Information System (CIS), Choices, DISCOVER®, System of Interactive Guidance and Information (SIGI PLUS®), and Virginia Career VIEW.

Career Information System (CIS)

The Career Information System (CIS) was developed in the College of Education at the University of Oregon (2003a). It is a comprehensive system that delivers national and localized information about occupations, employment, education and training to both students and adults. Over 7,000 schools and state agencies currently use CIS. It is the leader in state-based systems and is the basis for the career information delivery systems in fifteen states (University of Oregon, 2003b). CIS Operators (those licensed to use the CIS products) choose components from the system that best match the needs of their schools or agencies. Components of CIS include: content, exploration modules, delivery systems, documentation and writing guidelines, support materials, and utility software (University of Oregon, 2003c).

Content.   CIS content includes: databases with national information on occupations, occupation profiles, programs of study and training, schools, financial aid, job search, self-employment, keeping a job, and military employment. In addition it provides parallel databases for maintaining local information.

Exploration Modules.   CIS exploration modules allow users to sort information based on individual's needs, preferences, and abilities. Examples of exploration modules in CIS are the Occupation Sort, School Sort, Financial Aid Sort, and the IDEAS and Interest Profiler interest inventories. In addition users can connect results from other inventories to the CIS content by utilizing the Assessment Link. Results of the exploration can be saved via the CIS Portfolio.

Delivery Systems.   Users can access CIS through computers via computer software. It is currently available in three versions: Windows, Macintosh, and on the Internet.

Documentation and Writing Guides.   CIS documentation includes printed and on-line research papers and technical documentation on the use of the databases and software. In addition, writing guides are available that describe data sources, information analysis methods, and writing-style standards.

Support Materials.   On-line and printed user guides, teacher and counselor resources, and curriculum materials for use with the CIS Delivery Systems are also available. Support materials use graphics and illustrations to walk users through the various components of the system.

Utility Software.   Access Databases, Excel spreadsheets, and Word documents are converted into the CIS Delivery Systems through CIS Utility Software.

In 1999, National CIS changed its name to *intoCAREERS* (University of Oregon, 2003a). To date, it remains a unit within the College of Education at the University of Oregon where intoCAREERS works in collaboration with stakeholders in program development and direction.

Choices®

Choices® is one of the most widely used Career Information Delivery Systems. Bridges Transitions Inc., a Canada-based provider of career information services, training, and self-directed career and educational products and services, created the system (Bridges Transitions Inc., 2004a). Two versions are available: Choices®, geared towards high school to postsecondary users, and Choices® Explorer, designed for the middle-school to high-school student population (Bridges Transitions Inc., 2004b).

Choices® includes a variety of inventories such as the Basic Skills Survey, the Interest Profiler, and the Work Importance Locator. It contains information on colleges, technical schools, graduate schools, and occupations, including more than 200 career videos. It has as a financial aid search, an electronic portfolio, job-search activities, a resume builder and letter writer, and a customizable system manager. The network-ready software aligns to state and national career development standards. The system is also available in an online version. Choices® Planner is the Internet Version of Choices® (Bridges Transitions Inc., 2004b).

Choices® Explorer, designed for middle-school to high-school students, is an online, comprehensive career exploration system that allows users to explore college majors and future work. It contains a Career Finder that offers self-assessments of interests and skills and a Major Finder that guides students to the college majors in which they are interested. Additional features include peer written articles with interactive features, magazine-style articles, lesson plans, parent guides, and a student planner (Bridges Transitions Company, 2004b).

DISCOVER®

DISCOVER® is a career guidance and information system created by ACT, Inc. (2004)—a private, not-for-profit organization most widely known for its national college-entrance testing program. It combines a researched-based developmental guidance model with multiple delivery options. It is available in two separate versions—one for middle schools and the other for high schools, colleges, and adults.

The middle-school version is an Internet delivery-based program that uses photos, slide shows, and audio. It allows individuals to log-on at school and/or at home thereby enabling both parents/guardians and counselors to be involved in the process. Students learn about themselves by completing two separate inventories, the UNI-ACT Interest Inventory (for grades 6–9) and the Inventory for Work-Related Abilities (for grades 8–9). Once students complete the inventories, they are scored and the program suggests career areas for exploration. Students can also enter scores from other inventories that the program uses to propose career possibilities. Once students receive their lists of possible career options, the program enables them to explore a range of careers and occupations and obtain comprehensive information about the various careers of interest. With this information, they can begin preparing for their transition to high school by completing a customizable high school planner.

The version of DISCOVER® for high schools, colleges, and adults is available in both an Internet platform and a Windows® format on CD-ROM. This version provides the following features:

- Online and paper assessments of individuals' interests, values, and abilities
- The World-of Work map that organizes information about occupations into six clusters based on Holland's Hexagon
- Detailed information about hundreds of occupations in the current U.S. labor market
- A searchable file on majors, programs of study, and other educational options

- A school database that enables users to identify schools that match their interests
- A searchable financial aid/scholarship sources database (Windows® version only) that provides an estimate of federal eligibility
- Information on job search strategies, including resume and cover letter writing and interviewing skills
- Administrator reports that monitor and track individuals' career plans

DISCOVER® is available from licensed schools, businesses, organizations, and agencies for use with their students and/or clients.

System of Interactive Guidance and Information (SIGI PLUS®)

SIGI PLUS ® educational and career-planning software is a program for high-school students, college students, and adults that is based on the research of Educational Testing Service (ETS) (2004). The program is available via Windows® and the Internet and is licensed to institutions, states, One-Stop Career Centers, libraries, community-based organizations, and other such sites. This interactive system allows users to

- Evaluate work-related values, interests, and skills
- Create and search a list of occupations based on values, interests, and work skills, tech-prep clusters in high school (also referred to as 2 + 2 because it combines the last two years of high school with two years of community or technical college), and major fields of study in college
- Acquire up-to-date information and printouts on hundreds of occupations
- Evaluate different career options to determine best fit
- Determine education and training requirements for various occupational prospects
- Put career plans into action through goal-setting guidelines and job search skills

Individuals can complete the entire program or use portions of the program to obtain the information they need.

Virginia Career VIEW

Virginia Career VIEW (Vital Information for Education and Work) is the career information system for the Commonwealth of Virginia that provides information about educational and career opportunities (Virginia Department of Education, 2004). The online system is separated into four modules: careers, education, activity center, and professionals.

The career module contains interest assessments, career information, planning resources, and Internet resources and links. The education module provides classroom learning activities, educational and financial aid searches, practice tests, an online library, and career-information links. The activity center provides a wide range of

TABLE 4.1 *Virginia Career VIEW Modules*

Careers	Education	Activity Center	Professionals
Grades K–5	Grades K–5	Grades K–5	Software downloads
Grades 6–8	Grades 6–8	Grades 6–8	Publication downloads
Grades 9–12	Grades 9–12	Grades 9–12	Professional services
Adult	Adult		Guidance resources
			Bookstore

activities developed for each age bracket. The professional module allows users to download software and publications, access guidance information, checkout information from the resource library, and register for professional workshops. Each of the four modules is subsequently divided into subcategories as illustrated in Table 4.1.

Virginia Career VIEW is informative and free of charge for all students in Virginia. In addition, many of the resources and activities are available at no cost to the general public.

Informational Interviewing

Informational interviewing is the ultimate networking tool. It involves spending time with a professional in a highly focused conversation in order to gain valuable information that an individual can use to successfully choose or refine a career direction. Informational interviewing is different from a job interview. Where the purpose of a job interview is to land a new job, **informational interviewing** allows the client to conduct a screening process of the career and setting before applying for a job. Because of the exploratory nature of informational interviewing, candidates who are just beginning to explore career options find it especially helpful; however, the networking power of this process can certainly be beneficial to a wide variety of job seekers. Human service professionals need to share the many benefits of informational interviewing with their clients. Some of the many benefits include:

- *Network Building.* Informational interviewing provides clients with an opportunity to network with people in various career fields thereby allowing them to start or add to an existing network. In addition, **networking** helps clients gain important visibility.

- *Perspective Taking.* Informational interviewing gives clients an opportunity to learn about the skills needed to be successful in a given occupation. This information is often very up-to-date and allows clients to see how they may fit into a particular job.

- *Hidden Job Market Revelations.* This tool helps clients uncover the hidden job market, that is, those opportunities not advertised.

- *Professional Development.* Informational interviewing helps clients learn of the important skills needed for particular jobs. This crucial information can empower clients to obtain the needed education and skills in order to become an impressive job candidate.

- *Confidence Builder.* Unlike job interviews that are often anxiety provoking, informational interviewing is a more low-key process that allows clients to gain important confidence in their own interviewing skills. It can serve as an excellent dress rehearsal for the real thing.

In addition to sharing the benefits of informational interviewing with clients, human service professionals must teach the following "how to" steps to their clients.

- *Step 1: Assess.* Conduct a thorough assessment of your skills, interests, values, and abilities in order to identify occupations that may be a good fit for you. Research carefully the occupations of interest to you to learn as much about the field as possible prior to setting up the informational interview.

- *Step 2: Identify.* Identify people you would like to interview based on the assessment results obtained from Step 1. Some of the numerous means of identifying people to interview include talking with friends, family members, neighbors, teachers, and current or former employers. You can also find contacts through local schools, the phone book, Chamber of Commerce directories, and through a search of company and organization websites. You can find additional sources at local colleges through their Alumni offices or through their career development centers.

- *Step 3: Research.* Once you have identified a person to contact, research the company or organization meticulously. The more information you obtain about the occupation and organization, the better able you will be to formulate questions relevant to the company or position. Check for information in local newspapers, periodicals, and on company-sponsored websites.

- *Step 4: Prepare.* Prepare a list of questions that are important and appropriate to you. Questions that are important to you will convey your enthusiasm and motivation for the position and career. Possible questions you might ask include:

  - Describe a typical day at your job. What types of problems do you deal with? What are your typical duties, tasks, and responsibilities? How is your time divided among your various responsibilities?
  - How did you get started in this job? How did you prepare for it?
  - What was it about this type of work that interested you?
  - What do you most like about your job? What do you least like about it?
  - What personal satisfactions do you gain from this job?
  - What made you decide to work for this company/organization? What do you like most about this company/organization? What do you least like about this company/organization? Describe the working environment of this company/organization.
  - What is your outlook or opinion regarding the future of your job? What is your outlook or opinion regarding the future of this company/organization?
  - What are some of the changes that are occurring in this field?

- What are the advancement possibilities in this occupation? Describe your own professional development.
- What is the typical salary range for this occupation? (Do not ask contacts to disclose their salary, just the average compensation for the position.)
- Can you suggest ways for a person to obtain the experience needed to work in this field? What ways can an individual best prepare for this job?
- What advice do you have for someone interested in this field?
- Would you mind looking over my resume in order to assess my qualifications for entering this field? (Be sure to bring an updated copy of your resume with you.)
- Would you recommend another person that I can contact in order to get additional information about this occupation?

- *Step 5: Schedule.* Make contact with the individual you are interested in interviewing. A phone call or letter sent directly to the person is recommended. Be clear why you would like to meet with the person. The person you have contacted must understand that you are requesting an informational interview only, and your objective is not to secure a job. If the person trusts your motives, you will have a better opportunity of obtaining an informational interview. Be flexible with your schedule, and let the person know that you will only need 20–30 minutes for the interview. Most people are extremely busy, but they are willing to share some of their time if the time commitment is not great. After you schedule a date and time for the interview, follow-up with a letter to the person verifying and confirming the date and time.

- *Step 6: Interview.* Arrive at the interview 10–15 minutes a head of time. This first impression is critical, and arriving late can leave a negative impression of you. Be polite, friendly, and focus the interview on the person's career and the career field. Choose 10–15 questions to ask, and be respectful of the person's busy schedule. Do not take more time than you allotted. Be a good listener. Show that you are interested in the information that is being shared with you. When the interview is complete, leave a copy of your resume with the person and ask for the person's business card. This contact information will be necessary in order to send the person a thank-you letter. Thank-you letters should be well written and sent within 48 hours of the informational interview. The contact information can also be used to keep the person informed of your professional development.

- *Step 7: Evaluate.* Following the interview, document and analyze the information you have gathered. Be objective about what you have learned but be aware of personal feelings. Consult with other sources in order to verify your information. Ask yourself these questions: What have I learned? How does this job match my dream job? What information do I still need about the job? What is my plan of action?

Informational interviewing is a productive and helpful tool in acquiring occupational information and in establishing or strengthening a career network. Helping professionals would serve their clients well by teaching this valuable information-gathering tool to their clients. Although not previously mentioned, informational interviewing has been known to lead to job interviews and offers. Speaking from experience, my first graduate assistantship was acquired through informational interviewing, and two of my classmates subsequently received job offers through the informational interviewing process.

Job Shadowing

Human service professionals can introduce their clients to job shadowing experiences as a means of gathering valuable information regarding the real life, day-to-day activities involved in certain jobs. Through **job shadowing,** clients can discover whether or not they might enjoy certain jobs by observing the work environment, occupational skills, duties, and potential career options that come along with the job. Job shadowing involves individuals walking through a workday (or other period of time) as a shadow to a competent worker. The experience is temporary and unpaid, but it provides exposure to a work setting in a career area of interest to the client. Since job shadowing involves observation only, work skills are not acquired, which is perhaps one of the limitations of this option. However, it is a beneficial means of increasing career awareness.

Human service professionals can find job-shadowing opportunities by contacting businesses and organizations of interest directly. At times informational interviewing can lead to job-shadowing experiences. Many other prospects can be found on the Internet including "virtual job-shadowing" programs. In addition to providing information on where to find job-shadowing experiences, human service professionals should also share job-shadowing tips and guidelines with their clients in order to make the experience a positive one for all parties involved. Some of the tips include:

- If applicable, you should complete any application forms and/or essays and have a neatly prepared resume available.
- Many businesses have extremely busy schedules. Make sure you allow enough time to make any needed arrangements and be flexible. Call a day or two ahead of the scheduled visit in order to confirm the arrangement.
- Learn as much as you can about the company prior to the job-shadowing experience so you can ask well-thought-out questions during the experience. Individuals who ask well-thought-out questions during the job-shadowing experience have a better chance of being remembered favorably by the professional.
- Arrive at the shadowing experience on time and dressed professionally. Ask beforehand about dress code and other company policies that may affect your visit.
- Exercise business etiquette skills. Be polite and professional. Remember your host/hostess is doing you a favor.
- Customer privacy is very important, and you may be limited to where you can go and what you can see. Be mindful and respectful of this.
- During the shadowing experience, you can ask questions, however, you should spend the majority of time observing and listening.

- Even if you do not like the work or the professional you are shadowing, remain positive and pleasant. Although you might decide the job is not for you, you can still develop some valuable and important contacts.
- Always follow up each experience will a well-written thank you note to the professional whom you shadowed. This note should be sent within forty-eight hours from the experience.

The list of benefits from job-shadowing experiences is daunting. In addition to providing relevant career information, it is also a valuable networking tool whereby clients can strengthen their career networks of working professionals. Perhaps one of the greatest outcomes of this experience is the occasional job offer. Although this outcome is infrequent, it nonetheless has happened to quite a number of individuals. As you can see, job-shadowing experiences can be a wonderful way to motivate clients into reaching their career goals.

One-Stop Career Centers

One-Stop Career Centers, also known as CareerOneStop, is an amalgamation of Internet resources, job banks, and service providers located throughout the United States. CareerOneStop is a collection of electronic tools for job seekers, employers, and the workforce community. It operates as a federal–state partnership and is funded by grants to states. CareerOneStop is accessed through the Internet and includes the following components:

- *America's Job Bank.* This database allows job seekers to post their resumes and search for job openings. Job postings are updated daily and the existing database has over one million positions posted. Job seekers can search for a job using a list of job categories, entering keywords, and selecting a location. Employers can post job listings, customize their job orders, set up an automated search of potential candidates, and search through the database of over 400,000 resumes.

- *America's Career InfoNet.* This web-based program has an extensive online career resource library offering information on salary and wages, employment trends, occupational requirements, state demographic and economic information, as well as over 450 career videos.

- *America's Service Locator.* The service locator is a comprehensive database of service providers available through the Internet or by phone. The locator also directs the public to a wide range of services available in their locale such as job training, unemployment benefits, educational opportunities, programs for individuals with disabilities, seminars, and other job-related services.

One-Stop Career Centers offer valuable resources for human service professionals to assist them in providing career interventions. Numerous presentation notes and brochures are available for helping professionals that can make them more knowledgeable resources for their clients. Some of the resources available include: information on trends in workforce development; Federal initiatives; One-Stop staff competencies needed to implement One-Stop Career Centers and the Workforce Investment Act (WIA); and labor market information.

Evaluating Occupational Information

Knowing what type of occupational information is available and where to find it is not sufficient information for human service professionals. They must also know how to evaluate the quality of the information gathered and be able to share these criteria with their clients. In evaluating occupational information, we find it helpful to keep in mind the acronym ACCURATE. Occupational information should be *A*ccurate, *C*omparable, *C*redited, *U*nbiased, *R*elevant, *A*mple, *T*imely, and *E*xplicable.

Accurate occupational information is correct, real, reliable, valid, verifiable, and factual. It must contain concrete facts. It should be based on empirical data that can be validated through comparison with other sources. Accurate information is essential to career decision-making and planning. According to the National Career Development Association (NCDA) (1991), occupational information should be free from distortion caused by self-serving bias, sex bias, or out-of-date resources.

Comparable career information is organized in a consistent manner. Material presented in a uniform format will ease the comparison and contrast of the various types of information gathered.

Occupational information should be *credited*. Who wrote the information? Who published the information? Who sponsored the information? Occupational information should include answers to these questions along with applicable references.

Occupational information should be *unbiased*. It should neither encourage nor discourage individuals from selecting a specific field. What motivation is behind the information being produced and distributed? If it is for self-serving purposes, that is if the individual or organization has a vested interest in the decisions of the individuals receiving the information, the material is *biased* and should be viewed with caution.

Information should be *relevant* to the individuals who use the information to make career decisions. According to NCDA (1991) guidelines, occupational information should specify its intended audience such as elementary schools, high schools, colleges and universities, rehabilitation agencies, libraries, or other audiences. It should help reduce a person's uncertainty about a career by providing meaningful information to assist with career decision-making and planning. In addition, occupational information should be relevant to the locale of the readers. Therefore information should include state and local conditions.

Ample information is comprehensive. It includes all the important types of information essential for evaluating an occupational prospect. According to guidelines provided by NCDA (1991) with respect to content, occupational information should include:

- The duties and nature of the work including the purpose and importance of the work
- The work setting, conditions, and environment

- The preparation required for entry into the occupation
- Special requirements or considerations necessary for entrance into the occupation such as physical requirements, licensing/certification, personal criteria, and social and psychological factors
- Methods of entry and/or preferred avenues of entry into the occupation; current data on earnings and other benefits; the typical and optional advancement possibilities; the short- and long-range employment outlook
- Opportunities for experience and exploration including part-time work, internships, apprenticeships, cooperative work experiences, and volunteer options
- Occupations sharing similar requirements and attributes
- Additional sources of information such as professional associations, books, journals, and audiovisual materials

Timely career information is current, up-to-date, and applicable to the present time. Old information should be replaced with new information. According to NCDA (1991), to stay current information should be revised at least every three to four years. Although some occupational information such as some unskilled and semiskilled fields changes slowly, others such as many technical and skilled occupations change rapidly. You should check publication dates on information and view any information over five years old with caution.

Individuals accessing occupational information must be able to understand it before they can use it. *Explicable* career literature is easy to read and easy to comprehend. Because occupational information can sometimes be dry and dull, it should be presented in such a way that makes it interesting to the reader. Information should be unambiguous and data should be clearly explained and converted into words.

The breadth of occupational information is seemingly endless. However, much of the information may be of limited value to our clients. The ACCURATE acronym can serve as a valuable guide for helping professionals as they assist their clients in evaluating the appropriateness and value of career information used in decision-making and planning.

Summary

Human service professionals must be cognizant of the types and numerous sources of occupational information available for their use. Career information is available in a number of formats including print copies, Internet websites, videos, and through the individuals themselves. No one source will have all desired or needed information, so helping professionals must be knowledgeable about the various sources, skilled in searching a variety of resources, and competent in evaluating the quality of the information obtained. Once, human service workers have learned the essential skills of obtaining and evaluating occupational information, they can convey those skills to their clients, thereby enhancing their clients' career development and success.

Key Terms

Computer-assisted career guidance (CACG) systems
Guide for Occupational Exploration (GOE)
Informational interviewing

Job shadowing
O*NET® system
Occupational Outlook Handbook (OOH)
One-Stop Career Centers

Web Resources

Note that website URLs may change over time.

Choices® Career Information Delivery System
http://www.bridges.com/usa/product/index.htm

CareerOneStop
http://www.careeronestop.org

DISCOVER® Career Guidance and Information System
http://www.act.org/discover/index.html

O*NET® OnLine
http://online.onetcenter.org

Occupational Outlook Handbook
http://www.bls.gov/oco

SIGI PLUS® Educational and Career Planning Software
http://www.ets.org/sigi

Standard Occupational Classification System
http://www.bls.gov/soc

Virginia Career VIEW
http://www.vaview.vt.edu/index.htm

5

Initiating an Employment Campaign

Just the mere thought of looking for a job and all it entails can raise your blood pressure. Now, imagine coming to the search with a full plate of barriers—lack of marketable job skills, insufficient educational background or training, physical, developmental, and/or mental disabilities, problems with transportation, isolation, gaps in employment history, and/or job instability. Many of our clients are faced with these very obstacles. As human service professionals, you must be knowledgeable about the skills involved in initiating an employment campaign. Only after becoming skillful in this area can you truly help your clients to put their best foot forward and vie with confidence in the competitive world of work.

Initiating an employment campaign is far more than filling out a stack of applications and mass mailing resumes. It is a strategic process where proper planning can make the difference between *waiting* for a phone call and *hearing* the phone ring. Literally hundreds of books detail *best practices* for conducting a job search. We strongly encourage you to take advantage of the surplus of resources on this topic. The purpose of this chapter is to draw attention to some of the most important tips and guidelines for initiating a quality employment campaign. This chapter provides the helper with "Cliff Notes" of the countless resources available on this topic. The major themes we will address include: strategic job-search skills, job-search correspondence, resume writing, completing job applications, interviewing skills, and negotiating job offers. Since every first-rate employment campaign should begin with a well-developed and executed plan of action, we will begin with the strategic job search.

The Strategic Job Search

Basics of a Job Search

An effective job search goes beyond browsing through the Sunday paper's classified section; it involves a thorough assessment of the self, the position, the employer, and the job market. It is not until candidates have spent sufficient time in these exploratory stages that they are properly prepared to move forward with the employment campaign. The first stage in carrying out a strategic job search is "knowing thyself."

Know Thyself.   The job search process begins with a careful assessment of one's interests, values, personality, aptitudes, skills, and goals. A thorough self-assessment can assist individuals with career decisions and help candidates effectively market themselves to prospective employers by identifying personal strengths and by becoming aware of weaknesses. In this section we will provide brief descriptions and examples of the aforementioned attributes. For a thorough review of specific assessment instruments, see Chapter 3.

Interests.   Interests are those things that arouse an individual's attention and are frequently predecessors to skill development. You can assess interests by examining themes in your life, by identifying your ideal job through daydreaming activities and journal writing, and by completing a series of instruments and assessments. Examples of career interests include acting, painting, calculating, selling, researching, managing, fixing, traveling, and socializing.

Values.   Values are qualities that are important to you in your life and career. They are the fundamental beliefs that drive the decision-making process. Values are expressed in your thinking and subsequent behavior. Values can be measured by completing instruments designed to assess various types of values—personal, cultural, and professional.

Personal values are those values that one deems important. They are a set of principles one lives by and continually develops throughout life. Examples of personal values include altruism, creativity, pleasure, recognition, and wealth.

Cultural values are those values shared by a group of people and passed on from generation to generation. Cultural values are the expected ways of thinking and behaving based on the beliefs of a particular cultural group (e.g., people of Asian decent, African Americans, people of Latin decent, Native People) or subculture (e.g., gay/lesbian/bisexual population, people with disabilities, the elderly). Examples of cultural values include beliefs regarding the roles individuals play in the family and community (i.e., collectivistic vs. individualistic values); views regarding physical touching and proximity of individuals in public settings, and opinions regarding the meaning of direct eye contact (i.e., representing honesty in the individual vs. portraying disrespect).

Professional or work *values* are those values essential in career planning. When individuals express work values in their position, they will likely be fulfilled in the job, and the work will take on purpose and meaning. On the other hand, if the professional values are not met in the job, the individual is likely to become dissatisfied with the work. This dissatisfaction may lead to a variety of physical and mental health problems and to high, employee turnover rates. Examples of professional or work values include helping people, helping society, making decisions, influencing people, working alone, supervising others, and having job security.

Personality.   The term *personality* describes individuals' social traits, attitudes, motivational drives and needs, and adjustment. Professional helpers can use measures of personality to evaluate the support for or the opposition to a career decision (Zunker, 2002). Examples of personality traits include extraversion, insecurity, self-confidence, openness, and friendliness.

Aptitudes.   Aptitudes are specified proficiencies or the ability to acquire certain proficiencies. *Aptitude* can also be defined as a tendency, inclination, or capacity, to perform certain tasks. Aptitudes reflect the interaction of nature and the environment, and they predict the capacity to learn. In other words, individuals are born with certain capacities that might or might not be nurtured by the environment. Aptitudes are measured using two types of aptitude tests–multiaptitude tests batteries that measure a number of aptitudes and single tests that measure specific aptitudes (Zunker, 2002).

Skills.   Skills can be described as transferable, technical, or self-management. *Transferable skills*, also called functional skills, are those skills you have previously acquired in a job, activity, and through educational training, and are applicable to another job or activity. They are expressed as verbs and examples include analyzing, persuading, repairing, supervising, monitoring, constructing, and teaching.

    Technical skills also referred to as content skills, describe specific skills required to perform the unique duties of a particular job or activity. They are things you know and are expressed as nouns. Examples include drama, economics, maps, motorcycles, journalism, cameras, anatomy, and foreign language.

    Self-management skills are personal traits that express how well one performs a particular skill. They are expressed as adjectives and adverbs and are perhaps the skills in which prospective employers are most interested. Examples of self-management skills are thorough, sensitive, attentive, helpful, cooperative, accurate, efficient, and sincere.

Goals.   Goals are achievements by which individuals direct their energy (Lock, 2005). *Career goals* provide individuals with long-term visions of what they would like to achieve as it relates to a job, profession, or occupation. In career planning, **goal setting** is a process used to set the direction in one's life. It consists of deciding what you would like to achieve and then moving step-by-step towards accomplishing the goal.

    Knowing thyself is an essential ingredient in initiating an employment campaign. It is a process of identifying one's interests, values, personality, aptitudes, skills, and goals in order to determine which occupation and work situation may be a better fit for the individual.

Know the Position.   For human service professionals, knowing the position is an essential element in determining whether or not the position is a good match with their candidates' attributes. If possible, you should obtain a copy of specific job descriptions and information on the number of such positions filled annually. You may also find it helpful to learn how the position became available. Also gather information regarding the typical career paths within the organization that begin with this particular position. Information on the experiences, training, and other credentials needed in order to advance along with the career is also important. The job seeker should also investigate how the position fits into the company structure, the desired qualifications and responsibilities, and the salary range of the position.

Know the Employer.   An abundance of information regarding an employer, company, or organization that can be valuable to the job seeker is usually available. Learning about the types of products or services a company provides along with future plans for new products or services is important. The job seeker or professional should gather information on the size and growth of the organization over the past five years and the potential growth in the future, including plans for new branches. A financial profile, stock prices, and recent merger or takeover discussions can be helpful. Collect information on the company's organizational structure, including whether it is for profit, nonprofit, public, or private, and on competing companies. *Nonprofit* organizations are tax-exempt organizations that serve the public interest. Generally they must be charitable, educational, religious, literary, or scientific. They must utilize all revenue available after normal operating expenses to serve the public interest. Whereas *private companies* rely on obtaining more business in order to secure a healthier bottom line, nonprofit organizations often have limits on the number of clients they can serve. The job seeker should learn about the geographic location of the company along with the number of sites, the parent company, and relocation policies, if any. Other beneficial information includes the organizational philosophy and personnel policies, training programs, professional development opportunities, advancement policies, and diversity of the workforce along with the organization's policy statements on diversity.

Know the Job Market.   The quintessential source for information on the job market is the U.S. Department of Labor, Bureau of Labor Statistics. The bureau is the main fact-finding agency for the federal government in the wide-ranging area of labor statistics and economics. In addition to providing statistics regarding the occupational outlook of various fields and jobs, the bureau provides up-to-date information on inflation and consumer spending, wages/earnings/benefits, productivity and costs, safety and health, import/export price indexes, demographic characteristics of the workforce, and Census Bureau information (U.S. Bureau of Labor Statistics, n.d.).

Know Where to Find Information.   Job seekers who want more information on companies in which they are interested can use libraries, career resource centers, and the Internet in their search.

Library and Basic Reference Resources.   Public libraries as well as university and college libraries house a number of business and government directories, basic reference books, financial reports, government indexes, and workforce information. Examples of multi-industry, national business directories include *Dun's Million Dollar Directory, Standard & Poor's Register,* and the *Thomas Register of Manufacturers.* Industry-specific, national directories and state-specific directories include the index to *The Wall Street Journal* and Chamber of Commerce business directories. International industry information can be found in the following resources: *Directory of Corporate Affiliations, Directory of American Firms Operating in Foreign Countries,* and the *Directory of Foreign Firms Operating in the United States.*

Additional resources available in libraries include a number of periodicals for women and minorities. Examples of these include *Black Enterprise, Hispanic Engineer, Hispanic Career World, African-American Career World, Woman Engineer, Minority Engineer, Careers and the Disabled, Equal Opportunity, Workforce Diversity,* and *NAFE Magazine.*

Career Resource Centers. Located on the campuses of many universities and colleges, Career Resource Centers are often a vital source of career and employment information. Companies and organizations that participate in on-campus recruiting often send recruiting brochures, videos, and annual reports to the centers for student use. Employers expect individuals to review these materials prior to their interview. In addition to company information, career centers may also have a Career Resource Library that makes available a number of print, video, and online resources for self-assessment and occupational exploration, along with information on job-search strategies, writing a resume and cover letter, and developing interviewing skills. Career Resource Centers are often staffed with trained professionals who offer career development programs and counseling services. Although many of the programs and counseling services are only available to students of the university or college, many centers allow community members to access the resources available in the Career Resource Library.

The Internet. Many of the aforementioned resources are also available via the Internet. In addition, most companies and organizations have websites that offer company mission statements, annual reports, and information on products and services they provide. Search engines provide Internet users with a means of accessing information stored within databases. Some of the most popular search engines include *Lycos, HotBot, Yahoo!,* and *Google.*

Know Where to Look for Jobs. Job seekers who want to consider all possibilities must be knowledgeable about two job markets: the visible job market and the hidden job market.

Visible Job Market. One common question human service professionals ask their job-seeking client is, "Where have you looked for jobs?" Perhaps one of the most frequent responses clients provide is, "In the Sunday paper." Although the newspaper is a popular place to scan for jobs, it is certainly not the best use of one's energy. Helpers can serve their clients well by providing some factual information on the visible job market and teaching clients about the advantages of the hidden job market and how to access this essential source of potential job openings.

The **visible job market**, also known as the advertised job market, includes, but is not limited to those positions found through classified ads, employer hotlines, employer listings on employer websites, job banks including Internet recruitment sites, classified sections of professional and trade journals, professional association placement services, public and private employment agencies, career fairs, and bulletin boards. Some segments of the workforce utilize the visible job market for a large portion of their openings. The government regularly relies on employment hotlines and classified ads to announce position vacancies. The private sector often utilizes this source to advertise positions linked to high demand and low supply of workers and/or high demand and high turnover. Although this list appears extensive, the visible job market accounts for only 15 to 20 percent of all available positions and in many cases some jobs are never advertised.

Hidden Job Market.   Believe it or not, 80 to 85 percent of all positions are filled without employer advertising! These openings are often filled by candidates who come to an employer's attention via employees' recommendations, informational interviewing, job-shadowing experiences, referrals from reliable associates, or recruiters. The **hidden job market** is vast and can be accessed through networking contacts, alumni, mentors, newspaper articles, telephone books, temporary agencies, internships, job shadowing, informational interviews, professional and trade journal articles, part-time and/or summer employment, freelance work, industry and professional websites, and chamber of commerce directories, to name a few. The most successful approach to tapping into the hidden job market is through networking; however sending targeted resumes and reader-oriented cover letters, contacting employers by phone, and showing up at a company's door step, are also effective means of gaining entry into this resource. In other words, clients should leave no stone unturned.

A strategic job search consists of a careful self-assessment along with a thorough exploration of the position, the employer, and the job market. These techniques provide the necessary foundation for an effective employment campaign. Once clients have mastered them, the helping professional can then begin teaching the client the basics of job search correspondence—the next important step in a successful employment campaign.

Job-Search Correspondence

Purpose of Correspondence.   Letter writing is an art. A well-written letter can charm the reader whereas a poorly written letter can irritate and even bore the reader. The importance of job-search correspondence cannot be overstated. Often it is the first type of communication an employer will have with the job seeker, and as such, it makes the first impression, whether good or bad. Employers value high-quality communication skills in their employees, and job-search correspondence provides job seekers with opportunities to demonstrate their ability to write concisely, correctly, clearly, and accurately. Additionally, letters provide candidates with opportunities to communicate positively about their qualifications and desire for specific positions. A well-written letter can help the client to standout among competing candidates. The following section provides human service professionals with information on the basic letter format, an explanation of several of the most useful types of job correspondence, and sample letters that can be shared with clients.

Basic Letter Format. Job-search correspondences are business letters, which can be written in a number of formats, the most popular are the full block and modified block formats. A *full block* format tends to be the easiest format because the typist simply moves all elements of the letter flush with the left margin. Indenting is unnecessary because a blank line is left between paragraphs. The *modified block* format is less formal than the full block format. The paragraphs are not indented and a blank line is left between paragraphs. The return address, reference line, date, complimentary closing, and signature block are right of center. The remaining elements are flush with the left margin. The *two-column* format is a newer format. This layout provides an attractive way of matching up the employer's requirements with the candidate's qualifications. The two-column format is used for the text or body of the letter. All other elements are formatted using either the full or modified block style. For all formats, the basic elements of the letter remain the same. The elements include (in this order):

- *Letterhead/Return Address.* The letterhead provides the name and address of the person sending the letter. The phone number can also be included here, however, it is often placed in the final paragraph of text.

- *Date Line.* The month, date, and year are placed two to three lines under the return address with the month written out as in: January 22, 2007.

- *Inside Address.* The inside address appears two to three lines under the date line. The first line of the inside address includes the addressee's courtesy title (e.g., Mr., Mrs., Miss, Dr.) followed by his or her full name. Line two is the addressee's business title. Line three is the name of the organization. Line four is the street address and/or Post Office box. Line five contains the city, state, and full zip code.

- *Salutation.* The salutation begins two lines under the inside address and typically begins with the conventional greeting "Dear" followed by the title and name of the addressee and a colon. When the name of the addressee is unknown, you can use titles such as Director of Personnel, Search Committee, or Human Resource Director. You should avoid sexist salutations (e.g., Dear Sirs, Dear Gentlemen) and the salutation "To Whom it May Concern."

- *Text or Body.* The text or body of the letter begins two lines below the salutation. It is single spaced with one blank line left between paragraphs. Paragraphs are not indented. This section is usually divided into three to four separate paragraphs. The opening paragraph tells the addressee why the person sending the letter is writing, gives specific information about the position of interest to the letter writer, and tells how the writer learned of the position. Also when applicable, make specific reference to previous contact with the addressee. The next section is the main body of the letter and can be divided into two paragraphs if necessary. When applying for a position, candidates use this section to concisely describe their qualifications for the position, including specific skills and experiences. Letter writers should also include statements regarding their interest in the company and the position, and they should point out relevant information that may not be included in their resume. In the closing paragraph candidates should mention any enclosures attached to the letter (e.g., resume, application), should state the action expected from the addressee (e.g., phone call, scheduling an interview), and the action the letter writer will take (e.g., call in 10 days). Letter writers should give specific dates for stated actions and give specific instructions on the best way they can be contacted.

• *Complimentary Closing.* The complimentary closing appears two lines below the last line of the text or body of the letter. Examples of complimentary closings for job search correspondence include: Sincerely, Sincerely yours, Yours sincerely, Thank you, Respectfully, Respectfully yours, and Cordially. The word "truly" has become a cliché and should be avoided in business letters.

• *Signature Block.* The signature block appears four or five lines below the complimentary closing. It contains the signature of the writer, the full typed name of the writer, and the title of the writer, if applicable.

• *Enclosure Notation.* An enclosure notation reminds the reader of any enclosures that are included with the letter. It appears two lines under the signature block. Examples of enclosure notations include: Enclosure, Enc., Enclosures (2), 2 Enclosures, and Enclosures 2. You can indicate the types of enclosures, for example, Enclosures: Resume, application, letter of recommendation.

• *Courtesy Copy Notation.* If the letter is distributed to more than the addressee, you should add a courtesy copy notation two lines after the enclosure notation. This notation lists all people receiving the letter, including the addressee. Examples of courtesy copy notations include: cc, cc:, copy to, copies to.

• *Postscripts.* Postscripts are used sparingly to emphasize an exceptional piece of information. When a postscript is used, it is placed two lines below the courtesy copy notation; or if the cc is not used, it is placed two lines below the enclosure notation. If the enclosure notation is not used, the postscript is placed two lines under the signature block. The use of the initials PS or PPS is optional.

Now we will describe the various types of job correspondence and provide some sample letters.

Types of Job-Search Correspondence.   The letters job seekers write in their job search serve different purposes. In the following section, we will describe the following letter types: prospecting, invited, referral, reminder, interview appreciation, withdrawal, acceptance, and declining an offer.

Prospecting Letter.   The prospecting letter, also referred to as an uninvited letter, introductory letter, or letter of inquiry, allows job seekers to take a proactive approach to their job search. It is a great tool for uncovering the hidden job market as it introduces the job seeker to the employer. Job seekers use this type of letter when they are inquiring about possible employment opportunities (i.e., there is no job posting). In the letter job seekers should state their specific job interest and briefly describe how they meet the needs of the employer. Job seekers should close the letter with a statement regarding the action they expect from the addressee (e.g., phone call, scheduling an interview), along with the action the job seeker will take (e.g., call in one week).

Invited Letter.   Job seekers use the invited letter when responding to an advertised position. This type of letter allows a job seeker to speak to the requirements in the ad. The format of this letter is designed to promptly inform the employer that the letter writer possesses the job qualifications as stated in the job posting.

Referral Letter.   A referral letter is the product of networking and thus, is also referred to as a networking letter. The writer should prominently display, in the first line or two of the letter, the name of the person the employer knows. This letter is valuable because it grabs the employer's attention when someone the employer knows and respects is mentioned. As a result, the job seeker can gain a tremendous advantage over other candidates.

Reminder Letter.   Candidates should use the reminder letter when they have not received a response from the potential employer. In the letter they reiterate their interest in the position or job possibility, remind the employer of their previous contact, and add additional information that may heighten the employer's interest in them. The letter should be positive, enthusiastic, and upbeat. It should not be perceived as negative or nagging.

Interview-Appreciation Letter.   Candidates should use the interview-appreciation letter, also referred to as a thank-you letter, to express appreciation following an interview or meeting. Since in the majority of cases candidates do not use this tool, it sets those who do apart and above other candidates. In addition to expressing appreciation for the interview or meeting, job seekers should reemphasize their strengths and/or mention some characteristic of their experience or background that was not covered during the interview. Interview appreciation letters should be personable and warm, while maintaining a professional business-like style. They should be sent within 48 hours after the interview or meeting.

Withdrawal Letter.   When candidates accept a position with an employer, they must notify other employers with whom they made contact of their decision to withdraw applications from consideration during the selection process. Job seekers should express their appreciation for employers' time, consideration, and courtesy. They should provide a brief explanation for their decision, for example, candidates could state that they accepted a position with another company. They should never say that they accepted a better job.

Accepting-an-Offer Letter.   When accepting a job offer, candidates use this style of letter to inform the employer of their decision to accept the offer and to confirm the terms of employment. This letter serves as confirmation in writing and ensures that the candidate has no misunderstandings regarding employment.

Declining-an-Offer Letter.   Job seekers should use this type of letter to inform an employer that they are declining an employment offer. In the letter they should include a brief explanation of their decision in a very positive way. For example, candidates should never state that they have accepted a better job. The letter should convey the candidate's sincere appreciation and careful consideration of the offer. Remember, the object here is not to burn any bridges!

Sample Job-Search Correspondence.   The following three samples of job-search correspondence are each set up differently to illustrate the various letter formats. Figure 5.1 is an *invited letter* that uses the two-column format. Figure 5.2 provides a sample of an *interview-appreciation letter* that uses a full block format. Figure 5.3 presents a *declining-an-offer letter* in a modified block format. You should use these letters as models only and should not copy them. Job seekers must tailor their correspondence specifically to the individuals, employers, and/or positions they are seeking.

Electronic Job-Search Correspondence.   More and more often employers will request candidates to send cover letters and resumes via e-mail or to post the documents to the company's website. When sending job-search correspondence by e-mail, job seekers must follow the formatting and display-style instructions that the employer provides. If instructions are not provided, format the document as plain text, commonly known as ASCII (American Standard Code for Information Interchange) or RTF (Rich Text Format). This format will allow the document to be read by most computer software programs. The documents should be copied and pasted directly to the e-mail message and not sent as attachments because the recipient may not have the compatible software to open and read the attachments and/or may be concerned about computer viruses.

Tailor-Made Resumes

Spend a couple of minutes paging through your favorite magazine. Does anything catch your eye? Did you see articles that capture your attention and urge you to read on? Did ads stop you in your tracks and entice you to further explore the marketed product? On the other hand, were the articles and ads so boring, uninteresting, or unrelated to your interests and needs that you quickly turned the page without giving them more than a second of your time? It is helpful to view resumes in this fashion. Resumes are a selling tool. They are used to market skills and experiences so that prospective employers can see, at a glance, whether or not the job seeker has the necessary qualifications for the position the employer is trying to fill. If the resume is boring, uninteresting, and/or unrelated to the interests and needs of the employer, it will not get a second glance. In other words, the resume must communicate clearly and quickly that the candidate is qualified for the position.

Purpose of a Resume.   Resumes are advertisements, the purpose of which is to effectively sell candidates' most relevant and positive credentials to potential employers. Employers use resumes as screening tools to rule out applicants who do not meet the qualifications for a position and who do not present themselves professionally in

Sherry M. Westendorf
11 Highland Avenue
Anytown, USA 00000

August 9, 20XX

Mr. Edward Lopez
United Plastics, Inc.
1072 Colina Drive
Somewhere, USA 00000

Dear Mr. Lopez:

I was excited to read your advertisement for a Customer Service Representative at United Plastics, Inc. in the August 8, 20XX edition of the *Virginian Pilot*. I feel my education, experience, and skills align well with the requirements you are seeking.

Along with my enclosed resume, which provides a nice summary of my accomplishments and strengths, below, please find a list of your specific requirements for the position matched with my qualifications.

Your needs:	My qualifications:
High school diploma or GED	High school diploma. Graduated 10th out of a class of 185. Completed college certificate program. Graduated top in class.
At least 2 years customer service experience	Customer Service Rep for 7 years at Primo Mortgage Services. Received "Employee of the Year" award. Handled customer concerns and inquiries resulting in high client satisfaction.
Troubleshooting/problem solving skills	Skilled in multitasking. Developed new customer database which increased client contracts by 30%. Negotiated new printing contracts reducing overhead costs by 15%.
Able to supervise & work with minimal supervision	Trained 12 temporary employees and supervised 8 full-time employees. Worked in an autonomous environment 85% of the time.

I would appreciate the opportunity to meet with you to discuss my qualifications at your earliest convenience. I will contact you the week of August 16 to follow up. If you need additional information or have questions, please do not hesitate to contact me. I can be reached at (757) 555–1212 or via e-mail at yourname@somewhere.com. I appreciate your time and consideration in reviewing my credentials.

Respectfully,

Sherry M. Westendorf

Sherry M. Westendorf

Enclosure: Resume

FIGURE 5.1 *An Invited Letter in Two-Column Format*

Sherry M. Westendorf
11 Highland Avenue
Anytown, USA 00000

August 15, 20XX

Mr. Edward Lopez
United Plastics, Inc.
1072 Colina Drive
Somewhere, USA 00000

Dear Mr. Lopez:

Please accept my appreciation for the time and consideration you afforded me during my interview on August 14 for the Customer Service Representative position. After speaking with you and meeting some of your employees, I am even more convinced that my education, experience, and skills have thoroughly prepared me for a position at United Plastics, Inc.

Your thorough overview of the job responsibilities gave me a good understanding of your company and your expectations for the position you are seeking to fill. I am confident that my background and experience in customer service and my outstanding organizational skills could be valuable to United Plastics, Inc. Often described as energetic, dependable, and efficient, my personality would mesh perfectly with your company's culture.

I welcome the opportunity to work at United Plastics, Inc. and become part of its family. I look forward to hearing from you soon. If I can provide additional information or answer any questions, please do not hesitate to contact me at (757) 555–1212.

Sincerely,

Sherry M. Westendorf
Sherry M. Westendorf

FIGURE 5.2   *An Interview-Appreciation Letter in Full-Block Format*

writing. Effective resumes get the job seekers interviews, guide the interviewing process, and justify hiring decisions to others.

Ten Tips for an Effective Resume.   Far too many resumes are written as though the potential employer actually has the time to read every word, which is typically not the case. Employers usually spend only 20 to 30 seconds glancing over a resume; therefore, each resume must be clear, concise, and targeted to the specific needs of the employer. A well-written resume generates a positive impression of the job seeker's qualifications without raising questions or confusing the employer. The following 10 tips can strengthen resumes and keep them from landing in the nearest trash bin.

   1. *Target the Resume.*   When preparing a resume, consider what you would look for in a candidate if you were hiring for the target position. Your resume is not a personal history and therefore should not include irrelevant, personal information such as age, weight, height, marital status, sex, race, or salary history. Job seekers should research the

Sherry M. Westendorf
11 Highland Avenue
Anytown, USA 00000

August 15, 20XX

Mr. Edward Lopez
United Plastics, Inc.
1072 Colina Drive
Somewhere, USA 00000

Dear Mr. Lopez:

Thank you for the time and attention you and your company have devoted to considering me for the position of Customer Service Representative at United Plastics, Inc. I consider the interviewing process at your company to be one of the most professional and thorough I have experienced in my employment campaign.

After careful consideration, I must respectfully decline the invitation to join your company. Your offer was competitive and the projected work responsibilities were very attractive. However, I have decided that another opportunity better meets my qualifications and interests at this time. I want you to know, however, that if was a very difficult decision.

I have been very impressed with you and your company and have shared my positive experience with my family and friends. I wish you and United Plastics, Inc. continued success and I hope our paths will cross again in the future. Thank you once again for your courtesy and hospitality. I appreciate the personal time you have devoted to considering my application.

Cordially,

Sherry M. Westendorf

Sherry M. Westendorf

FIGURE 5.3 *A Declining-an-Offer Letter in Modified-Block Format*

organization and position and pay attention to the job requirements. The resume they prepare needs to be reader-oriented and include only information that highlights qualifications as reflected in the hiring company's needs. The resume should not include information over 10 years old with the exception of degrees granted. Chances are that skills performed and acquired 10 years ago are not as transferable as those performed and acquired more recently because of changes in technology and the world of work. Basically, employers are more concerned with the candidates' recent experience and less concerned with what they did a decade ago. The 10-year rule applies to the job departure date only, not the job start date. In other words, a candidate who has 15 years experience in one job but left the position only 6 years previously would include that job on the resume because the departure date was within the 10-year timeframe. The main point we are trying to make is resumes are not generic. Candidates should format a different resume for each and every position applied for, and each resume should be up-to-date, reader oriented, and include only information that is applicable to the job being sought.

2. *Select the Best Format.* Job seekers must choose the resume format that best suits their individual needs. The most popular resume formats are the chronological resume, the functional or skills resume, and the combination or hybrid/creative resume. The *chronological* format organizes information in a reverse chronological time sequence with the most recent education and experience placed first. The *functional* or *skills* format organizes qualifications according to skill areas. A resume using this format omits or de-emphasizes dates, employers, positions, and responsibilities. The *combination* or *hybrid/creative* format combines the benefits of both the chronological and the functional formats. In a combination resume, the job seeker first presents a summary of relevant skills, abilities, and accomplishments that is followed in reverse chronological order by job titles that support the skills, abilities, and accomplishments presented in the summary. We will present further information regarding these three resume formats the next section, "Resume Styles."

3. *Appearances Count.* Although the content of the resume is vital, the visual appearance is also important. The prospective employer is likely preoccupied with a number of other job responsibilities, and if the resume is packed full of important information but is cramped, crowded, and hard to read, the employer may not give it the time it deserves. For this reason, use indentations, bullet points, and a lot of white space; keep typefaces and format simple. Although highlighting important information is a good idea, calling attention to too much information can defeat the purpose of highlighting! Use business-like fonts such as Times New Roman or Arial, as opposed to child-like fonts such as Curlz or **Comic Sans**. Do not skimp on paper—use high quality stationery that looks like paper and not gift wrap and matching envelopes. Choose a professional color of paper such as white, ivory, buff, light tan, or gray. Stay clear of pastel blues, yellows, pinks, and greens, or any color with "neon" in the name.

4. *Honesty Is Essential.* People often want to present themselves in the most positive light, but information contained in the resume cannot be fiction. Be honest and accurate. Employers often use the resume as a means of evaluating the integrity of a candidate. Aside from any moral or ethical consideration, lying is just a bad idea and the candidate will likely get caught.

5. *Quantify and Use Power Words.* By using numbers and percentages to quantify information and power words to describe achievements and accomplishments, job seekers can create positive images in the minds of employers. Numbers and percentages add credibility to action statements—they describe how often and how well the candidate performed an activity. For example, compare these two statements: "Sold merchandise to customers." vs. "Consistently exceeded weekly sales quotas by an average of 35 percent." The first statement simply reveals what the candidate did, but the second statement describes how well the candidate performed the task. Use the digit form for all numbers and percentages included in the resume. Digits pop off the page and catch the eye of the reader. Power words, or action verbs, convey a confident and positive image. The stronger the word and the more active the voice, the more powerful its impact. Power words include supervised, managed, directed, launched, organized, planned, designed, and evaluated. Weak phrases include responsible for, duties include, assisted, and words beginning with "co" such comanage, cofacilitate, and codirect. The resume should be an accomplishment driven document!

6. *Avoid Wordiness.* Resumes should make sense at first glance. Employers become irritated when they have to read, reread, and read again just to decipher the document. Employers are not impressed by phrases that are nothing more than a mish mash of verbs, adjectives, and nouns. Consider the following poor example, "Effectively created a proactive business atmosphere by empowering and encouraging structured interaction among peers and subordinates resulting in an enhanced image of the department by upper levels of management." Use short action phrases that clearly describe accomplishments and achievements. Refrain from using personal and possessive pronouns on the resume.

7. *Prioritize the Content.* Place the most important component of your resume before less important components. Prioritize not only the order of categories (e.g., education before experience or vice versa), but also prioritize each and every action phrase based on their level of importance. Since employers on average only spend 20 to 30 seconds scanning a resume, they are likely to focus more on the top half of the resume and the first few action phrases. Because of this fact, job seekers must format their resume in such a way as to highlight its most relevant and important information.

8. *Less Is Best.* Job seekers should not make their resume an exhaustive history of everything they have done. Resumes are marketing tools that highlight *key* information. Simply stated, limit resumes to one page unless the applicant has a substantial, relevant recent work and education history in which case limit the resume to two pages. For the majority of situations, a one-page resume is recommended and preferred. The job seeker should pick and choose the most important, recent, and applicable components to include in the resume. Delete information that has absolutely no direct relationship to the career objective. In this sense, less is truly best.

9. *Be Consistent.* The entire resume document must be written in a consistent style. For example, verb tenses must remain consistent. Use present-tense verbs for current activities and past-tense verbs for past activities. Job titles, names of organizations, dates of employment, and other headings should be placed in the same order in each section. All items in the resume should employ parallel structure. If an action phrase begins with a verb, all the action phrases should begin with a verb. If a line ends with a period, all lines should end with a period. If a leader bullet is used before an action phrase, leader bullets should be used before every action phrase. A lack of consistency in the resume gives the impression that the job seeker lacks attention to detail.

10. *Fine Tune.* As the old saying goes, "You never get a second chance to make a first impression." Fine-tune your resume. Proof read every word on the resume for accuracy and have at least three other people read it. Verify dates, titles, addresses, spelling, grammar, and punctuation for accuracy. Many employers dismiss the candidate if one error is found on the resume. A poorly structured and written resume tells the employer a lot about the candidate—none of it is good! For some employers an error on a resume shows poor written communication skills, little attention to detail, and a lack of respect for the employer or position.

Resume Styles.   In this section we will describe the format and organization of the following resume styles: chronological, functional, combination, and electronic/scannable. We have also provided samples of chronological, functional, and combination resumes.

Chronological Resumes.   The chronological resume is the format most common and familiar to employers. Most employers prefer this style because it is fact based and easy to scan. Information is organized in reverse chronological order, placing the most recent education and experience first. This resume works best for individuals who have a solid work history and related skills. However, it also can accentuate employment gaps, and sometimes skills are difficult to spot. The chronological format has the following components, the order of which varies depending on each unique situation:

- *Heading/Contact Information.* Include name, address, phone number, and e-mail address.

- *Objective/Career Objective.* This objective is recommended by most employers. It should be a concise statement of the candidate's career goal. Avoid "philosophy of life" statements such as "To continue to grown and flourish in an empowering environment."

- *Education.* Include institutions granting a degree or certificate along with the city, state, degree name, and the month and year the degree or certificate was or will be granted. Identify any major or minor formal certificate program, or vocational training. Include GPA if it is favorable (i.e., 3.0 or above in major or overall for undergraduate study; 3.5 or above for graduate study). If the candidate worked substantial hours to fund education, consider adding a statement such as, "Financed 100 percent of education by working 30 hours per week/month while enrolled in school."

- *Experience/Work History/Professional Experience/Related Experience.* List the job title, company name, location (city, state), dates (not necessarily in this order). List each job separately, even if within the same organization. Include relevant co-ops, internships, summer and part-time positions. Do not categorize experiences as paid or unpaid. Use action phrases to describe skills, achievements, and accomplishments, and list in order of importance. Use numbers, percentages, and power words. Begin each phrase with a leader bullet.

- *Skills.* List second language skills, computer skills, professional skills, technical skills, laboratory skills, and additional skills relevant to the position.

- *Optional Items.* This category can include items such as academic and service honors and awards, memberships and associations, volunteer work, publications, presentations, conferences, vocational training, extracurricular activities, elected or non-elected offices held, positions of leadership, study abroad, clubs and organizations, and community activities.

- *References.* Furnished upon request (optional).

See Figure 5.4 for a sample chronological resume.

SHERRY M. WESTENDORF
11 Highland Avenue • Anytown, USA 00000
(757) 555–1212 • E-mail: yourname@somewhere.com

CAREER OBJECTIVE:
A customer service representative position utilizing strong communication, problem solving, and organizational skills coupled with 7 years supervisory experience.

EDUCATION:
Certificate of Achievement in Managerial Leadership   April 1998
My College, Somewhere, USA
- Graduated with honors and top in class of 63.

RELATED EXPERIENCE:
Customer Service Representative   May 1998 – May 2005
Primo Mortgage Services, Anytown, USA
- Managed customer concerns and complaints effectively resulting in an "Employee of the Year" award for establishing the highest level of customer satisfaction within the company.
- Supervised the performance of 8 full-time employees including the preparation and delegation of work schedules and daily tasks. Received outstanding supervisory evaluations for 7 consecutive years.
- Facilitated 3 new employee orientations and trained 12 temporary administrative assistants.
- Conferred with over 500 clients within 6-state region to determine mortgage needs. Increased company's contracts by 25% within 1 year.

Assistant to Department Manager   June 1996 – May 1998
Carefree Publications, Mytown, USA
- Promoted to position from administrative assistant within first 3 months of employment based on excellent work performance.
- Exceeded company standards by creating a new customer database, which increased client contact by 30% per month resulting in an additional $15,000 in annual product sales.
- Reduced overhead costs by 15% by negotiating new printing contracts for publications.

HONORS AND AFFILIATIONS:
- Chair, United Way Communications Committee: 1999 – Present
- Scholarship Recipient for Certificate Program at Anytown College: 1998
- Student Ambassador, Anytown College: 1998
- Volunteer, Habitat for Humanity: 1997 – Present

REFERENCES:
Furnished upon request.

FIGURE 5.4 *Chronological Resume*

Functional Resumes.   The functional resume is also referred to as the "problem-solving resume" because it highlights transferable skills and de-emphasizes a spotty work history. Many employers dislike the functional format because matching skill areas with the job titles, dates of employment, and level of responsibility can be difficult. This resume is best used when first entering the job market or when reentering after a long period of time. Following are the components of a functional resume. The order of the sections varies depending on individual circumstances.

- *Heading/Contact Information.* Include name, address, phone number, and e-mail address.

- *Objective/Career Objective.* The objective is recommended by most employers. It should be a concise statement of candidate's career goal. Avoid "philosophy of life" statements such as "To continue to grown and flourish in an empowering environment."

- *Summary of Experience/Skills.* List several relevant skill areas that demonstrate the abilities required for the position. Select functional/transferable skills as subheadings. Under each subheading, use short action phrases to describe related skills, achievements, and accomplishments in order of importance. Use numbers, percentages, and power words. Do not identify the employment or nonemployment situation where the experience was gained as this should be listed under the "Work History" section.

- *Education.* Job seekers will place the "education" section either before or after the "Work History" based on whether they choose to emphasize or de-emphasize education. If education was completed less than five years previously, the "Education" section can appear immediately following the "Career Objective" section. Otherwise Education should be placed after the "Summary of Skills" section or after the "Work History" section. Include institutions granting a degree or certificate, along with the city, state, degree name, and the month and year the degree or certificate was or will be granted. Identify any major or minor, formal certificate program, or vocational training. Include GPA if it is favorable (i.e., 3.0 or above in major or overall for undergraduate study; 3.5 or above for graduate study).

- *Work History.* List a brief record of employment history in reverse chronological order with the most recent job listed first. List job title, company name, location (city, state), dates (not necessarily in this order).

- *Optional Items.* This category can include items such as academic and service honors and awards, memberships and associations, volunteer work, publications, presentations, conferences, vocational training, extracurricular activities, elected or non-elected offices held, positions of leadership, study abroad, clubs and organizations, and community activities.

- *References.* Furnished upon request (optional).

See Figure 5.5 for a sample functional resume.

SHERRY M. WESTENDORF
11 Highland Avenue • Anytown, USA 00000
(757) 555–1212 • E-mail: yourname@somewhere.com

CAREER OBJECTIVE:
A customer service representative position utilizing strong communication, problem solving, and organizational skills coupled with 7 years supervisory experience.

EDUCATION:
Certificate of Achievement in Managerial Leadership   April 1998
My College, Somewhere, USA
- Graduated with honors and top in class of 63.

REPRESENTATIVE ACCOMPLISHMENTS:
Customer Service and Supervision
- Managed customer concerns and complaints effectively resulting in an "Employee of the Year" award for establishing the highest level of customer satisfaction within the company.
- Conferred with over 500 clients within 6-state region to determine mortgage needs. Increased company's contracts by 25% within 1 year.
- Supervised the performance of 8 full-time employees including the preparation and delegation of work schedules and daily tasks. Received outstanding supervisory evaluations for 7 consecutive years.
- Facilitated 3 new employee orientations and trained 12 temporary administrative assistants.

Troubleshooting and Problem Solving
- Exceeded company standards by creating a new customer database, which increased client contact by 30% per month resulting in an additional $15,000 in annual product sales.
- Reduced overhead costs by 15% by negotiating new printing contracts for publications.
- Promoted to position from administrative assistant within first 3 months of employment based on excellent work performance.

WORK HISTORY:
Customer Service Representative   May 1998 – May 2005
Primo Mortgage Services, Anytown, USA

Assistant to Department Manager   June 1996 – May 1998
Carefree Publications, Mytown, USA

HONORS AND AFFILIATIONS:
- Chair, United Way Communications Committee: 1999 – Present
- Scholarship Recipient for Certificate Program at Anytown College: 1998
- Student Ambassador, Anytown College: 1998
- Volunteer, Habitat for Humanity: 1997 – Present

REFERENCES:
Furnished upon request.

FIGURE 5.5 *Functional Resume*

Combination Resumes.   The combination resume is also referred to as the hybrid/creative format. It has gained popularity over the years because many people feel it is the most attractive and impressive way to present information. It showcases strong employment histories and transferable skills. This resume is best used when individuals have had several different types of jobs, need to condense many years of experience, and want to highlight many skills and accomplishments but find tying them together using another format, difficult. Under these circumstances, this format has been well received by hiring personnel. Components of the combination resume include:

- *Heading/Contact Information.* Include name, address, phone number, and e-mail address.

- *Objective/Career Objective.* This objective is recommended by most employers. It should be a concise statement of candidate's career goal. Avoid "philosophy of life" statements such as "To continue to grown and flourish in an empowering environment."

- *Education.* Include institution granting degree or certificate, city, state, degree name, and the month and year the degree or certificate was or will be granted. If applicable, identify major, minor, formal certificate program, or vocational training. Include GPA if favorable (i.e., 3.0 or above in major or overall if undergraduate; 3.5 or above for graduate).

- *Skill Areas and Experience/Work History/Professional Experience/Related Experience.* List in order of importance several relevant skill areas that demonstrate the abilities required for the position. Under each skill area list the experience that corresponds to the skill area. Include position title, company name, location (city, state), dates along with related action phrases to describe skills, achievements, and accomplishments. List action phrases in order of importance. Use numbers, percentages, and power words. Begin each action phrase with a leader bullet.

- *Optional Items.* This category can include items such as academic and service honors and awards, memberships and associations, volunteer work, publications, presentations, conferences, vocational training, extracurricular activities, elected or non-elected offices held, positions of leadership, study abroad, clubs and organizations, and community activities.

- *References.* Furnished upon request (optional).

See Figure 5.6 for a sample combination resume.

Electronic/Scannable Resumes.   Many companies and organizations are investing in state-of-the-art computer systems to increase efficiency in scanning, storing, and retrieving resumes. Many resumes are forwarded electronically through website postings and e-mails. When forwarding resumes to e-mail addresses, follow the same guidelines outlined previously for job correspondence. Specifically, individuals must follow the formatting and display style instructions the employer provides. If instructions are not provided, format resumes as plain text, commonly known as

SHERRY M. WESTENDORF
11 Highland Avenue • Anytown, USA 00000
(757) 555–1212 • E-mail: yourname@somewhere.com

CAREER OBJECTIVE:
A customer service representative position utilizing strong communication, problem solving, and organizational skills coupled with 7 years supervisory experience.

EDUCATION:
Certificate of Achievement in Managerial Leadership   April 1998
My College, Somewhere, USA
- Graduated with honors and top in class of 63.

CUSTOMER SERVICE AND SUPERVISION:
Customer Service Representative   May 1998 – May 2005
Primo Mortgage Services, Anytown, USA
- Managed customer concerns and complaints effectively resulting in an "Employee of the Year" award for establishing the highest level of customer satisfaction within the company.
- Conferred with over 500 clients within 6-state region to determine mortgage needs. Increased company's contracts by 25% within 1 year.
- Supervised the performance of 8 full-time employees including the preparation and delegation of work schedules and daily tasks. Received outstanding supervisory evaluations for 7 consecutive years.
- Facilitated 3 new employee orientations and trained 12 temporary administrative assistants.

TROUBLESHOOTING AND PROBLEM SOLVING:
Assistant to Department Manager   June 1996 – May 1998
Carefree Publications, Mytown, USA
- Exceeded company standards by creating a new customer database, which increased client contact by 30% per month resulting in an additional $15,000 in annual product sales.
- Reduced overhead costs by 15% by negotiating new printing contracts for publications.
- Promoted to position from administrative assistant within first 3 months of employment based on excellent work performance.

HONORS AND AFFILIATIONS:
- Chair, United Way Communications Committee: 1999 – Present
- Scholarship Recipient for Certificate Program at Anytown College: 1998
- Student Ambassador, Anytown College: 1998
- Volunteer, Habitat for Humanity: 1997 – Present

REFERENCES:
Furnished upon request.

FIGURE 5.6   *Combination Resume*

ASCII (American Standard Code for Information Interchange) or RTF (Rich Text Format). This format will enable the resume to be read by most computer software programs. Resumes should be copied and pasted directly to the e-mail message and not sent as attachments because the recipient may not have the compatible software to open and read the attachments and/or may be concerned about computer viruses.

In addition to accepting resumes electronically, many companies scan resumes into company computer systems in order to expedite their storage and retrieval. Scanners use optical character reading (OCR) programs that read the text of the resume when it is stored in a database. This information is then used to sort resumes in the databank. When employers are ready to hire, they can specify the skills, experience, or education needed for a position and retrieve and print resumes that match the selected characteristics. Many OCR programs, especially the older models, make errors when reading words or special characters such as italics, bullets, and underlining. As a result, resumes may look very different than the original copy. The scannable version of a resume needs to be formatted so that both older and newer scanning software programs can correctly scan it. The following guidelines should be used for formatting a scanner-friendly resume.

- Place only your name on the first line. Place your name and address on all pages of the document.
- Use standard san serif fonts in sizes between 10 and 14 points. Avoid flashy fonts and fonts where characters touch.
- Avoid using italics and underlining. Use bold or all-caps sparingly to emphasize information such as category headings.
- Avoid graphics, shading, vertical and horizontal lines, parentheses, brackets, and leader bullets.
- Do not compress space between letters or lines.
- Use key word phrases to describe skills, accomplishments, and experiences. Use nouns!
- The resume you submit should be a printed original. Avoid sending copies.
- Use plain, white $8\frac{1}{2} \times 11$ inch paper, printed on one side only.
- Do not fold, staple, or otherwise mutilate the document.
- Send a cover letter with your scannable resume. Often cover letters are scanned and stored with the resume.

In order to maximize potential employment opportunities, job seekers should prepare both a scannable resume and a standard resume. Candidates are urged to contact employers in advance to inquire about employers' use of scanning software.

Employment Applications

Employers primarily use the company application form (CAF) or the employer application form (EAF) as a means of screening applicants for part-time, entry-level, and blue-collar jobs. However, some companies and organizations require applications from all job applicants. Some companies request applications prior to an invitation for an interview; other companies request applications after the initial interview. Many employers prefer employment applications because they are helpful in standardizing the information they obtain from applicants. The employment application is a marketing tool and it helps employers decide who to call for an interview, and/or who is the best candidate for the position. When necessary for some clients, human service professionals can assist them in completing employment applications by helping them fill out the forms. In other cases, helping professionals can assist their clients by sharing the following valuable tips with them.

Prepare Ahead of Time. You can save effort and time if you plan ahead. You should create a fact sheet containing all the information that you will need to complete the application, such as employment history, addresses and phone numbers, and references. You should bring a resume, a photo ID, driver's license, and social security card.

Follow Instructions. Review the entire application prior to filling it out. Employers want you to follow their format and their instructions. By following instructions you show the employer that you really care about getting the job and that you *can* follow instructions.

Legibility Counts. First make a photocopy or print out an additional copy of the application to use as the rough draft. After you complete the draft, transfer the information onto the final copy. Impressions count and neatness plays a large role in leaving a positive first impression. Along with using correct spelling and grammar, *PRINT* neatly with a black or blue pen. You want the application to be easy to read. If your handwriting is too difficult to decipher, chances are good that the application will end up at the bottom of a trashcan. If a typewriter or word processor is available, consider typing the application. Because many companies use computers to scan and read applications, be careful not to bend, crease, or damage the application and make sure your application is clear, concise, easy to read, and properly formatted.

Tailor Answers. Focus your responses on the position for which you are applying. Just as you tailor each resume to a specific job, also tailor your applications to be reader oriented. Highlight not only what you have done, but also how well you have performed those tasks. Avoid compiling a list of duties and responsibilities, but instead, clearly communicate your skills. Do not undersell yourself. Convince the employer that you are the most qualified candidate for the position.

Avoid Leaving Blanks. You should avoid the temptation to write "see attached resume" on the application. Complete all sections; incomplete sections or blank boxes may give the appearance of laziness and a lack of interest on your part. Write "N/A" (not applicable) if necessary.

Be Honest. Tell the truth. You must refrain from lying on the application. Employers can easily confirm information you supply. Falsifying information will only count against you. However, you do not supply excessive detail about a past termination or firing. You should save more detailed explanations regarding a possible firing for the interview. The simple phrase "job ended" will suffice on the application. Remember, by signing the application, you are attesting to its accuracy.

Avoid Negative Information.   Providing negative information about former employers or jobs gives your potential employer a reason not to interview you. Create a good impression by using positive language. For example, when describing the reason for leaving a position use statements such as "opportunity for advancement," or "company downsizing."

Avoid Salary Requirements.   Some applications will ask you for salary requirements. Many employers use this section as a screening device. You do not want to be eliminated based on your response to this inquiry. It is best to fill in this section with "will discuss," "salary is negotiable," or "open."

Provide References.   When references are requested, you should always ask permission from your potential references prior to using their names. Choose your references carefully. A good reference can often lead to an interview or a job offer; a poor reference will often diminish your chance of securing the position. If you lack an employment history or have a minimal employment record, a mix of professional and character references such as teachers, family friends, ministers, former employers will work. If you are an experienced worker, professional references such as former or current employers and supervisors will be better able to describe your work skills and achievements.

Proofread.   After you complete the application, review it for accuracy. Let someone else read the application and give you honest feedback. Attention to these details is crucial. For some employers, one typographical or grammatical error is reason to eliminate you from consideration.

Keep Records.   Make a copy of the completed application for yourself (it is helpful to read over it prior to an interview). Keep records of where and when you have submitted applications.

Follow-up.   After you submit your application, ask the employer for information about the application process. When will applicants be contacted for interviews? How will applicants be contacted? Will applicants be notified when the position has been filled? If you do not hear from the employer within the designated time, follow-up with a phone call reiterating your interest in the position.

Companies use many different types of application forms, from the simple one-page format, to the comprehensive multipage layout. Some forms will be clear and easy to read, while others may appear faded and difficult to decipher. You should be prepared for all types of application forms and provide the same care and attention to detail to completing all forms regardless of their size and/or clarity.

Interviewing Strategies

A sound resume can land an interview, and a sound interview can land the job. Job interviews are the single most important aspect of the employment campaign, and human service professionals must possess expertise in interviewing strategies in order to effectively assist their clients with this essential element. Before we discuss interviewing tips, you need to be familiar with the various types of interviews and interviewing formats.

Types of Interviews.

In the section we will discuss two types of interviews: traditional interviews and behavioral interviews. Traditional interviews are often based on the candidate's resume and/or job application. Behavioral interviews are based on the premise that past performance and behaviors are good predictors of future performance and behaviors.

Traditional Interviews. In a traditional interview, the interviewer will likely use your application or resume to focus on areas of particular interest or relevance and to ask questions designed to provide a profile of your qualifications. You will have an opportunity to learn more about the company and the position in order to determine if the job is a good match for you. Examples of traditional interview questions include:

- Tell me about yourself.
- What will you bring to the job?
- Why should we employ you?
- Why do you want to work for us?
- What three major qualities do you possess?
- What personal characteristics do you possess that get in the way of your work?

Behavioral Interviews. Many employers view behavioral interviews, also referred to as performance-based interviews, as better predictors of future job performance, because they believe that a candidate's past job performance and behaviors are good predictors of the future. Prior to the interview, the employer determines what competencies are required for the job. Next, the interviewer develops questions that are designed to determine if job candidates possess the necessary skills to perform the job. Candidates are asked to demonstrate that they possess the necessary competencies by providing specific examples of past experiences. Examples of behavioral interview questions include:

- Can you give me an example of a situation where no procedure was in place and you had to make a decision?
- Can you describe a time when you persuaded someone to do something that initially did not appeal to him or her?
- Can you give me a specific example of a time when you had to keep costs down in your area or responsibility?
- Can you relate a personal story in which you did your best to resolve a customer complaint, but the customer still was not satisfied? What did you do?
- Can you describe a situation where you were criticized for the work you performed? How did you handle it?

In essence, behavioral questions are not hypothetical questions, but are questions that must be answered based on fact. An effective response to a behavioral-based question contains three major components. First, the response clearly and concisely describes the problem or situation. Second, it describes how the job seeker acted to resolve the problem. Third, it describes the results of the job seeker's action. Understanding and appreciating behavioral interviewing techniques can significantly help job seekers prepare for traditional interviews as well because they can give the traditional interviewer specific answers to hypothetical questions.

Interview Formats.   A job seeker might have many interviews during an employment campaign with different environments and circumstances. In this section, we will describe different interview formats including telephone, one-to-one, panel, and video-conferencing interviews.

Telephone Interviews.   More and more employers are using telephone interviews to prescreen potential interviewees and conduct actual interviews before inviting candidates for an on-site visit. Telephone interviews save money, take less time than an in-person interview, and allow employers to interview candidates from a wider geographical range. In most cases the employer notifies the candidate in advance and schedules the telephone interview. But in some cases, they do not give advance notice. Because telephone interviews are common and an important part of the selection process, candidates should use the following guidelines:

- *Expect Employers to Call at Any Time and Be Prepared.* If you expect an employer's call, make sure the message on your voice mail or answering machine is suitable and professional. Answer the phone in a professional manner with no silly comments or loud music in the background. Keep a list of the jobs you have applied for by the phone along with a copy of your resume, a calendar, pen and paper, and a list of questions you would like to ask the employer.

- *Telephone First Impressions Count.* If you expect a telephone interview, be aware of how you sound. Practice the interview with a friend and record your answers on a tape recorder. During the interview, eliminate all distractions. If possible, conduct the telephone interview while glancing into a mirror. Seeing yourself in a mirror will allow you to adjust your posture and enthusiasm during the interview. Ask specific questions about the position before answering any questions. You can then gear your responses to questions towards the needs of the employer and the requirements of the position.

One-to-One Interviews.   As the name suggests, the one-to-one interview is a meeting between the potential candidate and the employer. It is designed to exchange information about the candidate and the employer and to discuss the job opening. Tips for the one-to-one interview include:

- *Build Rapport.* Rapport between the candidate and employer is essential and will guide interactions.

- *Relax.* Usually the interview begins with small talk between the employer and the candidate. Be natural, relaxed, and responsive to the employer's comments about general topics such as the weather or traffic.

- *Show Enthusiasm and Interest.* Employers are not interested in hiring someone who shows little enthusiasm or interest for the position during the interview. Both verbal and nonverbal communication should reflect the job seeker's motivation and interest in the company and job.

- *Maintain Eye Contact.* For some cultures, direct eye contact has negative connotations and may be viewed as disrespectful. However, for many employers, eye contact is viewed as a sign of the candidate's assertiveness, confidence, and honesty. With that being said, eye contact should be natural and show interest. Candidates should not stare at the interviewer for the duration of the interview. This can easily make the employer uncomfortable.

Panel Interviews. Panel interviews are becoming more popular because of the time-saving feature that allows the people involved in the hiring decision to meet as a group to interview, and later discuss, each candidate. Because candidates often view panel interviews as the most anxiety-producing type of interview, they can use the following tips to help them remain calm, stay positive, and effectively handle the interviewing situation:

- *Bring a "Cheat Sheet" to the Interview.* Bring a list of highlights you would like to mention during the interview. This list should be an outline of significant assets you could bring to the position. A more comprehensive "cheat sheet" would be a professional portfolio. Professional portfolios are visual presentations of candidates' work that provide evidence of their skills and abilities. A portfolio can include samples of projects, evaluations, letters of recommendation, resumes, certificates, awards, professional goal statements, and training/education activities, to name a few.

- *Get to Know the Panel.* The candidate should ask for the participants' names and write them down according to their seating order. Refer to the individuals by their names throughout the interview. Use names to cross reference current questions with previous questions thereby linking the panel members' questions with one another. During the interview, jot down notes on each person's specific questions, concerns, and comments. The candidate can use these annotations to guide the interview and to personalize the thank-you letters sent to each panel member following the interview.

- *Maintain Eye Contact.* Although the candidate should focus mainly on the individual asking the question, it is also imperative to make eye contact and speak with each member of the panel equally.

Video-Conferencing Interviews. Employers are using video conferencing more and more as a means of interviewing candidates in remote sites around the country and world. This format utilizes a computer and/or television monitor, a camera, and a microphone. Many universities and organizations have the necessary software and technical capabilities to conduct video-conferencing interviews. Candidates can use the following tips to guide the process:

• *Rehearse.* Practice video-conferencing by getting a video camera and taping a mock interview. Reviewing the video will allow you to study your body movement and speech rate so that you can make modifications as needed.

• *Speak Slower than Normal.* Viedo-conferencing has a split-second delay between the voice transmission and the picture transmission. By speaking slower, you will make the delay between your voice and your moving mouth, less noticeable.

• *Limit Body Movements.* Rapid body movements may distract the viewer and appear blurred. To avoid this effect you must control body movements and expressions.

Tips for an Effective Interview.   Human service professionals can help their clients prepare for a job interview by sharing with them the following interviewing tips.

Preinterview Preparation.   Before showing up for the interview, you must do your homework. Research the company and the position and if possible, find out about the people you will meet for the interview. Conduct a thorough assessment of your skills, experiences, abilities, and accomplishments as they relate to the requirements for the position for which you are interviewing. Practice the interview by role-playing and rehearsing answers to a number of traditional and behavioral-based interview questions. Keep answers concise, under two minutes, and relevant to the job. Know the exact place and time of the interview and know the interviewer's full name and the correct pronunciation and title.

Clothing Guidelines.   When it comes to interviewing dress codes, different industries have different expectations. Candidates should dress like others do in the organization but lean towards the more formal. In most situations, conservative dress is the safest, most acceptable standard of dress for an interview. Although the clothes will not get the candidate the job, dress that is messy, untidy, and/or inappropriate can have a negative impact on the candidate. General clothing guidelines for women include:

• Conservative, simply tailored suit or dress (solid dark blue or gray is best)
• Long-sleeved shirt/blouse in white or pastel
• Conservative hosiery with no runs
• Clean and polished conservative shoes
• Little or no jewelry
• Moderate makeup and minimal cologne or perfume
• Clear or conservative colored nail polish, if any is worn
• Clean, manicured finger nails
• Neat, well-groomed hair style
• No visible body piercing (nose rings, eyebrow rings, tongue piercing, etc.)
• One set of earrings only
• Portfolio or briefcase

Clothing guidelines for men include:

- Clean, conservative pressed shirt and suit
- Silk necktie with a conservative pattern
- Dark, clean and polished shoes with dark socks
- Empty pockets—no bulges or jingling coins or keys
- Neatly groomed and clean, conservative hair;
- No visible body piercing (earrings, nose rings, eyebrow rings, tongue piercing, etc.);
- Neat and trimmed facial hair, if any (note: facial hair is sometimes viewed as a negative, especially beards)

Answering Questions.   When answering questions, you should present yourself in the best possible light. Maintain good eye contact, be positive, and demonstrate enthusiasm and interest in the position and company. Use active listening skills, and adapt your responses to the communication style of the interviewer. Make sure your nonverbal communication matches your verbal messages. Focus your answers to achievements that are relevant to the job and company. Do not answer questions with a simple yes or no. Provide explanations whenever possible. Answer all questions truthfully, succinctly, and frankly. Do not inquire about salary, benefits, vacation pay, or retirement packages during the initial interview. Always have some well-thought out questions to ask the employer that show your interest and enthusiasm for the job. At the conclusion of the interview, let the employer know if you are interested in the position and the company.

Handling Inappropriate Questions.   During an interview, the employer might ask an inappropriate question such as "How old are you?" or "Are you married?" Many times employers ask these questions innocently without realizing how they sound or how offensive the questions may be. Technically, it is inappropriate for an employer to ask any personal questions that are not job related.

So how should the candidate handle an inappropriate question? When asked an inappropriate question, you should be polite and try not to be defensive in your response. Here are some options:

- Indirectly avoid answering the question by responding positively about your qualifications for the position.
- Ask about the relationship of the question to the job.
- Refuse to answer the question; however, your choice of words is extremely important since some employers may perceive this as uncooperative.
- Answer the question directly but realize that you risk the chance that the answer may jeopardize your chance at getting the job.
- Deal with the concern behind the question and disclose partial information without compromising your rights.

The main point is that each candidate needs to determine how he or she will respond to inappropriate questions. If the candidate feels that he or she has been discriminated against on the basis of race, color, sex, religion, national origin, age, or disability, then the candidate should file a charge of discrimination with the U.S. Equal Employment Opportunity Commission (EEOC) (n.d.). The EEOC enforces laws that prohibit job discrimination and provides oversight and coordination of all federal equal employment opportunity regulations, practices, and policies.

Now that we have explored interviewing strategies, we will look at the final step of the strategic employment campaign, the process of evaluating and negotiating job offers.

Evaluating and Negotiating Job Offers

Once a job offer has been extended, the candidate must evaluate the offer and make a decision on whether or not to accept it. Most organizations will not expect the candidate to make an immediate decision, thereby allowing the individual to carefully evaluate the offer. The candidate must answer a number of questions when evaluating a job offer. Some of the critical questions include:

- Will you enjoy the job? Will the job be interesting? Does the job match your interests and skills? Is the job sufficiently challenging?
- Will you enjoy working with your coworkers and supervisor?
- Is there sufficient diversity in the organization?
- Will you enjoy the organization? Will the organization be a good match for you?
- What is the turnover rate for the position?
- Is the salary and benefit package competitive and fair?
- Are there opportunities for advancement? Will there be opportunities to learn new skills and expand?
- Will regular feedback and evaluations of your performance be provided?
- Are you comfortable with the hours you will be expected to work?
- Is the commute to and from work manageable?

Before accepting a job offer, candidates should have realistic expectations of what they want and need. If a job offer has been made and it appears perfect except for one or two things, candidates should consider negotiating with the employer. Although some items are nonnegotiable, often salary, benefits, working conditions, and future opportunities can be negotiated if the job seeker's expectations are realistic. When negotiating salary or other job features, the following six rules can guide the negotiation process and increase the likelihood of a favorable outcome.

• *Rule 1: Perform research on the salary range for the field in which you are interested.* Salary-range information is available from a number or sources including the U.S. Bureau of Labor Statistics, career centers, professional journals, and the Internet. Conducting research on the salary range provides you with the foundation needed to make informed decisions regarding the job offer.

• *Rule 2: Only discuss salary after you have been offered the job.* Never discuss salary unless you have been offered the job. Should the subject present itself, consider responding with "I'm sure we can come to a good salary agreement if I'm the right person for the job. What other areas can we discuss to help you decide that?"

• *Rule 3: Make them go first.* Once you have been offered the job and the employer asks you for your compensation requirements, a suitable response might be, "You are in a much better position to know how much I am worth to your organization, and I will consider any reasonable offer. What did you have in mind?

• *Rule 4: After hearing the figure or range, repeat the top figure and extend the range by approximately 5 to 15 percent.* After repeating the top figure and the extended range, be quiet for 30 seconds. This will give the employer time to process your statement and to respond.

• *Rule 5: Counter their offer with a researched response.* When negotiating a salary, aim for the top of your estimated salary range but be prepared to accept less. Some employers have formal pay structures or set, entry-level pay scales that are nonnegotiable. Most employers, however, try to hire above the minimum but slightly under the midpoint of the range. For example, you have just been offered $27,500 but you have sufficiently researched similar positions in the geographic area and the salary range is between $29,500 and $34,500, consider responding with, "I appreciate your offer, and I am very interested in the position. At present my salary requirements are negotiable within the range of $29,500 to $34,500. This range is based on research I conducted on salary ranges for this position. Is there any possibility of this?" The main point is to avoid being confrontational and to be reasonable in your approach.

• *Rule 6: Take time to think it over.* Most employers do not expect a decision at that moment. Take time to think it over. Consider responding with, "This sounds terrific! I think we've really got a solid match here. Would you jot all this down so we're clear, and I'll think about it and get back to you as soon as you need to know. When do you need my answer?" It is important to get the offer in writing. Many employers will send an official letter stating the position, start date, salary, location, and details of the benefit package. If the employer does not mention this, ask for a confirmation letter.

Many people focus solely on the salary and not on the range of benefits that are often part of the job package. Some benefit packages are worth 30 to 40 percent of the salary and are in addition to the salary. Examples of benefits include health care, dental care, disability insurance, vacation pay, paid holidays, tuition assistance, bonuses, childcare, stock options, and retirement plans. Even if the salary is nonnegotiable, often companies are open to and able to negotiate components of a benefits package.

Summary

Successful job seekers must have excellent information and exceptional job-search skills. Human service professionals can assist their clients by becoming competent in job search strategies, skilled in job-search correspondence and resume writing, knowledgeable about job applications, proficient in interviewing skills, and skillful in negotiating job offers. Initiating an employment campaign involves a lot of hard work, and clients become discouraged at times. Helpers can provide the support, knowledge, and expertise necessary to help alleviate feelings of frustration in their clients. By helping clients remain focused, flexible, open minded, and persistent, human service professionals can make the employment campaign an effective one.

Key Terms

Goal setting
Hidden job market

Visible job market

Web Resources

Note that website URLs may change over time.

U.S. Equal Employment Opportunity Commission
http://www.eeoc.gov/index.html

JobWeb® Website of Career Development and Job Search Information
http://www.jobweb.com/default.asp

Monster Jobs
http://www.monster.com

Salary.Com
http://www.salary.com

6

Career Intervention Program Planning, Implementation, and Evaluation

The need for career intervention programs continues to intensify, as one-to-one sessions between helping professionals and clients become increasingly cost ineffective. The workload of human service professionals coupled with time constraints and funding issues makes planning for career intervention programs all the more imperative. Successful career intervention programs require careful planning, strategic implementation, and thorough evaluation. Without first establishing a solid plan, implementation and evaluation are not feasible. We will begin then by presenting the steps for career intervention program planning.

Steps for Planning Career Intervention Programs

Prior to implementing a career intervention program, human service professionals must thoroughly plan the program in order to ensure a higher level of program quality. When planned successfully, career intervention programs can reach a considerable number of people and do so cost-effectively (Niles & Harris-Bowlsbey, 2002). A basic model for program planning consists of the following four steps: (1) define the population, (2) conduct a needs assessment, (3)establish goals and objectives, and (4) design the program.

Define the Population

In order to effectively design a career intervention program, human service professionals must first have a clear understanding of the **population** for whom the program is intended. They must have a clear picture of the people who will be receiving the career services (Niles & Harris-Bowlsbey, 2002). Helping professionals must plan interventions for various populations including single parents and displaced homemakers; new immigrants; welfare-to-work recipients; individuals with disabilities;

corrections/probation population; the working poor; victims of domestic violence; displaced/dislocated workers; the homeless; the elderly; veterans; and substance abuse clients. In addition to defining the population based on its shared group affiliation (i.e., victims of domestic violence) individual characteristics can also provide valuable information. Examples of individual characteristics include the gender, age, ethnicity, race, socioeconomic status, ability, religion, and sexual orientation of the clients. In other words, helpers must be able to answer the question, "Who are our clients?"

Conduct a Needs Assessment

Defining Needs Assessment.   Human service professionals cannot design an effective career intervention program without first being cognizant of the needs of the population for whom the intervention is intended. The purpose for a **needs assessment** is to identify gaps in services by exploring consumer perceptions of problems and goals and to determine whether or not needs are currently being met by existing programs and interventions (Lewis & Lewis, 1983). In other words, the term *need* is used as a noun to describe a discrepancy between what should be and what actually is. Needs assessments serve to create dialogue among agency personnel, clients, and community members; clarify client needs; and encourage the design of interventions to meet those needs. Needs assessments should contain detailed information on the agency and the population it serves, data on similar programs and services offered in the community, and information on the needs of those clients who will be served by the career intervention program.

Methods for Conducting Needs Assessments.   In order to get a true picture of the need for a career intervention program, human service professionals must use a combination of information gathering techniques. Four such techniques include analyzing historical data, surveying target groups, conducting focus groups, and utilizing consultants.

Historical Data.   Historical data can provide relevant information about the agency, the community, and other related services, as well as gaps in services. Helpers can find this information by reviewing records and reports from earlier needs assessments, examining previous reports and data on earlier interventions, and analyzing past community planning documents in comparable areas.

Survey Target Group.   Surveys involve asking a number of predetermined questions by using questionnaires or through face-to-face interviews using interviewing forms. In order to make generalizations about the career intervention needs of the client population, the professional must survey a significant number of individuals. Questions posed to the **survey target group** should generate information regarding unique characteristics of the group and potential career intervention needs. The target group can offer their perspective on their career concerns as well perceived gaps in the career services that the agency currently provides.

Conduct Focus Groups. Whereas surveys identify key issues and concerns, focus groups provide greater insights into the main issues and concerns that the survey identified. **Focus groups** bring together groups of 10 to 15 people with similar concerns and situations to discuss shared interests and concerns, and in this case, to discuss needs (First Nations and Inuit Health Branch, 2000; Niles & Harris-Bowlsbey, 2002). Experienced or trained moderators who are well versed in group process skills and in the methods used to get participants' reactions should facilitate the focus groups (Krueger & Casey, 2000). The professional helper should conduct group discussions several times with similar types of participants so that moderators can pinpoint themes and trends. Following the completion of the focus groups, the human service professional should carefully analyze the information in order to provide clues as to how a program, intervention, and/or agency is perceived.

Hire Consultants. Sometimes it is helpful to hire a consultant to make recommendations regarding the needs for the career intervention program. **Consultants** are experts who bring a greater level of knowledge regarding the population and needs of others in comparable settings (Niles & Harris-Bowlsbey, 2002). Consultants, who are often outside the organization or agency, learn about the agency and the population it serves by observing them. What they learn about the agency and the population through observation is shared with the agency. Consultants are most useful when the organization has no expertise in the area of needs assessment, the organization's prior attempts to meet their clients' needs were unsuccessful, organizational leaders want an objective perspective, outside funding sources request that the organization bring in a consultant, or the agency wants a consultant to lend credibility to a decision that has already been made. Consultants can be located by contacting professional associations; searching through nonprofit directories; consulting the Yellow Pages under "consultant;" calling a local university or college and speaking with human resources, training and development, or the business administration department; and by contacting area corporations who have community service programs (McNamara, 1999).

Regardless of the methods used for collecting data for the needs assessment, the quality of the data depends on what is asked and how it is asked. Survey questions must be worded carefully so that individuals in the survey can easily understand them and provide the type of information the agency needs.

Establish Goals and Objectives

The results of the needs assessment become the basis for writing measurable goals and objectives. Goal statements provide maps to the entire design of the career intervention program and guide the evaluation process. A straightforward way to remember the key ingredients to writing first-rate goals is to remember the acronym MAPS. Goals must be **M**easurable, **A**ction-oriented, **P**ractical, and **S**pecific.

Goals must be *measurable*. Planners use measurable goals to determine exactly what needs to be accomplished and when the goals have been reached. Goals must be *action-oriented*—they must state the activities that will produce the desired effects—and practical. *Practical* goals are realistic to achieve given the resources available to the agency. Finally, goals must be *specific* in order to effectively guide the planning process. Sound goal statements are not vague. They must be broken down into manageable steps or objectives that provide step-by-step action plans to follow in order to achieve specific goals. The action plan also provides a means of tracking progress towards the goals.

The development of goals and objectives serves as the blueprint for the design of the program and provides the foundation for subsequent program evaluations. Achieving program goals requires the attention and persistence of the human service professional, and the ongoing process necessitates frequent reviews, reevaluations, and revisions.

Design the Program

Following the development of program goals and objectives, human service professionals can begin the task of designing the career intervention program. Using the results of the needs assessment and subsequent program goals and objectives as guides, human service professionals can make impressive decisions on program design. In designing the program, helpful questions to pose include: What is the content of the program? How will the program be delivered? What resources are needed? How will funding resources be located?

Determine Program Content.   Program goals and objectives determine program content. Therefore, human service professionals must review program goals and objectives in order to determine how to address and achieve the desired goals (Niles & Harris-Bowlsbey, 2002). Determining the content of the career intervention program can be both challenging and rewarding. Challenges come when helpers try to determine what program components are relevant and beneficial. Rewards come from designing programs that are truly effective in meeting the career needs of specific populations that are being served. Helping professionals are confronted with a number of factors that impact the task of determining the scope of the content. Some of these factors include: the level of the content; the resources available; federal, state, and local government content requirements; and the pressure received from internal and external sources.

To more clearly explain the impact that various factors have on program content, we will focus on the impact of the federal, state, and local government. Often career interventions initiated by such policy makers reflect the need to reduce or alleviate social costs (e.g., lost wages, societal disruption, lost taxes). Government funding and support for career interventions can be found in a variety of areas that include: identifying and providing therapeutic assistance to persons whose behavior or lack of skills are problematic for them or for the larger society; providing encouragement and support for those who are not able to successfully care for themselves; and increasing the quality of individuals entering the workforce by strengthening workforce preparation, development, and training (Herr, 2003). Understanding the influence that various sources have on the content of the career intervention program can guide the human service professional in determining a scope of content that matches the needs and wants of the various constituents.

Choose Program Delivery Method.   After deciding on the program content, human service professionals must determine how to best deliver the widest variety of career services to as many people as possible in the most cost-effective way. The range of program delivery strategies is extensive. Choosing the best delivery strategy requires careful examination of the many possibilities and selection of the best strategy for enhancing the capacity of the agency to meet the needs of the clients. The most expensive delivery method is the one-to-one intervention. Although incorporating one-to-one interventions with other delivery methods is quite possible and often feasible, using other methods that are helpful, cost effective, and require less of a time commitment is often desirable. Additional examples of delivery methods include: incorporating career topics into existing courses offered at area schools; offering workshops at the helper's agency or at area agencies, schools, and corporations; utilizing career development software; creating and using websites that provide career development content; providing self-help materials such as inventories, workbooks, and occupational resources to individuals; and utilizing outreach strategies (Niles & Harris-Bowlsbey, 2002). We will now look at each of these program delivery methods in more detail beginning with the one-to-one intervention.

One-to-One Interventions.   Individual or **one-to-one interventions** provide direction, resolve barriers, and promote planfulness in individuals regarding their career development goals. Human service professionals work individually with clients for short or long periods of time providing academic and/or career counseling and advise. They can employ many different techniques when choosing this one-to-one approach. Examples of techniques include: administering a battery of inventories; providing college admissions testing and job placement testing; teaching job search, personal, and social preparation; designing portfolios and individual career plans; and providing referrals for external training (Wonacott, 2001). Because individual sessions provide personalized service, they are often the most costly and time-consuming delivery strategy.

Curriculum-Based Interventions.   Sometimes referred to as classroom instruction, **curriculum-based interventions** typically consist of group activities conducted in school that last for an extended period of time, ranging from a few weeks to several years. Curriculum-based interventions infuse career information and skills into the curriculum. Two of the more formal and comprehensive types of this delivery method include Tech Prep and School-Based Enterprises.

Tech Prep is a federally funded program that combines a minimum of two years secondary education with a minimum of two years postsecondary education in a nonduplicative, chronological course of study. The program combines academic requirements with technical courses and work-based learning experiences. The objective of Tech

Prep is to instill within individuals workplace skills that will allow them to successfully enter the job market, the military, or further their education. Tech Prep programs of study can lead to associate degrees, bachelor degrees, or to postsecondary certificates in a particular career field (Rouse, 1995; Tennessee Board of Regents, 2000).

School-Based Enterprises help to prepare students for the transition from school to work or from school to college. They provide first-hand work experience and opportunities to build and enhance management, leadership, and supervisory skills by allowing students to run actual small businesses. Student ownership of businesses builds confidence, improves interpersonal communication, and enhances team-building skills. Methods of instruction include just-in-time training and one-to-one tutoring and mentoring. School-Based Enterprises allow students to acquire occupational knowledge and to practice job skills in the same context used in the world of work. The money generated from the businesses is used to fund student organizations and/or to pay for materials, equipment, and other items necessary to improve or maintain a program or school (Sanderson, 1998; Wonacott, 2001).

Workshops.   Workshops are an excellent delivery method because they can cover various topics while reaching large numbers of clients. Some of the job-related topics that can be delivered using this format include: effective career planning, career decision making, career assessments, resume and cover letter writing, completing job applications, interviewing skills, job-search strategies, self-marketing and networking techniques, researching occupational sectors and fields, business etiquette, overcoming barriers to career success, using technology in career development, and compensation evaluation and negotiating.

Software.   Software is useful in a number of career-related activities such as career awareness, career growth, career exploration, career transition, skill and knowledge development, and career decision making. Such software is applicable to a number of settings that include: elementary, middle, junior high, and high schools; vocational schools; community and junior colleges; colleges and universities; job training programs; rehabilitation agencies; counseling agencies; correctional facilities; personnel offices; job placement services; libraries; resource centers; and the work place. Software is used for instruction, counseling, job search, and human resource development on a single-user computer or shared/networked computer (National Career Development Association, 2003a). The most useful career software programs have companion publications including user guides, coordinator manuals, implementation strategies, and evaluation reports (National Career Development Association (2003b)

Human service professionals are encouraged to meticulously evaluate career software programs prior to using it. According to the National Career Development Association (2003b), software should be evaluated on the following criteria: information in the program, career development process, user interaction, technical aspects of the software and materials, and support services.

Internet.   Career service professionals have embraced the Internet as a tool for career guidance, career advice, and career information. According to Bolles (2002), an estimated 100,000 career-related sites are available on the Internet. Internet sites vary in their focus and content. Some sites provide a wide range of career development services and others offer little more than job postings. The full implications of using the Internet for career interventions are still unfolding. Human service professionals can use the Internet to deliver career services to remote locations where clients live and work, thereby releasing helpers and clients from the constraints of space, time, and physical location (Watts, 2002). The need for face-to-face contact with the helper can be reduced because the Internet provides clients with a means of communicating with the practitioner via e-mail. Other online resources include discussion forums, chat rooms, online mentoring, bulletin boards, and message boards.

CareerOneStop is one of the most recognized Internet career intervention programs. CareerOneStop operates as a federal/state partnership funded by grants to states. It is a collection of electronic tools for prospective job seekers, employers, and the workforce community (CaeerOneStop, 2004). The Internet site for CareerOne-Stop includes three main components: (1) America's Job Bank, (2) America's Career InfoNet, and (3) America's Service Locator. America's Job Bank allows job seekers to post their resumes and search for job openings. Employer's can use this database to post job openings, search for resumes, and create customized job orders. America's Career InfoNet contains information on wage and employment trends and labor markets by state and provides millions of employer contacts. America's Service Locator is a comprehensive database that provides job seekers with referral information for a wide range of services available in the job seeker's area. The services, which are available via the Internet or by phone, include: unemployment benefits, job training, educational opportunities, seminars, youth programs, and programs for the disabled and elderly.

Human service professionals who choose the Internet as a program delivery method must ensure that this delivery mode is an appropriate means of meeting the needs of their clients. In addition, helpers must assess career-related Internet sites for accuracy and appropriateness in meeting each client's needs.

Self-Help Materials.   The intent of self-help or self-directed materials is to empower clients to learn to solve career concerns and make career-related decisions on their own. Self-help materials are available in a wide variety of forms including videotapes, books, cassettes, DVDs, CDs, online resources, and software. Before referring a client to self-help materials, the helper should evaluate the clients' level of readiness for career decision-making. According to Sampson, Palmer, and Watts (n.d.), individuals with high levels of readiness for career decision-making are the best candidates for self-help services.

Outreach.   Outreach programs, by definition, are designed to reach out to the community in a direct way. Such programs necessitate collaboration and effective communication between the human service professional and the community. Effective outreach programs embrace the community by building strong relationships with volunteers and partners and by addressing career development problems within the community through career program initiatives. This program delivery method speaks to the career needs of the community through creativity and innovation.

Outreach programs are often designed to assist those at-risk or less advantaged. Such programs can provide information on career development, career awareness, career decision-making and planning, as well as information on available resources. Outreach programs can be informal or formal and quite comprehensive. One such formal and comprehensive outreach program is GEAR UP (i.e., Gaining Early Awareness and Readiness for Undergraduate Programs). GEAR UP is a national outreach initiative that was implemented to provide academic support and information to low-income students and their parents in order to empower and encourage more young people to pursue postsecondary education. GEAR UP is funded by grants through the U.S. Department of Education. The program establishes strong partnerships in targeted schools and subsequently provides services and resources to students, parents, and teachers in an effort to improve students' academic performance and their college enrollment rates. Examples of GEAR UP programs for students include: tutoring, mentoring, after-school and weekend classes, summer enrichment academies, and teambuilding and conflict resolution programs. Programs for parents include: workshops on parenting skills and child development, and information on colleges and financial aid. Examples of programs for teachers include professional development and staff training that are employed to assist teachers in raising their expectations for all students (U.S. Department of Education, n.d.).

The preceding program delivery methods represent some of the most common modes of delivery and are offered as a sampling of the many existing possibilities. After choosing the delivery method, human service professionals must turn their attention to determining what resources are needed to deliver the full-blown career intervention program.

Determine Needed Resources.   When designing the career intervention program, human service professionals must ask themselves, "What resources are needed in order to put this plan into action?" For each goal and objective they write, they must consider the resources necessary to meet them. Here are some questions to consider:

- How many staff members will this take?
- How much staff time will be necessary?
- What equipment, materials, and supplies will be needed?
- How much is needed to cover printing costs, if any?
- What technical support and software is needed, if any?
- What additional costs will there be (e.g., refreshments, facility rental fees, incentives for clients to participate, consultant fees, subcontracting fees for specialized services, etc.)?

The cost analyses planning begins with a full-cost budget—the cost it would take to fund the program with everything your heart desires. Even if the initial "dream program" cannot be funded in its entirety, preparing a full-cost budget is a helpful exercise in developing budgets, making budget cuts, justifying expenditures, and setting priorities.

Including the projected benefit of the career intervention program to the agency in the cost analyses is also helpful. For example, if the career intervention program were expected to serve 50 clients in a group format, a cost comparison of the program to one-to-one sessions would help to support the need for the group intervention.

Locate Funding Resources.   Sometimes the human service professional will have to locate funding for career intervention programs. Funding for programs may be found through donations, government support, and/or grants. Examples of potential funding sources include:

- City or municipal councils often have budgets for community programs.
- Various service organizations such as Rotary, Lions, Kiwanis, Elks, Junior League, and the YMCA/YWCA may provide funding.
- Community charitable organizations such as the United Way as well as area churches, synagogues, and other faith or multicultural groups may be able to provide help.
- Local businesses such as banks, realtors, grocery stores, drug stores, retail establishments, and manufacturing industries often support community agencies. The area Chamber of Commerce Directory can provide contact information on local businesses.
- Local, state, and federal government assistance is sometimes available.

The local library can be a helpful resource for directories of grant-giving organizations and foundations to approach. In addition, many resources are available via the Internet.

Steps for Implementing Career Intervention Programs

After successfully planning the career intervention program, human service professionals can direct their attention to program implementation. Implementing the career intervention program consists of two steps: (1) marketing and promoting the program, and (2) delivering the program. Program marketing and promotion is a vital first step in program implementation.

Marketing and Promoting Career Intervention Programs

Before a career intervention program is delivered, it must be successfully marketed. A winning marketing plan increases awareness of the career intervention program, informs the constituents of the features and benefits of the intervention, and decreases potential resistance to the program. In order to accomplish these marketing objectives, human service professionals must develop a marketing strategy that outlines the game plan to accomplishing the marketing objectives. When developing the strategy, integrating the "4 Ps of marketing" into the plan is helpful. The 4 Ps of marketing, also known as the marketing mix, classify the controllable aspects of the marketing plan. These include: **P**roduct, **P**rice, **P**lace, and **P**romotion (Family Business Institute, Inc., 2004).

The first **P** symbolizes the *product*. This component focuses on the actual goods and/or services being offered. In this situation, the product is the career intervention program. Products should be described in terms of their features and benefits. Examples of features include the program's quality and exclusivity. A benefit might be the specific advantages of the career intervention program to clients and customers (e.g., strengthening career decision-making skills).

The second **P** represents the *price* of the program. Price is the amount, if any, that clients/customers will be charged. If the career intervention program is free, state this as well.

The third **P** denotes the *place*. Place provides information on where the career intervention program will be brought to the clients/customers such as the social service agency, school, or community center.

The final **P** stands for *promotion* of the program. How will the professional or agency promote the career intervention program so that clients become aware of it? Promotion is synonymous with communication. Promotion includes advertising, media selection, understanding the position of the intervention as it relates to similar programs, and selling the service.

Delivering Career Intervention Programs

Once the program has been effectively marketed and promoted, human service professionals can then deliver the career intervention program to their clients. First impressions are everything. The program must be of the highest quality and must not be delivered until it is in tip-top shape. If programs are delivered prematurely, customers' first impressions may lead to negative publicity and lack of future support. *Implementation fidelity*, also referred to as adherence or integrity, is a measure of whether or not the program is being delivered as it was planned in the original program design. According to Dane and Schneider (1998), professionals should consider the following four components when examining implementation fidelity: (1) adherence, (2) exposure, (3) quality of program delivery, and (4) participant responsiveness.

Adherence refers to whether or not the career intervention program is being delivered as it was intended or as it was written. *Exposure*, also referred to as dosage, examines the number of sessions delivered, the length of sessions, and the frequency in which program techniques and strategies were used. The *quality of program delivery* reports on the manner in which the human service professional, or other person, delivers the intervention by assessing the person's skill, enthusiasm, preparedness, and attitude in using the techniques and methods outlined in the program plan. *Participant responsiveness* examines the extent to which the program participants are involved in and engaged by the content and activities of the program.

Program integrity is linked to successful programming. Delivering programs that foster positive experiences will result in more positive outcomes for the clients, human service professionals, agencies, and stakeholders.

Steps for Evaluating Career Intervention Programs

The evaluation of career intervention programs has become increasingly essential as funding in human service agencies becomes more limited and accountability for programs more imperative. Effective program evaluations require knowledge of the following six topics: (1) reasons for evaluations, (2) types of evaluation, (3) evaluation tools, (4) components of an evaluation report, (5) the process of evaluating the evaluation process, and (6) program modification.

Reasons for Evaluations

Although some view program evaluation as a tedious and monotonous undertaking, if conducted collaboratively with stakeholders, the experience can foster group cohesion and a greater understanding of the purpose and need for the career intervention program. Program evaluations are used to:

- Clarify the purpose of the intervention
- Chart the progress of the program, and assess the effectiveness of the program in meeting goals and objectives
- Assist in making strategic decisions
- Aid in reassessing the direction of the program
- Help to determine if the program's outcomes can be attributed to the program itself or to other factors
- Facilitate program improvement through design modifications
- Provide information that can help outside decision makers (e.g., funding sources, community service boards, governmental agencies, etc.)

Types of Evaluations

Many different types of program evaluations are used; some are very formal and structured and others are less formal such as personal reflections of the program. Surveys, interviews, discussion, and/or statistical analyses of data can be used to make evaluations. Three of the most common types of evaluations include: process evaluations, outcome evaluations, and impact evaluations.

Process Evaluations.   Process evaluations, also referred to as *formative evaluations*, enhance the program by helping human service professionals understand it more fully. Process evaluations assist in accountability, provide information for program improvement, and help others to setup similar programs. Process evaluations measure how effectively a program was designed, implemented, and completed. It measures actions taken, decisions made, and procedures followed in developing the program, and it describes the services delivered, how the program operates, and the functions that the program carries out (Justice Research and Statistics Association, 2004). Process evaluations are descriptive and ongoing. They identify factors that facilitate or hinder the successful implementation of the program.

Outcome Evaluations.   Outcome evaluations, also known as *summative evaluations*, help to identify the results of a program's effort. In other words, outcome evaluations answer the question "What difference, if any, did the program make?" Outcome evaluations describe and document actual changes that took place as a result of the program based on the program's goals and objectives. They examine the extent to which desired changes have been achieved at the completion of the program. Typically, outcome evaluations involve comparison of certain measures taken prior to the implementation of the program with measures taken at the completion of the program. The resulting information may include both intended and unintended consequences. Successful outcome evaluations must include measurable objectives that allow for meaningful measurements and comparisons to be drawn. In addition, outcome evaluations require a well-planned and useful design in order to establish the effectiveness of the program. There are three types of outcome evaluations: initial, intermediate, and long term. The *initial* outcome evaluation provides the immediate results of the program. The *intermediate* outcome evaluation reports on the results that follow the initial outcome. The final type, the *long-term* outcome evaluation, provides information on the ultimate impact of the program as it relates to accomplishing its goal (Justice Research and Statistics Association, 2004). Because long-term outcome evaluations, also known as *impact* evaluations, sometimes provide unique barriers to evaluation, we will address this category of evaluation separately.

Impact Evaluations.   Impact evaluations are used to determine if a program has positively affected the overall severity of the problem being addressed. Impact evaluations are not as common in the human service field as process and outcome evaluations. One reason for this fact is the reality that impact evaluations often require measurement over long periods of time and change is sometimes slow or challenging to maintain. Another reason for underutilizing impact evaluations is that isolating the effects of a program from other extraneous variables, interventions, and strategies that can impact the population participing in the program is difficult. In other words, attributing change in the population to a specific intervention is extremely difficult. Impact evaluations are also costly, extensive, and require long-range commitments from agencies and program stakeholders.

Evaluation Tools

Human service professionals can choose from a wide range of evaluation tools. Sometimes evaluators get into the habit of using only the same one or two tools to collect their data. The choice of evaluation tools should be based on program goals and objectives and on the user's requirements. Helpers must sample a variety of tools for possible multiple measures and consider the advantages and disadvantages of each data collection method. By careful examination of the tools the helper can choose the options that have the greatest potential for providing the necessary information. Reeves (n.d.) recommends considering some of the following evaluation tools: anecdotal record forms, expert review checklists, focus group protocols, process review logs, implementation logs, interview protocols, and questionnaires. Although Reeves' (n.d.) suggestions refer to the evaluation of interactive multimedia designs, the tools represent a helpful mixture of instruments that easily adapt to career intervention programs, as illustrated in the following paragraphs.

Anecdotal Record Form. The anecdotal record form is used to record critical events that take place during the development and the implementation of the career intervention program. As opposed to "official statistics," this record provides "human stories" of important incidents that occur during the various stages of program design and execution. Each anecdote should be limited to a single incident, should contain factual descriptions of the reported incident, should include a description of the situation, should be written as soon as possible following the situation that occurred, and should include a separate statement describing interpretations or feelings about the incident.

Expert Review Checklist. The expert review checklist is a useful tool for both process and outcome evaluations. The checklist is given to experts in the field (e.g., career intervention experts). The form should include a guide to insure that the experts critique all the aspects of the career intervention program that the agency would like reviewed. The instrument can be in the form of a Likert-type survey that asks respondents to rate various aspects of the program.

Focus Group Protocol. Just as focus groups can be used for conducting needs assessments, they are also valuable means of conducting program evaluations. Focus groups can be used to collect useful data about clients' reactions to the career intervention program. The focus group protocol is the actual evaluation tool that consists of a list of questions regarding the program to be addressed during the focus group.

Process Review Log. A process review log, also referred to as a formative review log, is used for reviewing the program during its formative stages. It consists of three columns. The first column is used to indicate the precise part of the program that is being evaluated. The second column is used to record the evaluator's reactions, questions, comments, and/or suggestions. The third column is used to record the actions taken as a result of the feedback received from the reviewer (Reeves, n.d.).

Implementation Log.   An implementation log gathers information about the actual implementation of the program as compared to the planned implementation. The implementation log consists of four columns. The first column is used to described what was planned to happen during the implementation. Column two describes what actually happened. The third column is used to comment on the differences between the planned and actual implementation. The fourth column is reserved for additional questions, if any, regarding the content and implementation of the program.

Interview Protocol.   Interviews are used to collect data about clients' reactions to the career intervention program. The interview protocol is the evaluation tool used to collect such data. This tool is a type of survey activity and is completed systematically. The overall steps include: (1) organizing the survey team; (2) determining the goal of the survey; (3) selecting a representative sample; (4) generating a list of questions; (5) constructing the instrument; (6) testing the instrument; (7) administering the instrument; (8) analyzing the data; and (9) distributing and using the results.

Questionnaires.   Questionnaires are perhaps the singly most-used evaluation tool. In order to be an effective instrument, questionnaires must be well designed. They can take on many forms such as checklists, multiple-choice questions, rating scales, open-ended questions, and so on. The questionnaire should be designed in such a way that it provides the type of information that is helpful to the human service professionals and to the organization. It should not be too long or require a lengthy amount of time to complete. The wording of questions is very important and it is helpful to follow these guidelines: (1) consider the average reading level of the survey group; (2) make sure that the words used in the questionnaire have the same meaning for everyone; (3) only include a single idea in each question; (4) design questions to minimize the number of words in questions and answers; (5) ask questions as they appear in other studies if the intent is to compare results with another program; (6) be specific when asking questions about frequency or quantity; (7) do not bias questions—state questions neutrally; (8) do not use unfamiliar abbreviations, initials, or double negatives; (9) do not use general terms such as "many," "usually," "often," or "unhappy" (Austin, Cox, Gottlieb, Hawkins, Kruzich, & Rauch, 1982).

   Before using previously developed questionnaires, human service professionals should assess the instrument's prior use and soundness. In other words, helpers must gauge the instruments' reliability and validity. *Reliability* refers to the consistency of the instrument in accurately measuring the traits or factors. *Validity* refers to the degree to which a score is actually measuring what it is supposed to measure.

Evaluation Report

Once the evaluations have been completed, human service professionals must present the information in an evaluation report. According to Reeves (n.d.), evaluation reports are infamous for being lengthy volumes that nobody reads. He suggests dividing the evaluation report into two-page sections each containing the following four parts:

(1) an attention-getting headline; (2) a description of the key issues related to the headline; (3) a presentation of data related to the issues; and (4) a concise recommendation and/or summary of the findings. This type of report is more reader friendly and allows the reader an opportunity to focus on one section at a time thereby increasing the likelihood of impacting important future decisions.

Evaluating the Evaluation Process. Evaluating the evaluation process is just as critical as the evaluation itself. When assessing the evaluation process, the following questions are helpful:

- Are all stakeholders involved in the evaluation process?
- Are opportunities to reflect on program goals and objectives embedded into the evaluation process?
- Are the clients who are involved in the program also involved in the evaluation process?
- Are the needs of the community, funding resources, and the project itself being met through the evaluation process?

Evaluation is a process that guides program efforts from the very start. It continues throughout the various stages of the program and terminates only when all needed information has been obtained. Sound evaluation plans lead to successful career intervention programs.

Modify Program as Needed. Program evaluation should not be used to simply verify the success or failure of a program. If this were the case, then the so-called "successful" programs would run perfectly without ever having to hear from the stakeholders again. Conversely, the alleged "failure" would meet its demise without so much as a chance for a rescue. One of the beneficial aspects of program evaluation is that it provides agencies with crucial feedback so that the successful programs can become even more successful and the not-so-successful programs can be revamped and improved through suggested modifications and adjustments.

Summary

Career intervention program planning, implementation, and evaluation requires careful attention to the various components that shape successful programs. Human service professionals must begin by carefully planning the career intervention program by defining the population, conducting a needs assessment, establishing goals and objectives, and then designing the program. After the program has been planned, human service professionals can turn their attention to program implementation. Program implementation consists of effectively marketing, promoting, and then delivering the career intervention program. Once the program has been implemented, helpers must focus on program evaluations. Effective program evaluations consist of choosing the best types of evaluation, selecting the finest evaluation tools, and developing an evaluation report that provides essential data necessary to modify, strengthen, and enhance future programs.

Key Terms

Consultants
Curriculum-based interventions
Focus groups
Needs assessment

One-to-one interventions
Population
Survey target group

Web Resources

Note that website URLs may change over time.

CareerOneStop
http://www.careeronestop.org

GEAR UP
http://www.ed.gov/programs/gearup/index.html

National Association for Tech Prep Leadership
http://www.natpl.org

National Career Development Association
http://www.ncda.org/index.html

Career Development and Diverse Populations

Now that we have introduced you to the basics of career-development challenges, history, theories, assessments, occupational resources, employment campaigns, and the design, implementation, and evaluation of the career-development program, it is time for you to learn how to integrate this knowledge and apply it carefully and ethically to your work with clients. Part II describes the various populations with whom you will be working as a human service professional. First, you will get acquainted with single parents, displaced homemakers, and welfare-to-work clients. Then you will meet the working poor, victims of intimate partner violence, dislocated workers, and the homeless. Next, you will visit with older workers, offenders/ex-offenders, and those with physical and/or mental disabilities, and finally you will visit those clients with a chemical dependency, veterans, and the newly immigrated.

In each chapter you will meet a case-study client and explore the structural, individual, physical health, and mental health barriers to his or her career success. You will experience and see life through the client's eyes. Then you will delve into a career-development program model designed to move each group of clients toward full-time employment and self-sufficiency. Finally, you will revisit each client, applying the career-development program model to assist that client in finding employment and achieving self-sufficiency.

Your visits begin with the turn of the page.

7

Single Parents and Displaced Homemakers

Entering the Workplace after a Break of Several Years

Case Study: Beverly

Beverly is 42 and has one teenage child and two children in middle school, all three of whom are doing well in school. After 23 years of marriage, her husband asked for a divorce and moved out of the home. Because the amount of alimony and child support that Beverly now receives is not enough to meet the expenses of running a household, which includes rent, groceries, and utilities, she is returning to the workforce after a 17-year gap. Before the children were born, Beverly worked for two years in a cashier's position at a local clothing store and really enjoyed the job. She only left because she was laid off when the store went out of business. While receiving unemployment benefits, Beverly volunteered for her family physician, and by the time her unemployment benefits stopped, her doctor had offered her a part-time position answering telephones and handling insurance claims. Beverly remained in this position for three years until she discovered that she was pregnant. She decided to stay home with her first child and soon after, her second child and third child were born.

Beverly knows she needs to return to the workforce but is unsure where to start or what to do. Her children are supportive, but they have grown used to having a stay-at-home mom. Her mother and siblings live in another state, and although they are willing to provide emotional support from a distance, they are unable to offer financial assistance. While Beverly has considered relocating to be closer to her family, she lacks the financial resources for such a move and is unwilling to uproot the children who are involved with school and community activities. Beverly is also involved in a variety of community activities (PTA, Garden Club, and hospital volunteer) that she may have to give up in order to return to the workforce.

The Single Parent and Displaced Homemaker Population

According to the U.S. Census Bureau (2003), over 12 million or 32 percent of all families with children under the age of 18 are **single-parent** families. This number has increased steadily since 1970 when single parents headed only 3.8 million or 13 percent of all families. While the percentage of single-parent families maintained by the mother has decreased from 86 percent in 1990 to 82 percent in 2002, the percentage maintained by the father has risen from 14 percent in 1990 to 18 percent in 2002. In fact, the number of single-father families has increased fivefold since 1970. Twenty percent of male, single parents are either unemployed or otherwise not in the workforce compared to almost 29 percent of single, female parents who are unemployed or otherwise not in the workforce (U.S. Census Bureau, 2002a). Fifteen percent of male single-parent families live in poverty compared to almost 31 percent of female single-parent families (U.S. Census Bureau, n.d.).

Displaced homemakers are more difficult to identify, because defining them is more complex. Once limited to homemakers between the ages of 35 and 64 (Office of Technology Assessment, 1985), a displaced homemaker is now defined as "one who has been dependent on the income of another family member but is no longer supported by that income, is unemployed or underemployed, and is experiencing difficulty in obtaining or upgrading employment" (U.S. Department of Labor, 2000, p. 49318). This newer definition removes the age requirement. You should note that not all single parents are displaced homemakers nor are all displaced homemakers single parents. Displaced homemakers can be either male or female, as well as separated, divorced, or widowed. Thus, determining the exact number of displaced homemakers is a difficult task. Thirty-eight percent of single fathers have never married, 41.4 percent are divorced, 16.4 percent are separated, and 4.2 percent are widowed. In mother-maintained families, 43.1 percent of single mothers have never married, 34.7 percent are divorced, 17.8 percent are separated, and 4.4 percent widowed (U.S. Census Bureau, 2002b). According to Fields and Casper (2001), in March 2000 almost 27 million people between the ages of 15 and 65 were separated, divorced, or widowed, and an additional 13 million were over the age of 65.

Barriers to Career Success

Structural Barriers

Affordable Childcare.   In 2002, approximately 13.4 million single parents had custody of over 21 million children under the age of 18. More than 84 percent of these custodial parents were mothers (Grall, 2003). Between 1993 and 1997, the number of single parents working full time and year-round rose from 46 percent to 51 percent. During the same period, the number of single parents receiving public assistance decreased to 34 percent (U.S. Census Bureau, 2000). Reliance upon childcare is paramount to employment success for single, working parents. Seventy-nine percent of children less than three years of age, 90.7 percent of children ages 3 to 5, and 59.4 percent of children ages 6 to 11 who lived in a single-parent home where the parent was employed were in childcare (U.S. Census Bureau, 2000).

Finding affordable and dependable childcare is not an easy task, and a lack of affordable childcare can hinder a single parent's ability to obtain *and* keep a job (Employment Training Project, 1996; U.S. General Accounting Office, 2004). Inflexible work schedules that require overtime or travel may impact a parent's ability to find childcare at certain hours and during times of emergency such as a child's illness. Single parents are frequently faced with choosing between a higher-paying job with inflexible hours that might require the use of an unknown childcare provider and a lower-paying job that comes with a lower cost of working because more regular childcare opportunities are available (Stone, 1997). Unfortunately, not all parents have the opportunity to make such a choice, and they have to deal with their fear of child abuse and poor quality childcare because it is all that they can afford. Jobs that require worker relocation also impact childcare because workers have to spend time searching for childcare in a new location. Often workers lack the social connections in the new location to find childcare quickly, cheaply, and easily (Seguino & Butler, 1998). School closings alone can wreak havoc with the work schedule of a single parent who has to have back-up childcare during times of inclement weather and school holidays.

Elder Care and Informal Caregiving. According to the U.S. Census Bureau (1996), life expectancy is expected to increase from 75.9 years in 1995 to 82.0 years in 2050. After the year 2010 when members of the baby-boom generation start to turn 65, the population of people ages 65 and over is expected to increase from 13.2 percent in 2010 to 20 percent by 2030. This change is an increase of 39.4 million elderly persons to 69.4 million by 2030. The elder population age 85 and older will be the fastest growing age group, doubling in size from 1995 to 2010, then increasing fivefold by 2050.

Approximately 52 million Americans or 31 percent of the adult population are informal caregivers (Older Women's League, n.d.). Almost 25 percent of American householders provide care to families or friends over the age of 50. Because formal long-term care and support do not meet the needs of many Americans, they rely on an informal network of unpaid care. Families provide **informal caregiving** for several reasons, ranging from commitment and duty, to social expectations and financial constraints. What does this caregiving have to do with single parents and displaced homemakers?

Despite their participation in the workforce, younger, single parents and displaced homemakers will find themselves increasingly responsible for **elder care** within their family unit. In 1997 seventy-three percent of the informal caregivers for family and friends over the age of 50 were women. Women who must balance the need to provide caregiving with that of childcare find it difficult to maintain full-time employment. While some financial resources for childcare are available to single parents and displaced homemakers, elder care does not have the same resources. Single parents and displaced homemakers who are handling caregiving duties often face similar barriers as those with childcare responsibilities. Inflexible schedules and the need to travel and work overtime prove difficult for parents working this "third shift" at home. As elder care in the home becomes increasingly common, women in particular may find themselves taking care of their elder parents for a period of time that is longer than they spent rearing their own children (Older Women's League, n.d.). While some workplace policies include family caregiving, they tend to focus on childcare and omit issues of elder care (Medjuck, Keefe, & Fancey, 1998).

Transportation. Single parents are more likely to have fewer economic resources and live in low-income households in poor neighborhoods with limited access to a variety of resources than two-parent households (Bruin & Cook, 1997). Transportation is one resource that might be a barrier to career success for single parents and displaced homemakers. Rural communities seldom have local, public transportation. Single parents and displaced homemakers in these communities who do not own a vehicle or know how to drive will need employment within walking distance until they are able to purchase a car or obtain a driver's license (Seguino & Butler, 1998).

Workplace Discrimination. Age discrimination and gender bias are two forms of workplace discrimination that often plague single parents and displaced homemakers.

Age Discrimination. Those trying to reenter the workplace after several years may face age discrimination as they compete with younger workers for jobs. Workers age 55 and older sometimes find themselves combating myths such as older workers perform at a lower level, are less able to learn, are entitled to stop work after the age of 55, and take more sick leave (Paul & Townsend, 1993).

Gender Bias. Myths about single parents such as single parents will take more sick leave than nonparents and single mothers, in particular, will be more likely to take sick leave than single fathers sometimes exert influence on hiring decisions. Still another myth is that female employees will take more leave time for elder care than will their male and nonparent counterparts (Doress-Worters, 1994).

Gender bias may even impact workplace evaluations, keeping single parents and displaced homemakers, but women specifically, from advancing due to the "glass ceiling." Men are often viewed as aggressive, forceful, decisive, and independent. Women are characterized as helpful, sympathetic, kind, and concerned about others. These stereotypical behaviors have become the norm, the unspoken guidelines for acceptable workplace behavior; workers who deviate from these norms often find workplace advancement to be difficult because of their "lack of fit." Work is expected to take precedence over family matters, and overtime and travel become linked to promotions (Heilman, 2001). Workers who do not fit the norms because they need to balance the demands of the workplace with those of the family may find workplace success to be almost out of their reach. Displaced homemakers entering the workplace after several years of unemployment may not even be aware of these "unspoken rules" of workplace behavior.

The gender wage gap also affects single parents and displaced homemakers. Forty-one years after the **Equal Pay Act of 1963,** women are making 75.5 cents for every dollar earned by men (Institute for Women's Policy Research, 2004). While this gap is narrower than it was in 1960 when women earned 60.7 cents to every dollar earned by men, the slowed pace of increase since the early 1990s has raised concerns that women may not reach pay equity with men (Institute for Women's Policy Research, 2003). Over the long run, this disparity is even more pronounced. Rose and Hartman (2004) discovered that women workers in their prime earning years of 26 to 59 make only 38 percent of what men earn. Their research showed that across the 15 years of the study the average working woman earned only $273,592, while the average working man earned $722,693. These figures show a gap of 62 percent, or a gap more than twice as large as the 25-percent gap in earnings frequently reported. Even when single mothers and female displaced homemakers find employment, they seldom earn what a male earns, making their financial independence more difficult to achieve. Work patterns are often a key to earnings, and female, single parents and displaced homemakers often have fewer years of work experience, fewer work hours per year, fewer work hours per week, frequently leave the labor force, and earn less than their male counterparts (U.S. General Accounting Office, 2003). According to Barko (2000), "if men and women were paid equally, more than 50 percent of low-income households across the country—dual earner as well as single mother—would rise above the poverty line" (p.61).

Single parents and displaced homemakers may also have a difficult time finding jobs at a living wage. Jobs that offer higher-paying wages are often accompanied by such requirements as travel and overtime—job requirements that are often problematic for this population. Still other high-paying jobs may require relocation, and not every worker can easily move. Relocation requires additional financial assistance, even when it is accompanied by a moving stipend, and many single parents and displaced homemakers lack such funds. An inability to balance the workplace requirements with those of the family may result in a single parent accepting a lower-paying job that does not have health benefits (Seguino & Butler, 1998). This population, however, strongly needs medical benefits for their children, and public assistance may be a viable alternative for some single parents on an emergency basis (Stone 1997).

Sex-Role Stereotyping. Society still views employment and parenting through the lens of sex-role stereotyping. According to Etaugh and Folger (1998), full-time employment of fathers, as compared to part-time employment, often enhances other people's perceptions of the fathers' professional competence. Fathers who reduce their work hours are devalued and often seen as less professionally competent. While both fathers and mothers are often viewed as less nurturing when they are employed full-time, working mothers are viewed as even less nurturing than working fathers. Because nurturance is viewed as a more typical component of a woman's personality than of a man's, full-time working mothers are often viewed as deviating from their expected gender role. Stone (1997) notes that society gives women conflicting messages about motherhood and career, thus making it difficult for them to reconcile work and motherhood. Single parents, despite their gender, have no choice but to deviate from these gender-role expectations.

Individual Barriers

Lack of Marketable Job Skills and Work Experience.   A lack of marketable job skills may also serve as a barrier to career success for single parents and displaced homemakers. Single parents often lack the time and financial resources necessary to complete additional training and coursework that would make them more competitive in the workforce. Newly single parents or displaced homemakers may also lack marketable job skills such as computer competency, because they have been in the home for several years rather than in the workforce. Although they may have developed skills in homemaking through volunteer activities or even through past work experience, the lack of current experience in paid work, little or outdated education, and/or little or no source of income can be significant handicaps to finding employment. Securing a well-paying job when one lacks current marketable skills is not an easy task. Often single parents and displaced homemakers are forced into lower paying jobs while they try to gain the skills necessary to obtain a better job (Employment Training Project, 1996; Fields, 2003; U.S. General Accounting Office, 1994, 2003, 2004; Office of Technology Assessment, 1985; Vosler & Robertson, 1998).

Lack of Support System.   Single parents and displaced homemakers need a variety of supports to help them become successfully employed. Grandparents often serve as childcare providers for working single parents, sometimes raising the children themselves while the parent relocates to find better employment. In 2002, 5.6 million children (8 percent of all children) were living in households with a coresident grandparent. Ten percent of children under the age of 6, 7 percent of children ages 6 to 11, and 6 percent of children ages 12 to 17 lived in a household with a grandparent. At least 65 percent of these children had one parent living in the household (Fields, 2003). Grandparents are not the only people providing support for single parents and displaced homemakers. Other unmarried people may be sharing resources and providing support for each other (Bullough, 1998).

Federal support providing financial assistance for childcare, transportation, education, and training for displaced homemakers began in 1976 with amendments to the Vocational Education Act. In 1984 Congress strengthened the **Carl D. Perkins Vocational Education Act of 1984** in an attempt to serve the eligible population of two to four million (Office of Technology Assessment, 1985). State funds were the main support for displaced homemaker programs in 1984, but these funds were replaced when the **Workforce Investment Act of 1998 (WIA)** replaced the Carl D. Perkins Act. Very little funding is available at this time to directly meet the needs of displaced homemakers who must qualify for funding resources under other definitions such as dislocated workers or single parents (U.S. Department of Labor, 2000). Unfortunately, many displaced homemakers may not qualify for assistance because their income loss is recent, and their income before they became displaced was too high (Office of Technology Assessment, 1985).

Another barrier to success for this population is the lack of peer support or social groups. Single parents and displaced homemakers often spend so much time meeting the needs of their families and employers that they seldom take time to search for supports for themselves. Whether support is available through their work, community, family, or friends, single parents and displaced homemakers find that emotional support often eases the transition to independence and reinforces the universality of their situation (Bruin & Cook, 1997; Seguino & Butler, 1998; Office of Technology Assessment, 1985; Vosler & Robinson, 1998; Ward & Spitze, 1998). According to Burden (1986), single fathers often rely on the person they are dating to provide emotional support. Single mothers tend to rely on their sons for emotional support. Single fathers also report larger support networks than do single mothers.

While widows often benefit from social support, this benefit varies based on the type of support and the widow's stage of grieving. Bankoff (1983) suggests that widows in the first phase of grieving—the "crisis-loss" phase—benefit more from emotional support from family members than from friends and neighbors. At this point, the widow is in a state of chaos while she tries to adjust to the loss of the central person in her life. Widows in this phase tend to withdraw from reality and become unresponsive to human relationships. Once they have entered the second phase—the transition phase—widows often need a different type of social support other than intimacy. This support, which comes from the friends, provides widows with the opportunity to talk about important personal problems with their support network. Now that the intensity of the grief has decreased, widows start to reorganize and rebuild social relationships. Families providing too much emotional support for widows in this second phase, however, can make the widows' transition to their new roles more difficult. Until widows have reached the second stage of grieving, they may not be able to deal with issues of employment and job search. In the third phase of widowhood, widows start to rebuild their lives and new identity as a single rather than married person (Bankoff, 1983).

Divorce.   Marriage and divorce trends have shifted over the past 30 years. In 1970 the median age for a first marriage was 23.2 years for men and 20.8 for women. By 2000, the mean age had increased to 26.8 for men and 25.1 for women. On the whole, the number of single men and women (never married and divorced) in 2000 has increased since 1970. The married population has decreased proportionately from almost 60 percent of the women in 1970 to 52 percent in 2000 (Fields & Casper, 2001). Although some literature links the increase in divorce rates to the increase of women's full-time employment (Schoen & Urton, 1979; Spitze, 1988), other research suggests that women may consider work as a type of insurance policy against future divorce (Greene & Quester, 1982). Still other research connects divorce to changing gender roles (Davis, 1984). Hou and Omwanda (1997) suggest that participation in the female labor force was a leading factor in divorce rates prior to 1969, but they note that this factor has changed over time. While not all households that experience a divorce become poor, divorce is frequently associated with the beginning of poverty (Davis & Weber, 1998). According to the U.S. Census Bureau (2002b), over 3 million single-parent families were below the poverty level. Divorced and separated male, single parents headed 48 percent of those families in poverty. Divorced and separated female, single parents headed 43.4 percent of the single-parent families in poverty. Widows headed 3.8 percent of the single-parent families in poverty, and widowers headed 5.3 percent of those single-parent families below the poverty line. Displaced homemakers who go through a divorce after 20 or 30 years of marriage are particularly at risk for being in poverty. Often they are too young to qualify for Social Security, and they seldom qualify for public assistance because their income loss is so recent. Also they may be unwilling or unknowledgeable enough to ask for assistance (Office of Technology Assessment, 1985). The transition to divorce or widowhood is associated with more negative effects for women than it is for men (Marks & Lambert, 1998).

Child Support.   According to the U.S. Census Bureau (2000), in 2000 only 56 percent of custodial parents had child support agreements as compared to 1992 when 54 percent of custodial parents received child support (Scoon-Rogers & Lester, 1995). Davis and Weber (1998) link entry into poverty directly to a decrease in or lack of child support. They explain that child support is one of the five main routes out of poverty. Out of the 79 million custodial parents awarded child support in 2002, only 44.8 percent received their full payments. Forty-five percent of single, custodial mothers received full child support as compared to 39 percent of single, custodial fathers. Although the proportion of single, custodial parents living in poverty declined from 33.3 percent in 1993 to 23.4 percent in 2001, the number of custodial parents in poverty is still almost four times higher than the rate for married couple families in 2001. The poverty rate of custodial mothers dropped from 36.8 percent in 1993 to 25 percent in 2001, but it was still higher than the poverty rate for custodial fathers at 14.7 percent. The 3.1 million custodial parents who received full child support payments in 2001 had an average family income of $32,300 with a poverty rate of 14.6 percent. Eighty-five percent of custodial parents receiving full child support payments had **joint custody** or child visitation arrangements with the noncustodial parents (Grall, 2003).

Death of Spouse.   Morgan's (1981) study of widowhood at midlife showed that women who have been poor all of their lives are more likely to become widowed than women who have not been poor. Consequences differ, however, for widows and widowers. In traditional divisions of labor, women tend to rely on their husbands to provide a variety of services including income. Death of a spouse often means a decrease of income for the widow, but also a loss of services such as household repairs. Males who lose spouses, however, often lose childcare and homemaking services.

Physical Health Barriers

Since employers are the primary source of health insurance coverage, the availability of such coverage often motivates people to choose one job over another. Single parents and displaced homemakers are no exception. In fact, the need for quality medical and health insurance is particularly important for this group. Eighty-six percent of children living in single-mother households were covered by health insurance, as compared to 82 percent of children living in single-father households. Children living with divorced mothers were more likely to have health insurance coverage than were those living with never married mothers. Health coverage increases as family income increases, but children living in households receiving public assistance were more likely to be covered by health insurance than those who were not in public assistant households (Fields, 2003). Since participation in public assistance programs often includes health coverage, low-income single parents sometimes have to decide between working part-time for little pay but still qualifying for health insurance through public assistance or working full time for little pay but no longer qualifying for health coverage because of earning too much money (Seguino & Butler, 1998).

Children with Disabilities.   Parents with special needs children often leave the labor force or reduce their working hours because of the additional time they need to care for these children. Low-income single parents in particular face this barrier to success because of the prevalence of disabilities in this population (Loprest & Acs, 1996). Although **Supplemental Security Income (SSI)** provides limited cash assistance to some low-income adults and children with disabilities, in 1996 welfare reform restructured the definition of "disabilities" to exclude children with less severe disabilities. Therefore, many low-income single parents have lost the financial assistance that helped them care for their disabled children and now have to enter the workforce, despite the childcare limitations that may pose a barrier to success. The care of a child with a disability can also negatively impact the parent's participation in the workforce if the child needs specialized childcare services, medical assistance, special diets, or even transportation. When single parents provide the sole economic support for the family, the need for an income to relieve the financial burden of the child with disabilities becomes very important. Parenting a child with disabilities can be taxing because of the need to balance childcare demands with the needs of the employer.

Personal Health and Disabilities.   Lee, Oh, Hartmann, and Gault (2004) found that low-income single mothers were almost twice as likely to have a disability, as were married mothers. Twenty-one percent of single mothers had some form of disability as compared to 11 percent of married mothers. Thirteen percent of low-income single mothers had a severe disability as compared to 6 percent of low-income married mothers. Fifty-six percent of low-income single mothers reported physical disabilities, 36 percent reported mental disabilities, and 21 percent reported communication disabilities (Lee, Oh, Hartmann, & Gault, 2004). When women with disabilities enter the workforce, their health limitations often affect their ability to remain employed (Earle & Heymann, 2002).

Children of adolescent parents are at risk for disabilities, poor physical health, and abuse. These problems contribute to barriers to career success for their mothers, who are also at an increased risk for physical health problems, depression, and addictions such as smoking, alcohol, and other drug use (Vosler & Robertson, 1998).

According to the Older Women's League (n.d.), women often provide 50 percent more hours per week than men in informal caregiving, and they tend to do so for longer periods of time, often putting their own health at risk. Almost one-third of those women who provide informal caregiving consider their health as fair to poor. Forty-four percent report some type of physical strain due to caregiving activities, combined with frequent illness.

Are married people healthier than single people? Waite (1995) states that married people live longer, have better physical health, and are more psychologically healthy than are unmarried people. In addition, other studies demonstrate that young married adults are happier and have less substance abuse issues than single adults. While problematic levels of alcohol use drops during a seven-year time period for single and married young adults, the levels drop more sharply for young married adults (Horwitz, White, & Howell-White, 1996). Unhappily married, employed women have been found to have higher blood pressure at home as compared to happily married employed women (Carels, Sherwood, Szczepanski, & Blumenthal, 2000).

Mental Health Barriers

In normal conditions of life, people occupy more than one role, sometimes sharing roles with other family members such as spouses. However, single parents seldom have someone with whom to share roles, and they must take on multiple roles. Along with participating in the workforce, they parent, provide elder care, and serve in their communities, often at the same time. Research is relatively new on the cumulative impact of multiple roles on the psychological well-being of employed women (Doress-Worters, 1994). Adult daughters are more frequently becoming the caregivers of older parents at the same time that employment of middle-aged women is growing. These increased demands on the female employee often result in emotional stress. Forty-four percent of female informal caregivers who provide caregiving for someone over the age of 65 are concerned about their ability to juggle caregiving with their other responsibilities as compared to 27 percent of male informal caregivers. Thirty-three percent of female caregivers report concern about not having enough time for themselves as compared to 26 percent of male caregivers. Twenty-eight percent of female caregivers report concern about having enough time with their children compared to 20 percent of male caregivers (Older Women's League, n.d.). Male caregivers are more likely to provide services than they are to provide hands-on care; female caregivers are likely to do both, combining managed services with hands-on care. The more hours that female caregivers spend in the workforce, the less hours they spend in hands-on elder care, and they take a more service-management approach resembling that of the male caregiver. This suggests that employment may be more influential than gender on roles (Finley, 1989).

Working parents in general have been identified as being at risk for role overload, but single working mothers in particular have an increased risk for poorer physical health and emotional well-being. Single working mothers are also at risk for depression, decreased self-esteem, and stress (Carels et al., 2000; Marks & Lambert, 1998; Seguino & Butler, 1998). Widows and divorced single mothers are also at risk for depression, stress, and anxiety (Carels et al., 2000; Hou & Omwanda, 1997; Marks & Lambert, 1998). Being married and staying married does not enhance young, adult women's mental health with regards to depression (Horwitz et al., 1996). Marks and Lambert (1998) found that midlife men who remained separated or divorced over a five-year period experienced less of an increase in depression and hostility than did younger men. Jones (1991) reported that a job loss affected a man's mental health status more than a woman's mental health status.

A study by Horwitz et al. (1996) examined the effect of marriage on the mental health of 18-, 21-, and 24-year-old men and women who either remained unmarried or married and remained married over seven years. Their findings suggest that young adults who marry and stay married have higher levels of well-being than those who remain single. For example, married men and women are less depressed and have fewer alcohol problems than their single counterparts. Men who marry and stay married showed less depression. Men with children and less income were more likely than women to show depression.

Career Development Program Model: Single Parents and Displaced Homemakers

A career development program for use with single parents and displaced homemakers requires an individualized approach to address each client's needs and barriers with respect to the goal of long-term employment. Because of the varied backgrounds presented by this group of clients—divorced, never married, separated, male/female, parent/nonparent—human service professionals must take great care to look at each client separately and design a series of interventions that will enhance the client's career success. Our program has three major components: the applicant pool, the individual success plan (ISP), and the program evaluation that we explain in further detail in the following sections. Figure 7.1 is a graphic model of the career development model.

Applicant Pool

From the applicant pool that includes all single parents and displaced homemakers, intake personnel determine which clients fit the criteria for participation in a specific program and which do not. For example, public assistance programs offer a variety of services that target low-income, single parents, thus referrals for those programs may better meet their specific needs (See Chapter 8). Depending upon the funding source, grants may have certain requirements that applicants must meet to receive services. For example, some grants may only serve single parents or displaced homemakers who are seeking entry into a nontraditional field of work.

Individual Success Plan

Developing an Individual Success Plan (ISP) provides clients a personal approach to career development. The fact that a job is available and a single parent or displaced homemaker possesses the skills for it does not mean that the job is "affordable." Seguino and Butler (1998) suggest that single parents need to measure both the benefits and the costs of taking a job. By developing an ISP, human service professionals can help clients determine the best approach to full employment for them. Each single parent and displaced homemaker brings a different combination of factors to the job

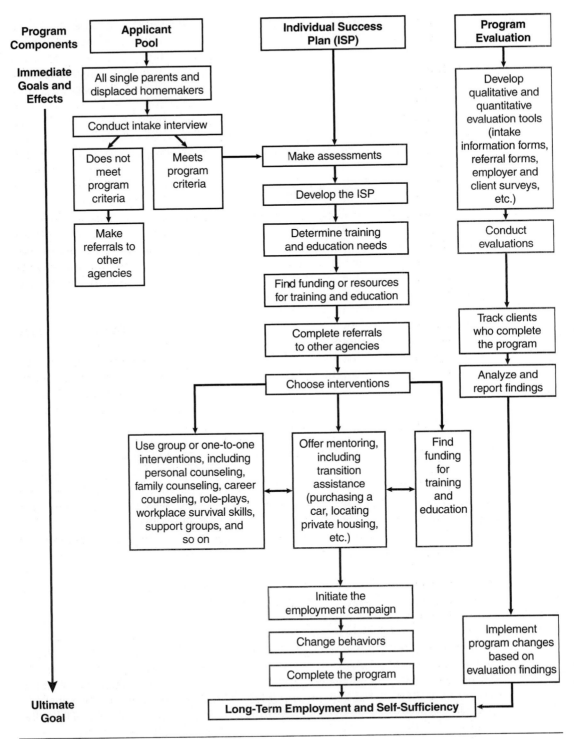

FIGURE 7.1 *Career Development Program Model: Single Parents and Displaced Homemakers*

search, and the ISP can address each of those factors, fostering a personalized approach for each client.

Make Assessments. In Chapter 3 we provided a variety of career-related assessments human service professionals can use based on their clients' needs and background. Starting with a traditional intake interview, helpers can identify clients' needs and decide whether or not employment is the best course of action at this time. During the interview, the client and human service professional will examine the family-survival strategies currently in use to determine their appropriateness. Exploring the costs and benefits of employment during the personal interview not only helps to assess whether a job is "affordable" for the client, but it also facilitates other decision-making. For example, creating a basic needs budget with the clients can help them assess what level of wages they need to meet the family/individual's minimal material needs. Table 7.1 contains a list of assessments appropriate for use with the single parent and displaced homemaker population in designing an ISP. Although we encourage the use of several assessments, human service professionals must be careful to use the assessments that best fit the needs of their clients. (See Chapter 3 for additional details on each assessment.)

Develop the ISP. After the client and the human service professional complete the assessments, they can develop the ISP. Using information gathered from the traditional intake interview, the assessments, and from discussions with the client, human service professionals can gain insight into values, job interests, career goals, and possible barriers to their client's career success. Human service professionals must allow clients to help create their ISPs as much as possible to encourage their participation in the career development process.

Determine Training and Education Needs. Using the results from the assessments, human service professionals and clients next need to determine what type of education and training, if any, is needed to help clients reach their goals. Clients who have not finished high school may need to complete a General Equivalency Diploma (GED) prior to or during the job search or other training. Other clients may need to explore the possibility of college or a variety of training programs, depending upon their needs. Depending upon the length of time that they have been out of the workforce, clients may need to brush-up their skills, or they may need exposure to different jobs to help them make their decisions. Depending upon individual circumstances, some clients may need to find employment immediately and put education plans on hold until they have a steady income. By giving clients a long-term goal, human service professionals can help clients understand that they are not "stuck" in a job. Having a plan to move into a job that meets their goals may make the transition to employment easier. Assessments may point out life skills such as budgeting, nutrition/health, balancing work with family, choosing child/elder care, stress management, and time management that clients need to strengthen. Allowing clients to choose which life skills they will strengthen first helps to empower them in this time of great flux by allowing them to make decisions.

TABLE 7.1   *Career-Related Assessments for Use with Single Parents and Displaced Homemakers*

Title	Source
Ability Tests	
Career Key*	Jones, L. K., & Jones, J. W. (2000). *Career key.* Raleigh, NC: Author.
Motivated Skills Card Sort	Knowdell, R. (2002, June). *Motivated skills card sort.* San Jose, CA: Career Research & Testing.
O*NET Ability Profiler*	O*NET Consortium (2003, April). *O*NET ability profiler.* Washington, DC: Author.
Elevations Manual Card Sort System	Scully, H. (2003, August). *Elevations manual card sort system.* Roseville, CA: Author.
WorkKeys	ACT, Inc. (1993). *Workeys assessments.* Iowa City, IO: ACT.
Interest Inventories	
Career Explorer CD-ROM*	JIST Works (2004). *Careerexplorer CD-ROM.* Indianapolis, IN: Author.
Leisure to Occupations Connection Search	McDaniels, C., & Mullins, S. R. (1999). *The leisure to occupations connection search.* Indianapolis, IN: JIST Works.
Occupational Interests Card Sort	Knowdell, R. (2002, June). *Occupational interests card sort.* San Jose, CA: Career Research & Testing.
O*NET Interest Profiler*	O*NET (n.d.) *O*NET interest profiler.* Washington, DC: Author.
Self-Directed Search, Forms CP, R, & E	Holland, J. L. (1990). *Self-directed search form CP: Career planning.* Lutz, FL: Psychological Assessment Resources. Holland J. L. (1994). *Self-directed search form R.* Lutz, FL: Psychological Assessment Resources. Holland, J. L. (1996). *Self-directed search form E* (4th ed.). Lutz, FL: Psychological Assessment Resources.
Transition-to-Work Inventory	Liptak, J. J. (2004). *Transition-to-work inventory.* Indianapolis, IN: JIST Works.
Voc-Tech Quick Screener	JIST Works (2002). *Voc-tech quick screener.* Indianapolis, IN: Author.
Personality Inventories	
Keirsey Temperament Sorter II	Keirsey, D. (1998, May). *Please understand me II.* Del Mar, CA: Prometheus Nemesis Book.
Vocational Preference Inventory	Holland, J. L. (1985). *Vocational preference inventory (VPI).* Lutz, FL: Psychological Assessment Resources.

TABLE 7.1   Continued

Title	*Source*
Value Inventories	
Career Values Card Sort	Knowdell, R. (1998, June). *Career values card sort.* San Jose, CA: Career Research & Testing.
O*NET Work Importance Locator and Profiler*	O*NET Consortium (n.d.). *O*NET work importance locator and profiler.* Washington, DC: Author.
Values-Driven Work Card Sort	Career Action Center. (n.d.) *Values-driven work card sort.* Menlo Park, CA: Prodigy Press.
Work Orientation and Values Survey	Brady, R. P. (2002). *Work orientation and values survey.* Indianapolis, IN: JIST Works.
Career-Development Inventories	
Career Attitudes and Strategies Inventory	Holland, J. L., & Gottfredson, G. D. (1994). *Career attitudes and strategies inventory.* Lutz, FL: Psychological Assessment Resources.
Career Beliefs Inventory	Krumboltz, J. D. (1991). *Career beliefs inventory.* Mountain View, CA: CPP
Career Decision Scale	Osipow, S. H., Carney, C. G., Winer, J. L., Yanico, B. J., & Koschier. M. (1987). *Career decision scale* (3rd ed.). Lutz, FL: Psychological Assessment Resources.
Career Thoughts Inventory	Sampson, J. P., Peterson, G. W., Lenz, J. G., Reardon, R. C., & Saunders, D. E. (1996). *Career thoughts inventory.* Lutz, FL: Psychological Assessment Resources.
Career Transition Inventory	Heppner, M. J. (1991). *Career transition inventory.* Columbia, MO: Author.
My Vocational Situation	Holland, J. L., Daiger, D., & Power, P. G. (1980). *My vocational situation.* Mountain View, CA: CPP.
Overcoming Barriers Card Sort Game Kit	Harney, E. E., & Angel, D. L. (1999). *Overcoming barriers card sort game kit.* Hacienda Heights, CA: WorkNet Solutions.
Salient Beliefs Review: Connecting Spirit to Work	Bloch, D. (2003). *Salient beliefs review: Connecting spirit to work.* Indianapolis, IN: JIST Works.
Vocational Exploration and Insight Kit	Holland, J. L., Birk, J. M., Cooper, J. F., Dewey, C. R., Dolliver, H., Takai, R. T., & Tyler, L. (1980). *The vocational exploration and insight kit.* Mountain View, CA: CPP.

* Use only if client is computer literate.

Find Funding or Resources for Training and Education.   Funding or resources for some training and education may be available through the local One-Stop Career Centers of the Workforce Investment Act, depending upon the client's income level and qualifications. Community colleges and universities often have tuition assistance through grants and scholarships, and in some cases they offer programs that target the single-parent/displaced homemaker population. Other local agencies, along with businesses, community colleges, training and education grants, community organizations, and clubs may also provide training programs either free or at reduced cost. Human service professionals need to be familiar with local programs and various funding sources to better help their clients secure the training and education they need for success.

Complete Referrals to Other Agencies.   Interagency cooperation is important at this point, because some clients may need referrals for issues such as medical care, mental health care, childcare and transportation assistance, elder care, and life skills. Other clients may have more immediate needs such as food and shelter. Certain barriers to employment may necessitate referral, too. As before, human service professionals need to be aware of community resources that can help their clients.

Choose Interventions.   The career development program model for the single parent and displaced homemaker has three categories of interventions: one-to-one interventions, training and education, and mentoring. These interventions may be offered simultaneously or in phases, depending upon the individual needs of clients as well as the requirements of the local agency. Some clients may need all three interventions while others may only need one or two of them. The helping professional should take into consideration that certain clients may respond better to small groups than to an individualized approach.

Using Group or One-to-One Interventions.   In some instances, counseling is needed to help clients transition into self-sufficiency. This intervention may involve personal, career, and family counseling; and it could include role-plays and support, or psycho-educational groups. Clients may be referred elsewhere for services that are not available at the home agency. Personal and family counseling could address such issues as grief, stress, anxiety, self-esteem, and/or depression. Support groups, process groups, or career groups can augment the personal counseling for those clients who are ready for a group format (Creamer, Duggan, & Kidd, 1999; Duggan & Jurgens, 2005). For example, single parents often benefit from being in a group with other single parents who are also learning to balance home, family, and work obligations. Male, single parents in particular can benefit from a group setting to decrease the isolation of being a single, working father. Both male and female displaced homemakers can benefit from a group approach that decreases their isolation by allowing them to discover that they are not alone in their situation, be it death of a spouse or divorce. Career exploration interventions could include job shadowing or even workplace survival skills.

Providing Training and Education.   Although training and education were mentioned earlier with respect to funding, they are also interventions. Clients who need to find work immediately in order to pay the bills may have to delay their education and training. They may need encouragement to continue their training and education while on the job. Providing classes in life-skills training and education may fall under this intervention as well for clients who need additional help with budgeting, money management, stress reduction, time management, parenting skills, taxes, automobile repair, and household maintenance (Office of Technology, 1985). Human service professionals need to encourage single parents and displaced homemakers to choose the training and education that meets their needs, thus empowering them in their decision-making.

Offering Mentoring.   Some clients may need mentoring assistance in addition to other interventions. Mentors assist clients in the transition to self-sufficiency, a process that can last for several weeks or years. Mentors might help clients who need assistance locating a dependable form of transportation; learning how to make household repairs; locating affordable, safe childcare or elder care; or locating housing. Mentors could be from an agency or they could be trained volunteers who have developed a strong network within the community to assist clients in their transition. As helpers outside an agency, mentors help clients with their integration into the community.

Initiate the Employment Campaign.   The employment campaign begins at different times for different clients, depending on their needs and goals. Some clients may need to start their employment campaign immediately, whereas others may have time to complete work-related activities before starting the campaign. Eliminating barriers to employment success before initiating a job campaign is the best approach, but some clients will have to work on several activities at once. The latter event emphasizes the need for intensive case management by the human service professional. In the next section we provide an overview of considerations for single parents and displaced homemakers during the employment campaign. For additional details, see Chapter 5.

The Strategic Job Search.   In this phase, human service professionals use information gathered from the assessments and the intake interview to help clients integrate their values with their goals in order to facilitate the job-search process. By stressing the impact of clients' values on employment choices, human service professionals can help clients choose employment that better matches their needs and personalities. Better choices will allow for a more comfortable placement that in turn may result in less stress in the future. Clients who have been out of the workforce for several years will need to develop their own network of job contacts. Other job possibilities clients can explore include working at home or starting a business. Providing job-search classes or referring clients to small business classes offered by the local Chamber of Commerce can be useful at this stage.

Job-Search Correspondence.   Clients may find that correspondence techniques have changed since they last used them, so refresher training will probably be necessary. Clients must learn how to create letters of application along with thank-you letters following an interview. They may need practice writing letters that accept or decline a job offer. Clients find that role-playing these situations is helpful. As clients gain more job experience, they will hone these skills on their own, but clients who have been out of the workforce for several years will need help.

Tailor-Made Resumes.   Clients entering the workforce after a break of several years may feel that they have no job skills to offer an employer. They may benefit by preparing a functional resume to organize their job experience according to their skills. This type of resume can increase clients' self-esteem, because it enables them to see that they have job skills despite taking a break from the workforce. Clients who have a work history but need to seek better employment may be better served by using a chronological resume to stress their steady employment. Some clients may choose to use electronic resumes, depending upon their job interests, relocation possibilities, or their own technology skills. Creating a resume will help *all* clients organize and better understand themselves, allowing them to focus more on their strengths, instead of their weaknesses.

Interviewing Strategies.   Self-esteem can impact interviewing skills; with this in mind, helpers can use role-playing in possible types of interviewing situations to help their clients who may need to attend a Job Fair where interviews are more spontaneous and less structured. Role-playing those types of situations would also help clients prepare for the interview. Some clients may need help in crafting answers to some common interview questions. Human service professionals can videotape clients during mock interviews and then critique the interview with the client. This technique gives clients an opportunity to see themselves as others see them. Clients who have been out of the workforce for a while or for those who are moving into a new career may need tips on appropriate interview attire.

Change Behaviors.   Participation in career development programs is designed to help clients diminish their barriers to career success and to facilitate their move to self-sufficiency. Some clients may need job search and resume assistance but may not need to make behavioral changes. Other clients may need to learn new behaviors that will help them enter the workforce. Still others clients may need to learn new behaviors in order to maintain their physical, mental, and family health while they enter the workplace. Some clients require more intensive assistance than others to decrease their barriers to employment success. Although clients' specific needs and/or behavioral changes will vary with each person's ISP, all clients will have had an opportunity to improve their interpersonal and work-related skills, along with whatever other skills they originally targeted for change.

Complete the Program.   Clients who complete the program are those who have met the program criteria, completed their assessments, developed their ISPs, completed the training and education that were detailed in their ISPs, and exhibited behavioral changes that lead to employment. Clients who drop out at any time during the process, need to be advised of the ramifications of their decision—they will probably lose funds and other forms of support. Some clients may have to cycle through several of the program stages at a later time as they move from low-skill employment to employment requiring more advanced skills.

Achieve Goal of Long-Term Employment. The client's final goal is long-term employment and self-sufficiency. What is long-term employment? Each agency needs to create a working definition of *long-term employment* for program evaluation purposes. Generally, when clients have been employed and self-sufficient for at least a year and are able to fully support themselves and their family members, they can be considered self-sufficient with long-term employment. While some clients may return to the agency for assistance, most clients just need help at that time and are now on their way to self-sufficiency.

Program Evaluation

The program evaluation process has several sublevels: developing tools, tracking program completers, conducting the evaluation, analyzing and reporting findings, and implementing program changes. Human service professionals need to develop a variety of tools to evaluate their program. Figure 7.1 is a flow chart for the career development program model for single parents and displaced homemakers. The text in each box in the figure is a factor that needs to be measured. The tools needed for measuring will vary with the agency, but general tools would include a database of client information, intake sheets, case files, tracking sheets, and referral sheets. The program staff also needs to construct paper-and-pencil surveys or telephone surveys for clients who complete the program and their employers. They must determine a way to track their clients and keep that information current. The program staff will also need to decide when to evaluate a program and what type of evaluation is best. The staff also needs to consider how they will collect, analyze, and report the information. Once the staff has made these decisions, they need to create a timeline for the entire program evaluation process that shows every item to be accomplished, the deadline by which it is to be accomplished, and who is responsible for the evaluation. Once the evaluation information is collected, then the input can be used to strengthen the current program. For additional information on program evaluation, see Chapter 6.

Revisiting the Case Study: Beverly

Conduct an Intake Interview

The intake interview should explore Beverly's educational and work history; her interests, values, and views on role expectations, employment, and family. The human service professional should delve into Beverly's feelings regarding the divorce and her financial arrangements. These factors are extremely important because she needs to support herself and her three children while she helps the children to adjust to the divorce in a healthy manner. The helper should also determine whether or not Beverly has childcare or elder care responsibilities. She may need referrals for care services and/or elder care along with family counseling. The professional needs to explore personal supports with Beverly and determine if they are meeting her needs.

A review of Beverly's job history, despite its age, is also important. Although she has not worked outside of the home in 17 years, the helper needs to explore Beverly's previous jobs—what she enjoyed or did not enjoy—and determine how they apply to finding work now. The helper also needs to examine Beverly's volunteer history to see what skills are transferable from those experiences and what job networks she may already have in place. Another important part of the intake interview is to create a working budget to determine Beverly's current needs. Based on those needs, the helper determines how quickly Beverly needs to start work and whether or not she has enough time to pursue additional education and training before initiating the employment campaign.

Make Assessments

Because Beverly has been out of the workplace for so long, she will need to complete a variety of assessments. If she possesses basic computer skills, she could start with the Career Key (Jones, 2000) to help her match her abilities and interests to occupations and then review job descriptions through the *Occupational Outlook Handbook: 2006–2007* (U.S. Department of Labor, n. d.). She could also use either one of two card sorts for ability assessment: Motivated Skills Card Sort (Knowdell, 2002a) or Elevations Manual Card Sort (Scully, 2003). Cards sorts are useful when working with undecided clients, female clients who may have stereotypical thoughts about occupations, and clients who are interested in controlling their own decision-making (Zunker & Osborn, 2000). Since the goal is to empower Beverly as much as possible, using card sorts seems a natural choice. In choosing interest inventories, the human service professional needs to once again consider whether or not Beverly has the technology skills necessary to use the Career Explorer CD-ROM (JIST Works, 2004). If she does, this inventory would allow her to explore occupations based on her interests and linking her directly to job information. Since Beverly is a displaced homemaker, the Leisure to Occupations Connection Search (McDaniels & Mullins, 1999) or the Transition-to-Work Inventory (Liptak, 2004) would be useful because both match interests to possible jobs using leisure activities. She could also use The Occupational Interests Card Sort (Knowdell, 2002b) to clarify her high-appeal jobs and careers along with her degree of readiness, her skills, and the education she needs. Exploring Beverly's values through interviews or assessment is also important. Possible assessments that are appropriate to help her clarify her values include: Career Values Card Sort (Knowdell, 1998a), Values-Driven Work Card Sort (Career Action Center, n.d.), and the Work Orientation and Values Survey (Brady, 2002). Career development issues also need examination. The Career Decision Scale (Osipow et al., 1987) will help identify career decision-making difficulties she may have, and the Career Transitions Inventory (Heppner, 1991) will help explore her career motivation or readiness, confidence, perceived support, internal/external control, and independence/interdependence. As mentioned in Chapter 3, human service professionals should not give every assessment to every client. They should choose assessments that meet the client's needs and provide information that cannot be obtained using other methods.

Determine Barriers to Success

Beverly has a number of barriers that might impact her career success. One barrier is affordable childcare. Although one child is a teenager, the younger two children are in middle school and may need some sort of after-school care. Beverly will also have to find someone to stay with her children when they are ill if she is unable to take sick leave from work. Beverly's age and the length of time since she was last employed will also impact her career success because some employers may view her as less marketable because of those factors. Although Beverly has family, they are not close physically, and she cannot rely on them to help out in emergencies. Finding a job at a living wage may be difficult as well, especially since Beverly needs to support a family of four and her child support and alimony are not enough to meet expenses. She lacks a current education and may need to upgrade what skills she possesses.

Choose Interventions

Using One-to-One Interventions.

One-to-one interventions for Beverly need to explore issues of self-esteem, transition-related issues such as her return to the workplace after 17 years, and her need to balance work and family. Helping Beverly prepare her children for her return to work is also necessary. Role-playing various transition-related situations will give Beverly the self-confidence she needs to start this new phase of her life. Creating a family budget is also necessary to determine how quickly she will need to find employment. The budget will also give Beverly the opportunity to explore whether she should stay in her current home or relocate to save expenses. Issues of child support and alimony must be addressed as well. If Beverly's ex-husband is not current on his support, the human service professional will need to help her contact Child Support Enforcement. Support groups may also help Beverly transition into this new phase of life.

Beverly does have a work history, although it happened 17 years previously. The human service professional can review that period of her life with her to explore what she enjoyed and what she did not enjoy as a beginning to the career development work. Identifying Beverly's transferable skills from her jobs in retail and the doctor's office, along with those skills she gained volunteering and homemaking, will help determine what additional skills she needs in order to become marketable in today's workforce. By examining the support network that is already in place, she can see how to utilize it in other areas. For example, her volunteer work with the PTA, garden club, and local hospital has already provided her with a job network; she merely needs to learn how to use it. As part of career development work the human service professional needs to review the results of Beverly's assessments and use her values, goals, and interests to determine the best way to integrate all of her information into a career plan that meets her needs. If Beverly needs to start working before she has the necessary training and education to pursue her career choice, then she and the human service professional need to explore her past work experience to determine if it offers job possibilities for her and if the job would meet her budget needs.

Finding Funding for Training and Education.   Once Beverly has identified her career goals, she and the human service professional need to determine how to best meet those goals. If she needs more training and education (she will probably at least need some computer training), then obtaining funding for it is the next step. Depending upon where Beverly is in the divorce process, she may be able to arrange for her ex-husband to cover education and training. If not, then the human service professional will have to look at community funding sources such as the local One-Stop Career Center, community colleges, training and education grants, and community organizations and clubs.

Using Mentoring.   Since Beverly has not worked in 17 years, she will need mentoring to help her through her next year. This mentoring, coupled with support groups, will help ease her transition from full-time homemaker and mother into full-time employee and mother. Other topics that might arise during this first year include car maintenance, home repair, and other related issues.

Initiate the Employment Campaign

After Beverly has determined her career emphasis, the human service professional can help her with the job search, letters of application, resume writing, and interviewing skills. Beverly may be able to use her volunteer network as a source for job leads, and she can certainly use her volunteer experience on her resume. Her job search will need to stay local until she feels better able to relocate. Beverly can use her network to enter the hidden job market, and the human service professional can help her to expand that network. Beverly can use a functional resume to emphasize her transferable skills, and role-playing interviews will help her develop the self-confidence she needs to reenter the job market.

Conclusion

Thirty-two percent of all families are single-parent families. While the percentage of single-mother families has decreased from 86 percent in 1990 to 82 percent in 2002, the percentage of single-father families has risen from 14 percent in 1990 to 18 percent in 2002. Twenty-nine percent of single-female parents are unemployed as compared to 20 percent of single-male parents. Fifteen percent of single-father families live in poverty compared to almost 31 percent of single-mother families. Although more difficult to count, displaced homemakers are still growing because of the increased divorce rate and increased longevity. Many single parents and displaced homemakers live below the poverty level and need assistance in finding employment.

The newly separated, divorced, and widowed persons need assistance as well if they are to transition into self-sufficiency. Several changes can be made to assist this particular population. Some recommended policy changes would help the single parent and displaced homemaker population in transition to self-sufficiency. Family friendly policy changes include:

- More childcare subsidies for low-income families
- Work site childcare
- Sick leave to cover time parents spend with sick children, elder care, etc.
- Innovative elder care programs
- Increased job flex/job share opportunities

A recommended change in case management policy is the addition of elder care referral services.

Economic and workforce policy changes include:

- Availability of more jobs to allow families to live above the poverty line
- Increased funding for training and education for displaced homemakers
- Decreased pay inequities
- Equitable workplace evaluation policies

Summary

The number of single parents and displaced homemakers is increasing, and they face specific barriers to their career success. The most common barriers include childcare, elder care, and a lack of job skills that result from being out of the workforce. Other barriers such as physical and mental health, poverty, and workplace discrimination also affect the ability of this population to successfully transition into the workforce and maintain their employment. A career development model presents the development of an Individual Success Plan for each participant. The ISP includes assessments of career abilities, interests, barriers, and values; interagency referrals; interventions such as counseling, training and education, and mentoring. The ISP is followed by an employment campaign that leads to long-term employment and self-sufficiency.

Key Terms

Carl D. Perkins Vocational Education Act of 1984	Joint custody or shared legal custody
Displaced homemaker	Single parent
Equal Pay Act of 1963	Supplemental Security Income (SSI)
Informal caregiving	Workforce Investment Act of 1998 (WIA)

Web Resources

Note that website URLs may change over time.

Older Women's League
http://www.owl-national.org

Single Parents' Network
http://singleparentsnetwork.com

Women Work!
http://www.womenwork.org

8

Welfare-to-Work Clients

Transition to Independence

Case Study: Annie

Annie is a 35-year-old single mother of three boys. One son is 17 and lives in a group home in another city several hours away. The second son, Mark, age 7, is enrolled in a local elementary school. A younger son, Steven, age 5, is in Head Start. Annie dropped out of school in the 7th grade and is not interested in returning for additional education. She has only one year of eligibility remaining out of her five-year temporary assistance for needy families (TANF) cap and has been sanctioned in the past for non-participation in work activities. Although Annie wants to work so she "don't have to report my business to nobody," she does not have a steady work history and is unsure of how to find a job. Over the years she has worked one month as a fast food cook, six weeks as a farm worker picking cotton, and most recently, three months cleaning her church weekly. The last job ended a few months earlier. When she was cleaning the church, she also cleaned houses for a few church members, but those jobs ended after only a few visits. Annie also worked for one week as a housekeeper at a local hotel, but quit when the manager questioned the quality of her work and her lack of teamwork. Although Annie does not live in public housing, her rent is subsidized through the local housing agency. Her house is located outside of the city at the end of a road where the closest house is a mile away. She lives within two miles of the house where she was born. Her father still lives in the family home, but her mother died several years ago. Annie has very little contact with her father. Her son Mark was just removed from the school bus for starting a fight, so she now has to drive him to and from school each day. Mark recently brought a Game Boy (a gift from Annie's father) to class, but his teacher confiscated it, saying that Mark could pick it up from her on the last day of school. When Annie went to the school to talk to the teacher about the Game Boy, the teacher refused to give it to her, stating that doing so would undermine her authority with the students. Annie then threatened to "punch her lights out." The teacher has now taken out a restraining order against Annie.

Personal Responsibility and Work Opportunity Reconciliation Act

In August 1996 President Clinton signed into law the Personal Responsibility and Work Opportunity Reconciliation Act (PRWORA), creating the transitional block grant program **Temporary Assistance for Needy Families (TANF)** while phasing out the **Aid to Families with Dependent Children (AFDC)** programs currently in place. PRWORA increased states' power over welfare policies while emphasizing employment and self-sufficiency. Federal funds were capped at five years over a lifetime to one family and were coupled with the requirement to sign a self-sufficiency contract outlining employment requirements. Recipients of TANF funds who failed to comply with the contracts soon found themselves sanctioned and unable to receive their monthly compensation. The first group of recipients was given two years to become self-sufficient, requiring them to overcome, in many instances, a lifetime of barriers to employment success.

The Welfare-to-Work Population

The typical TANF recipient is a single-mother head of household, approximately 31 years of age. She and her two children receive food stamp assistance, and her average monthly cash and cash-equivalent assistance is $351. *Cash-equivalent* assistance includes, but is not limited to housing, transportation assistance, and **Medicaid.** She has one or two children, at an average age of 7.8 years (Administration for Children and Families, 2004).

Welfare reform also affects legal immigrants since PRWORA legislation has sharply decreased their eligibility for benefits (Kurz, 1998; Wilkins, 2002). Despite Congress eventually restoring food stamp benefits to a limited number of legal immigrants, many are still ineligible for any form of assistance. Adult immigrants who are not disabled along with any immigrant who entered the United States after August 22, 1996, are currently ineligible for food stamps or cash assistance (Wilkins, 2002).

Over two million families received TANF assistance in 2001, as compared to five million families in fiscal year 1994. Forty percent of TANF families had one child; 10 percent had more than three children. Thirty-nine percent of TANF families were African American, and 30 percent were White. Twenty-six percent of the TANF families were Hispanic, 2.1 percent Asian, and 1.3 percent Native American. Whereas independent studies often show that over half of TANF families leave the welfare program because of employment, agencies are often unaware that clients have become employed and close their cases for other reasons. Other reasons TANF families leave assistance programs include they have reached their state time limit, transferred to a Tribal program and failed to cooperate with agency requirements and were sanctioned. One out of every four TANF families had non-TANF income averaging $593 per month per family (Administration for Children and Families, 2004). Despite the decline of welfare use nationally and the rules restricting access for legal immigrants, the number of immigrants and limited-English speakers using welfare comprise a large segment of the current TANF population. For example, immigrants comprise nearly one-third of the caseload in California and New York and one-fifth in Texas (Tumlin & Zimmermann, 2003).

Barriers to Career Success

As the number of potential barriers to employment increase, the likelihood that a person will find employment decreases. In fact, TANF recipients reporting seven or more barriers have only a 5 percent likelihood of working 20 hours each week (Wilkins, 2002). Most welfare recipients who experience potential barriers to employment do work, although they do so irregularly (Olson & Pavetti, 1996). Some potential barriers (physical and mental health problems, domestic violence, lack of transportation) are more numerous than others (drug or alcohol use and a lack of understanding of work customs), yet many welfare recipients possess a combination of barriers that affect their ability to find and maintain work (Loprest, 2003; Olson & Pavetti, 1996; Zedlewski & Alderson, 2001). Although many welfare recipients are able to find and maintain employment, others are not and often cycle back and forth between work and welfare assistance (Harris, 1993, 1996). Welfare recipients who do not deal with their barriers may lose their assistance for failure to meet the PRWORA requirements, whether or not they have a means of financial support. Identifying and understanding barriers to successful employment will help human service professionals address the needs of their clients while their clients transition from welfare dependence to self-sufficiency.

Structural Barriers

Affordable Childcare. Access to affordable and dependable childcare is one of the primary barriers faced by TANF recipients (Administration for Children and Families, 2004; East, 1999; Kalil, Born, Kunz, & Caudill, 2001; Zedlewski, 2002). Since TANF has a **"work first"** emphasis, parents who may not have previously needed childcare must now quickly find affordable and safe childcare, a difficult task for many people, not just welfare recipients. While an increased subsidy is sometimes available for childcare, a lack of dependable childcare still exists. A lack of trust in local childcare providers combined with lengthy waiting lists for childcare is still an issue for many recipients (Zedlewski et al., 2003). In most cases, parents first must pay for childcare and then be reimbursed. Evening and weekend work schedules pose a childcare problem since few providers are available at those times. While family and friends are sometimes a source of childcare assistance, a lack of trust still frequently interferes. Finding childcare that allows parents to attend classes is often problematic because childcare may not be subsidized unless the welfare recipient is working. Some mothers believe their job is to be home with their children and do not want to work until their children reach school age (Hill & Kauff, 2002).

Transportation.   A lack of access to transportation affects many welfare recipients, whether rural or urban (Danziger et al., 1999; Kalil et al., 2001; Zedlewski, 1999; Zedlewski et al., 2003). In one study almost half of the respondents reported that they lacked a driver's license or access to a car, affecting their ability to gain employment (Danziger et al., 1999). Welfare recipients in small towns frequently report access to transportation as a barrier to work unless they can find employment within walking distance (Holzer & Danziger, 1998; Zedlewski et al., 2003). With access to public transportation women in urban settings appear to have an increased likelihood of finding and maintaining employment (Harris, 1996). Some TANF recipients who claim to have few local job opportunities report that they cannot leave their areas because they will lose family-support networks, and they are unable to afford the transportation to look elsewhere. Local fast-food jobs simply do not provide the necessary income, yet the recipients lack access to the transportation that is necessary to reach better-paying jobs that are further away (Zedlewski et al., 2003). Working imposes transportation costs that are often burdensome in money and time, and workers with very little money often have to make hard choices between paying for childcare, transportation, food, or rent.

Availability of Jobs at a Living Wage.   The lack of unskilled jobs that pay above minimum wage also obstructs employment for welfare recipients who often need higher-paying jobs in order to earn above the poverty level (Hershey & Pavetti, 1997; Kurz, 1998; Zedlewski, 1999). Health and other benefits (i.e., sick leave, paid vacation) are a necessity for this population, yet benefits are seldom available in entry-level jobs for which many welfare recipients qualify. Due to PRWORA regulations, TANF recipients are often encouraged to accept employment regardless of whether or not the work pays a living wage and provides the necessary fringe benefits. Since TANF recipients are not the only people applying for the higher-paying jobs, they are less likely to be hired when competing against equally or more skilled workers (Holzer & Danziger, 1998). Employment is determined by skill requirements and by the industry, resulting in limited employment options for the welfare-to-work population (Holzer & Stoll, 2003).

Local Economy.   Labor market constraints affect employer demand for welfare recipients. The willingness of employers to provide workplace amenities or supports to welfare recipients (i.e., childcare, transportation assistance, training) and to allow policy interventions on behalf of recipients is influenced by labor market constraints as well (Holzer, 1999; U.S. Department of Health and Human Services, 2000). The local economy also impacts the availability of training and the type of worksite activities that agencies develop for TANF recipients (U.S. Department of Health and Human Services, 2000). Temporary and seasonal jobs are often available, but the irregular earnings in the jobs make meeting expenses difficult for TANF recipients (Hill & Kauff, 2002). Andersson, Lane, and McEntarfer (2004) found that the industries and firms for which TANF recipients work, the characteristics of their coworkers, and the neighborhoods in which the recipients live affect the likelihood they will exit from low-wage status.

Job Instability. Early employment instability contributes to low levels of employment for female, high-school dropouts. Primary determinants of job stability include cognitive skills (measured by math test scores), current or previous experience and job tenure, and job characteristics (i.e., starting wages, occupation, and industry). Job instability among female, high-school dropouts strongly relates to fertility history and marital status (Holzer & LaLonde, 1999).

Perceptions of Job Discrimination. Perceptions by employees of employer discrimination may also hinder employment (Danziger et al., 1999; Rice, 2001). Fifty percent of respondents in two separate studies reported that they had experienced at least one occurrence of discrimination (Danziger et al., 1999; Wilkins, 2002). Welfare recipients who reported discrimination were less likely to work more than 20 hours a week. They provided examples such as they were refused a job, fired from a job, or not promoted in a job because of their gender, race, or welfare status; and their current or most recent supervisor made racial slurs, insulting remarks about their gender, or insulting remarks about welfare. Being harassed at work is another example of discrimination. TANF recipients are often equipped to diffuse discrimination, and they often choose between quitting to avoid discrimination and ignoring the discrimination to remain employed (Wilkins, 2002).

Welfare Disincentives. Some aspects of the welfare-to-work programs lack flexibility, which is a very important component to helping clients transition to self-sufficiency. For example, federally mandated, state work-participation rates limit the variety of acceptable activities for TANF recipients. Unfortunately, job skills programs and education-related activities, such as English as a second language (ESL) and General Equivalency Diploma (GED), while extremely important for recipients with few skills, do not always count as acceptable work activities. Although vocational education does count, very few TANF recipients qualify for such training. Those who do qualify are limited to no more than 12 months of training. This restriction means that recipients' educational activities must be pursued on top of the work requirements and on their own time and with their own resources. Immigrants, who are in even more need of education and training seldom qualify if they receive TANF funds. Two-parent families face even more disincentives to being placed in employment and training because they count toward states' two-parent rates and toward their family rates. Immigrants in particular are at a disadvantage because they are more likely to be in two-parent families than are U.S. citizens (Tumlin & Zimmermann, 2003).

Another disincentive to work is rent rules linking rent to income. As welfare recipients' incomes increase, so does their rent (Reingold, Van Ryzin, & Ronda, 2001). Health coverage (i.e., Medicaid eligibility) is also tied to income. Coverage frequently ends when TANF recipients earn just above poverty level. Requiring recipients to repeat job searches or training programs that did not lead to employment in the past in order to receive a small amount of TANF funds proves very discouraging. Recipients who are unable to meet the work requirements often give up the program, relying on shelters, family members, and friends for assistance (Zedlewski et al., 2003). Native Americans do not do well under welfare regulations, even though in many cases the tribal government is responsible for the distribution of funds. Despite the fact that federal funding to increase employment participation has increased, most tribes lack the required matching funds to qualify for the additional monies (Walters et al., 2001).

The application process often deters people who are eligible from applying for cash assistance, thus decreasing the likelihood that they will receive the training and education that could lead to improved employment (Zedlewski, 2002). People often view applications for Medicaid, TANF, and Food Stamps as being too complex and requiring them to take time off from work in order to complete the process. Some people think the applications are lengthy and require a reading level they do not possess (U.S. General Accounting Office, 2004). Another disincentive is that the rigor of the actual application process differs from state to state. Some states require no up-front documentation, and others require multiple intake interviews in several different locations, fingerprinting, home visits, workforce orientations, and daily job-search classes, all of which are part of a 30-day qualifying process. The difficulty of the application process is increased further by the diversity of immigrant groups who speak dozens of different languages (Holcomb, Tumlin, Koralek, Capps, & Zuberi, 2003).

Housing Stability.   Not having stable, affordable housing is another serious barrier to employment for low-income families (Olson & Pavetti, 1996). TANF recipients living in homeless and domestic-violence shelters face this barrier constantly (Hill & Kauff, 2002; Kurz, 1998). Still others live with family or friends, moving frequently (Zedlewski et al., 2003). Evictions occur as one landlord sells to another and as cities decide to raze low-income housing to make way for more lucrative projects (Montoya & Atkinson, 2002).

Individual Barriers

Education.   Few jobs exist for those with little or no education (Zedlewski, 2002). People with low levels of education (i.e., did not graduate from high school or earn a GED) have been negatively linked to employment (Olson & Pavetti, 1996; Zedlewski & Alderson, 2002; Zedlewski et al., 2003). Lack of a high-school diploma alone may not be a rigid barrier to unemployment, but employers may be less willing to hire a high-school dropout who possesses other barriers such as few work skills, transportation and childcare problems, and depression (Danziger et al., 1999). Studies show that education increases the wages of women following welfare exit (Harris, 1996), so providing education for welfare recipients could greatly benefit them. Lack of education, coupled with limited English skills, serves as a deterrent to employment for many immigrants (Wilkins, 2002; Zedlewski, 1999).

Lack of Marketable Job Skills and Work Experiences.   Limited job and academic skills impact welfare recipients in several ways. The most obvious affect is that of relegating them to low-paying jobs, irregular hours, and few, if any, benefits. These low skills may be indicative of a learning disability or even contribute to issues of low self-esteem (Olson & Pavetti, 1996). A gap sometimes exists between the job skills an employer expects and the actual job skills of the welfare recipients, resulting in their inability to perform certain tasks due to the lack of job-specific experience or training (Holzer & Danziger, 1998).

According to Zedlewski (2002), the majority of female TANF recipients have had no work experience in the past three years and that minimal work experience significantly reduces work activity (Danziger et al., 1999; U.S. Department of Health and Human Services, 2000; Zedlewski, 2002; Zedlewski et al., 2003). Lack of early job experience may cause employment difficulties to persist over time. In fact, restricted early work experience for high-school dropouts often results in low transition rates into employment along with high transition rates out of employment (Holzer & LaLonde, 1999). Immigrant TANF recipients often have even less job experience than the native-born recipients may have (Tumlin & Zimmermann, 2003).

Welfare recipients with less education and work experience frequently have a difficult time staying employed once they do find a job (Bartik, 2000). Their inability to keep a job causes gaps in their employment history, which in turn makes them less likely to be hired (Zedlewski, 1999).

Lack of Work-Readiness Skills. Some TANF recipients are not "work ready" and do not understand or follow workplace norms or behaviors. They previously may have lost jobs because they did not understand the need for punctuality or the negative effects of absenteeism; they took longer breaks than needed; they did not correct a problem pointed out by a supervisor; they refused to do tasks not mentioned in the job description; or they argued with their supervisor or misunderstood authority in the workplace (Danziger et al., 1999; Hershey & Pavetti, 1997). While these problems are not a significant barrier for all welfare recipients, they still need to be addressed (Danziger et al., 1999). Other research suggested that job-skill problems contribute less to job loss than do a lack of social skills or a lack of social decision-making and life skills (Hershey & Pavetti, 1997).

Lack of Support System. Welfare recipients frequently lack support systems that could help them in the transition to self-sufficiency. Some recipients lack the support network necessary to find jobs and be job-ready (Bartik, 2000a; Wilkins, 2002). Others lack the support necessary to assist them with transportation or emergency childcare (Zedlewski et al., 2003). Some are unaware of available community supports or lack spiritual support (Holcomb et al., 2003; Reingold et al., 2001).

Physical Health Barriers

Personal and Family Illness. Health limitations can be a serious barrier for many welfare recipients. Illnesses of single mothers and their children frequently account for work absenteeism (Olson & Pavetti, 1996). Younger mothers are sometimes unaware of how to assess the seriousness of a child's illness and may stay home needlessly. Still other mothers lack the support network that they need to find someone trustworthy to stay with an ill child and allow the parent to work. When children are seriously ill, multiple trips to the doctor or emergency room require parents to miss work. Single mothers may hesitate to look for employment, fearing that working would interfere with their ability to meet their child's medical needs. Few jobs allow the flexibility needed to care for sick children, and health benefits and/or sick leave are seldom available to ease the financial burden of life with a sick child.

Children with Disabilities.   Parents of children with disabilities face an even greater barrier to employment success. Women who have children with special needs often rate their own health as poor due to the stress of balancing the care of a child with special needs with finding work. Families who have a child with a disability are more likely to have a family member go hungry or go without medical care (Olson & Pavetti, 1996).

Personal Health and Disabilities.   Poor health is another explanation for the lack of employment among TANF recipients (Zedlewski & Alderson, 2002; Zedlewski et al., 2003). They often have a high rate of physical ailments and are more likely to lose jobs than those without health problems (U.S. General Accounting Office, 2001; Hill & Kauff, 2002; Sweeney, 2000; Zedlewski et al., 2003). Physical, developmental, or learning disabilities also impact the ability of TANF recipients to transition to self-sufficiency (Olson & Pavetti, 1996; Wilkins, 2002). Recipients with severe disabilities may not be able to seek employment at all, and those with minor disabilities may only be able to work a limited number of hours or intermittently. Still other recipients may want to work but are unable to do so without jeopardizing their Medicaid coverage. As many as one-fourth to one-half of TANF recipients who have been sanctioned for noncompliance report that they were unable to comply due to their disability, health condition, or illness (Sweeney, 2000).

Mental Health Barriers

Mental health issues often heavily affect social functioning that results in lower work-force participation rates, fewer work hours, and reduced earnings (Jayakody & Stauffer, 2000; Kalil et al., 2001; Olson & Pavetti, 1996; Wilkins, 2002; Zedlewski, 1999). The reverse is also true: Continued unemployment can negatively affect a person's mental health and has been connected to such issues as depression, low self-esteem, and alcohol abuse (Dooley, 2003; Montoya, Bell, Atkinson, Nagy, & Whitsett, 2002; Murphy & Athanasou, 1999; Nordenmark & Strandh, 1999; Raver, 2003). Poor economic resources are highly correlated with mental health. Low-income, single mothers tend to have higher rates of psychiatric disorders (i.e., major depression, general anxiety disorder, panic attacks, agoraphobia) than do higher-income, single mothers (Jayakody & Stauffer, 2000; Rosen, Spencer, Tolman, Williams, & Jackson, 2003). Research by Jayakody and Stauffer (2000) indicates that a person who had a psychiatric disorder in the previous year has a 25 percent less likelihood of working. As the mental health of TANF recipients improves, however, they become more successful in seeking and gaining employment (Montoya et al., 2002). Human service professionals must understand the effect of mental health barriers in order to meet the needs of clients in transition from welfare to work.

Depression.   Several factors contribute to depression in low-income families. Stressful life events such as a change in financial status and residence; family-related events (i.e., pregnancy, getting a new family member, separation from a mate, increase in responsibility for a family member); and lack of assistance for childrearing, along with unsatisfactory childcare arrangements are often found in low-income women at risk for depression. Depression has been found in first-time welfare recipients (Kalil et al., 2001) as well as long-term recipients (Jayakody & Stauffer, 2000; Raver, 2003). In fact, depression is frequently exacerbated when combined with other barriers such as dissatisfaction with housing, lack of transportation, and childcare (Kalil et al., 2001). Emotional support from family and friends as well as ties to the religious community, however, can reduce the depressive symptoms (Kalil et al., 2001).

Self-Esteem.   Low self-esteem is particularly prevalent in welfare recipients (East, 1999). Research suggests a positive connection between employment and self-esteem (Dooley & Prause, 1997); thus, self-esteem seems to be an important determinant for women on welfare (East, 1999). Welfare recipients who have attended college reported an increase in self-esteem (Rice, 2001).

Substance Abuse.   The PRWORA mandates refusal of benefits to anyone who is convicted of a drug-related felony and requires recipients to sign a Personal Responsibility Agreement pledging to abstain from illegal drug use. Despite this mandate, substance abuse is frequently cited as a major barrier that prevents recipients from leaving welfare and securing employment. Therefore, substance abuse among welfare recipients has attracted a great deal of attention (Danziger et al., 1999; Grayson, 1999; Jayakody & Stauffer, 2000; Kalil et al., 2001; Metsch, Pereyra, Miles, & McCoy, 2003; Montoya et al., 2002). Substance-abuse problems prevent welfare recipients from undertaking the tasks necessary to find employment and often affect their ability to maintain employment later (Metsch et al., 2003; Mulia & Schmidt, 2003; Olson & Pavetti, 1996). Long-term welfare recipients are more likely to have substance-abuse problems that those who are first-time recipients (Grayson, 1999). Substance-abuse treatment does have a positive effect on later employment and subsequent earnings (Metsch et al., 2003).

In a study by Morgenstern, McCrady, Blanchard, McVeigh, Riordan, & Irwin, (2002), substance-dependent welfare recipients reported that they have not worked during the previous three years. They also reported more difficulties with transportation, childcare, and stable housing than did nonabusing welfare recipients. Many reported symptoms of depression and post-traumatic stress disorder (PTSD), coupled with severe domestic violence (i.e., being beaten, threatened with a weapon) and legal problems such as being under investigation by child protective services. Substance-dependent welfare recipients also reported high-risk sexual activity during the previous six months (i.e., unprotected sex with a partner who is not a mate, unprotected sex with a partner who injects drugs, and unprotected sex in exchange for money or drugs) (Wilkins, 2002; Zedlewski, 1999). Substance abusers reported higher rates of barriers such as domestic violence, mental health problems, and fewer job skills (Morgenstern et al., 2002).

Domestic Violence.   Women involved in abusive relationships often have difficulty regularly attending classes and work because of threatening and bullying behavior by their partners, both at home and at work. According to Raphael (1995, 1996), direct and indirect interference with work can include behaviors such as keeping the victim awake all night before a job interview, deliberately disabling the family car, failing to show up as promised for childcare or transportation, and harassing the victim at work. Undermining the victim's confidence along with attempting to force the victim to feel guilty about childcare arrangements also impact the victim's ability to find and maintain employment. TANF recipients often report that incidents of domestic violence increase as they seek education, training, and/or work. Low-income, battered women respond in many different ways to abuse. Some struggle to work while others work but are unable to sustain employment over time (Tolman & Raphael, 2000). Still other women are unable to find jobs at all. Domestic-violence victims may experience emotional and/or physical problems that could impact their ability to maintain employment. Abused women often suffer from chronic health problems, depression, low self-esteem, and PTSD (Gerdes, 1997). Past and present domestic violence may affect employability differently. While domestic violence victims may suffer emotional effects for some time after leaving an abusive situation, they may not have the same safety and logistical issues faced by those who are currently being abused (East, 1999; Olson & Pavetti, 1996; Wilkins, 2002).

Post-Traumatic Stress Disorder (PTSD).   Gerdes (1997) suggested that the lives of many long-term welfare recipients are characterized by repeated exposure to traumatic events such as violence, poverty, and uncertainty. Therefore, PTSD may well affect the interactions of welfare recipients with their human service workers as well as with coworkers or employers (Gerdes, 1997; Strauser & Lustig, 2001). In Gerdes' (1997) ethnographic study, welfare recipients report feeling worried, stressed, powerless, pressured, trapped, isolated, lonely, and helpless, which are feelings also reported by Vietnam veterans with PTSD. Gerdes also suggested that the punitive relationship between those who administer welfare funds and long-term recipients may replicate prior abusive relationships due to the prolonged contact with their case worker and their increasing dependence on the case worker for assistance. PTSD affects such areas of vocational functioning as short-term memory, concentration and persistence, adaptability, and social interaction (Strauser & Lustig, 2001). Women with PTSD and substance-abuse difficulties tend to have less monthly income, work fewer days, and hold a full-time job for a shorter period of time. They are less likely to hold a driver's license. They have more legal problems, fewer friends, and higher rates of exposure to serious accidents. They also reported higher incidents of vaginal rape and aggravated assault (Back, Sonne, Killeen, Dansky, & Brady, 2003).

Career Development Program Model: Welfare-to-Work Population

A career development program for use with welfare-to-work clients needs an individualized approach that addresses each client's barriers to success. The ultimate goal is the long-term employment of the client. Our program has three major components: the applicant pool, the Individual Success Plan (ISP), and the program evaluation. Each component will be explained in further detail. Figure 8.1 is a graphic model of the career development program.

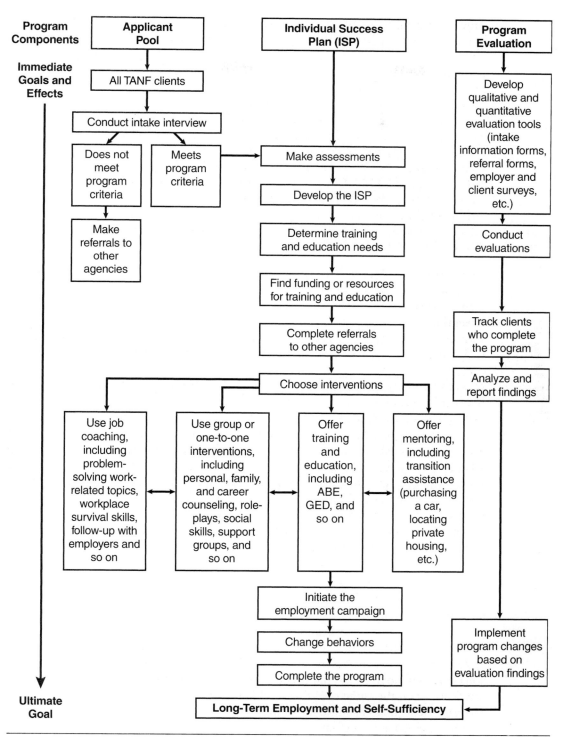

FIGURE 8.1 *Career Development Program Model: Welfare-to-Work Population*

Applicant Pool

The applicant pool includes all TANF recipients. Intake interview personnel determine which clients fit the criteria for program participation and which do not. For example, not all TANF recipients are required to participate in the Work First program. They may be exempt from the work requirement if they (1) are pregnant or have a child under the age of 18 months; (2) are disabled or caring for a family member who is severely disabled; (3) are under the age of 16 or over the age of 65; (4) qualify for the **Family Violence Option (FVO)**; (5) are head of "child only" families (those where the child, not the caretaker, is receiving the TANF funds); (6) are awaiting SSI eligibility determination because of an impairment; (7) are refugees, asylees, or a member of similar classes of legal immigrants; or (8) qualify for a temporary mental or physical exemption (U.S. General Accounting Office, 2001, 2003; Tolman & Raphael, 2000). Exempt TANF recipients then would not meet the career development program's entrance criteria and would need to be referred elsewhere for assistance. Those recipients who meet the criteria are required to participate in the career development program for creation of their ISP.

Individual Success Plan

The Individual Success Plan (ISP) provides a personal approach to career development while meeting the documentation requirements of PRWORA and the Workforce Investment Act (WIA). Congress passed the WIA in 1998 to begin unifying the current, fragmented employment and training system to better serve job seekers and employers. The WIA provides for three levels of services: *core, intensive,* and *training.* Services at one level serve as a prerequisite to moving to the next level. This tiered approach allows for flexibility at the local level, where the locality has the power to establish *gateway* activities that lead from the core to the intensive and training levels. Any core service, such as an initial assessment or job search, could serve as a gateway activity. The intensive services could include the development of the ISP, individual counseling, and career planning offered either through the local One-Stop Career Center or through another agency (U.S. Department of Labor, 2000; U.S. General Accounting Office, 2003a). The key is to determine at a local level what intensive or training services are required to move the client to employment. In the case of TANF recipients who are already employed, the locality can determine whether intensive or training services are needed to help the employed client retain or obtain self-sufficient employment (U.S. Department of Labor, 2000). The first step in providing intensive services to the welfare-to-work population is to make comprehensive assessments that identify each client's unique set of barriers to employment. After identifying each barrier, the human service professional is then better able to provide appropriate interventions, eventually resulting in the long-term employment of the client.

Make Assessments.   As mentioned in Chapter 3, a variety of career-related assessments based on the client's reading level may be used in this step. Creating individual files on each client using a file system such as the Individual Employment Plan (Ludden & Maitlen, 2002) allows the human service professional to more easily track each program participant during the intake interview and future sessions, thus meeting the WIA requirements for PRWORA. While the human service professional can learn a great deal from a client during a traditional intake interview, PRWORA requires documentation to prove the existence of certain barriers. Assessments combined with the intake interview provide that documentation (U.S. Department of Labor, 2000). Table 8.1 lists assessments that are appropriate for use with the welfare-to-work population to develop an Individual Success Plan. While using several assessments is encouraged, human service professionals need to be careful to limit their choices based

TABLE 8.1 *Career-Related Assessments for Use with the Welfare-to-Work Population*

Title	*Source*
Ability Tests	
Ability Explorer	Harrington, J. C., & Harrington, T. F. (1996). *Ability Explorer.* Itasca, IL: Houghton Mifflin.
Motivated Skills Card Sort	Knowdell, R. (2002, June). *Motivated skills card sort.* San Jose, CA: Career Research & Testing.
O*NET Ability Profiler*	O*NET Consortium (2003, April). *O*NET ability profiler.* Washington, DC: Author.
WorkKeys	ACT, Inc. (1993). *Workkeys assessments.* Iowa City, IO: ACT.
Interest Inventories	
Career Exploration Inventory 2	Liptak, J. (2002). *Career exploration inventory 2.* Indianapolis, IN: JIST Works.
Guide for Occupational Exploration Interest Inventory	Farr, M. (2002). *Guide for occupational exploration interest inventory* (4th ed.). Indianapolis, IN: JIST Works.
Occupational Interests Card Sort	Knowdell, R. (2002, June). *Occupational interests card sort.* San Jose, CA: Career Research & Testing.
Self-Directed Search, Forms E, & R	Holland J. L. (1996). *Self-directed search form E* (4th ed). Lutz, FL: Psychological Assessment Resources. Holland, J. L. (1996). *Self-directed search form R* (4th ed.). Lutz, FL: Psychological Assessment Resources.
Transition-to-Work Inventory	Liptak, J. J. (2004). *Transition-to-work inventory.* Indianapolis, IN: JIST Works.
Values Tests	
Career Values Card Sort	Knowdell, R. (1998, June). *Career values card sort.* San Jose, CA: Career Research & Testing.
Work Orientation and Values Survey	Brady, R. P. (2002). *Work orientation and values survey.* Indianapolis, IN: JIST Works.
Career Development Inventories	
Barriers to Employment Success Inventory	Liptak, J. (2002). *Barriers to employment success inventory* (2nd ed.) Indianapolis, IN: JIST Works.

(Continued)

TABLE 8.1   Continued

Title	Source
Career Attitudes and Strategies Inventory	Holland, J. L., & Gottfredson, G. D. (1994). *Career attitudes and strategies inventory*. Lutz, FL: Psychological Assessment Resources.
Career Beliefs Inventory	Krumboltz, J. D. (1991). *Career beliefs inventory*. Mountain View, CA: CPP.
Career Transitions Inventory	Heppner, M. J. (1991). *Career transition inventory*. Columbia, MO: Author.
Job Search Attitude Inventory	Liptak, J. (2002). *Job search attitude inventory* (2nd ed.). Indianapolis, IN: JIST Works.
My Vocational Situation	Holland, J. L., Daiger, D., & Power, P. G. (1980). *My vocational situation*. Mountain View, CA: CPP.
Overcoming Barriers Card Sort Game Kit	Harney, E. E., & Angel, D. L. (1999). *Overcoming barriers card sort game kit*. Hacienda Heights, CA: WorkNet Solutions.
Vocational Decision-Making Interview	Czerlinsky, T., & Chandler, S. (1999). *Vocational decision-making interview*. IN: JIST Works.
Miscellaneou	
Elevations® Manual Card Sort System	Scully, H. (2003, August). *Elevations manual card sort system*. Roseville, CA: Author.
Individual Employment Plan	Ludden, L. L., & Maitlen, B. (2002). *Individual Employment Plan*. Indian apolis, IN; JIST Works.
Vocational Exploration and Insight Kit	Holland, J. L., Birk, J. M., Cooper, J. F., Dewey, C. R., Dolliver, H., Takai, R. T., & Tyler, L. (1980). *The vocational exploration and insight kit*. Mountain View, CA: CPP.

*Use only if client is computer literate.

on the reading level and need of the client. (See Chapter 3 for additional details on each assessment.)

Develop the ISP.   Once the assessments are completed, the next step is the development of the ISP. By incorporating information gained from the intake interview, from discussions with the client, and from the assessments, the human service worker assists the client in identifying specific barriers to employment success. Next, the professional and the client incorporate values into the planning process and identify personal and career goals. Human service professionals need to develop these plans in collaboration with clients to help them take ownership (East, 1999; U.S. Department of Labor, 2000; McDonald, 2002). Clients taking an active role in the creation of these plans are empowered and more likely to move toward self-sufficiency. Together, the client and worker determine what barriers to address first and set a timeline for accomplishing each goal. By setting mini goals to meet along the way, clients can see what progress they are making, while allowing for the revision and redesign of the plan as necessary.

Determine Training and Education Needs.   With assessment results in front of them, the human service worker and client determine what type of training and education the client needs to reach his or her goals. Clients who dropped out of school may need to complete an **Adult Basic Education (ABE)** program or a **General Equivalency Diploma (GED)** prior to or during the job search or other training. In some cases education can be included as an acceptable activity, depending on the section of the country, the determined need for the education, and whether or not the client is already participating in other job-skills training. Clients who have already completed high school or have a GED may qualify to immediately enter a training program offered through the community college or a local proprietary school.

For clients with more experience, reviewing the interest inventory's results will help identify career leads and any necessary training and education. Other clients may need more exposure to different jobs or even basic job skills before they would qualify for the various careers available. Training and education are determined by the job openings with local employers, the economy, and by the funding available through the local One-Stop Career Center that is tasked with collaborating with local agencies, metropolitan planning organizations, childcare agencies, and nonprofit and community partners. Program providers will coordinate and integrate activities and information to provide a coherent system accessible to businesses and clients alike (U.S. General Accounting Office, 2003a).

Assessment results will likely dictate other areas where training and education is necessary such as life skills. These skills can be offered to clients in small groups or in one-on-one counseling that will allow for a more individualized fit. Providing clients with a list of possible training and educational group topics (i.e., nutrition and health, building family strengths, balancing work with family, stress management, time management, money management) from which to choose continues to empower them to take responsibility for their life choices and ownership in their successes.

Find Funding or Resources for Training and Education.   Eligible adults have access to training resources through **Individual Training Accounts (ITAs)** arranged through One-Stop Career Center. These accounts supplement financial aid already available through other institutions, or, if no financial aid is available, these accounts may cover the cost of all training. The Workforce Investment Act provides limited funding for training, however. Individuals who are unable to obtain grant assistance from other sources to pay for their training and those who need financial assistance beyond that which is available through grants may qualify for some financial assistance through WIA funds. The case manager will be responsible for coordinating those funds as well as the available services. To access these funds, the client will need to be referred for training by the local One-Stop Center once all other funding has been exhausted (U.S. Department of Labor, 2000; U.S. General Accounting Office, 2003a).

Grants and scholarships are available to help low-income students afford tuition at local community colleges or two-year intuitions. Other local agencies, businesses, or organizations may offer financial support as well. The human service worker needs to become familiar with the various funding streams in the community to better assist the client in obtaining training and education (U.S. Department of Labor, 2000; McDonald, 2002).

Life-skills training is provided in a variety of settings and through several different agencies, often at no cost. Coordination and case management are necessary to guarantee that clients receive the skills they need and have requested.

Complete Referrals to Other Agencies.   Interagency cooperation and intensive case management are crucial during this stage to allow for a more holistic approach to addressing the needs and barriers of TANF recipients and their families (East, 1999; Hill & Kauff, 2002; U.S. General Accounting Office, 2001, 2003a; Wilkins, 2002). During the development of the ISP, the client or worker may identify certain behaviors or events that require referral to another agency. Clients who are victims of domestic violence, for example, need referrals to the local domestic violence shelter. Other referrals might address medical, substance-abuse, or mental health issues. Clients may need funding for childcare, transportation, and housing along with referrals for Supplemental Security Income (SSI); **Special Supplemental Nutrition Program for Women, Infants, and Children (WIC Program)**.

Choose Interventions.   The welfare-to-work career development model has four categories of interventions: job coaching, group or one-to-one counseling, mentoring, and training and education. The human service worker may offer these interventions concurrently or in phases, depending upon the individual needs of the client as well as the requirements of the local agency. Some clients may need all four interventions while others may only need one or two. Certain clients may respond better to small groups and others to an individualized approach, which the helper needs to take into consideration.

Using Job Coaching.   Also known as supported employment, *job coaching* is a frequent intervention in rehabilitation counseling (Hagner, Rogan, & Murphy, 1992). Job coaching can be modified to work with TANF recipients to help them learn the necessary workplace and social skills that can overcome barriers to success (Holzer & LaLonde, 1999; Wilkins, 2002). The *job coach* can be an agency employee or a trained volunteer who addresses problem solving with work-related topics, explores workplace survival skills, and meets with employers about their TANF recipient employees. Since maintaining employment is frequently a barrier to success, the job coach's overall task is helping the client transition into the workforce (Bartik, 2000; Zedlewski, 1999). Coaching includes meeting regularly with the client both on or off the job site to deal with the client's concerns before they affect employment. Such concerns could include how to handle being late or absent from work, how to problem-solve to find back-up transportation or childcare, and how to deal with anger on the job. Topics addressed by the job coach do not include the skills training provided by the employer. The employer meets regularly with the job coach and is available to meet with the coach and the client as needed. If an employer hires several TANF recipients, they could meet in group sessions, but the individual sessions need to continue.

Using Group One-to-One Interventions.   In some instances, counseling is needed to help clients transition into self-sufficiency. This intervention involves personal, family, and career counseling. It may include role-plays and support groups. It may be a service that is referred elsewhere. Personal and family counseling would address such issues as substance abuse, domestic violence, PTSD, or depression. Since the thrust of PRWORA is "work first," clients may decide to seek personal or work goals that they cannot achieve where they are currently employed, and they need assistance to reach those goals. Career exploration interventions could include job shadowing, unpaid internships, and even field trips to local businesses, organizations, and agencies (U.S. Department of Labor, 2000; Wilkins, 2002).

Providing Training and Education.   While training and education are a step in developing the ISP, as mentioned previously, they are also interventions. Clients need encouragement to continue training while on the job as well as to pursue and upgrade their education. The human service worker may need to help them find training and education that will assist them in their current jobs or to find ABE or GED classes. Arranging community work experience placements could help provide social skills and training for clients who are unable to secure employment immediately and could also provide clients with references and entry-level forms of networking. Training also occurs on the job, and research has shown that working next to higher-wage employees often allows low-wage employees to gain industry-specific skills that could help them advance later (Andersson, Lane, & McEntarfer, 2004). Providing life-skills training and education to clients both in a class format and individually occurs during this stage. Referred to as *self-reliance education,* these life-skills classes (i.e., time, stress, or money management; parenting skills; balancing work and family commitments) allow participants to select and attend the classes they feel fit their ISP goals and will increase their self-sufficiency (Duncan, Dunnagan, Christopher, & Paul, 2003). A Job Club could be a part of the education component, as could support groups. Clients who are employed yet uncomfortable with a job-coach approach could opt to attend these skills-training classes instead of working with a job coach.

Offering Mentoring.   Once clients have been employed for at least a year, they may be ready for the next level of services—providing transition assistance, such as teaching clients how to open a bank account, buy a car, or locate private housing. Once clients have a steady income and have adjusted to the workplace, they often need help taking these next steps to self-sufficiency. The mentor can be an agency employee or a trained volunteer who develops networks with local businesses and community organizations to provide these services to clients. Such networks include bank employees who are willing to guide clients through the process of opening their first bank accounts. Another useful contact is a local car dealership that is willing to help clients establish credit and develop a payment plan for purchasing affordable and safe transportation. Enlisting the aid of a local mechanic could prove helpful as well. Still other contacts are landlords or realtors willing to walk clients through the process of renting or buying a home. The mentor would develop a network of such contacts for the clients to use, facilitate meetings, and offer whatever other assistance clients need at the time.

Initiate the Employment Campaign.   The employment campaign begins at different times for different clients, depending on where they are in the TANF process. Some

clients who are long-term TANF recipients may have to begin their employment campaign immediately, whereas other clients may have time to complete several work-related activities before beginning the campaign. Obviously, eradicating barriers before initiating a job campaign is the best approach, but since that is not always possible, clients will often be working on several activities at once, which requires intensive case management. The next section provides an overview of considerations for welfare-to-work clients during the employment campaign. For additional details, please see Chapter 5.

The Strategic Job Search.   Information gathered from the assessments and from the intake interview is used in this phase to help clients explore the importance of values and goals in the job-search process. Human service professionals need to help clients understand the importance of setting goals and developing a plan to meet those goals. Clients may also need reminding that they do not have the skills for the jobs of their choice and will need to work toward developing those skills. Helping clients plan and see that every step they take is leading them closer to their employment goal is extremely important. In the meantime, they need to determine whether or not their values are consistent with the jobs they are considering. Once clients better understand themselves, they can begin to understand career choice as it relates to education and skills. By understanding the employer's needs the client can learn how to anticipate and meet those needs. The job market varies with the location, and the human service worker can help clients navigate through the market by knowing what is available and who is hiring through the networks they have developed. Local employment agencies can assist with this task. Some TANF clients may not be familiar with the various methods of researching a job and will need assistance with this task. The importance of creating a network to find jobs cannot be stressed too heavily, and clients must be encouraged to use those networks already in place (U.S. Department of Labor, 2000; Livermore & Neustrom, 2003; McDonald, 2002). Clients can take job-search classes and volunteer to work in the community.

Job-Search Correspondence.   While most TANF recipients will not need to write letters of application, they will need to write interview thank-you letters. Also, rather than teaching them to write a letter accepting or declining an offer, role-playing these situations will help them better understand the process. Once clients have more job experience and are applying for higher-level positions, they can learn the other letter-writing procedures.

Tailor-Made Resumes.   Most TANF recipients will use a functional resume to organize their job experience according to their skills. Using this type of resume will increase their self-esteem and empower them to see that they do possess job skills, something they may not have considered in the past. Creating a resume also helps clients organize and better understand themselves and allows them to focus more on their strengths than on weaknesses.

Interviewing Strategies.   Interpersonal skills are often a weakness in the welfare-to-work population. The service worker can use role-playing of the various types of interview situations from easy to difficult, and from panel to telephone to help clients develop interview skills. Helping clients craft answers to some of the common interview questions will empower them as well. Videotaping clients during mock interviews and then critiquing the interviews provide clients with an opportunity to see themselves as others see them. Interview attire needs to be addressed. A client may not be aware of appropriate dress for an interview or that the attire may vary depending upon the job.

Change Behaviors.   Participation in a career development program is designed to help clients change behaviors that may be keeping them from self-sufficiency. Although specific behavior changes will vary with each person's ISP, all clients will have an opportunity to improve their interpersonal and work-related skills, along with whatever other skills they originally targeted for change. A behavior change should be reflected in clients' ability to find and to maintain a job, eventually moving toward self-sufficiency.

Complete the Program.   Clients who complete the program are those who have met the criteria for the program, developed their ISP, completed the training and education detailed in their ISP, and exhibited behavior changes leading to employment. Although clients can drop out at any time during the process, the service worker must advise them that they will probably lose their TANF funds. Some clients may have to cycle through several of stages of the program later as they move from low-skill employment to employment requiring more advanced skills.

Achieve Goal of Long-Term Employment.   The final goal for the client is long-term employment and self-sufficiency. The program must provide a working definition of *long-term* because the WIA does not provide one. Generally, when clients have been without TANF funds and other forms of public assistance (housing, Medicaid, **food stamps,** WIC), for at least a year and they are able to fully support themselves and their family members, they can be considered self-sufficient with long-term employment.

Program Evaluation

The program evaluation process has several sublevels: developing tools, tracking clients who complete the program, conducting the evaluation surveys, analyzing and reporting findings, and implementing program changes. The program staff and human service professionals need to develop a variety of tools to evaluate their program. Figure 8.1 is a flow chart for the career development program model for use with welfare-to-work clients. The text in each box in the figure is a factor that needs to be measured. Evaluation tools can include such items as a database of client information, intake interview sheets, case files, tracking forms, and referral forms. The program staff must also construct paper-and-pencil surveys or telephone surveys for clients who complete the program and their employers and decide how to track program clients and keep their information current. Another important task for the staff is to decide when to evaluate the program. For example, they can evaluate the programs and their participants at several points in the program: midway, upon completion, six months after completion.

While constant evaluation can be time consuming, the input is invaluable for the program. Evaluating midway provides data for making program adjustments in time to help the current participants. Evaluating participants immediately after the program is valuable, but it may not show how employable clients may actually be until they are hired. In deciding when to evaluate, the human service worker must consider the mobility of clients and the ability of the program to track them. The staff can survey employers who hire program participants at different times as well, perhaps six weeks and again at six months after hiring. The staff also needs to consider how they will collect, analyze, and report the information. Once the program staff has made these decisions, they need to create a timeline for the entire program-evaluation process showing every goal to be accomplished, the deadline for accomplishing them, and the person who is responsible. Once the evaluation information is collected, the input can be used to strengthen the current program.

Revisiting the Case Study: Annie

Conducting an Intake Interview

During the intake session the human service worker explored Annie's educational and work history; her interests and values; and her views on employment, education, and family. Discovering why she dropped out of school in the seventh grade was very important, because her oldest child was not born until Annie was 18. She may have an undiagnosed learning disability that has affected her self-esteem and, possibly, her social skills. The helping professional will have to be sensitive in exploring the reason that Annie's eldest son was living in a group home elsewhere. Since both Annie and her middle child have exhibited problems with anger, the eldest child may have a similar problem. Based on that information, Annie may need referral for anger management and family counseling as part of her services. The service worker will need to explore personal supports with Annie to determine whether she needs childcare assistance. Annie has her own transportation, which is a big benefit, but the service worker may want to explore its reliability.

Make Assessments

The human service professional will use the lower-reading level assessments with Annie. One possibility is the Ability Explorer (Harrington & Harrington, 1996), because it is written on a fifth-grade reading level and includes ability areas not measured by traditional aptitude measures. Another appropriate assessment is either of two card sorts for ability assessment: Motivated Skills Card Sort (Knowdell, 2002a) or Elevations Manual Card Sort (Scully, 2003). Despite the numerous computer-based assessment versions available, the service worker would avoid using them because of Annie's lack of computer skills. The Self-Directed Search, Form E (Holland, 1996a) would be an appropriate interest inventory to use with Annie since it is written at a lower reading level and links users to jobs requiring lower reading levels. If her scores are low with little differentiation, then Knowdell's (2002b) Occupational Interests Card Sort is useful for linking interests to possible jobs. The values assessment used would depend upon whether Annie responds better to card sorts or paper-and-pencil tests. If Annie feels comfortable with paper-and-pencil tests, then the Job Search Attitude Inventory (Liptak, 2002c) would be useful as a pre-post measure of Annie's attitudes and motivation.

Determine Barriers to Success

Based on the intake interview, Annie demonstrated some weaknesses with her social skills, anger in particular. The human service professional needs to address childcare options for her five- and seven-year old sons, as well as her level of education, coupled with her work skills and history. Depending on why she dropped out of school in the seventh grade, she may be referred for an assessment for learning disabilities. The Job Search Attitude Inventory (Liptak, 2002b) will detail other barriers for exploration and discussion. The human service worker should address these barriers to employment and incorporate Annie's personal and career goals and her values when they co-create Annie's ISP.

Choose Interventions

Using Job Coaching.   Because of her sketchy work history and some of her past work-related experiences, Annie would be a strong candidate for job coaching. Depending upon her self-esteem, however, she may prefer not to have a human service worker involved in her work life. In fact, her earlier comment "don't want to have to report my business to nobody" demonstrates that she may not feel comfortable with a job coach. The human service worker needs to address this problem and respect Annie's wishes if she is to feel empowered to make her own choices and to grow. The human service worker needs to explore the benefits and drawbacks of having a job coach with Annie to help her make her decision.

Using Group or One-to-One Interventions.   Anger plays an important part in Annie's life, and the human service worker needs to address how it affects her relationships with others (i.e., son's teacher, employers, coworkers). Her adjustment to her oldest son living in a group home may be connected to her anger, as may her family of origin. Other topics for counseling include self-esteem and possible depression. Process groups or career groups might help Annie learn to trust others as she explores her barriers to success (Creamer, Duggan, & Kidd, 1999; Duggan & Jurgens, 2005).

Finding Training and Education.   Annie's work in fast food and in housekeeping show some existing job skills that may need to be improved to ready her for a full-time job. Since she only has one year remaining of her total five-year TANF cap, finding full-time employment quickly is the main goal. Annie will not have time for training courses prior to work but will need on-the-job training instead. The human service worker needs to use a job network to help place Annie as soon as possible in a job that provides skills training. While ABE classes would be ideal, Annie will have to complete them either as part of her job or on her own time. Social-skills training combined with life-skills classes are paramount now, and if at all possible, Annie should be active in a group session that allows her an opportunity to practice new skills in a safe setting. Parenting skills, adjusting to a new job, balancing work and family, proper nutrition, and handling money are definite topics for inclusion.

Offering Mentoring. Even though Annie has not worked for a full year, she will need mentoring to help her through her last year on TANF. This mentoring, coupled with her life-skills classes, will prepare her to be on her own. She already has her own transportation and can remain in subsidized housing for several years, but she needs help in adjusting to life without public assistance.

Initiate the Employment Campaign

To allow her as much time as possible to adjust to being on her own, Annie needs a fast job search with a great deal of support. The human service worker needs to use a professional network to find Annie a job with an employer who understands TANF recipients and is willing to provide on-the-job training for Annie to help her adjust. If no positions exist within the professional network, then Annie will need a functional resume and a great deal of role-playing to practice interviewing and responding to a variety of job-related scenarios.

Conclusion

The welfare reform bill of 1996 stresses self-sufficiency and the requirement of work, centered on the assumption that welfare recipients function similarly to the rest of the population, thus are capable of supporting themselves and their family. To this end, human service professionals are tasked with assisting TANF clients in dealing with barriers to employment and empowering clients to reach their full potential. Changes need to be made, though, to better help the welfare-to-work population in its transition. The following recommended policy changes would assist the welfare-to-work population in transition to self-sufficiency. Childcare changes include:

- More infant care and care for toddlers
- Refundable childcare credits at the federal level
- Increased funding and improved access to childcare subsidies, especially more generous childcare subsidies to provide alternative childcare when the client's primary childcare falls through

- Childcare subsidies for clients seeking an education
- Childcare for clients while attending job-skills classes, therapy sessions, and so on
- Provision of evening, night, and weekend childcare

Changes in transportation policies that would be useful include:

- Promotion of a better transportation infrastructure
- Increased access to subsidized driving classes
- Fuel subsidies

Suggested changes in case management policy include:

- A service provider team approach (agency, TANF workers, and case managers) to monitor the intervention or service delivery
- Increased networking with local employers and community organizations to develop a mentoring system

Summary

The Personal Responsibility and Work Reconciliation Act (PRWORA) of 1996 created a transitional block grant program, Temporary Assistance to Needy Families (TANF). The TANF program emphasizes employment and self-sufficiency by providing a five-year lifetime cap for funds for families. This means that TANF recipients have very little time to ready themselves for the workforce, forcing them to overcome a lifetime of barriers to employment success. As the number of barriers to employment increases, the likelihood of becoming employed decreases. The most common barriers include: lack of childcare, access to transportation, physical and mental health problems, domestic violence, education, social skills, and work skills. Many clients face a combination of these barriers rather than one or two. A career development model presents the development of an Individual Success Plan for each participant that includes assessments of career abilities, interests, barriers, and values; interagency referrals; interventions such as job coaching, counseling, training/education/ life-skills classes, and mentoring; followed by an employment campaign that leads to long-term employment and self-sufficiency.

Key Terms

Adult Basic Education (ABE)
Aid to Families with Dependent Children (AFDC)
Family Violence Option (FVO)
Food stamps
General Equivalency Diploma (GED)

Medicaid
Special Supplemental Nutrition Program for Women, Infants, and Children (WIC)
Temporary Assistance to Needy Families (TANF)
Work first

Web Resources

Note that website URLs may change over time.

Child Care Development Block Grant
http://www.ucc.org/justice/welfare/childcare.htm

Department of Health and Human Services
http://www.hhs.gov

Nutritional Assistance Programs
http://www.fns.usda.gov/fns

Office on Violence Against Women
http://www.usdoj.gov/ovw

Workforce Investment Act (WIA)
http://www.usdoj.gov/crt/508/508law.html

9

The Working Poor

Poverty Despite a Paycheck

Case Study: David and Marla

David and Marla, both in their twenties, live in a small apartment with their three children ages three, five, and six. David has worked as an exterior housepainter for several years, a carpenter's helper for three years, then as a landscape maintenance worker for two years. During that time Marla stayed home with the children during the day and worked part time in the evenings at a video rental store while David watched the children. While life was not extremely difficult financially, David and Marla often struggled with paying all of their bills on time each month, and they sometimes chose to delay paying one bill in favor of paying others. David also tries to meet his child support obligations for his son by a previous marriage ($250 month) whether or not the other bills are paid. David's father is disabled and unable to work, so David gives him money whenever he can.

Now Marla stays home with the children because David often comes home too late to watch them, allowing her to go to work. Childcare costs $600 a month, which is more than the $400 that Marla was able to bring home in a month. David's work hours changed when he took a construction job as a framer when their car broke down. He now walks two miles to the closest bus stop, catches a bus at 6 A.M., arrives at the construction site by 7 A.M., and works 8–9 hours a day. He often does not return home until after 8 P.M. He brings home between $400 and $450 each week. Since Marla is home alone with the children, she calls on her sister who has a car but lives across town to take her to the grocery store as necessary.

David wants to find a job inside that is more consistent because his current work is weather-dependent. For example, constant rains last month reduced his work to only one or two days each week, drastically reducing his pay for the month. As a result, David and Marla had to once again choose which bills to pay and which to delay. David also wants a job with benefits that will provide health care for his wife and children. Both he and Marla have high-school diplomas, but no additional education.

The Working Poor Population

The working poor, often referred to as **low-wage** workers or low-income workers, work hard but struggle to make ends meet. While not all of the working poor meet the **federal poverty threshold** guidelines for being poor, many of them are close enough that illness, a major car repair, or a job layoff can push them into poverty. According to the 1997 National Survey of America's Families (NSAF), one in six nonelderly Americans live in families where the adults work on average at least half of the time but whose incomes fall below 200 percent of the federal poverty level. In 2001, 32.9 million people, 11.7 percent of the population, lived at or below the official poverty level, an increase of 1.3 million since 2000 (U.S. Department of Labor, 2003). Two-thirds of these Americans were members of families with children and two or more adults. The primary earner in these families often works full time, year round. Despite this full-time employment, the income of the working poor is often so low that it becomes difficult for them to sustain a life with what many Americans view as a minimally adequate standard of living because they suffer from an **income deficit** (Acs, Phillips, & McKenzie, 2000).

In 2000, the median household income was $42,100. The median income was $51,800 for family households and $25,400 for nonfamily households (U.S. Census Bureau, 2000b). Almost one out of five American workers reported being paid less than eight dollars an hour in 2001, or $17,000 a year for those who worked full time (Jencks, 2004). The 2006 official poverty threshold is $20,000 for a family of four, and the standard low-income cutoff for this family (i.e., 200 percent of the FPL), is $40,000. Out of this income, families need to pay for shelter, utilities, food, and clothing, along with any costs of working outside the home, such as transportation and childcare. On a national basis, low-wage earners making 200 percent or less than the FPL are three times more likely to have problems paying the rent, mortgage, or utility bills than are families with higher incomes (Acs et al., 2000). Between 1997 and 1999 employment rates for low-income adults ages 25 to 54 held steady, while the income rate for low-income single parents rose four percent (Zedlewski, 2000). Between 2000 and 2002, however, this rate shifted as the median income for single-mother families fell by one percent per year (Economic Policy Institute, 2004a).

Effect of the Economy on the Working Poor

According to the Economic Policy Institute (2004b), Americans lost more than 1 million jobs between March 2001 and August 2003. In fact, the United States lost manufacturing jobs for 41 consecutive months from August 2001 to January 2004. Families in the lower one-fifth income bracket lost 4.1 percent in earnings, while families in the highest one-fifth income bracket experienced only a 0.9 percent decrease in earnings. The increase in the unemployment rate from 4 percent in 2000 to 5.6 percent in 2002 is coupled with a 2.2 percent decline in family income for middle-class families and a 2.9 percent decline for those families in the poorest one-fifth bracket. The number of the unemployed who are classified as long-term unemployed—those who have been out of work for 27 consecutive weeks—rose to 22.1 percent in 2003, the highest number since the 1980s. Long-term unemployment increased 198 percent between 2000 and 2003. Long-term unemployed Americans with bachelors' degrees increased by 299 percent (Economic Policy Institute, 2004c).

Median family income declined $1,300 from 2000–2002 with almost 80 percent of that decline due to a decrease in the number of working hours per year. Minority families lost income between 2000 and 2002 at three times the rate of nonminority families (Economic Policy Institute, 2004a). Between 1995 and 2000, the poverty rate fell by 2.5 percent. The 2001 recession and the resulting loss of jobs ended the poverty drop of the 1990s. By 2002 the poverty rate was at 12.2 percent and the twice poverty rate was at 30.5 percent. These rates mean that 34.6 million people were officially poor, and 87.2 million people lived in households with a mean family income of less than two times the poverty threshold. In 2002, 18.8 percent or 4.4 million children under the age of six were poor. Almost 36 percent of African American children and 29 percent of Hispanic children were in this category (Economic Policy Institute, 2004c).

Measures of Poverty

Working poor is a broad-spectrum term that implies a distribution of people's well-being rather than a finite definition. This spectrum demonstrates that the composition of poverty varies by the severity of the poverty. For example, the number of **severely poor** rose from 12.6 million in 2000 to 13.4 million in 2001. Almost 41 percent of the working poor in 2000 and 2001 were classified as severely poor. Over 12 million of the working poor were classified as **nearly poor** in 2000 and 2001, which is 4.4 percent of the poor population (Proctor & Dalaker, 2003).

Entry into and Exit from Poverty

Poverty may be long term, but in many instances, people cycle into poverty and out of poverty with poverty spells lasting from one to three years. McKernan and Ratliff (2002) suggest that specific factors are associated with entry into poverty. For example, changes in employment and earnings are more likely to be associated with entry into poverty than are changes in household structure. Other events common to entry into poverty include the shift to a female head of household. The birth of a child to an unmarried woman and dropping out of school also affect entry into poverty (McKernan & Ratliff, 2002).

More than one single path may lead out of poverty. Changes in household composition, disability status, increases in educational attainment, and labor supply are connected with exiting poverty. Individuals who experience a combination of these events are more likely to exit poverty. Employment gains by the head of the household, spouse, or other household member are of equal importance in helping individuals exit poverty. A person who is head of the household and receives an advanced degree (associate's degree or higher) is 27 percent more likely to exit poverty (McKernan & Ratliff, 2002). In married-couple families, 28.6 percent were more likely to exit poverty as compared to other type families where 12.2 percent were likely to exit poverty. Whites were most likely to exit poverty at 25.7 percent, followed by Hispanics at 18.4 percent and African Americans at 13.2 percent (Eller, 1996).

Characteristics of the Working Poor Population

In a study of 2000 applicants for early Head Start, Wall and associates (2000) identified three groups of working poor: military, civilian, and immigrant families. Sixty-six percent of military families were likely to have two biological parents compared to 31 percent of civilian families and 25 percent of immigrant families. Forty-four percent of immigrant families had a mother alone, and 30 percent had a mother with a partner, friends, or relatives. Sixty-three percent of civilian families had a mother alone. Fifty-six percent of immigrant mothers and 66 percent of military mothers were likely to be married compared to 21 percent of civilian mothers. The average age of U.S. civilian mothers tended at 25 years of age to be younger compared to U.S. military mothers at 27 and immigrant mothers at 30 years of age. The average age of military fathers tended to be younger at 26 years of age compared to civilian fathers at 28 and immigrant fathers at 34 years of age. There parents also differed with respect to education. Sixty-three percent of military mothers were likely to have a college education compared to 26 percent of civilian mothers and 18 percent of immigrant mothers. Fifty-eight percent of civilian mothers were likely to have a high-school education, and 16 percent were likely to have less than a high-school education. Only 23 percent of immigrant mothers had a high-school diploma.

Almost 41 percent of minority working families are considered low-income as compared to 20 percent of nonminority working families. Almost 35 percent of low-income working families have a parent without a high-school degree. About 52 percent of low-income working families live in housing that costs more than one-third of their income, and 36.7 percent have an **uninsured** parent (Waldron, Roberts, & Reamer, 2004).

Job Characteristics.   The median hourly wage for low-income working families is $7.55, less than half of that for high-wage working families ($16.67). Low-income families are less likely to have additional wage earners than are **higher income** families. Almost 86 percent of nonprimary earners in higher-income families provided additional earnings for their families as compared to 69.1 percent of nonprimary earners in lower-income families. These secondary workers in low-income families are also more likely to work fewer hours than those secondary earners in higher-income families. Differences in job quality also exist between low-income workers and high-income workers. Almost 75 percent of low-income workers work during regular business hours of 6 A.M. to 6 P.M. as compared to 83 percent of high-income workers. Only 69.2 percent of low-wage earners were with their current employer for more than one year, whereas 86.3 percent of high-income earners had been with the same employer for over a year. Just over 54 percent of low-income earners had **employer-sponsored medical insurance** as compared to 88.6 percent of the high-income earners (Acs et al., 2000).

Families and Unrelated Individuals.   The number of families in poverty increased from 6.8 million in 2001, a 9.2 percent poverty rate, to 7.2 million in 2002, a 9.6 percent poverty rate. The poverty rate for married-couple families increased from 4.9 percent (2.8 million families) in 2001 to 5.3 percent (3.1 million families) in 2002. The number of families in poverty with a female head of household with no spouse present rose from 3.5 million in 2001 to 3.6 million in 2002, but the 26.5 percent poverty rate remained the same. These families comprised half of all those in poverty in 2002. The number of male heads of household with no spouse present did not increase in number or in poverty rate over that same time period, but remained at 564,000 in number at a 12.1 percent poverty rate (Proctor & Dalaker, 2003). Families in poverty cite finances as their greatest stress, because working poor families are often unable to provide basic necessities such as health care and dental care. Still other families in poverty are unable to educate their children or protect them from drug-ridden neighborhoods (Abramovitz, 1991).

The number of *unrelated individuals*—people not living with any relatives—living in poverty also increased between 2001 and 2002. In 2001, 9.2 million unrelated individuals were living in poverty; the number rose to 9.6 million in 2002. The 3.8 million men in poverty in 2001 increased to 4 million in 2002. The number of women in poverty rose from 5.4 million in 2001 to 5.6 million in 2002 with women accounting for 58.2 percent of all unrelated individuals in poverty in 2002 (Proctor & Dalaker, 2003).

Housing. According to Burman and Kravitz (2004), families earning less than $10,000 spend 81 percent of their income on housing as compared to families earning between $10,000 and $20,000 who spend 43 percent of their income on housing. Families earning more than $200,000 only spend 9 percent of their income on housing. Families who cannot spend 81 percent of their income on housing are often forced to live in severely dilapidated buildings. Seventeen percent live in crowded conditions. Over 67 percent of those with **critical housing needs** are renters and are almost evenly split between 42.8 percent non-Hispanic whites and 52.8 percent minorities. More than half of the working poor with critical housing needs who rent live in central cities as compared to most homeowners who tend to live in the suburbs and in rural areas (Harkness & Newman, 2004).

Lack of Health Insurance. In 2003 nearly 45 million people or 15.6 percent of Americans were uninsured, up from 15.2 percent or 43.6 million people in 2002. The number of people covered by employer-offered insurance dropped from 175.3 million or 61.3 percent in 2002 to 174 million or 60.4 percent in 2003 (DeNavas-Walt, Proctor, & Mills, 2004). Low-wage workers are less likely to have insurance offered through work and often cannot afford to purchase private insurance. In 1996, 54.3 percent of low-income working families had employer-provided health insurance compared to 88.6 percent of all high-income working families (Acs et al., 2000). The median living wage in 2000 for employees receiving health insurance was $8.19 per hour, almost 60 percent above the federal minimum wage of $5.15 per hour that year (Bartik, 2002). When finances force families to choose between health insurance, medical care, food, or housing, often health insurance and medical care are the first cut from the family budget (Long, 2003; Neumark, 2002).

Food Costs. Families who earn less than $10,000 a year spend 52 percent of their earnings on food. Those families who earn between $10,000 and $20,000 per year spend 25 percent of their income on food (Burman & Kravitz, 2004). Many families who meet the federal guidelines for poverty also qualify for food stamps and Special Supplemental Nutrition Program for Women, Infants, and Children (WIC), yet less than half of working families eligible for assistance participate (Fishman & Beebout, 2001).

Barriers to Career Success

Structural Barriers

Affordable and Dependable Childcare.
One important barrier to career success for the working poor is that of finding affordable and dependable childcare (Bartik, 2000; Bassuk, Mickelson, Bissell, & Perloff, 2002; Kinglsey & Pettit, 2003; Zedlewski, 2002; Zedlewski & Bader, 2004). For many employees, keeping their job depends on finding childcare that is affordable, dependable, and safe; matches their work schedule; and improves their job satisfaction. Abramovitz (1991) cited the lack of dependable and safe childcare as one reason why single parents often choose public assistance over low-wage jobs. Brown and McIntosh (2003) suggested that the childcare is tied to job satisfaction in the low-wage service sector. Over 24 percent of those people who recently left Temporary Assistance to Needy Families (TANF) reported having used government childcare benefits during their first three months off of TANF (Loprest, 2002). Those who used the governmental childcare benefits were less likely to return to TANF. Only 19.5 percent of those who received governmental assistance with childcare returned to TANF as compared to 27.7 percent of families without this help. Whereas in the past, parents were able to manage childcare and employment by delaying employment until their children were able to attend school, delaying employment is no longer an option for low-wage families. This situation means an increase of reliance upon kin and nonkin childcare support. Finding childcare that is both affordable and safe, however, often proves to be difficult. Low-income families often have more children than do higher-income families. Forty-three percent of low-income families have three or more children as compared to 22.9 percent of higher-income families. For low-income families affordable and dependable childcare is extremely important (Acs et al., 2000).

Transportation.
Access to transportation is often a barrier to employment success for both the inner city poor (Bartik, 2000) and the rural poor where the lack of public transportation often results in increased transportation expenses for workers (Robertson & Donnermeyer, 1997; Waldron et al., 2004). Public transportation is often inadequate, and few jobs are available within walking distance of housing developments (Iceland, 2003; Kim & Mergoupis, 1997). Transportation conditions often make it difficult for those in poverty to work full time and even serves as a disincentive for workers to extend their working hours (Lambert, 1998). Lack of affordable and stable public transportation also impacts the use of after-school care (Nash & Fraser, 1998). Families themselves have cited poor transportation as a barrier to their career success (Nelson et al., 2003). Small, low-interest loans for automobile purchases or repairs have increased workers' long-range financial stability (Raschick, 1997).

Deindustrialization: Employment Shifts and Wage Bias. Much research attributes the decline in the economic future of less-skilled workers to an increase in the demand for higher-skilled workers. One possible reason for this trend is the increased outsourcing of jobs to countries with a large low-wage and low-skill workforce. Outsourcing allows companies to move the low-skill-intensive components of production to countries with lower wages while keeping the high-skill-intensive components of production stateside. Once the low-skill activities are complete, the goods are imported back from the low-wage countries to be completed and sold in the United States. Less-competitive firms, often low tech and with a high number of low-skilled workers, are often squeezed out of business as the imported goods become cheaper than locally produced goods (Anderton & Brenton, 1998). The United States has lost 2.7 million manufacturing jobs since 2000 (Koehler & Hagigh, 2004). Labor experts at Cornell and the University of Massachusetts-Amherst predicted a loss of 406,000 jobs to other countries during 2004 alone (Bronfenbrenner & Luce, 2004).

Skill-biased technological change has also impacted the shift of jobs because labor-saving technical progress has reduced the demand for less-skilled workers (Anderton &Brenton, 1998). Welfare reform has been linked to the increasing number of low-skilled workers, because former welfare recipients compete with those already employed, thus the workforce outweighs the demand for low-skilled jobs and eventually decreases wages for all (Acs et al., 2000; Hout, 1997). Therefore, finding a full-time job no longer guarantees an escape from poverty. Immigration also affects jobs and wages when low-skilled immigrants are willing to work for lower wages than native workers (Hout, 1997).

The shift from higher-paying, unionized, manufacturing jobs to an expanding service and retail job market has also impacted the availability of low-skilled jobs. This shift has created more employment opportunities with nonstandard work schedules that often require late hours and weekend work (Presser, 1999). Unfortunately, even some of these newly created service jobs are now moving offshore by taking customer-call centers and data-entry facilities to other nations where wage levels are lower (Koehler & Hagigh, 2004). According to a study by the University of California Berkley, almost 14 million service jobs in the United States or 11 percent of all U.S. occupations are in danger of being exported (Bardhan & Kroll, 2003).

Individual Barriers

Education. The level of educational attainment varies among the working poor. In 1996 over 45 percent of the heads of household of working poor families had a GED or high-school diploma, 22.4 percent had less than a high-school education, 21.5 percent had completed some college, and 10.4 percent were college graduates. In comparison, the heads of household of higher-income families in 1996 reported the following educational attainment: 36 percent were college graduates, 35 percent possessed a high-school diploma or GED, 24.7 percent completed some college, and only 4.3 percent did not complete high school (Acs et al., 2000). Kim (1998) suggested that lack of skills and education impact the ability of members of the working poor to find more lucrative employment, primarily because of the decreasing number of jobs available for those with limited skills and education. Educational gains have been linked with exits from poverty because of the increased likelihood of higher-wage employment that accompanies an increase in educational attainment (McKernan & Ratcliffe, 2002). Few jobs allow employees to arrange their working schedules to accommodate an educational plan (Secret & Green, 1998).

Family Responsibilities.   Family responsibilities often impact the ability to work full time (Kim, 1998). Single parents, however, are not the only people who curtail work hours to meet family needs. Less-flexible jobs and positions with fewer benefits affect the low-income worker who is trying to balance work with family responsibilities (Phillips, 2004). While employees in higher-paying jobs often have the flexibility to rearrange their work schedule to respond to family needs and crises, employees in low-paying jobs often lack that freedom (Secret & Green, 1998).

Lack of Marketable Job Skills.   Juhn (1999) proposed that two types of skills determine wages: physical skills and cognitive skills. Employees with cognitive skills are hired for high-wage, high-skilled jobs; and workers with physical skills are hired for low-wage, low-skilled jobs (Juhn, 1999). As the number of low-skilled jobs decreases, the need for employees to possess more skills increases. Bardhan and Kroll (2003) suggested that as jobs lost to outsourcing are replaced by higher-wage jobs, workers will need to improve their education and skills to be competitive. Bartik (2000) suggested that soft skills, such as an employee's ability to be on time for work as well as the ability to get along with coworkers and supervisors, are also beneficial to obtaining and keeping employment. Workers who have references from former employers that attest to these skills are more easily hired than workers without such references. Completing training programs with ties to local employers is also beneficial in the job search (Bartik, 2000). Language skills are also necessary for employment. Both native-born and immigrant workers with low literacy skills are at a disadvantage because they lack the English skills required for higher-skilled jobs (Booth-Kewley, Rosenfield, & Edwards, 1993; Lerman, 2000; McNichol & Springer, 2004).

Physical Health Barriers

Illness.   The health status of household members can affect the number of hours they work if a household member misses work due to illness, injury, or a disability (Johnson & Crystal, 1996; McKernan & Ratcliffe, 2002). The Family and Medical Leave Act of 1993 provides eligible employees with up to 12 workweeks of protected leave during a 12-month period, but this leave is often unpaid. Family illness or childbirth often results in a loss of time from work and reduced income for families who lack family-care policies (Phillips, 2004). Low-wage earners in their 50s and early 60s are more likely to suffer from a major illness than are younger, low-wage earners (Johnson & Crystal, 1996).

Substance Abuse.   Research linked unemployment and underemployment (i.e., involuntary part-time employment and employment at poverty wages) with alcohol abuse and found that underemployment increased the likelihood of binge drinking by

85 percent (Dooley & Prouse, 1997b). Robertson and Donnermeyer (1997) found that those employed in blue-collar professions were more likely to report drug-related mental health problems than those who were employed in other professions or not employed at all.

Mental Health Barriers

The increase in family stress has been attributed to the declining standard of living as families cite financial worry as the greatest cause of stress (Abramovitz, 1991). Economically stressed parents have little time for leisure and often have to juggle expenses for food, housing, and medical expenses (Long, 2003). Lack of time for leisure combined with the financial strain of poverty takes it toll on physical as well as mental health leading to cardiovascular disease and other illnesses (Johnson & Crystal, 1996). According to Bassuk et al. (2002), kin and nonkin support is extremely important to the mental health of extremely poor women. Conflict with members of their support network, in particular with siblings and/or their mother, was found to be highly predictive of adverse mental health outcomes. When extremely poor women experience conflict with kin, depression often results (Bassuk et al., 2002). Long-term unemployment has also been linked to depression (Broman, Hamilton, Hoffman, & Mavaddat, 1995). Both underemployment and job dissatisfaction are linked to depression (Robertson & Donnermeyer, 1997; Secret & Green, 1998).

Career Development Program Model: The Working Poor Population

A career development program for use with low-wage or working poor clients involves an individualized approach that addresses each client's needs and barriers with the ultimate goal being long-term employment. Because of the varied backgrounds presented by this group of clients (parent/nonparent/family/single adult), human service professionals need to look at each client separately in developing a series of interventions to enhance the client's career success. Our program has three major components: the applicant pool, the Individual Success Plan (ISP), and the program evaluation. Each component will be explained in detail. Figure 9.1 is a graphic model of the career development program.

Applicant Pool

The Applicant Pool includes any client with a family income at or below 200 percent of the federal poverty threshold. After the intake interview, staff personnel will then determine which clients fit the criteria for program participation and which do not. For example, low-income, working poor clients with housing difficulties may need assistance from local homeless shelters or from a Housing and Urban Development program (see chapter 12). Victims of domestic violence may be better served by referral to a shelter offering domestic-violence-related services (see Chapter 10).

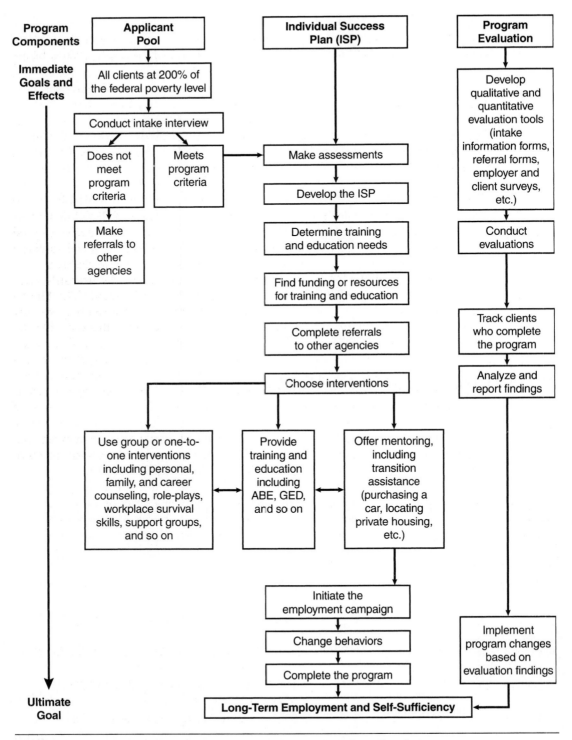

FIGURE 9.1 *Career Development Program Model: Working Poor Population*

Individual Success Plan

Developing an Individual Success Plan (ISP) provides a personal approach to career development. Just because a job is available and a low-wage earner is only working 25 hours a week does not mean that the job is "affordable" nor does it mean the client is able to work full time. Because the low-wage and working poor population consists of single parents, single adults, two-parent families, and extended families, human service professionals need to view clients as individuals while determining how to best meet their needs. Developing an ISP can help clients determine the best steps for them. Also, each client brings a different combination of factors to the job search, and the ISP can address each of those factors while fostering a personalized approach for the client.

Make Assessments.   When working with clients, human service professionals need to consider not only the clients' career, educational, and training needs, but also their medical needs. The financial stresses created by living in poverty are not conducive to good physical or mental health, both of which impact clients' success in finding and holding a job. Thus, the ISP needs to include ways to address these issues as well as a career.

Chapter 3 provides a variety of career-related assessments the human service professional can use depending on the client's needs and background. The human service professional will start with a traditional intake interview that can help identify these needs and determine the best course of action for the client at this time. During the interview, the client and human service professional will examine survival strategies currently in use to determine their appropriateness. Again, the diverse backgrounds of these clients cannot be overemphasized. One client may have an eighth grade education and another may have completed several years of college, so human service professionals need to be very careful in matching assessments to the client. Table 9.1 is a list of assessments appropriate for use in designing an ISP with clients who are low-wage earners. As mentioned in Chapter 3, using several assessments is encouraged, but human service professionals need to be careful to use the ones that best fit the needs of their clients. (See Chapter 3 for additional details on each assessment.)

TABLE 9.1   *Career Related Assessments for Use with the Working Poor Populations*

Title	Source
Ability Tests	
Ability Explorer	Harrington, J. C., & Harrington, T. F. (1996). *Ability Explorer*. Itasca, IL: Houghton Mifflin.
Career Key*	Jones, L. K., & Jones, J. W. (2000). *Career key*. Raleigh, NC: Author.
Motivated Skills Card Sort	Knowdell, R. (2002, June). *Motivated skills card sort*. San Jose, CA: Career Research & Testing.
O*NET Ability Profiler*	O*NET Consortium (2003), April). *O*NET ability profiler*. Washington, DC: Author.
WorkKeys	ACT, Inc. (1993). *Workkeys assessments*. Iowa City, IO: ACT.

(Continued)

TABLE 9.1   Continued

Title	Source
Interest Inventories	
Career Exploration Inventory 2	Liptak, J. (2002). *The career exploration inventory: A guide for exploring work, leisure, and learning* (2nd ed). Indianapolis, IN: JIST Works.
CareerExplorer CD-ROM*	JIST Works. (2004). *Careerexplorer CD-ROM.* Indianapolis, IN: Author.
Guide for Occupational Exploration Interest Inventory	Farr, M. (2002). *Guide for occupational exploration interest inventory* (4th ed.). Indianapolis, IN: JIST Works.
Leisure to Occupations Search	McDaniels, C., & Mullins, S. R., (1999). *The leisure to occupations connection search.* Indianapolis, IN: JIST Works.
Occupational Interests Card Sort	Knowdell, R. (2002, June). *Occupational interests card sort.* San Jose, CA: Career Research & Testing.
O*NET Career Interest Inventory*	JIST Works. (2002). *O*NET career interests inventory.* Indianapolis, IN: Author.
O*NET Interest Profiler	O*NET Consortium (n.d.) *O*NET Interest profiler.* Washington, DC: Author.
Self-Directed Search, Forms CP, R, & E	Holland, J. L. (1990). *Self-directed search form CP: Career Planning.* Lutz, FL: Psychological Assessment Resources; Holland, J. L. (1994). *Self-directed search form R.* Lutz, FL: Psychological Assessment Resources; Holland J. L. (1996). *Self-directed search form E* (4th ed). Lutz, FL: Psychological Assessment Resources. Holland, J. L. (1996). *Self-directed search form E* (4th ed.). [Audiotape]. Lutz, FL: Psychological Assessment Resources.
Transition-to-Work Inventory	Liptak, J. J. (2004). *Transition-to-work inventory.* Indianapolis, IN: JIST Works.
Voc-Tech Quick Screener	JIST Works (2002) *Voc-Tech Quick Screener.* Indianapolis, IN: Author
Wide Range Interest and Occupation Test	Glutting, J. J. & Wilkinson, G. (2003). *Wide range interest and occupation test* (2nd ed.). Wilmington, DE: Wide Range.
Value Inventories	
Career Values Card Sort	Knowdell, R. (1998, June). *Career values card sort.* San Jose, CA: Career Research & Testing.
O*NET Career Values Inventory*	JIST Works (2002). *O*NET career values inventory.* Indianapolis, IN: Author.
O*NET Work Importance Locator and Profiler*	O*NET Consortium (n.d.). *O*NET work importance locator and profiler.* Washington, DC: Author.
Values-Driven Work Card Sort	Career Action Center. (n.d.) *Values-driven work card sort.* Menlo Park, CA: Prodigy Press.

TABLE 9.1   Continued

Title	*Source*
Work Orientation and Values Survey	Brady, R. P. (2002). *Work orientation and values survey.* Indianapolis, IN: JIST Works.
Career Development Inventories	
Barriers to Employment Success Inventory	Liptak, J. *Barriers to employment success inventory* (2nd ed.) Indianapolis, IN: JIST Works.
Career Attitudes and Strategies Inventory	Holland, J. L., & Gottfredson, G. D. (1994). *Career attitudes and strategies inventory.* Lutz, FL: Psychological Assessment Resources.
Career Beliefs Inventory	Krumboltz, J. D. (1991). *Career beliefs inventory.* Mountain View, CA: CPP.
Career Decision Scale	Osipow, S. H., Carney, C. G., Winer, J. L., Yanico, B. J., & Koschier. M. (1987). *Career decision scale* (3rd ed.). Lutz, FL: Psychological Assessment Resources.
Career Thoughts Inventory	Sampson, J. P., Peterson, G. W., Lenz, J. G., Reardon, R. C., & Saunders, D. E. (1996). *Career thoughts inventory.* Lutz, FL: Psychological Assessment Resources.
Career Transition Inventory	Heppner, M. J. (1991). *Career transition inventory.* Columbia, MO: Author.
Job Search Attitude Inventory	Liptak, J. (2002). *Job search attitude inventory* (2nd ed.). Indianapolis, IN: JIST Works.
My Vocational Situation	Holland, J. L., Daiger, D., & Power, P. G. (1980). *My vocational situation.* Mountain View, CA: CPP.
Overcoming Barriers Card Sort Game Kit	Harney, E. E., & Angel, D. L. (1999). *Overcoming barriers card sort game kit.* Hacienda Heights, CA: WorkNet Solutions.
Salient Beliefs Review: Connecting Spirit to Work	Bloch, D. (2003). *Salient beliefs review: Connecting spirit to work.* Indianapolis, IN: JIST Works.
Vocational Exploration and Insight Kit	Holland, J. L., Birk, J. M., Cooper, J. F., Dewey, C. R., Dolliver, H., Takai, R. T., & Tyler, L. (1980). *The vocational exploration and insight kit.* Mountain View, CA: CPP.
Miscellaneous	
Elevations ® Manual Card Sort System	Scully, H. (2003, August). *Elevations manual card sort system.* Roseville, CA: Author.
Individual Employment Plan	Ludden, L. L., & Maitlen, B. (2002). *Individual employment plan.* Indianapolis, IN: JIST Works.
Vocational Decision-Making Interview	Czerlinsky, T., & C handler, S. (1999). *Vocational decision-making interview.* Indianapolis, IN: JIST Works.

*Use only if client is computer literate.

Develop the ISP.   Once the client completes assessments, the client and human service professional will develop the ISP. By incorporating information gained from the intake interview, discussions, and assessments, the human service worker will assist the client in identifying specific barriers to employment success. The human service professional needs to explore issues of mental and physical health and make referrals where necessary. After helping clients recognize their possible barriers to career success, the human service professional needs to integrate clients' values and career and personal goals into the planning process. Helping clients take an active role in developing their ISP empowers the clients and helps them move toward self-sufficiency. Together, the client and human service professional will determine what barriers the client will address first, and they will make a timeline for meeting each goal. Setting mini goals for clients to meet along the way will help them see what progress they are making, while allowing for a redesign of the ISP as necessary.

Determine Training and Education Needs.   The human service professional and client will explore next what type of training and education the client needs to reach the client's goals by using assessment and intake interview results. Clients who have dropped out of high school may need to complete an Adult Basic Education (ABE) program or a General Equivalency Diploma (GED) prior to or during the job search or other training. When possible, the human service professional needs to help clients locate jobs that provide workers with the flexibility to attend school, gain additional training, and meet their family-based responsibilities. When on-the-job-training is not available, clients who completed high school or have a GED may qualify to immediately enter a training program offered through the community college or a local proprietary school.

Reviewing the results of the interest inventories will provide career leads for possible training and education for the more experienced clients. Considering *future* jobs should be a priority for the human service professional and the client at this time as part of the training considerations. Technology skills in particular are important skills to develop. Human service professionals need to help clients avoid training that perpetuates low skills, obsolete technologies, and low-wage jobs; instead, they should emphasize matching skills development and support with *local* economic opportunities. Goozner (2004) suggested that the modern American factory worker now needs to be able to read, work in teams, compute, solve problems, and be willing to take on many more tasks during a typical day in order to be competitive with workers in other nations who work for less money. The new American worker then needs to work ten times smarter and know how to work in a modernized environment filled with robots and other technological advances. Helping low-wage earners prepare for these new jobs is crucial to their success.

Assessment results will possibly suggest other topics such as life skills for training and education. Life skills can be offered to clients in small groups or in one-on-one sessions, allowing for a more individualized fit as necessary. Providing clients with a list of possible training and educational group topics (i.e., nutrition and health, building family strengths, balancing work with family, stress management, time management, money management, parenting skills) from which to choose continues to empower them to take responsibility for their life choices and ownership in their successes.

Find Funding or Resources for Training and Education.   Money is scarce for low-wage earners who seldom have the luxury of being able to meet all of their financial needs at once. In many instances, these workers may earn too much money to receive financial assistance available to other clients, so locating funding sources for education and training is crucial. Human service professionals, therefore, need to familiarize themselves with their local resources. Federally funded One-Stop Career Centers provide funding for training and education for eligible adults through Individual Training Accounts arranged through One-Stop. These accounts supplement financial aid already available through other intuitions, or when no financial aid is available, these accounts may cover the cost of all training. In some instances clients may have outstanding educational loans or may have used federal financial aid in the past to obtain training and dropped out prior to finishing. These individuals will need other sources of funding to pay for their training, and those who need financial assistance beyond that available through grants may qualify for some financial assistance through Workforce Investment Act funds. The case manager will be responsible for coordinating those funds as well as the available services. To access these funds, the client will need to be referred for training by the local One-Stop center once all other funding has been exhausted (U.S. Department of Labor, 2000; U.S. General Accounting Office, 2003a). Families that qualify can be referred to the local Family Self-Sufficiency program for assistance in job training, education, and life skills. Life-skills training and education are often available in a variety of settings and at no cost. Again, meeting the goals set forth in the ISP will require the human service professional to serve as a case manager to coordinate these efforts.

Complete Referrals to Other Agencies.   As mentioned previously, referring qualifying families to local **Family Self-Sufficiency (FSS)** programs needs to be the first step in the ISP whenever possible. Interagency cooperation is necessary to assure that clients' needs are met for food and shelter, medical care, mental health, and education and training. A holistic approach to the working poor addresses the interaction of all of these factors rather than concentrating on just finding better employment for the client. Human service professionals need to familiarize themselves with their local providers for all support services and refer clients accordingly to create the best assistance program possible to meet clients' individual needs. While developing the ISP, the client or worker may identify certain behaviors or events that necessitate referral to another agency. Clients who are victims of domestic violence, for example, need referrals for domestic violence services. Medical referrals may be needed along with those for mental health issues or substance abuse. Clients may need funding for childcare and transportation along with referrals for the following: Supplemental Security Income (SSI), Special Supplemental Nutrition Program for Women, Infants, and Children (WIC Program), **Earned Income Tax Credit (EITC)**, Temporary Assistance for Needy Families (TANF), food stamps (FS), National School Lunch Program (NSLP), Transitional Medicaid Assistance (TMA), and **State Children's Health Insurance Program (SCHIP)**.

Choose Interventions.   The career development model for the working poor population has three categories of interventions: one-to-one interventions, training and education, and mentoring. The client and human service professional can determine whether an individual or group approach is best, and these interventions may be offered concurrently or in phases, depending upon the individual needs of the client as well as the requirements of the local agency. Some clients may need all three interventions while others may only need one or two. Again, the need for an individualized approach cannot be stressed too much due to the diverse backgrounds of low-wage earners.

Using Group or One-to-One Interventions.   One-to-one intervention is sometimes necessary to help clients transition into self-sufficiency. This intervention involves personal and family counseling, combined with career development. It might include role-plays and support groups. Clients may be referred elsewhere for these services or kept in house. Personal and family counseling would address such issues as substance abuse, domestic violence, and depression. Clients who are eligible for TANF benefits must abide by the guidelines of that program, which may mean that they will have to go to work before addressing other issues of support, training, or education. Depending upon the clients' past exposure to work, their career exploration interventions could include job shadowing, unpaid internships, and even field trips to local businesses, organizations, and agencies (U.S. Department of Labor, 2000; Wilkins, 2002).

Providing Training and Education.   Clients often need encouragement to continue training and education while on the job. Helping clients prepare for careers that are not obsolete and for careers that will bring them higher wages and more stability will be paramount, and technology skills need to be included in the training whenever possible. Clients with little job experience may benefit from community work experience placements that provide social skills and training, along with references and entry-level forms of networking. Training occurs on the job as well, and research has shown that working next to higher-wage employees often allows low-wage employees to gain industry-specific skills that could help them advance later (Andersson, Lane, & McEntarfer, 2004). Life-skills training and education, whether in a class format or individually, also occur during this stage. These life-skills classes (i.e., time, stress, or money management; parenting skills; balancing work, education, and family commitments) allow participants to select and attend the classes that they feel fit their ISP goals and will increase their self-sufficiency (Duncan, Dunnagan, Christopher, & Paul, 2003).

Offering Mentoring.   Several levels of mentoring need to be offered to low-wage earners. Clients who are currently employed in a stable position may need transition assistance in locating private, safe housing, buying a car, or opening a bank account. Other clients may need mentoring on the job to help them adjust to new employment demands. The mentor can be an agency employee or a trained volunteer with networks to local businesses and community organizations that provide these services to clients. Such networks could include bank employees who are willing to guide clients through the process of opening their first bank accounts. Another useful contact is a local car dealership that is willing to help clients establish credit and develop a payment plan to purchase affordable and safe transportation. Enlisting the aid of a local mechanic could prove helpful as well. Still other contacts are landlords or realtors willing to walk clients through the process of renting or buying a home, as well as the variety of housing transition programs available for the homeless. Homeowners may need assistance in home maintenance and in home repair. The mentor would develop a network of such contacts for clients to use and would facilitate meetings and offer whatever other assistance clients need at the time.

Initiate the Employment Campaign.   The employment campaign is determined by the needs and goals of the clients. Some clients may need to begin their employment campaign immediately, whereas others may have time to complete work-related activities before beginning the campaign. Eliminating barriers to employment success before initiating a job campaign is the best approach, but some clients will have to work on several activities at once. These clients will need intensive case management by the human service professional. This next section provides an overview of considerations for low-wage earners during the employment campaign. For additional details, please see Chapter 5.

The Strategic Job Search.   Labor market intermediaries can help low-wage earners connect with employers who need low-skilled workers but are having a difficult time finding workers using traditional hiring practices. These intermediaries or *job placement assistants* need to carefully and correctly match the employer's needs to the employee's needs, sending only workers who already possess the necessary skills for the job (Holzer, 2000). Employer studies report that employers put a great deal of trust in referrals, whether the referrals are from current employees, friends, or acquaintances (Henley, 2000). Informal referrals work primarily through a social network. Job candidates within the network find their job search facilitated by networking. Those outside of the network find their job search at a disadvantage. An important component of job search is helping clients develop an informal network of job contacts with people already in the field in which the client wants to work (Henley, 2000).

Human service professionals can use the information collected from the assessments and intake interview to help clients explore the impact of their goals and values on the job-search process. Some clients may need help setting goals and developing a plan to meet those goals. Other clients may need support in developing the skills that they need to begin in the jobs of their choice. Helping clients plan and understand that every step they take in the employment campaign leads them closer to their goal of employment and self-sufficiency is important. Meanwhile, clients will want to explore whether or not their values will be in line with each of the jobs they are considering. Once they better understand themselves, they can begin to understand what their career choice entails with respect to education skills.

Another key to employment success is for the employee to understand the employer's needs. The human service professional must help clients anticipate employer's needs and be better able to meet them. The job market varies with the location, and the human service worker can help the client navigate through the market by knowing what is available and who is hiring through previously developed networks. Local employment agencies and local One-Stop Career Centers can help with this task. Job search classes could be used here.

Job-Search Correspondence.   Many jobs will not require a letter of application, but some will. Clients seeking such jobs will need to learn how to write letters of application, as well as referral letters, reminder letters, and interview appreciation letters. Along with teaching clients how to write a letter accepting or declining an offer, role-playing these situations will help clients better understand the process and give them a chance to practice their interpersonal skills in a safe environment.

Tailor-Made Resumes.   The resume format a client uses will vary with the client and with the job. Clients who possess a great deal of experience will be able to use a chronological format. Other clients who lack job experience or a stable job history will need to use functional resumes that organize their job experiences according to their skills. Creating resumes also helps clients organize and better understand themselves, allowing them to focus more on their strengths instead of their weaknesses. Clients can prepare resumes individually or in a class session, according to the needs of each client and the requirements for each job.

Interviewing Strategies.   Interpersonal skills are sometimes a weakness (again, depending upon the client), so role-playing the various types of interview situations from easy to difficult, and from panel to telephone will help clients improve their skills. Helping clients craft answers to some of the common interview questions will empower them as well. Videotaping clients during mock interviews followed by a critique of the interview provides them with an opportunity to see themselves as others see them. Human service professionals also need to address interview attire. Clients may not be aware that the attire may vary depending upon the job. If clients are moving into a job that differs substantially from jobs they previously held, clients may be unaware of differences in work and/or interview attire. Refer clients to a clothing closet if they lack the appropriate work or interview attire.

Change Behaviors.   Participation in the career development program for the working poor is designed to help clients change behaviors that previously may have kept them from long-term employment and self-sufficiency. Although the specific behavior changes will vary with each person's ISP, all clients moving through this program will have had an opportunity to improve their interpersonal and work-related skills, along with whatever other skills they originally targeted for change. Other behavior changes they may make include upgrading education and obtaining training in a field in which they can work for a living wage.

Complete the Program.   Clients who entered the program, developed their ISPs, completed the training and education that were detailed in their ISPs, and have located new jobs at a living wage are considered to have completed the program. At any time during the process clients can drop out, but they must be made aware that by doing so they put their education and training along with their eligibility for other types of assistance at risk. Some clients may have to cycle through several steps of the program later as they move from low-skill level employment to employment requiring more advanced skills.

Achieve Goal of Long-Term Employment.   The final goal for the client is long-term employment and self-sufficiency. Program staff will need to determine the working definition of *long-term* employment for use in this program. Generally, when clients have moved into stable, high-wage jobs and are no longer receiving public assistance (TANF, housing, Medicaid, food stamps, WIC, SCHIP), for at least a year, and they are able to fully support themselves and their family members, they can be considered self-sufficient with long-term employment.

Program Evaluation

Program staff will first need to determine what type of evaluation to use: process evaluation, outcome evaluation, or impact evaluation. The program evaluation component has several sublevels: developing tools, tracking clients who complete the program, conducting the evaluation, analyzing and reporting findings, and implementing program changes. Human service professionals need to develop a variety of tools to evaluate their program. Figure 9.1 is a flow chart for the career development program model for use with the working poor. The text in each box in the figure is a factor that needs to be measured. Evaluation tools can include such items as a database of client information, intake interview sheets, case files, client tracking forms, and referral forms. Program staff must also determine what tools they need to develop just for evaluation purposes such as paper-and-pencil surveys or telephone surveys for clients and their employers, a method of tracking clients who complete the program and keeping their information current. The staff also needs to determine when and how often to evaluate the program. For example, programs and their participants can be evaluated at several points in the program: midway, upon completion, and then one year after completing the program. While this constant evaluation can be time-consuming, the input is invaluable for the program. In making decisions involving when to evaluate the staff needs to consider the mobility of clients and the ability of the program staff to track them. The staff may survey employers who hire program participants at different times as well, perhaps six weeks and again six months after hiring. The staff also needs to consider how the information will be collected, analyzed, and reported. Once the program staff has made these decisions, they need to create a timeline for the entire program evaluation process that shows every task to be accomplished, the deadline by which it is to be accomplished, and who is responsible for accomplishing the evaluation. Once the evaluation information is collected, the input can be used to strengthen the current program. For complete descriptions of all segments of the evaluation process, refer to Chapter 6.

Revisiting the Case Study: David and Marla

Conduct an Intake Interview

During the intake interview session, the human service professional needs to explore both David and Marla's medical, financial, educational, and employment histories; their interests and values; and their views on employment, education, and family. Exploring all family members' medical histories is very important since erratic income may have impacted purchasing choices. The professional helper should not overlook the stresses of living with unstable income, possibly leading to inadequate nutrition, clothing, and medical attention.

The helper and clients need to consider finances including any debts the clients may have incurred during lean times. Because David's pay is irregular, the family may be behind on several bills. David and Marla will need to meet those obligations, so exploring those debts and working to keep them from being turned over to collection agencies is very important. If these debts have been given to collection agencies, the human service professional needs to explore various methods of repayment, and possibly consider bankruptcy, along with making the necessary referrals. Setting up a budget will help David and Marla better plan to meet all financial obligations. The budget should include David's child-support payments along with any financial assistance he provides for his father.

Does this family have a critical housing need? Since David and Marla currently live in a small apartment, the human service professional may need to determine if their apartment meets local standards or if they need to look for better housing elsewhere.

The human service professional also needs to address transportation issues. While David is currently able to use public transportation, he may find it difficult to reach work on time if bus routes or schedules change. A change in work hours could impact his access to transportation as well. The human service professional should help the family explore repairing the car or finding a replacement vehicle thereby increasing their independence and ability to find higher-paying work. Marla also needs transportation for emergencies and for basic shopping. While she does not need her own car, Marla does need to have some type of contingency plan for emergencies in case her sister or her sister's car is unavailable.

Since both David and Marla finished high school but have no college coursework, the human service professional may want to explore other training possibilities for David as well as for Marla. David has mentioned a desire to work indoors—doing what? What are his interests? What type of activities has he enjoyed in the past? Marla's interests need to be explored as well. Just because she recently has stayed home with the children does not mean that she has no career dreams or aspirations. Does either of them want to stay home with the children? If both choose to work, then childcare becomes necessary. What is the family cost of both parents working? Obviously they need to consider the cost of childcare for three children that may require Marla to either find higher-wage employment or to wait until one or more of the children are in school so that she could work during the day with reduced childcare expenses. Having one parent stay at home may be more feasible for the family than dealing with the emotional and financial costs of childcare. Honoring their values and views of family life is extremely important as the human service professional helps move this family toward self-sufficiency.

Make Assessments

The human service professional needs to help both David and Marla explore their career options as separate clients and to give the assessments individually to maintain confidentiality. Doing so will empower David and Marla to share their knowledge as they make plans. Determining David and Mary's level of comfort with technology is the first step. While Marla may have used a computer in her job at the video store, David's previous jobs most likely have not provided him with much technology experience. The O*NET Ability Profiler (O*NET Consortium, 2003a) would help both David and Marla identify their strengths and the areas in which they might want to receive additional training along with pinpointing occupations to fit those strengths. WorkKeys (ACT, 1993) may also help David better see his current skills and how they might transfer to other jobs. Marla could also complete WorkKeys or the Career Key (Jones & Jones, 2000).

Completing interest inventories could provide career change options for both David and Marla. For instance, David could complete the GOEII (Farr, 2002) to identify which of 14 interest areas has the most appeal for him. Marla could complete the Leisure to Occupations Connection Search (McDaniels & Mullins, 1999) or the Transition to Work Inventory (Liptak, 2004). Since she does not have as much work experience as David, the Leisure to Occupations Connection Search will help her explore her levels of activity and skills in a variety of leisure activities. If David and Marla are comfortable with computers, they could also complete the O*NET Career Interests Inventory (JIST Works, 2002a) to identify work-related interests, what they consider important on the job, and their abilities. They could also use the Self-Directed Search (Holland, 1990, 1994, 1996a, 1996b). If neither David nor Marla want to pursue additional education, they could complete the Voc-Tech Quick Screener (JIST Works, 2002c) to help them match their interests and goals with jobs for which they can train in a short period of time. The human service professional needs to be careful, however, not to perpetuate the low-wage work that David has been doing, but to help him secure higher-level skills that will result in higher-paying, stable employment.

Exploring the couples' values is another component in career assessment. Finding careers that support their values makes for a better fit between worker and job. Workers' experience increased job satisfaction when their values are similar to the values of the job. They could use the Career Values Card Sort (Knowdell, 1998a) to quickly help them prioritize their values with regards to the areas of time freedom, job tranquility, creative expression, work under pressure, power, and technical competence. The O*NET Career Values Inventory (JIST Works, 2002b) could also help them identify work groups that include their values while pinpointing specific jobs they can explore later. Depending upon their computer skills, David and Marla may want to use the O*NET Work Importance Locator and Profiler (O*NET Consortium, n.d.b) or the Values-Driven Work Card Sort (Career Action Center, n.d.) to help them clarify values and identify possible occupations.

Career-development inventories will help the clients identify what aspects of their personal growth could hinder them in obtaining and keeping a job. This assessment component is particularly important for David who is trying to move from a low-wage job to a higher-wage job that requires a different skill set. Available in both a pencil-and-paper format and online, the Barriers to Employment Success Inventory (Liptak, 2002a) will help David and Marla identify personal, physical and psychological, career planning, job-seeking skills, along with education and training barriers that might hinder their employment. This inventory will also help them develop action plans to overcome those barriers. The Career Attitudes and Strategies Inventory (Holland & Gottfredson, 1994) will help them assess the likelihood of job stability while clarifying situations that could lead to future career problems. Other career-development inventories appropriate for David and Marla to use include the Career Beliefs Inventory (Krumboltz, 1991), the Career Decision Scale (Osipow et al., 1987), the Career Thoughts Inventory (Sampson et al., 1996), the Career Transition Inventory (Heppner, 1991), the Salient Beliefs Review (Bloch, 2003), or the Vocational Exploration and Insight Kit (Holland et. al., 1980). The human service professional does not need to administer all of these inventories but needs to select inventories based on the presenting client's needs.

Determine Barriers to Success

Based on intake discussion and assessment results, David and Marla are faced with several possible barriers to career success: transportation, education and training, and childcare. While transportation will help David maintain employment, upgrading his skills and education are the first step to a higher-wage job. Childcare becomes a barrier if Marla chooses to return to work.

Choose Interventions

Using Group or One-to-One Interventions.   The human service professional determines interventions based on David and Marla's ISPs. They may include social skills, family counseling, and a variety of referrals for other assistance. The human service professional will address both David's barriers to employment success and Marla's should she decide to return to work. If Marla chooses to remain at home caring for their children, she may find that support groups with other stay-at-home moms are useful and that forming some sort of play group can give her a needed break and foster social skills in the children. Helping David and Marla find affordable transportation and develop a budget are other interventions. The human service professional could find them financial counseling for their debts and refer them for any programs for which the family may qualify: Family Self- Sufficiency, Section 8 housing, food stamps, WIC, Medicaid, and SCHIP.

Finding Training and Education.   Both David and Marla have work experience. David has worked in several laborer positions over the past few years. After they determine what is best for their family—should both parents go to work full time, should one work and one stay at home, and what is the most effective in a cost-benefit analysis—David and Marla need to explore possible jobs and available training that fit with their career aspirations and their needs. Finding funding for them is extremely important because they have little money for education and training at this point. The human service professional can refer them to the local One-Stop Career Center and to the local community college, depending on their training needs. Although David has worked steadily, he has worked in laborer-type positions and now wants to change careers. Helping him look for a higher-wage, stable position would be a quicker way to employment than retraining, but this decision needs to be based on local job availability and whether the high-wage jobs match his skills. Marla's work history, while only part-time at a video store, provides her with some retail and interpersonal skills and possibly some computer skills that may be useful in a variety of workplace settings. Exploring how interested Marla is in working, however, is very important and needs to be a family decision made after creating a budget and examining all of the possibilities.

Using Mentoring.   David and Marla may need only limited amounts of mentoring because they have been somewhat self-sufficient in the past. Once they have established a budget, completed their education and training, secured reliable transportation, located health coverage, and found stable employment, they may only need minor assistance in adjusting to their new lives. They may require mentoring services for purchasing and/or repairing a car and adjusting to new careers. They may also need mentoring while they balance their training and education for any new job with family life and current employment.

Initiate the Employment Campaign

Once David and Marla have decided who will work and have completed the required training and education, they will need to initiate their employment campaign. While eliminating all of their barriers to employment success before beginning the campaign is the best approach, it may not be possible. Instead, the human service professional may need to provide case management as David and Marla locate transportation and complete education and training to decrease their barriers. Helping them develop their job-search network, their resumes, and their correspondence is part of this component. While they have worked in the past, both David and Marla have to address several gaps on their resumes. David may need to use a functional resume because he is changing careers and the skills he previously developed may prove beneficial to a new job. If Marla chooses to return to work, then she could either use a chronological or a functional resume depending upon whether she continues in retail or changes jobs. The concern here is to help them find employment to meet the needs of a five-member family.

Conclusion

Human service professionals are frequently tasked with assisting low-wage earning clients in finding stable, high-wage employment and dealing with their clients' additional barriers to employment in order to help them reach their full potential. Following are some recommended policy changes that would assist low-wage earners in their transition to self-sufficiency. Economic, community, and workforce changes would include:

- Revise the office measure of poverty to reflect the complex nature of poverty
- Raise minimum wage to a living wage
- Enact policies to create more jobs at a living wage and increase household incomes
- Raise unemployment benefits to allow job seekers to wait for high-wage jobs
- Provide tax credits to employers who hire disadvantaged job seekers
- Provide subsidies for inner-city business development accompanied by enhancements to public services
- Expand programs to help small- and medium-sized manufacturers modernize to help the United States hold on to the high-wage end of manufacturing
- Develop workforce development policies to address poor information in the low-wage labor market and a lack of adequate work readiness of many inner-city residents
- Complete more research on the effect of welfare reform on the availability of low skills jobs
- Build a strong macro economy at both the state and federal levels
- Return jobs to America that have been outsourced to other countries
- Support childcare and parental leave policies, keeping in mind the shift toward 24-hour cities
- Rebuild troubled communities by building affordable housing and increasing housing subsidies
- Increase affordability of houses by (1) lowering interest rates, (2) requiring a lower down payment for home purchasers, and (3) providing a down payment subsidy to home buyers
- Improve opportunities for home ownership among minority populations
- Provide small, low-interest loans for car purchase or repairs

Changes to medical/mental health policies would include:

- Provide comprehensive and integrated treatment approaches from health care, mental health and substance-abuse agencies
- Fund primary health care grants to provide comprehensive health care with a focus on the continuity of preventive care

Organizational policy changes would include:

- Increase benefit levels and participation in food stamps, EITC, TANF, WIC, Medicaid, SCHIP, and FSS programs
- Increase basic support services
- Educate low-wage earners on the availability of EITC, TANF, food stamps, Medicaid, WIC, and SCHIP

- Involve low-wage earners in local Family Self-Sufficiency programs
- Screen candidates better by employment agencies before sending them to a job interview
- Match work-ready candidates to positions

Changes to education policies would include:

- Increase access to education for children of working poor to stem adult problems
- Improve accessible and affordable training for the lower-skilled workers
- Reexamine high school and college curricula to make sure institutions are training workers to meet the jobs of the future.

Summary

Low-wage workers or the working poor struggle to make ends meet, often despite being employed full time. Those who may not meet the federal definition of 200 percent of the federal poverty threshold are still often close enough that a major illness, car repair, or job layoff can push them into poverty. In 2001, 32.9 million people or 11.7 percent of the population lived at or below the federal poverty level, an increase of 1.3 million people since 2000. Low-wage earners (those making 200 percent or less than the federal poverty threshold) are three times more likely to have problems paying rent, mortgage, or utility bills. Fifty-two percent of low-wage earners live in housing that costs more than one-third of their income. The working poor is comprised of military, civilian, and immigrant families. Military families are more likely to have two biological parents and more education. Housing for low-wage earners is frequently substandard, and they frequently spend anywhere from 25 percent to 52 percent of their incomes on food. The career development model to use with the working poor has an Individual Success Plan that includes career-related assessments of abilities, interests, barriers, and values; interagency referrals; interventions such as one-to-one interventions, training and education, and mentoring; followed by an employment campaign leading to long-term employment and self sufficiency.

Key Terms

Critical housing needs
Earned income tax credit (EITC)
Employer-sponsored medical insurance
Family Self-Sufficiency (FSS)
Federal poverty threshold
Higher income

Income deficit
Low-wage income
Nearly poor
Severely poor
State Children's Health Insurance Program (SCHIP)

Web Resources

Note that website URLs may change over time.

Federal Poverty Guidelines
http://aspe.os.dhhs.gov/poverty

America's Second Harvest
http://www.secondharvest.org

Economic Policy Institute
http://www.epinet.org

Fair Labor Standards Act
http://www.dol.gov/esa/whd/flsa

How the Census Bureau Measures poverty
http://www.census.gov/hhes/poverty/povdef.html

National Jobs for All Coalition
http://www.njfac.org/index.html

State Children's Health Insurance Program
http://www.cms.hhs.gov/schip

Survey of Income and Program Participation (SIPP)
http://www.sipp.census.gov/sipp/sipphome.htm

10

Victims of Intimate Partner Violence

Working Towards a New Life

Case Study: Georgia and Robert

Georgia, a stay-at-home mom with a 10-year-old daughter, has been married to Robert for 11 years. She was within a year of completing courses toward a business degree at a local community college when her husband was severely injured in a car accident on his way to work. During the first month after Robert's accident, Georgia had the following schedule: put their daughter on the school bus every morning, then attended a morning class, went to the hospital to be with Robert, then home to meet her daughter at the bus, then to her evening class, leaving her daughter with a neighbor. On weekends, Georgia and her daughter spent the day with Robert in the hospital. This pattern continued until Georgia brought Robert home from the hospital when physical therapy was added to the already tight schedule.

Even with the hectic scheduling required, Georgia still managed to work toward her education, one class at a time. Meanwhile, Robert's recovery was not going as well as expected, leaving him in a wheelchair. Despite this turn of events, Georgia wanted to finish her coursework, graduate, and then transfer to a local college to complete her bachelor's degree. Robert, however, was not yet able to return to work, and the family needed a paycheck, so Georgia dropped out of the community college and started looking for work to pay the bills. While she has "book" knowledge from her community college classes, she has very little job experience other than babysitting and working as a fast-food cashier while she was in high school.

Before Robert left the hospital, the hospital social worker helped Georgia apply for TANF funds for herself and her daughter as well as SSI for Robert, but the three of them were having a difficult time adjusting to their change in income. Before his accident Robert was making $45,000 a year. The family now lives on approximately

$800/month with $500 in food stamps. The landlord, however, volunteered to decrease the rent until the family could "get on their feet again," even built a ramp for Robert's wheelchair, and has been lowering cabinets and countertops to make it easier for Robert to adjust to his new life. Since the landlord reduced the rent, the local housing agency was able to cover it through Section 8 assistance, taking away one of their bills.

Since Georgia just started receiving TANF benefits, she has two years in which to complete workforce training and find a job. After talking with her caseworker, Georgia decided to drop her community college classes and enter a respiratory therapy program through the local hospital with the hope that it will lead to gainful employment after graduation.

Now that Robert is home and has completed some life-skills training as part of his therapy he agreed reluctantly to take care of their daughter after school and in the evenings while Georgia attended classes. During the day while their daughter is in school, however, Robert's friends have come over, bringing videotapes, food, and beer. One day the daughter came home to find Dad passed out in his wheelchair. She called Georgia at the hospital where she was in class. Robert had revived by the time Georgia came home and brushed the whole incident off as an accident. This pattern continued, and one evening when Georgia came home late from class, Robert was waiting for her in the front yard. Swinging a baseball bat from his wheelchair, he smashed her car's headlights and windshield. Although a neighbor called the police, when the police arrived they decided that Robert could not have done this damage because of his disability.

Robert apologized and swore that this would never happen again. He promised to try harder and explained how much he loved Georgia. All went well for a few weeks until Georgia had to study for an exam. Robert came into the room where she was studying, ripped her notes and books from her hands, and screamed at her. He accused her of not wanting to spend time with him. When she explained that she loved him but she had to study for this exam so she can do well, complete the program, and eventually get a job to support them, Robert grabbed her around the neck and started choking her. He only stopped when their daughter ran into the room, begging him to stop. Again, he apologized and promised this will never happen again.

The Victims of Intimate Partner Violence Population

A person is physically abused every six seconds in the United States by a spouse, common-law spouse, boyfriend/girlfriend, or ex-spouse. Between 1996 and 2001 75 percent of the victims of violent family crimes were female, and 83 percent were between the ages of 18 and 65 (Federal Bureau of Investigation, 2003). According to results from the National Violence Against Women Survey (NVAWS), nearly 7.8 million women reported having been **raped** by an intimate partner at some time in their lives, with some respondents reporting multiple, intimate-partner rapes during the preceding year. Over 22 percent of respondents reported having been physically assaulted by an intimate partner at some time in their lives. Women who were physically assaulted during the past year reported an average of 3.4 separate assaults, a rate of 44.2 assaults for every 1000 women. Over 4 percent of women reported having been stalked. Over 36 percent of the women who reported having been raped by an intimate partner also sustained additional physical injuries, and 44.5 percent of women who had been physically assaulted were injured as well. Their injuries ranged from scratches, bruises, and welts to broken bones, lacerations, chipped or broken teeth, head or spinal cord injuries, or internal injuries (Tjaden & Thoennes, 2000b).

Women are not the only victims of **intimate partner violence (IPV).** Estimates indicate that more than 371,000 men are stalked by an intimate partner, and 834,000 men are raped and or physically assaulted by an intimate partner each year (Tjaden & Thoennes, 2000b). Male victims average 2.5 assaults per year by an intimate partner (Tjaden & Thoennes, 1998). As with women, much of the violence perpetrated against men was chronic in nature, with male victims of intimate physical assault reporting 4.4 assaults by the same partner (Tjaden & Thoennes, 2000b). Because male victims are less likely to call the police, however, these numbers may well be inaccurate (Kelly, 2003).

Effects of Economic Distress

A study by the U.S. Department of Justice found that violence against women occurred more often and was more severe in economically disadvantaged neighborhoods. Women in these neighborhoods were twice as likely to be victims of intimate partner violence than were women in more affluent neighborhoods. Those women in economic stress and struggling with financial issues in their own relationships were at even greater risk of IPV (Benson & Fox, 2004). Almost 50 percent of the women receiving TANF funds cited **domestic violence** as a factor in their need for financial assistance (National Network to End Domestic Violence, 2004). Abusive partners are likely to have experienced unemployment, whether they live in an urban or a rural community (Bowlus & Seitz, 2002; Krishnan, Hilbert, & VanLeeuwen, 2001). One study found that women whose male partners experienced two or more periods of joblessness in five years were three times more likely to be in violent relationships than were women whose partners had stable jobs. Couples who reported financial strain were also three times as likely to have a violent relationship than were couples under low levels of financial strain (Benson & Fox, 2004).

Cycle of Violence

Violent events often follow a predictable pattern, cycling through three stages with violence often increasing with each cycle (Walker & Lurie, 1994).

1. *Tension-Building.* During the first stage, the victim is compliant as the batterer experiences increased tension. As minor conflicts arise, the victim minimizes them and denies anger. The batterer starts to take more and more control as the victim begins to withdraw.

2. *Battering.* In the second stage, violence erupts as the batterer becomes unpredictable and throws objects at the victim, hits, slaps, kicks, chokes, abuses the victim sexually, or uses weapons. Often no one witnesses the abuse, and once the attacks begin, the victim can do little to stop them. The victim feels helpless and trapped. The batterer is highly abusive and the victim is traumatized.

3. *Honeymoon.* In the third stage the batterer feels repentant, apologizes and promises that he or she will "change" and will never abuse the victim again. The victim feels confused, guilty, and responsible for the abuse. The batterer continues to manipulate the victim, possibly bringing gifts to persuade the victim to forgive the batterer and consider reconciliation. The batterer may even enter treatment in an attempt to prove that he/she will change.

Learned Helplessness

Walker (1984) proposed that repeated battering diminishes the victim's capability to leave the battering relationship. Repeated abuse results in victims becoming passive and feeling that they can do nothing to stop the abuse. Whether or not victims have control over the battering, as long as victims *perceive* they have no control, then learned helplessness results because the victims no longer see their options. The cyclical nature of abuse exacerbates the learned helplessness, and many victims do not believe they are in violent relationships (Brown, 2004). Victims who remain in violent relationships are more likely to show signs of learned helplessness than those who leave a violent relationship or who have never been in one (Walker, 1984).

Economics of Intimate Partner Violence

The costs of IPV on women are estimated to exceed $5.8 billion, including $4.1 billion in the direct costs of mental and physical health care (Centers for Disease Control and Prevention, 2004). Victims of IPV use the emergency room more often, see doctors more often, and use prescriptions more often than nonvictims. On average, a domestic violence victim acquires $1,775 more in medical costs than does a nonvictim (Partnership for Prevention, 2002).

Intimate partner violence also impacts workplace economics. Employers reported losing between $3 and $5 billion every year in lower productivity, absenteeism, higher turnover, and health/safety costs associated with battered workers. In addition, businesses lose $100 million in lost wages, absenteeism, and sick leave along with 1.7 million lost workdays each year due to domestic violence (American Institute on Domestic Violence, 2001). Ninety-one percent of corporate leaders believe that domestic violence impacts both the private lives and the working lives of their employees. Sixty-six percent of corporate leaders identified domestic violence as a major social issue, and 68 percent put it on par with terrorism as a major issue affecting modern society (Liz Claiborne, Inc., 2002).

Birth Control, Pregnancy, and Reproductive Health Issues

Intimate partner violence is linked to teen pregnancy as well as birth control sabotage. Women who have been sexually abused are more likely than nonabused women to report that their partners had stopped them from using contraception or had refused to use a condom to prevent disease (Groves, Augustyn, Lee, & Sawires, 2004; McKean, 2004b; Shane & Ellsberg, 2002). One Chicago study of low-income adolescent mothers found that 66 percent of the abused mothers had experienced birth control sabotage, compared to 34 percent of nonabused women (Center for Impact Research, 2002). IPV is also linked to sexually transmitted disease (STD) and HIV transmission, miscarriages, and risky sexual health behaviors (Moore, 1999). Women who experience IPV are more than three times as likely to have gynecological problems than are nonabused women. Such problems can include chronic pelvic pain, vaginal infection, vaginal bleeding, sexual dysfunction, painful menstruation, pelvic inflammatory disease, urinary tract infections, and infertility (Shane & Ellsberg, 2002). Complications of pregnancy (low-weight gain, first and second trimester bleeding, infections, and anemia) are also higher for abused women (McFarlane, Parker, & Soeken, 1996).

Barriers to Career Success

Structural Barriers

Societal Beliefs.   Societal beliefs that foster role and gender stereotypes can be barriers to employment for members of the IPV population as well as to the gay men and lesbian population. We present some of the issues of role and gender stereotyping, homophobia, and cross-cultural insensitivity in the following sections.

Role and Gender Stereotyping.   Individuals with gender-stereotyping attitudes are more likely to blame the victim and less likely to see the seriousness of IPV incidents (Berkel, Vandiver, & Bahner, 2004; Willis, Hallinan, & Melby, 1996). One study of physicians showed that 30 percent of the physicians held victim-blaming attitudes towards victims of spousal abuse (Garimella, Plichta, Houseman, & Garzon, 2000). People who exhibit gender-stereotyping attitudes are also more likely to endorse rape myths (Burt, 1980). Batterers often blame their victims for the batter's own abusive behaviors and their personal problems. Victims are conditioned to accept such battering behaviors through gender stereotypes and accepted cultural norms (Native American Circle, 2001). One of the commonalities amongst battered women is the belief in the traditional female role stereotypes (Walker, 1984). Gender stereotypes also impact male victims of IPV. Masculine society norms state that a man should not be (or appear to be) vulnerable; therefore, a male should be able to defend himself against another male. If a man seeks help from an outside source, then the man is often viewed as weak and vulnerable. Similarly, society decrees that women should not exhibit violence toward a man or a woman. These same norms state that women are to be nurturing and docile. According to society's expectations, therefore, women can be abused by men but not by other women (Potoczniak, Mourot, Crosbie-Burnett, & Potoczniak, 2003). Human service professionals who lack a clear understanding of IPV and who accept society's gender stereotypes and cultural norms may well find themselves blaming the victim for ongoing abuse or for not leaving a violent relationship. They may also be unable to recognize abuse in nonheterosexual couples (Logan, Walker, Cole, & Leukefeld, 2002).

Homophobia.   Many individuals view domestic violence as including only male abusers/female victims. However, heterosexual females are not the only population to experience IPV. Research shows the IPV occurs at equal rates in lesbian, gay, bisexual, transgendered, adolescent, and adult populations (Rennison, 2001). Rates of violence are higher in male than in female same-sex relationships (Greenwood et al., 2002; Groves et al., 2004). Twelve National Coalition of Anti-Violence Program member organizations reported a 13 percent increase in the number of domestic violence incidents reported since 2002 (NCAVP, 2004). Homophobia negates the reality of lesbian and gay men's lives, including the existence of gay male and lesbian relationships, and, in particular, domestic violence. Fear of facing homophobic responses may be keeping gay, lesbian, bisexual, and transgendered individuals from reporting domestic violence or seeking assistance (Parry & Wright, 2001).

Cross-Cultural Insensitivity.   Intimate partner violence affects people from all demographic groups, despite gender, culture, race, socioeconomic status, sexual and gender identity, immigration status, religious affiliation, age, and ability (Groves et al., 2004). Because abuse is a sensitive and private issue, providing culturally relevant care for victims of IPV is critical. Victims of IPV deal with multiple issues simultaneously including limited resources, homophobia, language barriers, acculturation, racism, and accessibility issues. Human service professionals need to acknowledge that every victim of IPV will experience the abuse in culturally different ways. Human service professionals also need to be aware of their own cultural perspectives and how they may differ from those of their abuse-victim clients as they strive to communicate effectively and in a culturally sensitive way.

Access to Quality Health Care.   Increasing health care costs affect access to services, but particularly for individuals who lack financial resources. Even insured patients are now paying more out-of-pocket money for health care, and as costs continue to rise, some health care purchasers will be forced to drop their coverage, increasing the number of uninsured (Family Violence Prevention Fund, 2002). Delivering quality health care to victims of IPV becomes more and more difficult as costs increase, yet these patients often have a high need of medical attention. Even victims who have the financial resources for health care may be unable to access health care due to their abuse.

Lack of Resources to Assist Victims.   Although most shelters offering shelter to victims of IPV have services for married women with children, other victims of IPV who need similar services are often excluded. These victims include older women, lesbians, teens, and males. We discuss the needs of these other groups in the next section.

Older Victims of IPV.   Older women are frequently underrepresented in the shelters for abuse victims and are unfamiliar with these services that have only been offered within the past 25 years. Older women often view shelters and services as available only for younger, married women, instead of older, single or separated women (Intimate Partner Abuse and Relationship Violence Working Group, n.d.).

Lesbian and Transgendered Victims of IPV.   Few services exist for lesbian women who are victims of IPV. Since standard shelters are primarily sensitive to male threats to their residents, a lesbian may not feel safe since her female abuser may also have access to the shelter. Another shelter-based concern for lesbian victims of IPV is that services are generally geared toward heterosexual relationships, and they may not meet the specialized needs of lesbians (Intimate Partner Abuse and Relationship Violence Working Group, n.d.). Very few shelters provide transgendered male-to-female battered-victim services since the shelters often view such individuals as men (Intimate Partner Abuse and Relationship Violence Working Group, n.d.).

Teen Victims of IPV.   Teen victims of IPV find alternative housing to be very difficult to secure, because many domestic-violence shelters are not licensed to take in adolescents and are unable to house them unless the teens are emancipated. Some states require parental consent before a minor can stay in a domestic-violence shelter (Marcy & Martinez, 2000). Another structural barrier for teen victims concerns their exclusion from the Family Violence Option (FVO). Teen mothers who are unable to live at home due to IPV may be required to meet all TANF requirements without access to the waivers that provide services for adult victims of IPV (Kurz, 1998).

Male Victims of IPV.   Male victims are at an even greater disadvantage because few domestic violence shelters accept single males or even males with children, and other types of shelters may not offer the necessary transitional programs for domestic-violence victims (Potoczniak, Mourot, Crosbie-Burnett, & Potooczniak, 2003). The lack of support for male, domestic-violence services is not due to a lack of need but to an unwillingness to accept that women could batter men (Kelly, 2003).

Ethnic Minority Victims of IPV.   Ethnic minority victims face a variety of issues affecting their services. Ethnic minority women often find shelters staffed by white women who do not speak the victim's language. Fear of deportation, unfamiliar food, lack of transportation, and separation from one's culture impact their ability to receive and use shelter services (Intimate Partner Abuse and Relationship Violence Working Group, n.d.)

Shelters and Safe Housing.   Forty-four percent of cities surveyed cited domestic violence as a primary cause of homelessness (U.S. Conference of Mayors, 2003).

Victims who leave their abusers need some form of alternative housing, yet domestic-violence shelters are often full. The average stay at a shelter is normally 30 days, but families often need six to ten months to secure affordable housing (National Network to End Domestic Violence, 2004). Purchasing or renting affordable housing is not always a solution either. In 1995, only 56 percent of families could afford to purchase a moderately priced house in their community, meaning they could either afford to purchase a house with cash, or they qualified for a 30-year conventional mortgage with a 5 percent down payment (Savage, 1999). Victims of IPV often lack the financial resources to purchase housing and in many cases would not qualify for financial assistance to help them secure housing. Victims who move into shelters or live with friends have an added barrier as they now lack a permanent address and telephone number that are critical contact information for job applications. Employers sometimes view job candidates without a permanent address as risky and unstable, poor candidates for a position.

Law and Enforcement.   As of 2000, states had gender-neutral statutes that permit local jurisdictions to decide how each statute is to be enforced on a case-by-case basis (Potoczniak et al., 2003). As of 2000, however, several states still excluded lesbian, gay, bisexual, and transgender individuals in their domestic-violence legislation (Jablow, 2000).

Individual Barriers

Lost Productivity.   Victims of IPV often lose time from everyday activities such as household chores and employment. Thirty-five percent of adult female victims who were stalked, 21 percent who were raped, and 17 percent who were physically assaulted reported losing time from paid employment. Women who have been raped by an intimate partner lost an average of 8.1 days from paid employment and 13.5 days from household chores. Those who were victims of physical assault by an intimate partner lost on average 7.2 days from employment and 8.4 days from household chores. Women who had been stalked by an intimate partner lost on average 10.1 days from employment and 12.7 days from household chores (Tjaden & Thoennes, 2000b).

Perception of Victims as Problem Employees.   Intimate partner violence also takes place at work, not just in the home. Harassing telephone calls, a stalker in the business's parking lot, or an angry partner or spouse who attacks the employee in the office impacts the entire organization. Estimates show that IPV costs businesses $5 billion each year (Johnson & Indvik, 1999). Many of the so-called "problem employees" who have difficulty arriving to work on time, are frequently absent from work, or who may have trouble focusing on their tasks, may well be victims of intimate partner violence. Batterers may be sabotaging their victims' work by turning off their alarm clocks to make them late for work; not delivering work-related messages; inflicting black eyes, bruises, or cigarette burns to embarrass the victims into staying home; destroying items that victims need for work or training; keeping the victims up all night; neglecting to get the car repaired; feigning illness to keep the partner at home; stealing the victim's car keys; harassing the victim at work (telephone calls, e-mails, visits); or refusing to baby-sit at the last minute (Burt, Zweig, & Schlichter, 2000; U.S. General Accounting Office, 1998; Johnson & Indvik, 1999; McKean, 2004b). Victims of IPV miss time from work due to injuries, depression, embarrassment, or appointments with lawyers and doctors. Many women have lost at least one job as a direct result of the violence (Friedman, Tucker, Neville, & Imperial, 1996). Also women victims of abuse have experienced more unemployment spells and greater job turnover than non-victims of IPV (U.S. General Accounting Office, 1998; Lloyd & Taluc, 1999; McKean, 2004a).

Lack of Marketable Job Skills and Work Experience.   Victims of IPV who live in impoverished neighborhoods or in very rural areas may lack the marketable skills necessary to find and keep a job (Cole, 2001; Goldberg, 2002; NAC, 2001; Sable, Libbus, Huneke, & Anger, 1999). In some cases, the batterers do not allow the victims to work, limiting their ability to be self-supporting (Kurz, 1998; Sable et al., 1999). One study stated that one-third of the victims surveyed reported that their batterers would not allow them to work (Shepard & Pence, 1988).

Isolation and Lack of Support Networks.   Victims who have lived in poverty for a length of time will likely have a support network that is also impoverished and shares the same barriers to employment success (Cole, 2001). Many victims of IPV, however, have been deftly isolated from any physical and social support networks and have no job contacts or network through which to obtain assistance (Intimate Partner Abuse and Relationship Violence Working Group, n.d.; Kurz, 1998; Logan, Walker, Cole & Leukefeld, 2002). Familiar, informal support from family and friends may not be available for victims in rural settings, requiring that victims develop more formal networks to succeed (Krishnan et al., 2001). Gay, lesbian, bisexual, and transgendered victims of IPV find themselves even more isolated than the standard IPV victim due to their sexual orientation (Parry & Wright, 2001).

Affordable and Dependable Childcare.   As with several other populations, childcare may be a barrier to employment success for victims of IPV. Finding safe and secure daycare is very important for these clients who may be concerned about their partners taking the children without permission or waiting for them at the daycare. Victims of IPV need to explore their legal options to determine the law regarding their partners' access to the children.

Physical and Mental Health Barriers

Injuries.   More than 1.8 million of the nearly 4.5 million physical assaults cause injuries, over half a million of which necessitate medical care (Tjaden & Thoennes, 2000a). Women who are unemployed or employed part time and who were injured during the previous year are at increased risk of injury from intimate partner violence.

Victims who leave the abuser after a previous injury are also at an increased risk of future injury. Perpetrators with a history of drug or substance abuse are more likely to reinjure the victim in the future (Crandall, Nathens, Kernic, Holt, & Rivara, 2004; Hilton et al., 2004). Women who are raped or physically assaulted by current or former partners are more likely to be injured in a future assault (Tjaden & Thoennes, 2000a). Securing a protective order, however, decreases the chance of future injury (Crandall et al., 2004).

Thirty-one percent of the adult women who were injured during their most recent intimate-partner rape received some type of medical care (ambulance/paramedic services, physical therapy, or treatment in a hospital emergency room). Twenty-eight percent of adult, female victims of physical assault who were injured also received some form of medical treatment. More than three-quarters of physical-assault and rape victims received medical attention in a hospital setting. Almost 44 percent of the rape victims and 33 percent of the physical-assault victims were admitted, spending one or more nights in the hospital (Tjaden & Thoennes, 2000b).

Physical Health.   Coker, Smith, Bethea, King, and McKeown, (2000) have linked psychological IPV with a variety of physical health outcomes. These adverse physical outcomes include a disability preventing the victim from working, migraines, chronic pain, arthritis, stammering, chronic pelvic pain, stomach ulcers, spastic colon, and frequent indigestion, constipation, and diarrhea. Management of other chronic conditions such as asthma, diabetes, or hypertension is often made more difficult due to IVP (Groves et al., 2004).

Disabilities.   Survivors of IPV may experience many forms of physical and **emotional abuse** that cause disabilities. A single act of violence can cause long-lasting trauma to the victim or observer; repeated acts of IPV can cause significant psychological distress resulting in post-traumatic stress disorder, depression, mood disorders, and dissociative anxiety, as well as physical injuries that may qualify as disabilities under the Americans with Disabilities Act. Once victims qualify as having a disability, the workplace will need to provide reasonable accommodations to help them perform their jobs. Such accommodations can include a more private workplace to avoid distractions, flexible schedules due to physical or mental health needs, time away from work for therapy, unpaid leave of absence to recover from abuse, job restructuring, job coaching, or job transfers (Job Protections and Accommodations for Disabilities Caused by Domestic Violence, 2001).

Mental Health.   Intimate partner violence is also connected to a variety of mental health concerns. Low self-esteem manifests in the workplace as well as in the home and often leads to low-productivity and low morale (Centers for Disease Control and Prevention, 2004; McKean, 2004b; Moe & Bell, 2004). Repeated belittling, constant criticisms, humiliation, and "put-downs" by the abuser constantly erode a victim's self-esteem, eventually causing the victim to believe the abuser. Research identified low self-esteem in the victim as a precursor to repeated violence (Logan et al., 2002). Feelings of low self-esteem may lead victims to substance abuse to help them cope with the negative feelings about themselves (Lawrence, Chau, & Lennon, 2004; Miller & Downs, 1993). Victims of IPV also deal with depression, anxiety, anger, and hypervigilance related to post-traumatic stress disorder (Groves et al., 2004; Hattendorf & Tollerud, 1997; Intimate Partner Abuse and Relationship Violence Working Group, n.d.). The ongoing violence of living under psychological abuse leads to a high incidence of suicide and suicide attempts (UNICEF, 2000). Psychological abuse also contributes to eating disorders (Family Violence Prevention Fund, 2002; Groves et al., 2004; Intimate Partner Abuse and Relationship Violence Working Group, n.d.).

Career Development Program Model: Victims of Intimate Partner Violence

Designing a career development program for use with victims of intimate partner violence calls for an extremely individualized approach. Victims of battering bring a variety of needs and barriers, each of which must be addressed with the ultimate goals being both long-term safety and employment of the client. Our program has three major components: the applicant pool, the Individual Success Plan (ISP), and the program evaluation. Each component will be explained in additional detail. Figure 10.1 is a graphic model of the program.

Applicant Pool

The applicant pool includes any client who is suspected of being or who reported being a victim of violence perpetrated by a spouse, ex-spouse, current or former boyfriend or girlfriend. In some cases, the human service professional may suspect a client is a victim although the client has not self-identified. The professional needs to be careful, however, not to *assume* that clients who fit certain stereotypes are victims of IPV. This needs to be balanced with the need to not overlook symptoms of possible IPV. The human service professional will then determine which clients fit the criteria for program participation and which do not, being careful to consider client safety as the overriding concern.

Individual Success Plan

Make Assessments. The first step in working with a victim or suspected victim of IPV is to assess the client's level of safety and his or her needs with regards to abuse. The following four-step general guide will help entry-level human service professionals assess the initial level of client risk once IPV is suspected or reported.

(*NOTE*: In no way is this information to substitute for professional training in IPV. This information is provided only as a general guide. The authors strongly urge all human service professionals to obtain training in this area before working intensively with victims of IPV).

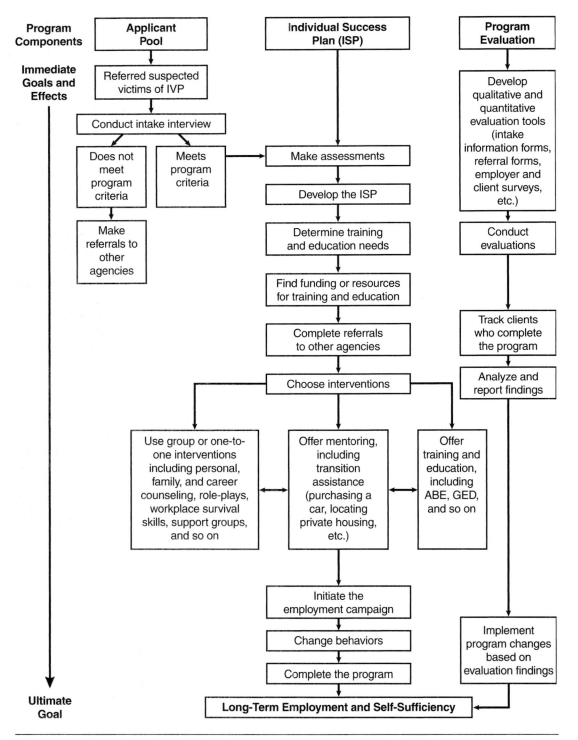

FIGURE 10.1   *Career Development Program Model: Victims of Intimate Partner Violence*

1. *Assess the Immediate Safety Needs.* Explore the immediacy of danger to the client. Find out where the abuser is currently and where the abuser will be when the client leaves your agency. Determine whether or not the client has a safe, alternative form of housing.

2. *Assess the Pattern of Abuse and Its History.* Explore the tactics used by the abuser, along with the type of abuse—**cyberstalking** and **stalking, economic or financial abuse, emotional or psychological abuse, physical abuse, sexual abuse, spiritual abuse, and verbal abuse,** and so on). Questions to ask the client include the following: How long has this been happening? Has your partner harmed you or forced you sexually? Has your partner threatened you? Has your partner harmed others or threatened to harm others? Has your partner harmed himself/herself or threatened to do so? Has your partner ever threatened you with a weapon or threatened to use one? If so, what type of weapon? How often has this happened? Do you currently have or have you taken out a restraining order on your partner? Has your partner ever violated a **temporary restraining order** or **emergency injunction**? Does your partner control your finances, children, access to family and friends, or transportation? Does your partner ever appear at your place of employment or call you at work? Have you ever lost a job due to the activities of your partner? Has your partner's treatment of you changed over time? If so, how? The client's responses will help you to ascertain the possibility of future violence. Threats indicate future intentions and need to be considered significant in determining the pattern and history of abuse. Repeated restraining orders may indicate a violent disposition.

3. *Assess the Connection Between the IPV and Client Health.* Explore the impact of the abuse on the client's psychological, physical, emotional, and economic well-being and determine the abuser's amount of control over the client. Questions to ask the client include the following: Have your injuries ever required you to go to an emergency room or clinic or see a doctor for treatment? How would you describe your eating patterns? How would you describe your sleeping patterns? How would you describe your physical health? What changes, if any, have you noticed in your physical health? What changes, if any, have you noticed in your moods? How have your mental and physical health impacted your employment? What medications are you currently taking? Do you ever miss a dose of medication due to the abuse? If so, how often does this happen? The client's responses will help you determine what effect the abuse is having on the client's current physical and mental health, along with employment, useful for later referrals.

4. *Assess the Client's Access to Support Resources.* The client may be unaware of local support services or resources. If so, the human service professional needs to provide appropriate referral information. Questions to ask the client include the following: Have you tried to access community resources (shelter, etc.) in the past? If so, what happened? What resources are you familiar with? Are family or friends aware of your situation? If not, would you feel comfortable talking with them about it? While some clients may have a support network in place, others may not. Exploring clients' relationships with family members and friends can help clients begin to establish a personal resource network.

If human service professionals determine that the clients are in immediate danger, then they need to take steps immediately to secure the client's safety. Such steps can include contacting a local shelter or domestic-violence hotline, along with providing the client with a list of appropriate resources and assisting the client in making the necessary contacts. If the client decides to return to the abuser, the human service professional needs to respect that decision and not try to force the client to leave his or her abuser.

A variety of IPV assessments and screening forms can be used in addition to the steps outlined. Human service professionals need to be careful, however, to follow agency guidelines in dealing with any suspicion of violence. In many cases, the human service worker must complete specific screening forms prior to referring a client for other services. It is incumbent on the human service professional to be familiar with local referring agencies and their policies.

After completing the initial intake interview to determine the risk of IPV, the human service professional and client need to determine the most appropriate career-related assessments, according to the client's reading level and needs. We cannot emphasize enough that *intimate partner violence occurs across all age groups, socioeconomic groups, religious groups, races, cultures, genders, and sexual orientations.* Therefore, human service professionals need to take into consideration other information about the client that may be gleaned during the intake interview and combine it with the IPV assessment to develop the best ISP possible for the client. For example, if the client is currently homeless, then the information on assessments from Chapter 12 needs to be incorporated into designing the ISP. If the client is a single parent or displaced homemaker, then the human service professional needs to refer to the assessments noted in Chapter 7. If the client is newly immigrated, then this chapter should be blended with the assessment information provided in Chapter 17. Table 10.1 lists assessments that are appropriate for use with IPV victims.

Develop the ISP.   Once the assessments are completed, the next step for the human service professional and the client is to develop the ISP, incorporating information gained from the intake interview, discussions, and the assessments. Identifying barriers to the client's employment success is very important here, because IPV frequently impacts one's work history. Next incorporate the client's values into the planning process as the human service professional and client identify the client's personal and career goals. Victims of IPV need an opportunity to take ownership of their ISPs, and encouraging them to make their own decisions is extremely important to their growing independence. For some clients, providing input for an ISP may be the first opportunity they have had to make a decision in a place of safety where their opinion really matters. Clients taking an active role in the development of these plans are empowered and more likely to move toward self-sufficiency. Together, the client and human service worker will determine what barriers to address first and will construct a timeline by which each goal will be accomplished. Setting mini goals to meet along the way will help clients see what progress they are making and will allow for revision and redesign of the plan as necessary.

TABLE 10.1 *Career-Related Assessments for Use with Victims of Intimate Partner Violence*

Title	Source
Ability Tests	
Career Key*	Jones, L. K., & Jones, J. W. (2000). *Career key*. Raleigh, NC: Author.
Motivated Skills Card Sort	Knowdell, R. (2002, June). *Motivated skills card sort*. San Jose, CA: Career Research & Testing.
O*NET Ability Profiler*	O*NET Consortium (2003, April). *O*NET ability profiler*. Washington, DC: Author.
WorkKeys	ACT, Inc. (1993). *Workkeys assessments*. Iowa City, IO: ACT.
Interest Inventories	
CareerExplorer CD-ROM*	JIST Works (2004). *Careerexplorer CD-ROM*. Indianapolis, IN: Author.
Leisure to Occupations Connection Search	McDaniels, C., & Mullins, S. R. (1999). *The leisure to occupations connection search*. Indianapolis, IN: JIST Works.
Occupational Interests Card Sort	Knowdell, R. (2002, June). *Occupational interests card sort*. San Jose, CA: Career Research & Testing.
O*NET Interest Profiler*	O*NET Consortium (n.d.) *O*NET interest profiler*. Washington, DC: Author
Self-Directed Search, Forms CP, R & E	Holland, J. L. (1990). *Self-directed search form CP: Career planning*. Lutz, FL: Psychological Assessment Resources. Holland J. L. (1994). *Self-directed search form R*. Lutz, FL: Psychological Assessment Resources. Holland, J. L. (1996). *Self-directed search form E* (4th ed.). Lutz, FL: Psychological Assessment Resources.
Transition-to-Work Inventory	Liptak, J. J. (2004). *Transition-to-work inventory*. Indianapolis, IN: JIST Works.
Voc-Tech Quick Screener	JIST Works (2002). *Voc-tech quick screener*. Indianapolis, IN: Author.
Personality Inventories	
Keirsey Temperament Sorter II	Keirsey, D. (1998, May). *Please understand me II*. Del Mar, CA: Prometheus Nemesis Book.
Vocational Preference Inventory	Holland, J. L. (1985). *Vocational preference inventory* (VPI). Lutz, FL: Psychological Assessment Resources.

(Continued)

TABLE 10.1   Continued

Title	Source
Value Inventories	
Career Values Card Sort	Knowdell, R. (1998, June). *Career values card sort.* San Jose, CA: Career Research & Testing.
O*NET Work Importance Locator and Profiler*	O*NET Consortium (n.d.). *O*NET work importance locator and profiler.* Washington, DC: Author.
Values-Driven Work Card Sort	Career Action Center. (n.d.) *Values-driven work card sort.* Menlo Park, CA: Prodigy Press.
Work Orientation and Values Survey	Brady, R. P. (2002). *Work orientation and values survey.* Indianapolis, IN: JIST Works.
Career-Development Inventories	
Career Attitudes and Strategies Inventory	Holland, J. L., & Gottfredson, G. D. (1994). *Career attitudes and strategies inventory.* Lutz, FL: Psychological Assessment Resources.
Career Beliefs Inventory	Krumboltz, J. D. (1991). *Career beliefs inventory.* Mountain View, CA: CPP.
Career Decision Scale	Osipow, S. H., Carney, C. G., Winer, J. L., Yanico, B. J., & Koschier. M. (1987). *Career decision scale* (3rd ed.). Lutz, FL: Psychological Assessment Resources.
Career Thoughts Inventory	Sampson, J. P., Peterson, G. W., Lenz, J. G., Reardon, R. C., & Saunders, D. E. (1996). *Career thoughts inventory.* Lutz, FL: Psychological Assessment Resources.
Career Transition Inventory	Heppner, M. J. (1991). *Career transition inventory.* Columbia, MO: Author.
My Vocational Situation	Holland, J. L., Daiger, D., & Power, P. G. (1980). *My vocational situation.* Palo Alto, CA: Consulting Psychologist Press.
Overcoming Barriers Card Sort Game Kit	Harney, E. E., & Angel, D. L. (1999). *Overcoming barriers card sort game kit.* Hacienda Heights, CA: WorkNet Solutions.
Salient Beliefs Review: Connecting Spirit to Work	Bloch, D. (2003). *Salient beliefs review: Connecting spirit to work.* Indianapolis, IN: JIST Works.
Vocational Exploration and Insight Kit	Holland, J. L., Birk, J. M., Cooper, J. F., Dewey, C. R., Dolliver, H., Takai, R. T., & Tyler, L. (1980). *The vocational exploration and insight kit.* Mountain View, CA: CPP.
Miscellaneous	
Elevations Manual Card Sort System	Scully, H. (2003, August). *Elevations manual card sort system.* Roseville, CA: Author.

*Use only if client is computer literate.

Determine Training and Education Needs.   Next, the human service professional and client need to determine what type of training and education the client needs to reach the client's goals. Clients who dropped out of high school may need to complete an Adult Basic Education (ABE) program or a General Equivalency Diploma (GED) prior to or during the job search or other training. If the client receives TANF benefits, then the Family Violence Option may apply. In such cases the human service professional needs to help the client explore that option to provide extended time to receive TANF benefits. Clients who have already completed high school or have a GED may qualify to enter immediately a training program offered through the community college or a local proprietary school. Clients who have attended college in the past may choose to finish a previously started college degree.

For the more experienced clients, the interest inventory results will provide career leads for the necessary training and education. Clients who lack work experience and have been extremely isolated during their abuse will need more exposure to different jobs or even basic job skills before they can consider the various careers available. The human service professional also will want to help the client explore the possibility of relocation. Does the client need to relocate now? Later? Can the client stay local and remain safe? Does the client need to begin work immediately, or does he or she have some time and the support necessary to pursue education and training first? Clients who have the necessary support to complete training and education in the fields of their choice need to do so. Other clients, however, may not be as fortunate and will need to find immediate employment and put their career goals on hold for a while. For them, the job openings with the local employers, the economy, and the funding available through the local One-Stop Career Center will determine their training and education. Starting work immediately does not mean these clients need to give up their career goals. However, human service professionals need to help these clients find a way to work toward achieving those goals while dealing with current employment.

Assessment results will likely dictate other topics of possible education and training as well as life skills. Clients who have not had access to their finances in the past may suddenly find themselves struggling to learn how to create a budget, pay bills, and balance a checkbook. Others may need to learn how to choose good daycare. These skills can be offered to clients in small groups or one-on-one, allowing the client to choose what is the best fit for him or her. To empower clients, the human service professional can provide a list of possible training and educational group topics (i.e., nutrition and health, building family strengths, balancing work with family, stress management, time management, money management) and allow the client to choose. Giving clients the opportunity to make choices, however small, continues to empower them to take responsibility for their life choices and ownership in their successes.

Find Funding or Resources for Training and Education.   Human service professionals need to familiarize themselves with local resources that provide funding for training and education. Federally funded One-Stop Career Centers, for example, provide funding for training and education for eligible adults through Individual Training Accounts arranged through One-Stop. These individual accounts supplement financial aid already available through other intuitions, and when no financial aid is available, these accounts may cover the cost of training or education. Clients who do not qualify for assistance from other sources to pay for their training and those who need financial assistance beyond that which is available through grants may qualify for some financial assistance through Workforce Investment Act funds. The human service professional may need to serve as case manager to coordinate both funds and services. The client will need to be referred for training by the local One-Stop once all other funding has been exhausted (U.S. Department of Labor, 2000; U.S. General Accounting Office, 2003a). The human service professional will likely be able to find a variety of sources of free, life-skills training and education but will need to provide case management to coordinate these efforts.

Complete Referrals to Other Agencies.   Victims of IPV need interagency cooperation to insure that their needs are met for safe shelter, medical care, mental health care, and education and training. A holistic approach to IPV addresses the interplay of all of these factors rather than concentrating on just finding shelter for the client. Human service professionals need to be familiar with their local providers for all support services and refer the client accordingly to create the best assistance program possible to meet the client's individual needs. While developing the ISP, the client and human service professional may identify certain events or behaviors that require a referral to another agency. Clients may need medical referrals for any injuries or for substance-abuse or mental health issues such as depression, anxiety, anger management, or post-traumatic stress disorder. Clients may need funding for childcare and transportation along with referrals for Supplemental Security Income (SSI); Special Supplemental Nutrition Program for Women, Infants, and Children (WIC Program); and housing. Still other clients may need assistance due to disabilities. The human service professional serves as case manager to guarantee that all client needs are met.

Choose Interventions.   The career development program model for victims of IPV has three categories of interventions: one-to-one interventions, training and education, and mentoring. The client and the human service professional together determine whether the best approach is that of group or individual interventions, and these interventions may be offered concurrently or in phases, depending upon the individual needs of the client as well as the requirements of the local agency. Some clients may need all three interventions while others may only need one or two. Again, the need for an individualized approach cannot be stressed too much due to the diversity of this population.

Using Group or One-to-One Interventions.   In some instances, one-to-one interventions are necessary to help clients who are victims of IPV transition into self-sufficiency. This intervention involves personal and family counseling, combined with career development and might include role-plays and support groups. Clients may be referred elsewhere for these services or kept in house. Personal and family counseling would address such issues as substance abuse, domestic violence, PTSD, depression, and family violence. Clients who are eligible for TANF benefits will need to abide by the guidelines of the program. They will likely be given extended benefits due to the Family Violence Option. Depending upon the amount of exposure the clients have had to work in the past, their career exploration interventions could include job shadowing and informational interviews. At first some clients may prefer individual counseling rather than group work while exploring their barriers to career success. Still other clients may prefer to explore the effects of their nonviolent sabotage in a group setting as a way to decrease the isolation they may be feeling. Human service professionals must explore clients' views and values regarding career and homemaking, along with their perceived barriers to success, because victims of IPV have frequently had their views and values ignored or denigrated. They also need to consider the influences of parents, family, and spouse. Support groups may be extremely beneficial for victims of IPV, because they will find that they are not alone and others have been through similar circumstances.

Providing Training and Education.   In addition to being in the ISP development, training and education are also interventions. Some clients may need encouragement to continue training while on the job and to pursue and upgrade their education. Encouragement is even more important when clients are living in shelters and need to be empowered in their decision-making. Community work experience placements could help provide social skills and training for those clients who are unable to secure employment immediately. This experience could also be a source for references and an entry-level form of networking. Life-skills training and education either in a class format or individual setting occur during this stage. These life-skills classes allow participants to select and attend the classes that they feel fit their ISP goals and will increase their self-sufficiency (Burt et al., 2002; U.S. Conference of Mayors, 2002). Victims of IPV may also need workplace survival skills. Clients who have not been allowed to work in the past may feel they are incapable of holding a job or that no one will hire them. Others may have a job history but may have lost several jobs due to IPV. Workplace survival skills could give them the necessary confidence to enter or reenter the workplace, knowing that they have job skills to offer an employer. Clients who choose to pursue education may need additional assistance during this time as they learn to be independent and realize that they are capable of learning and being successful.

Offering Mentoring.   Mentoring is a very important intervention to use with victims of IPV. Many victims have been isolated, and working with a mentor will help them adjust more smoothly during the transition to self-sufficiency. Others have learned to depend upon their partners to provide for everything they need. They may need assistance in learning that that they can meet their own needs without the help of their partners. Due to their isolation, these clients may need help in opening a bank account, locating transportation, finding an apartment, or even adjusting to dating. A mentor can assist them in all of these areas as needed.

Initiate the Employment Campaign.   Not all clients who are victims of IPV will initiate their employment campaigns at the same time. While eliminating barriers to employment success before initiating a job campaign is the best approach, this approach is not always possible. Clients who have no other forms of support and are unable to stay in a domestic violence shelter may have to look for a job and deal with their barriers to employment success at the same time. Clients who work on several activities at once will need intensive case management. The next section provides an overview of considerations for victims of IPV during their employment campaign. For additional details, see Chapter 5.

The Strategic Job Search.   Human service professionals can use the information collected from the assessments and from the intake interview to help clients explore the impact of their values and goals on the job-search process. Some clients may need help setting goals and developing a plan to meet those goals. Other clients may need reminding that they do not yet have the skills to begin in the jobs of their choice, and they will need to work toward obtaining those skills. Helping clients make plans and understand that every step they take leads them closer to their goal of employment and self-sufficiency is extremely important. Meanwhile, clients need to explore whether or not their values will be in line with each of the jobs they are considering. Once clients better understand themselves, they can begin to understand the career choice process and the education and skills it entails. Another key to clients' employment success is for them to understand their employer's needs. This realization helps clients anticipate and meet those needs. The job market varies with the location, and the human service worker can help clients navigate through the market by knowing what is available and who is hiring through previously developed networks. Local employment agencies can assist with this task, as can local One-Stop Career Centers. Clients can take job-search classes here and become involved in community and volunteer work as necessary. Victims of long-term IPV may be fearful of entering the workplace, and that fear may in fact hinder their job search. Human service professionals can help clients deal with those fears and help them ease into the work world. Clients who may have disabilities will need to be aware of the jobs that best meet their needs such as jobs that are free of distractions, have a modified work schedule, or require special devices. (See Chapter 15 for more information on disabilities in the workplace).

Job-Search Correspondence.   Some jobs will not require a letter of application, but many jobs will. Clients seeking such jobs will need to learn how to write letters of application, as well as referral letters, reminder letters, and interview appreciation letters. Along with teaching clients how to write a letter accepting or declining an offer, role-playing these situations will help clients better understand the process and give them a chance to practice their interpersonal skills.

Tailor-Made Resumes.   The resume format used will vary with the client. For example clients who possess a great deal of job experience will be able to use a chronological format. Clients who lack job experience or a stable job history will need to use functional resumes that organize their job experiences according to their skills. Abusers spend a great deal of time telling victims of IPV about their weaknesses; often these victims feel they have no strengths because all they heard about was their weaknesses. Creating resumes will help clients organize their life and work experience and better understand themselves thereby allowing them to focus more on their strengths instead of their weaknesses. Resume writing can be done individually or in a class session, according to the needs of each client.

Interviewing Strategies. Role-playing the various types of interview situations from easy to difficult and from panel to telephone can greatly benefit victims of IPV. Helping clients craft answers to some of the common interview questions will empower them as well. Videotaping clients during mock interviews followed by a critique of the interview provides clients with an opportunity to see themselves as others see them. Clients who have not worked before or those who suddenly left their abusers may not have appropriate work attire, much less interview attire, so the human service professional may need to refer clients to a local clothes closet.

Change Behaviors. Participation in the career development program for victims of IPV is designed to help clients change behaviors that may keep them from long-term employment and self-sufficiency. The primary behavior change here, however, is leaving the abuser and learning to believe and to trust in one's self. Although the specific barriers to employment success will vary with each person's ISP, all clients moving through this program will have had an opportunity to improve their education and work-related skills, along with other skills they originally targeted for change. Behavior changes sometimes take place slowly, but eventually these changes will manifest in the clients' ability to find and to maintain a job and housing as they eventually move toward self-sufficiency.

Complete the Program. Clients who entered the program, developed their ISPs, completed the training and education that were detailed in their ISPs, located permanent safe housing, and exhibited behavior changes leading to employment are considered to have completed the program. At any time during the process clients can drop out of the program, but the human service professional needs to advise them that their decisions may impact their housing and their eligibility for other types of assistance. Victims of IPV often cycle in and out of domestic violence shelters, returning to their abusive relationship in between. Long-term victims of IPV often have more experience being abused than being self-sufficient, and they may need several tries to gain full-time, stable employment. Some clients may have to cycle through the program several times until they gain the self-assurance to leave the abuser permanently.

Achieve Goal of Long-Term Employment and Self-Sufficiency. The final goal of the ISP is long-term employment and client self-sufficiency. The program staff will need to determine the working definition of *long-term* employment. Generally, clients could be considered self-sufficient with long-term employment when they have left their abusers and moved into more permanent, safe housing; no longer receive any public assistance such as TANF, housing, Medicaid, food stamps, or WIC, for at least a year; and are able to fully support themselves and their family members.

Program Evaluation

The program staff will first have to determine what type of evaluation is appropriate: process evaluation, outcome evaluation, or impact evaluation. The program evaluation component has several sublevels: developing tools, tracking clients who complete the program, conducting the evaluation, analyzing and reporting findings, and implementing program changes. Human service professionals need to develop a variety of tools to evaluate their program. Figure 10.1 is a flow chart for the career development program model for use with victims of IPV. The text in each box in the figure is a factor that needs to be measured. Measuring tools can include such items as intake interview sheets, domestic-violence screening forms, database of client information, case files, tracking sheets, and referral sheets. The program staff may also need to create other tools for evaluation purposes such as paper-and-pencil surveys or telephone surveys for clients who complete the program and their employers. The staff also needs to decide when to evaluate. For example, programs and their participants can be evaluated at several points in the program: midway, upon completion, and one year after program completion. While this constant evaluation can be time-consuming, the input is invaluable for the program. Decisions involving when to evaluate need to consider the mobility of clients and the ability of the program staff to track them. Employers who hire program participants may be surveyed at different times as well, perhaps six weeks followed by six months after they hire clients in the program. The staff also need to decide how they will collect, analyze, and report the data. After the program staff has made these decisions, they will need to construct a timeline for the entire program evaluation process that shows every item to be accomplished, the deadline for accomplishing it, and who is responsible. Once the staff collects the evaluation information, they can use the input to strengthen the current program. For complete descriptions of all parts of the evaluation process, see Chapter 6.

Revisiting the Case Study: Georgia and Robert

Conduct an Intake Interview

In most cases the human service professional will be working only with the victim of IPV. For the purpose of this case study, then, we will only address Georgia's needs. During the intake interview, the human service professional must first complete a risk assessment of Georgia's situation and make the necessary referrals. If Georgia is ready to leave Robert, then the human service professional will help Georgia and her daughter find shelter. If Georgia is not yet ready to leave Robert, then the professional needs to help Georgia create a safety plan to use during the next incident of violence (Walker & Lurie, 1994). This safety plan will help Georgia recognize the danger signs that the battering is escalating, and that it is time for her and her daughter to leave. This plan involves helping Georgia design a foolproof escape route, including detailed floor plans of her home, noting where the abuse generally occurs, and the exits available to her (i.e., windows, doors, fire escapes) before the violence erupts. This plan also addresses what items Georgia will need to take and where she will go. For more information on creating a safety plan, see *Abused Women and Survivor Therapy: A Practical Guide for the Psychotherapist* (Walker, 1994).

The human service professional's next task is to explore Georgia's medical, financial, educational, and employment histories, her interests and values; and her views on employment, education, and family. Georgia has been placed under a great deal of stress due to Robert's accident and now the abuse. As a result, the case worker needs to consider Georgia's physical, mental, and emotional health, including whether Georgia or her child have any unmet medical needs. Since their income has been greatly reduced, Georgia may have chosen to spend money on food rather than on any of her or her daughter's health-related needs. The human service worker needs to explore the stresses on Georgia of adjusting to her partner's accident, his ensuing disability, and the abuse, as well.

Other issues that Georgia and her case worker need to consider are finances and the family's debts. Georgia may be legally responsible for part of any debt that she and Robert have incurred, so exploring those debts and working to keep them from being turned over to collection agencies is very important. If these debts have been given to collection agencies, the human service professional needs then to explore various methods of repayment and possibly consider bankruptcy, as well as make any necessary referrals. Setting up a budget will help Georgia better plan to meet all financial obligations.

Since Georgia finished high school and is close to completing her degree from a community college, the human service professional will want to help Georgia determine her best course of action: complete the associate's degree in business or complete the respiratory therapy program at the local hospital. They should consider the questions: Which program would best meet Georgia's needs? Which career really interests her? Under the FVO, Georgia qualifies for extended time on TANF, so now is the time to decide on the best career path for Georgia.

Make Assessments

Why did Georgia choose a business degree program? Why did she choose a respiratory therapy program? Exploring the answers to these questions is important, because Georgia's answers will help her understand her own decision-making process. By completing several career assessments, Georgia will see options that she may not have previously considered. If Georgia has some computer experience from her community college courses, Career Key (Jones & Jones, 2000) and O*Net Ability Profiler (O*NET Consortium, 2003) could help her identify occupations that fit her strengths. Since Georgia is a displaced homemaker, the Leisure to Occupations Connection Search (McDaniels and Mullins, 1999) could also help her connect leisure activities to possible career choices as could the Transition-to-Work Inventory (Liptak, 2004). The O*NET Work Importance Locator and Profiler (O*NET Consortium, n.d.b) could assist Georgia in connecting her work values to careers. The Barriers to Employment Success Inventory (Liptak, 2002a) is especially appropriate for Georgia because it identifies clients with low self-esteem and substance-abuse problems, which are common in victims of IPV. The Career Attitudes and Strategies Inventory (Holland & Gottfredson, 1994) could help Georgia assess the likelihood of career stability while clarifying situations that could lead to potential job problems. The Career Beliefs Inventory (Krumboltz, 1991) would be helpful to Georgia as a victim of IPV as it provides suggestions that help overcome barriers while strengthening the values that are not barriers to employment success. Creating a career genogram would help Georgia see the impact of work on her family members and herself, and the impact of family values regarding work, education, and vocational patterns. Human service professionals do not need to give every assessment, and they should carefully choose assessments that best meet the needs of the individual client.

Determine Barriers to Success

Lack of safe, stable housing is an extremely important barrier for Georgia to overcome. If she and her daughter do not have a safe place to stay, employment success will be much more difficult to attain. Once Georgia decides on her career goals, she will need to pursue the necessary training and education to achieve that goal. At the same time, she may be dealing with mental health issues caused by the IPV (i.e., depression, anxiety, PTSD). Other barriers to her success include affordable childcare and transportation. The human service professional needs to address these barriers to employment success along with any others that surfaced during the intake interview and assessment process.

Choose Interventions

Using Group or One-to-One Interventions.   In one-to-one interventions for Georgia the human service professional needs to explore the areas of self-esteem, stress, and abuse, along with transition-related issues such as her shift in career goals and her need to balance work, education, and family. Role-playing various transition-related situations will give Georgia the self-confidence she needs to start this new phase of her life. With the help of the human service worker, Georgia needs to create a family budget to determine how quickly she will need to find employment. The budget will also allow Georgia the opportunity to explore how she can best meet her expenses while working towards independence for herself and her daughter. Also, Georgia must consider issues of child support. If Robert is unable or unwilling to go to work to provide financial support, then the human service professional may need to help Georgia contact Child Support Enforcement or another agency to help obtain financial support for her daughter.

Support groups may also be useful in helping Georgia transition into this new phase of life. Being with other victims of IPV who are facing some of the same problems will help decrease Georgia's isolation while allowing her to be part of a group. Group members could participate in role-plays to help Georgia practice new behaviors. Her daughter may need assistance as well, depending on the amount of IPV she has witnessed.

Despite having been a stay-at-home mother, Georgia has some transferable skills from both her time running a household and her coursework in the community college. By identifying her transferable skills, Georgia will be able to decide what additional skills she needs to become more marketable in today's workforce and to see that she does possess skills despite not having worked outside of the home. Georgia may also have a support network already in place, and exploring that network would help her see how it can be utilized in other areas. The human service professional will need to review Georgia's assessment results and use her values, goals, and interests to determine the best way to integrate all of the information about Georgia into a career plan that will meet her needs.

Finding Training and Education.   Once Georgia has identified her career goals, she and the human service professional need to determine how to best meet those goals. Whether she decides to complete her business degree, the respiratory therapy program, or a new program, Georgia will need to meet with an academic advisor to develop a plan to complete her coursework as quickly as possible in accordance with her needs. The human service professional needs to assist Georgia in finding the necessary funding to complete her education and training, whether through the local One-Stop Career Center, the community college, training and education grants, community organizations, or clubs.

Using Mentoring.   Because Georgia has no work history since high school, she will likely need some level of mentoring until she has completed her education and training and has worked for at least a year. During this time the mentor can assist Georgia in securing affordable childcare, reliable transportation, and affordable housing (if necessary).

Initiate the Employment Campaign

Once Georgia has determined her career emphasis, has completed the requisite training and education, and has decided whether or not to relocate, then the human service professional can help her with the job search, letters of application, resume writing, and interviewing skills. Georgia can use a functional resume to emphasize her transferable skills, and role-playing interviews will help her develop the self-confidence she needs to enter the job market.

Conclusion

Intimate partner violence (IPV) cuts across all demographic groups, races, socioeconomic groups, cultures, religions, and sexual orientations. In the United States, a person is physically abused every six seconds by his or her spouse, common-law spouse, ex-spouse, boyfriend/girlfriend, or ex-boyfriend/girlfriend. Nearly 7.8 million women reported having been raped by an intimate partner at some time in their lives, and nearly 22 percent reported having been assaulted by an intimate partner. More than 371,000 men reported having been raped by an intimate partner, and 834,000 reported physical assault by an intimate partner. Despite the prevalence of IPV, more resources need to be developed to fit the diverse needs of this population. Some recommended policy changes would help victims of IPV. Changes in economic, community, and workforce policies would include:

- Increase education on IPV through workplace and schools
- Develop worksite domestic violence policies
- Inform women of need for protective orders

Changes in physical and mental health policies would include:

- Improve the documentation used in medical records to include photographs of injuries suspected to be the result of intimate partner violence
- Give counselors more autonomy to determine whether parental notification of mental health counseling is in the best interest of the minor (when otherwise not provided for by law as in cases of rape and sexual assault), or extend the number of counseling sessions that do not require parental consent

Organizational policy changes would include:

- Provide services for battered men
- Classify IPV as major public health and criminal justice concerns in the United States
- Develop violence-prevention strategies that focus on how victims can protect themselves from intimate partners
- Provide financial assistance for women in poverty
- Expand transitional living services to include minors, and create partial emancipation so that minors can seek shelter without parental consent in cases of family or domestic violence
- Educate service providers, officials, and teens about their rights and responsibilities concerning the issue of teens and domestic violence
- Provide services in the language of the clients

Summary

Victims of intimate partner violence can be found in all populations and they face specific barriers to career success. The most common barriers include lack of safe and stable housing and a lack of marketable skills and work experience, either from being out of the workforce or from having their work interrupted by incidents of IPV. Other barriers, such as physical and mental health, and poverty also affect the ability of IPV victims to successfully transition into the workforce and maintain their employment.

The career development model to use for victims of IPV has an Individual Success Plan that includes assessments of career-related abilities, interests, barriers, and values; interagency referrals; interventions such as one-to-one interventions, training and education, and mentoring; followed by an employment campaign that leads to long-term employment, self-sufficiency, and freedom from abuse.

Key Terms

Cyberstalking
Domestic violence
Economic or financial abuse
Emotional or psychological abuse
Injunction
Intimate partner/spousal abuse or intimate partner violence (IPV)
Physical abuse

Rape
Sexual abuse
Spiritual abuse
Stalking
Temporary restraining order or emergency injunction
Verbal abuse

Web Resources

Note that website URLs may change over time.

General Information

American Institute on Domestic Violence
http://www.aidv-usa.com

Coalition of Labor Union Women Center for Education and Research
http://www.cluw.org

Corporate Alliance to End Partner Violence
http://www.caepv.org

Domestic Violence Institute
http://www.dviworld.org

Legal Momentum
http://www.legalmomentum.org

National Coalition Against Domestic Violence
http://www.ncadv.org

National Domestic Violence Hotline
http://www.ndvh.org

National Network to End Domestic Violence
http://www.nnedv.org

National Resource Center on Domestic Violence
http://www.nrcdv.org

National Work-Life Alliance
http://www.worklifealliance.org

Native American Circle, Ltd.
http://www.nativeamericancircle.org

Safe@Work Coalition
http://www.safeatworkcoalition.org

The American Bar Association's Commission on Domestic Violence
http://www.abanet.org/domviol/workviolence.html

The Family Violence Prevention Fund
http://endabuse.org

The Legal Aid Society—Employment Law Center
http://www.las-elc.org

Violence Against Women Act of 1998
http://www.now.org/issues/violence/vawa/vawa1998.html

Violence Against Women Online Resources
http://www.vaw.umn.edu/library/bwjp

Violence Literature Database Search
http://ibs.colorado.edu/cspv/infohouse/violit/keywords.php?table=violit

Workplace Violence Research Institute
http://www.noworkviolence.com/index.htm

*Resources for Members of
Minority Groups*

Abuse and Women with Disabilities
http://www.vawnet.org/Domestic Violence/
Research/VAWnet Docs/AR_disab.pdf

**Asian and Pacific Islander Institute on
Domestic Violence**
http://www.apiahf.org/apidvinstitute/default.htm

**Domestic Abuse Helpline for
Men and Women**
http://www.batteredmenshelpline.org/index.html

Gay Men's Domestic Violence Project
http://www.gmdvp.org

**Institute on Domestic Violence in
the African American Community**
http://www.dvinstitute.org

Men Stopping Violence
http://www.menstoppingviolence.org/index.php

MenWeb
http://www.batteredmen.com

**National Latino Alliance for the
Elimination of Domestic Violence**
http://www.dvalianza.org

11

Displaced or Dislocated Workers

Through No Fault of Their Own

Case Study: Martina and Michael

Martina and Michael are in their forties and live in a small home in a rural area with their four children, ages 7, 10, 14, and 17. Since he graduated from high school, Michael has worked as a millwright for 25 years in the local paper mill. This is the only job he has ever had, and he just received written notification that the mill is closing in 60 days. The notice cites escalating costs for energy, wood, transportation, and chemicals, coupled with difficult market conditions as the reason for closing. Michael's wife, Martina, has been a **part-time employee** for several years at a local department store while her children are in school. When she asked her boss if she could change to full-time or at least work more hours due to the impending layoff, the store's owners told her that the store would be closing before the end of the year due to competition by a chain retail store that moved into the area.

Neither Michael nor Martina has any idea what to do at this point. Since the paper mill job has been his entire work experience, Michael feels untrained to do anything else, and at 42 is unsure of how to start over, especially since he does not want to leave the area and wants a job that is local. He is very angry that the mill is closing because his father had worked at the mill, and Michael's children had expected to do the same. As a teenager Martina had worked as a grocery store cashier. She then stayed at home with the children until two years ago when she started working at the department store for a little spending money. In her spare time she is a member of the women's auxiliary with the local hospital, a volunteer in the hospital's gift shop, vice president of the PTA, and president of the county flower and garden club. Martina and Michael have a small savings account, a monthly mortgage payment, a truck payment, and several credit cards. Their eldest son will graduate from high school in three months.

The Displaced or Dislocated Worker Population

According to the Workforce Investment Act (1998), displaced or dislocated workers fall into four categories:

1. Those who have been terminated or laid off or who have received a notice of termination or being laid off are eligible for unemployment compensation; or who have exhausted their unemployment compensation, have been employed long enough to be able to demonstrate a connection to the workforce to those at the local One-Stop Career Center, and are unlikely to return to a previous occupation
2. Those who have been terminated or laid off or who have received a notice of termination or being laid off due to permanent closure or substantial layoff at the place of employment, or are employed at a facility where the employer has announced that the facility will close within 180 days
3. Those who have been self-employed but are now unemployed due to general economic conditions
4. Those who have been displaced homemakers

Since displaced homemakers were discussed in Chapter 7 of this text, we will concentrate here on the first three categories of displaced or dislocated workers.

Demographics

The U.S. Bureau of Labor Statistics (2005) reported that in April 2005, 7.7 million people were unemployed, an unemployment rate of 5.2 percent down from 5.5 percent in April 2004. Twenty-one percent of those unemployed in April 2005 were classified as **long-term unemployed.** An additional 1.5 million people were marginally attached to the workforce during that time (i.e., they were available for work and had looked for work but were not actively involved in job search for four consecutive weeks.) Over 390,000 of these workers were not looking for work because they believed that no jobs were available for them. The remaining marginally attached workers reported not looking for work due to school attendance or family responsibilities (U.S. Bureau of Labor Statistics, 2005).

According to the Trade Act Participant Report (2004), dislocated or displaced workers were 55 percent female compared to 45 percent male. Forty-one percent of all dislocated workers were between the ages of 30 and 45; 32 percent were between the age of 45 and 55. Nineteen percent of the workers did not have a high school diploma, compared to 52 percent who possessed a diploma or its equivalent, 18 percent who had taken some college courses, and 4 percent who were college graduates. These workers are 64 percent white, 17 percent African American, 12 percent Hispanic/Latino, 3 percent Asian, and 1 percent Native American. Eighty-two percent of the workers received occupational training, 15 percent received remedial training, and 3 percent received on-the-job training through **Trade Adjustment Assistance Reform Act of 2002** programs, spending an average of 53.91 weeks in training. Sixty-three percent of the workers completed their training. Eighty percent of Trade Act participants received a trade readjustment allowance, 21 percent received a waiver from training, 9 percent received transportation allowance, 2 percent received a subsistence allowance, 1 percent received job-search allowance, and 1 percent received a relocation allowance.

Occupational and Unemployment Data

Dislocated workers come from a variety of occupations. In 2004, more than 8.1 million people over the age of 16 were unemployed. Almost 2 million of these workers had been employed in sales and office occupations such as administrative support. The next largest group is 1.6 million displaced workers in service occupations such as health-care support, protective service, food preparation and serving; building and grounds cleaning and maintenance; and personal care and service. Almost 1.4 million of the unemployed had most recently worked in production, transportation, and material moving occupations, followed by 1.3 million unemployed in the management, professional, and related occupations. This latter group includes occupations in management; business and financial operations; computer and mathematics; architecture and engineering; life, physical, and social science; community and social services; legal; education, training, and library; arts, entertainment, sports, and media; and healthcare practitioners. Almost 1.1 million displaced workers were in occupations in natural resources, construction, and maintenance (i.e., farming, fishing, and forestry; construction and extraction; and installation, maintenance, and repair) (U.S. Bureau of Labor Statistics, n.d.a).

Types of Layoffs and Length of Unemployment

Over 1 million of these unemployed workers were on temporary layoffs, and over 900,000 were classified as permanent job losers (U.S. Bureau of Labor Statistics, n.d.b). Of those workers on temporary layoff, 53.3 percent were unemployed less than 5 weeks; 30.6 percent were unemployed between 5 and 14 weeks; 10.3 percent were unemployed between 15 and 26 weeks; and 5.8 percent were unemployed for 27 weeks or more. Permanent job losers demonstrated different rates. Only 23.6 percent were unemployed less than 5 weeks as compared to 26.8 percent unemployed from 5 to 14 weeks, 19.3 percent unemployed between 15 and 26 weeks, and 30.3 percent were unemployed for 27 weeks or longer (U.S. Bureau of Labor Statistics, n.d.c). Thirty percent of unemployed full-time workers were unemployed for 5 or less weeks, 29.2 percent were unemployed from 5 to 10 weeks, 10 percent were unemployed from 11 to 14 weeks, 16.8 percent were unemployed from 15 to 26 weeks, 10.1 percent were unemployed from 27 to 51 weeks, and 13.9 percent were unemployed more than 51 weeks (U.S. Bureau of Labor Statistics, n.d.c).

Occupation impacts the length of time a dislocated worker is unemployed. Workers in durable good manufacturing average 14.2 weeks of unemployment, those in public administration average 13.6 weeks, those in nondurable goods manufacturing average 13 weeks, those in information average 12.5 weeks, and those in financial activities average 11.2 weeks of unemployment. Those in leisure and hospitality return to the workplace more quickly, averaging 8.2 weeks of unemployment, those in agriculture and mining average 8.3 weeks, those with no previous work experience average 8.9 weeks, and those in education and health services average 9 weeks of unemployment (U.S. Bureau of Labor Statistics, n.d.d).

Stages of Job Loss

Bradley (1990) identifies five stages of job loss: denial, anger, bargaining, depression, and acceptance.

1. *Denial.* Long-term employees frequently respond with shock and denial to a job loss, sometimes refusing to believe that they have just lost their jobs. Normally this stage is short term, as reality sets in. Some dislocated workers will continue to believe that the layoff is not happening or will only be temporary. "No! This can't be true. They won't really let me go."

2. *Anger.* Once workers understand they are really losing their job, they frequently feel betrayed and abandoned by their employer. This anger is often displaced at family members, and other dislocated workers may *scapegoat* by taking their anger out on family members. "After all I've done for this company, and they're still going to let me go."

3. *Bargaining.* At this stage the worker realizes that the job is being lost, so he or she tries to bargain for one last time. "If you give me just one more chance, I'll work hard and help the company turn a profit." "If you let me finish this one project I'm working on, I'll be ready to leave the company."

4. *Depression.* In this stage the worker realizes the job is lost and often feels overwhelmed and hopeless. Workers often want to be alone, withdrawing from everyday activities and contact with family, friends, and coworkers. This lethargy makes the job search more difficult as the worker lacks the motivation to search for a new job and feels unwanted and useless. "No one's going hire me now. I don't know how to do anything else. All my friends are from work. I just don't know anything else."

5. *Acceptance.* The worker in this stage realizes that the job is truly over and starts making plans for the future. "I don't really like being replaced by technology, but I can't change it. I need to move on and look for another job."

While many dislocated workers move through all five stages, some workers become stuck in one of the first four stages and find it difficult to move toward acceptance of their job loss. Those workers who are stuck in an earlier stage may either choose not to job search or may choose ineffective job-search methods or coping skills that reinforce their maladaptive beliefs.

Job-Search Methods

Dislocated male workers use a variety of job-search methods with many using more than one method. Of workers who had lost jobs and/or completed temporary or **part-time employment** 65.4 percent contacted the employer directly for jobs, 53.9 percent sent out resumes or filled out applications, 25.7 percent used a public employment agency, 21.1 percent used friends or relatives, 19.8 percent placed or answered ads, and 10.3 percent used a private employment agency. People who left their job followed a similar pattern in job-search methods as did reentrants.

Dislocated female workers tended to vary only slightly from the pattern for male workers. Sixty-four percent of dislocated female workers contacted the employer directly, 57.5 percent sent out resumes or completed applications, 27.2 percent used a public employment agency, 21.6 percent placed or answered ads, 19.5 percent used friends or relatives, and 10.2 percent used a private employment agency (U.S. Bureau of Labor Statistics, n.d.e).

Reemployment

Almost 65 percent of the long-term employed who were displaced in 2003 were reemployed as of January 2004. Sixty-five percent of workers between the ages of 20 to 24 and 69 percent of workers between the ages of 25 to 54 reported reemployment. Only 56 percent of workers between the ages of 55 to 64 and 24 percent of workers over the age of 65 were reemployed at that same time. Men had the edge on reemployment: 68 percent of men were reemployed compared to 61 percent of women. Fifty-one percent of long-term workers who were displaced from full-time wage and salary jobs and reemployed in similar positions reported earnings lower than those on the lost job. Almost one-third reported earning losses of 20 percent (U.S. Bureau of Labor Statistics, 2004c).

Barriers to Career Success

Structural Barriers

Affordable Quality Labor Abroad.   At the same time that American schools are being criticized for the erosion of education (Couturier & Scurry, 2005), the quality of education abroad is increasing rapidly (National Science Board, 2000). In 1999, China graduated three times as many engineers as the United States. Engineering graduates in China account for 44.3 percent of all undergraduate degrees compared to engineering graduates in the United States who only accounted for 5.1 percent of undergraduate degrees awarded (National Science Board, 2000). As the number of science and engineering graduates who are U.S. citizens is decreasing, the global competition for technical expertise is increasing. Foreign-born engineers and scientists who are educated in the United States are frequently recruited by their home countries, and they receive competitive salaries, benefits packages, stock options, and housing. As these graduates leave the United States, the talent pool in the United States dwindles, decreasing the ability for the remaining labor pool to compete with those in other countries (Koehler & Hagigh, 2004).

Labor abroad is often more affordable than it is in the United States. A surplus of labor coupled with the low cost of living in underdeveloped nations allows companies to reduce labor costs by as much as 90 percent (Koehler & Hagigh, 2004). In some case federal legislation such as the **North American Free Trade Agreement (NAFTA)** allowed companies to relocate jobs and/or trade to Mexico and Canada. This outsourcing of jobs permits companies to move the low-skill-intensive components of their production to other countries with lower wages and to keep the high-skill-intensive components local. When the low-skill components are complete, the U.S. company imports them back from the low-wage countries, then they complete and sell their product. This practice frequently squeezes out less-competitive firms that are often low tech and have a high number of low-skilled workers as the imported goods become cheaper than locally produced goods (Anderton & Brenton, 1998). The United States has lost 2.7 million manufacturing jobs since 2000 (Koehler & Hagigh, 2004). Labor experts predicted a loss of 406,000 jobs to other countries during 2004 alone (Bronfenbrenner & Luce, 2004).

Advance Notification of Plant Closings and Layoffs.   Employees who receive advance notice of layoffs tend to begin their job searches before their layoff begins. Those who expect to be recalled, however, are less likely to job search before the layoff. Preunemployment job search decreases as the levels of benefits available after layoff increase (Burgess & Low, 1998; Kodrzycki, 1998). In fact, workers who receive no severance pay tend to find jobs more quickly than their counterparts who receive benefits (Kodrzycki, 1998). In some instances those with unemployment benefits who find a job within a year of their displacement have an increased chance of part-time employment as opposed to full-time employment (McCall, 1997).

Confusing Unemployment Terminology.   The entire process of being "laid off" can be very confusing for the dislocated worker. Confusing terminology combined with the need for the worker to fit into certain categories in order to qualify for assistance can make job displacement a bewildering experience. Dislocated workers often need help navigating this terminology maze. For example, workers are considered to have a **constructive discharge** when their resignation or retirement is involuntary due to harassment or other pressure by the employer. A worker may be part of a **mass layoff** when the workforce reduction is not due to a plant closure if anywhere between 50 and 499 employees or 33 percent of the total full-time staff are laid off during a single month at a single site of employment. A **single site of employment** may be a single location or a group of adjacent locations that form a campus, industrial park, and so on. The site may include separate buildings that are not necessarily connected but may be in reasonable proximity and share staff and equipment. For workers who travel, the single site of employment includes the worker's home base from which the work is assigned or to which workers report. An **employment loss** is not quite as simple as the phrase sounds. An official employment loss can be the termination of employment, a layoff lasting for six months or longer, or a 50 percent reduction in work hours during each month of any six-month period (U.S. Department of Labor, 2003c).

Supportive Services.   Various supportive services are available for dislocated or displaced workers, including rapid-response services, unemployment insurance, severance benefits, and other services such as help with childcare and transportation.

Rapid-Response Services. Dislocated or displaced workers need to be informed *quickly* of services linking them to new jobs. Workers need immediate assistance to help them cope with the impeding or current loss of their job to better plan how to support themselves during job search and/or retraining with their limited financial resources (U.S. Department of Labor, 1994). While the **Worker Adjustment and Retraining Notification (WARN) Act of 1989** provides guidelines regarding provision of rapid-response services for dislocated employees, this act does not apply to all companies or even to all employees at the same company (U.S. Department of Labor, 2003c). Small-scale layoffs may even pass unnoticed in some communities (U.S. Department of Labor, 1994).

Unemployment Insurance and Severance Benefits. While both benefits provide income support for those who have lost their jobs, they have some basic differences. Unemployment insurance reflects social goals by providing general protection to those who have lost their jobs while taking hardship under consideration. Such benefits are often more generous for those with larger families, and benefits are sometimes capped for those with larger pay prior to job loss. Unemployment insurance and benefits end, however, when workers obtain new employment.

Severance pay is not set by law, thus it varies across employers. Severance pay does not vary according to worker need, and it is often based on job tenure. In some states, severance pay affects the amount of unemployment insurance a worker receives or even when the unemployment insurance begins. Unlike unemployment insurance, dislocated workers can receive severance pay whether or not they have started new employment (Kodrzycki, 1998). Because unemployment insurance lowers the cost of unemployment, many recipients reduce the intensity of their job search until the benefits are close to expiring (Burgess & Lowe, 1998; Kodrzycki, 1998). Therefore, more generous benefits or benefits provided for a longer period of time lead to fewer displaced workers returning to work quickly. Workers with fewer benefits have to return to work more quickly than their counterparts, possibly taking jobs at lower wages or in other fields in order to return to work before their benefits expire.

Other Services. Displaced or dislocated workers often need a variety of other support services in addition to response services and insurance. Dislocated workers may need transportation assistance, which is frequently unavailable in rural areas (Schweke, 2004). When jobs leave the city and move to the suburbs, displaced workers who live in the inner city may also lack transportation to a new job (Immergluck, 1998). Depending upon the female dislocated worker's marital status, she may or may not need childcare support and elder care support (U.S. Department of Labor, 1994; Schweke, 2004). Women who decide to enter nontraditional jobs often still face some barriers in doing so (Schweke, 2004). As workers run through their unemployment benefits and their savings, evictions and foreclosures are likely (U.S. Department of Labor, 1994; Schweke, 2004).

Individual Barriers

Financial Status. Displaced or dislocated workers frequently experience a financial crisis due to a lack of income coupled with extensive financial obligations. Job-search costs often serve as a barrier to employment to dislocated workers who live in economically segregated, urban areas, especially for workers dealing with long commute times (Immergluck, 1998). Dislocated workers in general report financial hardship during periods of unemployment, including inability to pay bills, increasing credit card debt, missing mortgage payments, accepting public assistance, or difficulty in feeding and clothing the family (Broman, Hamilton, Hoffman, & Mavaddat, 1995). Extended joblessness could result in homelessness, increased medical problems due to lack of health care, and bankruptcy.

Job Stability and Earnings vs. Marital Stability.   Ahituv and Lerman (2004) explored the connections between job instability, wages, and marriage by reviewing data from the Bureau of Labor Statistics' National Longitudinal Survey of Youth 1979, a survey of 9,964 young men and women who were ages 14 to 22 when they were first interviewed in 1979. Survey respondents were reinterviewed annually until 1994, then semiannually until 2004 (U.S. Bureau of Labor Statistics, 2004d). Ahituv and Lerman found that job instability combined with having a high number of jobs often resulted in lower wage and marriage rates. Their findings also suggested that marriage augments job stability and improves wage rates (Ahituv & Lerman, 2004).

Job Tenure.   Job tenure, also referred to as position tenure or seniority on the job, affects severance packages, which in turn affects reemployment. For example, nonunion workers with 20 years or more on the job received between four and seven weeks more severance pay than workers with less than 20 years service. This allowed them more time to job search to find jobs with wages comparable to those of the lost job (Kodrzycki, 1998). Reemployment wages for workers for unionized jobs decrease as the number of years on the job increases (Kuhn & Sweetman, 1999). Dislocated workers with long tenure at their previous jobs frequently suffer large pay cuts when compared to other workers who enter a different occupation or industry (Kletzer, 1998).

Education and Training.   Juhn (1999) proposed that wages are determined by two types of skills: physical skills and cognitive skills. Industries with low-wage, low-skilled jobs hire workers with physical skills, and industries with high-wage, high-skilled jobs hire workers with cognitive skills (Juhn, 1999). In fact, workers with less education have greater fluctuations in earning and more job turnover (Fitzgerald, 1999). As the number of low-skilled jobs decrease due to outsourcing, the need for employees to possess more skills increases. Bardhan and Kroll (2003) suggested that as jobs lost to outsourcing are replaced by higher-wage jobs, workers will need to improve their education and skills to be competitive.

A 1995 study by Broman and colleagues of dislocated autoworkers reported that long-term unemployment had a more severe impact on less-educated workers as compared to more-educated workers, and on less-educated African Americans in particular. When severance packages include provisions for basic education courses to improve reading, writing, mathematics, and computer literacy, displaced workers who lack a GED and earn lower salaries are more likely to enroll in such courses compared to workers who do not receive a severance package or who are more educated. Even so, few dislocated workers who are high-school dropouts take advantage of the general education courses, opting for training instead (Kodrzycki, 1998). Enrollment in education and training classes sometimes has little effect on the starting pay of new jobs, although enrollment did increase the chances that workers who changed their lines of work would move into jobs with better long-term possibilities (Kodrzycki, 1997). Employees with more education and training often have higher career aspirations and are less likely to be satisfied with or remain in part-time or unstable employment (Moss, Salzman, & Tilly, 2005). Some research suggested that the impact of education may reflect the worker's ability to look toward the future rather the past (Broman et al., 1995). Programs such as STRIVE report 80 percent job-placement rates for workers who have completed their training and education programs (Schweke, 2004). Since displaced or dislocated workers frequently have occupational skills in obsolete fields or in areas that are not in demand in the current economy, additional training and education are often necessary for reemployment (U.S. Department of Labor, 1994).

"Soft" Skills.   While job displacement can occur in any field or industry and with workers of any educational background, dislocated workers from manufacturing plants or other work sites with site-specific cultures may find themselves missing certain prevocational skills necessary for new employment positions. Referred to as *workplace behavior skills* or *soft skills* (Schweke, 2004; Worksystems, Inc. 2004), these skills include workplace dress and behaviors, work attitudes, communication skills, working as a team, motivation, and the ability to adapt to varied work cultures (U.S. Department of Labor, 1994). Dislocated workers who do not possess these skills face an additional hurdle to reemployment when seeking jobs outside their field or jobs that differ from their previous positions.

Physical Health Barriers

In 2003, 60.2 percent of the population was covered by an employment-based health insurance plan, a decline from 69.2 percent in 2002. Government-provided health insurance (including but not limited to **Medicaid, Medicare,** and military health care) increased from 25.7 percent in 2002 to 26.6 percent in 2003, leaving 15.6 percent of the population with no health insurance (DeNavas-Walt, Proctor, & Mills, 2004). Many employers offer severance packages to their full-time workers who are laid off, and these packages often include an extension of group health insurance, sometimes beyond the federally mandated limits (Kodrzyck, 1998). However, the disparity between those workers who receive severance packages and those who do not is significant. Part-time workers, for example, seldom receive severance packages or health insurance. Dislocated workers who seek medical care without coverage through insurance or **Consolidated Omnibus Budget Reconciliation Act (COBRA)** may face action by a collection agency due to nonpayment of medical bills, may not see a doctor even when ill, and may avoid filling prescriptions (Schweke, 2004). Dislocated workers may be able to extend or even receive health care through such entities as **Employment Benefits Security Administration (EBSA),** COBRA or **Health Insurance Portability and Accountability Act of 1996 (HIPPA)** (U.S. Department of Labor, 2004). Such methods are expensive as the displaced workers now have to pay full price for medical coverage that may have been free while they were employed.

Unemployment and underemployment have been linked with alcohol abuse, with underemployment increasing the chance of binge drinking (Dooley & Prause, 1997b). While women are more likely to be depressed, anxious, and stressed, they are less likely to resort to drinking than are their male counterparts. In fact, women and married workers are less likely to drink than the unmarried (Broman et al., 1995). While substance abuse often decreases once the unemployed or underemployed improve their employment situation, employment is not necessarily a cure for substance abuse. Dislocated workers who seek assistance through Workforce Investment Act (1998) programs, however, qualify for drug- and alcohol-abuse counseling and referrals as needed.

Mental Health Barriers

Long-term unemployment has been linked to a number of mental health issues. Depression has been studied in dislocated autoworkers, Mexican Americans, and in dislocated workers in general (Broman et al., 1995; Catalano et al., 2000; U.S. Department of Labor, 1994). Such depression can lead to sexual problems and lethargy as the workers withdraw from everyday activities along with family and friends. Dislocated workers may even find it difficult to concentrate, thus impacting their ability to find a job or even believe that they can be employed again (U.S. Department of Labor, 1994). Anger that is related to communication during the transition and the workers' distrust and perception of fairness frequently accompanies layoffs. This distrust and anger can affect the workers' ability to commit to future employers (Wanberg, Bunce, & Gavin, 1999). Dislocated or displaced workers also experience anxiety, especially those who have experienced repeated episodes of unemployment (Broman et al., 1995). They also experience other indicators of stress such as irritability, domestic violence, and behavioral symptoms such as increased eating, smoking, or drinking (U.S. Department of Labor, 1994). Loss of self-esteem and low self-confidence also often affect dislocated workers (Wanberg et al., 1999; U.S. Department of Labor, 1994).

Career Development Program Model: Displaced or Dislocated Workers

Displaced or dislocated workers need a career development program that will move them quickly into their new job, while individually addressing each client's needs and barriers to success. The ultimate goal is the long-term employment of the client. Because of the varied educational, skill, and employment backgrounds presented by this group of clients, human service professionals need to consider each client separately in developing a series of interventions to enhance the client's career success. Our program has three major components: the applicant pool, the Individual Success Plan (ISP), and the program evaluation. Each component will be explained in detail. Figure 11.1 is a graphic model of the career development model.

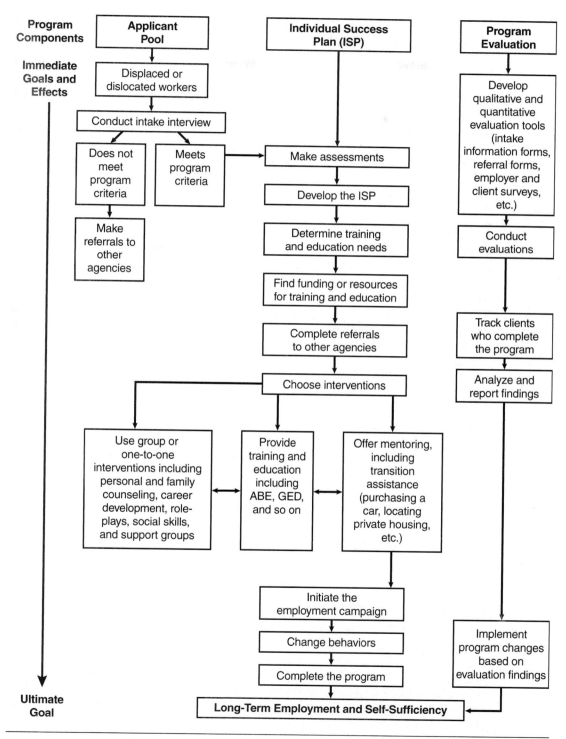

FIGURE 11.1 *Career Development Program Model: Displaced or Dislocated Workers*

Applicant Pool

The applicant pool includes any clients who have been displaced from their most recent job. Intake personnel will then determine which clients meet the criteria for program participation, and they will refer those who *do not* meet the criteria to other agencies. For example, low-income or working poor clients with housing difficulties may need assistance from local homeless shelters or from a Housing and Urban Development program (see Chapter 12). Clients with chemical dependency issues should be referred for substance treatment before addressing career development issues (see Chapter 16). They may refer displaced or dislocated workers who are recent veterans to Veteran's Affairs (see Chapter 17).

Individual Success Plan

Creating an Individual Success Plan (ISP) offers a personal approach to career development. Displaced or dislocated workers come from a variety of educational, skill, and work backgrounds, so great care needs to be taken to consider each worker as an individual and to help that worker move into a *stable* job paying equal or better than the displaced job. Developing an ISP with clients can help them determine the best steps to take. Also, as dislocated workers bring a different combination of factors to the job search, the ISP can address each of those factors while providing a personalized approach for each client.

Make Assessments.   Human service professionals need to consider more than just the clients' career, educational, and training needs; the clients' stage of job loss impacts all of these. The stress of knowing that they are about to lose their jobs or that their financial supports will soon be extinguished are not conducive to either good physical health or mental health, and both can impact clients' success in finding and holding a job. Thus, the ISP needs to address these issues as well as career.

Chapter 3 provides an assortment of career-related assessments to be used according to clients' needs and background. Beginning with a traditional intake interview the human service professional can help identify these needs and determine the best course of action for the client at this time. During the interview, the client and human service professional will examine survival strategies currently in use to determine their appropriateness. Other issues they will explore include unemployment insurance benefits and severance pay and the length of time that remains before those subsidies expire. Again, the diverse backgrounds of these clients must be considered. One client may have a high school education, and another client may have a bachelor's degree, so human service professionals need to be very careful in matching assessments to the client. Table 11.1 is as list of assessments appropriate for use in designing an ISP with displaced or dislocated workers. Using several assessments is encouraged, but human service professionals need to be careful to use the ones that best fit the needs of their clients. (See Chapter 3 for additional details on each assessment.)

TABLE 11.1 *Career-Related Assessments for Use with Displaced or Dislocated Workers*

Title	Source
Ability Tests	
Career Key*	Jones, L. K., & Jones, J. W. (2000). *Career key.* Raleigh, NC: Author.
Motivated Skills Card Sort	Knowdell, R. (2002, June). *Motivated skills card sort.* San Jose, CA: Career Research & Testing.
O*NET Ability Profiler*	O*NET Consortium (2003, April). *O*NET ability profiler.* Washington, DC: Author
WorkKeys	ACT, Inc. (1993). *Workkeys assessments.* Iowa City, IO: ACT.
Interest Inventories	
Career Exploration Inventory 2	Liptak, J. (2002). *Career exploration inventory 2.* Indianapolis, IN: JIST Works.
CareerExplorer CD-ROM*	JIST Works (2004). *Careerexplorer CD-ROM.* Indianapolis, IN: Author.
Guide for Occupational Exploration Interest Inventory	Farr, M. (2002). *Guide for occupational exploration interest inventory* (4th ed.). Indianapolis, IN: JIST Works.
Leisure to Occupations Connection Search	McDaniels, C., & Mullins, S. R. (1999). *The leisure to occupations connection search.* Indianapolis, IN: JIST Works.
Occupational Interests Card Sort	Knowdell, R. (2002, June). *Occupational interests card sort.* San Jose, CA: Career Research & Testing.
O*NET Career Interests Inventory	JIST Works. (2002). *O*NET career interests in ventory.* Indianapolis, IN: Author.
O*NET Interest Profiler*	O*NET Consortium (n.d.) *O*NET interest profiler.* Washington, DC: Author.
Self-Directed Search, Forms CP, Form R, & Form E	Holland, J. L. (1990). *Self-directed search form CP: Career planning.* Lutz, FL: Psychological Assessment Resources. Holland J. L. (1994). *Self-directed search form R.* Lutz, FL: Psychological Assessment Resources. Holland, J. L. (1996). *Self-directed search form E* (4th ed.). Lutz, FL: Psychological Assessment Resources.
Transition-to-Work Inventory	Liptak, J. J. (2004). *Transition-to-work inventory.* Indianapolis, IN: JIST Works.
Voc-Tech Quick Screener	JIST Works (2002). *Voc-tech quick screener.* Indianapolis, IN: Author.
Wide Range Interest and Occupation Test	Glutting, J. J., & Wilkinson, G. (2003). *Wide range interest and occupation test* (2nd ed.). Wilmington, DE: Wide Range.
Value Inventories	
Career Values Card Sort	Knowdell, R. (1998, June). *Career values card sort.* San Jose, CA: Career Research & Testing.

(Continued)

TABLE 11.1   Continued

Title	*Source*
O*NET Career Values Inventory*	JIST Works (2002). *O*NET career values inventory.* Indianapolis, IN: Author.
O*NET Work Importance Locator and Profiler*	O*NET Consortium (n.d.). *O*NET work importance locator and profiler.* Washington, DC: Author.
Values-Driven Work Card Sort	Career Action Center. (n.d.) *Values-driven work card sort.* Menlo Park, CA: Prodigy Press.
Work Orientation and Values Survey	Brady, R. P. (2002). *Work orientation and values survey.* Indianapolis, IN: JIST Works.
Career-Development Inventories	
Career Attitudes and Strategies Inventory	Holland, J. L., & Gottfredson, G. D. (1994). *Career attitudes and strategies inventory.* Lutz, FL: Psychological Assessment Resources.
Career Beliefs Inventory	Krumboltz, J. D. (1991). *Career beliefs inventory.* Mountain View, CA: CPP.
Career Decision Scale	Osipow, S. H., Carney, C. G., Winer, J. L., Yanico, B. J., & Koschier. M. (1987). *Career decision scale* (3rd ed.). Lutz, FL: Psychological Assessment Resources.
Career Thoughts Inventory	Sampson, J. P., Peterson, G. W., Lenz, J. G., Reardon, R. C., & Saunders, D. E. (1996). *Career thoughts inventory.* Lutz, FL: Psychological Assessment Resources.
Career Transition Inventory	Heppner, M. J. (1991). *Career transition inventory.* Columbia, MO: Author.
My Vocational Situation	Holland, J. L., Daiger, D., & Power, P. G. (1980). *My vocational situation.* Mountain View, CA: CPP.
Overcoming Barriers Card Sort Game Kit	Harney, E. E., & Angel, D. L. (1999). *Overcoming barriers card sort game kit.* Hacienda Heights, CA: WorkNet Solutions.
Salient Beliefs Review: Connecting Spirit to Work	Bloch, D. (2003). *Salient beliefs review: Connecting spirit to work.* Indianapolis, IN: JIST Works.
Vocational Exploration and Insight Kit	Holland, J. L., Birk, J. M., Cooper, J. F., Dewey, C. R., Dolliver, H., Takai, R. T., & Tyler, L. (1980). *The vocational exploration and insight kit.* Mountain View, CA: CPP.
Miscellaneous	
Elevations ® Manual Card Sort System	Scully, H. (2003, August). *Elevations manual card sort system.* Roseville, CA: Author.
Individual Employment Plan	Ludden, L. L., & Maitlen, B. (2002). *Individual employment plan.* Indianapolis, IN: JIST Works.
Vocational Decision-Making Interview	Czerlinsky, T., & Chandler, S. (1999). *Vocational decision-making interview.* Indianapolis, IN: JIST Works.

*Use only if client is computer literate.

Develop the ISP.   Once the client and human service professional have chosen and completed the assessments, the next step is to develop the ISP. The human service professional assists the client in identifying specific barriers to employment success by integrating information obtained through the intake interview, assessments, and discussions. The human service professional will need to explore issues of mental and physical health and make referrals where necessary. After helping clients identify their possible barriers to career success, the human service professional needs to help clients integrate their values, career, and personal goals into the planning process. Helping clients take an active role in creating these plans empowers them and assists them in moving toward self-sufficiency, which is particularly important for workers who have just been laid off. The human service professional and the client work together to determine which barriers to include in the ISP, and then they create a timeline for meeting each goal. Setting mini goals to meet along the way will help clients see their progress and will allow for a redesign of the ISP as necessary.

Determine Training and Education Needs.   The level of formal education the client has completed may not accurately indicate whether or not basic skills remediation is needed. College graduates may need to brush up on skills they may not have used recently in order to succeed in training. Workers who lack a basic education may have picked up their basic skills through jobs or other experiences (U.S. Department of Labor, 1994). Thus the human service professional must carefully explore the need for education and training without making assumptions regarding their clients' needs. In some cases clients may not be ready to accept that they need additional training and education until they have completed a lengthy job search and failed to obtain reemployment at a similar wage level. Workers with the least education and the fewest transferable skills are often hesitant to enter classroom-based training because of their previous lack of success (U.S. Department of Labor, 1994). Other clients may not immediately see the need to improve their soft skills. Human service professionals need to respect their clients' wishes while they help clients move toward career success even if that means allowing clients to enter the job search before they are ready.

Reviewing the results of the interest inventories' provides career leads for possible training and education. Consideration of *future* jobs, however, needs to be foremost in the minds of both the human service professional and the client in deciding what training programs and skills to pursue. Technology skills, in particular, are important skills to develop. Human service professionals must help clients avoid training that maintains obsolete technologies and unstable jobs; instead they need to emphasize the match of skills development and support with *local* economic opportunities. Goozner (2004) proposed that the modern American factory worker now needs to be able to read, work in teams, compute, solve problems, and willing to take on many more tasks during a typical day in order to be competitive with workers in another nation who can work for less money. The American worker needs to work ten times smarter and know how to work in a modernized environment filled with robots and other technological advances. Helping the displaced or dislocated worker prepare for and transition into these new jobs is vital.

Assessment results may suggest other topics for training and education such as life skills. Human service professionals can offer life-skills training to clients in small groups or one-on-one sessions to meet individual client's needs. Providing clients with a list of possible training and educational group topics (i.e., stress management, time management, money management) from which to choose continues to empower them to take responsibility for their life choices and successes.

Find Funding or Resources for Training and Education.
Under the WARN Act (1989), eligible companies provide 60 days notice of job layoffs that gives the company and the **State Rapid Response Dislocated Worker Unit** time to coordinate services to provide on-site information about the employment and retraining services available (U.S. Department of Labor, 2003c). Trade Act Assistance may also provide funding for education and training. Federal financial-aid packages often cover training classes provided through local community colleges. The dislocated workers' severance packages may provide funding for retraining and education as well (Kodrzycki, 1998). Those workers whose employers were not covered under WARN (1989) or who do not provide severance packages for dislocated workers are eligible for funding for training and education through the federally funded One-Stop Career Centers of the Workforce Investment Act (1998).

Complete Referrals to Other Agencies.
Individuals who are unable to obtain grant assistance from other sources to pay for their training and those who need financial assistance beyond that which is available through grants may qualify for some financial assistance through Workforce Investment Act funds. For these workers, the case manager will be responsible for coordinating Act funds as well as the available services. To access these funds, the local One-Stop center will need to refer the client for training once all other funding has been exhausted (U.S. Department of Labor, 2000; U.S. General Accounting Office, 2003). The human service professional can refer qualifying families to the local Family Self-Sufficiency program for assistance in job training, education, and life skills. Life-skills training and education are often available free in a variety of settings. Other services requiring referrals include medical coverage and counseling.

Choose Interventions.
The career development program for the displaced or dislocated worker has three categories of interventions: one-to-one interventions, training and education, and mentoring. The client and human service professional decide whether an individual or group approach is best. The human service professional can offer interventions concurrently or in phases, depending upon clients' needs and agency requirements. Some clients may need all three interventions while others may only need one or two. Again, an individualized approach is necessary because of the diverse backgrounds of displaced or dislocated workers.

Using Group or One-to-One Interventions.   One-to-one interventions are often needed to help clients transition into self-sufficiency. These interventions could include personal and family counseling combined with career development, and they might include role-plays and support groups. The case worker may refer clients elsewhere for these services or keep them in house. Personal or family counseling would address such issues as depression, anxiety, and substance abuse.

Providing Training and Education.   Soon-to-be dislocated workers often need encouragement to continue their training and education while still on a job that they know will soon end. Even workers whose jobs have already ended and who are receiving unemployment insurance and severance pay may need encouragement to pursue education and training. Helping these workers prepare for stable careers that will bring them similar or higher wages is extremely important. The training program should include technology skills whenever possible. Displaced or dislocated workers with limited job experience may benefit from job shadowing along with community, work experience placements that help provide social skills and training and entry-level forms of networking. Life-skills training and education, whether provided in groups or individually, also occur during this stage. These life-skills classes (i.e., time, stress, or money management; balancing work, education, and family commitments) allow participants to select and attend the classes that they feel fit their ISP goals and will increase their self-sufficiency (Duncan et al., 2003).

Offering Mentoring.   Many displaced or dislocated workers will not need mentoring and can skip this intervention entirely. However, workers who have limited skills may need to take advantage of these services, possibly including mentoring on the job to help them adjust to new employment demands.

Initiate the Employment Campaign.

The employment campaign is determined by clients' needs and goals. Some clients may need to begin their employment campaign immediately, whereas others may have time to complete work-related activities before beginning the campaign. Eliminating barriers to employment success before initiating a job campaign is the best approach, but since that is not always possible, some clients must work on several activities at once, emphasizing the need for intensive case management by the human service professional. The following sections provide an overview of considerations for the employment campaign for displaced or dislocated workers. For additional details, see Chapter 5.

The Strategic Job Search.   As mentioned previously, motivating dislocated workers to begin their job search while they are still employed and/or receiving benefits may be difficult, especially with the time constraints of working full time and trying to search for employment. Research, however, showed that on-the-job searches reduced the length of time that workers were unemployed, sometimes, eliminating it all together (Burgess & Low, 1998, 1992). For this reason, workers need encouragement to begin their job searches as soon as possible. Helping clients develop an informal network of job contacts with people already in the fields where clients plan to work is an important component of the job search, particularly for dislocated workers changing fields (Henley, 2000). Another issue for clients to consider is the geographical area of their job search. Workers with higher skills tend to job search more broadly geographically while lower-skilled workers tend to job search closer to home (Immergluck, 1998; Simpson, 1987).

To avoid possible mismatches between specific job opportunities and the capabilities of dislocated workers, human service professionals need to guide workers toward exploring job openings in new, growing fields of work. This exploration can take place individually, in small groups, or through job classes. Many dislocated workers have not had to search for a job for many years, so they may need to be refreshed on all aspects of the reemployment campaign.

Job-Search Correspondence.   While many jobs will not require a letter of application, some will. Clients need to learn how to write letters of application, as well as referral letters, reminder letters, and interview appreciation letters. Along with learning how to write a letter accepting or declining an offer, clients can role-play these situations in order to better understand the process. Role-playing also gives them a chance to practice their interpersonal skills in a safe environment.

Tailor-Made Resumes.   The resume format a client uses will vary with the client and the job. Clients who possess a great deal of experience will be able to use a chronological format. Clients who lack job experience in their chosen field will need to use functional resumes that organize their job experiences according to their skills. Creating resumes also helps clients organize and better understand themselves and allows them to focus more on their strengths instead of their weaknesses. Clients can prepare their resumes individually or in a class session, according to the needs of each client.

Interviewing Strategies.   Dislocated workers with long job tenures may need to strengthen their interpersonal skills before interviewing. Role-playing the various types of interview situations from easy to difficult and from panel to telephone is a useful intervention. Helping clients craft answers to some of the common interview questions will empower them as well. Videotaping clients during mock interviews and then critiquing the interviews provide clients with an opportunity to see themselves as others see them. If clients are moving into jobs that differ substantially from jobs they previously held, clients may be unaware of requirements for work and interview attire. Referrals to a clothing closet may be necessary for clients who lack the appropriate work or interview attire.

Change Behaviors.   A career development program is designed to help clients change behaviors that may have previously kept them from long-term employment and self-sufficiency. However, displaced or dislocated workers have been employed and self-sufficient, and they may only need assistance to enter new fields of work. Some workers may have responded to layoffs with anger, depression, anxiety, or substance abuse, and they may need help changing related behaviors. Although the specific behavior changes will vary with each person's ISP, all clients moving through this program will have had an opportunity to improve their interpersonal and work-related skills, and other skills they originally targeted for change.

Complete the Program.   Clients who have entered the program, developed their ISPs, completed the training and education that were detailed in their ISPs, and located reemployment at the same or similar wage of their previous job can be considered as having completed the program. At any time during the process, clients can drop out, but they need to be aware that their decisions probably will have a negative impact on their education and training and their eligibility for other types of assistance.

Achieve Goal of Long-Term Employment.   The clients' final goal is that of long-term reemployment in a stable position. The program staff will need to determine the working definition of *long-term* employment for use in this program. The main goal of the program is to help dislocated workers find new employment in stable fields, leaving behind all severance and unemployment benefits.

Program Evaluation

The first task the program staff faces is to determine what type of evaluation to use: process evaluation, outcome evaluation, or impact evaluation. The program evaluation component of the program has several sublevels: developing tools, tracking clients who complete the program, conducting the evaluation, analyzing and reporting survey findings, and implementing program changes. Human service professionals need to develop a variety of tools to evaluate their program. Figure 11.1. is a flow chart for the career development program model for displaced or dislocated workers. The text in each box in the figure is a factor that needs to be measured. These tools can include such items as a database of client information, intake interview sheets, case files, tracking sheets, and referral sheets. The program staff also needs to develop tools just for evaluation purposes: paper-and-pencil or telephone surveys for clients who complete the program and their employers and a method of tracking program clients and keeping their information current. The staff needs to determine when and how often to evaluate. While constant evaluation can be time-consuming, the input is invaluable for the program. In making decisions involving when to evaluate, the staff needs to consider the mobility of clients and the ability of the staff to track them. Employers who hire program participants may be surveyed at different times as well, perhaps six weeks and again six months after hiring. The staff also needs to consider how the information will be collected, analyzed, and reported. Once the program staff has made these decisions, they need to create a timeline for the entire program-evaluation process that shows every task to be accomplished, the deadline for accomplishing it, and the people responsible for accomplishing the evaluation. Once the evaluation information is collected, then the input can be used to strengthen the current program. For complete descriptions of all segments of the evaluation process, refer to Chapter 6.

Revisiting the Case Study: Martina and Michael

Conduct an Intake Interview

During the intake interview session, the human service professional needs to explore the medical, financial, educational, and employment histories of both Martina and

Michael along with their interests and values; and their views on employment, education, and family. Exploring the medical histories of all family members is important in helping the couple plan their spending over the next few months. Since both qualify as dislocated workers, the human service professional needs to help both clients work through their stages of job loss.

Martina and Michael need to consider their finances to avoid going further into debt. Because Michael has 60 days notice, the couple has the ability to curb spending now, while planning how to use any severance pay and unemployment benefits. Martina and Michael will want to meet any financial obligations they have incurred already, but they need to avoid taking on any new debt. By setting up a budget they will be better able to decide how to meet all financial obligations during this time of transition. The family must make every effort to retain medical coverage so they need to explore those options as well.

Since both Martina and Michael finished high school but have no college coursework, the human service professional will want to explore other training and education possibilities for them. Some questions to ask Michael include: What were some of your career dreams in the past? What interests or intrigues you? What type of activities do you enjoy? The human service professional needs to explore Martina's interests as well. Just because until recently Martina has stayed home with the children does not mean that she has no career dreams or aspirations. If both Michael and Martina choose to work full time, then after-school childcare may become necessary. For that reason they need to determine the family cost of both parents working full time. Obviously the cost of childcare for the younger children needs to be considered, and it may require that Martina seek higher-wage employment if she plans to work when the children are not in school. Honoring this couple's values and views of family life is extremely important as the human service professional helps move them toward reemployment.

Make Assessments

Martina and Michael need to explore their career options as separate clients. The human service professional needs to have them complete the assessments individually to maintain their confidentiality, thus empowering the couple to share their knowledge as they make plans. Determining their comfort level with technology is the first step. While Martina may have used a computer-based cash register in her job at a department store, Michael's millwright experience may not have afforded him much technology experience. Depending upon the level of automation at the paper mill, Michael may have experience with computer-controlled machine tools to fabricate parts but may lack other computer skills. The human service professional will want to research millwrights thoroughly in the *Occupational Outlook Handbook* to better understand the skills that Michael brings to the next employer. Millwrights can work either independently or as part of a team, often consulting with computer or electronics experts, engineers, electricians, and manufacturer's representatives to install machinery at the mill, so Michael's soft skills need to be explored as well. The O*NET Ability Profiler (O*NET Consortium, 2003) would help both Martina and Michael identify their strengths and the areas in which they might want to receive additional training along with pinpointing occupations to fit those strengths. WorkKeys (ACT, 1993) may also help Michael better see his current skills and how they might transfer to other jobs. Martina could also complete WorkKeys or the Career Key (Jones & Jones, 2000).

Results from the interest inventories could provide career change options for both Martina and Michael. For example, Michael could complete the GOEII (Farr, 2002) or the CEI2 (Liptak, 2002b) to identify what interest area most appeals to him. Martina could complete the Leisure to Occupations Connection Search (McDaniels & Mullins, 1999) or the Transition to Work Inventory (Liptak, 2004) to explore her levels of activity and skills in a variety of leisure activities. If both Michael and Martina are comfortable with computers, they could also complete the O*NET Career Interests Inventory (JIST Works, 2002a) to pinpoint work-related interests, what they consider important on the job, and their abilities. The Self-Directed Search (Holland, 1990, 1994, 1996a, 1996b) would also be useful with these clients. If neither wants to pursue additional education, they could complete the Voc-Tech Quick Screener (JIST Works, 2002c) to help them match interests and goals to jobs for which they can train in a short period of time. The human service professional needs to be careful, however, to steer both clients toward stable employment that will meet their financial needs.

Exploring the couples' values is another component in career assessment. Michael and Martina need to choose careers that support their values. A better fit between them and their jobs can lead to increased job satisfaction because of the similarity between their values and the values of the job. The Career Values Card Sort (Knowdell, 1998) could be used to quickly help them prioritize their values with regards to the areas of job tranquility, time freedom, work under pressure, creative expression, power, and technical competence. In addition, the O*NET Career Values Inventory (JIST Works, 2002b) could help them identify work groups that include their values while pinpointing specific jobs for further exploration. Depending once again upon their computer skills, Marina and Michael may want to use the Values-Driven Work Card Sort (Career Action Center, n.d.) or the O*NET Work Importance Locator and Profiler (O*NET Consortium, n.d.b) to help clarify values and identify possible occupations.

Michael and Marina also need to complete career-development inventories to help identify what aspects of their personal growth could hinder their ability to obtain and keep a job. This assessment component is particularly important because Michael may be moving from one field to another field that requires a different skill set. Available in both a pencil-and-paper format and online, the Barriers to Employment Success Inventory (Liptak, 2002a) will help Michael and Martina identify career planning, personal, physical, psychological, job-seeking skills, along with education and training barriers that might impede their employment and will help them develop action plans to overcome those barriers. Other values inventories for consideration include the Career Beliefs Inventory (Krumboltz, 1991), the Career Decision Scale (Osipow et al., 1987), the Career Thoughts Inventory (Sampson et al., 1996), the Career Transition Inventory (Heppner, 1998), the Salient Beliefs Review (Bloch, 2003), or the Vocational Exploration and Insight Kit (Holland et. al., 1980). The human service professional does not need to administer all of these inventories but needs to select inventories based on the clients' needs.

Determine Barriers to Success

Michael and Martina are faced with several possible barriers to career success: education and training and childcare. Upgrading Michael's skills and education is the first step to a stable, high-wage job that is necessary to support a family of six. Childcare becomes a barrier if Martina chooses to work full time. Soft skills may or may not be a barrier, depending upon Michael's position as a millwright, but these skills should not be overlooked.

Choose Interventions

Using Group or One-to-One Interventions.   Based on Michael and Martina's ISPs, one-to-one interventions may include social-skills training, family counseling, and a variety of referrals for other assistance. Michael's barriers to employment success would be addressed, as would Martina's should she decide to pursue full-time work somewhere other than the department store. One concern that needs to be addressed is Michael's anger over losing his job, which could impact both his treatment of his family, friends, and colleagues as well as his ability to detach from his current job. Helping Michael move through the stages of a job loss will be very important for him and it will help Martina as well. Developing a budget, financial counseling for any debts incurred, and referrals for any programs for which the family may qualify are other interventions the couple may need.

Finding Training and Education.   After they determine what is best for the family (i.e., should both parents go to work full time, should one work and one stay at home, and what approach is most effective in a cost-benefit analysis?), Martina and Michael will want to explore possible jobs and the available training that fit with their career aspirations and desires. Since the entire paper mill is closing, finding training and education for Michael should not be difficult if the mill provides the services required by the WARN Act (1989). The emphasis here needs to be on helping Michael look into training and education *now* rather than waiting until the job ends or until unemployment benefits are nearly finished. Martina may qualify for displaced homemaker services for help with education and training (see Chapter 7). Referring Martina to the local One-Stop Career Center and to the local community college would be good places to start, depending on her training and education needs. While Michael has worked steadily, he has worked in only one position—installing and repairing heavy machinery and equipment, including testing for proper installation. While these are transferable skills, Michael may want to explore other training and education options to update these skills. Helping him look for similar positions would be a quicker way to reemployment, but this decision needs to be based on local job availability and whether these local jobs match his skills and are stable positions. Martina's work history, while only part time at a department store, provides her with some retail and interpersonal skills and possibly some computer skills that would be useful in a variety of workplace settings. Exploring how interested she is in working, however, is very important and needs to be a family decision made after creating a budget and examining all of the possibilities.

Using Mentoring.   Martina and Michael may need only limited amounts of mentoring, if any, as they have been self-sufficient in the past. Once they have established a budget to reduce living expenses until finding reemployment, have completed any education and training, and have found stable employment, they may only need minor assistance in adjusting to their new lives. Areas that may require mentoring could include adjusting to a new career and any effects on the family. They may also need mentoring while balancing the training and education for any new job with family life and current employment.

Initiate the Employment Campaign

Michael will need to initiate his reemployment campaign before his job ends. Hopefully he will be able to move directly from one job to the other without any break in employment. If this is not possible, then he will need to initiate this campaign as soon as his job ends or after completing any education and training he undertakes. Martina faces similar decisions. While eliminating all of their barriers to employment success before beginning their campaigns is the best approach, it may not be possible. Instead, the human service professional may need to provide case management as Michael and Martina complete their education and training and participate in the interventions they chose to decrease their barriers. Helping them develop their job-search network, their resumes, and their correspondence is part of the employment campaign effort. Michael may be able to use some of his contacts from work, but he has coworkers who are also looking for reemployment, so the quicker he makes contact, the better. Michael may need to use a functional resume as he is changing careers and has some transferable skills that may prove beneficial to a new job.

Martina has a strongly developed network through her volunteer work that she will need to learn how to access to develop her job contacts. If Martina chooses to look for work, then she could either use a chronological or a functional resume depending on whether she continues in retail or changes jobs. The concern here is to help them find reemployment to meet the needs of a six-member family.

Conclusion

Human service professionals are frequently tasked with assisting displaced or dislocated workers find stable employment with wages that are similar to those of their previous positions and deal with any barriers to employment. Some recommended policy changes would help workers transition to reemployment before they become displaced and after they are displaced. Changes in economy, community, and workforce would include:

- Create an early warning system that enables the state, regions, and localities to anticipate important economic events rather than reacting to them
- Encourage states to develop economic plans to retain companies

- Increase the pressure to comply with WARN
- Increase the amount of funds targeted for displaced or dislocated workers through the WIA
- Develop policies that encourage companies to remain in the United States rather than relocate
- Provide long-term unemployment benefits to decrease the impact of dislocation on the local economy as well as on workers and their families
- Create funding subsidies for hiring the state's jobless, including displaced employees
- Develop programs to decrease the number of mortgage delinquencies and fore-closures
- Increase the availability of on-site reemployment services
- Encourage flexibility by cross-training employees
- Provide community-wide crisis intervention through support groups, retraining, and education

Changes in medical and mental health policies would include:

- Decrease the cost of COBRA
- Provide increased subsidies for medical coverage
- Establish spousal support groups

Education policy changes would include:

- Develop policies that improve K–16 education and lifelong training
- Provide alternative forms of training that are not classroom based
- Provide separate computer classes for older workers

Summary

Displaced workers, also known as dislocated workers, are those who have worked in their chosen field for a period of time who through no fault of their own lose their jobs due to company shut-downs or company relocations. Job displacement often comes as a complete surprise. Almost 8 million people were unemployed in April 2005 (U.S. Bureau of Labor Statistics, 2005) resulting in an unemployment rate of 5.2 percent that is down from 5.5 percent in April 2004. Twenty-one percent of those unemployed in April 2005 were classified as long-term unemployed. An additional 1.5 million people were marginally attached to the workforce during that time (i.e., they were available for work and had looked for work but were not actively involved in job search for four weeks prior to the report). These numbers are expected to increase as jobs continue to be outsourced to other countries and as developments in technology affect those jobs that remain stateside. Displaced or dislocated workers may need assistance moving through the five stages of job loss—denial, anger, bargaining, depression, and acceptance—and frequently face education and training barriers as they often need to change fields to become reemployed. A career development program that helps displaced or dislocated workers find reemployment includes an Individual Success Plan developed through assessments of career interests, abilities, values, and barriers to identify necessary referrals and training and education. Interventions appropriate for use with this population include one-to-one interventions, training and education, and mentoring.

Key Terms

Consolidated Omnibus Budget Reconciliation
    Act (COBRA) of 1986
Constructive discharge
Employee Benefits Security Administration
    (EBSA)
Employment loss
Health Insurance Portability and Accountability
    Act of 1996 (HIPPA)
Long-term unemployed
Mass layoff
Medicaid

Medicare
North American Free Trade Agreement-
    Transitional Adjustment Assistance
    (NAFTA-TAA)
Part-time employee
Single site of employment
State Rapid Response Dislocated Worker Unit
Trade Adjustment Assistance Reform Act
    of 2002
Worker Adjustment and Retraining Notification
    Act (WARN)

Web Resources

Note that website URLs may change over time.

Department of Labor's Layoff Services
http://www.doleta.gov/layoff

E-Laws: Employment Laws Assistance for Workers and Small Businesses
http://www.dol.gov/elaws

Employee Benefits Security Administration
http://www.dol.gov/ebsa

Free Trade Agreement and Trade Beneficiary Countries
http://www.doleta.gov/tradeact/
2002act_freetradeagreements.cfm

Trade Adjustment Assistance Reform Act of 2002
http://www.doleta.gov/tradeact/directives/
107PL210.cfm

12

The Homeless Population

No Place to Call Their Own

Case Study: George and Mary

George and Mary have been married for 20 years and have five children, ages 15, 13, 10, 8, and 3. George has worked as a maintenance supervisor for a low-income housing project for the past five years. Before that he did carpentry, roofing, and drove a dump truck for the city. George completed high school but has no additional education. Mary, also a high-school graduate, worked part time at a help-desk for a local computer distributor until a year ago. While the older three children were doing well in school, the fourth child was diagnosed with severe Attention Deficit Hyperactivity Disorder (ADHD) that required medication and a reduction in outside stimulation. To accommodate the doctor's orders, Mary gave up her part-time job to home school this child. While Mary's job loss did have some financial impact on the family, they were able to meet their rent and other expenses each month with George's salary, although little money remained once all of the bills were paid.

Then Mary received a telephone call from George's employer who explained that George had just been taken to the hospital due to labored breathing and chest pains. After two angioplasties and a week in the hospital, the cardiologist released George who returned home, newly diagnosed with diabetes, hypertension, and with 20 percent damage to his heart. While he was home recovering, the housing project changed management, and a new manager brought in a new supervisory staff and released all former employees. Once George recovered from his heart attack, but before his unemployment benefits expired, he searched for a new job. Because of his age, his medical history, and his lack of skills, the job search was unsuccessful. George then decided to stay home leaving Mary to work part time while she looked for full-time employment. During this time they ran up the credit on two high-interest credit cards to help make ends meet. They missed several rent payments, and their landlord, at first sympathetic to their plight, sent them an eviction notice that left Mary, George, and their five children on the streets. After losing all of their possessions in the eviction other than what fit in their van, the family moved to the local campground for the summer while Mary continued to work part time. At the end of the season when the campground closed, they lived in their van and frequented a local soup kitchen. They soon moved into a local shelter, but they were unable to stay as a family unit due to lack of space. George and the two sons stayed on one side of the shelter, while Mary and the three daughters stayed on the other side. The family was forced to leave, however, when the child with ADHD became uncontrollable. Once again they were living in the van.

The Homeless Population

Definition and Demographics

The Stewart B. McKinney-Vento Homeless Assistance Act of 1999 defines a homeless person as:

> an individual who lacks a fixed, regular, and adequate nighttime residence, or has a primary nighttime residence that is a publicly operated shelter, an institution providing temporary shelter, or a public or private place not designed for the accommodation of human beings. (p. 6)

Even with the assistance of a public law, defining the term *homeless* is not as simple as it may seem. Homelessness is in most cases a temporary situation not a permanent one, and each program that works with the homeless population uses a different definition. A better way to think of the homeless population is to consider the number of people who are homeless over time instead of the number of homeless people. How do we *count* the homeless? This task is just as difficult as that of defining the term homeless. How do we count those who do not have a stable residence? Or those who live in their cars? Or those who live on the streets? Or those who live in tents? The easiest way to count the homeless population is to count the number of people who live in shelters or on the streets and who access soup kitchens. However, this method only includes those people who are easy to reach and is most likely an underestimation because most shelters are full or unavailable, which leaves few options for those who lack a stable residence.

During the late 1990s, between 2.3 to 3.5 million people reported having been homeless for some time during a one-year time period. During a typical year, between 900,000 and 1.4 million children and their families are homeless. One out of every 10 poor people in America faces homelessness at some point during the year (Burt, 2001). According to the U.S. Conference of Mayors (2002), 88 percent of the 27 cities surveyed reported a 19 percent increase in requests for emergency shelter over the past year. Requests for shelter for homeless families increased by 20 percent. Requesting shelter, however, did not guarantee shelter. Thirty percent of requests for shelter by homeless people overall and 38 percent of requests by homeless families went unmet in 2002. These figures do not include the rural population that often have no or few homeless services (Burt & Aron, 2001). Seventy-one percent of the people using homeless-assistance programs live in the cities, 21 percent live in suburban or urban fringe areas, and 9 percent live in rural areas (Burt, 2001). Very little difference exists ethnically between the homeless families and single, homeless adults. Between 40 and 41 percent of the homeless are Northern European and African American, 11 to 12 percent are Hispanic, 6 to 8 percent are Native American, and 1 percent are from other ethnic backgrounds.

How poor are the homeless? According to Burt et al. (1999), single, homeless clients reported a mean income of $348 during a 30-day period, which is only 51 percent of the 1996 federal poverty level of $680/month for one person. Homeless families reported an average income of $475 during the same 30-day time period, which is 46 percent of the 1996 federal poverty level of $1,023/month for a family of three. In 1995, single, homeless clients reported only 12 percent of the average monthly income of all American households ($2,840) in the month before being interviewed, and homeless families received only 17 percent.

Reasons for Homelessness

The lack of affordable housing is the most often cited reason for homelessness (National Coalition for the Homeless, 2003; U.S. Conference of Mayors, 2002). Other reasons include mental illness and the lack of needed services, substance abuse and the lack of needed services, domestic violence, unemployment, low paying jobs, prison release, problems paying rent or utilities, poverty, downturn in the economy, changes and cuts in public assistance programs, and limited life skills (Burt et al., 1999; Hill & Stanley, 1990; National Coalition for the Homeless, 2003: Shin & Gillespie, 1994; U.S. Conference of Mayors, 2002; Wasson & Hill, 1998). Still other reasons for homelessness include having lived in a foster home, institution, or group home and having run away from one's residence for a week or more (Burt et al., 1999; Wasson & Hill, 1998).

Patterns of Homelessness

Several studies note patterns of homelessness. Nolan, Magee, and Burt (2004) found that among a group of female, single parents in a supportive housing program, almost one-third reported that they had been homeless for the first time as a child. These mothers reported an average of four homeless episodes totaling almost four years over their lifetime. Ninety-three percent of these single mothers had been homeless in the past. Findings from the National Survey of Homeless Assistance Providers and Clients also identified patterns of homelessness (Burt et al., 1999). Forty-nine percent of the homeless clients were in the first episode of homelessness at the time of the survey. Thirty-four percent of the clients had been homeless at least three times. Twenty-eight percent of the homeless episodes lasted three months or less, yet 30 percent of respondents had been homeless two or more years. Patterns of homelessness also differ between single adults and families. While both groups were equally likely to be in their first homeless episode, 34 percent of the families were in a short homeless episode compared to 15 percent of the single adult homeless.

Homeless families are surprisingly mobile. Forty-four percent reported a move to another community while they were homeless. Out of this group, 61 percent were living in the same state, and 37 percent had left the state where they first became homeless. Seventy-one percent of homeless families remained in the same community compared to 54 percent of single, homeless adults. Homeless families primarily move between their own residence, their friends or other family members, and homeless shelters. (Wasson & Hill, 1998). The four most common reasons for leaving their original community were (1) no jobs in the community, (2) no affordable housing, (3) evicted and/or asked to leave their housing, and (4) lack of services for the homeless (Burt, et al. 1999).

Barriers to Career Success

Describing a *typical* homeless person is another difficult task. Intact families can be homeless, as can single-parent families and single adults. The head of the household may or may not be working. Some people become homeless because their local factory closed, and they lost their job. Others have unstable work histories. Still others may be migrant workers, political refugees, "street people," or disaster victims. Some have been homeless off and on since they were children. Some are homeless due to an inability to pay a rent increase demanded by a new landlord. Still others are homeless to avoid abuse. Some homeless people have substance-abuse problems, but many do not. Others have mental illness problems, yet not all homeless do. Human service professionals need to understand exactly what barriers are keeping their clients from being successfully employed in order to help them get off and stay off of the streets. They also need to consider the combination of barriers, while keeping in mind that every homeless person is an individual facing different barriers from those of the next homeless person.

Structural Barriers

Availability of Stable Jobs at a Living Wage.   Research concurs that providing more jobs at a living wage will decrease the number of homeless (Aron & Sharkey, 2002; Burt et al., 2002; Hopper & Baumohl, 1998; Lindsey, 1998; U.S. Conference of Mayors, 2002). Many available jobs are low-wage and lack the benefits that are necessary for workers with families. The higher-wage, factory-based jobs often lack the stability necessary to provide continuous support and result in frequent layoffs (Burt, 2001; Burt et al., 2004; Wasson & Hill, 1998). Low-wage jobs provide few rewards for legitimate work, so some people accept other more viable, yet illegal, forms of employment for support, starting a downward spiral that leads to homelessness (Burt, 2001; Cohen & Stahler, 1998).

Local Economy.   Many factors influence homelessness, including a downturn or weakening of the economy (Burt et al., 1999; Burt et al., 2004; Jacobs, 1990; Lindsey, 1998; Rossi, 1994; Sowell, Bairan, Akers, & Holtz, 2004; U.S. Conference of Mayors, 2002). As local manufacturing companies relocate to other countries, former employees are left jobless, and the entire community is negatively affected. The general shift away from manufacturing toward a knowledge-based economy leaves few jobs available for those who now need them. This shift is particularly problematic in areas that are single-industry based. When that industry collapses, bankruptcies and foreclosures follow.

Lack of Adequate and Affordable Housing.   As the cost of living continues to rise and housing becomes even less affordable, both low- and middle-income families find it more difficult to meet their basic needs (Aron & Sharkey, 2002; Burt & Aron, 2001; Burt et al., 2004; Hopper & Baumohl, 1994; Lindsey, 1998; U.S. Conference of Mayors, 2002). In 1995, only 56 percent of families could afford to purchase a moderately priced house in their community compared to 60 percent in 1988. These families could either afford to purchase a house with cash, or they qualified for a 30-year conventional mortgage with a 5 percent down payment. Only 10 percent of renters could afford to purchase a home in 1995. Families who rent were often disqualified for several reasons including lack of down payment, excessive debt, or insufficient income. Almost 48 percent of families who rent were disqualified due to excessive debt and insufficient income to qualify for a mortgage. Several factors affect the affordability of homes. Almost 74 percent of married couples with no children under the age of 18 could afford to buy a house compared to 56 percent of married couples with children under the age of 18. Thirty-six percent of male and 22 percent of female heads of house families could afford to purchase a house in 1995. The median age of renters who were unable to afford to purchase a home is 36 years compared to 48 years for those who could afford a home purchase. Other families who could not afford to purchase a home in their community had a median age of 39 (Savage, 1999). A shortage of available homes forces people to either live beyond their means, thus existing from paycheck to paycheck, or to relocate to find affordable housing, possibly losing their jobs in the process. Several **housing choice voucher** programs are available through the **Department of Housing and Urban Development (HUD)**, but suitable *available* housing is often still limited. Those who move into shelters or live in their cars have an added barrier as they now lack a permanent address and telephone number, which are critical contact information for job applications. Employers sometimes view job candidates without a permanent address as risky, unstable, and not good candidates for a position. Yet, without a job, how is the applicant to afford a place to live?

Lack of Support Services.   Childcare and transportation are among the support services necessary to help the homeless return to work (Aron & Sharkey, 2002; Burt et al., 2002; Jacobs, 1990; Popkin et al., 2004; Sowell et al., 2004; U.S. Conference of Mayors, 2002). Many workers need affordable childcare for times other than the traditional 9 to 5 shift and after-school programs. Some workers need to learn how to locate good childcare and to trust childcare providers (Nolan et al., 2004). They may need other critical support services such as meal programs for children and families and housing assistance (U.S. Conference of Mayors, 2002). Emergency shelters, food and clothing, and showers are also important (Luck et al., 2002). Providing such support helps the homeless secure employment and transition into the workplace. Having their support systems in place can help prevent poor people from becoming homeless and ensure that those who do become homeless are only homeless once and for a short period of time (Aron & Sharkey, 2002).

Poverty.   Poverty is a direct link to homelessness as little affordable housing exists for those living at or below the poverty level (Burt et al., 2002). The 2003 poverty threshold for a single adult under the age of 65 was $9,573 a year. For a single parent, one-child family the threshold was $12,682 and for a two-parent family with two children the threshold was $18,660 (U.S. Census Bureau, 2004). In 2002 and 2003 median annual income was holding steady at $43,318, after two years of decline. The official poverty rate in 2003 was 1.5 percent or 35.9 million people (DeNavas-Walt, Proctor, & Mills, 2004). Poverty combined with a lack of affordable housing often results in between five and ten percent of poor people experiencing homelessness within a year. Extreme poverty (income at less than half the federal poverty level) is one of the most important predictors of homelessness (Burt, 2001). Poverty brings its own set of barriers to career success (i.e., social isolation, physical health, and mental health), and these barriers also need to be considered.

Organizational Barriers

Designed as places to sleep, eat, and take care of bodily hygiene, emergency shelters attempt to replicate the basic functions of a home, although on a temporary basis. Unfortunately, shelters may also become a barrier to employment as they become more institutionalized (Stark, 1994). Shelters often have strict rules to control the physical and social environment and to protect the institution from the chaos that sometimes results from numerous people living under one roof, all trying to manage their own lives. Residents are told when to eat, sleep, and shower; when to leave; and when to return. Residents lose their dignity, pride, and self-esteem because they have lost control over their lives. In the case of homeless families, children often have difficulty viewing their parents as authority figures when their parents are not allowed to make their own decisions. The role of a shelter resident, then, often conflicts with people's other roles in life such as parent, spouse or partner, and employee. Parents have no control over the food their children eat, the television their children watch, or when their children go to sleep because these decisions are made by shelter employees who begin to assume the parenting role. Since not all shelters have family housing, some families are divided by gender and stay on different sides of the shelter. Unmarried couples often find themselves separated except on weekends. Residents who are employed but whose work hours conflict with shelter policies often find it difficult to maintain their jobs and shelter residency at the same time.

Individual Barriers

Education.   The education barrier for the homeless often begins when they are children. Homeless children face several barriers to education that eventually impact their career success as adults. Homeless families often lack the documents necessary to prove residency for school enrollment. As a result, school systems turn away students until the situation is resolved. Once allowed to enroll in public school, many homeless children have a difficult time participating in federal and local programs due to their transience (Da Costa Nunez & Collignon, 1997; Pawlas, 1994). Although homeless children tend to have lower-academic performance than their peers with homes, their performance on tests of cognitive ability is comparable. Homeless children frequently score lower on math, reading, and spelling skills, but perform equally well on tests of verbal and nonverbal intelligence. Twenty percent of homeless children were held back a grade compared to 8 percent of children with homes, and 8 percent of homeless children were in special education classes compared to 1 percent of their counterparts. Rubin et al. (1996) suggested that academic performance of homeless children was affected both by maternal depression and the length of time they have spent homeless.

Aron and Sharkey's (2002) comparison of faith-based nonprofit agencies, secular nonprofit agencies, and governmental agencies reported similar needs among clients with regards to education. All three types of programs found their clients needed ESL, GED, basic literacy, family literacy, and adult education. Adult education was the most needed intervention among clients with 17.2 percent in faith-based nonprofit agencies, 18 percent in secular nonprofit agencies, and 16.4 percent in government agencies needing the service. Researchers agreed on the importance of providing education as a support service to help the homeless obtain higher-wage jobs (Aron & Sharkey, 2002; Burt, 2001; Burt et al., 2004; Jacobs, 1990; Popkin et al., 2004). According to Burt et al. (1999), 53 percent of parents in homeless families had less than a high-school education, 21 percent had completed high school, and 27 percent had some type of education beyond high school. Thirty-seven percent of single, homeless clients had less than a high-school education, 36 percent completed high school, and 28 percent had some type of education beyond high school.

Lack of Marketable Skills and Unstable Work Experience.   A lack of marketable skills and little work experience also impacts the ability of the homeless population to find high-paying, stable employment (Burt et al., 1999; Burt et al., 2002; Burt et al., 2004; Jacobs, 1990, Lindsey, 1998). Many need additional job training (Aron & Sharkey, 2002; Jacobs, 1990; Lindsey, 1998; Oliveira & Goldberg, 2002). Many of the higher-wage jobs for which the members of this population do qualify (i.e., factory, assembly-line) lack the stability necessary to provide permanent employment (Burt, 2001; Wasson & Hill, 1998). Many members of this population have experienced job layoffs due to the economy, and the increased number of job layoffs contributes to an erratic employment history (Burt et al., 2004; Rossi, 1994).

Lack of Life Skills.   In their National Survey of Homeless Assistance Providers and Clients, Aron and Sharkey (2002) reported that more than 50 percent of faith-based nonprofit, secular nonprofit, and governmental agencies had clients in need of money management skills. Between 37.6 percent of governmental agency clients and 51 percent of secular nonprofit agency clients needed conflict-resolution skills. Approximately 33 percent of agency programs reported clients needing household skills. Between 21.1 percent of governmental agencies and 29.4 percent of secular nonprofit agencies reported clients who needed parenting skills. Some programs reported that over

60 percent of their clients needed and participated in life-skills programs (Burt et al., 2004). Other programs reported that clients requested assistance in developing their life skills (Sowell et al., 2004).

Physical Health Barriers

Physical health care programs offered through shelters, soup kitchens, and other facilities frequented by the homeless often provide health screenings, immunizations, acute health care, and other services addressing physical health care. According to Aron and Sharkey (2002), governmental agencies oversee less than 15 percent of all homeless assistance programs in the United States, yet they are responsible for 59 percent of physical health programs. Burt and Aron (2001) reported providers estimated that 64,000 homeless used health services on an average day in February 1996. Burt et al. (1999) reported that 55 percent of the homeless have no health insurance; 48 percent have chronic health conditions (diabetes, cancer, high blood pressure, or arthritis); 26 percent have acute infectious conditions such as coughs, colds, bronchitis, tuberculosis, pneumonia, or sexually transmitted diseases; 8 percent have acute noninfectious conditions such as skin ulcers, lice, or scabies; and 3 percent have HIV/AIDS. In one study, over 71 percent of the homeless had seen a medical doctor within the past year, and 30.7 percent had been hospitalized due to illness or injury. Twenty-nine percent of the homeless reported that they had taken prescription medications during the previous month. Fifty-three percent of the homeless rated their health as good or excellent compared to that of other people their age, and 23 percent reported that their health had worsened over the past two years (Harris et al., 1994). According to the American Academy of Pediatrics (1996), homeless families are likely to have poor nutrition and little access to health care, and they often use emergency rooms for acute health problems. Continuity of care in this population is nonexistent. Young people who live on the streets frequently have "survival" sex. They exchange sex for shelter, food, protection, or drugs and have as a result a high incidence of HIV/AIDS (American Academy of Pediatrics, 1996).

Mental Health Barriers

A variety of mental health issues serve as barriers to employment for homeless people. Clients report depression, stress, low self-esteem, and anxiety (Bassuk et al., 2002; Holleman, et al., 2004; Popkin et al., 2004; Sowell et al., 2004). Still others report suicidal thoughts, anger, and PTSD (Bassuk et al., 2002; Burt et al., 2004; Lindsey, 1988).

Substance Abuse. People who live as part of a family unit are less likely to have mental health problems or substance-abuse problems that could contribute to their homelessness (Shin & Gillespie, 1994). Between 27 and 32 percent of faith-based nonprofit, secular nonprofit, and governmental agencies provide substance-abuse education to their clients, 20 to 26 percent provide clinical, alcohol and drug assessment, and approximately 20 percent provide alcohol and drug testing (Aron & Sharkey, 2002).

The residential instability of this population, however, makes it difficult to treat substance abuse (Cohen & Stahler, 1998). Sixty percent of clients in a study by Harris et al. (1994) reported drinking in the previous 30 days, and 33 percent reported that they used alcohol daily. Thirty-one percent had completed an alcohol-abuse treatment program in the past, and almost 64 percent of the clients had been in treatment within the past six months. Almost 31 percent were current drug users who reported using marijuana during the previous month. Over 11 percent of all respondents reported using cocaine or heroin during the previous month.

Adverse Childhood Experiences.   Twenty seven percent of homeless clients in a study by Burt et al. (1999) reported that they had been placed in foster care, a group home, or other institutional setting prior to the age of 18, often resulting in multiple placements. Twenty-nine percent reported that they had been abused or neglected as a child, and 33 percent had run away from home. Twenty-two percent reported that they had been forced to leave home for at least 24 hours before the age of 18, and 21 percent reported that their first experience of homelessness occurred prior to age 18. Clients in Cohen and Stahler's (1998) study of crack-using, African-American, homeless men reported exposure during childhood to both physical and emotional interpersonal violence. Such interpersonal violence ranged from physical abuse by their parents or guardians to witnessing the murder of a close friend or relative. Long-standing dysfunctional patterns of family abuse have been noted by a variety of researchers (Holleman et al., 2004; Lim, Andersen, Leake, Cunningham, & Gelberg, 2000; Ng & McQuistion, 2004; Rossi, 1994; U.S. Conference of Mayors, 2002).

Domestic Violence.   Thirty percent of homeless-shelter programs focused primarily on domestic violence (Aron & Sharkey, 2002). Faith-based shelters were less likely to have any special focus; only 5.2 percent focused on domestic violence. In a study examining causes for homelessness, Lindsey (1998) found that those staying in domestic-violence shelters were more likely to view leaving an abusive relationship as their reason for being homeless than were clients staying in other types of shelters. See Chapter 10 for additional information on victims of domestic violence.

Career Development Program Model: The Homeless Population

A career development program for use with homeless clients requires an individualized approach to address each client's needs and barriers to career success. The ultimate goal is the long-term employment of the client. Because of the varied backgrounds presented by this group of clients (parent/nonparent, family/single adult, employed/unemployed), human service professionals need to look at each client separately in developing a series of interventions to enhance the client's career success. Our program has three major components: the applicant pool, the Individual Success Plan (ISP), and the program evaluation. Each component will be explained in additional detail. Figure 12.1 is a graphic model of the career development program.

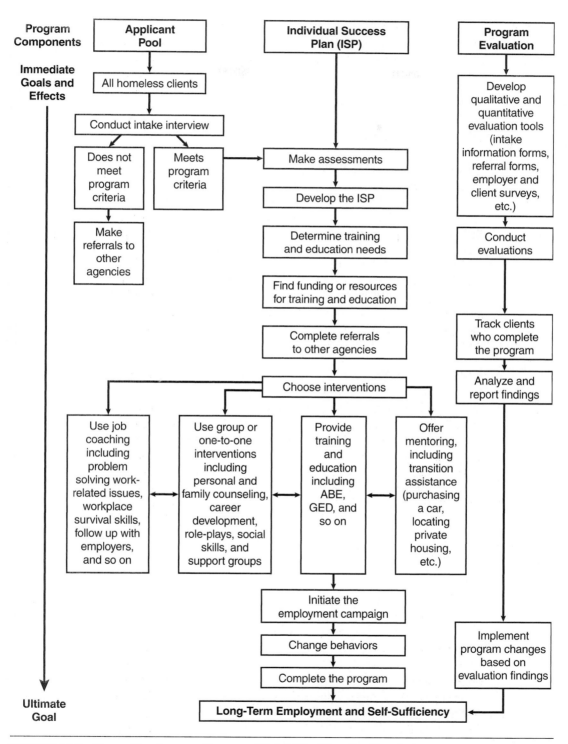

FIGURE 12.1 *Career Development Program Model: The Homeless Population*

Applicant Pool

The applicant pool includes any client who "lacks a fixed, regular, and adequate night-time residence, or has a primary nighttime residence that is a publicly operated shelter, an institution providing temporary shelter, or a public or private place not designed for the accommodation of human beings" (Stewart B. McKinney Homeless Assistance Act of 1999, p. 6). Program staff will then determine which clients fit the criteria for program participation and which do not. For example, public assistance programs offer a variety of services that target low-income, single parents, so referrals for some clients to those programs may better meet their specific needs (see Chapter 8). Referral of victims of domestic violence to a shelter offering domestic violence-related services may better serve those clients (see Chapter 10).

Individual Success Plan

Developing an Individual Success Plan (ISP) provides a personal approach to career development. Just because a job is available and a homeless client possesses the skills for that job does not mean that the job is "affordable," nor does it mean the client is ready to go to work. Since the homeless population is comprised of single parents, single adults, two-parent families, and unescorted minors, human service professionals need to view clients as individuals and determine how to best meet their needs. Developing an ISP can help clients determine the best step for them. Also, each homeless client brings a different combination of factors to the job search, and the ISP can address each of those factors while fostering a personalized approach for each client.

Make Assessments.   When working with any client, but with homeless clients in particular, the human service professional needs to consider more than just the clients' career and housing needs, but they must also consider their medical needs. Life on the street is not conducive to good physical or mental health, both of which impact clients' success in finding and holding a job. Thus, the ISP needs to include ways to address these issues as well as career issues.

Chapter 3 provides a variety of career-related assessments that can be used, based on clients' needs and background. A traditional intake interview can help identify a client's needs and indicate whether or not employment should be the first course of action for the client at this time. Because of the high incidence of repeat homeless experiences, some clients may be less secure than others because their lives are centered primarily on day-to-day survival rather than on the same 9-to-5 routine followed by some human service professionals. During the interview, the client and human service professional will examine survival strategies currently in use to determine their appropriateness. Again, the diverse backgrounds of these clients cannot be overemphasized. Since one client may have a sixth-grade education and another client may have completed several years of college, human service professionals need to be very careful in matching assessments to the client. Table 12.1 follows is a list of assessments appropriate for use in designing an ISP with clients who are homeless. Using several assessments is encouraged, but human service professionals must make sure that they use assessments that best fit the needs of their clients. (See Chapter 3 for additional details on each assessment.)

TABLE 12.1 *Career-Related Assessments for Use with the Homeless Population*

Title	Source
Ability Tests	
Ability Explorer	Harrington, J. C., & Harrington, T. F. (1996). *Ability explorer.* Itasca, IL: Houghton Mifflin.
Career Key*	Jones, L. K., & Jones, J. W. (2000). *Career key.* Raleigh, NC: Author.
Motivated Skills Card Sort	Knowdell, R. (2002, June). *Motivated skills card sort.* San Jose, CA: Career Research & Testing.
O*NET Ability Profiler*	O*NET Consortium (2003, April). *O*NET ability profiler.* Washington, DC: Author
WorkKeys	ACT, Inc. (1993). *Workkeys assessments.* Iowa City, IO: ACT.
Interest Inventories	
Career Exploration Inventory 2	Liptak, J. (2001). *Career exploration inventory 2.* Indianapolis, IN: JIST Works.
CareerExplorer CD-ROM*	JIST Works (2004). *Careerexplorer CD-ROM.* Indianapolis, IN: Author.
Guide for Occupational Exploration Interest Inventory	Farr, M. (2002). *Guide for occupational exploration interest inventory* (4th ed.). Indianapolis, IN: JIST Works.
Leisure to Occupations Connection Search	McDaniels, C., & Mullins, S. R. (1999). *The leisure to occupations connection search.* Indianapolis, IN: JIST Works.
Occupational Interests Card Sort	Knowdell, R. (2002, June). *Occupational interests card sort.* San Jose, CA: Career Research & Testing.
O*NET Career Interests Inventory*	JIST Works. (2002). *O*NET career interests inventory.* Indianapolis, IN: Author.
Self-Directed Search, Forms CP, R, & E	Holland, J. L. (1990). *Self-directed search form CP: Career planning.* Lutz, FL: Psychological Assessment Resources. Holland J. L. (1994). *Self-directed search form R.* Lutz, FL: Psychological Assessment Resources. Holland, J. L. (1996). *Self-directed search form E* (4th ed.). Lutz, FL: Psychological Assessment Resources.
Transition-to-Work Inventory	Liptak, J. J. (2004). *Transition-to-work inventory.* Indianapolis, IN: JIST Works.
Voc-Tech Quick Screener	JIST Works (2002). *Voc-tech quick screener.* Indianapolis, IN: Author.
Value Inventories	
Career Values Card Sort	Knowdell, R. (1998, June). *Career values card sort.* San Jose, CA: Career Research & Testing.
O*NET Career Values Inventory*	JIST Works (2002). *O*NET career values inventory.* Indianapolis, IN: Author.

(Continued)

TABLE 12.1   Continued

Title	Source
Values-Driven Work Card Sort	Career Action Center. (n.d.) *Values-driven work card sort.* Menlo Park, CA: Prodigy Press.
Work Orientation and Values Survey	Brady, R. P. (2002). *Work orientation and values survey.* Indianapolis, IN: JIST Works.

Career-Development Inventories

Title	Source
Barriers to Employment Success Inventory	Liptak, J. J. (2002). *Barriers to employment success* (2nd ed.). Indianapolis, IN: JIST Works.
Career Attitudes and Strategies Inventory	Holland, J. L., & Gottfredson, G. D. (1994). *Career attitudes and strategies inventory.* Lutz, FL: Psychological Assessment Resources.
Career Beliefs Inventory	Krumboltz, J. D. (1991). *Career beliefs inventory.* Mountain View, CA: CPP.
Career Thoughts Inventory	Sampson, J. P., Peterson, G. W., Lenz, J. G., Reardon, R. C., & Saunders, D. E. (1996). *Career thoughts inventory.* Lutz, FL: Psychological Assessment Resources.
Career Transition Inventory	Heppner, M. J. (1991). *Career transition inventory.* Columbia, MO: Author.
Job Search Attitude Inventory	Liptak, J. J. (2002). *Job search attitude inventory* (2nd ed.). Indianapolis, IN: JIST Works.
My Vocational Situation	Holland, J. L., Daiger, D., & Power, P. G. (1980). *My vocational situation.* Mountain View, CA: CPP.
Overcoming Barriers Card Sort Game Kit	Harney, E. E., & Angel, D. L. (1999). *Overcoming barriers card sort game kit.* Hacienda Heights, CA: WorkNet Solutions.
Reading-Free Vocational Interest Inventory: 2	Becker, R. L. (2000). *Reading-free vocational interest inventory: 2.* Columbus, OH: Elburn.
Vocational Exploration and Insight Kit	Holland, J. L., Birk, J. M., Cooper, J. F., Dewey, C. R., Dolliver, H., Takai, R. T., & Tyler, L. (1980). *The vocational exploration and insight kit.* Mountain View, CA: CPP.

Miscellaneous

Title	Source
Elevations ® Manual Card Sort System	Scully, H. (2003, August). *Elevations manual card sort system.* Roseville, CA: Author.
Individual Employment Plan	Ludden, L. L., & Maitlen, B. (2002). *Individual employment plan.* Indianapolis, IN: JIST Works.
Vocational Decision-Making Interview	Czerlinsky, T., & Chandler, S. (1999). *Vocational decision-making interview.* Indianapolis, IN: JIST Works.

*Use only if client is computer literate.

Develop the ISP. Once the assessments are completed, the human service professional and the client create the ISP. By incorporating information gained from the intake interview, from discussions, and from the assessments, the human service worker assists the client in identifying specific barriers to employment success. As mentioned previously, the human service professional must address issues of mental and physical health and make referrals where necessary. After helping clients recognize their barriers to career success, the human service professional needs to integrate clients' values into the planning process along with personal and career goals. Allowing clients to take an active role in the creation of these plans empowers them and assists them in moving toward self-sufficiency. Together, the client and worker determine what barriers to address first and they construct a timeline that lists each goal to be accomplished. They set mini goals for the client to meet along the way that will help the client see what progress is being made and will allow for revision and redesigning of the plan as necessary.

Determine Training and Education Needs. Aron and Sharkey (2002) reported that almost 52 percent of clients in governmental-based agencies needed job-skills assessments compared to 49.7 percent of clients receiving assistance from secular nonprofit agencies and 42.4 percent from faith-based nonprofit agencies. With assessment results in front of them, the human service worker and client then explore what type of training and education the client needs to reach his or her goals. Clients who dropped out of school may need to complete an Adult Basic Education (ABE) program or a General Equivalency Diploma (GED) prior to or during the job search or other training. In some cases clients may complete their education while they receive training and even after they have obtained a job. Clients who completed high school or have a GED may qualify to immediately enter a training program offered through the community college or a local proprietary school.

For the more experienced clients, reviewing the interest inventories' results will provide career leads for the necessary training and education. Other clients may need more exposure to different jobs or even basic job-skills training before they can consider the various careers available. Training and education are determined by the job openings with the local employers, the economy, and by the funding available through the various local supports.

Assessment results will likely dictate other areas of necessary training and education such as life skills. These skills can be offered to clients either in small groups or one-on-one, allowing for a more individualized fit as necessary. Providing clients with a list of possible training or educational group topics (i.e., nutrition and health, building family strengths, balancing work with family, stress management, time management, money management, parenting skills) from which to choose helps to empower clients to take responsibility for their life choices and ownership in their successes.

Find Funding or Resources for Training and Education. Several different federal grant programs help local agencies to provide services and funding, including funding for job training and education and financial assistance for housing. Human service professionals need to familiarize themselves with those local resources. Federally funded One-Stop Career Centers, for example, provide funding for training and education for eligible adults through Individual Training Accounts arranged through One-Stop. These accounts supplement financial aid already available through other intuitions, or when no financial aid is available, these accounts may cover the cost of all training. Individuals who are unable to obtain grant assistance from other sources to pay for their training and those who need financial assistance beyond that which is available through grants may qualify for some financial assistance through Workforce Investment Act funds. For these individuals, the case manager will be responsible for coordinating those funds and the available services. To access these funds, the local One-Stop center must refer the client for training once all other funding has been exhausted (U.S. Department of Labor, 2000; U.S. Government Accounting Office, 2003a). Life-skills training and education are often available in a variety of settings and at no cost. Again the human service professional must coordinate these efforts.

Complete Referrals to Other Agencies.   Interagency cooperation is necessary to assure that clients' needs for food and shelter, medical care, mental health, and education and training are met. A holistic approach to the state of the homeless addresses the interplay of all these factors rather than concentrating on only finding food and shelter for clients. Human service professionals need to be aware of the local providers for all support services and must refer clients accordingly to create the best assistance program possible for their clients. While developing the ISP, the client and professional may identify certain behaviors or events that require referral to other agencies. For example, clients who are victims of domestic violence need referrals for domestic-violence services. Other referrals a client may need could include medical, substance-abuse or mental-health issues. Clients may need funding for childcare and transportation along with referrals for Supplemental Security Income (SSI); Special Supplemental Nutrition Program for Women, Infants, and Children (WIC Program); and housing.

Choose Interventions.   The career development program for the homeless population has four categories of interventions: job coaching, one-to-one interventions, training and education, and mentoring. The human service professional and the client together can determine whether an individual or a group approach is best. These interventions may be offered concurrently or in phases, depending upon the individual needs of the client as well as the requirements of the local agency. Some clients may need all four interventions while others may only need one or two. Again, the need for an individualized approach cannot be stressed too much due to the diversity of the homeless population.

Using Job Coaching.   Also known as supported employment, job coaching is a frequent intervention in rehabilitation counseling (Hagner, Rogan, & Murphy, 1992; Wittenburg & Favreault, 2003). Job coaching can be modified to help homeless clients learn the necessary workplace and social skills to overcome barriers to success. The job coach can be an agency employee or a trained volunteer. The job coach addresses problem solving with work-related topics, explores workplace survival skills, and meets with employers about their employees. Since employment retention is frequently a barrier to success, the job coach's overall task is helping the client transition successfully into the workforce (Burt, 2001; Burt et al., 2004; Wasson & Hill, 1998). This task includes meeting regularly with clients both on and off the job site to address clients' concerns before they affect employment. Such concerns could include how to deal with anger on the job, how to handle childcare or transportation difficulties, or how to handle being late or absent from work. The topics the job coach addresses do not include the skills training that the employer provides. The employer meets regularly with the job coach and is available to meet with the coach and the client as needed.

Using Group or One-to-One Interventions.   In some instances, one-to-one interventions are necessary to help clients transition into self-sufficiency. This intervention involves personal and family counseling combined with career development. It might also include role-plays and support groups. The case manager may refer clients elsewhere for these services or keep them in house. Personal and family counseling would address such issues as substance abuse, domestic violence, PTSD, depression, and family violence. Clients who are eligible for TANF benefits must abide by the guidelines of that program, which may mean that clients will have to go to work before addressing other issues of support. Depending upon the degree of work exposure clients have had in the past, their career exploration interventions could include job shadowing, unpaid internships, and even field trips to local businesses, organizations, and agencies (U.S. Department of Labor, 2000; Wilkins, 2002).

Providing Training and Education.   In addition to being a step in the career development program, training and education are also interventions. Clients may need encouragement to continue their training while on the job and to pursue and upgrade their education. Encouragement is even more important when clients are living in shelters and need to be empowered in their decision-making. Placing clients in community-work positions could help them develop social skills and provide training for those clients who are unable to secure employment immediately. These placements could also provide references and entry-level forms of networking. Clients also receive training on the job, and research has shown that working next to higher-wage employees often gives low-wage employees an opportunity to gain industry-specific skills that could help them advance later (Andersson, Lane, & McEntarfer, 2004). Life-skills training and education, whether given in a class format or individually, occur during this stage. These life-skills classes (i.e., time, stress, or money management; parenting skills; balancing work and family commitments) allow participants to select and attend the classes that they feel fit their ISP goals and will increase their self-sufficiency (Burt et al., 2002; Duncan et al., 2003; U.S. Conference of Mayors, 2002). A Job Club and support groups could also be a part of the education component. Clients who are employed but are uncomfortable with a job-coach approach could opt to attend these skills-training classes instead of working with a job coach.

Offering Mentoring.   After clients have been employed for several months in a stable position, they may be ready for the next level of intervention services—providing transition assistance such as teaching clients how to locate private housing, buy a car, or open a bank account. Once clients have a steady income and have adjusted to the workplace, they may need help taking these next steps to self-sufficiency. The mentor can be an agency employee or a trained volunteer who develops networks with local businesses and community organizations to provide these services to clients. These important networks could include bank employees who are willing to guide clients through the process of opening their first bank accounts. Another useful contact is a local car dealership that is willing to help clients establish credit and develop a payment plan so they can purchase affordable and safe transportation. Enlisting the aid of a local mechanic could prove helpful as well. Still other contacts are landlords or realtors who are willing to walk clients through the process of renting or buying a home, as well as people who can help with the variety of housing transition programs available for the homeless. The mentor would develop a network of such contacts for the clients to use and would facilitate meetings and offer whatever other assistance clients need at the time.

Initiate the Employment Campaign.   The employment campaign begins at different times for different clients, depending on their needs. Chronic homeless clients might have to address other barriers to career success first, but clients who qualify for public assistance through TANF may need to begin their employment campaign immediately. While eliminating barriers to employment success before initiating a job campaign is the best approach, this approach is not always possible. Some clients may have to work on several activities at once, which will require intensive case management. The next sections provide an overview of considerations for homeless clients during their employment campaign. For additional details, see Chapter 5.

The Strategic Job Search.   Secular nonprofit agencies report that 41.9 percent of their clients need assistance with their job search, compared to 40.6 percent of governmental agency clients and 39.3 percent of faith-based nonprofit agency clients (Aron & Sharkey, 2002). Human service professionals can use the information collected from the assessments and from the intake interview to help clients explore the importance of their values and goals on the job-search process. Some clients may need help setting goals and developing a plan to meet those goals. Other clients may need reminding that they do not yet have the skills for the jobs of their choice, and they must work toward developing those skills. Clients should understand that every step in their plan leads them closer to their goal of employment and self-sufficiency. In their job search clients should explore whether or not their values are in line with each of the jobs they are considering. Once clients better understand themselves, they can begin to understand the career choice itself and the education and skills it entails. Another key to employment success is understanding the employer's needs, and clients must learn how to anticipate and meet those needs. Because the job market varies with the location, human service workers can use their networks to help clients navigate the local job market. To help the case worker must know what jobs are available and who is hiring. Local employment agencies and local One-Stop Career Centers can help with this task. Clients can use job search classes here, and they can become involved in community and volunteer work.

Job-Search Correspondence.   While some jobs will not require a letter of application, many jobs will. Clients seeking such jobs should learn how to write letters of application, as well as referral letters, reminder letters, and interview appreciation letters. Along with teaching clients how to write a letter accepting or declining an offer, human service workers can use role-playing to help clients better understand the interview process and to give them a chance to practice their interpersonal skills.

Tailor-Made Resumes.   The resume format a client uses will vary with the client. For example, clients who have a great deal of work experience and are in their current homeless episode due to downsizing will be able to use a chronological format. Clients who lack job experience or a stable job history will need to use functional resumes to organize their job experiences according to their skills. Creating resumes also helps clients to organize their work experience and better understand themselves, which will allow them to focus more on their strengths instead of their weaknesses. Clients can complete their resumes individually or in a class session.

Interviewing Strategies.   Interpersonal skills are sometimes a weakness in the homeless population (again, depending upon the client), so they would benefit from role-playing the various types of interview situations, from easy to difficult and from panel to telephone. Helping clients craft answers to some of the common interview questions will empower them as well. Videotaping clients during mock interviews followed by a critique of the interview provides clients with an opportunity to see themselves as others see them. The human service worker should stress appropriate interview attire because clients may not be aware of the necessity to dress professionally or that the attire may vary depending upon the job. Clients may not have appropriate work attire, much less interview attire, so referrals to clothing closets may be necessary for both.

Change Behaviors.   Participation in the career development program for the homeless is designed to help clients change behaviors that may have previously kept them from long-term employment and self-sufficiency. Although specific behavior changes will vary with each person's ISP, all clients moving through this program will have had an opportunity to improve their interpersonal and work-related skills and other skills they originally targeted for change. When clients' behaviors change, hopefully, the change will show in clients' ability to find and hold a job and find permanent housing, as they eventually move toward self-sufficiency.

Complete the Program.   Clients who entered the program, developed their ISPs, completed the training and education that were detailed in their ISPs, located permanent housing, and exhibited changes in behavior that led to employment are considered to have completed the program. At any time during the process, clients can drop out of the program, but they need to be aware that their decisions may negatively impact their housing and their eligibility for other types of assistance. Chronic homeless people often have more experience with being homeless than of being self-sufficient, and they may need several tries to gain full-time, stable employment. Some clients may have to cycle through several steps of the program later as they move from a low-skill level employment to employment requiring more advanced skills.

Achieve Goal of Long-Term Employment.   Clients' final goal is that of long-term employment and self-sufficiency. The program staff will need to determine the working definition of *long-term* employment. Generally, when clients have moved from their shelter into permanent housing and are no longer receiving public assistance (TANF, housing, Medicaid, Food Stamps, WIC), for at least a year, and they are able to fully support themselves and their family members, they could be considered self-sufficient with long-term employment.

Program Evaluation

The first task of the program staff will be to determine what type of evaluation is appropriate: process evaluation, outcome evaluation, and/or impact evaluation. The program evaluation component has several sublevels: developing tools, tracking clients who complete the program, conducting the evaluation, analyzing and reporting findings, and implementing program changes. Human service professionals need to develop a variety of tools to evaluate their program. Figure 12.1 is a flow chart for the career development program model for use with the homeless population. The text in each box in the figure is a factor that needs to be measured. Measuring tools can include such items as anecdotal interview record forms, client information, intake sheets, case files, tracking sheets, logs, interview protocols, and questionnaires. The program staff also needs to decide what other tools should be developed just for evaluation purposes. For example, the staff may need to construct paper-and-pencil or telephone surveys for clients who complete the program and their employers and determine how to track clients and keep their information current. Another important task for the staff is to decide when to evaluate. For example, programs and their participants can be evaluated at several points in the program: midway, upon completion, then one year or more later. While this constant evaluation can be time-consuming, the evaluation input is invaluable for the program. When making decisions involving when to evaluate, the staff needs to consider their ability to track clients. The staff may also survey at different times employers who hire program participants, perhaps six weeks after they hire clients and then six months later. The staff also needs to consider how they will collect, analyze, and report the information. Once the program staff has made these decisions, they need to create a timeline for the entire program evaluation process that shows every item the client should accomplish, the deadline for doing so, and the person responsible. Once the evaluation information is collected, the input can be used to strengthen the current program. For complete descriptions of all segments of the evaluation process, refer to Chapter 6.

Revisiting the Case Study: George and Mary

Conduct an Intake Interview

During the intake interview session, the human service professional needs to explore the housing, medical, financial, educational, and employment histories of both George and Mary along with their interests and values; and their views on employment, education, and family. Finding a shelter where the family can stay together as a family unit is the first step. This family has been each other's support for several months, and allowing them to live together as a family strengthens their familial bonds and will help empower them during this crisis. Helping them arrange for emergency housing would be the start to getting them back on their own feet as a family unit without the stigma of living in a shelter where they cannot even live together.

The human service professional needs to explore medical needs of George and Mary along with those of the child with ADHD. Because the stress of being the sole bread winner has fallen on Mary's shoulders since George's heart attack, her physical, mental, and emotional health needs must also be considered. Making sure that all medication prescriptions have been filled and that they are being taken correctly is important. Since the family has such a reduced income, they may well have to choose to buy food over medications. Determining the remainder of the family's medical needs is also important. The child with severe ADHD may have some other disabilities or needs that should be addressed. The human service worker should not overlook the stresses of living in a tent for several months, possibly without adequate nutrition, clothing, and medical attention. To reduce the possibility of future homelessness, the human service professional should explore how the family is adapting as a whole to being homeless and see to it that all children are receiving their education.

The human service professional needs to consider finances and the family's debts. When George and Mary were evicted, they were behind on their rent and probably were behind on other bills as well, including the credit cards with high-interest rates. Once they are employed, they will have to meet those obligations, so it is important to explore those debts and work to keep them from being turned over to collection agencies. If the debts have gone to collection agencies, then they must explore various methods of repayment and possible bankruptcy, and the case worker should make necessary referrals. Setting up a budget will help George and Mary better plan to meet all financial obligations.

Since both Mary and George finished high school but have no college education, the human service professional may want to explore other training possibilities for them. Because George was working full time until his heart attack, his self-esteem may be affected because he is unable to work. Retraining for another job would help him emotionally as well as financially. Exploring whether or not one of the parents still needs to stay home with their child who has ADHD is also important. The human service professional should explore the feasibility of after-school programs for the younger children and the level of disability of the child with ADHD to determine what type of program would best meet the needs of the children and family. Caring for a child with ADHD can be very wearing, and depending upon the extent of George or Mary's ability to handle stress, finding some sort of affordable childcare may benefit the entire family. The human service professional should consider the questions: What are George and Mary's dream occupations? What have they enjoyed doing? Does one of them want to stay home with the children? What are their plans for the children? Do they see college in their children's future? What is the family cost of both parents working? Having one parent stay at home may be more feasible for the family than dealing with the emotional and financial costs of childcare. Honoring George and

Mary's values and views of family life is extremely important as the human service professional strives to help this family start anew on the road to self-sufficiency.

Make Assessments

The human service professional must take great care to treat George and Mary as separate clients although part of a unit. They must complete the assessments individually to maintain their confidentiality, and each client will decide what to discuss with the other. Although Mary is computer literate because of her job at the help desk for a local computer distributor, the human service professional will need to determine George's comfort level with the computer. The Career Key (Jones & Jones, 2000) would be a good place for Mary to begin because it utilizes her computer skills and would help her explore her interests, skills, and values while linking her directly to the *Occupational Outlook Handbook* (U.S. Department of Labor, n.d.) for career exploration. If George has the computer skills, then this assessment would be appropriate for him as well. Another option they could use for exploring abilities would be Knowdell's (2000) Motivated Skills Card Sort that helps pinpoint the functional-transferable skills central to their career satisfaction and success. Working with this card sort will help George and Mary explore their motivations to use these skills or develop and strengthen others. The O*NET Ability Profiler (O*NET Consortium, 2003) might be useful in helping George and Mary to identify their strengths and the areas in which they want to receive additional training along with identifying occupations to fit those strengths. Because George has a skilled-labor background, WorkKeys (ACT, 1993) may help him recognize his current skills and see how he can transfer them to other jobs despite his medical history.

The knowledge George and Mary gained from interest inventories can be useful because George may be considering a career change, and Mary is looking for full-time employment. They would find the CareerExplorer CD-ROM (JIST Works, 2004) useful to pinpoint their job interests and link them to *Occupational Outlook Handbook* (U.S. Department of Labor, n. d.) to review job descriptions on-line. The case worker must consider George's technology skills before giving him a computer-based assessment to avoid giving him a task he cannot complete and chance weakening his self-esteem. If the case worker chooses a more traditional form of assessment, the Guide for Occupational Exploration Interest Inventory (Farr, 2002) could match Georges's interests to O*NET job titles in a paper-and-pencil format. Another assessment to consider is the Leisure to Occupations Search (McDaniels & Mullins, 1999) because both Mary and George are, in a way, displaced homemakers who now have to upgrade their job skills. While the human service professional would not want to use all of these assessments, if George and Mary want to explore other career options, the Self Directed Search Form R (Holland, 1996) or Form CP (Holland, 1990) as well as the Transition to Work Inventory (Liptak, 2004) would help to assess their career interests. The Transition to Work Inventory (Liptak, 2004) would help them identify interests they have developed at home that could lead to a possible job. They might investigate opening their own business, an option that could one day allow them to work from the home and be with the children.

Helping George and Mary explore their value system will assist them in choosing not just a career, but also a specific job that will fit with those values. The Career Values Card Sort (Knowdell, 1998a) would help them to prioritize their values in five minutes. Using the Values-Driven Work Card Sort (Career Action Center, n. d.) they could explore their values as part of a work situation while looking at organizational values.

Using career-development inventories, George and Mary can explore any factors that might hinder their personal growth and impact their ability to maintain a job. The Barriers to Employment Success Inventory (Liptak, 2002a) identifies personal, physical and psychological, career planning, job-seeking skills, and education and training barriers to career success, including low self-esteem and substance abuse. The Career Attitudes and Strategies Inventory (Holland & Gottfredson, 1994) helps to identify the likelihood of job stability while exploring job satisfaction, interpersonal abuse, work involvement, family commitment, skill development, risk-taking style, dominant style, geographical barriers, and career worries. If the human service professional detects any negative thinking in career problem-solving and decision-making with George or Mary, then the Career Thoughts Inventory (Sampson et al., 1996) can be useful. How motivated are George and Mary to find employment? How confident are they in their ability to find employment? Depending on what information surfaced through the intake interview and other discussions, Heppner's (1998) Career Transition Inventory may help the clients explore other barriers to their career success. Depending on successful use of previous card sorts, George and Mary could use the Overcoming Barriers Card Sort Kit (Harney & Angel, 1999) to help them learn to think like an employer while they identify their own barriers.

Determine Barriers to Success

A lack of stable housing is an extremely significant barrier. George and Mary need a safe roof over their heads and an opportunity to live as a family unit again. Finding more permanent housing is the first item on their list, but it remains a barrier until they succeed. Without a stable residence, they have no permanent address to put on job applications, and education for their children becomes more difficult to access. Without an education, the children become increasingly likely to become homeless again as adults.

Based on intake discussions, George may have several barriers to employment, none of which have to be permanent. Probably the first barrier is his medical condition. Just how ill is he? How much can he really do? These are questions that an assessment by a medical professional can help answer. The medical assessement will determine to what degree his health is a barrier to employment. Because his work history consists primarily of labor jobs, George will definitely need more training and possibly education to find another job that fits with his medical condition. His state of mind, in particular his level of self-esteem, is an important consideration. Having been the main breadwinner for many years, he may not be adjusting well to Mary in that role while he stays at home.

Mary has barriers of her own. As a displaced homemaker of sorts, she is now responsible for making enough money to support a family of seven—a tall order for any breadwinner. On top of this she needs a job that provides medical coverage, sick leave, and other such benefits. Having been a stay-at-home-mom for several years, she may harbor some resentment about having to work full time. She may have some well-founded fears about leaving her husband every day while she goes to work. She may also need more skills and education to move into a full-time job.

Childcare and transportation may be barriers as well. While some of the children are old enough to stay at home without parental supervision after school, the younger ones are not. Some type of childcare or after-school programs may be necessary for the younger two children. In particular, the child diagnosed with severe ADHD needs to be reevaluated to determine what other treatments might be possible and helpful. If the child truly needs to be home-schooled due to the severity of the ADHD, then this could be another barrier for the family. Finding suitable programs for this child will become a priority. Since they only have the van, transportation may be a barrier for them as they find a way to survive with one vehicle.

George and Mary's financial status is another possible barrier to employment. Depending upon the size of any outstanding bills, George and Mary may be dealing with garnisheed paychecks and possible bankruptcy. Making sure they can afford continued medical treatment and prescriptions is another financial obligation. They will need to set up a budget to address these obligations and determine the best approach for paying their debt. They may discover that it is more efficient for one of them to stay home than for both to work and pay for childcare and/or after-school programs. They need to investigate additional avenues of support as part of this exploration.

The human service professional needs to address these barriers to employment success along with any others that surfaced through the assessments and to create separate ISPs for George and Mary. Both ISPs, then, would address these barriers to employment while incorporating their personal and their career goals and values.

Choose Interventions

Using Job Coaching.   George and Mary may not need job coaching because they both have had successful careers in the past. They appear to have the necessary social skills and workplace skills, so any job coaching would be short-lived and utilized to make sure they adjust to their new jobs. Their primary interventions will be in the other categories of one-to-one interventions, education and training, and mentoring.

Using Group or One-to-One Interventions.   Helping the family adjust to this new life will be the main focus of this intervention. This family has experienced several crises one right after the other: a child diagnosed with a disability that required Mary to stay at home thus losing her income; George's heart attack and subsequent diagnoses of diabetes, hypertension, and heart damage; Mary's return to work after she had been a stay-at-home mom for several years; and then eviction, life in a homeless shelter, separation of the family; and life in their family van. The children have been pulled way from their friends, school, and activities, and thrust into a world where they wonder where they will sleep and eat. Now they will have to adjust to either one or both parents working full time, a new place to live, and a new community. To address these problems, family therapy and support groups for the parents and children are important interventions to help this family adjust and to serve as a preventative for future barriers to success. Other family-based interventions may include, but are not limited to, referrals for financial and legal counseling, along with referrals for any assistance programs for which the family may qualify such as Family Self-Sufficiency, Section 8 housing, SSI for the child, food stamps, Medicaid, and WIC.

Upon considering George's view of his medical problem, the human service worker may suggest support groups for both him and Mary. By having George spend time with other heart attack victims with similar amounts of heart damage, he will see that he is not alone and that he would be able to do some jobs. Mary may need support to help her deal with her fear of losing her husband and with the loss of their home and her way of life, coupled with whatever resentments she may possess.

Finding Training and Education. Both George and Mary have been employed, and George has a solid work history for at least five years. After they determine what is best financially for the family (i.e., should both parents go to work full time, should one work and one stay at home), George and Mary need to explore possible jobs and available training that fit with their career aspirations and needs. Once they have a home and can live as a family, they will want to begin the training and education they need to become self-sufficient. Finding funding is paramount because they have no money to spare for education and training at this point. The local One-Stop Career Center and the local community college are good places for them to start, depending on their training needs. George has supervisory skills from his years as a maintenance supervisor, carpentry and roofing skills, and driving skills. While he may not be able to do much physical labor, he could still supervise in some capacity. Helping him find a position that is consistent with his medical condition would be a quicker way to employment than retraining, but this decision belongs to George and Mary. Mary's part-time work history provides her with some office skills and computer background that may be useful in a variety of workplace settings. The case worker should explore how interested Mary is in doing this type of work. Since she is currently employed, Mary will need to continue until she can either find improved employment, increase her job skills and move elsewhere, or until George resumes the main responsibility for family support. Again, this family decision must be made by George and Mary after they create a budget and examine all of their possibilities.

Using Mentoring. Mentoring might not be necessary to help George and Mary in their transition since they have been self-sufficient in the past. After they have established a budget, obtained medical assistance, made their decisions, and found stable housing and employment, they may need only minor assistance in adjusting to their new lives.

Initiate the Employment Campaign

Once George and Mary have found stable housing (whether temporary or permanent) and have decided who will work, they will initiate their employment campaign.

Obviously eliminating all of their barriers to employment success before they begin the campaign is the best approach but that may not always be possible. Instead, the human service professional may need to provide case management as George and Mary work to find childcare or after-school programs, housing, and other services to lessen the effect of their barriers. Helping George and Mary develop their job-search network, their resumes, and their correspondence is part of this campaign. While they have worked in the past, both George and Mary have some gaps on their resumes, and they will need to consider this when developing their resumes. If George searches for supervisory positions, he will probably be able to use a chronological resume due to his stable job history. If he changes careers, he may opt for a functional or skills resume. Mary has more current job experience, and she can also use a skills resume. The goal here is to help them find employment that meets the needs of a seven-member family with some medical problems.

Conclusion

One out of every 10 poor people in America faces homelessness at some point during the year (Burt, 2001). As the cost of living continues to rise, both low- and middle-income families are finding it more and more difficult to meet their basic needs and housing becomes even less affordable. In 1995 only 56 percent of families could afford to buy a moderately priced house in their own community. Only 10 percent of renters could afford to purchase homes. Most were disqualified because of no down payment, excessive debt, or insufficient income. A shortage of available and affordable homes combined with a shortage of living-wage jobs results in homelessness. Human service professionals are frequently tasked with helping homeless clients find stable housing while dealing with their additional barriers to employment. Some recommended policy changes would help homeless families and single adults in their transition to self-sufficiency. Changes in economic, community, and workforce policies would include:

- Raise minimum wage to a living wage
- Enact policies to create more jobs at a living wage and increase household incomes
- Rebuild troubled communities by building affordable housing and increasing housing subsidies
- Increase affordability of houses by (1) lowering interest rates, (2) requiring a lower down payment for home purchasers, and (3) providing a down payment subsidy to home buyers
- Improve opportunities for home ownership among minority populations

Changes in medical or mental-health policies would include:

- Provide comprehensive and integrated treatment approaches for health care, mental health, and substance-abuse agencies

- Fund primary health care grants to provide comprehensive health care for all homeless people with a focus on the continuity of preventive care

Organizational policy changes would include:

- Increase benefit levels and participation in food stamps
- Increase basic support services
- Provide community-based care for the disabled
- Involve the medical profession in development of national guidelines for health and safety standards for temporary residences that house the homeless
- Coordinate services for the homeless

Education policy changes would include:

- Increase access to education for children of homeless to reduce their likelihood of homelessness as adults
- Create communities of learning for adults and children

Summary

The homeless population, while difficult to define and measure, is growing constantly. They may live in tents, in cars, on the streets, under bridges, or in shelters. They are all ages, all ethnicities, and all education levels. Homelessness is attributed to several factors: lack of affordable housing, lack of jobs at a living wage, mental illness, substance abuse, domestic violence, prison release, unemployment, limited life skills, poverty, difficulties in paying rent and utilities, and changes or cuts in public assistance programs. The homeless population comes with several patterns: some people being homeless repeatedly, some only once, and others move from friend to friend. All of these characteristics serve as barriers to employment and need to be addressed in order to help the homeless client move to self-sufficiency. A career development program model presents the development of an Individual Success Plan for each participant that includes assessments of career abilities, interests, barriers, and values; interagency referrals; interventions such as job coaching, one-to-one interventions, training and education, and mentoring; followed by an employment campaign that leads to long-term employment.

Key Terms

Department of Housing and Urban Development (HUD)

Housing choice vouchers

Stewart B. McKinney-Vento Homeless Assistance Act

Web Resources

Note that website URLs may change over time.

Beyond Shelter
http://www.beyondshelter.org

Center for Urban Community Services
http://www.cucs.org

Corporation for Supportive Housing
http://www.csh.org

Health Care for the Homeless Information Resource Center
http://www.bphc.hrsa.gov/hchirc

Homebase: Center for Common Concern
http://www.homebaseccc.org

Homes for the Homeless: Institute for Children and Poverty
http://www.homesforthehomeless.com

National Alliance to End Homelessness
http://www.naeh.org

National Center for Homeless Education
http://www.serve.org/nche

National Center on Family Homelessness
http://www/familyhomelessness.org

National Coalition for Homeless Veterans
http://www.nchv.org/index.cfm

National Coalition for the Homeless
http://www.nationalhomeless.org

National Healthcare for the Homeless Council
http://www.nhchc.org

National Law Center on Homelessness and Poverty
http://www.nlchp.org

National Resource Center on Homelessness and Mental Illness
http://www.nrchmi.samhsa.gov

The Partnership for the Homeless
http://www.partnershipforthehomeless.org

U.S. Department of Health and Human Services
http://www.hhs.gov

U.S. Department of Housing and Urban Development
http://www.hud.gov/offices/cpd/index.cfm

13

Older Workers

Choosing Work Over Retirement

Case Study: Wayne

Lorna and Wayne had retirement all planned: Lorna would retire from her administrative assistant job two years before Wayne was due to retire. They would use her **pension** to pay off the last of their bills, leaving them almost debt free when Wayne retired a few years later. They then planned to spend most of their time traveling around the country in their camper, visiting all of the places of their dreams. Every night they thumbed through magazines marking the various places they wanted to visit: the Grand Canyon, the Blue Ridge Parkway, the California Redwoods, Natchez Trace Parkway, and Route 66, to name a few. They made plans for Tom, their adult child with disabilities, to move in with his sister Susan and her family when Lorna and Wayne had both retired. Wayne's mother, although elderly, was living independently and would not be a particular concern because Wayne had siblings who could help her if needed. Unfortunately, Lorna died of lung cancer several years before she would have retired, and she left Wayne with her hospital bills and the sole responsibility for caring for an elderly parent and an adult child with disabilities.

Dealing with the adult child with disabilities proved to be very difficult for Wayne as he struggled with how to meet his son's needs while he dealt with his own grief for Lorna. Then Wayne's mother was hospitalized with a stroke. The doctors wanted her to move into assisted living, but she refused and demanded to be returned to her home. Although Wayne's siblings help with their mother as they can, Wayne is worried that she will have another stroke, and no one will be able to take care of her and help her obtain medical treatment.

Then Wayne retired at age 55 from his job of 30 years at the local shipyard. For the first few months, Wayne adjusted to his new life, although it was not the life he had originally planned. His daughter Susan announced that she could no longer take responsibility for her brother because she was now working full time, had three young children, and lacked the resources to care for him. While Tom can care for himself at home, for example, dress himself and fix sandwiches, he has had minimal training and experience that would help him be self-sufficient. Wayne discovered that retirement was not what he expected. Even though he receives survivor's benefits from Lorna's social security, money is still very tight. Wayne tried to decrease his expenses by selling his pickup truck and buying a smaller, more economical car. He sold the camper and even considered selling his mortgage-free home to buy a smaller one and save some of the money. In spite of his efforts, Wayne still had trouble making ends meet and decided to search for a job. Wayne has a high-school diploma and prior to his job at the shipyard, he worked as a house painter, a carpenter, and a roofer. He then attended a local community college and completed an electrician's program that helped him obtain his job at the shipyard.

The Older Worker Population

Description

In 2002, according to the U.S. Census Bureau, more than 59 million individuals were ages 55 or older, and 55 percent of them were women (Smith, 2003). By ethnic distribution, almost 52 percent of Native Americans and Alaskan Natives, 51 percent of Asian/Pacific Islanders and Hispanics, 47 percent of Blacks, and 42 percent of Whites were between the ages of 55 and 64. Their living arrangements and marital status varied with age. While 74 percent of men between the ages of 55 and 64 were likely to be married and living with their spouses, only 63 percent of women between 55 and 64 were married and living with their spouses. Eighty-four percent of those ages 55 to 64 had completed high school, and 31.1 percent of the men had completed a college degree compared to 21.5 percent of the women. Men were also more likely to be employed than were women. Seventy-seven percent of men ages 55 to 59 and 57.2 percent of those ages 60 to 64 were in the civilian workforce. More than 63 percent of women ages 55 to 59 and 44.3 percent of those ages 60 to 64 were employed. While the poverty rate was only 9.4 percent among those ages 55 to 64, 10.3 percent of the women were below poverty level compared to 8.4 percent of the men (Smith, 2003). Overall, however, earnings have increased for those in white collar jobs (U.S. General Accounting Office, 2001).

Workforce Projections

Projections show that almost 65 percent of individuals ages 55 to 64 will be working in 2015, and 63 percent will be working in 2025. Sixty-nine percent of **older workers** in 2015 will be men and almost 63 percent will be women (Fullerton, 1999). In 2000, 18.5 million older workers were in the workforce, and this number is expected to grow to 31.9 million by 2015. In 2000, 30 percent of all persons in the labor force were over the age of 55, and by 2015, this number is expected to rise to 37 percent. By 2015 older workers will comprise almost 20 percent of the total labor workforce. This growth of older workers is spurred by the increased number of older women in the labor force (U.S. General Accounting Office, 2001).

The older population is expected to grow as the *baby-boom* generation reaches retirement age. According to the U.S. Bureau of the Census estimates, by 2019 the total U.S. population age 55 and older will have increased from 21 percent to almost 29 percent (Day, 1996). The Bureau of Labor Statistics projected that the total labor-force growth will decrease from an annual rate of 1.1 percent between 1990 and 2000 to an annual rate of 0.7 percent between 2000 and 2025 (Fullerton, 1999). This trend will impact both employers and the economy as businesses stand to lose experienced key employees due to retirement. These retirements will create shortages in skilled workers and in management positions. Encouraging older workers to work longer could lessen the effect of these events and improve their economic well-being (Butrica, Johnson, Smith, & Steuerle, 2004).

Occupations of Older Workers

Older workers are employed in a broad group of occupations, and they are more likely than younger workers to be in white-collar or management positions. In 2000, for example, almost 62 percent of older workers were in **white-collar occupations** compared to 58.5 percent of workers between ages 30 to 39. Some professions such as teaching and nursing have an increasing number of older workers. By 2008 the number of teachers over the age of 55 is expected to increase from 13 to 19 percent, and the number of nurses or related professionals over the age of 55 is expected to increase from 12 to 18 percent. Twenty-five percent of older workers were in **blue-collar occupations,** and 13.2 percent were in **service occupations.** While workers of all ages tend to shift away from physically demanding jobs, this shift becomes more obvious as workers age (U.S. General Accounting Office, 2001).

Computer Skills of Older Workers

Many older workers use computers and the internet both at home and at work. Fifty-six percent of individuals between ages 55 to 64 reported using a computer at home compared to 70 percent ages 35 to 44. Almost 50 percent of those 55 to 64 reported having internet access compared to almost 63 percent of those ages 35 to 44 (U.S. Bureau of the Census, 2001a). Almost 56 percent of individuals ages 55 to 64 used the computer for word processing, 89 percent for internet, 83 percent for e-mail, 47.5 percent for playing games, and 30.7 percent for spreadsheets (U.S. Bureau of the Census, 2001c). Almost 54 percent of workers ages 55 to 64 reported using a computer and 38.5 percent reported using the internet at work. This compares to 58 percent of workers ages 35 to 44 who reported using a computer at work and almost 43 percent who reported using the internet at work (U.S. Bureau of the Census, 2001b). While at work, 71.5 percent of older workers used computers primarily for internet and e-mail, 66.3 percent used them for word processing, 57.5 percent for spreadsheets, and 41.7 percent for scheduling (U.S. Bureau of the Census, 2001d). In contrast, in 1992 only 18.6 percent of older workers reported working with computers (Johnson, 2004).

Job Loss and Reemployment

Thirty-one percent of older workers compared to 24 percent of younger workers are likely to lose their jobs because of plant closures or plant relocations. Seventeen percent of older workers compared to 22 percent of younger workers are likely to lose their jobs due to lack of work. Although younger workers are more likely to lose their jobs than are older workers, job loss has a greater impact on older workers. Older workers often have longer tenure in their jobs, and they experience a larger loss of earnings and benefits upon reemployment (Couch, 1997). The potential loss of health-care benefits due to job loss can be devastating for older workers because of the link between aging and greater health problems (Rogowski & Karoly, 2000).

Older workers often have a difficult time finding a new job (Chan & Stevens, 1999; U.S. General Accounting Office, 2001). In fact, 57 percent of older workers who lose their jobs retire either fully or partially following the job loss. Workers who are not ready to retire frequently seek transitional or bridge employment, often at lower pay. Once these workers retire, however, they seldom reenter the labor force. In 2000, more than 760,000 individuals over the age of 55 were unemployed and looking for work while 248,000 individuals had fully retired yet wanted to return to work. Thus almost a million individuals over the age of 55 did not have jobs but wanted to work (U.S. General Accounting Office, 2001).

Job-search time for older workers parallels that of younger workers. The median job-search time is four weeks for workers between ages 40 to 54 and ages 55 to 64. Workers between ages 55 to 74, however, average 12 weeks between jobs compared to workers from ages 40 to 54 who average 10.7 weeks and those from 19 to 39 who average 8.4 weeks between jobs (U.S. General Accounting Office, 2001).

Several job-related factors determine reemployment for older workers: the level of compensation, blend of wages and benefits, skill requirements, work hours, and working conditions. Businesses whose wages are related to work-specific experience hire fewer older workers and instend tend to hire from within the company. Such firms are often more likely to encourage the early exit of older workers through pension plans and retirement benefits. Fewer older workers are hired for jobs that require extensive computer training, perhaps due to the false assumption that older workers have a difficult time learning new skills and adapting to new technologies. Also fewer older workers are hired for jobs that require night- and evening-shift work (Hirsch, Macpherson, & Hardy, 2000).

Retirement Trends

Surveys of older workers reported a preference for gradual retirement (Ruhm, 1995). Postcareer employment offers a less demanding option for those who want to continue to work, and it often makes for a smooth transition into retirement for many workers. Some workers who voluntarily leave their **career job** to open a small business or work part time are dismayed by the realities of long hours, insufficient work, or too little income. Disenchantment is common in those who have suffered a job loss and are forced to reenter employment (Ruhm, 1995).

Many workers choose to delay retirement. Forty-four percent of almost 2,000 global executives surveyed plan to continue working past the age of 64. Two-thirds of executives reported that they planned to retire later than they thought they would three years ago. When asked why, respondents claimed that their employers had inadequate retirement benefits programs. Even more surprising was the finding that over 60 percent of the firms had no plans in place to retain the skills and knowledge that might be lost upon the retirement of the **baby boomers** (Marshall & Heffes, 2005).

"Bridge" Jobs and Career Paths of Older Workers

Older workers frequently seek alternative employment arrangements such as "phased retirement" or "bridge" employment. *Phased retirement* means that workers stay with a career job, but gradually phase from full-time to part-time employment or part-year employment over several years until they fully retire. *Bridge employment* refers to workers who leave full-time career jobs for jobs that are part time or out of their career field before retiring (Committee for Economic Development, 1999; U.S. General Accounting Office, 2001, 2003a; Herz, 1995; O'Leary & Wandner, 2000). In the United States, for example, almost half of all workers between the ages of 55 and 65 use a **bridge job** before fully retiring (U.S. General Accounting Office, 2003a). Types of bridge jobs include, but are not limited to consulting or contract work, part-time work, seasonal work, job sharing, compressed work weeks, and mentoring of new and younger workers (Agarwal & DeGroote, 1998; U.S. General Accounting Office, 2001; Penner, Perun, & Steuerle, 2002; Yeandle, 2005). Still other older workers become **career changers** and change their careers entirely after retirement (Yeandle, 2005).

Barriers to Career Success

Structural Barriers

Work Disincentives.   The current employee compensation system was designed to get rid of long-term, high-cost employees and replace them with younger, relatively less-expensive employees (Penner, Perun, & Steuerle, 2003). Unfortunately, the retiring long-term employees take with them knowledge, skills, and experience that younger workers lack and often leave the companies at a loss (Marshall & Heffes, 2005). Many older workers would prefer to work a few years longer, but several aspects of current benefits and taxes provide strong work disincentives.

Tax Laws.   Current tax laws often serve as a disincentive to work for older workers who may not want to enter full retirement. For example, the current tax rate on work increases rapidly with age and often workers choose early retirement because of it. Also, by the time some workers turn 65, they can make almost as much money in retirement as they did working full time. Even so, the longer they work past retirement age, the greater their benefits will be when they *do* retire (Butrica et al., 2004). Other tax laws impact retirement funds. Employees normally pay regular income tax when they withdraw funds from retirement plans. But current employees who withdraw funds before specified ages may pay additional taxes unless they lock themselves into withdrawals in the form of lifetime annuity payments. Employees who quit their job after age 55 and then withdraw funds are not required to pay this extra tax (Penner et al., 2002).

Phased Retirement.   A lack of available phased-retirement programs that provide flexible employment options is also a disincentive for workers who would prefer to gradually transition into retirement rather than make the abrupt move from full-time employment into full-time retirement (Committee for Economic Development, 1999; Penner et al., 2003). Benefit plans that penalize delayed retirement often persuade workers to retire early as do subtle institutional pressures (Penner et al., 2002).

These practices also serve as disincentives to hiring older workers for new jobs. Older workers who remain on the new job for five years tend to cost their employers more in pension and health benefits than younger workers who possess the same qualifications and skills (Penner et al., 2002). To offset these costs, employers often limit wage growth at older ages (Butrica et al., 2004). Sometimes rehiring a worker who has just retired is the only way an employer can legally allow that employee to move to phased retirement (Penner et al., 2003). Flexible hours and financial benefits, reducing workloads through part-time schedules, and job sharing are options that employers sometimes provide in an effort to help retain older workers. Many employers, however, can not afford the cost of such options (U.S. General Accounting Office, 2001).

Health Benefits.   Health policies for workers between ages 55 to 59 can cost more than twice that for workers between ages 20 to 44. Currently, private insurers must pay health costs before Medicare will start to contribute. Workers with employer-sponsored health benefits may have to relinquish their Medicare benefits if they work past the age of 65. Because Medicare does not pay as generously as privately-sponsored insurance, having Medicare as a secondary insurance does not enhance coverage. For those who use Medicare as their primary health-care coverage, however, its loss due to working past age 65 can leave older workers with no coverage at all (Butrica et al., 2004). In cases where Medicare provides secondary coverage, workers tend to give up thousands of dollars in Medicare benefits every year just to work past age 65. One way around this problem is to take a job that offers no health incentives at all. The guidelines for **Employee Retirement Income Security Act of 1974 (ERISA)** and Age Discrimination in Employment Act of 1967 (ADEA) also inadvertently make it difficult for older workers to work past retirement by imposing regulations on benefits and taxes (Penner et al., 2003). The **Older Workers Benefit Protection Act of 1990** amends several sections of the ADEA to prohibit employers from denying benefits to older employees. Employers may reduce benefits based on age only if the cost of providing reduced benefits to older workers is the same as the cost of providing benefits to younger workers.

Perpetuation of Stereotypes. The **Age Discrimination in Employment Act of 1967 (ADEA)** prohibits age discrimination in employment for persons 40 years of age or older. ADEA promotes the employment of older persons based on their ability rather than age, helping employers and workers find ways of responding to problems that arise from the impact of age on employment. This act applies to federal, state, and city governments and to private businesses with more than 20 employees that engage in interstate commerce. It also sets standards for employer-provided benefits and pensions. Despite ADEA, employers' stereotypical attitudes and views of older workers often discourage their continued participation in the labor force. Some employers have negative perceptions about the productivity of older workers and see them as less flexible, less adaptable, less energetic, and less enthusiastic than younger workers, simply due to their age. Other employers feel that older workers are liabilities who have higher accident rates and are more expensive to employ because of their higher salaries and increased benefits. Another employers' stereotypical view is that older workers are less interested than younger workers in training and learning new skills (Agarwal & DeGroote, 1998; U.S. General Accounting Office, 2001; Gibson, Zerbe, & Franken, 1993; Paul & Townsend, 1993). Research, however, disproves these beliefs.

Lack of Geographical Mobility. Older workers are often established in marriage and family and own their home, which might affect their willingness and ability to relocate to find new employment (Mazzerole & Singh, 1999). Their inability to relocate requires older workers to limit their job search to local areas, impacting their likelihood of finding a new job that meets their needs.

Lack of Support Services. Older workers frequently lack experience and skills in job searching that their younger counterparts may have had an opportunity to develop. When older workers need assistance with job search or additional training, they are often placed in programs designed for the general population rather than one that addresses the needs of the older worker. Older workers who use segregated workshops that offer counseling and a placement component that provides individualized assistance enables them to be more independent in their job search and reinforces their self-esteem and motivation (Human Resources Development Canada [HRDC], 1999). Employers often inadvertently target younger workers with their brochures and campaigns, and older workers are often unaware that job openings exist. Providing placement services that partner with local businesses and provide computer- and internet-based job searches would help match older workers with the available jobs (Committee for Economic Development, 1999).

The Workforce Investment Act of 1998 provides basic job-search assistance for older workers, but an older worker's desire to work only part time or the need to look for higher wages may discourage a program administrator from enrolling the worker in other more specific services such as training. While anyone may receive core services such as job-search assistance, WIA enrollment is required for more intensive services and training. Of those workers age 55 and older who received job-search assistance through WIA, only half received training (U.S. General Accounting Office,

2003a). Older workers who qualify for dislocated worker assistance must be unable to find a job leading to self-sufficiency in order to qualify for training. The definition of *self-sufficiency*, however, is left to the discretion of each workforce investment board, with self-sufficient jobs paying anywhere from $8.50/hour in Maryland to $16.39/hour in Louisiana. The lower the wage used to define self-sufficiency, the easier it is for older workers to be hired. This wage discrepancy increases the difficulty for the older worker who needs training (U.S. General Accounting Office, 2002).

Individual Barriers

Computer and Technology Skills vs. Physical Job Demands. Displacement of workers because positions are eliminated happens frequently in high-tech companies (Aaronson & Housinger, 1999). Older workers in particular are likely to experience reemployment problems when they lose jobs with high-tech industries, because as the degree of technology increases, the chances of finding reemployment decreases. Older workers who are college graduates are more likely to work with computers than are noncollege graduates. The college graduates reported that their jobs are stressful and require intense concentration and good eyesight. Occupations that require more computer skills tend to attract fewer older workers because of the mistaken belief that older workers cannot learn additional computer skills beyond those they already possess (U.S. General Accounting Office, 2001). Older workers with less education, however, tend to have more physically demanding jobs that require good eye sight and intense concentration but fewer computer skills (Johnson, 2004).

Other Skills. Older workers with job tenure have experience and many industry-specific skills that have led to higher wages in their current jobs. However, such skills may not transfer to new jobs, and the displaced older worker may have to take a job for less wages. This situation is repeated in cases when older workers with industry-specific skills change industries (Aaronson & Housinger, 1999). Long-term unemployment may lead to a depreciation of skills. Skills might decline 30 percent during the first year of unemployment for white-collar workers and 10 percent per year for blue-collar workers (Keane & Wolpin, 1997).

Caregiving. Workers over the age of 55 frequently care for frail, elderly relatives, which often requires flexible working arrangements for the older worker. Older workers who once dealt with their children with disabilities are now dealing with their adult children with disabilities. Tension in the workplace may result because supervisors assumed that childcare duties would lessen as workers aged. In fact such duties may even increase as the child matures into adulthood (Yeandle, 2005).

Physical Health Barriers

Individuals between ages 55 to 70 are better able to work today than they were in the past, and their health status has generally improved overall (Johnson & Steuerle,

2003). In fact, many people leave the workforce long before health issues make it necessary for them to leave (Steuerle, Spiro, & Johnson, 1999). Most individuals reach age 65 without health issues posing a major employment problem. Workers over the age of 55 tend to have slightly lower absentee rates from work, and those who miss work tend to do so for illness or injury rather than personal or family commitments. Older workers also have lower work injury or accident rates than younger workers. They are, however, more likely to suffer permanent disabilities and fatalities (Committee for Economic Development, 1999). One-half of older workers who experienced health impairments or illness remained with their current employers, and one-third received some type of accommodation for their impairments. Such accommodations can include a shorter work day, special equipment, more breaks, or a change in work duties (Daly & Bound, 1996).

Some older workers suffer from work-related illnesses. In 1999, estimates of physician-diagnosed pesticide illnesses per year in farm workers were between 10,000 to 20,000 instances. These cases are believed to be underreported because farm workers are hesitant to seek medical care for financial reasons, and they fear retaliation by their employers (U.S. General Accounting Office, 2000).

Stress-Related Illness. While the physical demands of work may be decreasing for older workers, evidence shows that jobs are now more demanding and more time-consuming than they once were (National Institute for Occupational Safety and Health [NIOSH], 1999). These nonphysical demands may push the older worker into an early retirement whether or not the jobs require physical strength and stamina. While 20 percent of older workers reported that their jobs involved a lot of stress, 16 percent strongly agreed that their jobs had become more difficult. College-educated older workers were more likely to work in stressful jobs than older workers who lack a college degree (Johnson, 2004).

Blue-collar workers, however, are more likely than white-collar worker to have such stress-related illnesses as musculoskeletal disorders, respiratory diseases, and diabetes (U.S. General Accounting Office, 1999). Blue-collar workers are 58 percent more likely to have arthritis, 42 percent more likely to have chronic lung disease, and 30 percent more likely to have problems with either a foot or a leg. They are also more likely to suffer from asthma and diabetes. Other physical ailments that affect both blue-collar and white-collar older workers include back problems, cancer (other than skin), heart problems, kidney or bladder problems, stomach or intestinal ulcers, and strokes (Petersen & Zwerling, 1998).

Lower-Limb Muscle Strength. Older workers' decrease in exercise and activity in retirement affects their lower-limb muscle strength and possibly leads to future muscle deterioration in the lower legs. Increases in household, leisure, and sporting physical activity levels after retirement are often not sufficient to compensate for the loss of daily activity that workers experienced when they were employed full time (Bryant, Trew, Bruce, Kuisma, & Smith, 2005). Older workers who retire for several months and then return to the workforce may find themselves unable to move as well as they did preretirement, possibly affecting their performance on the new job.

Alcohol.   Older women tend to live longer than men and are less likely to be financially independent, which are factors associated with at-risk drinking in older adulthood. While women of all ages have less muscle mass, making them more susceptible to the effects of alcohol, older women in particular have an age-related decrease in the amount of body fat that increases the effect of mood-altering chemicals in the body. Decreased body mass coupled with prescribed medications for physical ailments can be problematic. Liver enzymes that metabolize alcohol and other medications tend to deteriorate with age in both genders, but when compared with younger adults and with older men, older women are at increased sensitivity to alcohol (Blow & Barry, 2002).

The effect of retirement on drinking is the subject of much debate. Retirement is sometimes accompanied by a loss of status and a feeling of social marginalization because people who once identified themselves through their work roles are now dealing with role loss. Retirees sometimes use drinking to cope with these adjustments. Retirees who already drink and may possibly be heavy drinkers suddenly find themselves with more time to drink and fewer social consequences if they do (Bacharach, Bamberger, Sonnenstuhl, & Vashdi, 2004). Older individuals who retire and then return to work may find it difficult to adjust to work if they have started to drink more heavily.

Mental Health Barriers

Aging can affect a person's self-esteem in a variety of ways. How people feel about themselves is often reflected in how they feel about their bodies. The body changes that accompany aging may exacerbate feelings of low self-esteem for older workers who struggle to accept themselves while trying to decrease the gap between who they think they ought to be and who they perceive themselves to be. Women in particular face a loss of self-esteem as they age (McQuaide, 1998). Self-esteem is also connected to a person's work roles. A job loss can increase older workers' insecurity and pessimism and make their motivation and perseverance to find a new job sometimes difficult to sustain (Human Resources Development Canada, 1999). Self-esteem also influences workers' attitudes toward retirement because workers with high self-esteem tend to view retirement more positively than do those with low self-esteem (Mutran, Reitzes, & Fernandez, 1997). Work provides a sense of accomplishment and responsibility, and workers who retire will need to find a nonwork-based method to meet those needs through volunteer work, family involvement, and other social outlets (Committee for Economic Development, 1999). Depression in older workers often influences attitudes toward retirement. Workers who are depressed are often more negative about retirement, but for workers who continue to work, depression appears to have no affect on their attitude toward retirement (Mutran et al., 1997). Older workers may move through the stages of job loss just as dislocated workers do (see Chapter 11), so human service professionals need to be aware of those stages: denial, anger, bargaining, depression, and acceptance (Bradley, 1990).

Career Development Program Model: The Older Worker Population

A career development program for older workers requires a personalized approach that addresses each client's needs and barriers to the work situation—full-time, part-time, or bridge employment. Human service professionals need to consider each client separately as they develop a series of interventions to enhance the client's career success. Our program has three major components: the applicant pool, the Individual Success Plan (ISP), and the program evaluation. Each component will be explained in additional detail. Figure 13.1 is a graphical model of the career development program.

Applicant Pool

The applicant pool includes any client who is an older worker between ages 55 to 64 and who is searching for full-time, part-time, or bridge employment. Intake personnel will determine which clients fit the criteria for program participation and which do not. For example, clients with chemical-dependency issues may be better served with a referral for substance treatment before they address career development issues (see Chapter 16). Clients who are displaced or dislocated workers and are veterans may need to be referred to Veteran's Affairs (see Chapter 17).

Individual Success Plan

By creating an Individual Success Plan (ISP) the human service professional will address the client's various educational, skill, and work backgrounds, while considering each client as an individual who needs a *stable* job that meets specific employment needs. The development of an ISP can help clients explore the best plan for them. Also, because older workers bring a different combination of factors to the job search, an ISP can address each of those factors and provide a personalized approach for each client.

Make Assessments. Human service professionals need to consider more than just the clients' career, educational, and training needs: the clients' employment goals impact all of these. The client needs to explore all available options, whether they include full-time employment, part-time employment, bridge employment, or even a new career. If the worker is dislocated, then the requirements for displaced or dislocated workers apply (see Chapter 11). If the older worker has been forced to retire, the worker may be experiencing one of Bradley's (1990) stages of job loss. Thus, the ISP needs to address these issues as well as the career.

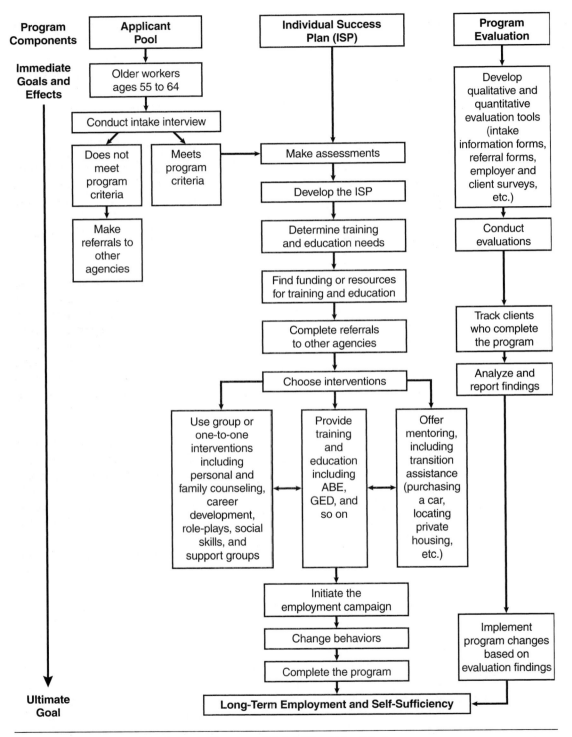

FIGURE 13.1 *Career Development Program Model: The Older Worker*

Chapter 3 provides an assortment of career-related assessments to use based on clients' needs and background. Beginning with a traditional intake interview, the human service professional can explore the client's needs and determine the best course of action at this time. During the interview, the client and human service professional will examine current survival strategies to determine their appropriateness. Other issues they will explore include the client's health coverage and other benefits. They will create a budget to help the client better examine financial needs and resources. The service worker will consider the diverse background as well as the employment goals of the client: Does the client have a high-school education or a bachelor's degree; want to work full time; want bridge employment in another field, and so on? The human service professional must be very careful to match assessments to the client. Table 13.1 is a list of assessments that are appropriate for use in designing an ISP with older workers. Using several assessments is encouraged, but human service professionals need to be careful to use those that best fit the needs of their clients. (See Chapter 3 for additional details on each assessment.)

Develop the ISP. Once clients complete their assessments, the next task is to create the ISP. The human service professional will integrate information from the intake interview, assessments, and discussions and help clients identify specific barriers to employment and will tailor clients' ISP to meet the specific objective of part-time, full-time, or bridge employment. The human service professional will need to explore issues of mental and physical health and make referrals when necessary. After clients identify possible barriers to career success, the human service professional needs to help them integrate their values and career and personal goals into the planning process.

Determine Training and Education Needs. As with the dislocated worker (Chapter 11), the level of formal education completed by older workers may not accurately indicate whether or not basic-skills remediation is needed. College graduates may need to improve skills they have not used recently, and workers who lack a basic education may have learned basic skills through jobs or other experiences (U.S. Department of Labor, 1994). Other workers may decide to change to fields that require skills they possess but have not had an opportunity to use. Therefore, the human service professional should carefully explore the need for education and training without making assumptions regarding the client's skills and abilities. Workers with the least education and the fewest transferable skills are often hesitant to enter classroom-based training because they lack previous success (U.S. Department of Labor, 1994). Other clients may not immediately see the reason to improve their soft skills. Human service professionals must respect the client's wishes while helping the client move toward career success.

While exploring the results of the various career-related assessments will provide career leads for possible training and education, the human service professional and client must concentrate on employment goals in deciding what training programs and skills to pursue. Human service professionals should help clients avoid training that maintains obsolete technologies and unstable jobs; instead they need to emphasize the

TABLE 13.1   *Career-Related Assessments for Use with the Older Worker Population*

Title	Source
Ability Tests	
Career Key*	Jones, L. K., & Jones, J. W. (2000). *Career key.* Raleigh, NC: Author.
Motivated Skills Card Sort	Knowdell, R. (2002, June). *Motivated skills card sort.* San Jose, CA: Career Research & Testing.
O*NET Ability Profiler*	O*NET Consortium (2003, April). *O*NET ability profiler.* Washington, DC: Author.
WorkKeys	ACT, Inc. (1993). *Workkeys assessments.* Iowa City, IO: ACT.
Interest Inventories	
Career Exploration Inventory 2	Liptak, J. (2002). *Career exploration inventory 2.* Indianapolis, IN: JIST Works.
CareerExplorer CD-ROM*	JIST Works (2004). *Careerexplorer CD-ROM.* Indianapolis, IN: Author.
Guide for Occupational Exploration Interest Inventory	Farr, M. (2002). *Guide for occupational exploration interest inventory* (4th ed.). Indianapolis, IN: JIST Works.
Leisure to Occupations Connection Search	McDaniels, C., & Mullins, S. R. (1999). *The leisure to occupations connection search.* Indianapolis, IN: JIST Works.
Occupational Interests Card Sort	Knowdell, R. (2002, June). *Occupational interests card sort.* San Jose, CA: Career Research & Testing.
O*NET Career Interests Inventory*	JIST Works. (2002). *O*NET career interests inventory.* Indianapolis, IN: Author.
O*NET Interests Profiler	O*NET Consortium. (n.d.). *O*NET interest profiler.* Washington, DC: Author.
Retirement Activities Card Sort Kit	Knowdell, R. (1998, June). *Retirement activities card sort kit.* San Jose, CA: Career Research & Testing.
Self-Directed Search, Forms CP, R, & E	Holland, J. L. (1990). *Self-directed search form CP: Career planning.* Lutz, FL: Psychological Assessment Resources. Holland J. L. (1994). *Self-directed search form R.* Lutz, FL: Psychological Assessment Resources. Holland, J. L. (1996). *Self-directed search form E* (4th ed.). Lutz, FL: Psychological Assessment Resources.
Transition-to-Work Inventory	Liptak, J. J. (2004). *Transition-to-work inventory.* Indianapolis, IN: JIST Works.
Voc-Tech Quick Screener	JIST Works (2002). *Voc-tech quick screener.* Indianapolis, IN: Author.
Wide Range Interest and Occupation Test	Glutting, J. J., & Wilkinson, G. (2003). *Wide range interest and occupation test* (2nd ed.). Wilmington, DE: Wide Range.
Value Inventories	
Career Values Card Sort	Knowdell, R. (1998, June). *Career values card sort.* San Jose, CA: Career Research & Testing.
O*NET Career Values Inventory*	JIST Works (2002). *O*NET career values inventory.* Indianapolis, IN: Author.

TABLE 13.1   Continued

Title	Source
O*NET Work Importance * Locator and Profiler	O*NET Consortium (n.d.). *O*NET work importancelocator and profiler.* Washington, DC: Author.
Values-Driven Work Card Sort	Career Action Center. (n.d.) *Values-driven work card sort.* Menlo Park, CA: Prodigy Press.
Work Orientation and Values Survey	Brady, R. P. (2002). *Work orientation and values survey.* Indianapolis, IN: JIST Works.
Career-Development Inventories	
Barriers to Employment Success Inventory	Liptak, J. J. (2002). *Barriers to employment success* (2nd ed.). Indianapolis, IN: JIST Works.
Career Attitudes and Strategies Inventory	Holland, J. L., & Gottfredson, G. D. (1994). *Career attitudes and strategies inventory.* Lutz, FL: Psychological Assessment Resources.
Career Beliefs Inventory	Krumboltz, J. D. (1991). *Career beliefs inventory.* Mountain View, CA: CPP.
Career Decision Scale	Osipow, S. H., Carney, C. G., Winer, J. L., Yanico, B. J., & Koschier. M. (1987). *Career decision scale* (3rd ed.). Lutz, FL: Psychological Assessment Resources.
Career Thoughts Inventory	Sampson, J. P., Peterson, G. W., Lenz, J. G., Reardon, R. C., & Saunders, D. E. (1996). *Career thoughts inventory.* Lutz, FL: Psychological Assessment Resources.
Career Transition Inventory	Heppner, M. J. (1991). *Career transition inventory.* Columbia, MO: Author.
Job Search Attitude Inventory	Liptak, J. J. (2002). *Job search attitude inventory* (2nd ed.). Indiaanapolis, IN: JIST Works.
My Vocational Situation	Holland, J. L., Daiger, D., & Power, P. G. (1980). *My vocational situation.* Mountain View, CA: CPP.
Overcoming Barriers Card Sort Game Kit	Harney, E. E., & Angel, D. L. (1999). *Overcoming barriers card sort game kit.* Hacienda Heights, CA: WorkNet Solutions.
Salient Belief Review: Connecting Spirit to Work	Bloch, D. (203). *Salient beliefs review: Connecting spirit to work.* Indianapolis, IN: JIST Works.
Vocational Exploration and Insight Kit	Holland, J. L., Birk, J. M., Cooper, J. F., Dewey, C. R., Dolliver, H., Takai, R. T., & Tyler, L. (1980). *The vocational exploration and insight kit.* Mountain View, CA: CPP.
Miscellaneous	
Elevations® Manual Card Sort System	Scully, H. (2003, August). *Elevations manual card sort system.* Roseville, CA: Author.
Individual Employment Plan	Ludden, L. L., & Maitlen, B. (2002). *Individual employment plan.* Indianapolis, IN: JIST Works.
Vocational Decision-Making Interview	Czerlinsky, T., & Chandler, S. (1999). *Vocational decision-making interview.* Indianapolis, IN: JIST Works.

*Use only if client is computer literate.

match of skills development and support with *local* economic opportunities. Assessment results may suggest other areas for training and education such as life skills. Clients can receive life-skills training in small groups or in one-on-one sessions that allow for a more individualized fit. The human service professional may want to provide clients with a list of possible training or educational group topics (i.e., money management, time management, stress management) from which to choose. Making choices empowers clients to take responsibility for their life choices and ownership in their successes.

Find Funding or Resources for Training and Education.   Older workers who lose employment due to plant closure or outsourcing may qualify for education and training assistance under the WARN Act (1989) and/or the Trade Adjustment Assistance Reform Act (2002). Those who consider taking community college classes may qualify for federal financial aid or other grant programs. Older dislocated workers may qualify for severance packages that provide funding for retraining and education (Kodrzycki, 1998). Older dislocated workers whose employers were not covered under WARN (1989) or who do not provide severance packages for dislocated workers are eligible for funding for training and education through the federally funded One-Stop Career Centers of the Workforce Investment Act (1998). Older workers who retire and then return to work also qualify for general assistance through the Workforce Investment Act (1998) although they will need referrals for additional training and education. Those with limited financial resources may qualify for education and training through their local **Senior Community Service Employment Program (SCSEP).**

Complete Referrals to Other Agencies.   As with other clients, the case manager will be responsible for coordinating those funds and services for the older worker. To access these funds, the local One-Stop center will need to refer the client for training once all other funding has been exhausted (U.S. Department of Labor, 2000; U.S. General Accounting Office, 2003b). Life-skills training and education are often available free of charge in a variety of settings. Other services appropriate for older workers include referrals for medical coverage, elder care, disabilities, and various mental health issues. Older workers who are considering opening their own business may want to contact their local chamber of commerce for small business assistance.

Choose Interventions.   The career development program for the older worker has three categories of interventions: one-to-one interventions, training and education, and mentoring. Once the client and human service professional have decided whether to use an individual approach, a group approach, or a combination of the two approaches, then they can begin the interventions. Interventions may be offered concurrently or in phases, depending upon the client's needs and the agency requirements. Some clients may need all three interventions while others may need only one or two. Again, an individualized approach is necessary.

Using Group or One-to-One Interventions.   One-to-one interventions are often needed to help older workers transition into reemployment. These interventions could include personal and family counseling with a focus on increasing the older worker's confidence and self-efficacy to find another job. Other interventions might include role-plays and support groups. Clients may go elsewhere for these services or stay in house. Personal or family counseling would address such issues as financial planning, depression, stress, and substance abuse.

Providing Training and Education. Older workers who have been warned of impending dislocation may need encouragement to pursue training and education while still on a job that they know will soon end. Even workers who have retired or want to seek part-time or bridge employment may need encouragement to pursue education and training. The human service worker can help these workers prepare for continued employment that will help them transition into retirement. Life-skills training and education, whether provided in group format or individually, also occurs during this stage. These life-skills classes (i.e., time, stress, or money management; balancing work, education, and family commitments) allow participants to select and attend the classes they feel fit their ISP goals and will increase their self-sufficiency (Duncan, Dunnagan, Christopher, & Paul, 2003).

Offering Mentoring. Many older workers will not need mentoring and can skip this intervention entirely. However, workers who have limited skills may need to take advantage of these services and possibly include mentoring on the job to help them adjust to new employment demands.

Initiate the Employment Campaign. Clients' employment goals will determine the nature of the employment campaign. Some clients may decide to begin their employment campaign immediately, and others may want to complete work-related activities before they begin their campaigns. Eliminating barriers to employment success before initiating a job campaign is the best approach, but since that is not always possible, some clients will work on several activities at once, which emphasizes the need for intensive case management by the human service professional. The next sections provide an overview of considerations for an employment campaign for older workers. For additional details see Chapter 5.

The Strategic Job Search. Once older workers decide whether they want to pursue full-time employment, part-time employment, or bridge employment, and whether or not they want to change fields, they can begin their job search. Some older workers may need help in developing an informal network of job contacts with people who are already in the field in which clients plan to work. Clients need to consider the geographical area of their job search. In many instances, workers with higher skills tend to job search in a broader geographical area while lower-skilled workers tend to job search closer to home (Immergluck, 1998; Simpson, 1987). However, older workers with mortgages and ties to their communities may need to limit their job search geographically (Mazzerole & Singh, 1999). Many older workers have not had to search for a job for many years, so they may need to be refreshed on all aspects of the employment campaign.

Job-Search Correspondence.   Clients will need to learn how to write letters of application, as well as referral letters, reminder letters, and interview appreciation letters. Along with teaching clients how to write a letter accepting or declining an offer, the human service professional can use role-playing of these situations to help clients better understand the process and give them a chance to practice their interpersonal skills in a safe environment.

Tailor-Made Resumes.   The resume format a client uses will vary with the client and the job. Clients who possess a great deal of experience will be able to use a chronological resume. Clients who lack job experience in their chosen field will need to use a functional resume that organizes their job experiences according to their skills. Creating resumes also helps clients organize their experiences and better understand themselves, allowing them to focus more on their strengths instead of their weaknesses. Clients can write their resume individually or in a class session.

Interviewing Strategies.   Older workers with long job tenures may need to strengthen their interpersonal skills before interviewing. For these workers role-playing the various types of interview situations from easy to difficult and from panel to telephone can be useful. Helping clients craft answers to some of the common interview questions will empower them as well. Videotaping clients during mock interviews then critiquing the interviews provide clients with an opportunity to see themselves as others see them. Clients who move into jobs that differ substantially from previous jobs may be unaware of differences in work and/or interview attire. The human service professional can refer clients who lack the appropriate work/interview attire to a clothing closet.

Change Behaviors.   Participation in the career development program for older workers is designed to help clients change behaviors that may have previously kept them from long-term employment and self-sufficiency. Older workers who have been employed and self-sufficient may only need assistance in entering new fields of work or in finding new employment. Other workers may have responded to retirement with anger, depression, anxiety, or substance abuse. Although specific behavior changes will vary with each person, all clients who move through this program will have an opportunity to improve their interpersonal and work-related skills and other skills they originally targeted for change.

Complete the Program.   Clients who entered the program, developed their ISPs, completed the training and education that were detailed in their ISPs, and located reemployment that meets their employment goals are considered to have completed the program. At any time during the program clients can drop out, but they need to be aware that their decisions may impact their education and training and their eligibility for other types of assistance.

Achieve Goal of Stable Employment. The final goal is employment that meets the needs of older workers through full-time, part-time, or bridge employment. The program staff will need to determine the working definition of *employment* for use in this program. The main goal here is to help older workers meet their goals and find stable employment in the fields they choose that result in a graceful transition into retirement.

Program Evaluation

The program staff will need to choose the type of evaluation process that is best suited to their program: process evaluation, outcome evaluation, or impact evaluation. Human service professionals need to develop a variety of tools to evaluate their program. Figure 13.1 is a flow chart for the career development program model for the older worker. The text in each box in the figure is a factor that needs to be measured. Some evaluation tools include a database of client information, intake interview sheets, case files, tracking sheets, and referral sheets. Other tools necessary for program evaluation my include paper-and-pencil surveys or telephone surveys for the clients who complete the program and their employers and a method of tracking clients and keeping that information current. After developing the tools, the staff must decide when to collect information for evaluation and how to collect, analyze, and report it. Once the program staff has made these decisions, they need to create a timeline for the entire program evaluation process that shows every evaluation task to be accomplished, the deadline for accomplishing the task, and the persons responsible for making the evaluation. Once the evaluation information is collected, the input can be used to strengthen the current program. For complete descriptions of all segments of the evaluation process, refer to Chapter 6.

Revisiting the Case Study: Wayne

Conduct an Intake Interview

During the intake interview the human service professional should explore Wayne's medical, financial, educational, and employment history; his interests and values; and his views on employment, education, and family. Exploring Wayne and Tom's medical histories is important to help Wayne plan his spending while he is job searching. In particular, the human service professional needs to consider the impact of Lorna's death on Wayne, along with the "death" of their retirement plans. Since lung cancer is often connected to smoking, Wayne's own medical and smoking history now becomes extremely important. Other issues they should explore during the intake interview include the emotional issues of job loss; the possibility that Wayne's son, Tom, either will be living on his own or in some type of group home; and the need to find in-home care for Wayne's mother.

The human service professional and Wayne need to consider his finances and how to avoid going further into debt. Because Wayne has already started to pare down his living expenses, he has a better idea of his financial needs and thus his employment needs. He will want to meet any financial obligations he has already incurred, but he needs to avoid taking on any new ones. By making a budget, Wayne can help insure that he is able to meet all financial obligations during this transition time.

Since Wayne has a high-school diploma and some community college course work, the human service professional should explore other training and education possibilities based on Wayne's employment needs. Questions to help Wayne make decisions include: What do you want to do? Do you want to return to full-time employment, part-time employment, or bridge employment? Do you want to stay in the electrician's field or change fields? Would you consider opening your own business or serving as a consultant? What were some of your career dreams in the past? What interests or intrigues you? What type of activities have you enjoyed?

Make Assessments

As Wayne and the human service professional explore Wayne's career goals and employment needs, they will need to determine what assessments are most appropriate. Determining his comfort level with technology is the first step. Wayne's experience as an electrician in the shipyard may not have afforded him much technology experience. The human service professional should explore Wayne's job description in detail to determine what transferable skills he has and what additional skills he may need to meet his employment goals. Shipyard electricians sometimes work independently, but they primarily work as part of a team. They often consult with supervisors and electronics technicians, so Wayne's soft skills need to be explored as well. The O*NET Ability Profiler (O*NET Consortium, 2003) would help Wayne identify his strengths and possible training options and pinpoint occupations that fit those strengths. WorkKeys (ACT, 1993) may also help him better see his current skills and how they might transfer to other jobs. The human service professional might also use the Retirement Activities Card Sort Kit (Knowdell, 1998b) to explore Wayne's pastimes to aid in his transition from formal employment to a meaningful retirement lifestyle and to help him determine whether a return to employment is necessary.

Results from the interest inventories could provide career-change options as well. Wayne could complete the GOEII (Farr, 2002) or the CEI2 (Liptak, 2002b) to identify which areas of interest most appeals to him the most. If he is comfortable with computers, Wayne could also complete the O*NET Career Interests Inventory (JIST Works, 2002a) to pinpoint work-related interests, what he considers important on the job, and his abilities. If Wayne decides not to pursue additional education, he could complete the Voc-Tech Quick Screener (JIST Works, 2002c) to help him match interests and goals with a job for which he can train in a short period of time. The human service professional needs to be careful, however, to steer him toward stable employment that will meet his financial needs, his employment goals, and allow him to receive his pension.

Exploring Wayne's values is another component in career assessment. Wayne needs to consider careers that support his values because a better fit between the worker's values and the values of the job leads to increased job satisfaction. The Career Values Card Sort (Knowdell, 1998) could quickly help Wayne prioritize his values with respect to job tranquility, time freedom, work under pressure, creative expression, power, and technical competence. The O*NET Career Values Inventory (JIST Works, 2002b) could help him identify work groups that promote his values and pinpoint specific jobs for further exploration. Depending once again upon his computer skills, Wayne may want to use the Values-Driven Work Card Sort (Career Action Center, n.d.) or the O*NET Work Importance Locator and Profiler (O*NET Consortium, n.d. b) to help clarify his values and identify possible occupations.

Wayne can use the results of career-development inventories to help identify aspects of his personal growth that could hinder his ability to get and keep a new job. Although he has an established work history, Wayne may have developed some barriers to reemployment that could affect a new position. This assessment process is particularly important because Wayne may be moving from one field to another that will require a different skill set. Available in both a pencil-and-paper format and online, the Barriers to Employment Success Inventory (Liptak, 2002a) will help him identify career planning, personal, physical, psychological, job-seeking skills barriers, along with education and training barriers that might impede his reemployment, and it will help him develop action plans to overcome those barriers. The human service professional should not administer all of these inventories but should select inventories based on the presenting client's needs.

Determine Barriers to Career Success

Wayne is faced with several possible barriers to career success: structural barriers such as the need to keep both his and Lorna's retirement pensions and individual barriers such as being responsible for his son and mother. Depending upon how long Wayne has been retired, he may have developed some physical barriers related to lack of exercise, coupled with possible mental health issues such as depression or anger regarding Lorna's death. "Soft" skills may or may not be a barrier, depending upon Wayne's duties as a shipyard electrician, but the importance of these skills should not be overlooked.

Choose Interventions

Using Group or One-to-One Interventions.

Based on Wayne's ISP, one-to-one interventions may include social-skills training and a number of referrals for other assistance. These interventions should address Wayne's barriers to employment success and could include possible referrals for help for his adult son with disabilities. One concern is to help Wayne deal with any unresolved grief over Lorna's death as well as the loss of his job due to retirement. Helping him move through the stages of both grief and a job loss can take place in either an individual session or in a group setting. Developing a budget and financial counseling along with referrals to any programs for which he and his son or mother may qualify are interventions that would help Wayne. Other interventions appropriate for his use include role-plays that address his barriers, combined with role-playing to practice new behaviors. Individual and group work may also help Wayne deal with any self-esteem or age issues, examine norms and combat stereotypes, and improve his coping skills.

Finding Training and Education.   After deciding what is best for himself and his family, Wayne may want to explore possible jobs and available training that fit with his career aspirations and desires. He could start with a referral to the local One-Stop Career Center and to the community college, depending on his training and education decisions. Although Wayne has worked steadily, he has worked primarily in only one position as a shipyard electrician. While he probably has transferable skills, Wayne may want to explore other training and education options to update them. Helping Wayne look for similar positions would be a quicker way to reemployment, but he must base his decision on available local jobs and whether these local jobs match his skills and are stable positions.

Using Mentoring.   Wayne may need only limited if any mentoring services because he has been self-sufficient in the past. He should focus his budget on reducing living expenses until he finds stable reemployment and completes any education and training. He may need only minor assistance in adjusting to his new life. Most of his mentoring needs will involve helping his son adjust, especially if Tom moves to a group home situation.

Initiate the Employment Campaign

While eliminating all of the barriers to employment success before beginning the campaign is the best approach, this may not be possible. Instead, the human service professional may need to provide case management as Wayne completes education and training and participates in the interventions designed to decrease his barriers. Helping him develop his job-search network, a resume, and any correspondence is part of this component. If Wayne changes careers, he may want to use a functional resume as he has some transferable skills that may prove beneficial to a new job. If he is able to arrange a return to his old job, the human service professional would want to encourage Wayne to consider a job redesign to meet his new needs, perhaps one with more flexibility in its hours and duties.

Conclusion

Human service professionals are frequently tasked with helping older workers locate stable employment to meet their employment goals and helping clients deal with any barriers to employment. Some recommended policy changes would assist older workers in their transition into retirement. Changes in economic, community, and workforce policies would include:

- Reconsider human resource policies
- Explore the possibility of redesigning jobs to meet the needs of older workers while increasing the ease of moving into part-time or bridge employment, including flexible work arrangements and job sharing

- Provide career-long training for all workers
- Work to eradicate persistent and damaging stereotypes about older workers' performance at work and negative attitudes from line managers about the potential of older workers
- Reconsider the need for forced retirement
- Allow older workers to have higher limits on their income

Changes in education policy would include:

- Create separate computer classes tailored to older workers
- Provide career training for those nearing retirement

Summary

Older workers are those between ages 55 to 64, who have worked in their chosen field for a period of time, and they then either lost their jobs due to retirement or through company shut-downs or relocations. Often employed in a broad group of occupations, older workers are more likely to be in white-collar or management positions than are younger workers. While workers of all ages tend to shift away from physically demanding jobs, this shift becomes more obvious as workers age. Thirty-one percent of older workers compared to 24 percent of younger workers are likely to lose their jobs due to plant closures or plant relocations. Seventeen percent of older workers compared to 22 percent of younger workers are likely to lose their jobs due to lack of work. Although younger workers are more likely to lose their jobs than are older workers, the job loss has a greater impact on older workers who have more difficulty finding a new job. Older workers often have greater tenure in their jobs and often experience a larger loss of earnings and benefits upon reemployment. The potential loss of health-care benefits due to job loss can be devastating for older workers because of the link between aging and increased health problems. Fifty-seven percent of older workers who lose their jobs retire fully or partially following a job loss. Reemployment for older workers is determined by several job-related factors: the level of their compensation, a combination of wages and benefits, skill requirements, work hours, and working conditions. Businesses whose wages are related to work-specific experience will hire fewer older workers, instead they choose to hire from within. Older workers frequently seek alternative employment arrangements such as phased retirement or bridge employment. The career development program model designed for older workers includes the development of an Individual Success Plan that uses assessments of career abilities, interests, values, and barriers; interagency referrals; interventions such as one-to-one interventions, training and education, and mentoring; and an employment campaign leading to reemployment and self-sufficiency.

Key Terms

Age Discrimination in Employment Act of
    1967 (ADEA)
Baby boomers
Blue-collar occupations
Bridge job
Career changers
Career job
Employee Retirement Income Security Act of
    1974 (ERISA)

Older workers
Older Workers Benefit Protection Act of
    1990
Pension
Senior Community Service Employment
    Program (SCSEP)
Service occupations
White-collar occupations

Web Resources

Note that website URLs may change over time.

AARP
http://www.aarp.org

Administration on Aging (AoA)
http://www.aoa.dhhs.gov

Civil Service Retirement Services
http://www.opm.gov/retire

Equal Employment Opportunity Commission
http://www.eeoc.gov

Federal Employees Retirement System
http://www.opm.gov/retire

National Council on Disability (NCD)
http://www.ncd.gov

National Institute on Aging (NIA)
http://www.nia.nih.gov

**Senior Community Service Employment
Program (SCSEP)**
http://www.doleta.gov/seniors

Social Security Benefit Publications
http://www.ssa.gov/pubs

**The Age Discrimination in Employment Act
of 1967**
http://www.eeoc.gov/policy/adea.html

14

Offenders and Ex-Offenders: Getting a Second Chance

Case Study: Brian

Seventeen-year-old Brian comes in 10 minutes late, mumbling, and wearing baggy pants with a very large shirt. He is thin, walks with a slouch, and his unkempt red hair hangs below his shoulders. He has a court-ordered appointment following his most recent court appearance. Brian has also been ordered to attend anger management groups. Over the past two years, he has been in court over a variety of events, including, but not limited to shooting out a neighbor's window with a BB gun, trespassing on school grounds, threatening to destroy a friend's car, hitting his girlfriend's father, and possession of several ounces of marijuana. He was on house arrest from Thanksgiving through March. During this time he started GED classes. His latest court appearance was the result of being drunk and noisy in his front yard in April. His sole form of transportation is his girlfriend Brenda, who is also working toward her GED and who works part time delivering pizza. He mentions that they are sexually active and drink together and have also smoked pot and used crack a few times.

Brian has held two jobs. For one week he was a dishwasher, but that job ended when he called in sick to spend more time with Brenda. He worked (under the table) as a roofer's assistant carrying roofing materials up the ladder, but that job also lasted only a few weeks due to rain. When the rain ended, Brian did not return to the job. He lives with his mother who says that when he turns 18 in two months he will have to move out. He calls his dad periodically and visits with him when he can but is more interested in being with his girlfriend and his friends than in being with his dad.

The Offender And Ex-Offender Population

Description

United States residents over the age of 12 were victims of approximately 25.9 million crimes in 2003, 75 percent were property crimes, 24 percent were **crimes of violence,** and 1 percent was personal thefts (Adams & Reynolds, 2002). Although the number of serious **violent crimes** has decreased from 4,191,000 in 1993 to 1,829,700 in 2003 (U.S. Bureau of Justice Statistics [BJS], n.d. b.), the number of people convicted of crimes in federal courts and then imprisoned has increased steadily since 1980 (BJS, 2002). The number of **adults** in the correctional population has increased, and as of 2003, 6.9 million people were under some form of correctional supervision including prison, jail, **probation,** and **parole** (BJS, n.d. a). Four million citizens no longer have the right to vote, and one and one-half million children now have a parent in prison (Mears & Travis, 2004).

According to the U.S. Bureau of Justice Statistics, almost 14 percent or 2.1 million women are violent offenders (Greenfield & Snell, 2000). Seventy-five percent of violent female offenders committed **simple assault** as opposed to just over half of male offenders. An estimated 28 percent of violent female offenders are juveniles, and the arrest rate among female **juvenile offenders** is almost twice that of adult women offenders. Three out of four victims of violent female offenders were women, and 62 percent of the victims had a previous relationship with the female offender as an intimate, relative, or acquaintance as compared to 39 percent of violent male offenders. The number of female defendants who were convicted of felonies has been growing steadily since 1990, at more than twice the rate of increase in male defendants. Almost 60 percent of women in state facilities reported having been victims of physical or sexual abuse in the past. More than one-third reported that they had been raped by an intimate partner, and less than 25 percent of them had been abused by a family member (Greenfield & Snell, 2000).

Racial composition varies when comparing male and female offenders. African American, female offenders outnumber African American, male offenders by nearly 1.9 million. Minority offenders are 26.2 percent female compared to 25.9 percent male. Female offenders generally tend to be two and a half years older than male offenders, with African American females three years older than their male counterparts. Hispanic, female offenders who average 29.6 years old are the youngest group compared to white females who have the highest average age of 39.6 years (Greenfield & Snell, 2000).

One out of seven violent offenders is female, and women accounted for 1 in 50 offenders who committed a violent sex offense including rape and sexual assault. Nearly equal proportions of African American females and white females committed **robbery** and **aggravated assault,** and most simple assault female offenders were white. Fifty-three percent of violent, female offenders committed their offence while they were alone, and 40 percent committed their offence with other women. Only 47 percent of male offenders committed their offense while they were alone, and 51 percent were with other males. Almost 8 percent of violent, female offenders committed their offence with at least one male offender, while only 1 percent of violent, male offenders committed their offense while with a female offender (Greenfield & Snell, 2000).

Victim–Offender Relationships.   Over 60 percent of the murders committed by women were against an intimate partner or family member, compared to 20 percent of murders committed by men. This statistic means that 1 of 14 murders committed by females and 1 of 5 murders committed by males were against a victim who was a stranger to the offender (Greenfield & Snell, 2000).

Offenders as Parents.   Between 1976 and 1997 parents and stepparents murdered almost 11,000 children. One-half of those crimes were committed by mothers and stepmothers. Mothers were more likely to kill children during infancy, and 52 percent of the children killed were sons and stepsons. Men were more likely to kill children ages 8 and older. Women under the supervision of justice system agencies were the mothers of approximately 1.3 million minor children. Almost 72 percent of women on probation, 70 percent of those in local jails, and 59 percent of women in federal prisons had minor children, reporting an average of 2.11 children. Male inmates of state prisons fathered 1.1 million children under the age of 18, and 44 percent of the fathers resided with their children prior to imprisonment. Males in federal prison reported 15 times as many minor children as did women in federal prisons (Greenfield & Snell, 2000).

Criminal Histories.   While 65 percent of women in state prisons have criminal backgrounds, almost 77 percent of men reported prior offences. Thirty-eight percent of men have a juvenile history compared to 19 percent of women. Seventy percent of men have an adult criminal history compared to 60 percent of women. One in six women and 1 in 3 men have criminal histories spanning both juvenile and adult years. The number of convictions varies by gender as well. Men tend to have more convictions than women. Forty-three percent of men have three or more convictions compared to 33 percent of women. Women, however, are more likely to be on probation when their most recent offence occurred (Greenfield & Snell, 2000).

Reentry into Society

Approximately 630,000 individuals reenter the community every year. Whether or not the prisoner is released to some type of postprison supervision varies from state to state. In Massachusetts, for example, 58 percent of prisoners are released without any supervision, yet California only releases 3 percent of its prisoners without supervision. The likelihood of prison readmission from parole violations increases in states that have a high percentage of required supervisions (La Vigne, 2004). One in five women on probation or in local jails is under the age of 25 (Greenfield & Snell, 2000).

Adults on Probation.   Over 4 million adult women and men were on probation at the end of 2003; the number had grown 1.2 percent or an increase of 49,920 probationers during the year. Seventy-seven percent of probationers are male. The number of females on probation has increased slightly since 1995 from 21 percent to 23 percent. Fifty-six percent of adults on probation were white, 30 percent were African American, 12 percent were Hispanic, and the remainder was evenly divided between Native American/Alaskan Native and Asian/Pacific Islander. One-half of all people on probation had been convicted of a **felony.** Fifty-four percent had been directly sentenced to probation, 25 percent had received a suspended sentence, and 8 percent had been sentenced to incarceration followed by probation. Thirteen percent entered probation before their court proceedings ended (Glaze & Palla, 2004).

Supervision.   Seventy-one percent of convicted offenders were under active supervision where they were required to report regularly by mail, telephone, or in person to a probation authority. This number had dropped from 79 percent in 1995. By the end of 2003, 1 out of 9 adults on probation had absconded (failed to report for probation meetings and could not be found). This number represented an increase from 9 percent in 1995 to 11 percent in 2003 (Glaze & Palla, 2004). Almost 72 percent of women on probation have young children (Bloom & McDiarmid, 2000).

Offenses.   Forty-nine percent of all adults on probation had committed a felony, 49 percent a **misdemeanor,** and the remaining 2 percent had committed other infractions. Twenty-five percent had violated a drug law, and 17 percent were convicted of driving while intoxicated. Other offenses committed by adults on probation included 12 percent for larceny/theft, 9 percent for other assault, 7 percent for domestic violence, 6 percent for minor traffic violations, 5 percent for **burglary,** and 3 percent for sexual assault (Glaze & Palla, 2004). Seventeen percent of women were on probation for violence and drug trafficking, compared to 24 percent who were sentenced to local jails, 46 percent sentenced to state prisons, and 65 percent sentenced to federal prisons. Driving while intoxicated offences account for 18 percent of women on probation, 7 percent of those in local jails, and 25 percent of those in federal prisons (Greenfield & Snell, 2000).

Completion of Probation.   Fifty-nine percent of adults who left probation in 2003 successfully completed the terms of their probation. Five percent returned to incarceration with a new sentence, and 7 percent returned to incarceration for the same sentence. Thirteen percent had their probation sentences revoked without incarceration (Glaze & Palla, 2004).

Adults on Parole.   In 2003 the number of adults on parole increased as well, growing by 3.1 percent or 23,654 for a total of 774,588 on parole. Fifty-one percent of parolees were released to parole because of sentencing guidelines, up 10 percent from 1995. Ninety-five percent of parolees had felony convictions. In 2000 over 96,000 or 12.5 percent of adults on parole were women, a steady increase from 10 percent in 1995. Almost 41 percent of adults on parole were black while 40 percent or 309,900 were white. More than 18 percent or 136,000 adults on parole were Hispanic, and the remaining 11,200 were divided among other races (Glaze & Palla, 2004).

By the end of 2003, 84 percent of all parolees were under active supervision that required regular contact (telephone, mail, or visit) with their parole agency. Seven percent of parolees had absconded and could not be found. Out of all parolees discharged in 2003, only 47 percent successfully met the conditions of their parole, and 38 percent were returned to incarceration due to a parole violation or a new offense. Two out of every 5 adults on parole returned to incarceration. In 2003, 36 percent of adults on parole had committed drug offenses, compared to 28 percent who committed violent crimes, and 26 percent who committed property crimes (Glaze & Palla, 2004).

Juveniles and Young Adults

Approximately 200,000 juveniles and young adults (those under the age of 24) return home each year from secure juvenile correctional facilities or state and federal prisons (Travis, Solomon, & Waul, 2001). According to Snyder (2004), 88 percent of inmates released from juvenile facilities were male. Nineteen percent were 14 years old or younger. Thirty-six percent were age 17 or older. Thirty-nine percent were white, 39 percent were African American, and 17 percent were Hispanic. Mears and Travis (2004) identified seven distinctly different youth reentry pathways based on the legal status and age of young people at the time of their incarceration and their release:

1. Those youth who are incarcerated as juveniles (under the age of 17) in the juvenile justice system and released while they are still legally juveniles (under the age of 17).
2. Those youth who are incarcerated as juveniles (under the age of 17) in the juvenile justice system, then released as adults (i.e., age 18 or over). In many states, youth who are incarcerated in the juvenile justice system can be held until they turn 21.
3. Those youth who begin their incarceration in the juvenile justice system but are then transferred (still classified as juveniles) into the criminal justice system to complete their term of incarceration. This is sometimes referred to as custodial transfer. After this transfer, these youth are then released from the criminal system as juveniles (age 17 or younger).
4. Those youth who begin their incarceration in the juvenile justice system but are then transferred (still classified as juveniles) into the criminal justice system to complete their term of incarceration. This is sometimes referred to as custodial transfer. After this transfer, these youth are then released from the criminal system as young adults age 18 or older.
5. Those youth who are incarcerated as juveniles in adult prisons through transfer statues (laws allowing juveniles to be tried in criminal courts then placed in adult prisons upon conviction) and released while still juveniles (17 or younger).
6. Those youth who are incarcerated as juveniles in adult prisons through transfer statues (laws allowing juveniles to be tried in criminal courts then placed in adult prisons upon conviction) and released as young adults, age 18 or older.
7. Those young adults (age 18 or older) incarcerated in and released from the criminal justice system as adults (Mears & Travis, 2004).

Discussion of youth reentry into society is complicated for several reasons. First, states differ in their definitions of who is a juvenile and who is an adult. Another reason involves the length of time youth spend incarcerated. Many youth spend less than one year incarcerated in the juvenile justice system (Mears & Travis, 2004). They may, however, have been incarcerated repeatedly adding up collectively to one or more years of incarceration. Many youth released from the juvenile justice system will have spent approximately one-third of their adolescent life incarcerated (Snyder, 2004). Some researchers suggested that young people hold a different concept of time, so several months spent incarcerated may seem short to adults but an eternity to juveniles. Incarceration and reentry experiences may vary based on the youth's developmental stages, particularly if the juvenile is very young and has not reached the later stages of development. Incarceration may, in turn, affect a youth's development (Mears & Travis, 2004). Juvenile reentry is also affected by what happens *while* the youth is incarcerated. For example, the experience of a youth incarcerated for a short time who connects with a gang and becomes a part of a criminal organization could impact the youth's behavior after release (Snyder, 2004).

Youth Offenses and Commitment Time.   According to the Census of Juveniles in Residential Placement (CJRP), youth spend a mean of 17 weeks in residential facilities with 10 percent of all youth spending 72 weeks. Forty percent of the youth were charged with a violent offence, with a median 2-week stay, and 31 percent were charged with a property offence with a median 15-week stay. Fifteen percent of the youth committed a public-order offense with a median 11-week stay, and 9 percent committed a drug offense with a median 15-week stay. The median time spent in residential facilities differed across gender. The median stay in a facility for males was 17 weeks compared to 14 weeks for females. The length of stay also differed across ethnic groups. White youth stayed a median of 15 weeks compared to African American and Hispanic youth who both stayed a median of 18-weeks (Snyder, 2004).

Living Arrangements Prior to Commitment.   Fifty-four percent of youth staying in residential facilities come from single-parent homes where they often live with their mothers and 10 percent live with grandparents. These youth often have relatives who have been incarcerated, including a brother or sister (25 percent), a father (24 percent), mother (9 percent), or another family member (13 percent). Almost 20 percent of confined youth reported having at least two family members in jail or prison (Snyder, 2004).

Level of Education.   Incarcerated youth often have completed less education than their nonincarcerated counterparts. Fifty-eight percent of committed youth between ages 15 to 17 reported that they had not completed eighth grade, compared to 24 percent of other youth that age. Among those youth ages 18 or older, only 10 percent of those who were incarcerated had completed high school, and 23 percent had never started high school (Snyder, 2004).

Criminal History.   Many incarcerated youth reported a prior offence leading, at the very least, to probation. Eighty-three percent reported some type of placement history. Seventy percent reported a prior record for property crime, 33 percent reported a previous violent offence, and 22 percent reported a drug offence. Only 17 percent reported having never been sentenced to probation or incarceration (Snyder, 2004).

Postrelease Employment

Ex-offenders face a myriad of barriers to successful reentry into society. Over two-thirds of ex-offenders are rearrested within three years after release. Many of these rearrests are due to new crimes or technical violations of their release. While employment is often connected to successful reentry, many ex-offenders were unemployed before they entered the corrections system and remained unemployed after their release (La Vigne, 2004). Those who were employed prior to incarceration found that their earnings decreased anywhere from 10 to 30 percent upon release (Holzer, Raphael, & Stoll, 2003).

Barriers to Career Success

Structural Barriers

Geographic Location upon Release.   Ex-offenders often congregate in major metropolitan areas after their release, concentrating those who need assistance into areas that are poorly equipped to handle the influx of ex-offenders as they are already dealing with high rates of crime, poverty, unemployment, and homelessness, including high numbers of female head of households. Meeting the needs of ex-offenders requires these areas to stretch their already limited resources. In some cases, ex-offenders settle within a very concentrated geographical area, even further impacting already high-need communities. In 2001, for instance, 62 percent of all Illinois ex-offenders settled in Cook County where other Illinois counties received no more than 3 percent of the prisoner population. Fifty-three percent of the ex-offenders settled in Chicago with 34 percent returning to 6 neighborhoods. Thus communities experience prisoner reentry differently, often without additional resources moving to the areas that need them the most (La Vigne, 2004).

Employer's Attitudes.   Many employers are reluctant to hire ex-offenders (La Vigne, 2004). Some employers prefer to hire welfare recipients, employees without a GED, those with spotty work histories, and those unemployed for a year or more *before* they would hire an ex-offender (Holzer et al., 2003). Some employers are concerned that ex-offenders will not make good employees and will be unable to keep the job if they are hired (Bushway, 2003). Another employer concern is that they can be held legally liable for the actions of their employees (Solomon, Johnson, Travis, & McBride, 2004). Employers also often view ex-offenders as not trustworthy. Employers are often hesitant to hire someone without work experience who has committed a violent crime or recently was released from prison, and they are less hesitant to hire those charged with drug and property offences (Holzer et al., 2003). However, large firms are more likely to hire someone with a criminal record than are small firms (Employers Group Research Services, 2002). While the Small Business Job Protection Act of 1996 authorized the **Work Opportunity Tax Credit (WOTC)**, employers may be unaware of this financial incentive to hire from eight targeted groups of job seekers, including ex-felons who are members of a low-income family.

Employment Opportunities.   Some jobs are viewed as a better fit for ex-offenders than others. Manufacturing, construction, and transportation industries, for example, have little customer contact and are more likely to hire those with criminal backgrounds than others. Such industries often have a high number of unskilled jobs with high turnover, thus ex-offenders would add to their already unstable work history (Holzer et al., 2003). However, these blue-collar jobs are decreasing in the national economy while jobs that are legally closed to those with a felony conviction (elder care, childcare, criminal justice occupations, education, health care, customer contact, service industry, and security service) are increasing (Heinrich, 2000; Legal Action Center, 2000a).

Prison-Based Work Programs.   Several pieces of legislation have been enacted regarding prison-based work programs. The **Hawes-Cooper Act of 1929** (Public Law 669) created a Federal Prison Industries (FPI) to employ federal prisoners to make goods to sell to the federal government. This law authorized states to prohibit the acceptance of goods made by prisoners in other states, but it does not ban the transportation of such goods. A few years later the **Walsh-Healy Act of 1936** was enacted to prohibit prisoner labor on government contracts that exceed $10,000. This act stipulated that when prison contracts exceed $10,000, prison laborers are to be paid the prevailing wage. The Justice System Improvement Act of 1979 (Public Law 90-351) repealed some of the limitations imposed by Hawes-Cooper and provided prisoners with more work opportunities by linking them up with private companies. This Act authorized the **Prison Industry Enhancement (PIE) Certification Program** in an attempt to restore private sector involvement in prison industries, as long as certain conditions are met. The Crime Control Act of 1990 (Public Law 101–647) expanded this program to all 50 states.

UNICOR is the trade name for Federal Prison Industries. These industries provide job-skills training and employment to inmates confined within the Federal Bureau of Prisons. Through these industries, inmates produce market-price quality goods for sale to the federal government. UNICOR markets over 150 products and services in the following industries: clothing and textiles, office furniture, industrial products, electronics, fleet management and vehicular components, and recycling and service activities (Atkinson & Rostad, 2003).

Many prisons offer voluntary occupational training that provides real work opportunities in building and construction, indoor and outdoor maintenance, food service, horticulture, and various clerical support functions—all rich in postrelease employment opportunities. Some programs include academic skills coupled with life skills. There seems to be a disconnect, though, between these prison work programs and the realities of job-search and job-retention skills. Often such information is offered too late during the inmate's incarceration or in brief halfway-house transition programs, where training may be voluntary (McCollum, 1999).

Prison work in industries (i.e., prisoners employed by private companies) has been successful in reducing **recidivism,** but only 7 percent of state and federal inmates work in prison-industry programs (Atkinson & Rostad, 2003). A narrow segment of employers and organized labor, however, oppose such programs, citing unfair competition and worker displacement. Because of this opposition, legislation has placed several restrictions on these prison industries, effectively reducing the growth of prison industries (Solomon, Johnson, et al., 2004). Yet, employers of these inmates view them as a quality workforce and more productive than a nonoffender workforce might be. They often recommend prison workers to business associates (Atkinson & Rostad, 2003).

Legal Barriers. Ex-offenders face legal barriers to reentry including their criminal records, lack of public assistance, and stable housing.

Criminal Records. Applicants with criminal records receive one-half the job offers of those without criminal convictions (Pager, 2003). While it is illegal for employers to ban all applicants with criminal records, employers are allowed to consider the relationship between the conviction record and the job for which the applicant is applying. Some states have allowed ex-offenders to seal or expunge their criminal records if they have minimal criminal histories or have stayed out of the criminal justice system for a specified period of time (Mukamal, 2001). Many states make criminal history information available through the Internet. This access increases the ease by which employers can check employees' criminal information, and increases the likelihood that former offenders will be discriminated against on the basis of old or even minor convictions. In fact, the federal government and some states have dramatically increased the number of penalties for those with criminal convictions, in some instances, extending those penalties to people charged but never convicted (Samuels & Mukamal, 2004).

Public Assistance. In 1996, the federal welfare law included provisions restricting access to public benefits for those with drug-related convictions. States that do not enact legislation to opt out of or modify the ban must impose a lifetime ban on TANF and food stamps for all convicted of drug felonies since 1996. This ban does not apply to Medicaid or nonfederal assistance that states can provide through other programs. Single parents with drug convictions frequently find themselves ineligible for public assistance, yet they are not "job-ready," and require such services as substance-abuse treatment, job training, or education before they can enter the job market. These ex-offenders are unable to rely on public assistance to pay for food and housing while they become job-ready (Mukamal, 2001).

Housing. Finding a place to stay is one of the first obstacles that ex-offenders face upon their reentry into a community. Recent research shows that ex-offenders who do not find stable housing are more likely to return to prison (Metraux & Culhane, 2004), yet federal legislation such as the **Housing Opportunity Program Extension Act of 1996** (Public Law 104–120) requires that public housing agencies, those who provide section 8 housing, and other federally funded housing agencies deny housing to a variety of individuals with criminal backgrounds:

- Those who have been evicted from public housing, section 8, or federally assisted housing due to drug-related criminal activity are ineligible for public or federally assisted housing for three years after the date of the eviction.
- Any household with a member who is subject to the lifetime registration requirement as a sex offender is permanently ineligible for such housing.
- Any household with a member who was convicted of producing methamphetamine on public housing premises is permanently ineligible for such housing.
- Any household with a member who is currently abusing alcohol in such a way that it interferes with the health, safety, or the right to peaceful enjoyment of the premises' other residences is ineligible for such housing.
- Any household with a member who is illegally using drugs is ineligible for such housing (Legal Action Center, 2000b)

Prison Services.   Prisons have relatively few resources to address educational, vocational, physical health, and mental health needs of prisoners. Less that 20 percent of prisoners needing treatment receive it before release, approximately 25 percent receive some type of vocational training, and only 33 percent receive educational assistance. The length of prison terms is increasing, yet participation in prerelease programs has decreased, resulting in an increase in ex-offenders who are ill-prepared to reenter their communities and become self-sufficient (Lynch & Sabol, 2001).

Parole Supervision.   Very little is known as to whether parole supervision increases public safety or eases reentry transition. Parole supervision is used as a form of surveillance and as a social-service mechanism, and ideally it serves as a deterrent to keep parolees from committing new crimes (Solomon, Kachnowski, & Bhati, 2005). Research showed that less than half of parolees successfully completed their period of supervision without committing a new crime or violating a condition of their release (Hughes, Wilson, & Beck, 2001). However, an increasing number of ex-offenders are reentering the community without supervision. In many cases, these ex-offenders had committed less serious crimes, and the judge decided not to require postrelease supervision (Lynch & Sabol, 2001). Little is known, though, about recidivism rates among this population, and the unconditional release of prisoners varies from state to state (Travis et al., 2001). At least one study showed that parole supervision had little effect on the rearrest rate of released prisoners, and mandatory parolees had return rates similar to those who are unsupervised. Certain populations, however, benefit more from supervision. Individuals with few prior arrests, females, technical violators, and public-order offenders are less likely to be rearrested if supervised after their release. Low-level offenders (those who have several of the aforementioned characteristics) are even less likely to be rearrested when supervised. Supervision does not appear to improve rearrest outcomes for the more serious or violent offenders. Male, drug offenders have higher rearrest rates when they are released to mandatory supervision than when they are unconditionally released (Solomon et al., 2005).

Lack of Juvenile-Appropriate Services. Juveniles have different incarceration and postrelease needs than their adult counterparts. During the adolescent and teenage years, youth transition developmentally from child to adulthood, including physical, cognitive, social, and emotional conditions. In addition to facing the usual developmental challenges of adolescence, juvenile offenders face challenges in their transition into incarceration as well as their reentry into the community upon release. Altschuler and Brash (2004) suggested that reentry programs should be viewed more as reintegration programs that begin during confinement and continue postrelease. Such programs need to address all of the challenges facing youth. However, few programs in adult facilities meet the developmentally linked needs of youth offenders (Snyder, 2004). Multiple agencies and institutions lack systematic reintegration services. Such programs are critical in reducing crime and improving youth reentry (Altschuler & Brash, 2004). They need to provide independent living skills in addition to education, vocational training, and mental health services (Mears & Travis, 2004).

Individual Barriers

Education, Cognitive Skills, and Work Experience. The poor skills and work experience of many ex-offenders often conflict with the credentials and skills that are required by most employers for even the relatively unskilled jobs (Solomon, Johnson, et al., 2004). Almost 70 percent of offenders and ex-offenders are high-school dropouts (Travis et al., 2001). Although at one time inmates could used federal financial aid to pursue their postsecondary education while in prison, the **Violent Crime Control and Law Enforcement Act of 1994** (Public Law 103-322) made inmates ineligible to receive Pell Grants and other forms of financial assistance. Most offenders have not demonstrated that they are committed to holding a job and reporting every day for a substantial period of time. Thus, once ex-offenders obtain a job, *maintaining* that job for at least a year improves their likelihood of being hired by other employers and leads to better jobs (Bushway, 2003). Education needs for female offenders often differ from their male counterparts. Many adult women in the correctional systems are high-school graduates while 30 to 40 percent have attended some college. Juveniles, on the other hand have less education than their adult counterparts (Mears & Travis, 2004).

Family and Peers. Families are an important component of successful reentry. Families can provide emotional as well as physical support, and these relationships may help prevent relapse and recidivism. Not all families are functional, however, and child support and child custody can be specific challenges. Some ex-offenders have extensive family histories of incarceration, abuse, and substance abuse, any one of which can negatively impact attempts to reunite the family (La Vigne, 2004). Offenders are spending longer time in prison, which results in declining frequency of contact with family members (Lynch & Sabol, 2001). While some juveniles return to supportive families, others may not be able to do so if they have committed drug offenses and their parents live in public housing. In either case, a return to a family may not always be desirable. As Snyder (2004) pointed out, over half of all juvenile offenders have at least one family member who served a jail or prison sentence. From a developmental standpoint, reintegrating into peer networks is particularly important for juveniles but peer influence can be positive or negative, depending on the peers with whom the juvenile associates (Altschuler & Brash, 2004). Obviously, reintegration with delinquent peers can increase the likelihood of recidivism whereas connecting with nondelinquent peers can reduce that likelihood (Mears & Travis, 2004).

Lack of Employability Skills.   Ex-offenders often lack the employability or life skills they need to obtain and keep a job. McCollum (1999) suggested that skills such as learning why and how to get to work on time, dealing with criticism from a supervisor, working as a team member, and handling other job-related stresses such as locating childcare and dependable transportation require behavior modification and need to begin well in advance of the offender's reentry.

Physical and Mental Health Barriers

Problems with mental and physical health are often intertwined with one in five prisoners reporting a physical or mental health problem that affected their ability to work (Maruschak & Beck, 2001). Access to health care and any required medications, however, is limited for prisoners after their release, despite legislation such as the **Mentally Ill Offender Treatment and Crime Reduction Act of 2004** (La Vigne, 2004).

Communicable Diseases.   The National Commission on Correctional Health Care [NCCHC] (2002) reported that a high number of inmates suffer from infectious diseases such as AIDs, HIV, hepatitis C, and tuberculosis as compared to the general population. For instance, the prevalence of AIDs among inmates is six times that of the general population (Dean-Gaitor & Fleming, 1999). HIV infections among jail inmates are 8 to 10 times the prevalence in the general population, and HIV infections among the prison population are 4 to 6 times the prevalence in the general population. Hepatitis C is found 9 to 10 times as often in the corrections population. Tuberculosis disease is present in 7 percent of the correctional population, which is almost 17 times the prevalence in the general population. In addition, an estimated 2.6 to 4.3 percent of inmates have syphilis, 2.4 percent have chlamydia, and 1 percent has gonorrhea (NCCHC, 2002).

Chronic Diseases.   Inmates also often suffer from a variety of chronic diseases. Asthma is more prevalent in the corrections populations than in the general population. However, the prevalence of diabetes and hypertension are lower in the corrections population, probably because these diseases are more likely to afflict older individuals, and the corrections populations is generally younger (NCCHC, 2002).

Disabilities.   Ten percent of inmates reported having a learning disability, which is over three times the prevalence as reported in the general population. Twelve percent reported a vision or hearing problem, and 4 percent reported a speech condition that limited their ability to work. Many juveniles in the criminal justice system also have undiagnosed and untreated learning disabilities (Snyder, 2004). While such conditions may not contribute to criminal behavior, they do reduce the likelihood that ex-offenders will successfully transition into healthy and stable relationships and employment (Mears & Travis, 2004). Some estimates identified 12 percent of juvenile offenders as having a form of mental retardation and 36 percent as having learning disabilities (Mears & Aron, 2003). The juvenile justice system, however, lacks the resources necessary to address such disabilities when offering educational and vocational programming (Mears & Travis, 2004).

Mental Illness. Over 89 percent of the nation's private and public adult correctional facilities reported that they provided mental health services to their inmates. Almost 70 percent of state facilities reported screening inmates at intake, and 65 percent provided psychiatric assessments. Fifty-one percent reported providing 24-hour mental health care, 71 percent provided counseling and therapy by trained mental health professionals, 73 percent provided psychotropic medications for their inmates, and 66 percent assisted inmates in finding postrelease mental health care (Beck & Maruschak, 2001).

Mental health problems may contribute to the prevalence and frequency of illegal behaviors among some youth (Loeber, Farrington, Stouthamer-Loeber, & Van Kammen, 1998). One study, for example, found that 68 percent of incarcerated, male youths had a mental health disorder (Wasserman, MacReynolds, Lucas, Fisher, & Santos, 2002). Still another study suggested that the rate of mental health disorders for female juvenile offenders is higher than that of males. In this study, 66 percent of committed juvenile males had at least one diagnosable mental health disorder (comparable to that in the previously cited study), compared to 74 percent of the detained female juvenile offenders (Teplin, Abram, McClelland, Dulcan, & Mericle, 2002). This study also reported that the rates of diagnosable mental health disorders were higher for detained, white female juveniles than they were for detained, African American or Hispanic, female juveniles.

The NCCHC (2002) examined six mental illness diagnoses in the corrections population, and reported that the prevalence rates of many mental illnesses is higher in the criminal justice population than in the general population. Such mental illness included schizophrenia or other psychoses, major depression, bipolar (manic), dysthymia, post-traumatic stress disorder, and anxiety. Some estimates reported 8 to 16 percent of inmates have at least one disorder that requires treatment (Solomon, Waul, Van Ness, & Travis, 2004). Assessments of juvenile offenders include mental illness diagnoses of conduct disorder, oppositional defiant, suicide, panic disorder, PTSD, agoraphobia, social phobia, and obsessive compulsive disorder (Wasserman et al., 2002).

Substance Abuse. Substance abuse is a problem for both adult and youth offenders or ex-offenders. As such it is another barrier to success.

Adults. More than two-thirds of prisoners have histories of substance use, and almost one-third have served time for drug possession or sales (La Vigne, 2004). Almost half of the women in state prisons used drugs, alcohol, or both while committing the offence for which they had been incarcerated. Women were more likely to use drugs during the offence than were men. Forty percent of women reported that they had been under the influence of drugs compared to 32 percent of male inmates. Almost 60 percent of women in state prisons reported using drugs in the month before the offence, and 50 percent identified themselves as daily users. One in three women reported that they committed the offence that brought them to prison to obtain the money to support their drug use. Alcohol use was higher for males than for females. Over half of the women confined in state prisons reported drinking alcohol in the year before their current offence compared to two-thirds of male inmates. Twenty-five percent of male and female inmates reported being daily drinkers, yet 29 percent of women offenders and 39 percent of male offenders reported that they were under the influence of alcohol during their current offence (La Vigne, 2004).

Women substance abusers were more likely than their male counterparts to report that they had received substance-abuse treatment. Twenty percent of women substance abusers in state prisons reported they had received treatment since their incarceration as opposed to 14 percent of male substance abusers. Nearly one-third of both men and women substance abusers reported participating in voluntary programs such as Alcoholics Anonymous or Narcotics Anonymous since entering prison (Greenfield & Snell, 2000). Although treatment of offenders while incarcerated is often effective, substance-abuse treatment is not readily available (La Vigne, 2004). Linking drug treatment to aftercare is extremely important in helping ex-offenders successfully reintegrate into their communities (O'Brien, 2002).

Juveniles.   Juvenile offenders also reported substance abuse. Fifty-seven percent reported consuming alcohol at least once a week for the past month, and 32 percent reported being under the influence of alcohol when they committed their most recent crime. Most youth, however, were using drugs other than alcohol: 83 percent reported using drugs, and 63 percent used other drugs regularly. Eighty-one percent of incarcerated youth used marijuana compared to 51 percent of high-school seniors. Incarcerated youth have higher levels of substance abuse compared to nonincarcerated youth for other drugs. For example, 46 percent of incarcerated youth had used cocaine compared to 17 percent of nonincarcerated youth, 36 percent had used amphetamines compared to 23 percent, 29 percent had used LSD compared to 7 percent, 23 percent had used PCP compared to 9 percent, and 13 percent had used heroin compared to 1 percent. Youth offenders reported starting regular drug use at an early age: 11 percent started before age 10, 17 percent between ages 10 and 11, and 35 percent between ages 12 and 13. Thirty-five percent reported being under the influence of drugs when they committed their most recent crime (Snyder, 2004).

Career Development Program Model: The Offender or Ex-Offender Population

A career development program for offenders needs to integrate transitional services that address each client's needs and barriers with the ultimate goal being the successful reintegration of the client into the community through long-term employment. Offenders who participate in training programs *while in prison* are less likely to commit new crimes or violate the conditions of their release, and those participating in training programs are more likely to find postrelease employment (Bushway, 2003). Our program has three major components: the applicant pool, the Individual Success Plan (ISP), and the program evaluation. Each component will be explained in detail. Figure 14.1 is a graphic model of the career development program.

Applicant Pool

The applicant pool for this career development program contains any client who is an offender or ex-offender. Intake personnel will determine which clients fit the criteria for program participation and which do not and will refer clients for additional services as necessary. If this program assists those who have already been released from prison, then additional criteria will need to be established for ex-offenders in transition.

Individual Success Plan

The Individual Success Plan (ISP) provides a personal approach to career development. Offenders or ex-offenders have a variety of barriers to career success, so human service professionals need to continue to view each client as an individual and to help that client successfully transition into the community through finding a stable job. Involvement in developing the ISP can help clients take some control over their lives, empowering them to be successful.

Make Assessments.   Human service professionals need to consider more than just their clients' vocational and educational needs. They must consider their clients' criminal background, age, and stage of development. Chapter 3 provides an assortment of career-related assessments to be used according to the needs and background of the clients. A traditional intake interview can help identify these needs and clarify the best course of action for the client at this time. Again, the age, developmental level, and criminal justice backgrounds of these clients must be considered in choosing assessments, as well as their educational attainment and vocational training. One client may be a juvenile with a seventh-grade education and another might be an adult with a tenth-grade education, so human service professionals need to carefully match assessments to the client. Table 14.1 is as list of assessments appropriate for use in designing an ISP with offenders or ex-offenders. Using several assessments is encouraged, but human service professionals need to choose those that best fit the needs of their clients. (See Chapter 3 for additional details on each assessment.)

Develop the ISP.   After choosing and completing the assessments, clients and human service professionals will cocreate the ISP. First, they will identify specific barriers to employment success by integrating information obtained through the intake interview, assessments, and discussions. Human service professionals will also need to

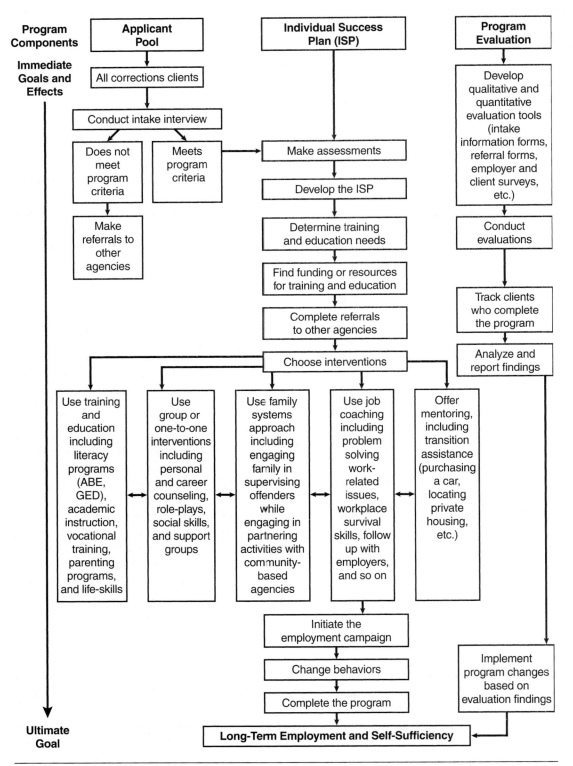

FIGURE 14.1 *Career Development Program Model: The Offender or Ex-Offender Population*

TABLE 14.1 *Career Related Assessments for Use with the Offender or Ex-Offender Population*

Title	Source
Ability Tests	
Ability Explorer	Harrington, J. C., & Harrington, T. F. (1996). *Ability explorer.* Itasca, IL: Houghton Mifflin.
Career Key*	Jones, L. L., & Jones, J. W. (2000). *Career key.* Raleigh, NC: Author.
Motivated Skills Card Sort	Knowdell, R. (2002, June). *Motivated skills card sort.* San Jose, CA: Career Research & Testing.
O*NET Ability Profiler*	O*NET Consortium (2003, April). *O*NET ability profiler.* Washington, DC: Author
WorkKeys	ACT, Inc. (1993). *Workkeys assessments.* Iowa City, IO: ACT.
Interest Inventories	
Career Exploration Inventory 2	Liptak, J. (2001). *Career exploration inventory 2.* Indianapolis, IN: JIST Works.
CareerExplorer CD-ROM*	JIST Works (2004). *Careerexplorer CD-ROM.* Indianapolis, IN: Author.
Guide for Occupational Exploration Interest Inventory	Farr, M. (2002). *Guide for occupational exploration interest inventory* (4th ed.). Indianapolis, IN: JIST Works.
Leisure to Occupations Connection Search	McDaniels, C., & Mullins, S. R. (1999). *The leisure to occupations connection search.* Indianapolis, IN: JIST Works.
Occupational Interests Card Sort	Knowdell, R. (2002, June). *Occupational interests card sort.* San Jose, CA: Career Research & Testing.
O*NET Career Interests Inventory*	JIST Works. (2002). *O*NET career interests inventory.* Indianapolis, IN: Author.
Self-Directed Search, Forms R, E, and E Audiotape	Holland J. L. (1994). *Self-directed search form R.* Lutz, FL: Psychological Assessment Resources. Holland, J. L. (1996). *Self-directed search form E* (4th ed.). Lutz, FL: Psychological Assessment Resources. Holland, J. L. (1996). *Self-directed search form E* (4th ed.). [Audiotape]. Lutz, FL: Psychological Assessment Resources.
Transition-to-Work Inventory	Liptak, J. J. (2004). *Transition-to-work inventory.* Indianapolis, IN: JIST Works.
Voc-Tech Quick Screener	JIST Works (2002). *Voc-tech quick screener.* Indianapolis, IN: Author.
Wide Range Interest and Occupation Test	Glutting, J. J., & Wilkinson, G. (2003). *Wide range interest and occupation test* (2nd ed.). Wilmington, DE: Wide Range.
Value Inventories	
Career Values Card Sort	Knowdell, R. (1998, June). *Career values card sort.* San Jose, CA: Career Research & Testing.

(Continued)

TABLE 14.1   Continued

Title	Source
O*NET Career Values Inventory*	JIST Works (2002). *O*NET career values inventory.* Indianapolis, IN: Author.
O*NET Work Importance Locator and Profiler*	O*NET Consortium (n.d.). *O*NET work importance locator and profiler.* Washington, DC: Author.
Career-Development Inventories	
Barriers to Employment Success Inventory	Liptak, J. J. (2002). *Barriers to employment success* (2nd ed.). Indianapolis, IN: JIST Works.
Career Attitudes and Strategies Inventory	Holland, J. L., & Gottfredson, G. D. (1994). *Career attitudes and strategies inventory.* Lutz, FL: Psychological Assessment Resources.
Career Beliefs Inventory	Krumboltz, J. D. (1991). *Career beliefs inventory.* Mountain View, CA:CPP.
Career Thoughts Inventory	Sampson, J. P., Peterson, G. W., Lenz, J. G., Reardon, R. C., & Saunders, D. E. (1996). *Career thoughts inventory.* Lutz, FL: Psychological Assessment Resources.
Career Transition Inventory	Heppner, M. J. (1991). *Career transition inventory.* Columbia, MO: Author.
Job Search Attitude Inventory	Liptak, J. J. (2002). *Job search attitude inventory* (2nd ed.). Indiaanapolis, IN: JIST Works.
My Vocational Situation	Holland, J. L., Daiger, D., & Power, P. G. (1980). *My vocational situation.* Mountain View, CA: CPP.
Overcoming Barriers Card Sort Game Kit	Harney, E. E., & Angel, D. L. (1999). *Overcoming barriers card sort game kit.* Hacienda Heights, CA: WorkNet Solutions.
Reading-Free Vocational Interest Inventory: 2	Becker, R. L. (2000). *Reading-free vocational interest inventory:2.* Columbus, OH: Elburn.
Vocational Exploration and Insight Kit	Holland, J. L., Birk, J. M., Cooper, J. F., Dewey, C. R., Dolliver, H., Takai, R. T., & Tyler, L. (1980). *The vocational exploration and insight kit.* Mountain View, CA: CPP.
Miscellaneous	
Elevations ® Manual Card Sort System	Scully, H. (2003, August). *Elevations manual card sort system.* Roseville, CA: Author.
Career Genograms	Gysbers, N. C., Heppner, M. J., & Johnson, J. A. (2003). *Career counseling: Process, issues, and techniques* (2nd ed.) Boston: Allyn and Bacon.
Individual Employment Plan	Ludden, L. L., & Maitlen, B. (2002). *Individual employment plan.* Indianapolis, IN: JIST Works.
Vocational Decision-Making Interview	Czerlinsky, T., & Chandler, S. (1999). *Vocational decision-making interview.* Indianapolis, IN: JIST Works.

*Use only if client is computer literate.

address issues of mental and physical health and make referrals when necessary. The next step is to help clients integrate their values and career and personal goals into the planning process. When feasible, human service professionals should involve the offenders' or ex-offenders' families in this stage so as to include the family's values and possible barriers to employment as well as those of the offender or ex-offender. Human service professionals and clients work together to determine what barriers to include in the ISP. They then create a timeline for meeting each goal and make sure that every goal is measurable and attainable. A well-developed program will motivate offenders to change by meeting their needs in all areas: education, training, life skills, social skills, mental health, and physical health.

Determine Training and Education Needs. Training and education are an important step to a successful transition into the community for offenders or ex-offenders that will enhance their potential productivity through specific skill-building programs or job training. Offenders or ex-offenders who dropped out of school, however, may be hesitant to enter classroom-based training because of a previous lack of success. Still other clients may not immediately see the need to improve their soft skills. Reviewing assessment results with clients will provide them with career leads for possible training and education in addition to other topics for training and education such as life skills. Offenders or ex-offenders can take life-skills training in small groups or one-on-one, allowing for a more individualized fit as needed.

Find Funding or Resources for Training and Education. Many correctional facilities provide ABE, GED, high-school classes, and postsecondary education. Such courses are often required for juvenile offenders. Adults are also able to take advantage of such services as available. While states often provide subsidies for juvenile education, these funds are frequently supplemented by voluntary, adult inmate contributions earned through prison work programs designed to encourage self-sufficiency. Inmates and ex-offenders who want to pursue postsecondary education can use WIA funding and private scholarships to cover the costs. Offenders or ex-offenders who are veterans can be referred to the local Incarcerated Veterans Transition Program for job-search activities and counseling, job-preparation training, classroom training, job placement, and follow-up services. Funding sources vary by state, so human service professionals need to be familiar with local organizations and funding sources. Some states have placed juvenile corrections under the Department of Human Services, further emphasizing youth reentry into society. Other states have shifted their resources to allow the funding to follow the youth back into the community (Mears & Travis, 2004). Postrelease training and education can be funded through federal as well as state programs. States that have pursued changes to TANF-based funding may provide TANF in addition to WIA funds and several grant programs that target the ex-offender population.

Choose Interventions. The career development program for offenders and ex-offenders has five categories of interventions: group or one-to-one interventions, training and education, family systems, job coaching, and mentoring. The client and human service professional consult to determine whether the best approach for the client is that of individual or group. Interventions may be offered concurrently or in phases, depending upon clients' needs and agency requirements. Some clients may need all five interventions while others may only need one or two. Again, an individualized approach is necessary due to the diverse backgrounds of offenders or ex-offenders.

Using Group or One-to-One Interventions.   One-to-one intervention is often needed to help offenders or ex-offenders transition into the community. These interventions include personal counseling combined with career development, and they may incorporate role-plays and support groups. Clients may be referred elsewhere for these services or kept in house, depending on the needs of the clients and the services available. Personal counseling would address such issues as depression, anxiety, and substance abuse. In some cases, offenders or ex-offenders may be eligible for unemployment benefits through the **Transitional Aid Research Project of 1963 (TARP)**, but this assistance is only available for the first year after release (Berk, Lenihan, & Rossi, 1980).

Providing Training and Education.   This component of the ISP includes literacy programs, academic instruction such as pre-GED, GED, and post-high-school education, as well as training needs. Offenders may participate in prison work programs or other available training programs to improve their potential productivity. Postrelease training programs, apprentice programs, life-skills classes, and reintegration programs are also offered in this component. Job-readiness programs help corrections clients improve their reliability. This population frequently needs to improve their self-presentation skills through interviews and resume writing. Offenders or ex-offenders may also need assistance in handling the logistical challenges that interfere with keeping a job such as transportation, childcare, and housing assistance.

Using a Family Systems Approach.   When feasible, families should be encouraged to help the offender reenter the community. In a functional system, families can provide emotional support for the ex-offender and can assist in supervising the ex-offender while the family is engaged in partnering activities with community-based agencies. The human service professional will want to encourage family members to participate in family counseling sessions to help them better understand the challenges both they and the ex-offender family member face.

Job Coaching.   The job coach's overall task is to help the offender or ex-offender transition into the workforce. The task includes meeting regularly with the client either on or off the job site to deal with job concerns before they affect employment. Such concerns could include how to handle being late or absent from work, how to problem-solve to find back-up transportation or childcare, and how to deal with anger on the job. Topics addressed by the job coach do not, however, include the skills training provided by the employer. The employer meets regularly with the job coach and is available to meet with the coach and the client as needed. If an employer hires several ex-offenders, then group sessions could also be integrated, but the individual sessions need to continue. The assistance provided by a job coach can lead to a better-qualified and self-confident employee.

Offering Mentoring.   While a job coach assists the client on the job, the mentor assists the client in the complete transition into the community, leading to self-sufficiency for the client. The mentor helps the client with the every day tasks of life: purchasing a car, locating private housing, opening a bank account, finding affordable childcare, and creating a new network of friends who are supportive of the ex-offender's reintegration goals.

Initiate the Employment Campaign.

The client's needs and goals determine the employment campaign. Some clients may need to begin their employment campaign immediately, whereas others may have time to complete work-related activities before beginning the campaign. Eliminating barriers to employment success before initiating a job campaign is the preferred approach, but it is not always feasible. Some clients may need to work on several activities at once, which will require intensive case management on the part of the human service professional. The next sections provide an overview of considerations for the employment campaign for offenders or ex-offenders. For additional details, see Chapter 5.

The Strategic Job Search.   Information gathered from the assessments and from the intake interview are used here as the offenders or ex-offenders explore the importance of values and goals in the job-search process. Clients may need to be reminded at this point that they do not yet have the skills to begin working in the job of their choice, and they will need to work toward developing those skills. Helping them plan and see that every step they take is leading them closer to their employment goal is extremely important. In the meantime, they need to determine whether or not their values will be met in each of the jobs they are considering. Once they better understand themselves, they can begin to understand the career choice itself and the education and skills it entails. Understanding their employer's needs helps clients better understand how to anticipate and meet those needs. The job market varies with geographical location, and the human service professionals can help clients maneuver through the local market by using their networks to find what is available and who is hiring. Local employment agencies can assist with this task. Job-search classes could be used here as well.

Job-Search Correspondence.   Many jobs will not require a letter of application, but clients should still know how to prepare these letters, along with referral letters, reminder letters, and interview appreciation letters. Also, rather than teaching clients to write a letter accepting or declining an offer, human service professionals can use role-playing these situations to help them better understand the process from the employer's point of view. As their job experience grows and they apply for higher-level positions, then they can learn the other letter-writing procedures.

Tailor-Made Resumes.   Offenders or ex-offenders who participate in prison work programs have recent job experience that allows them to use a chronological resume format.

Those who do not have recent experience can use a functional resume to organize their job experience according to their skills. Using this type of resume will increase clients' self-esteem and empower them to see that they do possess job skills, something they may not have considered in the past. Developing a resume also helps clients organize their experiences and better understand themselves, allowing them to focus more on their strengths, instead of weaknesses.

Interviewing Strategies.   Interpersonal skills are often weak in this population, so they would benefit from role-playing the various types of interview situations from easy to difficult, and from panel to telephone. Helping clients craft answers to some of the common interview questions will empower them as well. Videotaping clients during mock interviews followed by a critique of the interview will provide clients with an opportunity to see themselves as others do. The case worker should stress appropriate interview attire since these clients may not be aware of the necessity to dress professionally for an interview or that the attire may vary depending upon the job.

Change Behaviors.   Participation in this career development program is designed to prevent offenders or ex-offenders from being repeat offenders by helping them change behaviors that were keeping them from being productive self-sufficient citizens with long-term employment. Although specific behavior changes will vary with each person's ISP, all clients moving through this program will have had an opportunity to improve their interpersonal and work-related skills and other skills they originally targeted for change.

Complete the Program.   Offenders or ex-offenders who entered the program, developed their ISPs, completed the training and education that were detailed in their ISPs, and located gainful employment are considered to have completed the program. Another measure of successful program completion for this population is that they have not committed a new crime or violated conditions of their release. Depending upon program guidelines, offenders or ex-offenders might be able to leave the program, but they need to be aware that their decisions may impact their education and training and their eligibility for other types of assistance.

Achieve Goal of Long-Term Employment.   Long-term employment and self-sufficiency are the goals of this program. The program staff will need to determine the definition of *long-term* employment but, generally, when clients have been employed for at least a year, are fully able to support themselves and their family members, and are no longer receiving any form of public assistance, they could be considered self-sufficient with long-term employment.

Program Evaluation

Increasing federal requirements to demonstrate accountability and program success make program evaluation an essential element of this career development program model. The program staff needs to integrate program evaluation into every phase of the career development program from development to termination. Human service professionals need to develop a variety of tools to evaluate their program. Figure 14.1 is a flow chart for the career development model for the offenders and ex-offenders. The text in each box in the figure is a factor that needs to be measured. In addition to providing accountability for programs, evaluations help the staff determine if the program is meeting the needs of the clients and agency. Agency staff must determine what type of evaluations they will use (i.e., process, outcome, impact) and what evaluative instruments will help them gather the necessary information. After making these decisions, the program staff needs to develop a timeline for the entire evaluation process that includes deadlines and the people responsible for the evaluation. After the evaluation is completed, human service professionals can then present their data, findings, and recommendations in an evaluation report that provides suggestions for program modifications and improvement. For more detailed information regarding the evaluation process see Chapter 6.

Revisiting the Case Study: Brian

Conduct an Intake Interview

During the intake interview session, the human service professional needs to explore Brian's correctional, medical, financial, educational, and employment histories; his interests and values; and his views on employment. Other topics to explore include his substance-abuse history and his relationships with his parents and his girlfriend. Since Brian has not completed high school and appears to have little job training, the human service professional needs to explore other training and education possibilities for Brian. The case worker must keep in mind Brian's level of development as a juvenile and test for learning disabilities and for his reading level. Assessments can help identify his interests, values, and goals.

Make Assessments

Several career-related assessments could help Brian at this point. The Ability Explorer (Harrington & Harrington, 1996) that is written on a fifth-grade reading level would help identify Brian's ability areas (i.e., artistic, clerical, interpersonal, language, leadership, manual, musical/dramatic, numerical/mathematical, organizational, persuasive, scientific, social, spatial, and technical/mechanical). The O*NET Ability Profiler (O*NET Consortium, 2003) could help Brian identify his strengths and the areas where he may want additional training. Another possible assessment is WorkKeys (ACT, 1993). This assessment would provide Brian with a list of his skills matched to available jobs. Skills that need further work can be enhanced through completion of a series of modules. If Brian is willing to use the computer, he could also use Career Key (Jones & Jones, 2000) to explore his abilities.

Interest inventories would help Brian identify potential careers of interest. The Career Exploration Inventory 2 (Liptak, 2002) helps unemployed youth who read on a seventh-grade level explore and plan their work, leisure activities, and education and learning. The Guide for Occupational Exploration Interest Inventory (Farr, 2002) and the O*NET Career Interests Inventory (JIST Works, 2002) are also appropriate to use with Brian. Finally, the Transition to Work Inventory (Liptak, 2004) is designed to help the ex-offender and probation population in incarceration-to-work programs by matching interests to job options in 84 areas. If Brian has any learning disabilities, then the human service professional may want to use the Wide Range Interest & Occupation Test (Glutting & Wilkinson, 2003) to determine his career interests.

Brian may not have had an opportunity to explore his values, and several different assessments could help him do so. Depending upon Brian's level of computer literacy, the human service professional may suggest that Brian complete either the O*NET Career Values Inventory (JIST Works, 2002) or the O*NET Work Importance Locator and Profiler (O*NET Consortium, n. d.) that will help him examine how values relate to various jobs. If Brian is not interested in computer-based assessments, then the human service professional might want to use the Career Values Card Sort (Knowdell, 1998a) to identify factors that affect his career satisfaction.

Brian's barriers to career success can be explored using one of several different assessments. Barriers to Employment Success Inventory (Liptak, 2002) helps identify personal, physical and psychological, career planning, job-seeking skills, and education and training barriers. The Career Beliefs Inventory (Krumboltz, 1991) would also be appropriate to use with Brian, because it provides suggestions that could help him overcome his barriers, along with information on how to strengthen values that are not barriers.

Determine Barriers to Career Success

Brian currently faces several possible barriers to his successful reintegration into the community. One barrier is his interrupted education. He has completed some work toward the GED, but he needs to finish it. Doing so will improve his self-esteem and open doors to jobs that require at least a GED. The human service professional needs to determine what kept him from finishing the GED. Was he spending time with the wrong crowd? Was he not interested in school? Was he unable to do his school work? If Brian has an undiagnosed learning disability, it should be addressed through other assistance (See Chapter 15). His sexual activity and use of alcohol and drugs also need to be addressed (See Chapter 16). As evidenced by his mumbling, Brian's social skills may need polishing and he may also need job-ready clothing. Although she is currently part of his support system, possibly his primary support, Brian's girlfriend may not be particularly helpful. Despite pursuing her own GED and having both a car and a job, she shares his substance-abuse behaviors. Helping Brain gradually build a strong supportive network is extremely important to his successful reintegration into the community. His mother seems to offer little support, but his father may be able to help Brian, so encouraging Brian to maintain and possibly increase contact with his father could greatly benefit him. Brian has worked in the past, although not steadily, so the human service professional will need to help him turn his spotty work record into a more stable one. Although Brian currently has a place to live, that situation will change on his next birthday, so the human service professional needs to address housing with him before he becomes homeless. The goal is to prepare Brian for progressively increased responsibility and freedom in his reintegration.

Choose Interventions

Using Group and One-to-One Interventions.   Brian would benefit from substance-abuse counseling and vocational counseling. The substance-abuse counseling can help Brian control his anger and improve his self-esteem, while exploring any other motivations he may have to self-medicate. Personal counseling could address those issues as well. Individual counseling could give Brian a safe place for role-plays and an opportunity to work on social skills that could be continued in support groups, anger management groups, or other group formats. Assertiveness training may also be useful.

Using a Family Systems Approach.   A supportive family network will help hasten Brian's reintegration into the community. His mother does not appear able to help him in this way, so his case worker should involve Brian's father, friends, neighbors, and others who are interested in helping Brian succeed in creating a "supportive" family. Brenda cannot be removed from the network, but she should be encouraged to deal with her own problems so that she does not become a barrier to Brian's success.

Finding Training and Education.   Once the human service professional has assessed Brian's reading level and has developed his ISP, then the two of them can craft a strong education and training plan for Brian at this time. As previously mentioned, Brian needs to complete his GED, utilizing whatever disability services may be necessary to do so. Vocational and life-skills programs can give Brian the skills he needs for success. Balancing a checkbook, locating transportation, and finding housing are important life skills for Brian to possess.

Using Job Coaching.   Once Brian has secured a job, the job coach will help him maintain his job by working with Brian and his employer to help Brian stay successful in the workplace. The job coach will address problem-solving with work-related topics and will explore workplace survival skills, with the goal of helping Brian transition into the workforce. This job-coach assistance can help Brian become a better-qualified and self-confident employee who will not commit a new crime or violate conditions of his release.

Using Mentoring.   Brian's support network needs to include a mentor who is familiar with the issues of juvenile reentry and will work with Brain to help him become successful. This mentor might encourage Brian to find new friends, help him handle various problems as they arise, and even help him problem-solve with *non*work-related problems.

Initiate the Employment Campaign

When Brian and his human service professional deem him ready, they will initiate the employment campaign. Once Brian has more education and vocational training, he will be ready to look for a job that meets his goals and values. The human service professional can use his or her professional network to find Brian a job with an employer who understands ex-offenders and is willing to help Brian adjust to his increasing responsibilities as Brian works toward self-sufficiency. If no positions exist within the case worker's professional network, then Brian will need a functional resume and a great deal of role-playing to practice interviewing and responding to a variety of job-related scenarios.

Conclusion

As the population in the correctional system increases, the number of people who need assistance reentering the community after their release will also increase. Changes need to be made, though, to better help offenders or ex-offenders with their reentry process. Some recommended policy changes would assist this population in its transition to self-sufficiency. Changes in economic, community, and workforce policies would include:

- Bringing a public safety presence to low-income neighborhoods to encourage businesses to relocate
- Including communities and family networks in reentry initiatives
- Linking programs offered in prison to those available after release
- Reducing the legal barriers to employment for ex-offenders
- Increasing the number of prison work programs, along with the number of inmates who participate in such programs
- Reorienting the juvenile and criminal justice systems to focus on the reintegration of young offenders into society
- Developing reentry programs that reflect a youth-development perspective and that address the unique role of race/ethnicity and gender
- Providing opportunities for youth offenders to go to work rather than to jail
- Providing the resources necessary to address learning and other disabilities when offering educational and vocational programming

Changes to medical or mental health policy would include:

- Developing linkages to continue to provide mental and medical health care for offenders once they enter the community

Changes to education policies would include:

- Developing policies that improve K–16 education and lifelong training
- Providing alternative forms of training that are not classroom based

Summary

In the United States in 2003 residents over the age of 12 were victims of approximately 25.9 million crimes the majority of which were property crimes. Many of these offenders are parents with prior criminal backgrounds. Approximately 630,000 criminal offenders reenter the community every year, and almost one-third of those individuals are juvenile offenders. Ex-offenders face a variety of barriers to successful reentry into the community and employment. Ex-offenders tend to congregate in urban areas that already have high numbers of crime, poverty, unemployment, and homelessness.

Employers are not always willing to hire ex-offenders, and ex-offenders are legally barred from some specific jobs. Ex-offenders may not be eligible for public assistance or housing because of their offender status. Only 7 percent of inmates participate in prison work programs, so many ex-offenders lack the job skills necessary to secure postrelease employment. Juvenile offenders have even fewer opportunities to participate in programs before their release, and their different stages of development necessitate programs that are geared specifically to their needs and not to those of the adult offenders. The corrections population has a higher incidence of both medical and mental illnesses than the general population and ex-offenders frequently lack access to necessary medications after their release. Substance abuse is common among both adult and juvenile offenders. Career development program models designed to help this population attain long-term employment and self-sufficiency include an Individual Success Plan that assesses career abilities, interests, values, and barriers to success and uses several interventions: one-to-one interventions, family systems, training and education, job coaching, and mentoring.

Key Terms

Adult

Aggravated assault

Burglary

Crimes of violence

Felony

Hawes-Cooper Act of 1929

Housing Opportunity Program Extension Act of 1996

Justice System Improvement Act of 1979

Juvenile offender

Mentally Ill Offender Treatment and Crime Reduction Act of 2004

Misdemeanor

Parole or probation

Prison Industry Enhancement (PIE) Certification Program

Recidivism

Robbery

Simple assault

Transitional Aid Research Project of 1963 (TARP)

UNICOR

Violent crime

Violent Crime Control and Law Enforcement Act of 1994

Walsh-Healy Act of 1936

Work Opportunity Tax Credit (WOTC)

Web Resources

Note that website URLs may change over time.

American Correctional Association (ACA)
http://www.aca.org

Center on Juvenile and Criminal Justice
http://www.cjcj.org

Center for Law and Social Policy
http://www.clasp.org

Correctional Education Association (CEA)
http://www.ceanational.org

Corrections Connection
http://www.ceanational.org

**Gang Resistance Education and Training
(G.R.E.A.T.) Program**
http://www.great-online.org

**International Community Corrections
Association**
http://www.iccaweb.org

Juvenile Info Network
http://www.juvenilenet.org

**National Center on Education, Disability, and
Juvenile Justice (EDJJ)**
http://www.edjj.org

National Criminal Justice Reference Service
http://www.ncjrs.org

**Prison Industry Enhancement Certification
Program**
http://www.nationalcia.org/pieprog2.html

Reentry Policy Council
http://www.reentrypolicy.org

Safer Foundation
http://www.saferfoundation.org

UNICOR
http://www.unicor.gov/index.cfm

15

People with Physical and/or Mental Disabilities

An Empowerment Approach to Independence

Case Study: Theresa

Theresa is a 33-year-old, African-American, single mother of a 7-year-old son, Eddie. At age 27, approximately one year after giving birth to her son, Theresa began experiencing a variety of troubling symptoms including frequent urination, excessive thirst, irritability, fatigue, unexplained weight loss, and most alarming, blurry vision. After seeking medical attention, Theresa was diagnosed with type 2 diabetes.

Theresa's physicians stressed to her the importance of keeping her blood sugar and blood pressure under control. However, raising her son single-handedly and working full time as an administrative assistant at a law firm often took precedence over her own health needs. Theresa sometimes forgot to check her blood sugar and would often fail to take her medication. The effects of this neglect began to take its toll on Theresa's health. Theresa began to experience prickling sensations in her muscles and deteriorating vision. Upon careful examination, Theresa's physicians diagnosed her with neuropathy, a type of nerve disease, and proliferative retinopathy. *Proliferative retinopathy* is a serious eye disease in which blood vessels damaged as a result of the diabetes close off. In response to the blood vessels closing off, new blood vessels begin to grow in the retina. These new vessels are weak and can leak blood, thereby blocking vision. These new blood vessels can also cause scar tissue to grow. Once the scar tissue grows and then shrinks, it can distort the retina or pull it out of place.

Theresa's proliferative retinopathy was so severe that her retinas became detached, causing her to lose vision in both eyes. Following her physician's advice, Theresa opted for surgery to reattach her retinas. Unfortunately, the surgery was

335

unsuccessful as it is in about one-half of the cases. Although Theresa's neuropathy was treatable, her blindness was irreversible. Theresa was now faced with the realization that without the proper support, **assistive devices and technology,** and other needed accommodations, she could possibly lose her job. If she lost her job, how would she support herself and her son?

The Population of People with Physical and/or Mental Disabilities

Population Distribution

According to the 2000 U.S. Census, 49.7 million people in the United States over age 5 have a **disability,** making them the single largest minority group in the country. Approximately 5.2 million people with disabilities were between ages 5 to 20, which is 8 percent of the people in this age group. About 30.6 million people with disabilities were between ages 21 to 64. In this group 57 percent were unemployed. Of the roughly 14 million people who were 65 and over, 5.9 million or 42 percent were people with disabilities. Arkansas, Kentucky, Mississippi, and West Virginia had proportionately at 24 percent the highest rates of residents age five and over with a disability as compared to Alaska, Minnesota, and Utah that had at about 15 percent the lowest rates of disability.

The incidence of disability rises significantly as individuals reach their 60s and 70s. Surprisingly, advances in medical practice such as treatment of life-threatening diseases and the development of trauma centers has increased the incidence of disability in younger persons (The Center for an Assessable Society, 2000). Disability cuts across all socioeconomic backgrounds, geographic areas, and demographic characteristics.

Employment

In spite of accomplishments, unemployment among people with disabilities hovers at an embarrassing 70 percent, although nearly half of the people with disabilities are an employable age. This figure is even more distressing when compared to the nation's general unemployment rate which is at a thirty-year low of 3.9 percent (The Abilities Fund, 2005; American Association of People with Disabilities, n.d.). In addition, low-income adults with disabilities are less likely to be employed than other low-income adults. Therefore, individuals with disabilities will likely need to find other forms of cash support (Wittenburg & Favreault, 2003).

The Wall Street Journal reported in October 2000 that the current job-growth rate of 192,000 jobs per month has made jobs "easier than ever" to find (The Abilities Fund, 2005). However, our nation's largest minority, people with disabilities, remains virtually unaffected by this seemingly limitless employment opportunity, in spite of the fact that 67 to 78 percent of Americans with disabilities indicate that they want to work (American Association of People with Disabilities, n.d.; The Abilities Fund, 2005).

Earning Ability and Economic Effect on Society

Employment is not the only economic indicator where Americans with disabilities lag behind. Serious gaps in income and earnings also exist. According to The Abilities Fund (2005) one out of three adults with disabilities lives in very low-income households (very low-income households is defined as those with less than $15,000 annual income). The rate of adults without disabilities living in very low-income households is one out of eight. Compared with all low-income adults, adults with disabilities are more likely to report difficulties meeting certain needs including housing (e.g., rent, utilities, telephone) and food. People with mental health disabilities reported the most difficulties in meeting these needs. Approximately half of the individuals with poor mental health had difficulty paying their rent, mortgage, and utility bills (Wittenburg & Favreault, 2003).

Even when people with disabilities are employed, they earn substantially less than their nondisabled counterparts—roughly 76 cents to the dollar. Specifically, according to the U.S. Census Bureau's March 2001 supplement to the Current Population Survey (2004), the average earnings in 2000 of year-round, full-time workers, ages 16–64, with work disabilities was $33,109. Those without work disabilities earned an average of $43,269. The economic effects of disability are multiplied for those who also belong to other minority groups.

The economic effect of unemployment of Americans with disabilities in our society is considerable. According to the American Association of People with Disabilities (n.d.), the cost of direct government and private payments to support people with disabilities of employable age who do not have jobs is estimated to be $232 billion annually. In addition, another $195 billion in earnings and taxes are lost each year due to the unemployment of Americans with disabilities. By comparison, the United States annual budget deficit is approximately $200 billion.

Education

Seventy-two percent of individuals with work disabilities ages 16 to 64 had high-school diplomas or higher education in 2001. Only 11 percent of individuals ages 16 to 64 with work disabilities had college degrees or more in 2001 (U.S. Census Bureau, 2004). For certain clients, an **Individualized Family Service Plan (IFSP)** and/or an **Individualized Education Program (IEP)** can build the foundation for which future educational goals are met and exceeded.

Specific Disabilities

The U.S. Census Bureau, Public Information Office (2001) released a report titled "Americans With Disabilities: 1997," based on the Survey of Income and Program Participation. According to the report, among people 15 and over in 1997:

- 25 million had difficulty walking a quarter mile or climbing a flight of 10 stairs; 2.2 million used an ambulatory aid, such as a wheelchair; and 6.4 million used a cane, crutches, or a walker (6.4 million).
- About 18 million had difficulty lifting and carrying a 10-pound bag of groceries or grasping small objects.
- About 14.3 million had a mental disability, including 1.9 million with Alzheimer's disease, senility or dementia; and 3.5 million with a learning, or **hidden or invisible disability**.
- About 8.0 million had difficulty hearing what was said in a normal conversation with another person (even when wearing a hearing aid); of these, 800,000 were unable to hear what was said in a normal conversation.
- About 7.7 million had difficulty seeing the words and letters in ordinary newspaper print (even with glasses); of these, 1.8 million were unable to see words and letters in ordinary newspaper print.

Barriers to Career Success

Structural Barriers

Attitudes Toward People with Disabilities.   People with disabilities face many barriers every day—from physical impediments in buildings to systematic barriers in employment. However, the most difficult barriers to overcome are often the attitudes other people hold regarding people with disabilities (e.g., focusing on a person's disability rather than on the individual's abilities). The origins of attitudinal barriers are diverse. Some are born from ignorance or fear and some from misunderstanding or hate. Regardless of their origins, attitudinal barriers often keep people with disabilities from achieving their full potential. According to the U.S. Department of Labor, Office of Disability Employment Policy (2005) attitudinal barriers include:

- *Inferiority*. Because a person may be impaired in one of life's major functions, some people believe that individual is a "second-class citizen." However, most people with disabilities have skills that make the impairment a nonissue in the workplace.

- *Pity*. People feel sorry for the person with a disability, which tends to lead to patronizing attitudes. People with disabilities generally do not want pity and charity, just equal opportunity to earn their own way and live independently.

- *Hero Worship*. People consider someone with a disability who lives independently or pursues a profession to be brave or "special" for overcoming a disability. But most people with disabilities do not want accolades for performing day-to-day tasks. The disability is there; the individual has simply learned to adapt by using his or her skills and knowledge, just as everybody adapts to being tall, short, strong, fast, easygoing, bald, blonde, etc.

- *Ignorance*. People with disabilities are often dismissed as incapable of accomplishing a task without the opportunity to display their skills. In fact, people with quadriplegia can drive cars and have children. People who are blind can tell time on a watch and visit museums. People who are deaf can play baseball and enjoy music. People with developmental disabilities can be creative and maintain strong work ethics.

• *The Spread Effect.* People assume that an individual's disability negatively affects other senses, abilities or personality traits, or that the total person is impaired. For example, many people shout at people who are blind or do not expect people using wheelchairs to have the intelligence to speak for themselves. Focusing on the person's abilities rather than his or her disability counters this type of prejudice.

• *Stereotypes.* The other side of the spread effect is the positive and negative generalizations people form about disabilities. For example, many believe that all people who are blind are great musicians or have a keener sense of smell and hearing, that all people who use wheelchairs are docile or compete in paralympics, that all people with developmental disabilities are innocent and sweet-natured, and that all people with disabilities are sad and bitter. Aside from diminishing the individual and his or her abilities, such prejudice can set a standard too high or too low for individuals who are merely human.

• *Backlash.* Many people believe individuals with disabilities are given unfair advantages, such as easier work requirements. Employers need to hold people with disabilities to the same job standards as coworkers, though the means of accomplishing the tasks may differ from person to person. The **Americans with Disabilities Act of 1990 (ADA)** does not require special privileges for people with disabilities, just equal opportunities.

• *Denial.* Many disabilities are "hidden," such as learning disabilities, psychiatric disabilities, epilepsy, cancer, arthritis, and heart conditions. People tend to believe these are not bona fide disabilities needing accommodation. The ADA of 1990 defines *disability* as an impairment that "substantially limits one or more of the major life activities." Accommodating "hidden" disabilities that meet the above definition can keep valued employees on the job and open doors for new employees.

• *Fear.* Many people are afraid that they will "do or say the wrong thing" around someone with a disability. They therefore avert their own discomfort by avoiding the individual with a disability. As with meeting a person from a different culture, frequent encounters can raise the comfort level.

Attitudinal barriers just touch the surface of the various structural barriers that individuals with disabilities often encounter. Another structural barrier is associated with the career-matching process.

Career Matching. It is essential to match an individual's capabilities and interests with an employer's identified needs. A career-matching specialist helps employers identify the various roles the client with a disability can play in order to meet the employer's needs. However, a number of barriers may impede the career-matching process. Some possible career-matching barriers according to Stevens and Ibanez (2002) include:

- Career-matching team not knowing how to provide experience for a client who is lacking needed experience
- One-Stop Career Centers not familiar with matching the specialized career needs of an individual with a disability
- Career-matching team limiting career matches to known, available jobs, which may not match the individual's goals, dreams, and capabilities
- Career-matching team making career matches with an agency or organization that does not match the individual's preferences, needs, and capabilities
- Career-matching team making personal connections that are limited, burned out, or not willing to participate
- Career-matching team not matching the client's vision to the business used

In addition to the structural barriers associated with the career-matching process, individuals with disabilities often confront a myriad of barriers associated with workplace accommodations and access. The reason behind the lack of accommodations and access for individuals with disabilities has often been attributed to a common misconception regarding the cost of such accommodations to the employer.

Accommodations and Access in the Workplace.   A belief held by many employers is that workplace accommodations for people with disabilities are too expensive to be worthwhile. Because of this belief, the unavailability of workplace accommodations is another barrier to employment for people with disabilities. Ironically, most employment accommodations required by people with disabilities cost less than $650 with the average cost at around $200. Some of the most common employment accommodations that can make work possible for individuals with disabilities according to the U.S. Department of Labor, Office of Disability Employment Policy (2001) include: accessible parking or accessible, public-transit stop nearby; an elevator; adaptations to work stations; special work arrangements such as reduction in work hours, reduced or part-time hours, job redesign; handrails or ramp; job coach; specific office supplies; personal assistant; braille, enlarged print, special lighting, or audiotape; voice synthesizer, TTY Infrared System, or other technical device; and, reader, oral or sign language interpreter.

Accommodations and access minimize **environmental factors** that impede a person's career development and enable a person with a disability to enjoy an equal employment opportunity. When the lack of accommodations and access come into play, people with disabilities are often faced with severe barriers that present enormous obstacles for their career development. Systematic barriers often hidden within organizations cause other obstacles.

Systematic Barriers.   Systematic barriers are barriers that are masked within the practices and policies of an organization or agency. For example, an employer cuts off the opportunity to apply for a job for a person with a visual disability because the employer never produces job postings in alternative formats. Such a case is not necessarily intentional discrimination, but it is a course of action that may still result in a person with a disability not having the same opportunity for employment as a person without a disability. Following are two systematic barriers that impact people with disabilities: employment-specialist barriers and workplace culture barriers.

Employment Specialist.   Employment specialists work to support individuals with disabilities in the workplace. The specialist must know the specific skills required for the job, how the individual's skills compare to what is needed on the job, where the person can best learn the needed skills, how to support the person while the individual is learning the tasks, and when and how to fade support (Stevens & Ibanez, 2002). Possible barriers include employment specialists who lack specialized training and career options; are isolated on the job; are doing the job for the client; lack in-depth knowledge of the client; do not know how to fade supports so coworkers and other natural supports can kick into place; have poor links with clients' families; have too many responsibilities; do not know how to deal with unstructured or slow-work time, breaks, and social interactions; isolate the employee just by always being present; and experience high-turnover rates.

Workplace Culture.   Workplace culture can positively or negatively effect job success and satisfaction for the employee with a disability. *Workplace culture* refers to the way people typically do things at a specific organization. It includes the expectations people have for one another, the meanings behind actions and symbols, and what they value. Workplace culture can be seen in the way people dress, act, talk to one another, and celebrate in the workplace. For people with disabilities, learning the workplace culture can be very difficult, and the culture itself can produce significant barriers to employment success. The following is a list of barriers that can be attributed to workplace culture (Stevens & Ibanez, 2002):

- Potential employees with disabilities are unable to get through the "red tape" in order to compete for a job.
- Employee with the disability does not feel welcomed by other employees.
- Employee with the disability does not fit into the work culture and does not understand why.
- Employee is isolated and lacks connections with coworkers.

The following section addresses individual barriers that have been found to negatively impact the career development of people with disabilities.

Individual Barriers

Discouragement.   One of the most prevalent barriers that negatively impacts the employment of individuals with disabilities is discouragement from looking for work. According to the U.S. Department of Labor, Office of Disability Employment Policy (2001), people with disabilities cited the following as the most common reasons for being discouraged from looking for work: lack of available appropriate jobs, family responsibilities, lack of transportation, lack of appropriate information about jobs, inadequate training, fear of losing health insurance or Medicaid, and being discouraged from working by family and friends.

Financial Policies.   Approximately 7.5 million Americans with disabilities receive federal disability benefits. Although 72 percent of individuals with disabilities want to work, less than 1 percent of those receiving disability benefits fully enter the workforce (Brooke, 2002). This lack of participation in the workplace is due in part to disincentives in federal law. Some of the more common financial barriers prevalent in the lives of people with disabilities include:

- Inaccurate or lack of any information on how to preserve benefits while working
- Pressure for the client to "get any job"
- Ineffective focus on funding
- Poorly thought out funding plan that undercuts the client's ability to do the job (e.g., no funds for transportation)
- Lack of knowledge regarding funding choices

Clients with disabilities can be assisted financially through a number of federally supported programs such as **Plan for Achieving Self-Support (PASS), Ticket-to-Work and Self-Sufficiency Program,** and **Individual Development Accounts**. Next we will address another individual barrier, the lack of self-determination.

Lack of Self-Determination.   Self-determination has been recognized as a best practice in the education of individuals with disabilities since the early 1990s, when the **Individuals with Disabilities Education Act (IDEA)** mandated increased student involvement in transition planning. Research has shown that students with disabilities who left school more self-determined were more than twice as likely to be employed one year after graduation as their peers who were less self-determined. In addition, the more self-determined individuals earned significantly more. Three years after graduation, they were more likely to be living outside the family home and to have obtained jobs that provided benefits such as health coverage and vacation (Wehmeyer & Schwartz, 1997).

Various barriers can impede an individual's ability to develop self-determination. Among the most common of these barriers, according to Stevens and Ibanez (2002), are

- Lacking in choice, training, or supports given to individuals with disabilities and to their families
- Focusing on job goals as opposed to career and life planning
- Focusing on paperwork as opposed to people-driven plans
- Providing "one size fits all" rather than personalized plans
- Providing planning that forces choices unrelated to interests
- Working with staff who do not possess the skills and training to facilitate life planning the way it should be facilitated

- Being led by mandate-driven annual or six-month planning updates that can be overwhelming for agencies and clients
- Conducting meetings that last too long for the client and family (e.g., 3–5 hours)
- Passing the buck to the client's family members and friends to find jobs
- Providing "one-shot" planning
- Lacking strong follow-up plans

Promoting self-determination involves addressing the knowledge, skills, and attitudes that individuals will need to take more control and responsibility for their lives. Individuals with disabilities who are self-determined are more likely to succeed as adults. In addition, self-determined individuals are less likely to overwork their relationship networks.

Overburdened Relationship Networks. Relationship networks such as family can provide valuable employment support to individuals with disabilities. However, at times relationship networks may be stretched thin. For example, family members may volunteer to help their relative who has a disability out of a sense of duty or obligation even when other responsibilities are taxing the family members' time and energy. According to Stevens and Ibanez (2002) common barriers to relationship networks include burned-out networks as a result of employment planning that relies solely on relationship networks; lack of social or relationship networks due to the person with a disability living in isolation; "burned bridges" between relationship networks because of past crises; and unknown personal relationships.

Physical Health Barriers

Managing one's health is key to being able to fully participate in society through self-sufficiency and independence. However, for individuals with disabilities managing one's health can be a difficult and often overwhelming task. Disability is not a static condition. Individuals with disabilities are susceptible not only to chronic conditions found in the general population (i.e., usual consequences of aging or those associated with environmental hazards or lifestyle such as smoking) but also to health conditions secondary to their primary disability. **Secondary conditions** are those associated with the disablement process. For example, people with activity limitations reported having more days of pain as compared to individuals without such limitations (Centers for Disease Control and Prevention, 1998). Other physical health barriers include **systematic disabilities**. Systematic disabilities are health problems such as asthma, cancer, diabetes, and AIDS. These disabilities may require medication that can further affect the individual's health.

A primary reason for the increase of physical health concerns in persons with disabilities is that 28 percent of people with disabilities are likely to postpone or put off medical care compared to 12 percent of individuals without disabilities (National Organization on Disability, 2000). The major reason for not seeking the medical care they need is the lack of sufficient insurance and income.

About 90 percent of people with and without disabilities are likely to be covered by some form of health insurance. However, 28 percent of individuals with disabilities are likely to have special needs that are not covered by their health insurance as compared to 7 percent of people without disabilities (National Organization on Disability, 2000).

Even when people with a disability have an income, typically they have a lower income compared to individuals without a disability. In addition, a person who has a severe disability likely will earn even less than a person with a slight disability, which can lead to lower-quality health care services even if the person is covered by insurance.

Mental Health Barriers

Individuals with disabilities tend to experience more days of depression, anxiety, and sleeplessness and fewer days of vitality during the previous month than people without disabilities. Increased emotional distress, however, does not arise directly from the person's limitations. The distress is likely to stem from encounters with environmental barriers that reduce the individual's ability to participate in life activities and that undermine physical and emotional health (Centers for Disease Control and Prevention, 1998).

According to the Office of Disease Prevention and Health Promotion (2000), 31 percent of children and adolescents with disabilities reported being sad, unhappy, or depressed compared with 17 percent of children and adolescents without disabilities. In the adult population ages 18 years and older, 28 percent with disabilities reported negative feelings that prevented them from being active compared with 7 percent of people ages 18 and older without disabilities who experienced feeling of sadness and depression.

Secondary conditions can undermine the physical health and mental well-being of people with disabilities. A broad array of health promotion activities that focus on improving functioning across disabilities and across age groups can substantially improve the quality of life for individuals with disabilities (Office of Disease Prevention and Health Promotion, 2000).

Career Development Program Model:
People with Physical and/or Mental Disabilities

The career development program model for working with people with disabilities is structured to meet the myriad of career-related needs that this population often encounters. Their career success will depend on the careful development and implementation of a plan that takes into account the individual needs of each and every client. Human service professionals are likely to take on a number of important roles when working with individuals with disabilities—that of advocate, adjustment counselor, life-skills coach, mentor, and accommodations expert. To successfully serve this population, helpers must not only understand the unique needs of their clients, but they must also be well versed in the common vocabulary, laws, and terminology associated with this population including **International Classification of Impairments, Disabilities, and Handicaps (ICIDH-2); Medicare** and **Medicaid; Rehabilitation Act of 1973; Social Security Disability Insurance;** and **work limitations**. Figure 15.1 is a graphic model of the career development program.

Applicant Pool

The applicant pool will include any individual with a physical or mental impairment that substantially limits one or more of the individual's major life activities; any individual that has a record of such impairment; or any individual that is regarded as having such impairment. (Americans with Disabilities Act [1990] Definitions section, § 12102). The intake personnel will then determine whether or not the client fits the criteria for program participation. For example, if the client became disabled as a result of a work-related injury, the client may qualify for rehabilitation services through Worker's Compensation (WC). The human service professional must be aware of the types of assistance and range of services available to individuals with disabilities.

Individual Success Plan

The goal of the Individual Success Plan (ISP) is the long-term employment of the client with a disability. Successful employment rests on the development of an ISP that meets the individual needs of each and every client. These needs include, but are not limited to, identifying and reducing barriers to employment; matching the skills of the individual with the skills needed for the job; making reasonable workplace accommodations; and providing the support, training, and education the client needs for success. The ISP is a collaborative effort between the human service professional and the client. Although the client's needs are the driving force behind the plan, the human service professional provides the guidance, expertise, and support to move the client into employment or to assist the client in keeping his or her existing job.

Make Assessments. Because individuals with disabilities tend to experience a range of discouraging emotions (i.e., depression, anxiety, sleeplessness) as a result of encountering barriers that reduce their ability to fully participate in life, the human service professional must address these emotions along with career-related concerns and physical health issues. Many individuals with disabilities experience health conditions that are secondary to their primary disability such as severe pain associated with the disablement process (Centers for Disease Control and Prevention, 1998).

Once the human service professional has assessed and addressed the client's physical and mental health, they can begin to determine the best course of action for the client. For example, if the client is dealing with significant financial issues, the human service professional may need to help the client secure funding through state or federal agencies. After taking these steps the human service professional will begin to address the client's specific career-related issues.

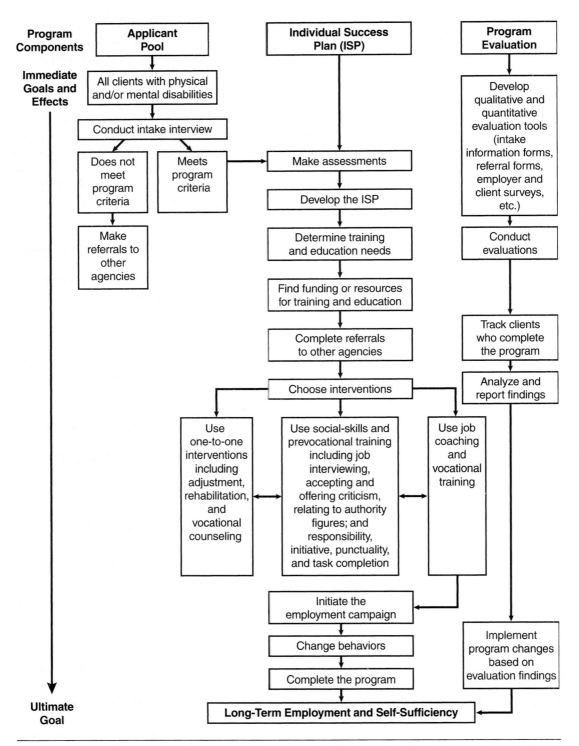

FIGURE 15.1   *Career Development Program Model: People with Physical and/or Mental Disabilities*

Depending on the nature of the client's career concerns, the human service professional will determine the number and type of assessments that are appropriate for the client. The following abbreviated list includes a variety of assessments that may be beneficial to the client with a disability. Because the range of disabilities is great, the number of available assessments mirrors the diverse needs of this group. Most of the assessments mentioned are not specifically developed for individuals with specific disabilities but may be appropriate inventories for certain clients. For example, clients with a **physical disability** may be able to successfully complete an interest inventory that focuses on the clients' interests as opposed to their physical abilities. Because the nature and degree of disability will vary from client to client, the human service professional *must* have knowledge and skill choosing and administering a wide range of career-related assessments. Expertise in selecting appropriate inventories will enable the helper to work with the client in developing a comprehensive and constructive ISP. Table 15.1 is a list of career-related assessments and inventories for use with individuals with disabilities. Although a battery of assessments is recommended, the human service professional must determine the best course of action based on the needs of each individual client. Chapter 3 provides an overview of many of the career-related assessments and inventories available to the helping professional.

TABLE 15.1 *Career-Related Assessments for Use with People with Physical and/or Mental Disabilities*

Title	Source
Ability Tests	
Ability Explorer	Harrington, J. C., & Harrington, T. F. (1996). *Ability explorer.* Itasca, IL: Houghton Mifflin.
Career Key*	Jones, L. K., & Jones, J. W. (2000). *Career key.* Raleigh, NC: Author.
Motivated Skills Card Sort	Knowdell, R. (2002, June). *Motivated skills card sort.* San Jose, CA: Career Research & Testing.
O*NET Ability Profiler*	O*NET Consortium (2003, April). *O*NET ability profiler.* Washington, DC: Author.
WorkKeys	ACT, Inc. (1993). *Workkeys assessments.* Iowa City, IO: ACT.
Interest Inventories	
Career Exploration Inventory 2	Liptak, J. (2002). *Career exploration inventory 2.* Indianapolis, IN: Author.
CareerExplorer CD-ROM*	JIST Works (2004). *Careerexplorer CD-ROM.* Indianapolis, IN: Author.
Guide for Occupational Exploration Interest Inventory	Farr, M. (2002). *Guide for occupational exploration interest inventory* (4th ed.). Indianapolis, IN: JIST Works.
Occupational Interests Card Sort	Knowdell, R. (2002, June). *Occupational interests card sort.* San Jose, CA: Career Research & Testing.
O*NET Interests Profiler*	O*NET Consortium (n.d.). *O*NET interest profiler.* Washington, DC: Author.

(Continued)

TABLE 15.1   Continued

Title	Source
Self-Directed Search Forms E and E Audiotape	Holland, J. L. (1996). *Self-directed search form E* (4th ed.). Lutz, FL: Psychological Assessment Resources. Holland, J. L. (1996). *Self-directed search form E* (4th ed.). [Audiotape]. Lutz, FL: Psychological Assessment Resources.
Transition-to-Work Inventory	Liptak, J. J. (2004). *Transition-to-work inventory.* Indianapolis, IN: JIST Works
Voc-Tech Quick Screener	JIST Works (2002). *Voc-tech quick screener.* Indianapolis, IN: Author
Wide Range Interest and Occupation Test	Glutting, J. J., & Wilkinson, G. (2003). *Wide range interest and occupation test* (2nd ed.). Wilmington, DE: Wide Range.
Personality Inventories	
Keirsey Temperament Sorter II	Keirsey, D. (1998, May*). Please understand me II.* Del Mar, CA: Prometheus Nemesis Book.
Vocational Preference Inventory (VPI)	Holland, J. L. (1985). *Vocational preference inventory (VPI).* Lutz, FL: Psychological Assessment Resources.
Value Inventories	
Career Values Card Sort	Knowdell, R. (1998, June). *Career values card sort.* San Jose, CA: Career Research & Testing.
O*NET Career Values Inventory*	JIST Works. (2002). *O*NET career values inventory.* Indianapolis, IN: Author.
Values-Driven Work Card Sort	Career Action Center. (n.d.). *Values-driven work card sort.* Menlo Park, CA: Prodigy Press.
Career Development Inventories	
Barriers to Employment Success Inventory	Liptak, J. J. (2002). *Barriers to employment success inventory* (2nd ed.). Indianapolis, IN: JIST Works.
Career Attitudes and Strategies Inventory	Holland, J. L., & Gottfredson, G. D. (1994). *Career attitudes and strategies inventory.* Lutz, FL: Psychological Assessment Resources.
Career Beliefs Inventory	Krumboltz, J. D. (1991). *Career beliefs inventory.* Mountain View, CA: CPP.
Career Decision Scale	Osipow, S. H., Carney, C. G., Winer, J. L., Yanico, B. J., & Koschier. M. (1987). *Career decision scale* (3rd ed.). Lutz, FL: Psychological Assessment Resources.
Career Thoughts Inventory	Sampson, J. P., Peterson, G. W., Lenz, J. G., Reardon, R. C., & Saunders, D. E. (1996). *Career thoughts inventory.* Lutz, FL: Psychological Assessment Resources.
Career Transitions Inventory	Heppner, M. J. (1991). *Career transition inventory.* Columbia MO: Author.

TABLE 15.1   Continued

Title	*Source*
Job Search Attitude Inventory	Liptak, J. J. (2002). *Job search attitude inventory* (2nd ed.). Indianapolis, IN: JIST Works.
My Vocational Situation	Holland, J. L., Daiger, D., & Power, P. G. (1980). *My vocational situation*. Mountain View, CA: CPP.
Overcoming Barriers Card Sort Game Kit	Harney, E. E., & Angel, D. L. (1999). *Overcoming barriers card sort game kit*. Hacienda Heights, CA: WorkNet Solutions.
Reading-Free Vocational Interest Inventory: 2	Becker, R. L. (2000). *Reading-free vocational interest inventory:2*. Columbus, OH: Elburn.
Salient Beliefs Review: Connecting Spirit to Work	Bloch, D. (2003). *Salient beliefs review: Connecting spirit to work*. Indianapolis, IN: JIST Works.
Vocational Exploration and Insight Kit	Holland, J. L., Birk, J. M., Cooper, J. F., Dewey, C. R. Dolliver, H., Takai, R. T., & Tyler, L. (1980). *The vocational exploration and insight kit*. Mountain View, CA: CPP.
Miscellaneous	
Career Genograms	Gysbers, N. C., Heppner, M. J., & Johnson, J. A. (2003). *Career counseling: Process, issues, and techniques* (2nd ed.). Boston: Allyn and Bacon.
Elevations ® Manual Card Sort System	Scully, H. (2003, August). *Elevations manual card sort system*. Roseville, CA: Author.
Individual Employment Plan	Ludden, L. L., & Maitlen, B. (2002). *Individual employment plan*. Indianapolis, IN: JIST Works.
Vocational Decision-Making Interview	Czerlinsky, T., & Chandler, S. (1999). *Vocational decision-making interview*. Indianapolis, IN: JIST Works.

*Use only if client is computer literate.

Develop the ISP.   Based on the information gained from the intake interview and from the administration of the career-related assessments, the human service professional and the client work together to create the ISP. This process involves a number of steps. First, based on the results of the assessments, clients explore occupational options by gathering career-related information on various occupational prospects. This information assists clients with their career decision-making process. Once they gather occupational information, clients explore their views and values in regards to their list of occupational prospects. Using this information, the client and helping professional clarify decisions and work together to establish the client's personal and career-related goals. These goals must be measurable, action-oriented, practical, and specific. Once they establish goals, they explore and address barriers to career success. After taking these steps the helper and client shift their focus to determine if the client needs training and education.

Determine Training and Education Needs.   Individuals with disabilities can often enhance their employment prospects through rehabilitation, training, and education. Many barriers to career success can be offset through programs geared specifically to help individuals with disabilities maintain or return to work. The largest program designed to assist such clients is Vocational Rehabilitation (VR)—a federal-state nationwide program that provides diagnostic and evaluation services, restoration, college or university training, business or vocational training, adjustment training, on-the-job training, counseling and guidance, job referral, job placement, transportation, maintenance, and a number of other services to adults with disabilities (Research Triangle Institute, 1998). Many of these services are arranged through agreements with local vendors. Funding for Vocational Rehabilitation comes from the federal government through the Rehabilitation Services Administration (RSA) Title I grants. The federal government funds approximately 78 percent of the VR program and each state supplies a minimum of 22 percent (Hayward & Schmidt-Davis, 2003).

To be eligible for VR services, the clients must have a work-limiting disability and show that they could become employable after receiving VR services. State VR agencies develop written plans to assess individuals' likely ability for employment. Benefits can be denied if state VR agencies can demonstrate that the client cannot benefit from the services. In many cases people needing VR services are on a long waiting list. The probability that a person will be accepted for services varies based on the applicant's age, race, sex, disability significance and type, education level, and other characteristics.

Additional state programs are available through the Workforce Investment Act of 1998. These programs integrate adult education and literacy, job training, and VR programs into a one-stop delivery system (Wittenburg & Favreault, 2003).

Adults with low income and with specific impairments, such as mental retardation, can also qualify for support from specialized systems that are geared toward assisting individuals with severe health conditions. Examples of these specialized support services include institutional care, supported employment/rehabilitation services, **Mental Retardation/Developmental Disability programs,** Plan for Achieving Self-Support (PASS), and social support. Many of these programs are monitored by state agencies or subagencies. Funding support for these programs comes directly from Medicaid, therefore clients must satisfy their state's Medicaid eligibility requirements in order to qualify for these services. The two largest providers of services are the Mental Retardation/Developmental Disability (MR/DD) program and the mental health system. MR/DD agencies provide clients with residential and social support, employment, after-school programs, family support, and other such services. The mental health system tends to provide services to a somewhat broader population with a range of mental disabilities. Qualified applicants receive services from state mental health agencies that are geared toward the treatment and the amelioration of symptoms (Wittenburg & Favreault, 2003).

Human service professionals must be well versed in the various types of programs and services available to help with the education and training of people with disabilities. Since the array of disabilities is infinite, helpers must be knowledgeable about specific disabilities and responsive to the individual education and training needs of each client.

Find Funding or Resources for Training and Education.   A variety of funding sources are available for individuals with disabilities. Some of the funding is provided through disability cash-transfer programs. These programs include Supplemental Security Income (SSI), Social Security Disability (DI), **Workers' Compensation (WC),** and **Veterans Administration programs**. These programs provide cash payments to individuals based on the program's criteria. For example, SSI provides monthly cash income to people under 65 who are blind or disabled. DI programs provide payments based on individuals' lifetime-average earnings covered by Social Security. Workers Compensation provides cash payments, rehabilitation services, and medical benefits to workers who experience work-related diseases or injuries. Veterans Administration programs grant disability compensation payments along with veterans' pensions to people over the age of 65 who served in the military or those under the age of 65 with a disability (Wittenburg & Favreault, 2003).

Additional cash transfer programs are available to low-income individuals and their families. Temporary Assistance for Needy Families (TANF) and **General Assistance** programs provide time-limited assistance. TANF grants cash benefits to needy families with children and general assistance programs provide temporary assistance to low-income clients, often targeting the elderly, individuals with disabilities, and children (Wittenburg & Favreault, 2003).

These funding sources provide cash-transfer payments to eligible clients. These funds can assist clients with costs-of-living expenses while they obtain the education, training, and skills necessary to succeed in the workplace. **State vocational rehabilitation, state Workforce Development systems,** Mental Retardation/Development Disability programs, and **state mental health systems** provide funding specifically earmarked for rehabilitation, education, and training.

A number of additional federally supported programs can help clients with disabilities by lessening their dependence on public assistance (i.e., PASS, Ticket-to-Work, Individual Development Accounts). Human service professionals must be familiar with the various funding sources including the eligibility requirements for each source.

Complete Referrals to Other Agencies.   Individuals with disabilities comprise an extremely diverse group of clients. The types of disabilities are quite varied and include a range of physical, mental, and **learning disabilities** that encompass both visible and hidden disabilities. Disabilities span across all categories (i.e., socioeconomic, gender, race, ethnicity, age, religion, etc.). Therefore, each client will have a unique set of circumstances and needs that will require the human service professional to work collaboratively with a variety of agencies, systems, and programs in order to best serve the client. For example, a client who suffered a disabling injury on the job would need to be referred to the company's Worker's Compensation program in order to receive needed rehabilitation services, medical benefits, and cash payments. A low-income client with a disability may need referrals for a variety of services to assist with daily-living expenses such as food purchases (i.e., food stamps) and housing (i.e., public housing subsidies).

Choose Interventions.   The career development model for clients with disabilities has three types of interventions: one-to-one interventions, social-skills and prevocational-skills training, and vocational training and job coaching. Based on the individual needs of the client, the human service worker can offer interventions in tandem with other interventions or independent of other interventions.

Using One-to-One Interventions.   Three important and effective types of one-to-one interventions appropriate for clients with disabilities are adjustment counseling, rehabilitation counseling, and vocational counseling. *Adjustment counseling* can aid clients who are newly disabled. Often such clients experience a range of emotions including grief over events such as the loss of independence, loss in their range of motion, loss of a job, and loss of a support network. Adjustment counseling can help such clients adapt to these changes through life-skills and personal-development training.

    Rehabilitation counseling can help individuals with disabilities become or remain self-sufficient and productive citizens. Rehabilitation counselors accomplish this task by addressing societal and individual barriers, building bridges and networks between the individual and the community, and by working closely with employers to modify work tasks and training options.

    Vocational counseling is used to help clients determine if certain jobs can be temporarily or permanently adjusted to meet their needs. If adjustments cannot be made, vocational counselors can investigate other options such as assessing the clients' skills for a new job or developing rehabilitation plans aimed at helping clients return to the workforce.

Using Social-Skills and Prevocational-Skills Training.   The acquisition and use of appropriate social skills is an integral element in job stability, and the lack of such skills can result in job losses. According to Elksnin and Elksnin (1991) social-skills deficit in young people with disabilities accounts for more jobs lost than for any other reason. The need for social-skills training becomes even more apparent when one recognizes the fact that most employers are unwilling to teach social skills to their employees. Social-skills training includes teaching job-interviewing skills, educating clients on how to appropriately accept and offer criticism, and preparing clients to properly relate to authority figures.

    Prevocational-skills training assists clients with the remediation of deficits in specific, work-related behaviors. Examples of prevocational-skill topics include attendance, responsibility, initiative, punctuality, care of materials, task completion, speed, following directions, and attention to detail. Prevocational-skills training can foster confidence and enhance the client's potential for success.

Providing Vocational Training and Job Coaching.   *Vocational training* is used to teach specific skills that clients need to enter a particular field. This type of training typically takes about 5 to 12 months and sometimes up to two years depending on the type of degree or certificate the client is working towards. Some of the most common vocational training is offered through a number of vocational-technical education programs and services at the state level. The programs, designed for youth and adults, are funded through federal grants awarded under the Carl D. Perkins Vocational–Technical Education Act Amendments of 1998 (Public Law 105-332).

Job-skills training can be enhanced through *job coaching*. Job coaches work in conjunction with the employee and employer until the employee can perform the duties and tasks of the job without assistance. The job coach can be a crucial support for the client with a disability. Job-coach services can significantly reduce the time and effort the employer spends on training the individual. This assistance can lead to a well-qualified, trained, and self-confident employee.

Once clients receive the interventions they need, the human service professional helps clients initiate the employment campaign, which is one of the most essential components of the ISP. A high-quality employment campaign can lead to the long-term employment of the client.

Initiate the Employment Campaign. Human service professionals play an integral part in the employment campaign of their clients with disabilities. The role of the helper varies with each individual client. Human service professionals serve as mentors, coaches, career specialists, and advocates for their clients. One of the most important tasks for the human service professional who is assisting clients with disabilities with their employment campaign is to help them anticipate reactions from employers and deal with such reactions in a positive, confident manner.

The Strategic Job Search. An important job-search service that human service professionals can provide to individuals with disabilities is helping them explore numerous career possibilities. Many individuals with disabilities receive advice on "stereotypical" career paths for people with disabilities (e.g., special education teacher, vocational rehabilitation assistant). Some may not believe they have many options because they have focused on their disabilities rather than their abilities. Helpers should help these clients expand their horizons and consider an array of positions that the clients may have seen as not possible or unlikely.

Job Applications. Employers use job applications as a tool to screen applicants who do not possess the necessary skills and qualifications and as a means to discover additional information about the candidate that may not be evident from the cover letter and/or resume. The employer often forms the first impression of the applicant from the job application. Human service professionals should help their clients with disabilities present information on the job application in the most professional manner. Job applications should be neat, accurate, complete, copied on quality paper, and submitted within the designated time frame.

Job-Search Correspondence. This correspondence is an essential component of the employment campaign. Cover letters, for example, are often the first point of contact between the client and the employer. Human service professionals should help their clients prepare strong, effective letters. For individuals with disabilities, the cover letter may be the first opportunity for them to disclose their disability. Of course, this disclosure is only recommended in certain circumstances. For example, clients may want to disclose their disability if they are applying for jobs with a state or federal agency that must comply with affirmative-action policies. Clients should also consider disclosing their disability if the job they are applying for directly relates to their experience as a person with a disability (e.g., a position as a vocational rehabilitation specialist). Finally, clients should disclose their disability if the disability is a requirement for the job (e.g., a job as an intake interviewer for a cancer treatment center that requires the applicant be a cancer survivor).

Human service professionals should also teach their clients the proper way to write other forms of job correspondence, such as reminder letters, interview appreciation letters, letters accepting and declining a job offer, and the other various forms of correspondence necessary for an effective employment campaign. Helpers must keep in mind the particular disability of the client when assisting with this crucial step. For some clients with learning disabilities, for example, the human service professional might need to proof each letter prior to mailing. Clients without word processing abilities cannot type their letter. In such cases the client can often dictate the letter to the helper who then types it. The human service professional should assess each client's needs individually with the goal of enhancing all clients' skills in producing effective job correspondence.

Taylor-Made Resumes.   The goal of the resume is to provide enough information about the job seeker to convince the employer that the candidate has the basic qualifications for the position thereby leading to an interview. The format for the resume depends on the experience, if any, of the candidate. Clients with steady work experience and related skills would likely utilize the chronological format. Those without work experience or with significant gaps in their employment history would be better served by using the functional format. The combination format would work well for clients who possess a solid work history and a number of transferable skills. In general in most situations people should not disclose their disability in their resume. When listing activities, some terms on the resume, such as attended a school for the Deaf or had memberships in certain clubs and organizations, may inadvertently be disclosing a client's disability. Questions and concerns that employers may have regarding a client's disability can be more effectively addressed during an interview. Of course, as previously mentioned, there will be certain situations when clients will want to disclose their disability to the employer in their cover letter.

For job seekers who use a TDD or TTY (Text Telephone) or other **auxiliary aids and services,** it is an individual decision whether or not to include the TDD/TTY phone number on the resume. If clients decide to include the TDD/TTY number, they should also include the number for the state relay service, which will assist the employers in contacting clients. Clients should also include a number for voice messages.

Interviewing Strategies.   For the majority of job seekers, the interview is the "make it, or break it" point. If the employer does not see a match between the company's needs and the skills and qualities of the job seeker, a job offer is unlikely.

Helpers can assist their clients prepare for an interview by making a list of possible interviewing questions, especially questions the client is likely to have trouble answering. For example, "I've noticed a gap in your employment history. What have you been doing during this time?" Next, the human service professional can conduct mock interviews with their clients to help them practice their delivery. For this particular population, a frequently posed question is whether or not individuals with disabilities should disclose their disability during the interviewing process. Disclosure is particularly difficult for clients with mental health/psychiatric disabilities because of the risk of discrimination. Based on their previous experiences, many individuals with mental health/psychiatric disabilities fear that disclosure of their disability will eliminate or reduce their job opportunities. This fear is well substantiated as stigma associated with psychiatric disabilities is well documented. According to a recent poll of 1,257 American adults, only 19 percent reported feeling "very comfortable" when meeting someone known to have a mental illness (i.e., **mental health/psychiatric disability**), compared with 59 percent feeling "very comfortable" when meeting someone in a wheelchair (U.S. Department of Health and Human Services, Substance Abuse and Mental Health Services Administration, n.d.). Disclosure of the disability is crucial during the interviewing process if accommodations and/or access to the building are necessary in order to do the job. Human service professionals should work with their clients to prepare them to handle difficult questions regarding their disability. Clients should be encouraged to talk about their abilities, not their disabilities. They should sell themselves on what they can do, not what they cannot do. Employers need qualified, capable people to fill positions, and human service professionals must work with their clients and prepare them to highlight their best skills. Teaching clients to answer such questions by disclosing how they have dealt with difficult situations in a positive, optimistic, way can be helpful. Clients should be honest and confident during the interviewing process. Clients should be advised to disclose information about their disability in a confident yet casual way towards the end of the interview or even at the time of the job offer. Again, the clients' focus during the interview should be on highlighting their abilities to do the job for which they are interviewing.

Many individuals with disabilities require special accommodations and/or access in order to perform the tasks of the job. Accommodations and/or access may be factors in the interviewing process as well. For example, clients who use wheelchairs will need access to buildings, designated parking, and possibly elevators. Human service professionals should work with their clients to determine what, if any, accommodation and access issues exist at the employer's location. If the building where the interview is to take place is not accessible, clients should be prepared to offer an alternative meeting site, just in case the employer needs some suggestions. These matters should be dealt with ahead of time. It will show the employer that the client is able to effectively deal with situations that may arise.

If clients need the assistance of a sign-language interpreter during the interview, human service professionals can help clients prepare for the interview by recommending that they follow these guidelines (Goldstein, Chun, & Winkler, 1994):

- After shaking hands with the employer, introduce the interpreter.
- Ask the employer if he or she has ever interviewed someone who uses an interpreter. If the employer has not, explain that the interpreter is there to facilitate communication, not to provide input into the interview.
- Explain that the best place for the interpreter to sit is next to the interviewer so that you can see both the employer and the interpreter at the same time. Confirm that this arrangement is all right with the employer before sitting down.
- Inform the employer that he or she should direct his or her comments to you and not to the interpreter.

A final subject regarding interviewing strategies for people with disabilities is clothing guidelines. Some people with disabilities find that they have problems with size, proportion, and shape. Human service professionals can help their clients choose the best color, line, and fabric for accentuating their best features. According to Goldstein, Chun, & Winkler (1994), the following clothing tips are helpful for people with disabilities:

- Clients who want to appear taller and thinner could wear vertical lines.
- Clients with scoliosis (curvature of the back) can wear diagonal lines that run opposite the curvature. This will visually lift a low shoulder and balance the scoliosis.
- For individuals who use a wheelchair, clean, uncluttered lines best show a seated figure.
- Individuals with cerebral palsy should choose an absorbent fabric, which can help to relieve the discomfort associated with salivating that may dampen the outfit.
- People who use crutches, artificial limbs, braces, or wheelchairs should choose fabrics for their strength in areas that take heavy wear.

Change Behaviors.   This career development program model is designed to change clients' negative and destructive behaviors to positive and constructive behaviors. One of the most important behavior changes that occur with this population is the movement from discouragement to encouragement. Individuals with disabilities often face obstacles that discourage them from seeking the skills, training, and education necessary to obtain long-term employment. Through tailored ISPs geared to meet the individual needs of each person, clients receive the counseling, training, education, and coaching necessary to empower them to reach their career-related goals.

Another important behavioral change that takes place is movement from lack of determination to self-determination. Self-determination is the byproduct of an ISP that addresses the knowledge, abilities, and attitudes clients need in order to have more control over their lives. Individuals with disabilities who are self-determined are more likely to succeed in life and in the workplace.

Complete the Program.   Clients who complete the program are those clients who entered the program, completed any necessary assessments, developed their ISPs, obtained needed education and training, participated in interventions, initiated an employment campaign, and obtained employment. For some clients it may be necessary to recycle through some of the phases of the ISP before they meet their career goals. For example, once a client obtains employment, additional training and education may be necessary in order for the client to update skills, to remain marketable or advance within the company.

Achieve Goal of Long-Term Employment.   The ultimate goal of the ISP is that of the long-term employment of the client. The definition of *long-term employment* will vary depending on the nature of the client's disability and the goals of the program and client. For clients with a chronic respiratory disease, long-term employment may be defined as employment that continues until the clients' health issues prohibit them from working. For clients who depend on Medicaid, SSI, and/or TANF, long-term employment may be defined by the degree of self-sufficiency clients exhibit after a designated period of time (e.g., one year).

Program Evaluation

An essential element of this career development program model is the program evaluation. The program staff should integrate the program evaluation within every phase of the career development program from development to termination. Human service professionals need to develop a variety of tools to evaluate their program. Figure 15.1 is a flow chart for the career development program model for people with physical and/or mental disabilities. The text in each box in the figure is a factor that needs to be measured. In addition to providing accountability for programs, evaluations serve as a means of determining if the programs are meeting the needs of the clients and agency. Agency staff must determine what type of evaluations they should use (i.e., process, outcome, impact) and what evaluative instruments (i.e., anecdotal record forms, expert-review checklists, focus-group protocols, process-review logs, implementation logs, interview protocols, questionnaires) will be most helpful in gathering the necessary information. Once the staff makes these decisions, a timeline should be developed that highlights the entire evaluation process including deadlines and the persons responsible for the evaluation. Once they have completed the evaluation process, human service professionals should present the data, findings, and recommendations in the form of an evaluation report. They can use this final report to provide suggestions for program modifications and improvement. For more detailed information regarding the evaluation process, see Chapter 6.

Revisiting the Case Study: Theresa

Conduct an Intake Interview

During the intake interview, the human service professional needs to explore with Theresa the possible emotional effects of her blindness (e.g., depression and anxiety), daily living concerns (e.g., bathing, preparing meals, dressing, getting around her home), concerns with functional activities (e.g., walking, lifting, standing, bending), and her employment concerns (e.g., work-related training, skill assessment). The first step is to address Theresa's potential for depression or other emotional effects from her blindness. As a single mother of a young son, Theresa may be experiencing bouts of depression and anxiety over issues related to raising her son. In addition to assisting Theresa with the emotional effects of her blindness, the human service professional should also assist her with adjusting to the financial impact of her blindness.

Make Assessments

Due to the recent onset of Theresa's blindness and to the impact it will have on her career direction, a battery of career-related assessments could provide her with a comprehensive picture of possible career options. Due to her disability, the human service professional must make certain that the assessments chosen are made for or are adaptable to a person without sight. The following inventories meet Theresa's unique needs.

The WorkKeys (ACT, 1993) offers several modules available in an audio or video format (e.g., writing, teamwork, observation, and listening). Other WorkKeys modules are available in a computer-based format (e.g., reading for information, applied mathematics, business writing, locating information, and applied technology). Special computer software can be installed in many computers that will enable individuals who are blind to use the computer. The *screen reader* is one example of such a program. A screen reader is a standard Windows application that runs alongside other computer programs and "tells" the computer user what is on the screen via a built in *speech synthesizer*. Another possible option to assess Theresa's work abilities would be the Career Key (Jones & Jones, 2000). The Career Key is an online assessment that can assess Theresa's skills, interests, values, and job appeal. Both these inventories would provide Theresa with means to assess her workplace skill levels.

To assess Theresa's interests, several assessments are available to her. The Career Explorer (JIST Works, 2004) is available in a CD-ROM version. The Self Directed Search (Holland, 1996) is available online and also in an audiotape format. Although the audiotape format would allow Theresa to hear the assessment, it also would require her to mark responses in a booklet. The human service professional would need to help her with that task. One additional interest inventory she could consider is the O*NET Interest Profiler (O*NET Consortium, n. d.). This inventory is available in a computerized format. It is not necessary to administer all three of the interest inventories. One interest inventory is likely to provide the type of information Theresa needs to help her with her career decision-making. The choice of assessment should depend on Theresa's needs, interests, and ability level (i.e., is she comfortable using a computer?).

The human service professional could administer the Keirsey Temperament Sorter II (Keirsey, 1998) to assess Theresa's personality. The Keirsey, which is available online, can provide Theresa with a better understanding of the direction of her energy, how she tends to gather information, how she tends to make decisions, and how she organizes her life.

The Values-Driven Work Card Sort (Career Action Center, n.d.) is available online and can be used to assess Theresa's work-related values and to explore her organizational and work-group values. Based on the results of this inventory, matches can be made between Theresa's work values and those values typically found in certain jobs.

To assess potential barriers to Theresa's career success, the helper could administer the Barriers to Employment Success Inventory (BESI) (Liptak, 2002). The BESI, available in an online format, identifies key barriers (i.e., personal, physical and psychological, career planning, job-seeking skills, and education and training) to obtaining and succeeding on a job.

The Elevations® Manual Card Sort System (Scully, 2003), available in an online version, can be used to supplement other inventories. In addition to measuring values, personality, career interests, and skills, Elevations® contains career research and action-planning components that may be helpful to Theresa.

The human service professional would suggest these inventories because of their online or audio capabilities. However, assessment choices for Theresa do not have to rest solely on the assessment's delivery mode. Human service professionals can choose from a variety of paper-and-pencil inventories and can serve as readers and writers for Theresa when necessary. The main point is to choose assessments based on their ability to meet Theresa's career development needs. For more detailed information on these inventories and on additional inventories, refer to Chapter 3.

Determine Barriers to Career Success

Theresa is likely to face a number of barriers that individuals who are blind experience, which may impact her employment success. Many of these barriers can be removed or reduced with support and accommodations. Attitudinal barriers (i.e., inferiority, pity, hero worship, ignorance, fear, etc.) that other people hold are potentially the most difficult for Theresa to overcome. These types of barriers, if unaddressed, can impede Theresa's career success.

Since her experience with vision loss is new, she is likely to face a number of barriers related to mobility and orientation such as getting around safely, performing personal hygiene tasks, preparing meals, and participating in recreational activities. Such barriers will likely impact her daily living activities.

Theresa may face a number of employment-related barriers including financial barriers, career-matching barriers, lack of accommodations and access, and systematic barriers integrated within company policies and practices. All the aforementioned barriers to career success are likely to negatively impact her self-concept and undermine her physical and emotional well-being making it difficult for her to fully participate in life activities. In addition to Theresa's barriers, the human service professional should address reactions of Theresa's son to her sudden blindness and help him with the adjustment process as well. For example, although in certain situations Theresa's son may need to be her "eyes," she must not become so dependent on him that his role shifts to that of a "parental child." The human service professional will need to address these barriers with Theresa and integrate a plan to overcome these obstacles within her ISP.

Choose Interventions

Using One-to-One Interventions.   Theresa may benefit from adjustment and vocational counseling. Because she is newly blind she is likely to experience a range of emotions that include anger, fear, confusion, and anxiety. Adjustment counseling can assist Theresa with the mourning over the loss of her vision and with the grieving she may be experiencing from other losses that often accompany the blindness (e.g., independence, job, confidence, driving, reading). Adjustment counseling can also provide Theresa with personal development or life-skills coaching. Theresa will need to do many daily-living tasks differently, and she must learn new skills. Adjustment counseling can provide the support and education that Theresa needs in her personal development. In addition to adjustment counseling, the human service professional could arrange a meeting between Theresa and a person with a similar background (i.e., blind and raising a family). This partnership could empower Theresa by showing her that given the proper tools, training, and support, she can continue to raise her son and provide him with a nurturing and loving environment.

Vocational counseling can help Theresa evaluate her abilities, skills, and interests and choose an appropriate course of action to pursue. Prior to losing her sight, Theresa worked as an administrative assistant at a law firm. The vocational counselor can explore the functional and transferable skills Theresa acquired in this position and can examine the possibility that she can return to her position at the law firm or seek a new position elsewhere. Regardless of her employment goals, Theresa will undoubtedly need additional training and education in order to reenter the workforce.

Because Theresa is newly blind, she would likely benefit from rehabilitation counseling. A rehabilitation specialist could work closely with Theresa by addressing barriers, building needed networks, and by working with employers to adapt and modify her work duties with her goal being that of increased independence and self-sufficiency.

Using Job Coaching.   The implementation of a job coach would be a crucial component to Theresa's program. Since she is newly blind, a job coach could train or retrain Theresa to perform the job-related tasks necessary for her job. Their eventual goal would be for Theresa to learn to perform these tasks without assistance.

Initiate the Employment Campaign

Once Theresa has participated in the interventions, the human service professional will work closely with her in initiating her employment campaign. Theresa must decide if she wants to return to her previous employer or seek new alternatives. If she decides to return to her previous employer, the human service professional must contact the law firm to determine the next steps in Theresa's employment process (e.g., address access and accommodation needs). Employers often benefit by retaining an employee who has become disabled. For example, it is usually as cost efficient for an employer to retain the employee with a disability as to recruit and train a new person. Should Theresa decide to seek new employment, she should explore both the hidden and visible job markets for possible career matches. Once career options are uncovered, the human service professional needs to help Theresa complete job applications, update her resume, and write job-correspondence letters. Because Theresa had a successful career prior to her disability, many of her abilities and skills may be transferred to a variety of work settings. The human service professional should help Theresa highlight her functional skills when she completes and formats these various documents.

Next, the helper would assist Theresa in preparing for the interviewing process by conducting mock interviews. Using mock interviews will allow Theresa to practice her responses to a variety of interviewing questions in a safe and nonthreatening environment.

Along with practicing interviewing skills, the human service professional should help Theresa access various workplaces and obtain needed workplace accommodations. Dealing with these issues ahead of time will show employers that Theresa is able to troubleshoot and adapt to similar situations that may arise. Careful implementation and monitoring of this employment campaign can lead to Theresa's long-term employment and in turn to her self-sufficiency.

Conclusion

Human service professionals are likely to work with clients experiencing a broad range of disabilities. Their work can be enhanced through a number of policy improvements. The following is a summary list of preventative and systemic recommendations for which human service professionals can advocate.

Recommendations that would enhance independence and quality of life include:

- Understand the causes of the disability
- Assess the quality of life
- Enhance technology for rehabilitation and assistance
- Improve the delivery of health and social care

Recommendations to reduce barriers include:

- Investigate new approaches for delaying disabilities
- Make the physical and social environment less challenging
- Design appropriate products and services
- Support the mental and physical well-being of the individual

Recommendations for conducting research include:

- Apply new technology to the treatment and control of diseases
- Increase research into diseases that are prevalent in the developing world
- Encourage a multinational approach to confronting disease
- Improve knowledge and understanding of genetic diseases

Policy changes to enhance health include:

- Improve health promotion and health care
- Reduce work-related exposure to damaging health agents
- Reduce physical and mental stress in the workplace

Summary

People with disabilities encompass the single, largest minority group in the United States. According to the 2000 U.S. Census, 49.7 million people over age 5 have a disability. Unemployment for individuals with disabilities is at a staggering 70 percent, although the majority of people with disabilities want to work. Earnings of this group are far below the earnings of individuals without disabilities—about 76 cents to the dollar. Although workers with disabilities share the same basic employment rights as workers without disabilities, additional employment rights under the Americans with Disabilities Act protect individuals with disabilities. Under this act it is illegal for employers to discriminate against individuals with disabilities for reasons related to their disabilities in all aspects of employment (e.g., job application procedures, hiring, firing, advancement, compensation, job training, etc.). Factors related to disabilities can serve as barriers to career success. This chapter presented a career development program model for working with people with disabilities. The model illustrates the development of an ISP, including assessment of clients' career interests, abilities, values, and barriers to career success; interagency referrals; and interventions such as one-to-one interventions, social-skills and prevocational-skills training, and vocational training and job coaching, all leading to the goal of long-term employment and self-sufficiency of the client.

Key Terms

Americans with Disabilities Act of 1990 (ADA)
Assistive devices and technology
Auxiliary Aids and Services
Disability
Environmental factors
General assistance
Hidden or invisible disability
Individual Development Accounts (IDAs)
Individualized Education Program (IEP)
Individualized Family Service Plan (IFSP)
Individuals with Disabilities Education Act
    (IDEA)
International Classification of Impairments,
    Disabilities, and Handicaps (ICIDH-2)
Learning disabilities (LD)
Medicaid
Medicare

Mental health/psychiatric disability
Mental Retardation/Developmental Disability
    Programs
Physical disability
Plan for Achieving Self-Support (PASS)
Rehabilitation Act of 1973
Secondary conditions
Social Security Disability Insurance (DI)
State mental health systems
State vocational rehabilitation
State Workforce Development systems
Systematic disabilities
Ticket-to-Work and
    Self-Sufficiency Program
Veterans Administration Programs
Work limitations
Workers' Compensation (WC)

Web Resources

Note that website URLs may change over time.

American Association of People with Disabilities
http://www.aapd-dc.org

Americans with Disabilities Home Page
http://www.usdoj.gov/crt/ada/adahom1.htm

National Institute on Disability and Rehabilitation Research
http://www.ed.gov/about/offices/list/osers/nidrr/index.html

Online Resource for Americans with Disabilities
http://www.disabilityinfo.gov

The Center for an Assessable Society
http://www.accessiblesociety.org

The National Organization on Disability
http://www.nod.org

U.S. Equal Employment Opportunity Commission
http://www.eeoc.gov

16

People with Chemical Dependency

A Fresh Start

Case Study: Carol

Carol is a 25-year-old daughter of an alcoholic father. Carol's father died of sclerosis of the liver when she was 15 years old. From an early age, Carol took on the role of the rebellious child. When she was 11 she began sneaking out of the house, drinking, running away from home, and having unprotected sex with older men. When she was 12, she was kicked out of her home by her parents and went to live with her aunt and uncle and their two children. Although she stayed in school, she continued her destructive lifestyle. Her high-school counselor referred her to the school's **Student Assistance Program (SAP)**, but Carol chose not to participate in the **intervention.** By the time she graduated from high school, many considered her a full-blown alcoholic, with a high **tolerance** for the **substance.** Her levels of **intoxication** would fluctuate throughout the week with few days of sobriety. After graduating from high school, she moved from her hometown in Kentucky to the resort community of Charleston, South Carolina where she began working in area bars. This environment perpetuated her drinking and her uncontrolled lifestyle. When Carol was 20, she became pregnant and married the father of her child, a 45 year-old man she met at one of the bars where she worked. Once married, she quit her job at a neighborhood bar to be a stay-at-home mother to her daughter. Her husband, a self-employed businessman, is a compulsive gambler and an alcoholic. Because he emotionally abused Carol by constantly degrading her, she left him after less than two years of marriage. Carol, now a single mother with a small toddler, stopped drinking four months ago with the exception of one **slip,** and she has been attending AA meetings. She has filed for divorce, moved in with a friend, and receives some child support from her husband. The support however, is irregular and Carol realized that she must obtain steady employment to support herself and her young daughter. Her highest level of education is her high-school diploma. Her work history is sporadic. She held jobs for an average of two or three months at a time then either quit or was fired. Carol has worked as a bartender, server, and hostess. She enjoys working with people and is viewed by others as social, fun, and popular.

The Population of People with Chemical Dependency

Description of Population

According to the U.S. Department of Labor (2005e), an estimated 14.8 million Americans are illicit drug users. Approximately 11 percent of youths ages 12 to 17 are illicit drug users with marijuana the most common drug of **use**. The highest rate of illicit drug use is roughly 20 percent and can be found among the young-adult population, ages 18 to 20. This drug-use rate is 8.7 percent for men compared to 4.9 percent for women.

The rate of heavy drinking at 13.3 percent is highest among young adults between ages 18 to 25, and it peaks around the age of 21 at 17.4 percent. Heavy drinking correlates compellingly with illicit drug use. Approximately 30.5 percent of the 12.4 million heavy drinkers are also illicit drug users (U.S. Department of Labor, 2005e).

Employment.   **Alcoholism** and illicit drug abuse causes immeasurable problems in the workplace. No workplace, regardless of its size or location, is protected from these problems. The majority of individuals who abuse drugs and/or alcohol are employed and bring their drug-abuse problems to work. Although the current rate of illicit drug use tends to be higher among the unemployed, the majority of illicit drug users are employed. Approximately 77 percent of the 12.3 million adults who use illicit drugs are employed. About 6.5 percent of full-time employees and 8.6 percent of all part-time employees are current, illicit drug users. The most widely abused drug among working adults is alcohol. Approximately 6.2 percent of full-time workers are heavy drinkers, and 38 percent of workers between ages 18 to 25 are binge drinkers (U.S. Department of Labor, 2005e).

White, non-Hispanic males, between ages 18 to 25, reported the highest rates of heavy drinking and illicit drug use among employed adults. Research has indicated that some industries tend to have higher incidences of **substance abuse** among employees than others. Demographic variations in substance-abuse problems among workers mirrors the demographic variations in substance-abuse problems across American society in general. Therefore, substance abuse is more likely to be prevalent in industries dominated by males and in work environments with large numbers of young workers (U.S. Department of Labor, 2005c). The rates of heavy drinking and illicit drug use by industry were reported as 19 percent for food preparation workers, waiters, waitresses, and bartenders; 14 percent for construction workers; 13 percent for service occupations; and 10 percent for transportation and material moving workers. Over 60 percent of adults reported knowing someone who arrived at work under the influence of alcohol or other drugs (U.S. Department of Labor, 2005e).

Although the focus in the medical community is often on alcoholics, light and moderate drinkers cause the majority of alcohol-related problems in the workplace. For example, hangovers, which are common in the work setting, are typically the result of having a half-dozen or fewer drinks at one sitting and can cost employers in poor job performance and absenteeism (Office of National Drug Control Policy, 2005).

Secondhand effects of alcohol use have also been studied. One study found that one-fifth of workers reported being injured, having to cover for a coworker, or needing to work harder due to another employee's drinking. Almost one-third of workers studied who considered their jobs to be hazardous reported experiencing some secondhand alcohol effects (Office of National Drug Control Policy, 2005).

Employment status is highly correlated with rates of substance abuse. According to the U.S. Department of Health and Human Services (2005), approximately 19.9 percent of unemployed adults ages 18 and older were current substance abusers compared with 10.5 percent of full-time employees and 11.9 percent of part-time employees. Of the 20.3 million substance abusers ages 18 and older in 2004, 15.7 million or approximately 77.6 percent were employed either full or part time.

Education.   According to the U.S. Department of Health and Human Services (2005), rates of substance abuse and **dependence** vary based on the users' level of education. In 2004, 9.1 percent of individuals ages 18 years and older who graduated from high school but did not attend any college, and 8.2 percent of those who graduated from college were substance-abuse dependent compared to 10.3 percent of individuals who were not high-school graduates and 10.5 percent of those with some college.

Economic Effects of Substance Abuse.   According to the Office of National Drug Control Policy (2001), the number of deaths attributed to drug abuse between 1993 and 1995 increased 5.3 percent annually. The number of deaths attributed to drug abuse between 1995 and 1997 declined 15.2 percent. The number of deaths between 1997 and 1998 declined less than one percent. The changes in number are largely due to HIV/AIDS patients which saw an increase in deaths between 1993 and 1995 and then abrupt reductions between 1995 and 1998. In order to calculate lost earnings due to substance abuse, the number of deaths for each age and sex category was multiplied by the estimated value of lifetime earnings. Based on these calculations, the overall costs in millions of dollars jumped from $69,421 million in 1992 to $98,467 million in 1998.

Workplace alcohol and drug abuse has a devastating impact on businesses, costing both employers and employees in obvious and less obvious ways. Some of the obvious costs include increased absences, errors, and accidents and less obvious costs include low morale and high illness rates. According to the U.S. Department of Labor (2005e) one in five workers report having to work harder, cover for a coworker, redo work, or were put in danger or injured as a result of a coworker's drinking. Approximately 40 percent of industrial fatalities and 47 percent of injuries are linked to alcohol use. It is estimated that alcohol and drug abuse cost American businesses about $81 billion in lost productivity annually—$37 billion is due to premature death and $44 billion due to illness. Roughly 86 percent of these combined costs are credited to drinking. Alcoholism causes approximately 500 million lost workdays per year. When compared to drug-free employees, substance abusers who are employed cost their employers approximately twice as much in worker compensation and medical claims (Office of National Drug Control Policy, 2005).

Of individuals who currently use illicit drugs, 9.3 percent have switched employers three or more times within the past year compared to 4.3 percent who do not use illicit drugs. In addition, 12.9 percent of illicit drug users have missed one or more workdays in the past month compared to 5 percent who do not use illicit drugs.

Eight percent of current, heavy alcohol users have switched employers three or more times over the past year compared to 4.4 percent who are not heavy drinkers. Similarly, 11.3 percent of current, heavy alcohol users have missed one or more workdays in the past month compared to 5.1 percent who are not heavy drinkers (U.S. Department of Labor, 2005e).

Small businesses tend to be the most vulnerable to workplace substance abuse. Not only do they tend to be the "employer-of-choice" for illicit drug users, they are also less likely to have programs in place to battle the problem. Many individuals who are current, illicit drug users cannot adhere to a drug-free workplace policy. As a result they tend to seek out businesses that do not have such policies. One injury or error caused by an employee who is impaired can ruin a small business. According to the U.S. Department of Labor (2005e), 44 percent of illicit drug users work for small businesses (1–24 employees). Forty-three percent work for medium-sized businesses (25–499 employees). While only 13 percent of illicit drug users work for large businesses (500 or more employees). Thirty-six percent of heavy drinkers work for small businesses, 47 percent work for medium businesses, and 17 percent work for large businesses.

The estimated number of individuals ages 12 and older in need of treatment for illicit drug problems was 7.7 million in 2002. This accounts for 3.3 percent of the total U.S. population. Of these 1.4 million, 18.2 percent received treatment for their abuse at a substance-abuse facility. In 1998, drug abuse cost the United States $143.4 billion. This cost was due to loss of productivity that was primarily related to incarceration, crime careers, drug-abuse related illnesses, and premature deaths (U.S. Department of Labor, 2005c).

Full substance-abuse **parity** to standard employee benefit plans range from an increase in premium rates of $0.14 per member/month for health care plans to $1.35 per member/month for fee-for-service plans. The estimated combined increase in premium rates is less that $8 per year or $0.66 per member/month (U.S. Department of Labor, 2005c). According to the U.S. Department of Health and Human Services (2005), the cost in medical and worker compensation claims for employed substance abusers is about twice that of their drug-free counterparts. Studies conducted by the Office of National Drug Control Policy (2001) estimated that the overall economic cost of drug abuse to society increased at a rate of 5.9 percent annually. By 1998 the economic cost of substance abuse was $143.4 billion.

Barriers to Career Success

Structural Barriers

Social Stigma.
Although both men and women with substance-abuse problems experience social stigma, key experts tend to believe that society, in general, views women who **misuse** drugs more harshly than men. Because of this, individuals with

substance-abuse concerns may have difficulty openly acknowledging their problems and their needs (Currie, 2001).

Reliable and Low-Cost Childcare.   Parents are likely to worry about finding appropriate and economical childcare while they are in treatment. This barrier is likely to impact women more than men (Currie, 2001).

Costs of Substance-Abuse Treatment.   Costs associated with treatment (e.g., transportation, childcare, direct fees for treatment) can make participation in treatment difficult for many substance-abuse clients. In addition, there is often no way to compensate for the loss of wages while substance abusers are in treatment (Currie, 2001).

Lack of Flexible Services and Accessible Program Information.   Many treatment services often lack the flexibility that is necessary to meet the real needs of clients. For example, the criteria for some treatment programs may prohibit individuals from entering treatment (i.e., some policies dictate the amount of time a person must be clean before entering the program). Other programs may not offer flexible scheduling (i.e., alternative treatment schedules, short-term programming). Such programs may not show consideration for the personal and working needs of the clients and their families (Currie, 2001).

Some clients may be unaware of treatment and program options available and what the various treatments and programs include. A number of programs lack effective outreach and publicity strategies to overcome this structural barrier (Currie, 2001).

Individual Barriers

Shame, Guilt, and Poor Motivation.   People who acknowledge substance-abuse problems often experience high levels of shame and guilt that are often associated with society's attitude towards people who have these problems. Society tends to stigmatize those who misuse drugs and/or alcohol (Beckman & Amaro, 1986; Copeland, 1997). Therefore, clients may experience feelings of shame and guilt for not meeting what they perceive to be society's expectations (Currie, 2001).

Individuals with substance-abuse problems face a number of individual barriers to career success including poor motivation. Poor motivation is often the by-product of abusers' repeated failures in their job-seeking efforts.

Fear of Losing Love and Support or of Being Isolated.   Some individuals with substance-abuse issues have difficulties recognizing problems with their substance misuse. In addition some people may have difficulty acknowledging the impact or severity of their substance abuse (Currie, 2001). One of the reasons individuals may have difficulty acknowledging substance-abuse problems and attempting treatment is their fear of losing the support and security of loved ones. This lack of support may be based on the family's shame or denial of the substance-abuse problem. For women, this fear may be exacerbated by their dependent relationships and their fear of isolation as a result of acknowledging their substance-abuse problems (Currie, 2001).

Fear of Losing Children.   Especially for women with substance-abuse problems, the fear of losing their children to their partners or to child welfare can serve as an immense barrier. For many women, the total responsibility for the children falls on them. Their fear of losing their children can prohibit clients from entering residential treatment because they may have to give up custody of their children and never get their children back (Currie, 2001).

Physical Health Barriers

According to the National Institute on Drug Abuse (2005d), drug abuse can weaken the immune system and can also lead to risky behaviors such as unsafe sex and needle sharing. These risky behaviors can increase the probability of acquiring HIV/AIDS, hepatitis, and other infectious diseases. Drugs that can lead to HIV, hepatitis, and other infectious diseases include heroin, cocaine, steroids, and methamphetamine.

Research has also shown a connection between substance abuse and harmful cardiovascular effects ranging from abnormal heart rate to heart attacks. Injecting drugs can lead to cardiovascular problems such as collapsed veins and bacterial infections of the blood vessels and heart valves. Drugs that can negatively affect the cardiovascular system include cocaine, heroin, inhalants, ketamine, LSD, marijuana, MDMA, methamphetamine, nicotine, PCP, prescription stimulants, and steroids (National Institute on Drug Abuse, 2005b).

Substance abuse has also been linked to respiratory problems. Cigarette smoking, for example, can cause bronchitis, emphysema, and lung cancer. Marijuana smoke can also cause respiratory problems. Other drugs can slow breathing, block air from the lungs, and exasperate asthmatic conditions. Drugs that can affect the respiratory system include cocaine, GHB (gamma hydoxybutyrate), heroin, inhalants, ketamine, marijuana, nicotine, PCP, and prescription opiates (National Institute on Drug Abuse, 2005n).

Substance abuse can lead to adverse effects on the gastrointestinal system including vomiting, nausea, and abdominal pain. Drugs that can cause gastrointestinal problems include cocaine, GHB, heroin, LSD, MDMA ecstasy, nicotine, and prescription opiates (National Institute on Drug Abuse, 2005c).

Drug use can have adverse effects on the musculoskeletal systems. Steroids, for example, used during childhood or adolescence can signal bones to stop growing at an earlier age than they may have stopped without the steroid use. This can lead to short stature in the individual. Other drugs may cause muscle cramping and weakness. Drugs that may affect the musculoskeletal system include inhalants, MDMA, PCP, and steroids (National Institute on Drug Abuse, 2005j).

Steroid use has also been linked to disruptions in the normal production of hormones in the body, causing both reversible and irreversible changes. These changes include testicle shrinkage and infertility in men and masculinization in women (National Institute on Drug Abuse, 2005e).

Some drugs can cause kidney damage or failure by directly or indirectly increasing body temperature and the breakdown of muscles. Drugs that may have adverse affects on the kidneys include heroin, inhalants, MDMA, and PCP (National Institute on Drug Abuse, 2005f). In addition, heroin, steroids, and inhalants can lead to significant damage to the liver (National Institute on Drug Abuse, 2005g).

Substance use can produce euphoric effects in the brain. In addition, some drugs can have severe negative consequences in the brain including seizures, strokes, and widespread brain damage. Some substances can also lead to memory loss and problems with attention and decision-making. Drugs that may lead to neurological problems include cocaine, GHB, inhalants, marijuana, MDMA methamphetamine, nicotine, prescription stimulants, and rohypnol (National Institute on Drug Abuse, 2005k).

Cigarette smoke has been linked to cancer of the mouth, neck, stomach, and lung, among others. Marijuana smoke also exposes the lungs to carcinogens that can cause precancerous changes to the lungs that often mirror those changes caused by cigarette smoke. Cigarettes, marijuana, and steroids all may cause cancer (National Institute on Drug Abuse, 2005a).

Prenatal drug exposure can have serious consequences on the unborn child. Although the full extent of the effects are not known, substance abuse may lead to premature births, miscarriages, low-birth weights, and various behavioral and cognitive problems. Substances linked to adverse prenatal effects include cocaine, heroin, inhalants, marijuana, MDMA, methamphetamine, and nicotine (National Institute on Drug Abuse, 2005m).

In addition to the impact drugs have on various body organs, some drugs produce large-scale body changes such as dramatic increases in body temperature and changes in appetite. These changes may negatively impact an individual's health. **Withdrawal** from drug use may also lead to a number of adverse health effects including mood swings, restlessness, changes in appetite and mood, fatigue, muscle and bone pain, insomnia, diarrhea, vomiting, and cold flashes. Drugs that may have universal adverse health effects include cocaine, heroin, inhalants, marijuana, MDMA, methamphetamine, nicotine, prescription central nervous system depressants, prescription opiates and stimulants, and steroids (National Institute on Drug Abuse, 2005l).

Finally, drug-related deaths have more than doubled since the early 1980s. According to the National Institute on Drug Abuse (2005i), more deaths, illnesses, and disabilities are caused from substance abuse than from any other preventable health condition. Today, it is estimated that one in every four deaths is attributable to alcohol, tobacco, and illicit drug use.

Mental Health Barriers

Chronic abuse of drugs can lead to long-lasting changes in the brain. These changes may cause depression, paranoia, aggression, and hallucinations. Drugs that may affect mental health include cocaine, inhalants, ketamine, marijuana, MDMA, methamphetamine, and prescription stimulants (National Institute on Drug Abuse, 2005g).

According to the U.S. Department of Health and Human Services (2005), 20.6 percent of adults with substance-abuse problems have serious mental illness compared to 8.3 percent of adults without substance-abuse problems. Among adults with serious psychological distress, 27.6 percent used an illicit drug during the past year compared with 11.8 percent of adults without serious psychological distress. Serious psychological distress was not soundly linked with current or past year alcohol use. However, there was a link between serious psychological distress and heavy alcohol use and binge drinking. In 2004, the rate of current alcohol use was 52.1 percent for adults with serious psychological distress compared to the 53.3 percent rate for those without serious psychological distress. Nonetheless, the rate of heavy alcohol use over the previous month among adults with serious psychological distress was 9.7 percent compared to the 7.0 percent rate among adults without serious psychological distress. Serious psychological distress was highly correlated with substance dependence or abuse. In 2004 approximately 21.3 percent of adults with serious psychological distress were dependent on or abused illicit drugs or alcohol compared to 7.9 percent of adults without serious psychological distress.

In 2004, 28.8 percent of individuals with major depressive episodes were more likely to have used an illicit drug in the past year compared to 13.8 percent without major depressive episodes. Researchers reported comparable patterns for specific types of illicit drug use over the past year including marijuana, cocaine, heroin, hallucinogens, inhalants, and the nonmedical use of psychotherapeutics (i.e., not referring to the medical use of **psychoactive** or **psychotropic drugs**). Also major depressive episodes are linked to heavy alcohol use. Among individuals with major depressive episodes, 9.2 percent were heavy alcohol users within the previous month compared to 6.9 percent of those without major depressive episodes (U.S. Department of Health and Human Services, 2005).

A link has also been found between suicide and substance-abuse disorders. According to the National Institute on Drug Abuse (2005i), males who attempted suicide had a significantly earlier onset of alcohol-abuse disorders and significantly more mood and disruptive behavior disorder symptoms when compared to males who did not attempt suicide. Females who attempted suicide had a significantly earlier onset and higher numbers of mood disorders and substance-abuse disorders when compared to females who did not attempt suicide. Refer to the American Psychiatric Association's (2000) ***Diagnostic and Statistical Manual of Mental Disorders, 4th Edition, Text Revision (DSM-IV-TR)*** for more comprehensive descriptions of mental disorders.

Career Development Program Model: People with Chemical Dependency

We must point out that the career development model we designed for clients with **chemical dependency** concerns is intended for clients in recovery. Clients who are current users should be referred to treatment prior to focusing on their career development concerns. With that said, some employers may be reluctant to hire a person in recovery due to preconceived notions that hiring such a person could adversely affect their business. For example, some individuals with a substance-abuse history have learned manipulative behaviors that have helped them get whatever they have needed. The client might use the same behaviors in the work setting or even in the helping relationship between the human service professional and the client. However, research has indicated that hiring an individual in recovery tends to present a low risk. The employers' lack of understanding about the nature of **addiction**, treatment, and recovery leads to their reservations in the hiring of people in recovery (U.S. Department of Labor, 2005b). The helping professional must work not only with the client who has substance-abuse concerns but also with employers to dispel their preconceived notions regarding clients in recovery. The career development program model for working with clients with chemical dependency issues is wide-ranging and takes into account the varied needs of this unique population. Figure 16.1 is a graphic model of the career development program.

Applicant Pool

The applicant pool consists of clients with chemical-dependency problems who need career development assistance. During the intake interview, the helping professional assesses whether or not each individual client meets the criteria set forth by the agency for program participation. For example, the agency may require that the client be in recovery for a specific amount of time prior to participating in the career development program. Once the client meets the participation conditions of the program, the human service professional moves toward the development of an Individual Success Plan (ISP) that meets the specific needs of each client.

Individual Success Plan

The helping professional develops the Individual Success Plan (ISP) to help clients achieve their goal of long-term employment. In order to achieve this goal, the helper must develop each ISP in collaboration with the client to meet the specific needs of each client with substance-abuse problems. In developing an ISP for this specific population, the human service professional needs to examine and reduce the specific barriers to career success that are common to this population, assess clients' skills and attributes and match them to specific career choices, and provide the education and training that are necessary for clients' employment objectives.

Make Assessments.   Clients with chemical-dependency concerns are likely to experience a range of emotions due to their substance abuse. These emotions can range from feeling shame and embarrassment to feeling fearful of losing support from loved ones. Such emotions can lead to poor motivation in finding employment. The human service professional must first evaluate the client's feelings in order to determine the best path to take in meeting the client's career development goals.

Following the initial assessment of the client, the human service professional switches focus to the client's specific career-related issues. The first step involves choosing and administering career-related assessments. Since this population is so diverse, the range of possible assessments is large, and helping professionals need to determine each client's specific needs and characteristics in order to select appropriate instruments. Depending on the results of this evaluation, the human service professional can choose from a variety of available assessments and a battery of assessments is often helpful. Table 16.1 is a sample of assessments that may be valuable in assessing clients with chemical-dependency issues. See Chapter 3 for detailed information on each of the following inventories.

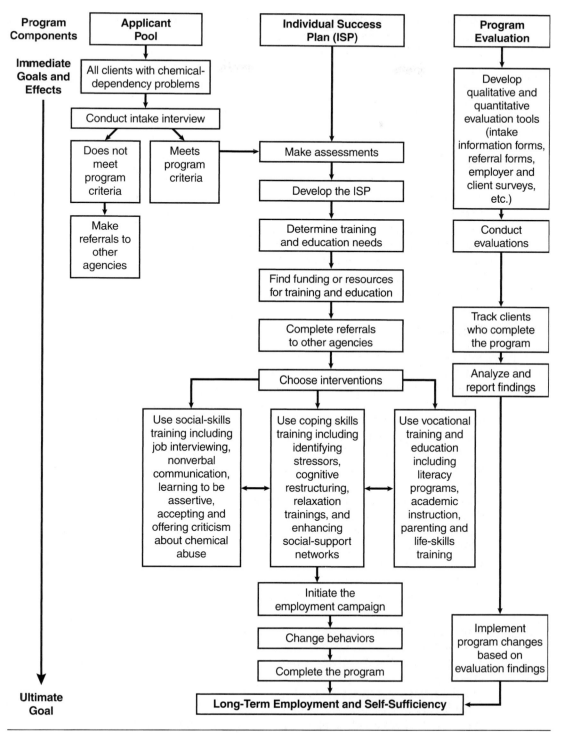

FIGURE 16.1 *Career Development Program Model: People with Chemical Dependency*

TABLE 16.1   *Career Related Assessments for Use with People with Chemical Dependency Problems*

Title	*Source*
Ability Tests	
Ability Explorer	Harrington, J. C., & Harrington, T. F. (1996). *Ability explorer.* Itasca, IL: Houghton Mifflin.
Career Key*	Jones, L. K., & Jones, J. W. (2000). *Career key.* Raleigh, NC: Author.
Motivated Skills Card Sort	Knowdell, R. (2002, June). *Motivated skills card sort.* San Jose, CA: Career Research & Testing.
O*NET Ability Profiler *	O*NET Consortium (2003, April). *O*NET ability profiler.* Washington, DC: Author.
WorkKeys	ACT, Inc. (1993). *Workkeys assessments.* Iowa City, IO: ACT.
Interest Inventories	
Career Exploration Inventory 2	Liptak, J. (2002). *Career exploration inventory: A guide for exploring work, leisure, and learning* (2nd ed.). Indianapolis, IN: JIST Works.
CareerExplorer CD-ROM*	JIST Works (2004). *Careerexplorer CD-ROM.* Indianapolis, IN: Author.
Guide for Occupational Exploration Interest Inventory	Farr, M. (2002). *Guide for occupational exploration interest inventory* (4th ed.). Indianapolis, IN: JIST Works.
Leisure to Occupations Connection Search	McDaniels, C., & Mullins, S. R. (1999). *The leisure to occupations connection search.* Indianapolis, IN: JIST Works.
Occupational Interests Card Sort	Knowdell, R. (2002, June). *Occupational interests card sort.* San Jose, CA: Career Research & Testing.
O*NET Career Interests Inventory*	JIST Works (2002). *O*NET career interests inventory.* Indianapolis, IN: Author.
O*NET Interests Profiler*	O*NET Consortium (n.d.). *O*NET interest profiler.* Washington, DC: Author.
Self-Directed Search Form E, R, & CP	Holland, J. L. (1996). *Self-directed search form E* (4th ed.). Lutz, FL: Psychological Assessment Resources. Holland J. L. (1994). *Self-directed search form R.* Lutz, FL: Psychological Assessment Resources. Holland, J. L. (1990). *Self-directed search form CP: Career planning.* Lutz, FL: Psychological Assessment Resources.
Transition-to-Work Inventory	Liptak, J. J. (2004). *Transition-to-work inventory.* Indianapolis, IN: JIST Works.
Voc-Tech Quick Screener	JIST Works (2002). *Voc-tech quick screener.* Indianapolis, IN: Author.
Wide Range Interest and Occupation Test	Glutting, J. J., & Wilkinson, G. (2003). *Wide range interest and occupation test* (2nd ed.). Wilmington, DE: Wide Range.

TABLE 16.1   Continued

Title	*Source*
Personality Inventories	
Keirsey Temperment Sorter II	Keirsey, D. (1998, May). *Please understand me II.* Del Mar, CA: Prometheus Nemesis Book.
Vocational Preference Inventory	Holland, J. L. (1985). *Vocational preference inventory (VPI).* Lutz, FL: Psychological Assessment Resources.
Value Inventories	
Career Values Card Sort	Knowdell, R. (1998, June). *Career values card sort.* San Jose, CA: Career Research & Testing.
O*NET Career Values Inventory*	JIST Works (2002). *O*NET career values inventory.* Indianapolis, IN: Author.
O*NET Work Importance Locator and Profiler	O*NET Consortium (n.d.). *O*NET work importance locator and profiler.* Washington, DC: Author.
Values-Driven Work Card Sort	Career Action Center. (n.d.). *Value-driven card sort.* Menlo Park, CA: Prodigy Press.
Work Orientation and Values Survey	Brady, R. P. (2000). *Work orientation and values survey.* Indianapolis, IN: JIST Works.
Career-Development Inventories	
Barriers to Employment Success Inventory	Liptak, J. J. (2002). *Barriers to employment success inventory* (2nd ed.). Indianapolis, IN: JIST Works.
Career Attitudes and Strategies Inventory	Holland, J. L., & Gottfredson, G. D. (1994). *Career attitudes and strategies inventory.* Lutz, FL: Psychological Assessment Resources.
Career Beliefs Inventory	Krumboltz, J. D. (1991). *Career beliefs inventory.* Mountain View, CA: CPP.
Career Decision Scale	Osipow, S. H., Carney, C. G., Winer, J. L., Yanico, B. J., & Koschier, M. (1987). *Career decision scale* (3rd ed.). Lutz, FL: Psychological Assessment Resources.
Career Thoughts Inventory	Sampson, J. P., Peterson, G. W., Lenz, J. G., Reardon, R. C., & Saunders, D. E. (1996). *Career thoughts inventory.* Lutz, FL: Psychological Assessment Resources.
Career Transitions Inventory	Heppner, M. J. (1991). *Career transitions inventory.* Columbia, MO: Author.
Job Search Attitude Inventory	Liptak, J. J. (2002). *Job search attitude inventory* (2nd ed.). Indianapolis, IN: JIST Works.
My Vocational Situation	Holland, J. L., Daiger, D., & Power, P. G. (1980). *My vocational situation.* Mountain View, CA: CPP.
Overcoming Barriers Card Sort Game	Harney, E. E., & Angel, D. L. (1999). *Overcoming barriers card sort game.* Hacienda Heights, CA: WorkNet Solutions.

(Continued)

TABLE 16.1   Continued

Title	Source
Reading-Free Vocational Interest Inventory: 2	Becker, R. L. (2000). *Reading-free vocational interest inventory: 2.* Columbus, OH: Elburn.
Salient Beliefs Review: Connecting Spirit to Work	Bloch, D. (2003). *Salient beliefs review: Connecting spirit to work.* Indianapolis, IN: JIST Works.
Vocational Exploration and Insight Kit	Holland, J. L., Birk, J. M., Cooper, J. F., Dewey, C. R., Dolliver, H., Takai, R. T., & Tyler, L. (1980). *The vocational exploration and insight kit.* Mountain View, CA: CPP.
Miscellaneous	
Career Genograms	Gysbers, N. C., Heppner, M. J., & Johnson, J. A. (2003). *Career counseling: Process, issues, and techniques* (2nd ed.) Boston: Allyn and Bacon.
Elevations® Manual Card Sort System	Scully, H. (2003, August). *Elevations manual card sort system.* Roseville, CA: Author.
Individual Employment Plan	Ludden, L. L., & Maitlen, B. (2002). *Individual employment plan.* Indianapolis, IN: JIST Works.
Vocational Decision-Making Interview	Czerlinsky, T., & Chandler, S. (1999). *Vocational decision-making interview.* Indianapolis, IN: JIST Works.

*Use only if client is computer literate.

Develop the ISP.   After the human service professional has administered, scored, and reviewed the career-related assessments, the helper works with the client to determine what occupational prospects are viable for consideration. The helping professional lists and gathers occupational information on each of the occupations the client chose for consideration. The client then explores personal values that relate to these occupational prospects. The client narrows his or her career decisions based on the information that is produced from this examination of values. The client and human service professional work together in creating the client's personal and career-related goals. As with all goals, they must be measurable, action-oriented, practical, and specific (see Chapter 6 for the details of goal setting). For example, a short-term goal for a client with a substance-abuse history might be to focus on job retention, particularly if the client has a sporadic work history. Once goals are established, the helper and client consider and address any potential barriers to career success. After they complete these steps, they shift their attention to determining any training and education the client needs.

Determine Training and Education Needs.   Helping professionals must have a number of resources and referrals available to meet the training and education needs of their clients with substance-abuse problems. Possible training may include "soft-skill" training that focuses on attendance and punctuality, appropriate attire, giving and receiving criticism about substance abuse, working collaboratively, and the importance of a strong work ethic. Education may be a combination of vocational and academic instruction coupled with life-skills training. Many community nonprofit agencies and community colleges offer a variety of skills-training and educational programs. Each client's individual situation will determine the type of training and education the client needs to reach his or her career-related goals.

Find Funding or Resources for Training and Education. The Substance Abuse and Mental Health Services Administration (SAMHSA) funds a number of discretionary grant programs. Many of these programs are related to substance-abuse prevention, however, some programs focus on social-skills and coping-skills training (U.S. Department of Health and Human Services, Substance Abuse and Mental Health Services Administration, 2005). Helping professionals are encouraged to research available programs in their geographical location.

Some clients may qualify for federal financial aid that can help clients cover a variety of school-related expenses including textbooks, tuition, general fees, supplies, room and board, and transportation. Qualification for financial aid is based on an individual's needs, not on grades. Three types of federal aid are available to qualified applicants: grants, work-study, and loans. *Grants* are monies that do not have to be repaid. *Work-study* consists of monies students earn while attending school. *Loans* are borrowed funds that the client repays with interest at a later date. Additional information on federal financial aid programs can be found by visiting the U.S. Department of Education's website at http://www.studentaid.ed.gov/students/publications/student_guide/index.html

Complete Referrals to Other Agencies. When working with clients who have chemical-dependency issues, the helping professional examines the individual needs of each client and determines the types of referrals that may be helpful. Helpers must be familiar with various community agencies, programs, and services that are available to assist clients with chemical-dependency issues achieve their goals of long-term employment. For example, human service professionals must have knowledge of and access to skills training, in-program support, placement, and skills upgrading programs available within the community for individuals with histories of substance abuse.

Choose Interventions. The career development model for clients with chemical-dependency issues consists of three kinds of interventions: social-skills training, coping-skills training, and vocational training and education. Interventions are selected based on the specific needs of each client and may be used independently or in combination with other interventions.

Using Social-Skills Training. When working with clients with a substance-abuse history, human service professionals need to empower their clients through social-skills training. Helping professionals must show clients the importance of not letting their past, chemical abuse bring down their future career possibilities. The social-skills training can include job interviewing skills, nonverbal communication skills, assertiveness training, and skill training in giving and receiving criticism about chemical abuse.

Mock interviews are beneficial for teaching clients how to effectively answer difficult interviewing questions, especially those that pertain to clients' erratic work history that was a result of substance abuse. Through practice clients can learn how to handle questions regarding employment gaps and how to focus on their achievements.

Human service professionals can teach their clients how to display appropriate and confident nonverbal behavior. Many clients with a substance-abuse history lack self-confidence and often display signs of shame and embarrassment. Their lack of self-confidence can result in self-fulfilled prophecies. In other words, clients who are critical of themselves may be likely to sabotage their employment interviews by projecting their lack of self-confidence. Helping professionals can assist their clients in creating an image of confidence through improvement of their nonverbal communication skills and identity management. *Identity management* is defined as communication strategies that individuals use to influence how other people view them (Adler, Proctor, & Towne, 2005).

Another important area to address with clients with chemical-dependency problems is assertiveness training. Clients can benefit from skill training that helps them appropriately express their needs, thoughts, and feelings, ask for information, stand up for their rights, and pursue their best interests in a nonjudgmental way that does not deny the rights of others (Adler, Proctor, & Towne, 2005; Beebe, Beebe, & Redmond, 2005). Beebe and colleagues (2005) recommend five steps for assertive behavior: (1) describe how you view the situation, (2) disclose your feelings, (3) identify how the other person's behavior effects you or others, (4) wait for a response, and (5) paraphrase both the content and feelings of the message. An assertive response seeks an empathic connection between the parties. Assertiveness training can help clients become competent communicators.

Finally, clients must be taught how to effectively give and receive criticism regarding their substance-abuse history. Teaching clients to respond nondefensively when others send critical messages can be an indispensable skill. Two strategies include teaching clients to seek additional information from the critic and, when appropriate, educating clients on how to agree with the critic. According to Adler and colleagues (2005), individuals can seek additional information from the critic in several ways: specifically, they can request more specific information from the sender; guess about the specifics of the criticism; clarify or amplify what they understand the critic to be saying; ask what the critic wants; ask about the consequences of clients' behavior; and finally, ask the critic if anything else is bothering him or her. At times soliciting additional information from the critic is not helpful, and in some cases, it may be useful to agree with the critic. Adler et al. (2005) proposed a variety of ways individuals can effectively agree with their critics including agreeing with the facts and agreeing with the critic's perception. In summary, teaching clients to use self-control and to think before responding to criticism can strengthen their social skills and can improve their probability of achieving their goals of long-term employment.

Using Coping-Skills Training. Clients with substance-abuse problems are likely to encounter stressors that may impede their career development. Human service professionals should work with their clients to identify these stressors and develop effective skills for dealing with them. Some possible coping skills include cognitive restructuring, relaxation training, and enhancing social-support networks.

Negative thinking can damage working and social relationships and undermine work performance. *Cognitive restructuring* is a technique used to help clients challenge negative thoughts and enable them to approach situations in a positive way. Through cognitive restructuring the helping professional works with the client to evaluate just how rational and legitimate are the client's thinking processes. When thinking processes are irrational and invalid, clients are given tools to alter their negative thinking. Mind Tools Ltd. (2005) offers the following steps for individuals to work their way through the cognitive-restructuring process:

1. Write down the situation that triggered the negative thoughts.
2. Identify the moods that were felt during the situation.
3. Write down any automatic thoughts that were experienced while feeling the mood.
4. Identify any evidence that supported the negative thoughts.
5. Identify any evidence that did not support the negative thoughts.
6. Identify balanced and fair thoughts regarding the situation.
7. Examine your mood and think about what you are going to do next.

Another valuable coping skill for clients with chemical-abuse concerns is relaxation training. Excessive stress can lead to a variety of physical and mental conditions. *Relaxation training* can help clients effectively deal with the unpleasant symptoms of stress. Some possible relaxation techniques include guided imagery, meditation, yoga, music/relaxation tapes, physical exercise, and deep-breathing exercises.

Finally, helpers can assist their clients in *enhancing social-support networks*. The health-enhancing effects of social support have been well documented over the years. Such support is crucial for clients with a substance-abuse history. Human service professionals should help their clients improve existing social networks, mobilize support from such networks, and train members of existing networks on ways to be more supportive to the client.

Providing Vocational Training and Education. The third type of intervention includes vocational training and education specifically selected to meet the needs of clients with chemical-dependency issues. This intervention may be a combination of vocational training and academic instruction. A range of skills-training and educational programs are available at many community-nonprofit agencies and community colleges. Vocational training is used to teach specific skills individuals need to enter certain occupations. Vocational training typically takes about 5 to 12 months and sometimes up to 2 years depending on the type of degree or certificate the client is working toward. The majority of vocational-training programs are offered through vocational-technical education programs and services at the state level.

Initiate the Employment Campaign.   Based on the individual needs and goals of each client, human service professionals work with their clients in determining and creating the employment campaign. One of the first steps in the campaign is often the elimination of employment barriers such as gaps in employment and blemished work histories. Some clients may not have the time and resources to complete many work-related activities prior to initiating an employment campaign. For these clients, human service professionals must often multitask by working with the client simultaneously on a number of job-related activities. The following sections summarize strategies for initiating an employment campaign for clients with chemical-dependency issues. For more specific details, see Chapter 5.

The Strategic Job Search.   Human service professionals and their clients utilize the data generated from the intake interview and the career assessments to investigate the role that the client's attributes, such as skills, interests, values, and goals play in the job-search process. For example, for clients who lack specific job skills, their discussion could focus on obtaining the necessary training and/or education needed for particular jobs. Although this process may seem overwhelming for some clients, the human service professional should help them see the big picture, such as long-term employment in their preferred field, which may help to alleviate some of these distressing feelings. Not until clients fully understand themselves can they begin to search for jobs that are good matches for their individual characteristics. Clients should also know the labor market and employer needs. Being able to recognize and respond to labor-market trends and employer needs will help clients find, secure, and retain long-term employment. Helping professionals can assist clients in navigating through this information and in developing and strengthening career networks.

Job Applications.   Employment applications are basically legal documents, and therefore they must be filled out honestly, completely, and accurately. If clients lie on a job application, they may be disqualified from consideration for a job, or if hired, they can be fired for falsifying information. Clients with an erratic employment history or a criminal record due to their former substance abuse may find answering some employment application questions difficult. Therefore clients must read employment applications carefully. The client should only answer what is asked. Additionally, by leaving questions blank, the client may suggest being dishonest by omission, so generally professional helpers should not advise clients to avoid answering certain questions all together. Human service professionals working with clients with a chemical-dependency history should gather a sample of employment applications from neighborhood employers to see how certain questions are posed. Helpers can then review these applications with their clients and help them complete the applications based on the their work history. Clients should be encouraged to bring copies of appropriate responses to questions with them when they are completing job applications. These responses will prevent the client from inadvertently omitting significant information or revealing more that what is asked (National Hire Network, 2005).

Job-Search Correspondence.   Although some jobs will not require a cover letter, job-search correspondence skills are an important component of the employment campaign.

Human service professionals should help their clients understand various forms of correspondence and prepare correspondence such as job-application letters, reminder letters, and letters of appreciation, to name a few.

Tailor-Made Resumes.   As with job applications, honesty is always the best policy when preparing a resume. Some clients with previous substance-abuse problems may have employment gaps. These clients should consider a functional resume instead of a chronological resume format. Clients should avoid resume templates because many templates highlight employment gaps by focusing on a chronological format. The helping professional should encourage clients to include jobs held while they were in rehabilitation. These jobs show employers that the clients used their time constructively and that they possess going-to-work skills. However, clients should never mention rehab as a reason for leaving a job or to fill gaps in their employment history (Giordani, 2005).

Interviewing Strategies.   As mentioned in the intervention strategies section, practice interviewing is the key to clients answering difficult questions with ease. Clients should be taught to convey that they accept responsibility for their past, express remorse when necessary, and show how they have changed. By stressing their current accomplishments such as obtaining formal training and education, clients are likely to overshadow blemishes in their work history.

Change Behaviors.   The career development program model for clients with chemical dependency is designed to help them reach their career-related goals through social-skills training, coping-skills training, vocational training and education, and programs and services specifically geared toward the needs of this population. These clients have a tendency to confront a variety of obstacles that can hinder their career development. Some of these obstacles include social stigma, shame and guilt over past substance abuse, poor motivation to look for employment, erratic work history, and a variety of physical and mental health concerns. This program model addresses these obstacles and empowers clients to overcome such barriers. Clients who move through this program are likely to improve their self-confidence through skill development that will lead them to their goal of long-term employment.

Complete the Program.   Clients who complete the program are those clients who entered the program, completed needed assessments, developed their ISPs, developed needed skills, completed training and education, initiated the employment campaign, and secured gainful employment. Because **relapse** rates are high within the substance-abuse population, clients who complete the program are also gauged by their ability to remain in recovery and to continue a substance-free existence. Clients need to know that a relapse of their chemical use may negatively impact their employment.

Achieve Goal of Long-Term Employment.   The overall goal of the ISP is the long-term employment of the client with chemical-dependency issues. Since the clients' ability to remain "clean" often impacts their ability to maintain employment, long-term employment and self-sufficiency for this population are often measured by the duration of employment coupled with the length of time a client remains substance-free. It cannot go unsaid that there remains an enormous need for more treatment programs and for the integration of workforce development into the long-term treatment modules of clients with substance-abuse concerns. Those clients who maintain employment for a year while remaining chemical-free are considered self-sufficient with long-term employment.

Program Evaluation

As with all career development models discussed in this text, program evaluation is an integral element. The staff should incorporate evaluative methods within every stage of the program, from the establishment of the program to termination. Without program evaluations, agencies could not determine whether or not the programs meet the needs of their clients. Programs that receive outside funding (e.g., grant funding) use evaluations to meet program accountability requirements. Agency human service professionals and staff members must determine what types of evaluations (i.e., process, outcome, impact) and evaluative instruments (i.e., anecdotal record forms, expert review checklists, focus group protocols, process review logs, implementation logs, interview protocols, questionnaires) will be the most helpful in obtaining needed information. Human service professionals need to develop a variety of tools to evaluate their program. Figure 16.1 is a flow chart for the career development program model for people with chemical dependency. The text in each box in the figure is a factor that needs to be measured. Once the staff makes their decisions, they must construct a schedule that includes all steps in the evaluative process, deadlines for meeting goals, and staff who are responsible for the evaluation. After the staff completes the evaluation process, they should gather their data, findings, and recommendations into a report that is distributed to stakeholders, agency representatives, and constituents. See Chapter 6 for additional information on program evaluation.

Revisiting the Case Study: Carol

Conduct an Intake Interview

During the intake interview, the helping professional should investigate Carol's recovery progress, her current financial situation (i.e., amount of child support she is receiving), childcare issues, and her interests, abilities, and values. Carol is currently living with a friend who may provide her with a temporary housing arrangement until she is better able to be self-sufficient.

Carol is likely to be experiencing a range of emotions due to her current situation including depression, anxiety, shame, guilt, embarrassment, fear of losing her child, and she may be poorly motivated to find employment. The human service professional should address the negative potential for these feelings and work with Carol to alleviate these sometimes debilitating emotions.

Make Assessments

The human service professional should administer a battery of assessments to Carol to aid her in exploring possible career options. The human service professional should work with Carol to determine what assessments can best serve her unique needs. Before choosing assessments, the human service professional should determine Carol's skill and comfort level with computer technology. The following are some suggested assessments that may be beneficial to Carol.

Providing Carol is comfortable using a computer the Career Key (Jones & Jones, 2000) and the O*NET Ability Profiler (O*NET Consortium, 2003) could help her assess her abilities. Interests could be measured through Hollands' (1990, 1994, 1996) Self-Directed Search. The Keirsey Temperment Sorter II (Keirsey, 1998) could be beneficial in assessing her personality. The O*NET Career Values Inventory (JIST Works, 2002b) would be a helpful measurement of Carol's values. The helping professional should compare the results of these various inventories with one another. Carol can use a significant overlap in results to determine the best possible career matches for her particular attributes.

The Barriers to Employment Success Inventory (Liptak, 2002a) could help Carol evaluate possible barriers that may impede her employment goals. Finally, the human service professional may want to help Carol develop a career genogram (Gysbers, Heppner, & Johnson, 2003). Because chemical-dependency issues are prominent in Carol's history, a career genogram that focuses on career paths can also trace chemical- abuse history within her family. This information can be a valuable resource for Carol during her recovery. For more detailed information on these inventories and on additional inventories, refer to Chapter 3.

Determine Barriers to Career Success

Carol is likely to have a number of barriers. Because she recently left her husband and is staying with a friend, childcare may be an issue. Helping Carol secure appropriate and inexpensive childcare might be a priority. Related to childcare issues is Carol's fear of losing child custody to her husband or to a child-welfare agency. Without the financial means to support herself and her child, this may be a legitimate fear.

Carol may have experienced social stigma because of her substance-abuse history, and as a result, she may be more inclined to keep her problems and needs concealed. The shame and guilt she is probably experiencing may also make her fearful of losing the support and security of loved ones.

Carol might be poorly motivated to find and secure gainful employment because of her sporadic work history. Her history of holding jobs for an average of a few months at a time can impede her job-seeking efforts.

Because Carol has a 34-year history of drinking coupled with promiscuous behavior, she may have physical and mental health concerns (i.e., STDs, kidney damage, liver damage, brain damage, mental illness). Due to the possibility of physical and/or mental health disorders, the human service professional should refer Carol for a physical and mental evaluation.

Choose Interventions

Using Social-Skills Training.

Carol would probably benefit from social-skills training, including assertiveness training. Assertiveness training could help Carol effectively overcoming her feelings of shame and guilt related to her previous substance abuse—feelings that can lead to nonassertive behavior. Assertiveness training could provide Carol with the verbal and nonverbal communication skills that she needs to boost her confidence in dealing effectively with a number of issues related to her career development.

Carol must also enhance her skills in giving and receiving criticism about her chemical abuse. Her sporadic work history is likely to be a topic of contention and Carol will need to learn how to effectively deal with condemnation. The human service professional should conduct mock interviews that could help Carol successfully address questions related to her complicated work history.

Using Coping-Skills Training.

Carol would likely benefit from relaxation techniques, because she has endured a number of stressors including an impending divorce, lack of financial resources, and childcare issues. Teaching Carol deep-breathing exercises and meditation techniques along with placing her on a physical-exercise regime can help to improve her mental and physical well-being.

Carol is in dire need of a social-support network. The helping professional can help her mobilize a support network including self-help groups (i.e., she is a member of AA), family members, and friends who have previously reached out to help her (i.e., her roommate). In some cases the helper may need to work with Carol's existing network on ways to be supportive during her transition.

Finding Vocational Training and Education.

Although Carol received her high-school diploma, she has no formal training or education beyond the twelfth grade. The fact that she has a high-school diploma will help her secure work while she explores additional training and educational possibilities. The human service professional should help Carol research various training and educational programs that are available within her community. Nonprofit agencies and community colleges would be a good place to start depending on the type of degree or certificate Carol has decided to pursue.

Initiate the Employment Campaign

After Carol completes her interventions, the human service professional should shift attention to Carol's employment campaign. Because Carol has a sporadic work history, one of the first steps in her employment campaign would be to assist her in answering difficult employment-application questions. Carol should be tutored on how to effectively complete employment applications, including instructing her to carefully read the applications and to answer only what she is asked. Carol might be helped if the human service professional gathered a number of employment applications from local businesses and reviewed them with Carol to assist her in answering specific questions related to her work history. When completing the actual application, Carol should bring a list of appropriate responses, which will prevent her from revealing too much information or unintentionally leaving out some.

Since she has a number of gaps in her work history, Carol would benefit most from a functional resume that would highlight her transferable and functional skills. The helper should also help Carol write effective cover letters and other job correspondence. Again, Carol should highlight her strengths and skills and not draw attention to employment gaps.

The human service professional should conduct mock interviews to help Carol answer problematic interview questions effortlessly. The helper should coach Carol on how to answer such questions by taking responsibility for her past actions and stressing her current achievements such as successfully completing formal education.

Developing and implementing an ISP that meets the individual needs of Carol can help her meet her goal of long-term employment that will provide her with a means of supporting herself and her young daughter. Her newfound independence can give her the confidence she needs to remain sober and continue to meet and exceed her career development and personal goals.

Conclusion

Human service professionals who work with clients with chemical dependency must be knowledgeable about the various issues and barriers this population often faces. They should address barriers such as sporadic work histories and physical and mental health problems. Helpers should show their clients unconditional, positive regard, which will boost the self-confidence of clients and help them overcome feelings of shame and guilt. With enhanced self-esteem clients are more likely to be successful in reaching their career development goals.

Human service professionals can work more effectively with clients who have substance-abuse problems by understanding the characteristics of workers in recovery and by advocating for them by conveying these characteristics to prospective employers. The following are some common characteristics of workers in recovery according to the U.S. Department of Labor (2005d):

- They have a chronic and possibly recurring disability and are watchful for threats to their commitment to a substance-free life.
- They have learned to recognize early warning signs and have the skills to prevent relapse.
- They are motivated to learn new skills and to apply themselves in new and productive ways.
- Those who have participated in treatment have better job and life skills as a result of their treatment experience.

- They have learned to develop and strengthen extensive professional and personal support networks as part of their commitment to remain drug free.
- They tend to be highly motivated to make up for past mistakes and lost time and as a result, tend to accomplish much in the workplace.
- They commit to the job because the work positively fills the gap created by giving up substance use.
- They tend to be team players who want others to succeed.
- They have overcome significant challenges in achieving recovery that translates to a determination to succeed in other areas of their lives such as employment.

Summary

Approximately 14.8 million Americans are illicit drug users with the highest rate of use found among the young adult population, ages 18 to 20. This substance-abuse rate is higher among men than among women. Therefore, substance abuse is more common in industries dominated by young, male workers. Although rates of illicit drug use tend to be higher among the unemployed, most individuals who abuse drugs and/or alcohol are employed and bring their substance-abuse problems to work. Therefore, no workplace, regardless of its size or location, is protected from problems associated with illicit drug use. Some of these problems include increased absences, errors, accidents, low morale, and high illness rates. The need for programs such as **Employee Assistance Programs (EAPs)** becomes all the more vital. This chapter presented a career development program model for working with clients with chemical-abuse issues. The model illustrates the creation of an Individual Success Plan using results from assessments of career abilities, interests, values, and barriers; interagency referrals; and interventions as such social-skills training, coping-skills training, and vocational training and education; followed by an employment campaign designed to help clients reach the goal of long-term employment and self-sufficiency.

Key Terms

Addiction	Parity
Alcoholism	Psychoactive drugs
Chemical dependency	Psychotropic drugs
Dependence	Relapse
Diagnostic and Statistical Manual of Mental Disorders, 4th Edition, Text Revision (DSM-IV-TR)	Slip
	Student Assistance Programs (SAPs)
Employee Assistance Programs (EAPs)	Substance
Intervention	Substance abuse
Intoxication	Tolerance
Misuse	Use
	Withdrawal

Web Resources

Note that website URLs may change over time.

Center for Substance Abuse Research (CESAR)
http://www.cesar.umd.edu

NAADAC The Association for Addiction Professionals
http://naadac.org

National Institute on Drug Abuse (NIDA)
http://www.nida.nih.gov

Substance Abuse and Mental Health Services Administration (SAMHSA)
http://www.samhsa.gov

The National Center on Addiction and Drug Abuse at Columbia University
http://www.casacolumbia.org/absolutenm/templates/article.asp?articleid=287&zoneid=32

17

Veterans

After They Serve Their Country

Case Study: Josh and Nadine

Josh and Nadine met in high school and married soon after graduation. While Nadine worked as a cashier at a local department store, Josh worked in construction, first as a roofer, then as a framing carpenter. They continued with these jobs for several years, and then Josh joined the navy, which he entered as a Seaman Apprentice (E-2). Now 20 years later, Josh is ready to retire at the rank of Chief Petty Officer (E-7) having served as a construction planner and estimator specialist (USN NEC 5915). Josh and Nadine have four children ages 7, 10, 15, and 20, and Nadine returned to work full time on the base as a commissary cashier once their youngest child started school. The family lived in base housing during the past 20 years and has recently moved into an apartment. The three younger children attend public school while the oldest attends the local community college. While in the navy, Josh deployed to several foreign countries, including Somalia, Saudi Arabia, and Iraq. As a concrete specialist, Josh has helped build piers, warehouses, and runways. Although he attended the navy's transition program, he is having a difficult time adjusting to life as a civilian, in particular trying to find a job that allows him to support his family of six.

The Veteran Population

Just who can be called a veteran? The U.S. Census Bureau (n.d.) proposed a three-part definition: a *civilian veteran* is someone who is 18 years or older who has served (1) in the armed forces (i.e., the U.S. Army, Navy, Air Force, Marine Corps, Coast Guard) or (2) in the Merchant Marine in World War II. (3) Those who have served in the reserves or in the National Guard are only classified as veterans if they have been called or ordered to active duty (in addition to their initial training and yearly summer camps).

Out of the almost 25 million veterans currently alive, almost 75 percent of them have served during an official period of conflict or war (U.S. Department of Veteran Affairs, 2005b). Approximately 1.7 million veterans are women; 2.3 million are African American; 1.1 million are Hispanic; 276,000 are Asian; 185,000 are Native American/Alaska Native; and 25,000 are native Hawaiian/Pacific Islanders (U.S. Census Bureau, 2005b). Over 2.1 million veterans are age 35 or younger; over 1.4 million are between ages 35 to 39; more than 6.1 million veterans are ages 40 to 54; over 3.4 million are ages 55 to 59; 2.4 million are 60 to 64; and 9.6 million are over the age of 65 (U.S. Census Bureau, 2005a). Six states are home to more than 1 million veterans: California with 2.3 million, Florida with 1.8 million, Texas with 1.7 million, New York with 1.2 million, Pennsylvania with1.1 million, and Ohio with 1.1 million (U.S. Bureau of the Census, 2005b).

As of 2003, 1.4 million Americans were on active duty in the army, 382,000 in the navy, 178,000 in the marines, and 375,000 in the air force. Almost 1.2 million are classified as military reserve personnel (U.S. Census Bureau, 2005a). At the time of this writing, veterans comprised 8 percent of the United States population, and active duty and reservists comprised an additional 12 percent. None of these numbers, however, reflect the current status of those serving in Iraq and Afghanistan.

Unemployment Rates

The unemployment rate of 4.7 percent of male veterans between ages 25 to 34 was lower than the 6.3 percent rate of their nonveteran peers in August 2003. The unemployment rate of veterans ages 35 to 44 at 3.8 percent was lower than the 4.8 percent rate of their nonveteran peers. Veterans ages 45 to 54 had a higher unemployment rate at 5.4 percent than their nonmilitary peers at a rate of 3.6 percent. Unemployment rates of female veterans differ from male veterans. Female veterans ages 25 to 35 had an unemployment rate of 8.2 percent versus 6.2 percent for their nonveteran female peers. The remaining age groups showed little difference (U.S. Bureau of Labor Statistics [BLS], 2004).

Unemployment rates for African American veterans were much lower than for their nonveteran peers with 4.8 percent unemployment among veterans and 11.3 percent among nonveterans as of August 2003. White veterans had an unemployment rate of 4.5 percent that was only somewhat lower than the 5.1 percent of their white nonveteran peers during this time period. Hispanic veterans and nonveterans had similar unemployment rates of approximately 7 percent (U.S. Bureau of Labor Statistics, 2004).

Disabled Veterans

Approximately 2.2 million veterans or 9 percent reported having a service-connected disability in 2003. The Department of Veterans Affairs assigns a disability rating between 0 and 100 percent in 10 percentage point increments to each veteran with a service-related disability. Almost 50 percent of disabled veterans reported a disability rated at 30 percent or less, and 21 percent reported a disability rated higher than 60 percent.

While the incidence of service-connected disabilities did not differ between those who served in World War II, Korea, and the Vietnam era and those who served in other periods, the severity of disabilities did vary. Twenty-one percent of veterans who had served in World War II, Korea, and Vietnam reported severe disabilities (60 percent or higher disability ratings). Only 14 percent of disabled veterans who served in other time periods reported a disability rating that high (U.S. Bureau of Labor Statistics, 2004).

Only 33 percent of those disabled veterans who had served in World War II, Korea, and Vietnam reported still being in the labor force in August 2003. This low-employment rate reflects not only their level of disability but also their age. Eighty percent of this group are age 55 or older. In comparison, 46 percent of the veterans from these service periods who did not report service-connected disabilities were employed. The unemployment rate for disabled veterans from these war-time periods was 3.5 percent. Veterans with service-connected disabilities from other service periods report different employment rates. For example, 75 percent of those with a service-connected disability were in the labor force, a similar participation rate to that of nondisabled veterans from those service periods (U.S. Bureau of Labor Statistics, 2004).

Veterans Recently Discharged from Active Duty

Almost 450,000 veterans were discharged from active duty between January 2000 and August 2003. Females accounted for 13 percent of those recently discharged, African American for 12 percent, and Hispanics for 9 percent. The labor-force participation rate for those recently discharged was 89 percent, with an unemployment rate of 6.9 percent. Twenty percent of discharged veterans had a service-related disability. Nearly 60 percent of those recently discharged veterans with a disability had a disability rating of 30 percent or higher compared with only 40 percent of veterans discharged between 1991 and 2000 (U.S. Bureau of Labor Statistics, 2004).

Military Discharge Versus Separation

Military members may receive a separation or a discharge from the military. A *discharge* cuts off all legal ties between the person and the military. A *separation*, on the other hand, is a more general term that includes discharges, release from active duty, a transfer to inactive reserves, and other changes of status. Separations may result in a transfer to reserve status for the remainder of the member's enlistment. Members may be discharged under a variety of conditions, including, but not limited to

- A physical problem that keeps the military member from performing his or her duties
- An inability to adjust to military life or meet the minimum standards of his or her training
- A conscientious objection due to deeply held moral, ethical, or religious beliefs
- Homosexual conduct or "don't ask, don't tell"
- Family hardships, such as family members or dependents experiencing severe financial, physical, or psychological problems

- Pregnancy or childbirth and parenthood
- Being the surviving son or daughter

Military members may also receive *punitive* discharges for bad conduct. Discharge papers report the type of discharge a person received as well as the reason for the discharge. The type of discharge, however, impacts the benefits available to the veteran (GI Rights Network, n.d.).

Veterans' Employment

Almost 16 percent of employed, disabled veterans work for the federal government compared to 6 percent of nondisabled veterans and 2 percent of nonveterans. Nearly 35 percent of male veterans were employed in management and professional occupations. Of the remaining employed, male veterans, 11.2 percent were in service occupations; 18.5 percent in sales and office occupations; 16.1 percent in natural resources (i.e., farming, fishing, and forestry), construction, and maintenance occupations; and 19.1 percent in production, transportation, and material moving occupations. Female veterans tend to be employed as follows: 43.2 percent in management and professional occupations; 16.3 percent in service occupations; 34.2 percent in sales and office occupations; 2 percent in natural resources (i.e., farming, fishing, and forestry), construction, and maintenance occupations; and 4.4 percent in production, transportation, and material moving occupations (U.S. Bureau of Labor Statistics, 2004).

Veterans' Education

The educational level of those in the military varies from commissioned officers to warrant officers to enlisted persons. As of September 2004, 99.3 percent of enlisted personnel had graduated from high school. Only 10.1 percent of enlisted personnel had completed two or more years of college compared to 48.2 percent of warrant officers and 98.6 percent of commissioned officers. College graduation rates were even more varied. Four percent of enlisted personnel, 28.6 percent of warrant officers, and 97.5 percent of commissioned officers were college graduates (U.S. Department of Defense [DOD], n.d.)

Transition Services

Veterans receive priority service through Employment Service and the Career One-Stop Center program and partners (Employment and Training Administration [ETA], 2005). A variety of other benefits programs have also been created to meet the needs of those in transition from military to civilian life. Some of the many assistance programs for veterans are as follows:

- *Disability Compensation.* Disability compensation is a benefit paid to veterans for injuries or illness suffered as a result of their active service. Compensation topics include prisoner of war, agent orange/other herbicides, exposure to radiation, Gulf War-related conditions, allowances for dependents, and incarcerated veterans (U.S. Department of Veteran Affairs, 2002)

- *Family and Survivor Benefits.* Benefits are available to some family members of disabled or deceased veterans. Benefits may include medical care, dependency and indemnity compensation, payments to the surviving spouse/parents/children, spina bifida benefits, death pension, education benefits, home loan guaranties, and the Montgomery GI Bill (U.S. Department of Veteran Affairs, 2002).

- *Home Benefits: VA Loan Guarantee.* Loan guarantees are made to eligible service members to purchase, repair, construct, or improve a dwelling that will be occupied by the veteran as a home (U.S. Department of Veteran Affairs, 2002).

- *Montgomery GI Bill.* This federal program provides educational benefits to those who enlisted after 1985, and also offers a program for members of the Selected Reserve and National Guard (U.S. Department of Veteran Affairs, 2002).

- *Registered Apprentice System.* This federal-state partnership provides registered apprenticeships that include on-the-job learning with theory-related instruction provided by various educational institutions and partners with the Department of Defense to provide training and credentials to veterans in transition (ETA, 2005).

- *Transition Assistance Program (TAP).* This federal program provides comprehensive 2–3 day workshops for exiting military members and their spouses on such topics as career exploration, methods of job search, preparing for job interviews, self-appraisal, and identification of other sources of support and assistance. Military members must attend TAP workshops within 12 months of separation or 24 months of retirement. The service member must have served on active duty for at least 180 days to participate in TAP. This requirement is waived, however, for those military members who are retiring or separating due to a disability (VETS Employment Services, n.d.b).

- *Veterans Education Assistance Program (VEAP).* This educational benefit program is for veterans who entered active duty after December 31, 1976 and before July 1, 1985, and who contributed to an educational fund (U.S. Department of Veteran Affairs, 2002).

- *Veterans Employment and Training Service (VETS).* Sponsored by the Department of Labor, VETS provides employment and training services to eligible veterans through the Jobs for Veterans State Grants Program that funds **Disabled Veteran Outreach Program (DVOP)** and **Local Veterans Employment Representatives (LVER)** (VETS Employment Services n.d.a).

- *Vocational Rehabilitation and Employment Benefits.* This benefits program assists veterans with service-related disabilities; provides services and assistance to prepare for, find, and keep suitable employment; and assists veterans in overcoming barriers to employment. It includes vocational-educational career counseling and vocational-training programs (U.S. Department of Veteran Affairs, 2002).

Homeless Veterans

While no accurate numbers exist as to the exact number of homeless veterans, the National Coalition for Homeless Veterans (2005) suggested that over 200,000 veterans are homeless on any given night and more than half a million are homeless at some point during the year. The Veterans Administration reported providing benefits and health care through **stand downs** to more than 100,000 homeless veterans each year; providing over 300 grants for transitional housing, service centers and vans for outreach; and providing transportation to service providers, including tribal government, state and local governments, and faith-based and other nonprofit community resources (U.S. Department of Veteran Affairs, 2005b, 2005c). Stand downs provided services to homeless veterans (i. e., food, shelter, clothing, health screenings, benefits counseling, and referrals for mental health services, housing, and employment services) through collaborating events that lasted 1–3 days and were sponsored by the Department of Veterans Affairs (Stand Down 2005, 2005). With annual estimates of 500,000 homeless veterans, 80 percent of these veterans lacked supportive services, and only 25 percent of homeless veterans reported having used homeless services provided through the Veterans Administration (National Coalition for Homeless Veterans, 2005).

Almost one-third of the homeless population are veterans. Still more veterans are considered to be near homeless because of poverty, lack of support from friends and family, and living in substandard housing or in cheap hotels (U.S. Department of Veteran Affairs, 2005a). Almost all homeless veterans are males; only 3 percent of homeless veterans are female. Homeless veterans are often older and better educated than the nonveteran homeless. Eighty-five percent of homeless veterans have completed high school or have a GED compared to 56 percent of nonveterans. Almost 45 percent of homeless veterans suffer some form of mental illness, and over 70 percent of homeless veterans reported some form of alcohol or drug-abuse problems (U.S. Department of Veteran Affairs, 2005a).

Selected Major Veterans' Legislation

Veterans' legislation is constantly being passed and updated. While the following list in no way includes all legislation pertaining to the military, it includes some of the most important pieces of veteran-related legislation:

• *National Defense Authorization Act of 1991* (Public Law 101–510). This act established the Transition Assistance Program (TAP) to provide benefits and services to military personnel and their spouses who will be separating from the military.

• *Uniformed Services Employment and Reemployment Rights Act of 1994* (Public Law 103–353). Also known as USERRA, this act provided reemployment protection for veterans and other employees who perform military service. It applies to voluntary as well as involuntary service and clarifies the rights and responsibilities of National Guard and reservists.

- *The Veterans Preference Act of 1944* (Public Law 85–857). This act provided preferential hiring status to veterans who are disabled or who may have served during certain time periods or military campaigns. It also entitles veterans to preference during reductions in workforce.

- *Veterans Employment Opportunities Act of 1998* (Public Law 105–339). This act authorized Veterans Workforce Investment Programs to meet the needs of newly separated military members and those with service-related disabilities who face significant barriers to employment.

- *Jobs for Veterans Act of 2002* (Public Law 107-288). This act revised veterans' employment and training benefits programs while increasing preferential status for hiring.

- *Vietnam Era Veterans' Readjustment Assistance Act of 1974* (Public Law 93–508). This act authorized affirmative action to employ and advance qualified veterans and disabled veterans. It prohibits employment discrimination based on veteran or disabled veteran status.

Barriers to Career Success

Structural Barriers

Communication and Societal Perspectives.   Veterans have spent their time in the military using military jargon and talking in acronyms that do not transfer easily into civilian communication. While other veterans understand the terms, most civilian employers and employees will not. Avoiding military jargon and references requires the veteran to concentrate on communicating in civilian terms rather than in military terms (Veterans Employment and Training Service, 2002.)

In some instances, employers have unrealistic expectations of veterans including expecting them to lack creativity, be rigid, and lack the knowledge of how to succeed in a civilian world. Civilian workers with military spouses often face the same stereotypes, and employers assume that the job applicant will relocate frequently due to the military spouse (Veterans Employment and Training Service, 2002).

Military Credentials.   Credentials earned in the military do not readily transfer into civilian credentials. Civilian credentials such as drivers' licenses and other certifications are obtained through the traditional path of education, training, and experience in the nonmilitary sector. Military-service members who need civilian-based certifications should determine what requirements they need for credentialing prior to transitioning. Those who do not take this step may face delays in obtaining employment (Veterans Employment and Training Service, 2002).

Individual Barriers

Type of Discharge.   When the veteran job applicant has little experience, employers often request military records, in particular they look for discharge papers and the discharge status. Veterans who received a bad conduct or other than honorable discharge may find it more difficult to obtain civilian employment if the employer asks to see discharge papers and is negatively influenced by the type of discharge. Employers may be unwilling to hire someone who found it difficult to adapt to the military (GI Rights Network, n.d.).

Military Culture. Riggio (2002) maintained that military members develop habits that meet their needs and help them adjust to their transition into the military. Veterans may need to change those habits, or examples of military culture as they transition out of the military. Military culture includes, but is not limited to, military housing, relocation every three years or less, deployments, knowing military rank and social structure, tax advantages, uniforms, acting according to military expectations, military traditions, exchange privileges, and having a mentor or resource person who tells the military member where to go or what to do. Military members who have lived on base will need to find housing and deal with rent, mortgages, and utility connection fees for the first time. Those who separate from the military and do not live near a military base will lose easy access to low-cost items from the exchange and will find it difficult to access their heath-care assistance through **Civilian Health and Medical Program of the Uniformed Services (CHAMPUS)** or TRICARE. Military members even transition from having scheduled meals that are provided for them three times a day to preparing meals themselves. The military culture differs greatly from the civilian culture, and the transition from one to the other can prove difficult for some veterans.

Family Adjustments. Transition to civilian life affects the families of military members as well. Families that needed time to adjust to a family member's frequent absences due to deployment must now adjust very quickly to having the family member at home. While the military member was gone, stay-at-home family members took on specific roles in that person's absence, and giving up those roles when the military member returns may not be easy or even desirable. Military parents will need to adjust to being with their children more frequently including taking on childcare responsibilities when they had not done so in the past. Other roles may change within the family that require almost a renegotiation of family roles during the transition process (Riggio, 2002).

Physical and Mental Health Barriers

The U.S. Department of Veteran Affairs [VA] (2005b) has identified a number of physical and mental health disabilities that may be related to the time a person served in the military. Former POWs (prisoners of war), for example, may suffer from frostbite-related organic conditions, posttraumatic osteoarthritis, heart disease, stroke, type 2 diabetes, a variety of nutritional deficiencies, irritable bowel syndrome, cirrhosis of the liver, psychoses, any of the anxiety states, and dysthymic disorder. Exposure of military members to Agent Orange and other herbicides has been linked to such illnesses as type 2 diabetes, non-Hodgkins lymphoma, prostate cancer, peripheral neuropathy, and chronic lymphocytic leukemia. Gulf War veterans may suffer from chronic fatigue syndrome, fybromyalgia, irritable bowel syndrome, skin disorders, headaches, muscle pain, joint pain, neurologic symptoms, menstrual disorders, abnormal weight loss, cardiovascular symptoms, sleep disturbances, anxiety disorders, and post-traumatic stress disorder (National Center for Post-Traumatic Stress Disorder, 2004; U.S. Department of Veteran Affairs, 2005b). Still other veterans may have lost their limbs, eyesight, or hearing while in the military. These disabilities are not limited to combat veterans, however, since noncombatants may have been similarly exposed during their military assignments (U.S. Department of Veteran Affairs, 2005b). Veterans may also suffer from depression, HIV/AIDS, pathological gambling, a substance abuse or chemical dependency, all of which may impact an individual's ability to find adequate work and maintain employment (Kausch, 2004; National Center for Post-Traumatic Stress Disorder, 2004; Smith, Schnurr, & Rosenheck, 2005; U.S. Department of Veteran Affairs, 2005c).

Career Development Program Model: The Veteran Population

In most instances veterans should be referred directly to the Department of Veterans Affairs for assistance. Some veterans, however, may be ineligible for assistance from the department and will need a program that meets their specific needs. The program should integrate transitional services that address each client's needs and barriers with the ultimate goal of successful reintegration of the veteran into the civilian community through long-term employment. Our program has three major components: the applicant pool, the Individual Success Plan (ISP), and the program evaluation. Each component will be explained in detail. Figure 17.1 is a graphic model of the career development program.

Applicant Pool

The applicant pool for this career development program includes any client who is a veteran. Intake personnel will determine which clients fit the criteria for program participation and will refer clients who do qualify to other agencies for additional services as necessary. If the program assists family members of veterans, the program staff will need to establish additional criteria for family members of veterans in transition.

Individual Success Plan

Developing an Individual Success Plan (ISP) provides a specialized approach to career development. Veterans and their families often face a variety of barriers to career success, so human service professionals need to view their clients as individuals and help them successfully transition from the military community into the civilian community through finding stable employment. Involving veterans in the development of their own ISPs can help them gain some control over their lives and empower them to be successful.

Make Assessments.   In addition to considering the veterans' career, education, and training needs, human service professionals need to consider the stage of job loss.

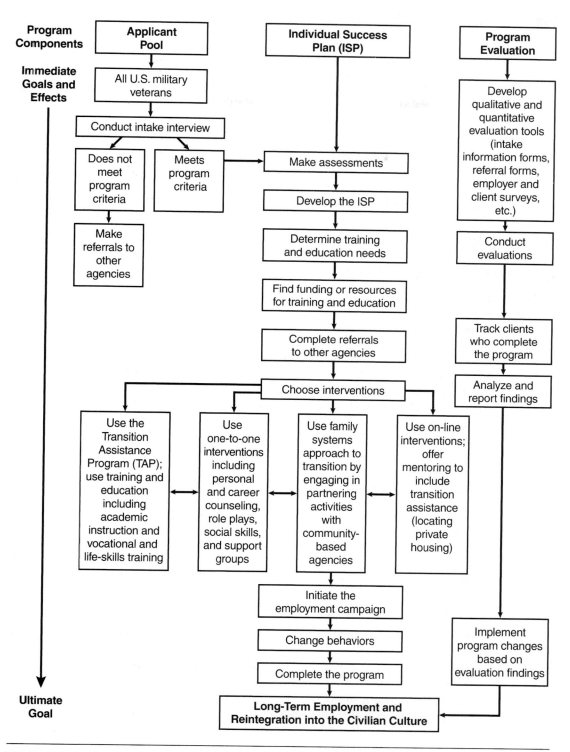

Program Components

Immediate Goals and Effects

| Applicant Pool | Individual Success Plan (ISP) | Program Evaluation |

All U.S. military veterans

Conduct intake interview

Does not meet program criteria

Meets program criteria

Make referrals to other agencies

Make assessments

Develop the ISP

Determine training and education needs

Find funding or resources for training and education

Complete referrals to other agencies

Choose interventions

Use the Transition Assistance Program (TAP); use training and education including academic instruction and vocational and life-skills training

Use one-to-one interventions including personal and career counseling, role plays, social skills, and support groups

Use family systems approach to transition by engaging in partnering activities with community-based agencies

Use on-line interventions; offer mentoring to include transition assistance (locating private housing)

Develop qualitative and quantitative evaluation tools (intake information forms, referral forms, employer and client surveys, etc.)

Conduct evaluations

Track clients who complete the program

Analyze and report findings

Initiate the employment campaign

Change behaviors

Complete the program

Implement program changes based on evaluation findings

Ultimate Goal

Long-Term Employment and Reintegration into the Civilian Culture

FIGURE 17.1 *Career Development Program Model: U.S. Military Veterans*

As with dislocated workers (see Chapter 11), veterans often work through stages of denial, anger, bargaining, depression, and acceptance in their transition to civilian life (Bradley, 1990). The stress of knowing that one is about to lose one's job (i.e., place in the military) or that one's financial supports will soon change often impacts the stress level of veterans and their families and possibly affects their success in finding and holding a job. Thus, the ISP needs to address these as well as career issues. Veterans also differ with respect to their work experiences and the length of time spent in the military. Twenty-year veterans, for example, will face different transition issues and possess different skills than those who leave the military after only two years.

Chapter 3 provides an assortment of career-related assessments that can be used according to clients' needs and background. A traditional intake interview can help identify their needs and clarify the best course of action for clients at this time. The education and vocational background of the client needs to be considered in choosing assessments. When working with veterans, one major skill-related issue is to identify military skills that transfer to civilian skills. Before administering any assessments, the human service professional will want to access a Military to Civilian Transferable Skills Identifier such as the one offered through the Department of Defense Vocational Rehabilitation and Employment Service's website (www.vba.va.gov/bln/vre/tsi/default.asp). Another useful site is the Skills Translator provided through Military.Com (www.military.com/Careers/Home). A similar tool is the Military Skills Translator on the Helmets to Hardhats website (www.helmetstohardhats.com), which links veterans to jobs in construction.

Table 17.1 is a list of assessments that are appropriate for use in designing an ISP with veterans. Using several assessments is encouraged, but human service professionals need to use only those that best fit the needs of their clients. (See Chapter 3 for additional details on each assessment.).

Develop the ISP.   After veterans have chosen and completed the assessments, the next step is to generate the ISP. Integrating information obtained through the intake interview, assessments, and discussions, the human service professional helps clients identify specific barriers to employment success, explores issues of mental and physical health, and makes referrals where necessary. Once clients have identified their barriers to career success, the human service professional will help them integrate their values, career goals, and personal goals into the planning process. Encouraging clients to take an active role in creating these plans empowers the clients and helps them move toward self-sufficiency, which is particularly important for those who have recently left the military. After identifying what barriers to include in the ISP, the human service professional will work with clients to establish a timeline for meeting each goal and will set mini goals to meet along the way that will help clients see their progress, while allowing for a redesign of the ISP as necessary.

Determine Training and Education Needs.   America's Career InfoNet provides several online services that are useful for veterans in this stage of their transition. This website's Workforce Credential Information Center provides links to several databases of military resources: COOL (Army Credentialing Opportunities On-Line), USMAP (United Services Military Apprenticeship Program), and DANTES (Defense Activity

TABLE 17.1 *Career Related Assessments for Use with the Veteran Population*

Title	*Source*
Ability Tests	
Career Key*	Jones, L. K., & Jones, J. W. (2000). *Career key.* Raleigh, NC: Author.
Motivated Skills Card Sort	Knowdell, R. (2002, June). *Motivated skills card sort.* San Jose, CA: Career Research & Testing.
O*NET Ability Profiler*	O*NET Consortium (2003), April). *O*NET ability profiler.* Washington, DC: Author.
WorkKeys	ACT, Inc. (1993). *Workkeys assessments.* Iowa City, IO: ACT.
Interest Inventories	
Career Exploration Inventory 2	Liptak, J. (2002). *Career exploration inventory: A guide for exploring work, leisure, and learning* (2nd ed). Indianapolis, IN: JIST Works.
CareerExplorer CD-ROM*	JIST Works (2004). *Careerexplorer CD-ROM.* Indianapolis, IN: Author.
Guide for Occupational Exploration Interest Inventory	Farr, M. (2002). *Guide for occupational exploration interest inventory* (4th ed.). Indianapolis, IN: JIST Works.
Leisure to Occupations Connection Search	McDaniels, C., & Mullins, S. R. (1999). *The leisure to occupations connection search.* Indianapolis, IN: JIST Works.
Occupational Interests Card Sort	Knowdell, R. (2002, June). *Occupational interests card sort.* San Jose, CA: Career Research & Testing.
O*NET Career Interests Inventory*	JIST Works. (2002). *O*NET career interests inventory.* Indianapolis, IN: Author.
Retirement Activities Card Sort	Knowdell, R. (1998). *Retirement activities card sort kit.* San Jose, CA: Career Research & Testing.
Self-Directed Search, Forms CP and R	Holland, J. L. (1990). *Self-directed search form CP: Career planning.* Lutz, FL: Psychological Assessment Resources. Holland J. L. (1994). *Self-directed search form R.* Lutz, FL: Psychological Assessment Resources.
Transition-to-Work Inventory	Liptak, J. J. (2004). *Transition-to-work inventory.* Indianapolis, IN: JIST Works.
Voc-Tech Quick Screener	JIST Works (2002). *Voc-tech quick screener.* Indianapolis, IN: Author.
Wide Range Interest and Occupation Test	Glutting, J. J., & Wilkinson, G. (2003). *Wide range interest and occupation test* (2nd ed.). Wilmington, DE: Wide Range.
Value Inventories	
Career Values Card Sort	Knowdell, R. (1998, June). *Career values card sort.* San Jose, CA: Career Research & Testing.
O*NET Career Values Inventory*	JIST Works (2002). *O*NET career values inventory.* Indianapolis, IN: Author.
O*NET Work Importance Locator and Profiler*	O*NET Consortium (n.d.). *O*NET work importance locator and profiler.* Washington, DC: Author.

(Continued)

TABLE 17.1   Continued

Title	Source
Values-Driven Work Card Sort	Career Action Center. (n.d.). *Values-driven card sort.* Menlo Park, CA: Prodigy Press.
Work Orientation and Values Survey	Brady, R. P. (2000). *Work orientation and values survey.* Indianapolis, IN: JIST Works.
Career-Development Inventories	
Barriers to Employment Success Inventory	Liptak, J. J. (2002). *Barriers to employment success inventory* (2nd ed.). Indianapolis, IN: JIST Works.
Career Attitudes and Strategies Inventory	Holland, J. L., & Gottfredson, G. D. (1994). *Career attitudes and strategies inventory.* Lutz, FL: Psychological Assessment Resources.
Career Beliefs Inventory	Krumboltz, J. D. (1991). *Career beliefs inventory.* Mountain View, CA: CPP.
Career Decision Scale	Osipow, S. H., Carney, C. G., Winer, J. L., Yanico, B. J., & Koschier. M. (1987). *Career decision scale* (3rd ed.). Lutz, FL: Psychological Assessment Resources.
Career Thoughts Inventory	Sampson, J. P., Peterson, G. W., Lenz, J. G., Reardon, R. C., & Saunders, D. E. (1996). *Career thoughts inventory.* Lutz, FL: Psychological Assessment Resources.
Career Transitions Inventory	Heppner, M. J. (1991). *Career transitions inventory.* Columbia, MO: Author.
My Vocational Situation	Holland, J. L., Daiger, D., & Power, P. G. (1980). *My vocational situation.* Mountain View, CA: CPP.
Overcoming Barriers Card Sort Game Kit	Harney, E. E., & Angel, D. L. (1999). *Overcoming barriers card sort game kit.* Hacienda Heights, CA: WorkNet Solutions.
Salient Beliefs Review: Connecting Spirit to Work	Bloch, D. (2003). *Salient beliefs review: Connecting spirit to work.* Indianapolis, IN: JIST Works.
Vocational Exploration and Insight Kit	Holland, J. L., Birk, J. M., Cooper, J. F., Dewey, C. R., Dolliver, H., Takai, R. T., & Tyler, L. (1980). *The vocational exploration and insight kit.* Mountain View, CA: CPP.
Miscellaneous	
Career Genograms	Gysbers, N. C., Heppner, M. J., & Johnson, J. A. (2003). *Career counseling: Process, issues, and techniques* (2nd ed.) Boston: Allyn and Bacon.
Elevations ® Manual Card Sort System	Scully, H. (2003, August). *Elevations manual card sort system.* Roseville, CA: Author.
Individual Employment Plan	Ludden, L. L., & Maitlen, B. (2002). *Individual employment plan.* Indianapolis, IN: JIST Works.
Vocational Decision-Making Interview	Czerlinsky, T., & Chandler, S. (1999). *Vocational decision-making interview.* Indianapolis, IN: JIST Works.

*Use only if client is computer literate.

for Non-Traditional Educational Support). Veterans who need to convert military experience into civilian certifications may want to begin with websites such as COOL, USMAP, and DANTES to better understand what steps they need to take to obtain those credentials and to find the necessary funding to cover those expenses.

Clients can obtain additional career leads for training and education by reviewing the results of the interest inventories. Technology skills, in particular, are important skills for veterans to develop. Human service professionals should help clients avoid training that maintains obsolete technologies and unstable jobs; instead they should emphasize the match of skills development and support with economic opportunities that meet clients' needs. Assessment results may suggest other topics for training and education. Clients can take life-skills training in small groups or in one-to-one sessions, allowing for a more individualized fit as needed. Providing clients with a list of possible training and educational group topics (i.e., parenting skills, house maintenance, stress management, time management, debt management) from which to choose continues to empower them to take responsibility for their life choices and ownership in their successes.

Find Funding for Training and Education.   Those who qualify for federal benefits for veterans may be eligible for educational benefits such as the Montgomery GI Bill, Veterans Education Assistance Program, or Survivors' and Dependents' Education Assistance. To determine their eligibility, clients can visit the GI Bill website (http://www.gibill.va.gov/) for additional information and to complete an electronic application. Other forms of tuition assistance may be available through the DANTES Tuition Assistance Program, as well as through the veteran's specific branch of the military. Veterans may also be eligible for funding for training and education through the federally funded One-Stop Career Centers of the Workforce Investment Act (1998).

Choose Interventions.   The Veterans Career Development Model has six categories of interventions: Transition Assistance Program (TAP), on-line interventions, one-to-one interventions, training and education, family systems approach, and mentoring. The client and human service professional consult to determine whether the best approach for the client is that of an individual or group intervention. The human service professional can offer the interventions concurrently or in phases, depending upon the client's needs and agency requirements. Some clients may need all six interventions while others may only need one or two. Again, an individualized approach is necessary due to the diverse backgrounds of veterans.

Using the Transition Assistance Program (TAP).   In 1989, the Department of Defense and the Department of Labor jointly conducted the first TAP to provide exiting service members with a variety of transitional services, including job-training assistance and counseling on VA benefits. Military members are encouraged to attend a three-day TAP seminar within one year of separation and two years of retirement from the military (U.S. Department of Veteran Affairs, 2005d). Professional, trained workshop facilitators from military family-support services; the state employment services; the Department of Labor; or VETS staff present the workshops, leading participants in personal appraisal, career decision making, job-search techniques, occupational and labor-market conditions, resume writing, cover-letter preparation, interviewing skills, and job-offer review (U.S. Department of Labor, 2002). As of 2002, TAP had assisted more than one million service members and their spouses (*TAP Participants Manual*, 2002). Members of the reserves and the national guard, however, may not have the opportunity to participate fully in TAP (U.S. Government Accounting Office, 2005).

Using On-Line Interventions.   Several online interventions have been developed to assist veterans in their transition into the civilian world. Career development centers assisting veterans can provide computers on site for the veterans to use, or human service professionals can demonstrate these and similar websites in workshops and provide a list of URLs for workshop participants to access later. The following list is a selected few of the many websites available to help the military transition into the civilian world:

- *Transition Assistance On-Line* (http://www.taonline.com/). This website provides transitioning military members and employers with a variety of transition-related services. Employers can post job ads that target military members specifically and search resumes. Those in transition can search job ads, post resumes, and explore business and educational opportunities for their postmilitary careers. This website also provides a transition assistance newsletter.

- *Military.Com* (http://www.military.com/). This website assists military members in all levels of military involvement by including military news updates and articles of interest to those in the military. This site includes a buddy finder, newsletters, discussion boards, and information on accessing and using education benefits, on-line education programs, a military-to-civilian job search, and unit home pages to name a few. After joining the website, members can access information available by type of service (i.e., army, navy, air force, marine corps, coast guard), including a section designed for military spouses.

- *The Department of Defense Job Search* (http://dod.jobsearch.org/). This website is associated with the Department of Labor's America's Job Bank. Operated and maintained by the Department of Labor, this website helps match veteran employees to military-friendly employers and provides links to other transition sites.

- *The Riley Guide* (http://www.rileyguide.com/vets.html/). This website is a directory of employment and career-related services on the internet that is designed for veterans and transitioning military personnel, including reactivated reservists and reassigned military personnel.

- *Military Spouse Resource Center* (http://www.milspouse.org/). This website is a resource library designed to assist military spouses with employment, education, and relocation information.

- *Corporate Gray Online* (http://www.GreenToGray.com/). This website provides free military assistance to veterans, matching job applicants with military-friendly employers nationwide.

- *Hire Vets First* (http://www.hirevetsfirst.gov/). This is a comprehensive career website that helps match employment opportunities with veterans. It contains sections for employees and for employers.

- *Vet Jobs.Com* (http://www.vetjobs.com/). This website is an internet job board that serves military veterans already in the work force, active-duty personnel in transition, and their families. Over 3,000 military-friendly employer companies use this site.

Using One-to-One Interventions. Veterans often need one-to-one interventions to help transition into the civilian world. These interventions could include personal counseling combined with career development and role plays. Clients may be referred elsewhere for these services or kept in house.

Finding Training and Education. Soon-to-be separated and retired military personnel often need encouragement to complete the training and education they need to obtain civilian certifications *prior* to entering the civilian world. Completing such programs prior to discharge will make a smoother transition and will allow veterans to move more quickly from military to civilian positions. Those veterans who do not complete their training and education prior to their transition will need encouragement to do so as soon as possible. Helping veterans prepare for stable careers that will bring them similar or higher wages than their military pay is extremely important. Technology skills should be included in the training whenever possible. Life-skills training and education, whether provided in group format or individually, also occur during this stage. These life-skills classes (i.e., time, stress, or debt management; balancing work, education, and family commitments) allow participants to select and attend the classes that they feel fit their ISP goals and will increase their self-sufficiency.

Using the Family Systems Approach. Transition affects family members as well as the veteran, so involving family and close friends in the transition process will help them better adjust to changes while they support the military member. The military person, in turn, needs to consider how these life changes will affect family members and take care to keep the family informed and involved in decision-making. In many instances, family members may attend transition classes and should be encouraged to do so. Helping the family focus is important to accomplish a successful transition. Some military members may need to stay with family or friends while they job search. Still other military members may need to leave their families behind while they relocate to find new employment. Family sessions where all family members (even the youngest) share their feelings about the transition will help with the adjustment (Riggio, 2002).

Offering Mentoring. Mentors can help veterans adjust more easily to their new lives as civilians. Mani (2001) suggested that women veterans who build networks and mentoring relationships increased their success when working in civil-service systems. Riggio (2002) recommended that a mentor and a good support team can lead a veteran to a successful transition. Some transition programs such as those that encourage veterans to start their own businesses provide mentoring as part of their services (Mikelson et al., 2004). Mentoring relationships can also be helpful with homeless veterans (Vet Center Homeless Veterans Working Group, 2005).

Initiate the Employment Campaign.   Some veterans may need to begin their employment campaign immediately, whereas others may have time to complete work- or certification-related activities before they begin their employment campaigns. Eliminating barriers to employment success before initiating a job campaign is the best approach, but since it is not always possible, veterans may need to work on several activities at once, which emphasizes the need for intensive case management on the part of the human service professional. This next section provides an overview of considerations for transitioning to civilian employment. See Chapter 5 for additional details.

The Strategic Job Search.   Some employers value the military experience of their employees and prefer to hire veterans whenever possible. Several previously mentioned websites will help match veterans to military-friendly employers. Some positions are filled through a competitive examination process. Human service professionals should also develop their own local network of military-friendly employers. As with any job search, the client and the human service professional need to work together to choose jobs that match the veteran's values, skills, education, and needs.

Job-Search Correspondence.   Veterans will need to learn how to write letters of application, as well as referral letters, reminder letters, and interview-appreciation letters. Along with teaching clients how to write a letter that accepts or declines an offer, human service professionals can role-play these situations to help clients better understand the process and give them a chance to practice their interpersonal skills in a safe environment.

Tailor-Made Resumes and Interviewing Strategies.   Veterans need to use a military-skills translator when they design their resumes to help them produce detailed job descriptions of their military activities. The resume and interview provide opportunities for veterans to turn their veterans' status into a strength. The *TAP Facilitator's Manual* (2002) suggested that veterans need to emphasize their leadership training, their ability to conform to rules and structure, their ability to work as both a team member and as a team leader, their ability to work in a diverse group, their ability to give and follow instructions, and their ability to work under pressure to meet deadlines. Still other strengths that many veterans bring to a job include an emphasis on safety, systematic planning, security clearance, and a minimized need for supervision. The human service professional can help veterans create resumes that emphasize these strengths and can provide opportunities to role play interviewing scenarios that allow veterans an opportunity to craft answers to common interview questions.

Change Behaviors.   Participation in this career development program is designed to help veterans successfully transition from the military world into the civilian world. Military members who have been successful in a military culture may still need help in reentering the civilian culture. While some veterans will transition with great ease, others may have more difficulty because of a lack or training and education, lack of family support, or a combination of mental and physical illnesses. Although specific behavior changes will vary with each person's ISP, all veterans moving through this program will have had an opportunity to improve their interpersonal and work-related skills and other skills they originally targeted for change.

Complete the Program.   Clients who have completed the program have entered the program, developed their ISPs, completed the training and education that were detailed in their ISPs, and have located civilian employment. At any time during the process, clients can drop out, but they must realize that their decisions may impact their education and training along with their eligibility for other types of assistance.

Achieve Goal of Long-Term Employment and Reintegration into the Civilian Culture.   The final goal in the transition process is long-term employment in a stable position, coupled with successful reintegration into civilian culture. The program staff will need to determine the working definition of *long-term* employment for use in this program. The main goal here is to help veterans find new employment in stable fields, while reentering the civilian world.

Program Evaluation

After the program staff determines what evaluation approach to use (i.e., process evaluation, outcome evaluation, or impact evaluation), they will need to decide how they will measure each component in the career development program and create the necessary tools to do so. Human service professionals need to develop a variety of tools to evaluate their program. Figure 17.1 is a flow chart for the career development program model for the veteran population. The text in each box in the figure is a factor that needs to be measured. Measurement tools can include a database of client information, intake sheets, case files, tracking sheets, referral sheets, and surveys. Once the staff decides when and how often to evaluate, they can begin to create a timeline that helps them better chart the evaluation process. The staff also needs to consider how they will collect, analyze, and report their program information. Once collected, the information can be used to strengthen the current program. For complete descriptions of all segments of the evaluation process, refer to Chapter 6.

Revisiting the Case Study: Josh and Nadine

Conduct an Intake Interview

During the intake interview session, the human service professional needs to explore the medical, financial, educational, and employment history of both Josh and Nadine; their interests and values; and their views on employment, education, and family. Although medical needs are covered by military benefits, Josh and Nadine must understand what those needs may be and how they might impact the job search/ employment process and affect the family in their transition. Although only Josh is leaving the military, the human service professional needs to explore how his lifestyle change will affect the entire family. For example, the children have known only a military life with its base housing and frequent relocations. While Josh did work in the civilian labor market for a few years before joining the military, that experience was 20 years ago, so his readjustment may take some time. Nadine's employment history includes civilian positions as well as her position on the base, so she may need assistance in securing civilian employment as well.

Josh and Nadine need to consider their finances to avoid going into debt during the job search and adjustment period. The couple may want to consider curbing their spending now to avoid incurring any large debt. Josh and Nadine will want to meet any current obligations and avoid taking on any new debt. By setting up a budget, they will be able to plan how they can meet all their financial obligations during this time of transition. Making sure the family has accessed all of the Veteran Affairs resources for which they qualify is very important at this point.

Since both Josh and Nadine finished high school but have no college coursework, the human service professional will want to explore certifications as well as other training and education possibilities for them. Josh should explore any skills from the navy that transfer to various civilian certifications. For example, he can do a quick search on America's Career InfoNet's Certification Finder that shows 11 possible certifications when searching with the keyword "concrete." As a concrete specialist, Josh may already possess the skills and/or experience necessary to obtain those certifications. Another quick search of Licensed Occupations on the same website using the same keyword results in 14 additional licensed occupations involving concrete. The human service professional should spend some time reviewing such findings to see how they interest Josh and apply to him personally, which is a very important step in his transition. Some questions for Josh include: What were some of your career dreams in the past? What interests or intrigues you? What type of activities have you enjoyed?

The human service professional needs to explore Nadine's interests as well. Just because Nadine has stayed home with the children until recently does not mean that she has no career dreams or aspirations. She might consider whether or not she wants to continue to work at the commissary.

Josh and Nadine should decide if they want to work full or part time. Josh's retirement benefits may make him eligible for only part-time employment. If they both decide to work full time, then after-school childcare may become necessary. They should also consider the family cost of both parents working full time. Obviously they need to consider the cost of after-school care for the younger children. Nadine and Josh may also need to consider higher-wage employment if both plan to work when the children are not in school. The couple should examine how they feel about relocating to find suitable employment for Josh. If they have to relocate to find work for Josh, then Nadine will also have to find new work. Honoring this couple's values and views of family life is extremely important as the human service professional helps this family transition from military into civilian life.

How is each family member reacting to Josh's retirement from the navy? Although transition into the civilian world is a huge step, the helper should remind the family of the many transitions they have already made, which might decrease the impact of this transition. For example, Josh and Nadine adjusted to Josh's entering boot camp, different duty stations, and promotions, to name a few. The family has adjusted to each location change, including changing schools, leaving friends, and making new friends. Helping family members see what they did in the past that helped them adjust to these transitions is empowering because they are reminded that they already possess the necessary skills to make this change. By examining what they did to make these transitions successful, the human service professional can guide the family members as they apply those skills to this experience, which will increase their chances of a faster and more successful transition. Honoring each family member's perspective on these changes is very important in order to help them take ownership of the process and feel a part of the family unit.

Make Assessments

Josh and Nadine need to explore their career options as separate clients and complete their assessments individually to maintain confidentiality. This separation empowers the couple to share their knowledge as they make plans. Before selecting assessments the helper should determine the couple's comfort level with technology. While Nadine may have used a computer-based cash register in her cashier position, Josh may not have had as much exposure to a computer as a construction planner. However, he may have some experience using a computer with blueprints and possibly using a computer to complete online documents and forms as a supervisor. The human service professional will want to help Josh research "construction planner and estimator specialist" thoroughly in a military to civilian translator and the companion civilian professions in the *Occupational Outlook Handbook* to better understand the skills that Josh brings to the next employer. Josh may have worked alone or as part of a team consulting with others in the construction field, so they need to explore his soft skills as well. Completing the O*NET Ability Profiler (O*NET Consortium, 2003) would help both Nadine and Josh identify their strengths and the areas in which they might want to receive additional training and pinpoint occupations to fit those strengths. WorkKeys (ACT, 1993) may also help Josh better see his current skills and how they might transfer to civilian jobs. Nadine could also complete WorkKeys or the Career Key (Jones & Jones, 2000).

Results from the interest inventories could provide career-change options for both Josh and Nadine. For example, Josh could complete the GOEII (Farr, 2002) or the CEI2 (Liptak, 2002b) to identify which interest area most appeals to him. Nadine could complete the Leisure to Occupations Connection Search (McDaniels & Mullins, 1999) or the Transition to Work Inventory (Liptak, 2004) to explore her levels of activity and skills in a variety of leisure activities. If both Nadine and Josh are comfortable with computers, they could also complete the O*NET Career Interests Inventory (JIST Works, 2002a) to pinpoint their work-related interests, what they consider important on the job, and their abilities. The Self-Directed Search (Holland,

1990, 1994) would also be useful with these clients. If neither wants to pursue additional education, they could complete the Voc-Tech Quick Screener (JIST Works, 2002c) to help them match their interests and goals with a job and to direct them to jobs for which they can train in a short period of time. The human service professional needs to be careful, however, to steer both clients toward stable employment that will meet their financial needs.

In the next step the couple will explore their values. Choosing careers that support their values will lead these clients to a better fit between them and their job and thus increase their job satisfaction because of the similarity between their values and those of the job. Josh and Nadine could use the Career Values Card Sort (Knowdell, 1998) to quickly help them prioritize their values with respect to job tranquility, time freedom, work under pressure, creative expression, power, and technical competence. In addition, they could use the O*NET Career Values Inventory (JIST Works, 2002b) to identify work groups that include their values and pinpoint specific jobs for further exploration. Depending once again upon their computer skills, they may want to use the Values-Driven Work Card Sort (Career Action Center, n.d.) or the O*NET Work Importance Locator and Profiler (O*NET Consortium, n.d.b) to help them clarify their values and identify possible occupations.

Career-development inventories can help Josh and Nadine identify those aspects of their personal growth that might hinder their obtaining and keeping a job. This assessment component is particularly important for Josh who may be moving from one field to another that requires a different skill set. Available in both a pencil-and-paper format and online, the Barriers to Employment Success Inventory (Liptak, 2002a) will help Josh and Nadine identify career planning, personal, physical, psychological, and job-seeking skills, along with education and training barriers that might impede their employment, and it will help them develop action plans to overcome those barriers. Other career development inventories for consideration include the Career Beliefs Inventory (Krumboltz, 1991), the Career Decision Scale (Osipow et al., 1987), the Career Thoughts Inventory (Sampson et al., 1996), the Career Transition Inventory (Heppner, 1991), the Salient Beliefs Review (Bloch, 2003), or the Vocational Exploration and Insight Kit (Holland et. al., 1980). The human service professional does not need to administer all of these inventories but should select inventories based on the presenting client's needs.

Determine Barriers to Career Success

Josh and Nadine possess several possible barriers to career success: age, education and training, lack of civilian experience, the need for appropriate housing, and childcare. Upgrading Josh's skills and education and/or exploring the path to possible certifications and licenses is an important step to help him find a stable, high-wage job, that he needs to support a family of six. Since this large family has moved from base housing into an apartment, finding an affordable house is also an important consideration. Josh's age may be a barrier because he is 20 years older than others who are competing for jobs that require his experience. For that reason he may need to consider a shift in his job search to decrease the lure of his youthful competitors. Childcare becomes a barrier if Nadine chooses to work full time, and Josh is unable to help with childcare duties. "Soft skills" may or may not be a barrier, depending upon Josh's position as a construction planner, but these skills should not be overlooked.

Choose Interventions

Using the Transition Assistance Program (TAP). Josh will have completed TAP prior to leaving the navy, but he may need additional assistance, particularly if his family was unable to attend classes with him. Topics for discussion during TAP include stress, personal appraisal, identifying strengths and weaknesses arising from military experience, skills analysis, determining work preferences, job search, interviews and resume writing, evaluating job offers, and transition support. Family members who did not attend TAP may need to review these items in another format, and Josh may need a periodic review as well.

Using On-Line Interventions. Josh and Nadine can access several on-line interventions to help them in their transition. America's Career InfoNet can provide information on necessary credentials and licenses, and sites such as Transition On-line can be useful as well. Websites that might be useful for Nadine as a military spouse include Military.Com and the Military Spouse Resource Center. The Department of Veteran Affairs website will provide the couple with medical information and links to various benefits-related forms.

Using One-to-One Interventions. Based on Josh and Nadine's ISPs, one-to-one interventions may include social-skills training, family counseling, and a variety of referrals for other assistance. The human service professional would address Josh's barriers to employment success, as well as Nadine's should she decide to pursue employment at this time. The helper should address the concern of housing, and Josh's difficulty in adjusting to civilian life. This transition and Josh's reaction to it impact his treatment of his family, friends, and colleagues as well as his ability to detach from the military. Helping Josh move through the stages of a job loss will be very important for him and will help Nadine as well. Developing a budget and providing financial counseling for any debts are interventions the human service professional can offer along with referrals for any programs for which the family may qualify.

Using the Family-Systems Approach. Josh is not alone in this transition—his family who is transitioning along with him are going through changes of their own. Family roles will change: Dad may be home more now, and the older children who may have had more independence and responsibility within the household because of Josh's absence may need to adjust to his newly reclaimed role as dad. Now that he is no longer deployed "fighting for his country," Josh's family may expect him to be more available to help with aging parents, childcare issues, even simple household repairs. The family unit may need new family rules that include Josh, because previous rules may have been crafted while he was less involved at home and more involved in the military. Josh's entire identify may have been that of Chief Petty Officer, and changing one's identify is neither quick nor effortless. Josh will need help from his family to redefine what his role is without the military. Exploring how each family member feels about Josh's leaving the navy after 20 years and the transition they must make will allow the family a chance to bond anew in the face of change.

Finding Training and Education.   After Josh and Nadine determine what is best for the family (i.e., should both parents go to work full time, should one work and one stay at home, and what choice is the most effective in a cost-benefit analysis), they will want to explore possible jobs and available training, certifications, and licenses that fit with their career aspirations and desires. Referring them to Veteran Affairs for education and training support, to the local One-Stop Career Center, and to the local community college would be good places to start, depending on their training and education needs.

Josh has several transferable skills, but he may no longer be interested in performing the physical labor and may be more interested in moving into management or inspections. He may want to explore other training and education options to update these skills. Helping Josh look for similar positions would be a quicker way to reemployment, but this decision needs to be based on local job availability and whether these local jobs match his skills and are stable positions.

Nadine's work history as a part-time cashier provides her with some retail and interpersonal skills and possibly some computer skills that are useful in a variety of workplace settings. However, exploring how interested she is in working is very important and needs to be a family decision made after they create a budget and examine all of the possibilities.

Offering Mentoring.   Finding a mentor for Josh can also help him make this transition. By joining professional organizations he can be in touch with possible role models and mentors to assist him. Informational interviews with possible employers can also help Josh find a mentor. Military.Com provides a buddy finder to help veterans find mentors in their chosen field, and the local VA Center may also be able to help. Family members may also need mentors. They might find another military family who has successfully transitioned into civilian life to guide them through the toughest times of the transition.

Initiate the Employment Campaign

Ideally Josh will explore certifications/licenses and training and education before he exits from the military. If so, his transition into civilian life will be faster and easier on the entire family. If he has not done so, then he will need to make time to pursue these items while job searching. He should initiate this campaign as soon as his time in the navy ends or after he completes any education and training. Nadine faces similar decisions. Eliminating all of their barriers to employment success before they begin the employment campaign is the best approach but may not be possible. Instead, the human service professional may need to provide case management as Josh and Nadine complete their education and training and participate in the interventions they chose to decrease their barriers. Helping them develop their job-search network, their resumes, and their correspondence is part of the employment campaign. Josh may be able to use some of his contacts from the Veteran Affairs, but he should quickly do so. On the other hand, Nadine may not have had an opportunity to develop a network and will need to learn how to develop job contacts. Josh may need to use a functional resume because he is changing careers and has some transferable skills that might prove beneficial to a new job. If Nadine chooses to look for work, then she could either use a chronological or a functional resume depending upon whether she continues as a cashier or changes jobs. The concern here is to help them find stable employment to meet the needs of a six-member family.

Conclusion

Human service professionals may work with veterans in a variety of settings, including a military-based agency or a civilian agency. An awareness of the barriers to success that veterans and their family members face in their transition to civilian life will assist professionals in better meeting their clients' needs. The following are some recommended changes that could help veterans and their family members transition more easily into civilian life:

- Increase opportunities for military members in the reserves to attend TAP or similar programs before release when they are based outside of the United States.
- Increase TAP from a 3–day workshop to a longer workshop, possibly 7–10 days in length.
- Improve integration of VETS-sponsored programs with those established by the Workforce Investment Act.
- Provide more opportunities for training and education while in the military.
- Provide civilian certifications and licenses to members before they leave the military.
- Increase the number of programs that assist homeless veterans.
- Collect more data on veteran's adjustment to civilian life that can provide opportunities for research on best practices.
- Update TAP manuals as the most recent dates from 2002.

Summary

Although exact numbers are not available for security reasons, as of 2003, 1.4 million Americans were on active duty in the army, 382,000 in the navy, 178,000 in the marine corps, and 375,000 in the air force. Almost 1.2 million were classified as military reserve personnel. A civilian veteran is someone 18 years or older who has served in the armed forces (i.e., U.S. Army, Navy, Air Force, Marine Corps, Coast Guard) or in the Merchant Marine in World War II. Those who have served in the reserves or in the national guard are only classified as veterans if they have been called or ordered to active duty (in addition to their initial training and yearly summer camps). Of the almost 25 million veterans currently alive, almost 75 percent of them have served during an official period of conflict or war. Approximately 1.7 million veterans are women; 2.3 million are African American; 1.1 million are Hispanic; 276,000 are Asian; 185,000 are Native American/Alaska Native; and 25,000 are native Hawaiian/Pacific Islanders. Over 2.1 million veterans are age 35 or younger, over 1.4 million are between ages 35 to 39, more than 6.1 million veterans are ages 40 to 54, over 3.4 million are ages 55 to 59, 2.4 million are ages 60 to 64, and 9.6 million are over the age of 65.

Generally, veterans are better educated and in many cases have lower unemployment rates than their civilian counterparts. Veterans do possess several barriers to career success, including translating their military skills into civilian skills, lack of traditional education and training, homelessness, stereotypical view of military members, type of discharge, military culture, and a variety of physical and mental illnesses stemming from their time in the military. Developing programs to assist veterans and their families in their transition will help increase their success as they reenter the civilian world. A career development program model for use with a veteran population contains an Individual Success Plan developed from the results of assessments of career abilities, interests, values, and barriers; interagency referrals; interventions, such as TAP, on-line interventions, one-to-one interventions, family systems approach, training and education, and mentoring; followed by an employment campaign designed to lead to successful reintegration into the civilian world, long-term employment, and self sufficiency.

Key Terms

Civilian Health and Medical Program of the
  Uniformed Services (CHAMPUS)
Disabled Veteran Outreach Program (DVOP)

Local Veterans Employment Representatives
  (LVER)
Stand downs

Web Resources

Note that website URLs may change over time.

Allied Veteran Education
http://www.education4va.com/LP/VE.asp

America's Career InfoNet
http://www.acinet.org

**Army Career and Alumni Program—Easing
the Transition from Soldier to Civilian**
http://www.acap.army.mil/default.cfm

Civilian Personnel On-Line: US Army
http://cpol.army.mil/library/permiss/63133.html

Corporate Gray Online
http://www.corporategray.com

The Destiny Group
http://www.destinygrp.com/destiny/index.jsp

Education Benefits—Veterans Benefits and Services
http://www.gibill.va.gov

GI Rights Hotline
http://www.objector.org/girights

Job Central—Veterans Employment Network
http://veterans.jobcentral.com/Veterans.asp

Job Transitioning for Vets and Former Military
http://www.quintcareers.com/former_military.html

Marine Corps Community Services
http://www.usmc-mccs.org/tamp/index.cfm

Military.Com
http://www.military.com

Military Exits
http://www.militaryexits.com

National Coalition for Homeless Veterans
http://www.nchv.org

National Center for Post Traumatic Stress Disorder: The War in Iraq
http://www.ncptsd.va.gov/topics/war.html

The Riley Guide
http://www.rileyguide.com/vets.html

Recruit Military
http://www.recruitmilitary.com

Transition Assistance Online
http://www.taonline.com

US Department of Defense
http://www.dod.gov

US Department of Veterans Affairs
http://www.va.gov

Veterans Employment and Training Service
http://www.dol.gov/vets/programs/main.htm

VET Guide
http://www.opm.gov/veterans/html/vetguide.asp

VETS Resource Connection
http://nvti.cudenver.edu/VETSResource2/Default2.htm

18

The Newly Immigrated Population

Home Away from Home

Case Study: Sandeep

Sandeep, a 35-year-old male, recently immigrated from India to California to join his two half brothers, who had **acquired-citizenship** status and had immigrated to the United States over 10 years ago for economic reasons. Sandeep left his wife and their 10-year-old daughter in India promising that he would send for them after he established a home for his family in America. Sandeep and his brothers were raised in a poor farming village located in Punjab, India. Upon arriving in California, his brothers began working as **migrant** farm laborers in fruit orchards earning minimum wage where they have been employed for the past 10 years. Neither Sandeep nor his two brothers finished secondary education while in India. All three struggle with the English language and speak their native language of Punjabi at home. Compounding these socioeconomic and language barriers is the severe prejudice the brothers face every day in the community in which they live. Many of the residents of the town are extremely hostile toward immigrants who look different, speak a different language, and act differently. Sandeep and his brothers have been spit at and told to "go back to India." Although they are not **deportable aliens** (i.e., illegal aliens)—his half brothers have acquired-citizenship status and Sandeep is a **conditional resident** who has applied for **adjustment to immigrant status**—they are often accused of being illegal **immigrants** and are sometimes stopped by officials and asked to provide **certificates of citizenship**. When they tried to defend themselves against these vicious attacks, they were labeled *troublemakers* and received threats of **deportation**. Sandeep does not want to follow in his brothers' footsteps and work as a farm laborer. Instead, his goal is to secure employment in one of the factories located in a nearby town. To do so would mean a 2-hour commute each day, but he believes that factory work would provide him with higher wages and better benefits thereby allowing him to send for his wife and daughter.

414

The Newly Immigrated Population

Description

According to Camarota (2004), approximately 34 million immigrants and **asylees** (both legal and illegal) are living in the United States. This number is the highest ever recorded and reflects an increase of 4.3 million immigrants since 2000. Over 14 million immigrants entered the United States during the 1990s (The Urban Institute, 2005). Data show that since 2000, approximately 6.1 million new immigrants (both legal and illegal) arrived from abroad. Of the 4.3 million increase since 2000, it is estimated that about 2 million are *illegal immigrants*. Immigrants now account for nearly 12 percent of the nation's population, reflecting the highest percentage in over 80 years. While this figure is lower than the historic high of 15 percent in 1990, it has more than doubled since 1970 when it reached a low of 5 percent (The Urban Institute, 2005).

The initial wave of immigrants arrived from Europe, but currently more than one-half of the immigrants come from Latin America and another one-third come from Asia. Historically, the majority of immigrants settled in California, New York, Texas, Florida, New Jersey, and Illinois. However, between 1990 to 2000, the immigrant population more than doubled across a wide band of states in the Midwest, Southeast, and the Rocky Mountain region, and the foreign-born population in the original six destination states decreased from 75 to 68 percent (The Urban Institute, 2005).

Nonimmigrant Versus Immigrant Classification.   **Nonimmigrant** classification describes any **alien** admitted to the United States by the **U.S. Citizenship and Immigration Services (USCIS)** for a specific purpose for a definite period of time (Bechtel International Center at Stanford University, 2004). Immigrant classification, also known as **permanent resident alien,** describes any alien who has been granted permission by the USCIS to remain in the United States permanently.

Undocumented Versus Documented Classification.   *Undocumented immigrants* are aliens or foreigners who are residing in the United States illegally. The *undocumented status* is a result of entering the United States illegally (e.g., not entering through a **port of entry**) or overstaying the **visa**. It is estimated that 4 out of 10 undocumented immigrants enter the United States on temporary visas as visitors, tourists, students, or **temporary workers** and stay after their visas expire (American Friends Service Committee, n.d.). Current statistics estimated the total undocumented immigrant population in the United States to be between 9 and 9.2 million although the actual number may be considerably higher based on an estimated 10 percent undercount of undocumented immigrants (Camarota, 2004). According to one source approximately 28 percent of the immigrants who live in the United States are undocumented (Grantmakers Concerned with Immigrants and Refugees [GCIA], 2001). See the glossary on the Companion website for classes of admission.

Employment

Although immigrants represent one in nine U.S. residents, they represent one in seven workers. In the 1990s, nearly one-half of all workers entering the workforce were immigrants (The Urban Institute, 2005). In 2004 nearly 21.4 million persons in the U.S. labor force were foreign born. From 2002 to 2004, the number of foreign-born workers in the United States grew by approximately 1.2 million and accounted for a little less than one-half of the total labor force growth during this period (U.S. Department of Labor, 2005).

Although some immigrants enter the United States with strong academic skills and credentials, many do not. Undocumented men have a labor-force participation rate of over 90 percent, and undocumented women have a labor-force participation rate of about 66 percent. Some hypothesized that the lower, labor-force rate for undocumented women may be the result of limited childcare and weaker, job-market opportunities for women (The Urban Institute, 2005).

The unemployment rate of foreign-born workers declined from 6.6 percent in 2003 to 5.5 percent in 2004. The declines reflected rates for both men and women. The unemployment rate for foreign-born men dropped from 6.2 to 5.0 percent and for foreign-born women from 7.1 to 6.3 percent. The unemployment rate for native-born men declined from 6.3 percent in 2003 to 5.8 percent in 2004, however, the rate for native-born women did not significantly change (U.S. Department of Labor, 2005).

In 2004, 26.5 percent of foreign-born workers were employed in management, professional, and related occupations compared to 36.3 percent of native-born workers in the same occupational category. Additionally, 22.8 percent of foreign-born workers were employed in service industries compared to 15.2 percent of native-born workers, and 18.4 percent of foreign-born workers were employed in office and sales occupations compared to 26.7 percent of native-born workers during this same period (U.S. Department of Labor, 2005).

The proportions of foreign-born and native-born workers employed in the manufacturing industry (i.e., production, transportation, material moving) from 2000 to 2004 reflect the downward trend in this field as a whole. In 2000, 20.4 percent of foreign-born and 13.8 percent of native-born workers were employed in the manufacturing industry. In 2004, 17.5 percent of foreign-born and 12.1 percent of native-born workers were employed in this industry (U.S. Department of Labor, 2005).

Immigrants are disproportionately employed in more hazardous industries such as construction, agriculture, manufacturing, and entertainment. However, they also encompass a large and growing share of certain highly skilled fields such as education, health care, and computer-related lines of work (The Urban Institute, 2005).

In addition to the disproportionately high rates of immigrants in dangerous work settings, many immigrants are *underemployed;* that is, they work in occupations that underutilize their skills. An example of underemployment in this population would be an immigrant who holds an engineering degree but works as a taxi cab driver. The result of underemployment is a catastrophic waste of expertise and potential.

Earnings

The immigrant population represents 20 percent of low-wage earners in the United States. *Low-wage earners* are defined as those earning below twice the minimum wage (See Chapter 9 on the Working Poor). Forty percent of low-wage immigrant workers are undocumented immigrants (The Urban Institute, 2005). As such the immigrant population is more vulnerable to poverty than the general population. According to census data, 36.3 percent of immigrant workers earn less than $20 thousand working full time, year round compared to 21.3 percent of native-born workers who earn less than $20 thousand annually working full time. Immigrants earning less than $20 thousand annually include 57.1 percent from Mexico and Central America, 22.4 percent from Asia, and 16.2 percent from Europe (American Friends Service Committee, n.d.).

Immigration status plays a central role in the earnings of foreign-born workers. Undocumented workers have little choice but to remain in occupations that pay minimum wage or below and have little or no benefits such as health insurance or pensions. Many of these jobs are seasonal or part time, forcing undocumented immigrants to work several jobs simultaneously in order to support their families (Grantmakers Concerned with Immigrants and Refugees, 2001b).

In 2004, the median weekly earnings of both male and female foreign-born, full-time workers were $502 compared to $664 for native-born workers. When comparing wages of men and women, foreign-born men earned $518 weekly compared to $749 for native-born men, and foreign-born women earned $473 compared to $585 for native-born women. Although earnings for both the foreign-born and native-born workers rose over the year, the increase for foreign-born workers was 2.7 percent compared to 3.3 percent for their native-born counterparts. The earnings gap narrows at higher education levels. For instance, in 2004 the median weekly salary of foreign-born, full-time workers with a bachelor's degree or higher was $943 compared to $994 for native-born workers with a similar education (U.S. Department of Labor, 2005).

Education

The distressing statistics regarding the employment and earnings of immigrants is primarily explained by a noteworthy decline in the educational attainment of immigrants relative to natives and by the needs of the U.S. economy. According to Camarota (2001), in every decade since 1970, the gap in the high-school completion rate between recent immigrants and natives has widened. In 2000, nearly three times as many recent immigrants as natives lacked a high-school education. In addition, immigrants who entered the United States in the 1990s were less likely to have completed high school when compared to immigrants who entered the United States before 1990.

Although it is true that a higher percentage of immigrants than natives have not completed high school, it is also true that a higher percentage of immigrants, when compared to natives, have earned graduate degrees. This pattern of the immigrant population either having very high or very low levels of educational achievement mainly reflects differences in the educational achievement of immigrants based on the country of origin. For example, according to Sneddon Little and Triest (2001), nearly 68 percent of immigrants from Mexico ages 25 to 64 have not completed high school, compared to approximately 11 percent of the native population in the same age group. Thirty-four percent of immigrants from other Latin American countries have a high-school education compared to 13.3 percent from Asia and the Middle

East; 12.4 percent from Europe, Australia, Canada, and New Zealand; and 6.2 percent from Africa. These figures are close to the high-school completion rate of natives. On the high end of the continuum of educational attainment, approximately 26 percent of natives have completed a four-year college degree, compared to less than 5 percent of the immigrants from Mexico and roughly 16 percent of the immigrants from other parts of Latin America. However, immigrants from Asia and Africa are more likely than native U.S. citizens to have completed a four-year college degree, and immigrants from outside Latin America are considerably more likely to hold graduate degrees.

Effect on the Economy

According to Smith and Edmonston (1997), immigration results in an increase in national output. In other words, immigration tends to benefit the U.S. economy overall. In addition, immigration tends to have little negative effect on the job opportunities and income of most native-born Americans, however, with some exceptions. For example, only in areas with high concentrations of low-paid, low-skilled immigrants are state and local taxpayers paying more on average to sustain the publicly funded services used by the immigrant population. It is estimated that immigrants add over $10 billion to the U.S. economy each year. Although some Americans pay more in taxes due to immigration, and some Americans without high-school educations have experienced lower wages due to competition generated by some newly arrived, lower-skilled immigrants, immigration for the most part has not weakened the U.S. economy. Overall, immigration increases the labor supply and tends to lower prices thereby enabling the vast majority of Americans to enjoy a healthier economy (Smith & Edmonston, 1997).

Barriers to Career Success

Structural Barriers

Discrimination.   Immigrants are faced with several barriers to their successful integration into American society including employment, computerized, housing, social service, and criminal-justice discrimination.

Employment Discrimination.   For the most part, immigrants built the United States, and the majority of U.S. workers today are descendents of immigrants. However, a staggering number of immigrants face egregious instances of employment discrimination in the hiring process. When promotions are being offered, employers discriminate against documented workers and exploit undocumented workers (AFL-CIO, 2005). Although Title VII of the Civil Rights Act protects against national origin discrimination, many employers refuse to hire someone who looks foreign or speaks with a foreign accent. These employers may also discriminate by demanding **green cards,** refusing to accept documents such as an Employment Authorization Document, which looks foreign, and insisting the applicant speak fluent English even in situations that are not related to the job (O'Connor, 2004). Other employers may resist hiring immigrants fearing that they will be taking "American" jobs.

Some employers discriminate against immigrants by exploiting them through low wages, poor working conditions, long hours, or by denying the immigrants their rights. Native-born workers are also subject to this treatment, but often the immigrants' cultural and linguistic isolation increases their vulnerability to exploitation and discrimination (Grantmakers Concerned with Immigrants and Refugees, 2001b).

Computerized Discrimination.   According to O'Connor (2004), *computerized discrimination* describes the bureaucratic intricacies of the U.S. Citizenship and Immigration Services (USCIS) and the U.S. State Department. The visa and quota systems are extremely complex making it incredibly difficult to navigate through the various forms, applications, fees, exemptions, checks, and reinstatements without expert assistance. The complexity of this system adds additional stress to the immigrant seeking a legitimate route to the United States.

Housing Discrimination.   Although federal and state fair-housing laws prohibit discrimination against housing based on country of birth or ancestry, housing discrimination against immigrants is a genuine problem. A number of studies have examined housing discrimination against the immigrant population. One study that examined discrimination in rental housing in Vermont found national-origin discrimination in both the non-Islamic and Islamic immigrant population. Specifically, discrimination was found in the following areas: not returning the immigrant's calls, not informing the immigrant of all available units, telling the immigrant that nothing was available when units were indeed available, presenting different rental terms and/or conditions, and discouraging the immigrant while encouraging natives (Meehan, 2004). Housing discrimination also places restrictions on immigrants with respect to land ownership (some states have a 10-year maximum) and the amount of land they can own. Other housing discrimination includes the unavailability of mortgage loans and the difficulty in establishing a credit history when references often are from another country. Immigrants have to pay federal and state taxes, but they are often inundated with procedures, paperwork, and bureaucracy when it comes to housing (O'Connor, 2004).

Social-Service Discrimination.   Lawful permanent residents (LPR) are eligible for some federal benefits but not for others. For example, lawful permanent residents are not eligible for food stamps or Medicaid for a period of five years following their declaration of residency. Due to the sponsorship requirement of many immigrants (i.e., a **sponsor** is a person willing to sign an "an affidavit of support" to provide financial support to the immigrant), immigrants who receive any type of government assistance may jeopardize their immigration status (O'Connor, 2004). As such, social-service discrimination against the immigrant population is widespread.

Criminal-Justice Discrimination.   Immigrants' residency can be terminated if they commit a felony, three or more misdemeanors, or do any number of things that may make them ineligible for U.S. citizenship (e.g., becoming a public charge or a member of certain organizations). Immigrants can be detained by USCIS without being charged with any offense for months or years, and if they have hearings, the hearings are sometimes held in secret and without the benefit of counsel. Such hearings can lead to **voluntary departure** or deportation. If the immigrant is deported, family members are often not notified of the **removal**. If the country to which the immigrants are being deported will not accept them, they can be held in a detention facility indefinitely (O'Connor, 2004).

Immigration Status.   For some immigrants their immigration status can present an enormous barrier. For example, some immigrants do not qualify for Medicaid and Medicare thereby limiting their access to health care. In cases of emergencies, undocumented immigrants may avoid seeking help from the police for fear of deportation or having their children removed from their custody.

Attitudinal Barriers.   Attitudes toward illegal immigrants tend to be harsher when compared to attitudes toward legal immigrants. According to the Public Agenda (2005), the majority of Americans polled felt that illegal immigrants should be deported immediately after being caught and should not be allotted court options.

   Americans tend to hold more favorable views of legal immigrants because such immigrants are seen as "playing by the rules." However, legal immigrants also experience varying levels of attitudinal barriers. Some surveys have reported that the general public believes that immigration lowers wages and weakens the national character (Public Agenda, 2005). Such harsh attitudes can certainly result in immigrants experiencing negative biases and prejudices by the general public.

Occupational Stereotyping.   Human service professionals must recognize their own biases and prejudices and how these attributes can lead to occupational stereotyping of their clients. Many immigrants are overrepresented in certain career fields. For example, Asian immigrants tend to be heavily represented in mathematics, engineering, and computer-science careers. In other words, they tend to gravitate toward scientific and theoretical careers while avoiding verbal-persuasive and social careers. The human service professional faces the danger of over generalizing by taking some occupational information regarding certain immigrant groups and applying that knowledge to each individual client. Such stereotyping might lead the helper to dissuade ethnic clients from pursuing certain occupations while prematurely introducing or stressing specific, conventional occupations to them (LeBlanc, 2002).

   In addition to the impact that occupational stereotyping by human service professionals can have on their clients, biases by employers can also influence clients' career development. For example, managers may apply occupational stereotypes when they make hiring decisions or when they determine which employee is best suited for a promotion (LeBlanc, 2002).

Access to Financial Resources.   According to Singer and Paulson (2004), immigrants are less likely than natives of the United States to utilize a wide range of financial services such as checking accounts, business loans, savings accounts, and home mortgages. Access to financial services has significant implications for immigrants' well-being and for the success of second-generation immigrants. Immigrants are frequently members of economically at-risk groups, and access to financial services might help them cope with financial insecurity and find pathways out of poverty. Unfortunately, however, immigrants' access to such services is often hindered by factors such as limited-English proficiency, low income, residential segregation, cultural diversity, little or no credit history, and/or insufficient experience with financial institutions. Access to financial institutions and resources is imperative for many immigrants whose earnings are often a vital source of income for their families back home. Therefore, transferred funds or remittances are essential financial transactions among many immigrants in the United States.

Individual Barriers

Language Barriers. Language barriers can present a multitude of problems for the newly immigrated. For those seeking employment, language barriers are possibly the greatest single barrier to employment success and may be one of the most difficult hurdles to overcome. Insufficient knowledge of the English language can make communication between the employer and the potential employee challenging. Even if immigrants can speak English at a fundamental level, they may not be able to adequately describe their skills to the employer. In addition to making it difficult to secure a job, language barriers can make it difficult for the newly immigrated to access and receive quality health care that meets their needs. A language barrier also impedes their pursuit of needed education and training.

According to the 2000 U.S. Census, the total limited-English-proficient population in the United States grew dramatically in the 1990s, increasing from almost 14 million to well over 21 million people. Of working-age adults (ages 18 to 64), the limited-English-proficient population expanded from 6 to 9 percent. Those with limited-English proficiencies now make up over 20 percent of adults in California and 16.6 percent of adults in New York and Texas (Tumlin & Zimmerman, 2003).

Adjustment Difficulties. Immigrants to the United States face the challenge of successfully adjusting to a new social environment. They are expected to value and preserve their own ethnic identity while simultaneously adjusting to the host society and often learning another language. This dual expectation that is experienced within the family and the host society can enhance acculturative stress and lead to decreased life satisfaction for immigrants (Rhee, Chang, & Rhee, 2003). Some immigrants become homesick and cease to function because of adjustment difficulties thereby impeding them in all phases of the employment-seeking process.

Self-Fulfilling Prophecy. Just as stereotyping by human service professionals can influence the services they provide, stereotyping can also lead clients to develop self-fulfilling prophecies or self-limiting guidelines. The *self-fulfilling prophecy*, a concept developed by American sociologist Robert King Merton (2004), is a person's belief or expectation, regardless of whether it is correct or not, that affects the outcome of a situation or how the person will behave. Social and occupational stereotypes that human service professionals and the public at large hold have the possibility of creating their own reality in the form of self-fulfilling prophecies in the immigrant client population (LeBlanc, 2002).

Insufficient Financial Resources.   Harsh living conditions, poverty, and despair lead many immigrants to flee their homelands for a shot at the "American dream." However, this dream often does not become a reality for immigrants. Once in America many immigrants face high-level unemployment and underemployment that only exasperates their limited financial resources. Insufficient financial resources impede immigrants' accessibility to vital services, housing, and to much needed employment opportunities.

Physical Health Barriers

Many immigrants in the United States confront some of the most dangerous work environments, yet they have the fewest resources to protect them. Immigrants are disproportionably represented in dangerous industries such as construction, agriculture, and manufacturing. Many find themselves working in hazardous occupations within those industries. Although they tend to be exposed to more dangerous working conditions, they also tend to be paid less and have less access to health care and insurance (Labor Occupational Health Program: University of California at Berkeley, 2005).

Immigrants tend to have a high-turnover rate and this high-turnover rate is related to high-injury rates. Most injuries to immigrants occur within the first year of employment. Higher-injury rates may be due to a number of factors. First, language and cultural factors may create barriers to receiving sufficient safety training. Second, immigrant workers may be less likely to report hazardous working conditions, because they fear they will lose their jobs. Third, immigrants may be concerned about their immigration status (whether legal or illegal), and that fear may prevent many from exercising their basic rights (Labor Occupational Health Program: University of California at Berkeley, 2005).

Mental Health Barriers

Immigrants may experience anxiety and frustration due to acculturation issues and difficulty finding work. *Acculturation*, as defined by Gysbers, Heppner, and Johnston (2003), is the process of learning the cultural values and customs of another culture while maintaining some degree of cultural affiliation to one's traditional culture. These acculturation issues can lead to acculturative stress. **Refugees** who migrate to the United States because of extreme political threats in their homelands tend to experience more trauma and less control over their immigration than voluntary immigrants (Meinhardt, Tom, Tse, & Yu, 1986; Rumbaut, 1985) Feelings of anxiety and frustration can lead immigrants to a loss of confidence or self-esteem. The loss of family and the lack of a support network may intensify these feelings and may also trigger feelings of loneliness and isolation in the client who has newly immigrated.

According to Vega and Rumbaut (1991), psychological stress associated with immigration tends to be more intense in the first three years after the immigrants' arrival in the United States. Although immigration and acculturation can bring subsequent stress and psychological distress, research does not suggest that immigration, in and of itself, results in higher levels of mental disorders. However, traumas experienced by immigrants from war-torn countries seem to result in high rates of post-traumatic stress disorder (PTSD) among these populations (Surgeon General's Report, 1999).

Both physical and mental health barriers are often aggravated when clients have limited-English-language proficiency. Miscommunication with physicians, counselors, human service professionals, and other helpers can limit immigrants' access to health care and threaten the quality of such care. Immigrants' inability to effectively communicate with health-care providers can lead to misdiagnoses, improper treatment, and misunderstandings on the part of the clients regarding what to do and where to go for assistance.

Career Development Program Model: The Newly Immigrated Population

The career development program model for the newly immigrated population is comprehensive and takes into account the diverse client population associated with this group. Because the life and work experiences of many immigrants often differ from that of the host society, the application of career interventions based on Western theories may be ineffective in working with the newly immigrated. In addition, the newly immigrated often experience culture-specific barriers to career development, and the human service professional must address such obstacles throughout the career-intervention process. Before we describe the career development program model, you should keep in mind some general guidelines when working with this population. According to Prince, Uemura, Chao, and Gonzales (1991), when working with the foreign-born client, helpers should (1) assess the client's comfort-level with the helping process based on the client's cultural attitudes regarding such interventions; (2) evaluate the client's cultural attitudes towards authority; (3) determine whether the client's culture is individualistic or collectivistic; (4) assess the client's cultural socialization regarding family, gender, and work roles; and (5) remain sensitive to barriers that may impede the client's employment prospects. Figure 18.1 is a graphic model of the career development program.

Applicant Pool

The applicant pool consists of newly immigrated clients who require career development assistance. Upon intake, the human service professional will determine whether or not the client meets the agency's conditions for participation in the program. For example, determining the client's immigration status (documented vs. undocumented, **legalized alien, national, permanent resident alien**) may be a precursor for agency services. Knowledge of the **preference system** of the **Immigration Act of 1990** and the **Immigration and Nationality Act** is crucial at this stage. Once helpers have established program participation criteria, they can shift their focus to the Individual Success Plan (ISP).

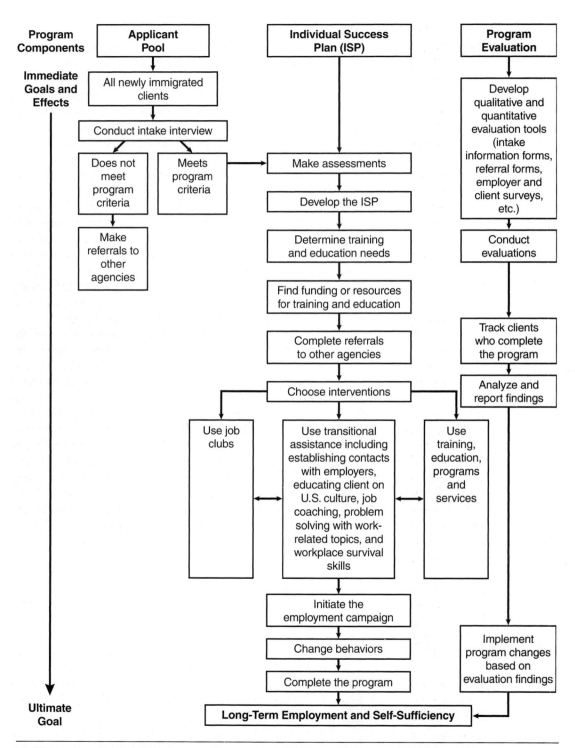

FIGURE 18.1   *Career Development Program Model: The Newly Immigrated Population*

Individual Success Plan

The Individual Success Plan (ISP) is created to help the client achieve the goal of long-term employment. In order to attain this goal, each ISP must be created in collaboration with the client and meet the specific needs of each newly immigrated client. For this particular population, the ISP should examine and reduce the specific barriers to career success that are common to this population, assess clients' attributes including transferable and functional skills and match these attributes to specific career options, and provide the education and training necessary for clients' employment goals.

Make Assessment.   Newly immigrated clients are likely to experience a range of emotions because of the acculturation process and their difficulty finding work. The human service professional should first evaluate clients' feelings of anxiety, frustration, loss of confidence, and other possible feelings in order to determine the best course of action. If clients do not have a support network in the United States, the helping professional may want to assist them in locating ethnic communities and resources that can help support them with the acculturation and adjustment process. For clients arriving in the United States through the **Diversity Lottery Program (DLP),** family members may be available for support (i.e., the DLP allows individuals to bring their spouse and any unmarried children under the age of 21 to the United States).

Once the client's initial assessment is completed and immediate needs met, the human service professional begins to attend to the specific career-related issues of the client. The first step in this process should be the administration of career-related assessments that are chosen to match the needs of each client. Since the newly immigrated population is so extremely diverse, the range of possible assessments is limitless. Helpers need to assess the client's English fluency and specific cultural characteristics before they select any instrument. For example, some clients who are able to read English may not interpret the words in the same manner as a native-born citizen. Helpers must take care to alleviate cultural biases that are related to the administration and evaluation of assessments. Depending on the results of this evaluation, the helper can choose from a variety of available assessments, and a battery of assessments is recommended. Table 18.1 lists possible assessments for the newly immigrated population. Those assessments that are available in another language, besides English, and/or may be especially helpful when working with the newly immigrated are marked with a dagger(†). For detailed information on each of the following assessments, see Chapter 3.

Develop the ISP.   Following the administration of the career-related assessments, the human service professional and client work together to create the client's ISP. First, they review the results of the assessments and the client explores occupational options by generating and gathering occupational information on occupational prospects that are of interest to him or her. The client can use the occupational information to make career-related decisions. After gathering occupational information, the client explores his or her views and values with respect to occupations of interest. Using the information that is generated from this examination, the client and helper refine decisions and collaborate to establish the client's personal and career-related goals. These goals must be measurable, action oriented, practical, and specific (see Chapter 6 for more on goal setting). After they establish goals, the human service professional and client examine

TABLE 18.1   *Career Related Assessment for Use with the Newly Immigrated Population*

Title	*Source*
Ability Tests	
Ability Explorer	Harrington, J. C., & Harrington, T. F. (1996). *Ability explorer.* Itasca, IL: Houghton Mifflin.
Career Key*	Jones, L. K., & Jones, J. (2000). *Career key.* Raleigh, NC: Author.
Motivated Skills Card Sort	Knowdell, R. (2002, June). *Motivated skills card sort.* San Jose, CA: Career Research & Testing.
O*NET Ability Profiler*	O*NET Consortium (2003, April). *O*NET ability profiler.* Washington, DC: Author.
WorkKeys	ACT, Inc. (1993). *Workkeys assessments.* Iowa City, IO: ACT.
Interest Inventories	
Career Exploration Inventory 2[†]	Liptak, J. (2002). *Career exploration inventory: A guide for exploring work, leisure, and learning* (2nd ed.). Indianapolis, IN: JIST Works.
CareerExplorer CD-ROM*	JIST Works (2004). *Careerexplorer CD-ROM.* Indianapolis, IN: Author.
Guide for Occupational Exploration Interest Inventory	Farr, M. (2002). *Guide for occupational exploration interest inventory* (4th ed.). Indianapolis, IN: JIST Works.
Leisure to Occupations Connection Search	McDaniels, C., & Mullins, S. R. (1999). *The leisure to occupations connection search.* Indianapolis, IN: JIST Works.
Occupational Interests Card Sort	Knowdell, R. (2002, June). *Occupational interests card sort.* San Jose, CA: Career Research & Testing.
O*NET Interest Profiler*	O*NET Consortium (n.d.). *O*NET interest profiler.* Washington, DC: Author.
Self-Directed Search, Forms E and E Audiotape[†]	Holland, J. L. (1996). *Self-directed search form E* (4th ed.) Lutz, FL: Psychological Assessment Resources. Holland J. L. (1996). *Self-directed search form E* (4th ed). [Audiotape]. Lutz, FL: Psychological Assessment Resources.
Transition-to-Work Inventory	Liptak, J. J. (2004). *Transition-to-work inventory.* Indianapolis, IN: JIST Works.
Voc-Tech Quick Screener	JIST Works (2002). *Voc-tech quick screener.* Indianapolis, IN: Author.
Wide Range Interest and Occupation Test[†]	Glutting, J. J., & Wilkinson, G. (2003). *Wide range interest and occupation test* (2nd ed.). Wilmington, DE: Wide Range.
Personality Inventories	
Keirsey Temperment Sorter II	Keirsey, D. (1998, May). *Please understand me II.* Del Mar, CA: Prometheus Nemesis Book.

TABLE 18.1 Continued

Title	*Source*
Vocational Preference Inventory	Holland, J. L. (1985). *Vocational preference inventory (VPI)*. Lutz, FL: Psychological Assessment Resources.
Value Inventories	
Career Values Card Sort	Knowdell, R. (1998, June). *Career values card sort*. San Jose, CA: Career Research & Testing.
O*NET Career Values Inventory*	JIST Works (2002). *O*NET career values inventory*. Indianapolis, IN: Author.
O*NET Work Importance Locator and Profiler*	O*NET Consortium (n.d.). *O*NET work importance locator and profiler*. Washington, DC: Author.
Values-Driven Work Card Sort	Career Action Center. (n.d.). *Values-driven card sort*. Menlo Park, CA: Prodigy Press.
Work Orientation and Values Survey	Brady, R. P. (2000). *Work orientation and values survey*. Indianapolis, IN: JIST Works.
Career-Development Inventories	
Barriers to Employment Success Inventory	Liptak, J. J. (2002). *Barriers to employment success inventory* (2nd ed.). Indianapolis, IN: JIST Works.
Career Attitudes and Strategies Inventory	Holland, J. L., & Gottfredson, G. D. (1994). *Career attitudes and strategies inventory*. Lutz, FL: Psychological Assessment Resources.
Career Beliefs Inventory	Krumboltz, J. D. (1991). *Career beliefs inventory*. Mountain View, CA: CPP.
Career Decision Scale	Osipow, S. H., Carney, C. G., Winer, J. L., Yanico, B. J., & Koschier. M. (1987). *Career decision scale* (3rd ed.). Lutz, FL: Psychological Assessment Resources.
Career Thoughts Inventory	Sampson, J. P., Peterson, G. W., Lenz, J. G., Reardon, R. C., & Saunders, D. E. (1996). *Career thoughts inventory*. Lutz, FL: Psychological Assessment Resources.
Career Transitions Inventory	Heppner, M. J. (1991). *Career transitions inventory*. Columbia, MO: Author.
Job Search Attitude Inventory	Liptak, J. J. (2002). *Job search attitude inventory* (2nd ed.). Indianapolis, IN: JIST Works.
My Vocational Situation	Holland, J. L., Daiger, D., & Power, P. G. (1980). *My vocational situation*. Mountain View, CA: CPP.
Overcoming Barriers Card Sort Game Kit	Harney, E. E., & Angel, D. L. (1999). *Overcoming barriers card sort game kit*. Hacienda Heights, CA: WorkNet Solutions.
Reading-Free Vocational Interest Inventory: 2	Becker, R. L. (2000). *Reading-free vocational interest inventory: 2*. Columbus, OH: Elburn.

(Continued)

TABLE 18.1   Continued

Title	Source
Salient Beliefs Review: Connecting Spirit to Work	Bloch, D. (2003). *Salient beliefs review: Connecting spirit to work.* Indianapolis, IN: JIST Works.
Vocational Exploration and Insight Kit	Holland, J. L., Birk, J. M., Cooper, J. F., Dewey, C. R., Dolliver, H., Takai, R. T., & Tyler, L. (1980). *The vocational exploration and insight kit.* Mountain View, CA: CPP.
Miscellaneous	
Career Genograms	Gysbers, N. C., Heppner, M. J., & Johnson, J. A. (2003). *Career counseling: Process, issues, and techniques* (2nd ed.) Boston: Allyn and Bacon.
Elevations ® Manual Card Sort System	Scully, H. (2003, August). *Elevations manual card sort system.* Roseville, CA: Author.
Individual Employment Plan	Ludden, L. L., & Maitlen, B. (2002). *Individual employment plan.* Indianapolis, IN: JIST Works.
Vocational Decision-Making Interview	Czerlinsky, T., & Chandler, S. (1999). *Vocational decision-making interview.* Indianapolis, IN: JIST Works.

*Use only if client is computer literate.
†Inventory is available in English and other languages.

and address any possible barriers to the client's career success. Once they complete these steps, they focus on determining any training and education the clients may need.

Determine Training and Education Needs.   Two of the most beneficial training and education options for the newly immigrated are language assistance and adult education. Human service professionals working with the newly immigrated should have available for their clients a number of referrals or options to help them learn to speak, read, and write in English. A number of English as a Second Language (ESL) classes are available for children and adults. These classes are designed to teach the English language to people who do not know English. These classes are also called English for speakers of other languages (ESOL) or English literacy classes. Many school districts and community colleges offer community education and public adult programs that may provide ESL classes and tutoring services. Some of these programs are free or are offered for a nominal fee. Large cities often offer private ESL classes with costs based on the number of hours of instruction. Public classes tend to be less expensive than private classes. Some religious groups, libraries, and community organizations offer ESL classes free of charge or at a low cost (U.S. Citizenship and Immigration Services, 2004a).

Many adults who are newly immigrated do not have a high-school education. Human service professionals must be knowledgeable about programs and services available to help their clients obtain the education they need. Clients age 16 and older who have not completed high school can enroll in Adult Secondary Education (ASE) classes that prepare them to earn a General Educational Development (GED) certificate. Many communities offer GED preparation classes at little or no cost. To earn the GED, the client must take and pass tests in five areas: reading, writing, social studies, science, and mathematics. Many employers in the United States consider the GED equivalent to a high-school diploma. In addition to GED classes, many public school systems and local community colleges offer adult education classes on a variety of subjects and provide skill training that can benefit clients in their jobs. Anyone can enroll in these classes, and they usually have low fees. Helpers should direct their clients to local community colleges and school systems for more information on possible courses and programs (U.S. Citizenship and Immigration Services, 2004a).

Find Funding for Training and Education.   A number of funding sources are available to assist immigrants and to provide support to organizations, programs, and projects that serve and work with immigrants and refugees. Some of the funding is determined by the immigration status of the client.

Some immigrants may qualify for federal financial aid to cover many school expenses including tuition, books, fees, room and board, supplies, and transportation. Students qualify for federal, financial aid based on needs not on grades. Three types of federal aid are available to qualified applicants: grants, work-study, and loans. *Grants* are funds that do not have to be repaid. *Work-study* is money that students earn while in school. A *loan* is borrowed money that is repaid with interest at a later date. Clients can get more information on federal, financial aid programs by visiting the U.S. Department of Education website at: http://www.studentaid.ed.gov/students/publications/student_guide/index.html (U.S. Citizenship and Immigration Services, 2004a).

Grantmakers Concerned with Immigrants and Refugees (2001a) publishes an online directory of funders who support immigrant and refugee issues. This funding directory provides information on 200 private, community, corporate, and public foundations that may provide support to organizations, projects, and programs serving or working with immigrants and refugees. The directory consist of a cross-section of foundations that support immigrant and refugee-related efforts within certain fields such as health care, arts, welfare, human rights, research, community development, and community organizing. This resource on the types of grants and areas of interest for a range of foundations across the country provides examples of grants that have been given in recent years to support programs that serve immigrant and refugee communities.

Complete Referrals to Other Agencies.   When working with the newly immigrated population, human service professionals must review the special circumstances that resulted in their clients' migration to the United States. The individual needs of each client will determine the types of referrals, that they might need. Helpers must be familiar with the various agencies, programs, and services that are available within the community to assist the newly immigrated in achieving their goals of long-term employment. For example, human service professionals must have knowledge of and access to school districts and community colleges that offer ESL courses and/or tutoring.

In addition, human service professionals must be well versed in the immigration-related vocabulary and processes (e.g., **entry visa**, green card, **inadmissible**, lawful permanent resident, **numerical limit, parolee, per-country limit**, preference system, **principal alien, refugee approvals** and **arrivals, resettlement, service centers, special immigrants, special naturalization provisions**, sponsor, **stateless, stowaway, subject to the numerical limit, Temporary Protected Status (TPS)**, temporary worker, **TN status, transient alien**, exempt form, **naturalization application, withdrawal**, etc.).

Choose Interventions.   The career development model for the newly immigrated population consists of three kinds of interventions: job clubs; transitional assistance; and training, education programs, and services. The human service professional and client choose interventions based on the individual needs of the client. Interventions may be used independently or in conjunction with other interventions.

Using Job Clubs.   For clients who come from collectivistic cultures, group interventions such as job clubs may be appropriate. *Job clubs* are small groups of people who come together to work on job-related concerns. The job clubs provide the newly immigrated with needed support, a place to air their concerns, and a means for learning about the U.S. labor market. Information provided via job clubs should be presented using a structured reading-discussion technique and up-to-date written and occupational video resources. This intervention helps to promote the reading and speaking of the English language. Because families are important components in the career development of many immigrants who come from collectivistic cultures, family members should be permitted to participate in job clubs when such participation is deemed helpful to the client. By recognizing the importance of the family, human service professionals show their respect for the role that family honor and loyalty play in the career decision-making process of their clients (Gysbers, et al., 2003; Zunker, 2002).

Using Transitional Assistance.   Transitions of any kind are often stressful. By any measure, immigration is one of the most stressful transitions an individual can experience. Immigration encompasses a variety of transition stressors. Most significantly, immigration removes individuals from their predictable and familiar environment and situations—community bonds, extended support network of families and friends, jobs, customs, living situations, and often language. Even though in some cases immigration may bring advantages in the form of economic rewards, social mobility, reunion with family and loved ones, and/or relief from religious or political persecution, immigration disruptions often trigger a variety of reactions including depression, anxiety, grief, and anger (Suárez-Orozco, 1998).

Human service professionals can assist with the transition process of the newly immigrated in a variety of ways. First, helpers can work to build bridges between the immigrants and employers. These bridges can provide access to new support networks, job opportunities, and to a range of services that may benefit the immigrants. For example, helpers can inquire about possible employment sites and part- and full-time, entry-level jobs that may provide viable work experience toward the client's tentative career options. These contacts can also provide valuable learning opportunities for the client.

Helpers can also arrange meetings between their clients and personnel specialists from businesses and industries. These specialists can provide clients with constructive feedback on qualifications (e.g., skills, training, education, etc.) they will need for success in a particular field. Human service professionals can also strengthen bonds between employers and clients by serving as information clearinghouses to potential employers. For example, some employers may be unfamiliar with immigration laws, procedures, and policies regarding the hiring of the newly immigrated. The human service professional can help alleviate potential uncertainties or confusions on the part of the employer by providing information regarding the hiring of the newly immigrated such as, **employer sanctions, Employment Authorization Document (EAD), labor certification,** visa information, benefits to the employer, and government agency information such as the U.S. Citizenship and Immigration Services/Immigration and Naturalization Service.

Second, human service professionals can provide immigrants with information regarding U.S. culture and the U.S. labor market that will enhance their knowledge and skills as they adapt to a new culture while simultaneously supporting the immigrants' culture-of-origin identity. Many of the newly immigrated do not understand the U.S. labor market or its expectations (e.g., need for additional training or education). Many immigrants lack the knowledge of how and where to obtain employment information and often do not understand the concept of career ladders. Some clients may not be aware of the importance of resume writing and interviewing skills. Interventions should focus on client-produced knowledge such as knowledge that requires the client to locate suitable role models and to develop networks. Client-produced knowledge enhances clients' personal involvement and self-efficacy in their career development.

Third, helpers can serve as job coaches by providing personal support to their clients and assisting them through the various stages of job seeking (e.g., assessing skills, completing job applications, formatting resumes and cover letters, contacting employers, meeting employers for the first time, signing contracts). Job coaches also work with employers and encourage them to hire immigrants, and they perform advocacy and mediation with employers and coworkers. Job coaches help clients with problem solving of work-related issues and support their clients even after employment begins for as long as the client needs the service.

Fourth, human service professionals can assist the new immigrant by sharing with their clients essential workplace survival skills. The following lists were extracted from the U.S. Department of Labor's (1991) report on essential workplace competencies for employee readiness in the U.S. workforce:

Resources: Identifies, organizes, plans, and allocates resources

- *Time:* selects goal-relevant activities, ranks them, allocates time, and prepares and follows schedules
- *Money:* uses or prepares budgets, makes forecasts, keeps records, and makes adjustments to meet objectives
- *Material and facilities:* acquires, stores, allocates, and uses materials or space efficiently
- *Human resources:* assesses skills and distributes work accordingly, evaluates performance and provides feedback

Interpersonal: Works with others

- *Participates as member of a team:* contributes to group effort
- *Teaches others new skills*
- *Services clients/customers:* works to satisfy customers expectations
- *Exercises leadership:* communicates ideas to justify position, persuades and convinces others, responsibly challenges existing procedures and policies
- *Negotiates:* works toward agreements involving exchange of resources, resolves divergent interests
- *Works with diversity:* works well with men and women from diverse backgrounds

Information: Acquires and evaluates information

- *Acquires and evaluates information*
- *Organizes and maintains information*
- *Interprets and communicates information*
- *Uses computers to process information*

Systems: Understands complex interrelationships

- *Understands systems:* knows how social, organizational, and technological systems work and operates effectively with them
- *Monitors and corrects performance:* distinguishes trends, predicts impacts on system operations, diagnoses deviations in systems performance, and corrects malfunctions
- *Improves or designs systems:* suggests modifications to existing systems and develops new or alternative systems to improve performance

Technology: Works with a variety of technologies

- *Selects technology:* chooses procedures, tools, or equipment including computers and related technologies
- *Applies technology to task:* understands intent and proper procedures for setup and operation of equipment
- *Maintains and troubleshoots equipment:* prevents, identifies, or solves problems with equipment, including computers and other technologies

The U.S. Department of Labor's (1991) report goes on to state that the following foundation skills and personal qualities are essential in order for individuals to perform the aforementioned workplace competencies:

Basic Skills: Reads, writes, performs arithmetic and mathematical operations, listens, and speaks

- *Reading:* locates, understands, and interprets written information in prose and in documents such as manuals, graphs, and schedules

- *Writing:* communicates thoughts, ideas, information, and messages in writing; and creates documents such as letters, directions, manuals, reports, graphs, and flow charts
- *Arithmetic/mathematics:* performs basic computations and approaches practical problems by choosing appropriately from a variety of mathematical techniques
- *Listening:* receives, attends to, interprets, and responds to verbal messages and other cues
- *Speaking:* organizes ideas and communicates orally

Thinking Skills: Thinks creatively, makes decisions, solves problems, visualizes, knows how to learn, and reasons

- *Creative thinking:* generates new ideas
- *Decision making:* specifies goals and constraints, generates alternatives, considers risks, and evaluates and chooses best alternatives
- *Problem solving:* recognizes problems and devises and implements plan of action
- *Visualizing:* organizes and processes symbols
- *Knowing how to learn:* uses efficient learning techniques to acquire and apply new knowledge and skills
- *Reasoning:* discovers a rule or principle underlying the relationship between two or more objects and applies it when solving a problem

Personal Qualities: Responsibility, self-esteem, sociability, self-management, integrity, and honesty

- *Responsibility:* exerts a high level of effort and perseveres towards goal attainment
- *Self-esteem:* believes in own self-worth and maintains a positive view of self
- *Sociability:* demonstrates understanding, friendliness, adaptability, empathy, and politeness in group settings
- *Self-management:* assesses self accurately, sets personal goals, monitors progress, and exhibits self-control
- *Integrity/honesty:* chooses ethical courses of action

Transitional assistance is a crucial intervention that requires knowledge and skills on the part of the helper. It should be noted that in certain cases human service professionals might not actually provide these services but rather refer clients to appropriate programs and agencies that provide transitional assistance.

Finding Training, Education Programs, and Services. The third type of intervention includes training, education programs, and services specifically selected to meet the needs of each newly immigrated client. Two of the most beneficial options for the newly immigrated are language assistance and adult education. Since we addressed these options previously, we will turn our attention to specific programs and services with which human service professionals must be knowledgeable when they work with the newly immigrated. Helpers must be familier with the following information on specific programs and on immigrant eligibility for governmental programs and services.

U.S. Citizenship and Immigration Services (USCIS), formerly known as the **Immigration and Naturalization Service (INS)** is a division within the Department of Homeland Security (DHS). The USCIS is responsible for the administration of immigration and **naturalization** adjudication functions and developing and implementing policies and procedures. Human service professionals working with the newly immigrated must be familiar with the various services available through USCIS, specifically with information on employment eligibility verification, hiring foreign temporary workers, naturalization, lawful permanent residency (LPR) including family and employment-related immigration, and foreign student authorization. The human service professional can supplement the following basic information regarding these services by looking for more detailed information on the USCIS website at: http://uscis.gov/graphics/index.htm.

Employers who hire persons to perform labor or services in exchange for wages or other remuneration must complete Form I-9 for each employee. Form I-9 verifies the employment eligibility of new employees by verifying that the employees are legally able to work in the United States due to citizenship or authorization to work (i.e., work visa).

Employers wishing to hire foreign workers to temporarily perform labor or services must file the Form I-129 petition. The I-129 consists of a petition and some supplemental forms that apply to various visa categories, the required payment, and initial evidence and documentation. Petitions should be filed at least 45 days prior to the employment start date but no more than 6 months in advance of the start date. The petitions are generally mailed to one of the USCIS Service Centers. If the petition is approved, the employer or agent is sent a Notice of Approval Form I-797. However, this approval does not guarantee visa issuance to an applicant, as applicants must also prove that they are admissible to the United States.

Naturalization is the process that awards U.S. citizenship to foreign-born individuals after such persons fulfill certain requirements. The official application form is the N-400 Application for Naturalization form. Applications are filed with various - N-400 Service Centers located throughout the country based on the residency location of the applicant. Requirements for naturalization include:

- *Age.* Applicants must be at least 18 years of age. Some exceptions are made for children born abroad to U.S. citizen parents and for adopted children of citizen parents.

- *Residency.* Applicants must have been lawfully admitted to the United States for permanent residency. Applicants must provide an I-551, Alien Residency Receipt Card, as proof of their residency.

- *Residence and Physical Presence.* Applicants must have resided in the United States as a **Lawful Permanent Resident (LPR)** for a minimum of five years prior to filing for citizenship with no single absence from the United States for more than one year. The applicant must have been physically present in the United States for a minimum of 30 months out of the previous 5 years and must have resided in a state or district for at least 3 months.

• *Good Moral Character.* Applicants must demonstrate that they have been persons of good moral character typically for five years, or three years if married to a U.S. citizen, or one year for Armed Forces expedite, prior to filing.

• *Attachment to the Constitution.* Applicants must demonstrate that they are committed to the principles of the Constitution of the United States.

• *Language.* Applicants must be able to read, write, speak, and comprehend words in ordinary usage in the English language. Exemptions for this requirement are made for certain individuals who have resided in the United States for 15 or more years and are over the age of 50 or 55 depending on their years of residency. Additional exemptions are made for individuals with certain disabilities, which affect the persons' ability to learn English.

• *United States Government and History Knowledge.* Applicants must demonstrate knowledge and understanding of U.S. History and Government. Exemptions and special consideration are made for individuals with certain disabilities, which affect their ability to learn U.S. History and Government and for those over age 65 who have been lawfully residing in the United States for over 20 years.

• *Oath of Allegiance.* Applicants must take an oath of allegiance and swear to support the Constitution and laws, relinquish any foreign allegiance and/or foreign title, and bear arms for the Armed Forces or perform services for the government when required. A modified oath is permitted for those who are able to establish their opposition to any type of service in the Armed Forces due to religious beliefs or teachings.

Human service professionals working with the newly immigrated must also be knowledgeable about the lawful permanent residency (LPR) green card application process. Individuals interested in becoming immigrants to the United States must go through a three-step application process. First, the USCIS approves the immigrant's petition, which is typically filed by an employer (Form I-140) or a relative (I-130 Petition for Alien Relative) of the applicant. Second, the State Department assigns a visa number to eligible applicants. Third, individuals already in the United States can apply to adjust their status to permanent resident after a visa number becomes available to them. Due to the limited number of immigrant visa numbers available each year, a time lag of several years may lapse between the time the USCIS approves the individual's immigrant petition and the time the State Department assigns an immigrant visa number. The *immigrant visa number* allows the person to permanently live and work in the United States.

The Immigration and Nationality Act provides two nonimmigrant visa categories for foreign students who want to study in the United States. The *F visa* is reserved for nonimmigrants wanting to pursue academic studies or language-training programs in the United States. The *M visa* is reserved for nonimmigrants wanting to pursue nonacademic or vocational studies in the United States. Schools must obtain approval to receive nonimmigrant students by filing a Petition for Approval Form I-17 with the

USCIS District Office. In addition, to the aforementioned visas, the **Visa Waiver Pilot Program (VWPP)** permits citizens of certain foreign countries to enter the United States for 90 days for business or pleasure.

Determining Immigrant Eligibility for Federal Programs.   A variety of federal programs are available for immigrants. Immigrants with permanent residencies may qualify for a number of federal public benefits including food stamps, Temporary Assistance for Needy Families (TANF), Medicaid, State Children's Health Insurance Program (SCHIP), and Supplemental Security Income (SSI).

The Food Stamp Program, operated by state and local welfare offices, provides coupons and Electronic Benefits Transfer (EBT) to low-income families to purchase food. TANF is a federal program that provides cash assistance to low-income families. Health insurance coverage is available through SCHIP in many states for all children, regardless of immigrant status, if their families meet the financial requirements. Supplemental Security Income is a cash benefit for individuals over 65, people who are blind, and people with disabilities. Those receiving SSI automatically receive Medicaid.

Following is a chart of immigrant eligibility for federal programs (National Conference of State Legislatures, 2004):

Food Stamps
- Legal immigrant children (benefits restored as of October 1, 2003)
- Legal immigrants with 5 years residence in the United States (benefits restored as of April 1, 2003)*
- Legal immigrants with 40 work quarters
- Refugees
- Elderly, resident in the United States on or before 8/22/96
- Disabled or blind immigrants, regardless of when they entered the United States
- Veterans, active military and their spouses and dependents

TANF
- Legal immigrants residing in the United States on or before 8/22/96 at state option
- Legal immigrants who enter the United States after 8/22/96: barred for first 5 years*
- Legal immigrants with 40 work quarters
- Refugees
- Veterans, active military and their spouses and dependents

Medicaid
- Legal immigrants residing in the United States on or before 8/22/96 at state option

---

*Sponsor-to-immigrant deeming will apply to legal immigrants who have signed a legally binding affidavit of support on or after December 19, 1997. The income and resources of the sponsor are counted as available to the immigrant when determining the immigrant's eligibility.

- Legal immigrants who enter the United States after 8/22/96: barred for first 5 years*
- Legal immigrants with 40 work quarters
- Refugees (eligible for first 7 years of residence)
- Veterans, active military and their spouses and dependents
- SSI recipients

State Children's Health Insurance Program (SCHIP)
- Legal immigrant children residing in the United States on or before 8/22/96
- Legal immigrant children who enter the United States after 8/22/96: barred for first 5 years*
- Refugees (eligible for first 7 years of residence)
- Children of veterans and active military (unmarried, dependent)

SSI
- Legal immigrant SSI recipients resident in the United States on or before 8/22/96
- Legal immigrants resident on or before 8/22/96 who are or become disabled
- Legal immigrants with 40 work quarters
- Veterans, active military and their spouses and dependents
- Refugees (eligible for first 7 years of residence)

States are required to have a verification process in place to verify the eligibility of aliens for the federal public benefits that the states administer. However, nonprofit charitable organizations are exempt from any of the requirements to determine, verify, or otherwise require proof of alien eligibility or status of individuals applying for or receiving such public benefits (Department of Health and Human Services, 2004).

A number of additional services and funding sources are available for individuals regardless of their immigration status on a state-by-state basis. Some of these include: Medicaid benefits for emergency services, Prenatal Care Assistance Program (PCAP), domestic violence counseling, food-pantry services, immunizations, HIV testing and counseling, child welfare and foster care services, public school education, school breakfast and lunch programs, short-term, noncash emergency disaster-relief, senior services, benefits under Title II of the Social Security Act (i.e., Old Age, Survivors, and Disability Insurance), protection of the Commission on Human Rights against discrimination, public library services, police protection, public transportation, and certain services provided by the Department of Health and Human Hygiene (City of New York, 2005; Moore, 1999).

Human service professionals should address the responsibilities of sponsors in providing support to immigrants. Many immigrants are required to have a sponsor or a person willing to sign an agreement to provide financial support to the immigrant. This agreement is called an *affidavit of support* (Form I-864) and is a legally enforceable agreement between the sponsor and the government by which the sponsor agrees to provide adequate support to maintain an immigrant at 125 percent of the Federal Poverty Level (FPL). In 1996 the Personal Responsibility and Work Opportunity

Reconciliation Act (PRWORA) and the Illegal Immigration Reform and Immigration Responsibility Act (IIRIRA) imposed greater legal liability on sponsors and made it more difficult for new immigrants to qualify for public benefits even after they have lived in the United States for five years. The new affidavits of support are legally binding until the sponsor dies or until the immigrant becomes a U.S. citizen, obtains 40 quarters of creditable Social Security coverage, leaves the United States and gives up Legal Permanent Resident (LPR) status, or dies (Schlosberg, 2000).

Human service professionals can assist the newly immigrated by becoming familiar with the eligibility requirements for the various state and federal programs and services. In addition, helpers must possess an understanding of the affidavit of support and the implications for the sponsor in providing adequate support to the immigrant.

Initiate the Employment Campaign.   Many newly immigrated clients may be unfamiliar with the conventional method of initiating an employment campaign in the United States. For example, they may be uncomfortable with the interviewing process or may not possess skills in formatting a resume to fit the expectations of U.S. employers. The human service professional is a vital resource in educating the newly immigrated on implementing an effective employment campaign.

The Strategic Job Search.   Having no "U.S. experience" can pose a barrier to the newly immigrated client's job search. To overcome this barrier, human service professionals can share with their clients the benefits of volunteer work. Although most people do not want to work for free, sometimes it can be beneficial for the newly immigrated to volunteer in order to gain experience, become familiar with the U.S. job market and employer expectations, and develop a network. Another helpful strategy includes assisting the newly immigrated with identifying transferable skills, employment barriers, and employment needs. In addition, clients could benefit from learning about the importance of personal presentation skills such as learning how to present their marketable, technical and soft skills (i.e., reliable, team player, positive attitude) to employers. Finally, the newly immigrated could benefit from information on requirements and procedures for applying for government-sponsored training, if applicable.

Job Applications.   For some newly immigrated clients, human service professionals will need to help them complete employment applications. This help will be especially important for clients who lack sufficient skills in the English language and/or are not familiar with the U.S. employers' expectations and requirements regarding the type of information clients should include in the job application. Since the employment application is often used as a prescreening device, first impressions matter. Applications should be easy to read, accurate and honest, complete, printed on quality paper, and submitted within the specified time frame.

Job-Search Correspondence.   Job-search correspondence is an important element in the employment campaign. For the newly immigrated, job-search correspondence may present some communication difficulties especially if the client lacks sufficient command of the English language. For clients who have limited-English proficiency, the human service professional must help with writing and/or proofreading the letter. In addition, the foreign-born clients may not be familiar with the business-style letter format that is standard in the United States. Helpers can assist the newly immigrated by teaching them basic letter formats and the types of job-search correspondence (i.e., prospecting letters, interview-appreciation letters, etc.) essential for an effective employment campaign.

Taylor-Made Resumes.   The primary goal of the resume is getting the client an interview. Employers are very busy and although they are eager to find good talent, they are just as eager to reduce the number of candidates' resumes to a manageable number. Human service professionals can help newly immigrated clients with resume writing skills by teaching them the basic resume formats (e.g., chronological, functional, combination, electronic/scannable) and by helping them to format an effective resume. For some newly immigrated, previous educational achievement may not be recognized in the United States. In such cases, clients should be taught how to stipulate the U.S. equivalent of the degrees, for example, degree is equivalent to U.S. Bachelor's degree in Sociology. The newly immigrated may also need assistance in clearly specifying their transferable skills in such a way that U.S. employers can easily match their skills with the requirements of the position. Finally, clients with limited English fluency will need help writing and proofing their resumes. This point cannot be over stressed. For many employers, one typo on a resume can make the difference between a candidate's resume leading to an interview and a candidate's resume ending up in the employer's trashcan.

Interviewing Strategies.   Perhaps the most difficult aspect of the employment campaign for many newly immigrated clients is the interviewing process. For some cultural groups, self-promotion is frowned upon and being humble is their cultural standard. The newly immigrated must be trained on basic interviewing skills including the types of interviews and interview formats, tips for an effective interview, clothing guidelines, and appropriate verbal and nonverbal behaviors.

One area of potential concern for the newly immigrated is handling illegal interviewing questions. Clients must be educated on U.S. discrimination laws and the various types of questions that are considered illegal as well as possible responses to such questions. Of particular significance are questions related to the client's nationality, race, and/or religion. The following are some questions, if asked, that might be viewed as illegal or inappropriate:

- Questions related to location of birthplace, nationality, ancestry, or descent of applicant, applicant's spouse, or parents (e.g., Garcia—Is that a Mexican name?).
- Questions related to race or color (e.g., Are you considered to be a member of a minority group?).
- Questions related to religion or religious days observed (e.g., Will your religion prohibit you from working on certain holidays?).

In many cases, untrained interviewers are asking illegal questions in an attempt to be friendly and learn more about the candidate's family, and so on. For that reason a defensive reaction on the part of the candidate could have a negative impact on the interviewing process, and the employer may view a defensive stance as a red flag for future interpersonal conflicts involving the candidate. Clients should be educated on the proper response to illegal questions. The following recommendations can be helpful: answer in brief and move on to the next topic, or ignore the question altogether and move on to a new topic of discussion. The interviewer may recognize the personal blunder and even appreciate the candidate's willingness to put it aside and move on. In cases where the question is truly blatant discrimination and offensive, clients should be told of their right to terminate the interview and walk out.

Videotaping mock interviews for review by the client can be extremely helpful to the newly immigrated client. Human service professionals can work with area employers and recruiters in setting up a videotaped mock interview program. This program would provide an opportunity for clients to practice their interviewing skills with actual employers in a nonthreatening environment. The first step of the mock interview lasts approximately 30 minutes. During this phase the employer conducts a videotaped mock interview. The second step consists of the employer and client discussing and critiquing the interview by viewing the videotape. This stage can also be videotaped thereby allowing clients to review the actual mock interview and the subsequent critique in order to strengthen their interviewing skills. The human service professional can role-play the interviewer if employers are not available.

Change Behaviors.   This career development program model is designed to help clients reach their career-related goals through training, education, and programs and services specifically geared towards the needs of the newly immigrated. This population often faces a number of obstacles that can impede their career development. Some of these obstacles include language barriers, adjustment difficulties, discrimination, and lack of familiarity with the U.S. culture and the U.S. labor market. This program model addresses these barriers and empowers clients to overcome such obstacles. Empowerment leads to self-confidence and self-reliance, two important behavior changes that are a byproduct of an ISP geared to meet the needs of the newly immigrated client.

Complete the Program.   Clients who complete the program are those who began the program, completed assessments, developed an ISP, completed needed training and education, participated in selected interventions, initiated an employment campaign, and secured employment. Some newly immigrated clients may need to recycle through some of the stages of the ISP to ensure that they achieve their career-related goals. For instance, some clients with limited-English-language proficiency may need to continue ESL or ESOL classes even after they secure employment. Continual work on language proficiency can enhance the client's career development opportunities in the future.

Achieve Goal of Long-Term Employment.   The overall goal of all ISPs is the long-term employment of the client. Because the newly immigrated encompass a wide range of employment possibilities that are often based on visa requirements and time limits, the long-term employment of this population may look very different from the long-term employment of other groups. For this population, long-term employment is often a reflection of the length of employment allowable by government regulations. Therefore, goal attainment may be the length of one's actual employment as compared to the total possible employment span permissible by immigration laws. This point is an important one in developing an ISP for the newly immigrated. Since time, or lack thereof, will most likely be an issue, the program is likely to begin in high gear and continue through a rapid progression of steps until steady employment is secured.

Program Evaluation

Program evaluation is a vital component of this career development model. As with all program evaluations, it is important to integrate evaluative methods within every stage of the program, from conception to termination. Evaluations allow agencies to determine if programs are meeting the needs of their clients and of their organization while demonstrating accountability for their programs. Human service professionals need to develop a variety of tools to evaluate their program. Figure 18.1 is a flow chart for the career development program model for the newly immigrated population. The text in each box in the figure is a factor that needs to be measured. Human service professionals and other staff members must decide on the types of evaluations (i.e., process, outcome, impact) and the sort of evaluative instruments (i.e., anecdotal record forms, expert review checklists, focus group protocols, process review logs, implementation logs, interview protocols, questionnaires) that will be the most beneficial in obtaining needed information. Following these decisions, they must create a timeline stipulating the evaluative process, deadlines, and the people responsible for the evaluation. After they complete the evaluation, the staff should present their data, findings, and recommendations to stakeholders and agency representatives and constituents. For additional information on program evaluation, see Chapter 6.

Revisiting the Case Study: Sandeep

Conduct an Intake Interview

The intake interview between the human service professional and Sandeep should explore Sandeep's adjustment difficulties, support system, and financial resources. Sandeep may be experiencing difficulties adjusting to a new social environment and to the fact that he had to leave his wife and daughter in India. Making this adjustment even more difficult is the fact that Sandeep and his brothers have faced severe prejudice by members of their California community. Sandeep needs to establish a support system, perhaps within the Punjabi community, that can help him manage feelings of anxiety and anger that he may be experiencing and can provide him with strategies for handling the extreme hostility of others. Because Sandeep left India for economic reasons, the human service professional should explore his financial resources. Being unemployed can only exasperate his limited financial resources, and the helper needs to investigate access to essential services.

Make Assessments

Because Sandeep has not finished high school and struggles with the English language, the human service professional must carefully choose assessments that Sandeep can understand and are not above his educational abilities. The human service professional must make certain that the assessments chosen can be adapted to meet Sandeep's language and educational level. For some instruments, a translator may be needed to help Sandeep understand terminology, instructions, and results. Working with a paraprofessional from the Punjabi community, Sandeep can access the needed translation services. The following inventories may match Sandeep's unique needs.

The Motivated Skills Card Sort (Knowdell, 2002a) can be used to pinpoint Sandeep's transferable and functional skills. Many immigrants are not aware that the skills they have developed in their native countries can translate to the U.S. work environment. This card sort can help Sandeep identify matches between his current skills and those he needs for his goal position at a nearby factory. The inventory can also pinpoint skills that will be important for him to develop in order to be successful in his new job.

To assess his interests, the Self-Directed Search (SDS) Form E or Form E Audiotape (Holland, 1996a, 1996b) may be helpful. The SDS Form E is designed for individuals who have a sixth-grade reading level. Because Sandeep has limited-English proficiency and did not finish secondary education, this version of the SDS might be beneficial. The audiotaped version, designed for individuals with limited-reading skills, may be a helpful alternative to the paper-and-pencil form.

The Vocational Preference Inventory (VPI) (Holland, 1985) would be a useful assessment to measure Sandeep's personality. Since the SDS was chosen to measure his interests, and both inventories utilize Holland's six personality types (i.e., RIASEC), Sandeep could easily link information gained from the SDS to information obtained on the VPI.

To assess Sandeep's work values, the Values-Driven Work Card Sort (Career Action Center, n.d.) could be helpful. This card sort is beneficial for career-changers and can provide Sandeep with a means to clarity his personal values, focus on organizational values, and explore work-group values. These three areas are extremely important to assess especially in a newly immigrated client who is in the process of acculturating into a new society.

Sandeep is likely to experience a number of barriers to career success. To assess and identify these key barriers to securing and succeeding on the job, the helping professional could administer the Barriers to Employment Success Inventory (BESI) (Liptak, 2002a). This inventory is designed for people with an eighth-grade reading level and may be well suited for Sandeep's limited-English-language proficiency and education.

One final assessment that may be helpful is Career Genograms (Gysbers, Heppner, & Johnson, 2003). Helping Sandeep create a career genogram can help him explore possible barriers (i.e., imbalances in learning and work) and family career messages (i.e., impact of work on various family members).

These inventories were suggested because of their lower-reading level and their ability to assess Sandeep's transferable skills along with his personality, work values, barriers to success, and interests. Human service professionals can choose from a variety of other possibilities. The main point is to choose assessments that are appropriate for meeting his career development needs and that give special attention to Sandeep's culture, his limited-English proficiency, and education. Refer to Chapter 3 for more detailed information on these and additional inventories.

Determine Barriers to Career Success

It is probable that Sandeep will be facing a number of barriers including discrimination, attitudinal barriers, language barriers, limited education, adjustment difficulties, insufficient financial resources, and physical health barriers. Sandeep has already experienced severe discrimination and prejudice in the community where he lives. Similar mistreatment will likely occur at his workplace in the form of low wages, poor working conditions, long hours, and harsh attitudes by coworkers and management.

His limited-English proficiency and education will possibly be the greatest barriers to his employment success. Lack of English proficiency can make communication between him and his employer difficult. His limited education can impact the type of work for which he is qualified and thus can negatively affect his salary.

Sandeep is likely to experience an array of adjustment difficulties stemming from leaving his family in India and moving to a new country with unfamiliar and sometimes even hostile people. These adjustment difficulties can lead to acculturative stress and decreased life satisfaction.

Sandeep's financial situation will undoubtedly present another barrier. While in India he lived in a poor farming village. His dire situation was the basis for his immigration to the United States. Although he is able to stay with his brothers in California, his brothers' financial state is not such that Sandeep can afford not to work.

Finally, because Sandeep's goal is to secure employment at a local factory, the possibility exists that this line of work will present him with physical health barriers due to dangerous work conditions. The human service professional will need to address all of these barriers with Sandeep and incorporate a plan to overcome them within his ISP.

Choose Interventions

Using Job Clubs.   Since Sandeep comes from a collectivistic culture, a job club could provide him with a means to air his concerns while he learns about the U.S. labor market. He can take advantage of the small group format of the job club to practice his English-speaking skills in a nonthreatening environment. Many job clubs permit family members to join. Allowing Sandeep's brothers to participate in the job club can help strengthen his family's support system.

Using Transitional Assistance.   The human service professional can help Sandeep with his transition to the United States by building bridges between him and the factory employers in the local community. For example, the helper can inquire about possible entry-level positions that would provide Sandeep with valuable work experience. The human service professional, or a paraprofessional from Sandeep's community, can also serve as a job coach to Sandeep. The job coach could work closely with Sandeep throughout the various stages of job seeking, from skill assessment to the signing of an employment contract. A job coach can also strengthen the bond between Sandeep and his employer by providing the employer with information regarding the hiring of the newly immigrated including visa information, documentation, and advantages to the employer.

Transition assistance for Sandeep can also take the form of information sharing regarding U.S. culture and the U.S. labor force. The human service professional could educate Sandeep on locating occupational information, developing career networks, finding appropriate role models, and acquiring essential workplace survival skills. Allowing Sandeep to take personal responsibility in securing information, contacts, and skills will enhance his self-esteem and self-efficacy in his career development.

Finding Training, Education Programs, and Services.   Due to Sandeep's limited-English-language proficiency, the human service professional must help him locate and enroll in an area ESL or ESOL English-literacy class. This intervention must take place prior to any additional training or education.

Following his English-literacy education, Sandeep should be enrolled in an ASE class that prepares him to earn his GED certificate. This certificate can provide him with the basic education needed for access to better employment options.

While Sandeep is getting this education, the human service professional should look into federal and nonprofit programs and services that would help him during his transition from unemployment to employment. Although Sandeep does not qualify for a number of federal programs because of his immigration status, the helper should explore nonprofit programs such as area food pantries and emergency relief services. In addition, since Sandeep and his brothers have experienced extreme hostility from the residents in their town, they should be given information regarding protection from the Commission on Human Rights against discrimination.

Initiate the Employment Campaign

Following Sandeep's participation in the interventions, the human service professional would help him initiate his employment campaign. First, they should contact the local factories. Since relationships between the industries and Sandeep were forged during the intervention stage, his contact at this point would be for the purpose of updating the employers on his progress with his education and training and inquiring about employment opportunities and the application process. Once he establishes employment prospects, the human service professional would help Sandeep fill out applications, format his resume, and write job-search correspondence. They would give special attention to highlighting Sandeep's functional and transferable skills.

In the next step the helper would arrange a videotaped mock interview with Sandeep to prepare him for the interviewing process. The helper should recruit a human resource person from one of the local factories to conduct the mock interview. This opportunity would provide Sandeep practice with his interviewing skills with an actual employer. The careful creation and implementation of Sandeep's ISP can lead to his long-term employment that in turn can provide him with a means to support his family thereby allowing him to reunite with his wife and daughter.

Conclusion

Human service professionals working with the newly immigrated should allow sufficient time for their clients to work through the various steps of the ISP and invite them to recycle through stages when doing so can enhance their career development. Helpers should also monitor each stage of the program to ensure that unanticipated barriers are addressed and that the newly immigrated clients' concerns are heard. Newly immigrated clients should be praised for their demonstrated skills and strengths. This praise can lead to clients' future job-seeking success. Finally, clients should be invited to return for additional assistance when such help is needed.

Working with the newly immigrated can be enhanced through a number of program and policy improvements. The following are suggested recommendations for which human service professionals can advocate.

Policy changes to improve access to training and education would include:

- Improve access to Adult Basic Education and ESL for immigrants
- Increase access to training opportunities for the immigrant population

Policy changes to provide more funding for community-based organizations (CBOs) would include:

- Expand funding to CBOs for adult-literacy services
- Increase cultural and linguistic competency training to CBOs

Policy changes to expand research and assessment on newly immigrated population would inclulde:

- Assess all new immigrant job seekers on English proficiency in order to establish the need for additional ESL programs
- Provide research funding for pilot projects that provide job-seeking services to the newly immigrated

Summary

The immigrant population in the United States has increased by 4.3 million since 2000 and now accounts for nearly 12 percent of the nation's population. Two million of the immigrant population in the United States are undocumented or illegal immigrants. Immigrants comprise 14.3 percent of U.S. workers, and although some immigrants enter the United States with strong academic skills and credentials, many do not. In 2000, nearly three times as many recent immigrants as natives lacked a high-school education. The unemployment rate of foreign-born workers was 5.5 percent in 2004. Immigration status plays a vital role in the earnings of the immigrant population, and undocumented workers are often forced to remain in occupations that pay minimum wage or below and have no benefits. Foreign-born workers earn, on average, 75.6 percent of the earnings of native-born workers. Factors related to the newly immigrated population can serve as barriers to career success. This chapter presented a career development program model for working with the newly immigrated. The model illustrates the creation of an Individual Success Plan that uses results from assessments of career abilities, interests, values, and barriers; interagency referrals; interventions such as job clubs, transitional assistance, and training, education programs, and services; and is followed by an employment campaign that leads to long-term employment and self-sufficiency.

Key Terms

Acquired citizenship
Adjustment to immigrant status
Alien
Asylee
Certificates of citizenship
Conditional resident
Deportable alien
Deportation
Deportment
Diversity Lottery Program (DLP)
Employer sanctions
Employment authorization
   Document (EAD)
Entry visa
Green card
Immigrant
Immigration Act of 1990
Immigration and Nationality Act (INA)
Immigration and Naturalization Service (INS)
Inadmissible
Labor certification
Lawful Permanent Resident (LPR)
Legalized alien
Migrant
National
Naturalization
Naturalization application
Nonimmigrant
Numerical limit, exempt from

Parolee
Per-country limit
Permanent resident alien
Port of entry
Preference system (Immigration Act of 1990)
Principal alien
Refugee
Refugee approvals
Refugee arrivals
Removal
Resettlement
Service centers
Special immigrants
Special naturalization provisions
Sponsor
Stateless
Stowaway
Subject to the Numerical Limit
Temporary Protected Status (TPS)
Temporary worker
TN status
Transient alien
U.S. Citizenship and Immigration Services (USCIS)
Visa
Visa Waiver Pilot Program (VWPP)
Voluntary departure
Withdrawl

Web Resources _____

Note that website URLs may change over time.

Center for Human Rights and Constitutional Law
http://www.centerforhumanrights.org

Cultural Orientation Resource Center
http://www.culturalorientation.net/index.html

Grantmakers Concerned with Immigrants and Refugees (GCIR)
http://www.gcir.org/index.htm

Life 360: The Immigrant Experience
http://www.pbs.org/opb/life360/locations/
immigrant/immigrant.htm

Living American.com
http://www.vidaamericana.com/english/
index.html

National Immigration Law Center
http://www.nilc.org

National Network for Immigrant and Refugee Rights
http://www.nnirr.org

The Urban Institute: America's Immigrants
http://www.urban.org/content/IssuesInFocus/
AmericasImmigrants/Immigrants.htm

U.S. Census Bureau: Immigration
http://www.census.gov/population/www/socdemo/
immigration.html

U.S. Citizenship and Immigration Services
http://uscis.gov/graphics/index.htm

U.S. Committee for Refugees and Immigrants
http://www.refugees.org

U.S. Department of Labor: Immigration
http://www.oalj.dol.gov/libina.htm

Division of Immigration Health Services
http://www.inshealth.org

Part III

Special Topics for the Human Service Professional

You now have a foundation in career development in addition to specific interventions to use when you offer career development services to a variety of populations. Your next task is to integrate a final round of knowledge—the ethics of the career development profession along with workplace issues that face human service professionals in the 21st century.

19

Ethical Issues in Providing Career Interventions

Case Study: Carmelita

Carmelita, a 31-year-old illegal immigrant from Mexico has been cleaning hotels in a resort community in North Carolina for the past seven years. She fled Mexico with her two children after her husband was killed in a car accident, because she found it difficult to earn enough money in her small Mexican village to support her family. Although she entered the United States on a visitor's visa, it has since expired. She is currently using a fabricated Social Security number.

Carmelita recently received word that her father in Mexico is dying from lung cancer. He has been given less than three months to live. Carmelita's mother died when Carmelita was just 10 years old after which time her father raised her by himself until she married at age 19. She is an only child and must now return to Mexico to care for her father. Although Carmelita has steady employment, her salary is barely enough to cover the rent of her small, one-bedroom apartment and the daily living expenses for a family of three. Therefore, she does not have enough money to fund the trip home to Mexico for her and her two children. In addition, because of her illegal immigrant status, she may be unable to return to the United States once she leaves. Recently a network of "friends" has assured her that if she secures enough money, they will help her reenter the United States. Carmelita needs a higher-paying job immediately and has learned of a number of new positions opening up at a local hospital. One custodial position pays twice as much as her current salary and offers a number of benefits. She has no resume and lacks strong interviewing skills. She came across a pamphlet advertising a "Job-Search Strategies Workshop" offered free of charge by a local nonprofit employment agency. You are the workshop facilitator. Carmelita meets with you before the start of the workshop and describes her dire situation. She is desperate to work at the local hospital and hopes that your expertise will provide her with the skills necessary to land the job. What is the ethical thing for you to do?

Ethical Language

Human service professionals often encounter situations in their professional lives that require ethical decision-making. Therefore, helpers must be knowledgeable about the ethical standards of their profession and competent in applying sound ethical decision-making skills. In order to make sound decisions, human service professionals must have a clear understanding of ethical language. In this section we will provide working definitions of some typical terms encountered when discussing the topic of ethics. Specifically, we will define the following terms: ethical standards, ethics, ethical, legal, and moral.

- *Ethical Standards.*   **Ethical standards** are sets of principles of conduct that guide individuals or groups through ethical or professional decision-making (National Organization for Human Services, 2004). Ethical standards provide guidelines of expected conduct, encourage excellence in practice, guide professionals in decision-making, and promote public understanding and confidence in the profession.

- *Ethics.*   **Ethics** refer to a set of standards or rules of right and wrong that prescribe what individuals ought to do, usually in terms of rights, obligations, benefits to society, fairness, or specific virtues. Ethics also refers to the explicit philosophical study of moral values and rules and to the development of one's ethical standards. In this case, ethics involves the constant effort of studying our own moral beliefs and conduct, and striving to ensure that we, and the institutions we help to shape, live up to such standards (Encyclopedia Britannica, 2004; Merriam-Webster Dictionary, 2004).

- *Ethical.*   To be **ethical** means to follow the dictates of a set of standards that a particular group has determined to be ethically right. For example, in the human service profession, ethical behavior means following the ethical standards of human service professionals as stipulated by the National Organization for Human Services.

- *Legal.*   **Legal** simply means of or pertaining to the law (Merriam-Webster, Inc., 2004). Laws are a combination of rules and principles of conduct that have been derived from court decisions, approved by the government, and established by local customs. Laws are enforced over a certain territory and must be obeyed by all persons within that territory.

- *Moral.*   **Moral** is related to the principles of right or wrong as they apply to an individual's behavior. For example, in ethical decision-making, moral could be defined as the firm conviction concerning justification of decisions reached after careful analysis of what is right or wrong.

The aforementioned list of terms and their definitions by no means covers the expanse of ethical language, but they begin to lay the foundation for the development of knowledge and skills relevant to ethical decision-making. Keep these terms in mind as we will turn our attention to understanding and recognizing ethical dimensions in providing career interventions.

Ethical Dimensions of Providing Career Interventions

Human service professionals are likely to face a number of common ethical conflicts when they provide career interventions. According to Niles and Harris-Bowlsbey (2005), three of the most significant ethical challenges facing practitioners who provide career services are as follows: the proper role of individuals who provide career interventions yet lack the standard credentials for counseling, whether all career services and interventions denote counseling relationships, and the appropriate use of Internet technology in providing career services.

- *Qualifications of the Helping Professionals.* Many individuals who provide career interventions have little or no formal training or education in the helping profession or in career development theory and practice. Professional organizations are concerned with the practice of delivering counseling interventions by helpers who lack proper credentials. However, counseling and psychology licensure laws do not prohibit providers who lack this formal training from providing some career interventions such as resume writing and job-search skill training. To address this concern, the National Career Development Association (NCDA) has developed training and credentialing guidelines for Career Development Facilitators (CDF) who are trained to provide certain career services under the supervision of a qualified career counselor.

- *Career Interventions and the Helping Professional.* Some career interventions are not considered "therapy" in the typical sense (i.e., resume development). Challenges arise when current ethical standards for the profession do not appropriately address many of the possible nontherapeutic scenarios that may arise when providing career interventions (e.g., a client visiting a career resource center and asking a human service professional to proofread a cover letter).

- *The Role of Internet Technology in Career Interventions.* The use of the Internet in providing career services is a topic that has provided much discussion in the career-counseling field. Because of its accessibility, the Internet has become a source of information for many individuals who may not have access to other sources of information. Because of its popularity, the National Career Development Association published guidelines for the use of Internet technology in delivering career services. Specifically, the guidelines stipulate that the Internet can be used to deliver occupational information, provide online searches of occupational databases, deliver interactive career planning and counseling services, and provide online job searches. These four reasons for the use of the Internet in delivering career services are subject to the ethical guidelines addressed by NCDA.

Although these ethical challenges are addressed in the ethical standards for the career counseling profession, a number of additional dimensions are not specifically addressed in the standards, but deserve attention. The following examples, derived from Spokane (1991), shed light on some additional ethical conflicts that human service professionals may face when delivering career interventions:

• *Pressure to See as Many Clients as Possible.*   Because of budget cuts, streamlining of services, and other circumstances, many helping professionals face extreme pressure from their agencies and supervisors to serve large numbers of clients. This pressure may result in "head counting" without giving much attention to the level of service a particular client needs. Although professionals must often respond to agency needs, the client's needs should determine the length and intensity of the career intervention.

• *Indiscriminate Testing.*   Sometimes practitioners use tests and assessments inappropriately (i.e., ordering a series of tests that are unnecessary). Practitioners should only administer or recommend tests and assessments that are necessary and appropriate for the needs of the client. In addition, the helping professional should provide the client with a list of the testing procedures and the cost, if any, of the assessment.

• *Informational Interviews.* As discussed previously in this text, informational interviews are a common tool used in gathering occupational information and in networking. Helping professionals sometimes use established businesses or contacts when they set up informational interviews for their clients. When doing so, human service professionals should obtain a written release from their client prior to discussing the client with any outside party.

• *Exaggerated Claims of Effectiveness.*   Although many career interventions result in positive outcomes for clients, some interventions may have negative results. Helping professionals should not guarantee positive outcomes, but they should provide clients with outcome research regarding the intervention's effectiveness. In addition, clients should be reminded that their commitment and effort to the intervention are significant predictors of positive outcomes.

• *Client Follow-Up.*   When clients miss one or more sessions without notifying the human service professional, a follow-up contact with the client should take place. Missing an appointment may be a sign of an obstacle that may impede the success of the intervention. Helpers should contact the client directly to discuss the situation and to problem solve, if necessary.

• *Note Taking and Record Keeping.*   Human service professionals should write brief postsession notes and retain copies of all the clients' test results, interpretations, correspondence, and reports. Court precedents have set liability limits to seven years after clients realize that they may have been harmed, so human service professionals should keep these records for an indefinite period of time. In addition, since records may be subpoenaed by the courts, human service professionals should ensure that all notes, comments, interpretations, and other written communication is professional and abides by the ethical standards of the profession.

• *When the Client Is the Organization but Individuals Are Counseled.*   When a human service professional is hired by an organization, a potential ethical dilemma may arise if the helper is asked to evaluate an individual within that organization for outplacement, career consultation, work-related psychological problems, or for a promotion. The dilemma occurs primarily in regards to ethical standards of the profession as they apply to the organization and to the individual. Human service professionals must be clear as to which standard should be applied first. Spokane (1991) recommended applying the standard to the individual case first and then to the organization, as confidentiality to the individual should be upheld, unless the client has in writing specifically granted the practitioner permission to discuss the case with the employer.

• *Referral.*   Human service professionals should practice only within the realms of their training, knowledge, and competence. When they are faced with clients and situations for which they do not possess the necessary skills, knowledge, and competencies, practitioners should have available for clients a list of diverse professionals (i.e., males and females, ethnic minority psychological and psychiatric professionals, etc.), to whom they can refere these clients. The list should also include some professionals who provide free services or services with sliding-scale fees.

• *Setting Fees.*   A common complaint in regards to setting fees is the practice of charging excessive fees for placement counseling or for assistance without regard for the services that are provided. Some of the career services for which human service professionals may typically bill include career consultation, organizational consultation, testing and scoring, on-site counseling, program evaluation, manuscript evaluation, supervision for interns or for trainees, videotaped mock interviews, resume preparation, report writing, expert testimony, and other professional activities. Although human service professionals have not stipulated exact fees, many services can be billed at the standard hourly rate for such services.

• *Third-Party Reimbursement.*   Some human service professionals may be licensed social workers or psychologists who are eligible for reimbursement from third-party insurers. Although career interventions are not typically reimbursable, some psychotherapy with a career focus may be reimbursable if the levels of psychic distress, depression, or anxiety call for an integrated approach to career intervention. However, it cannot be stressed enough that human service professionals know the limits of their training and refer clients whose presenting concerns exceed the helper's limits.

Human service professionals are likely to encounter a number of ethical and legal issues during their work. In order to avoid unethical practice in career interventions, helpers must be sensitive to the assumptions underlying their personal values, their client's values, the career interventions model, and the values being disseminated at the national level (Herr & Niles, 1988). What are your ethical values, and how do these values impact the ethical decisions you make?

Knowing Your Ethical Values

Almost every aspect of human behavior is influenced by personal values. *Values* are the intrinsic beliefs and feelings that guide or motivate our actions and attitudes. Values can be ranked in a way that defines what we treasure the most. In regards to decision-making, our values can determine how we will behave in certain situations. However, the terms ethics and values are not interchangeable. Whereas *ethics* are concerned with how a moral person would perform, *values* encompass the various beliefs and attitudes that determine how a person actually behaves. When values pertain to the attitudes and beliefs concerning what is right or wrong, they are referred to as *ethical values*. In other words, ethical values influence an individual's behavior and decision making with regards to what is right and wrong.

Virtually every day we are faced with making decisions that involve ethical values. Making informed, ethical decisions requires that human service professionals know and understand their own ethical value system and how this value system fits with those of an agency and/or a profession.

However, very few individuals stop and analyze their ethical values and the basis for them. Knowledge of one's own ethical value system requires ethical consciousness through deliberate and honest reflection. The Career Development Center at the University of Cincinnati (1997) provides the following questions for assessing your ethical values:

- What kinds of things do you think about when you are trying to determine right and wrong?
- Why do you think about these particular things?
- When you judge that something is right or wrong, what makes you certain about your judgment?
- Can you trace how your ideas of right and wrong have changed over time?
- Have you ever revised an opinion about what is right and wrong? Why?

As you have new experiences, your ethical values will be tested and retested; sometimes you will reaffirm your ethical values and other times you will revise them. Exercising your personal right and responsibility to make ethical choices can be challenging and demanding, as most difficult decisions are. However, making a conscious effort to think about and reflect on the ethical issues at hand before responding to them can serve to improve your ethical decision-making skills (University of Cincinnati, Career Development Center, 1997).

In addition to understand their ethical values, human service professionals must have the knowledge and skills to resolve ethical dilemmas. The following sections will highlight ethical standards for the profession and ethical and legal competencies that helpers should possess when they deliver career interventions. Along with this list, some models of ethical decision-making will be explored.

Ethical Standards

Helping professionals must use ethical principles when they make decisions and adhere to relevant ethical standards in order to increase the probability of performing ethically when they provide career interventions to their clients (Niles & Harris-Bowlsbey, 2005). The National Organization for Human Services adopted a set of ethical standards that govern the work of human service professionals. The American

Counseling Association (ACA) developed a set of general ethical guidelines for the counseling profession. The ACA standards provide a framework for many of the ethical guidelines developed by a number of ACA divisions. Division standards are used in conjunction with ACA guidelines and were created to shed light on unique circumstances that are found in various settings. The National Career Development Association (NCDA), a division of ACA, developed the ethical standards most relevant to providing career interventions. Following are reprints of the Ethical Standards of Human Service Professionals and the National Career Development Association Ethical Standards.

Ethical Standards of Human Service Professionals

The following is a reprint of the "National Organization for Human Services Ethical Standards of Human Service Professionals (Adopted 1996)." with permission from the National Organization for Human Services, Austin, TX.

Preamble

Human services is a profession developing in response to and in anticipation of the direction of human needs and human problems in the late twentieth century. Characterized particularly by an appreciation of human beings in all of their diversity, human services offers assistance to its clients within the context of their community and environment. Human service professionals and those who educate them, regardless of whether they are students, faculty or practitioners, promote and encourage the unique values and characteristics of human services. In so doing human service professionals and educators uphold the integrity and ethics of the profession, partake in constructive criticism of the profession, promote client and community well-being, and enhance their own professional growth.

The ethical guidelines presented are a set of standards of conduct which the human service professionals and educators consider in ethical and professional decision making. It is hoped that these guidelines will be of assistance when human service professionals and educators are challenged by difficult ethical dilemmas. Although ethical codes are not legal documents, they may be used to assist in the adjudication of issues related to ethical human service behavior.

Section I: Standards for Human Service Professionals

Human service professionals function in many ways and carry out many roles. They enter into professional-client relationships with individuals, families, groups and communities who are all referred to as "clients" in these standards. Among their roles are caregiver, case manager, broker, teacher/educator, behavior changer, consultant, outreach professional, mobilizer, advocate, community planner, community change organizer, evaluator and administrator.[1.] The following standards are written with these multifaceted roles in mind.

The Human Service Professional's Responsibility to Clients

Statement 1.   Human service professionals negotiate with clients the purpose, goals, and nature of the helping relationship prior to its onset as well as inform clients of the limitations of the proposed relationship.

Statement 2.   Human service professionals respect the integrity and welfare of the client at all times. Each client is treated with respect, acceptance and dignity.

Statement 3.   Human service professionals protect the client's right to privacy and confidentiality except when such confidentiality would cause harm to the client or others, when agency guidelines state otherwise, or under other stated conditions (e.g., local, state, or federal laws). Professionals inform clients of the limits of confidentiality prior to the onset of the helping relationship.

Statement 4.   If it is suspected that danger or harm may occur to the client or to others as a result of a client's behavior, the human service professional acts in an appropriate and professional manner to protect the safety of those individuals. This may involve seeking consultation, supervision, and/or breaking the confidentiality of the relationship.

Statement 5.   Human service professionals protect the integrity, safety, and security of client records. All written client information that is shared with other professionals, except in the course of professional supervision, must have the client's prior written consent.

Statement 6.   Human service professionals are aware that in their relationships with clients power and status are unequal. Therefore they recognize that dual or multiple relationships may increase the risk of harm to, or exploitation of, clients, and may impair their professional judgment. However, in some communities and situations it may not be feasible to avoid social or other nonprofessional contact with clients. Human service professionals support the trust implicit in the helping relationship by avoiding dual relationships that may impair professional judgment, increase the risk of harm to clients or lead to exploitation.

Statement 7.   Sexual relationships with current clients are not considered to be in the best interest of the client and are prohibited. Sexual relationships with previous clients are considered dual relationships and are addressed in Statement 6.

Statement 8.   The client's right to self-determination is protected by human service professionals. They recognize the client's right to receive or refuse services.

Statement 9.   Human service professionals recognize and build on client strengths.

The Human Service Professional's Responsibility to the Community and Society

Statement 10.   Human service professionals are aware of local, state, and federal laws. They advocate for change in regulations and statutes when such legislation conflicts with ethical guidelines and/or client rights. Where laws are harmful to individuals, groups, or communities, human service professionals consider the conflict between the values of obeying the law and the values of serving people and may decide to initiate social action.

Statement 11. Human service professionals keep informed about current social issues as they affect the client and the community. They share that information with clients, groups, and community as part of their work.

Statement 12. Human service professionals understand the complex interaction between individuals, their families, the communities in which they live, and society.

Statement 13. Human service professionals act as advocates in addressing unmet client and community needs. Human service professionals provide a mechanism for identifying unmet client needs, calling attention to these needs, and assisting in planning and mobilizing to advocate for those needs at the local community level.

Statement 14. Human service professionals represent their qualifications to the public accurately.

Statement 15. Human service professionals describe the effectiveness of programs, treatments, and/or techniques accurately.

Statement 16. Human service professionals advocate for the rights of all members of society, particularly those who are members of minorities and groups at which discriminatory practices have historically been directed.

Statement 17. Human service professionals provide services without discrimination or preference based on age, ethnicity, culture, race, disability, gender, religion, sexual orientation or socioeconomic status.

Statement 18. Human service professionals are knowledgeable about the cultures and communities within which they practice. They are aware of multiculturalism in society and its impact on the community as well as individuals within the community. They respect individuals and groups, their cultures and beliefs.

Statement 19. Human service professionals are aware of their own cultural backgrounds, beliefs, and values, recognizing the potential for impact on their relationships with others.

Statement 20. Human service professionals are aware of sociopolitical issues that differentially affect clients from diverse backgrounds.

Statement 21. Human service professionals seek the training, experience, education, and supervision necessary to ensure their effectiveness in working with culturally diverse client populations.

The Human Service Professional's Responsibility to Colleagues

Statement 22. Human service professionals avoid duplicating another professional's helping relationship with a client. They consult with other professionals who are assisting the client in a different type of relationship when it is in the best interest of the client to do so.

Statement 23. When a human service professional has a conflict with a colleague, he or she first seeks out the colleague in an attempt to manage the problem. If necessary, the professional then seeks the assistance of supervisors, consultants or other professionals in efforts to manage the problem.

Statement 24. Human service professionals respond appropriately to unethical behavior of colleagues. Usually this means initially talking directly with the colleague and, if no resolution is forthcoming, reporting the colleague's behavior to supervisory or administrative staff and/or to the Professional organization(s) to which the colleague belongs.

Statement 25.   All consultations between human service professionals are kept confidential unless to do so would result in harm to clients or communities.

The Human Service Professional's Responsibility to the Profession

Statement 26.   Human service professionals know the limit and scope of their professional knowledge and offer services only within their knowledge and skill base.

Statement 27.   Human service professionals seek appropriate consultation and supervision to assist in decision-making when there are legal, ethical or other dilemmas.

Statement 28.   Human service professionals act with integrity, honesty, genuineness, and objectivity.

Statement 29.   Human service professionals promote cooperation among related disciplines (e.g., psychology, counseling, social work, nursing, family and consumer sciences, medicine, education) to foster professional growth and interests within the various fields.

Statement 30.   Human service professionals promote the continuing development of their profession. They encourage membership in professional associations, support research endeavors, foster educational advancement, advocate for appropriate legislative actions, and participate in other related professional activities.

Statement 31.   Human service professionals continually seek out new and effective approaches to enhance their professional abilities.

The Human Service Professional's Responsibility to Employers

Statement 32.   Human service professionals adhere to commitments made to their employers.

Statement 33.   Human service professionals participate in efforts to establish and maintain employment conditions which are conducive to high quality client services. They assist in evaluating the effectiveness of the agency through reliable and valid assessment measures.

Statement 34.   When a conflict arises between fulfilling the responsibility to the employer and the responsibility to the client, human service professionals advise both of the conflict and work conjointly with all involved to manage the conflict.

The Human Service Professional's Responsibility to Self

Statement 35.   Human service professionals strive to personify those characteristics typically associated with the profession (e.g., accountability, respect for others, genuineness, empathy, pragmatism).

Statement 36.   Human service professionals foster self-awareness and personal growth in themselves. They recognize that when professionals are aware of their own values, attitudes, cultural background, and personal needs, the process of helping others is less likely to be negatively impacted by those factors.

Statement 37. Human service professionals recognize a commitment to life-long learning and continually upgrade knowledge and skills to serve the populations better.

Section II: Standards for Human Service Educators

Human Service educators are familiar with, informed by, and accountable to the standards of professional conduct put forth by their institutions of higher learning; their professional disciplines, for example, American Association of University Professors (AAUP), American Counseling Association (ACA), Academy of Criminal Justice Sciences (ACJS), American Psychological Association (APA), American Sociological Association (ASA), National Association of Social Workers (NASW), National Board of Certified Counselors (NBCC), National Education Association (NEA); and the National Organization for Human Services (NOHS).

Statement 38. Human service educators uphold the principle of liberal education and embrace the essence of academic freedom, abstaining from inflicting their own personal views/morals on students, and allowing students the freedom to express their views without penalty, censure or ridicule, and to engage in critical thinking.

Statement 39. Human service educators provide students with readily available and explicit program policies and criteria regarding program goals and objectives, recruitment, admission, course requirements, evaluations, retention and dismissal in accordance with due process procedures.

Statement 40. Human service educators demonstrate high standards of scholarship in content areas and of pedagogy by staying current with developments in the field of Human Services and in teaching effectiveness, for example learning styles and teaching styles.

Statement 41. Human service educators monitor students' field experiences to ensure the quality of the placement site, supervisory experience, and learning experience towards the goals of professional identity and skill development.

Statement 42. Human service educators participate actively in the selection of required readings and use them with care, based strictly on the merits of the material's content, and present relevant information accurately, objectively and fully.

Statement 43. Human service educators, at the onset of courses: inform students if sensitive/controversial issues or experiential/affective content or process are part of the course design; ensure that students are offered opportunities to discuss in structured ways their reactions to sensitive or controversial class content; ensure that the presentation of such material is justified on pedagogical grounds directly related to the course; and, differentiate between information based on scientific data, anecdotal data, and personal opinion.

Statement 44. Human service educators develop and demonstrate culturally sensitive knowledge, awareness, and teaching methodology.

Statement 45. Human service educators demonstrate full commitment to their appointed responsibilities, and are enthusiastic about and encouraging of students' learning.

Statement 46.   Human service educators model the personal attributes, values and skills of the human service professional, including but not limited to, the willingness to seek and respond to feedback from students.

Statement 47.   Human service educators establish and uphold appropriate guidelines concerning self-disclosure or student-disclosure of sensitive/personal information.

Statement 48.   Human service educators establish an appropriate and timely process for providing clear and objective feedback to students about their performance on relevant and established course/program academic and personal competence requirements and their suitability for the field.

Statement 49.   Human service educators are aware that in their relationships with students, power and status are unequal; therefore, human service educators are responsible to clearly define and maintain ethical and professional relationships with students, and avoid conduct that is demeaning, embarrassing or exploitative of students, and to treat students fairly, equally, and without discrimination.

Statement 50.   Human service educators recognize and acknowledge the contributions of students to their work, for example in case material, workshops, research, publications.

Statement 51.   Human service educators demonstrate professional standards of conduct in managing personal or professional differences with colleagues, for example, not disclosing such differences and/or affirming a student's negative opinion of a faculty/program.

Statement 52.   Human service educators ensure that students are familiar with, informed by, and accountable to the ethical standards and policies put forth by their program/department, the course syllabus/instructor, their advisor(s), and the Ethical Standards of Human Service Professionals.

Statement 53.   Human service educators are aware of all relevant curriculum standards, including those of the Council for Standards in Human Services Education (CSHSE); the Community Support Skills Standards; and state/local standards, and take them into consideration in designing the curriculum.

Statement 54.   Human service educators create a learning context in which students can achieve the knowledge, skills, values and attitudes of the academic program.

National Career Development Association Ethical Standards

The following is a reprint of the "National Career Development Associations' Ethical Standards (Revised 2003)" with permission from the National Career Development Association, Tulsa, OK.

These Ethical Standards were developed by the National Board for Certified Counselors (NBCC), an independent, voluntary, not-for-profit organization incorporated in 1982. Titled "Code of Ethics" by NBCC and last amended in February 1987, the Ethical Standards were adopted by the National Career Development Association (NCDA) Board of Directors in 1987 and revised in 1991, with minor changes in wording (e.g., the addition of specific references to NCDA members).

Preamble

NCDA is an educational, scientific, and professional organization dedicated to the enhancement of the worth, dignity, potential, and uniqueness of each individual and, thus, to the service of society. This code of ethics enables the NCDA to clarify the nature of ethical responsibilities for present and future professional career counselors.

Section A: General

NCDA members influence the development of the profession by continuous efforts to improve professional practices, services, and research. Professional growth is continuous through the career counselor's career and is exemplified by the development of a philosophy that explains why and how a career counselor functions in the helping relationship. Career counselors must gather data on their effectiveness and be guided by their findings.

1. NCDA members have a responsibility to the clients they are serving and to the institutions within which the services are being performed. Career counselors also strive to assist the respective agency, organization, or institution in providing the highest caliber of professional services. The acceptance of employment in an institution implies that the career counselor is in agreement with the general policies and principles of the institution. Therefore, the professional activities of the career counselor are in accord with the objectives of the institution. If, despite concerted efforts, the career counselor cannot reach agreement with the employer as to acceptable standards of conduct that allow for changes in institutional policy that are conducive to the positive growth and development of clients, then terminating the affiliation should be seriously considered.

2. Ethical behavior among professional associates (e.g., career counselors) must be expected at all times. When accessible information raises doubt as to the ethical behavior of professional colleagues, the NCDA member must take action to attempt to rectify this condition. Such action uses the respective institution's channels first and then uses procedures established by the American Counseling Association, of which NCDA is a division.

3. NCDA members neither claim nor imply professional qualifications which exceed those possessed, and are responsible for correcting any misrepresentations of these qualifications by others.

4. NCDA members must refuse a private fee or other remuneration for consultation or counseling with persons who are entitled to their services through the career counselor's employing institution or agency. The policies of some agencies may make explicit provisions for staff members to engage in private practice with agency clients. However, should agency clients desire private counseling or consulting services, they must be apprised of other options available to them. Career counselors must not divert to their private practices, legitimate clients in their primary agencies or of the institutions with which they are affiliated.

5. In establishing fees for professional counseling services, NCDA members must consider the financial status of clients and the respective locality. In the event that the established fee status is inappropriate for the client, assistance must be provided in finding comparable services of acceptable cost.

6. NCDA members seek only those positions in the delivery of professional services for which they are professionally qualified.

7. NCDA members recognize their limitations and provide services or only use techniques for which they are qualified by training and/or experience. Career counselors recognize the need, and seek continuing education, to assure competent services.

8. NCDA members are aware of the intimacy in the counseling relationship, maintain respect for the client, and avoid engaging in activities that seek to meet their personal needs at the expense of the client.

9. NCDA members do not condone or engage in sexual harassment which is defined as deliberate or repeated comments, gestures, or physical contacts of a sexual nature.

10. NCDA members avoid bringing their personal or professional issues into the counseling relationship. Through an awareness of the impact of stereotyping and discrimination (e.g., biases based on age, disability, ethnicity, gender, race, religion, or sexual preference), career counselors guard the individual rights and personal dignity of the client in the counseling relationship.

11. NCDA members are accountable at all times for their behavior. They must be aware that all actions and behaviors of a counselor reflect on professional integrity and, when inappropriate, can damage the public trust in the counseling profession. To protect public confidence in the counseling profession, career counselors avoid public behavior that is clearly in violation of accepted moral and legal standards.

12. NCDA members have a social responsibility because their recommendations and professional actions may alter the lives of others. Career counselors remain fully cognizant of their impact and are alert to personal, social, organizational, financial, or political situations or pressures which might lead to misuse of their influence.

13. Products or services provided by NCDA members by means of classroom instruction, public lectures, demonstrations, written articles, radio or television programs, or other types of media must meet the criteria cited in Sections A through F of these Ethical Standards.

Section B: Counseling Relationship

1. The primary obligation of NCDA members is to respect the integrity and promote the welfare of the client, regardless of whether the client is assisted individually or in a group relationship. In a group setting, the career counselor is also responsible for taking reasonable precautions to protect individuals from physical and/or psychological trauma resulting from interaction within the group.

2. The counseling relationship and information resulting from it remains confidential, consistent with the legal obligations of the NCDA member. In a group counseling setting, the career counselor sets a norm of confidentiality regarding all group participants' disclosures.

3. NCDA members know and take into account the traditions and practices of other professional groups with whom they work, and they cooperate fully with such groups. If a person is receiving similar services from another professional, career counselors do not offer their own services directly to such a person. If a career counselor is contacted by a person who is already receiving similar services from another professional, the career counselor carefully considers that professional relationship and proceeds with caution and sensitivity to the therapeutic issues as well as the client's welfare. Career counselors discuss these issues with clients so as to minimize the risk of confusion and conflict.

4. When a client's condition indicates that there is a clear and imminent danger to the client or others, the NCDA member must take reasonable personal action or inform responsible authorities. Consultation with other professionals must be used where possible. The assumption of responsibility for the client's behavior must be taken only after careful deliberation, and the client must be involved in the resumption of responsibility as quickly as possible.

5. Records of the counseling relationship, including interview notes, test data, correspondence, audio or visual tape recordings, electronic data storage, and other documents are to be considered professional information for use in counseling. They should not be considered a part of the records of the institution or agency in which the NCDA member is employed unless specified by state statute or regulation. Revelation to others of counseling material must occur only upon the expressed consent of the client; career counselors must make provisions for maintaining confidentiality in the storage and disposal of records. Career counselors providing information to the public or to subordinates, peers, or supervisors have a responsibility to ensure that the content is general; unidentified client information should be accurate and unbiased, and should consist of objective, factual data.

6. NCDA members must ensure that data maintained in electronic storage are secure. The data must be limited to information that is appropriate and necessary for the services being provided and accessible only to appropriate staff members involved in the provision of services by using the best computer security methods available. Career counselors must also ensure that electronically stored data are destroyed when the information is no longer of value in providing services.

7. Data derived from a counseling relationship for use in counselor training or research shall be confined to content that can be disguised to ensure full protection of the identity of the subject/client and shall be obtained with informed consent.

8. NCDA members must inform clients, before or at the time the counseling relationship commences, of the purposes, goals, techniques, rules and procedures, and limitations that may affect the relationship.

9. All methods of treatment by NCDA members must be clearly indicated to prospective recipients and safety precautions must be taken in their use.

10. NCDA members who have an administrative, supervisory, and/or evaluative relationship with individuals seeking counseling services must not serve as the counselor and should refer the individuals to other professionals. Exceptions are made only in instances where an individual's situation warrants counseling intervention and another alternative is unavailable. Dual relationships with clients that might impair the career counselor's objectivity and professional judgment must be avoided and/or the counseling relationship terminated through referral to another competent professional.

11. When NCDA members determine an inability to be of professional assistance to a potential or existing client, they must, respectively, not initiate the counseling relationship or immediately terminate the relationship. In either event, the career counselor must suggest appropriate alternatives. Career counselors must be knowledgeable about referral resources so that a satisfactory referral can be initiated. In the event that the client declines a suggested referral, the career counselor is not obligated to continue the relationship.

12. NCDA members may choose to consult with any other professionally competent person about a client and must notify clients of this right. Career counselors must avoid placing a consultant in a conflict-of-interest situation that would preclude the consultant's being a proper party to the career counselor's efforts to help the client.

13. NCDA members who counsel clients from cultures different from their own must gain knowledge, personal awareness, and sensitivity pertinent to the client populations served and must incorporate culturally relevant techniques into their practice.

14. When NCDA members engage in intensive counseling with a client, the client's counseling needs should be assessed. When needs exist outside the counselor's expertise, appropriate referrals should be made.

15. NCDA members must screen prospective group counseling participants, especially when the emphasis is on self-understanding and growth through self-disclosure. Career counselors must maintain an awareness of each group participant's welfare throughout the group process.

16. When electronic data and systems are used as a component of counseling services, NCDA members must ensure that the computer application, and any information it contains, is appropriate for the respective needs of clients and is nondiscriminatory. Career counselors must ensure that they themselves have acquired a facilitation level of knowledge with any system they use including hands-on application, search experience, and understanding of the uses of all aspects of the computer-based system. In selecting and/or maintaining computer-based systems that contain career information, career counselors must ensure that the systems provide current, accurate, and locally relevant information. Career counselors must also ensure that clients are intellectually, emotionally, and physically compatible with the use of the computer application and understand its purpose and operation. Client use of a computer application must be evaluated to correct possible problems and assess subsequent needs.

17. NCDA members who develop self-help, stand-alone computer software for use by the general public, must first ensure that it is initially designed to function in a stand-alone manner, as opposed to modifying software that was originally designed to require support from a counselor. Secondly, the software must include program statements that provide the user with intended outcomes, suggestions for using the software, descriptions of inappropriately used applications, and descriptions of when and how counseling services might be beneficial. Finally, the manual must include the qualifications of the developer, the development process, validation data, and operating procedures.

Section C: Measurement and Evaluation

1. NCDA members must provide specific orientation or information to an examinee prior to and following the administration of assessment instruments or techniques so that the results may be placed in proper perspective with other relevant factors. The purpose of testing and the explicit use of the results must be made known to an examinee prior to testing.

2. In selecting assessment instruments or techniques for use in a given situation or with a particular client, NCDA members must evaluate carefully the instrument's specific theoretical bases and characteristics, validity, reliability, and appropriateness. Career counselors are professionally responsible for using unvalidated information with special care.

3. When making statements to the public about assessment instruments or techniques, NCDA members must provide accurate information and avoid false claims or misconceptions concerning the meaning of psychometric terms. Special efforts are often required to avoid unwarranted connotations of terms such as IQ and grade-equivalent scores.

4. Because many types of assessment techniques exist, NCDA members must recognize the limits of their competence and perform only those functions for which they have received appropriate training.

5. NCDA members must note when tests are not administered under standard conditions or when unusual behavior or irregularities occur during a testing session and the results must be designated as invalid or of questionable validity. Unsupervised or inadequately supervised assessments, such as mail-in tests, are considered unethical.

However, the use of standardized instruments that are designed to be self-administered and self-scored, such as interest inventories, is appropriate.

6. Because prior coaching or dissemination of test materials can invalidate test results, NCDA members are professionally obligated to maintain test security. In addition, conditions that produce most favorable test results must be made known to an examinee (e.g., penalty for guessing).

7. NCDA members must consider psychometric limitations when selecting and using an instrument, and must be cognizant of the limitations when interpreting the results. When tests are used to classify clients, career counselors must ensure that periodic review and/or re-testing are conducted to prevent client stereotyping.

8. An examinee's welfare, explicit prior understanding, and agreement are the factors used when determining who receives the test results. NCDA members must see that appropriate interpretation accompanies any release of individual or group test data (e.g., limitations of instrument and norms).

9. NCDA members must ensure that computer-generated assessment administration and scoring programs function properly, thereby providing clients with accurate assessment results.

10. NCDA members who are responsible for making decisions based on assessment results, must have appropriate training and skills in educational and psychological measurement—including validation criteria, test research, and guidelines for test development and use.

11. NCDA members must be cautious when interpreting the results of instruments that possess insufficient technical data, and must explicitly state to examinees the specific purposes for the use of such instruments.

12. NCDA members must proceed with caution when attempting to evaluate and interpret performances of minority group members or other persons who are not represented in the norm group on which the instrument was standardized.

13. NCDA members who develop computer-based interpretations to support the assessment process must ensure that the validity of the interpretations is established prior to the commercial distribution of the computer application.

14. NCDA members recognize that test results may become obsolete, and avoid the misuse of obsolete data.

15. NCDA members must avoid the appropriation, reproduction, or modification of published tests or parts thereof without acknowledgment and permission from the publisher.

Section D: Research and Publication

1. NCDA members will adhere to relevant guidelines on research with human subjects. These include:

    a. Code of Federal Regulations, Title 45, Subtitle A, Part 46, as currently issued.

    b. American Psychological Association. (1982). Ethical principles in the conduct of research with human participants. Washington, DC: Author.

    c. American Psychological Association. (1981). Research with human participants. *American Psychologist, 36,* 633–638.

    d. Family Educational Rights and Privacy Act. (Buckley Amendment to P. L. 93–380 of the Laws of 1974).

    e. Current federal regulations and various state privacy acts.

    2. In planning research activities involving human subjects, NCDA members must be aware of and responsive to all pertinent ethical principles and ensure that the research problem, design, and execution are in full compliance with the principles.

    3. The ultimate responsibility for ethical research lies with the principal researcher, although others involved in research activities are ethically obligated and responsible for their own actions.

    4. NCDA members who conduct research with human subjects are responsible for the subjects' welfare throughout the experiment and must take all reasonable precautions to avoid causing injurious psychological, physical, or social effects on their subjects.

    5. NCDA members who conduct research must abide by the following basic elements of informed consent:

    a. A fair explanation of the procedures to be followed, including an identification of those which are experimental.

    b. A description of the attendant discomforts and risks.

    c. A description of the benefits to be expected.

    d. A disclosure of appropriate alternative procedures that would be advantageous for subjects.

    e. An offer to answer any inquiries concerning the procedures.

    f. An instruction that subjects are free to withdraw their consent and to discontinue participation in the project or activity at any time.

    6. When reporting research results, explicit mention must be made of all the variables and conditions known to the NCDA member that may have affected the outcome of the study or the interpretation of the data.

    7. NCDA members who conduct and report research investigations must do so in a manner that minimizes the possibility that the results will be misleading.

    8. NCDA members are obligated to make available sufficient original research data to qualified others who may wish to replicate the study.

    9. NCDA members who supply data, aid in the research of another person, report research results, or make original data available, must take due care to disguise the identity of respective subjects in the absence of specific authorization from the subject to do otherwise.

10. When conducting and reporting research, NCDA members must be familiar with, and give recognition to, previous work on the topic, must observe all copyright laws, and must follow the principles of giving full credit to those to whom credit is due.

11. NCDA members must give due credit through joint authorship, acknowledgment, footnote statements, or other appropriate means to those who have contributed significantly to the research and/or publication, in accordance with such contributions.

12. NCDA members should communicate to others the results of any research judged to be of professional value. Results that reflect unfavorably on institutions, programs, services, or vested interests must not be withheld.

13. NCDA members who agree to cooperate with another individual in research and/or publication incur an obligation to cooperate as promised in terms of punctuality of performance and with full regard to the completeness and accuracy of the information required.

14. NCDA members must not submit the same manuscript, or one essentially similar in content, for simultaneous publication consideration by two or more journals. In addition, manuscripts that are published in whole or substantial part in another journal or published work should not be submitted for publication without acknowledgment and permission from the previous publication.

Section E: Consulting

Consultation refers to a voluntary relationship between a professional helper and help-needing individual, group, or social unit in which the consultant is providing help to the client(s) in defining and solving a work-related problem or potential work-related problem with a client or client system.

1. NCDA members acting as consultants must have a high degree of self-awareness of their own values, knowledge, skills, limitations, and needs in entering a helping relationship that involves human and/or organizational change. The focus of the consulting relationship must be on the issues to be resolved and not on the person(s) presenting the problem.

2. In the consulting relationship, the NCDA member and client must understand and agree upon the problem definition, subsequent goals, and predicted consequences of interventions selected.

3. NCDA members must be reasonably certain that they, or the organization represented, have the necessary competencies and resources for giving the kind of help that is needed or that may develop later, and that appropriate referral resources are available to the consultant.

4. NCDA members in a consulting relationship must encourage and cultivate client adaptability and growth toward self-direction. NCDA members must maintain this role consistently and not become a decision maker for clients or create a future dependency on the consultant.

5. NCDA members conscientiously adhere to the NCDA Ethical Standards when announcing consultant availability for services.

Section F: Private Practice

1. NCDA members should assist the profession by facilitating the availability of counseling services in private as well as public settings.

2. In advertising services as private practitioners, NCDA members must advertise in a manner that accurately informs the public of the professional services, expertise, and counseling techniques available.

3. NCDA members who assume an executive leadership role in a private practice organization do not permit their names to be used in professional notices during periods of time when they are not actively engaged in the private practice of counseling.

4. NCDA members may list their highest relevant degree, type, and level of certification and/or license, address, telephone number, office hours, type and/or description of services, and other relevant information. Listed information must not contain false, inaccurate, misleading, partial, out-of-context, or otherwise deceptive material or statements.

5. NCDA members who are involved in a partnership or corporation with other professionals must, in compliance with the regulations of the locality, clearly specify the separate specialties of each member of the partnership or corporation.

6. NCDA members have an obligation to withdraw from a private-practice counseling relationship if it violates the NCDA Ethical Standards; if the mental or physical condition of the NCDA member renders it difficult to carry out an effective professional relationship; or if the counseling relationship is no longer productive for the client.

Procedures for Processing Ethical Complaints

As a division of the American Counseling Association (ACA) the National Career Development Association (NCDA) adheres to the guidelines and procedures for processing ethical complaints and the disciplinary sanctions adopted by ACA. A complaint against an NCDA member may be filed by any individual or group of individuals ("complainant"), whether or not the complainant is a member of NCDA. Action will not be taken on anonymous complaints.

For specifics on how to file ethical complaints and a description of the guidelines and procedures for processing complaints, contact:

ACA Ethics Committee
c/o Executive Director
American Counseling Association
5999 Stevenson Avenue
Alexandria, VA 22304
(800) 347-6647

Ethical Decision-Making Competencies, Models, and Influences

Isaacson and Brown (2000) developed a list of ethical and legal competencies that helpers should possess when providing career counseling interventions. Although these guidelines were developed primarily for career counselors, human service professionals can easily adapt the information to meet their particular needs in providing career interventions to their clients. According to Isaacson and Brown (2000), practitioners should demonstrate:

- Knowledge about the code of ethical standards of the American Counseling Association (ACA), the National Career Development Association (NCDA), the Council for Accreditation of Counseling and Related Educational Programs (CACREP), and other relevant professional organizations (i.e., National Organization for Human Services)
- Knowledge about current ethical and legal issues that impact the practice of providing career interventions
- Knowledge about ethical issues related to career interventions with minority groups including women, ethnic minorities, immigrants, individuals with disabilities, and the elderly
- Knowledge about current ethical and legal issues related to the use of computer-assisted career guidance
- Skill in applying ethical standards to career interventions, consultations, issues, and practices
- Skill in identifying situations involving the interpretation of ethical standards and the capacity to consult with supervisors and colleagues to determine appropriate and ethical courses of action
- Knowledge of state and federal laws relating to client confidentiality

Demonstrating knowledge in these areas is only one component of ethical decision-making. Human service professionals must also have knowledge of ethical decision-making models and of the influences to ethical decision-making. Only after helpers possess this knowledge, can they competently develop skills in applying this information to the ethical decision-making process. A number of approaches to solving ethical dilemmas exist.

We have highlighted two approaches to ethical decision-making. The first approach is an eight-step model developed by Corey, Corey, and Callanan (2002). The second approach, developed by Velasquez, Andre, Shanks, and Meyer (1996) demonstrates how values can be used in ethical decision-making. Following the discussion of these models, we address developmental influences on ethical decision-making.

Solving Ethical Dilemmas by Using an Eight-Step Model to Ethical Decision-Making

Sometimes the human service professional will find helpful a framework for analyzing and making ethical decisions. Corey, Corey, and Callanan (2002) developed a pragmatic, comprehensive approach to ethical decision making. Their eight-step approach follows:

Step 1: Identify the problem.
Step 2: Identify the potential issues involved.
Step 3: Review relevant ethical guidelines.
Step 4: Know relevant laws and regulations.
Step 5: Obtain consultation.
Step 6: Consider possible and probable courses of action.
Step 7: List the consequences of the probable courses of action.
Step 8: Decide on what appears to be the best course of action.

The model of Corey and colleagues underscores a practical, matter-of-fact approach to solving ethical dilemmas. The next model focuses on moral principles by appealing to values when resolving ethical conflicts.

Solving Ethical Dilemmas by Appealing to Values

According to Velasquez and associates (1996), the first step in solving an ethical dilemma is to get all the facts. Although an obvious step, it is often overlooked. Facts are important; they tell us what *is*. However, facts alone are not enough, and resolving an ethical issue also requires an appeal to values. In other words, we must also decide what *ought* to be. According to this model, once individuals ascertain facts, they must ask the following questions when trying to resolve ethical dilemmas:

- What benefits and what harms will each course of action produce, and which alternative will lead to the best overall consequences?
- What moral rights do the affected parties have, and which course of action best respects those rights?
- Which course of action treats everyone the same, except where there is a morally justifiable reason not to, or does not show favoritism or discrimination?
- Which course of action advances the common good?
- Which course of action develops moral virtues?

This method of ethical decision-making used to help identify the most important ethical considerations is not meant to provide an automatic solution to moral and ethical problems. Models of ethical decision making can be helpful to human service professionals faced with solving ethical dilemmas; however, much evidence supports the notion that the ability to make good ethical decisions may be influenced by the helper's level of ethical, moral and cognitive development (Neukrug, 2003). In the next section we will examine developmental influences on ethical decision-making.

Influences on Ethical Decision-Making

Developmental models of ethical decision-making focus on the influence that an individual's level of ethical, moral, and cognitive development has on the decision-making process. According to this view, lower-level thought tends to be characterized by dualistic (i.e., right vs. wrong), oversimplified, and rigid thinking when making ethical decisions. Conversely, higher-level thought tends to be more flexible, adaptable, complex, and more sensitive to the situation at hand (Cottone, 2001; Kohlberg, 1984; McAuliffe, Eriksen, & Associates, 2000; Neukrug, 2003; Pascarella & Terenzini, 1991). In other words, human service professionals with lower-level thought processes rigidly use the ethical standards to get the "right answer." They view authorities as having the answers and would unlikely recognize multiple alternatives or opinions. On the other hand, human service professionals with higher-level thought processes use the ethical standards as guidelines as opposed to using the codes as rigid rules. Higher-level thinkers take into account the circumstances surrounding the dilemma while utilizing a very reflective, decision-making process. This process would likely incorporate multiple alternatives or opinions. Both levels of thinkers may employ the same models of ethical decision-making. However, the approach the individuals would take in applying the models would be noticeably different even though they may both come to the same decision (Neukrug, 2003).

An Exercise in Ethical Decision-Making: Carmelita

To better illustrate how models of ethical decision-making and developmental variables influence the decision-making process, revisit the case of Carmelita on page 451, and respond to the question that we posed to you: What is the ethical thing for you to do? To help guide you through this process, it may be useful to answer the following questions that were developed by the Career Development Center at the University of Cincinnati (1997) p. 148.

- What are the practical considerations in this situation, for you and for others? *(Practical issues include risks, legal issues, and positive or negative consequences.)*
- What are the ethical dimensions of this situation? *(Ethical dimensions include things such as upholding or violating professional standards, judgments about what is right or wrong, and assessing your moral responsibility in a situation.)*
- Are there any conflicts between the practical issues and the ethical dimensions of this situation from your perspective?
- Are there any conflicts within the ethical dimensions from your perspective?
- What is the minimal action your values require of you in this situation?
- What supports or encourages an ethical action on your part?
- What prevents or works against an ethical action on your part?

No rules govern the way you should go about making ethical decisions. As you have new experiences, your values and your views will be tested and retested. At times you will reaffirm your stance, and at other times you may revise your ethical views. The major point is to possess the knowledge, competencies, and skills to make conscious, deliberate, and ethical decisions.

A discussion on ethics would not be complete without making this additional, important point. According to the research literature, most helpers are poorly informed about legal precedents and may use instinctual ethical values to guide their behavior in such situations. When ethical-legal conflicts occur, human service professionals should consult with a supervisor or colleague, seek legal counsel, and/or call the professional association that guides the profession. Although standards endorsed by professional associations are helpful in regard to ethical dilemmas, they are not necessarily helpful in regards to legal issues (Spokane, 1991).

Summary

Working through the ethical decision-making process requires an honest reflection of values and a complex combination of knowledge and skills. Human service professionals must have a keen understanding of the ethical codes of conduct that govern the profession as well as knowledge of the various decision-making models and developmental influences that impact decision-making. Possessing these skills and competencies will raise the helper's ethical consciousness thereby allowing him or her to make sound, ethical decisions.

Key Terms

Ethical

Ethical standards

Ethics

Legal

Moral

Web Resources

Note that website URLs may change over time.

Ethical Standards of Human Service Professionals
http://www.nohse.org/ethics.html

Markkula Center for Applied Ethics
http://www.scu.edu/ethics

National Career Development Association Ethical Standards
http://www.ncda.org/pdf/EthicalStandards.pdf

20

Workplace Issues for the 21st Century

Introduction

As with many workers, human service professionals often find it difficult to balance their roles as employees, parents, spouses, partners, students, and caregivers. Trying to balance work with family and personal needs can take a toll on all of us, and the stress can lead to absenteeism, declined job satisfaction, lower rates of workplace morale, and reduced satisfaction with family life. Diversity, workplace safety, supervision, and technology in the human service profession are other workplace issues applicable to the helping professional. In this final chapter we will address these topics and provide tips and strategies for effectively managing the many issues that impact the workplace of the human service professional.

Balancing It All

There are many outdated assumptions regarding the typical family, the 40-hour work-week, and the dispersion of domestic responsibilities among family members. Gone are the days when the typical family consisted of a full-time breadwinner (traditionally the male) and a stay-at-home spouse (traditionally the female) who was primarily responsible for the domestic tasks and childcare. In today's world, the traditional family structure has been replaced with a multitude of complex family structures ranging from single parent households, to **DINK**, to the **sandwich generation** (i.e., individuals who are sandwiched between their aging parents who need assistance and their own children). In addition, many mothers work outside the home out of economic necessity. These changes in family structure coupled with economic necessities have resulted in American workers reporting increased levels of stress (Knobloch-Fedders & Gorvine, 2003). The "balancing act" consists of balancing your career, your health, and your relationships.

Career

There are a number of factors related to career that contribute to an effective balance between career and personal life and family. According to Knobloch-Fedders and Gorvine (2003), individuals who work more than 45 hours per week tend to experience more conflict between work and family. Still, individuals who work less than 20 hours per week sometimes garner fewer benefits from their multiple roles—working less than 20 hours per week does not seem to result in improved physical health and marital satisfaction. Working between 20 and 45 hours per week tends to produce less conflict between work and family.

Along with the actual amount of hours spent each week at the workplace, scheduling also impacts employee satisfaction with work and family. When the work schedule is flexible and fits well with the individual's preferences, conflict between work and family tends to lesson and **burnout** is likely to decrease (Knobloch-Fedders & Gorvine, 2003). Many employers who recognize labor-market changes and the prospect of labor shortages have used flexible scheduling as a drawing card to secure workers. Such employers recognize that allowing employees the flexibility they need to balance their work with their family and personal lives can earn the organization long-term loyalty (JobQuality.ca, 2004).

Finally, workers' decision-making tends to impact the balance between work and family. When workers have control over decision-making as part of their jobs, they report healthier family relationships and less burnout (Knobloch-Fedders & Gorvine, 2003).

Although the balancing act between work and personal life can produce time pressures, family and work conflicts, and feelings of guilt, when the balance is done successfully, many benefits exist. For example, some people who perform multiple roles (caregiver, parent, worker, student, spouse, and partner) report greater levels of relationship satisfaction, physical health, and well-being. For dual-career couples (i.e., two-career couples), research has shown that positive involvement with the family offered protection from distress when their jobs became difficult. In addition, family members who consider work important tend to be more supportive of the other family member's need to balance work and family life (Knobloch-Fedders & Gorvine, 2003). To enhance the balance between work and family, dual-career couples should coordinate domestic and child care responsibilities and develop a schedule to spend free time together as well as individually. Other strategies include to get household help if you can afford it, lower your expectations of how clean and orderly your home should be, deal with problems as they happen, talk at regularly scheduled intervals and share your feelings, and be prepared to periodically evaluate both the career and the relationship (University of Cincinnati, Career Development Center, 1997).

Health

If you do not have your health, what do you have? It is quite apparent that health plays a vital role in the workplace. Employers are recognizing that absenteeism and the growing cost of health benefits can hurt the productivity and bottom line of any organization. Therefore, many organizations are requiring preemployment physicals and drug testing of new and current employees. In addition, many organizations are looking for ways to improve the health of their employees. Some businesses have established recreational centers for their employees and are offering special classes and courses to enhance their employees' physical and mental well-being. On another note, employers are also concerned with two factors that impact performance—weight and smoking. Some organizations are restricting their hiring to nonsmokers because studies have indicated that there is a significant relationship between smoking and absenteeism due to illness. In regards to weight, some organizations offer incentive programs to employees to lose and keep off the weight (University of Cincinnati, Career Development Center, 1997). It is quite clear that organizations are taking the health of their employees very seriously. Human service professionals should take note and recognize the importance of taking care of their health needs.

Relationships

For most individuals, maintaining social relationships is extremely important. Human beings need attachments, friends to confide in, and people to make them feel special. The balancing act can be enhanced through supportive social relationships, both inside and outside of work. According to Knobloch-Fedders and Gorvine (2003), workers who report supportive, friendly relationships with their colleagues tend to be more satisfied with their jobs and more able to maintain appropriate balance between their personal life and work. In addition support from family and friends outside of work tends to increase satisfaction with the family and with childcare decisions. This point is an extremely important one. Some people make decisions to reduce the amount of time they spend developing their social relationships in order to meet the demands of work and family. This strategy actually increases work-family conflict. People find sustaining happiness difficult if they are only living to go to work and return home each day. In other words, a lack of social relationships can actually hurt your job performance.

Diversity

Diversity means different. *Diversity* in the workplace means understanding and appreciating that which is different in every human being within the organization. Technological skills and communication skills have always been valued in the workplace. But competence to communicate and work effectively with people from diverse backgrounds, whether they are clients, colleagues, supervisors, or subordinates, is a qualification that many organizations prize. In fact, organizations are revising their agendas by giving priority to identifying and incorporating diverse people, perspectives, and skills into the workplace (University of Cincinnati, Career Development Center, 1997). Human service professionals must recognize the unique contributions that people with a variety of backgrounds, value systems, and perspectives make. As agencies and the clients they serve become more diverse, helpers will need to understand and relate to people who have different cultures, different values, and different styles of communication. Human service professionals need to be multiculturally competent. Multicultural skills are essential for a number of reasons, including client retention and enhanced treatment outcomes. Research has shown that when helpers practice multiculturalism, clients feel more understood and respected and positive treatment outcomes significantly improve (Obiakor & Schwenn, 1995; Zang & Dixon, 2001). The human service professional who can demonstrate these skills will be highly sought after; and those without these skills will be at a competitive disadvantage.

Workplace Safety

For many years human service professionals have faced a significant risk of job-related violence. Physical assaults represent a serious health and safety hazard within the human service industry. Not all assaults can be prevented, however, many can. In addition the severity of injuries sustained by employees can be reduced. Following is an overview of workplace violence in the human service profession as well as some strategies and tips for preventing and dealing with workplace violence.

Workplace Violence

Workplace violence includes any act of physical violence, threats of physical violence, intimidation, **harassment** including **sexual harassment,** or other disruptive or threatening behavior that occurs in the workplace. Violence in the workplace is an extremely serious health and safety issue. In its most severe form, homicide is the third-leading cause of fatal occupational injury in the United States. In 2001 there were 639 workplace homicides in the United States out of a total of 8,786 fatal work injuries. Workplace violence in the helping profession tends to differ from workplace violence in general. In other work settings such as retail establishments and taxicabs, violence is often related to robbery. In the human service settings, violence usually results from clients and sometimes from their family members who feel vulnerable, frustrated, and out of control. The Bureau of Labor Statistics (BLS) reported that there were 69 homicides in health services from 1996 to 2000. Although workplace violence resulting in homicides attracts most of the media's attention, the vast majority of workplace violence consists of nonfatal attacks. In 2000, 48 percent of all nonfatal injuries from occupational assaults and acts of violence in the workplace occurred in health care in the social services (Occupational Safety and Health Administration, 2004). Risks for violence in the workplace for human service professionals stem from several common factors (Department of Health and Human Services, Centers for Disease Control and Prevention, and the National Institute for Occupational Safety and Health, 2002; Occupational Safety and Health Administration, 2004):

- Working directly with volatile people, especially if they are under the influence of drugs or alcohol and/or have certain psychotic diagnosis or a history of violence
- The increasing number of people with acute and chronic mental illness being released from hospitals without follow-up care

- Working when understaffed, especially during times of high activity such as meal times, visiting hours, and when transporting clients
- The prevalence of handguns and other weapons among clients, family members, or their friends
- The availability of drugs or money at hospitals and clinics, making them likely robbery targets
- The increasing prevalence of gang members, drug or alcohol abusers, trauma patients, and distraught family members
- Long waits for service
- Working alone, often in remote areas with no backup or way to get help
- Poor environmental design
- Inadequate security
- Lack of staff training and policies for preventing and managing crises with potentially volatile patients
- Alcohol and drug abuse
- Access to firearms
- Unrestricted movement of the public
- Poorly lit rooms, corridors, parking lots, and other areas

In order to prevent violence in the workplace agencies should follow some general prevention strategies (Department of Health and Human Services, Centers for Disease Control and Prevention, & National Institute for Occupational Safety and Health, 2002; Occupational Safety and Health Administration, 2004):

- Create and disseminate a clear policy of zero tolerance for workplace violence, verbal and nonverbal threats, and related actions. Ensure that all workers, clients, and visitors are aware of this policy.
- Develop a comprehensive plan for maintaining security in the workplace. The plan should include establishing a liaison with law enforcement representatives and others who can help identify ways to prevent and alleviate workplace violence.
- Encourage employees to promptly report violent incidents and suggest ways to reduce or eliminate risks. Require records of all incidences to evaluate risks and to measure progress.
- Ensure that employees who report or experience workplace violence do not face retaliation.
- Develop emergency signaling, alarms, and monitoring systems. Install security devices such as cameras.
- Provide security escorts to parking lots at night.
- Design waiting areas to accommodate clients and family members who may have a long wait.
- Design staffing patterns to prevent staff from working alone.
- Provide workers with training to recognize and manage assaults and manage conflict.

In addition to the prevention strategies suggested for agencies, human service professionals should take the following precautions at the workplace (Department of

Health and Human Services, Centers for Disease Control and Prevention, & National Institute for Occupational Safety and Health, 2002):

- Evaluate each situation for potential violence whenever you enter a room or begin to relate to a client or family member.
- Be attentive and vigilant throughout the encounter.
- Do not isolate yourself with a potentially violent individual.
- Always maintain an open path for exiting between you and the potentially violent person. Do not let the person stand between you and the door.

When faced with impending violence, the human service professional should maintain behavior that diffuses the anger. Some suggestions include (Department of Health and Human Services, Centers for Disease Control and Prevention, & National Institute for Occupational Safety and Health (2002):

- Presenting a calm and caring attitude
- Refraining from matching the threats
- Acknowledging the person's feelings
- Avoiding behavior that may be interpreted as aggressive
- Refraining from giving orders

Despite the best prevention strategy, violence may still occur. Therefore agencies should be prepared to deal with such violence by promoting open communication and by developing written procedures for responding to and reporting acts of violence. In cases where the helping professional is threatened or assaulted, employers should offer and encourage counseling (Department of Health and Human Services, Centers for Disease Control and Prevention, & National Institute for Occupational Safety and Health, 2002).

Supervision

Human service professionals will likely find themselves in a supervisee role, a supervisor role, or in both roles simultaneously. Supervision occurs in the context of interpersonal relationships that are sometimes laden with conflict and difficulties. The manner in which the parties deal with and resolve it will determine whether the relationship continues to develop and expand or stagnate (Bernard & Goodyear, 1992). Conflicts between supervisors and supervisees tend to fall within three categories according to Moskowitz and Rupert (1983):

1. Conflicts between the supervisor and supervisee due to differences in theoretical orientation or in their views on suitable therapeutic techniques or approaches
2. Conflicts due to the supervisor's style of supervision (e.g., too much or too little autonomy)
3. Conflicts related to a personality clash between the supervisor and the supervisee

Corey and Corey (2003) recognized that there will be times when helpers will need to deal with supervision that is far from ideal. They offer the following courses of action for dealing with inadequate supervision:

- Recognize the qualities of an effective supervisor by becoming familiar with the "Ethical Guidelines for Counseling Supervisors" (Association for Counselor Education and Supervision, 1993). Take responsibility for getting the most from your supervisors, despite any limitations that may exist.
- Be willing to accept different styles of supervision. Learning how to function under a range of supervisory styles is beneficial to both the student and later the helping professional.
- Learn how to effectively solve problems in your supervision. Spend time thinking about what you need and want and find ways to directly ask for it.
- Develop a written contractual agreement between yourself and your supervisor. This agreement will increase accountability and will serve as informed consent, which should be a basic component of the supervisory relationship.

Technology

Technology provides a myriad of means by which human service professionals can assist their clients with career development issues. Technology can increase client access to information, resources, and services, while simultaneously saving time. In this final section we will discuss various ways that technology can be utilized to deliver career-related services to clients.

Telecounseling

The telephone has been used as a referral tool as well as a means for providing counseling. Telecounseling, also referred to as *teletherapy*, allows human service professionals to work with clients through off-site call centers, saving the client an office visit. Through telecounseling, helpers can work with their clients who phone in from home, the office, or from the road. Many career-related issues are being handled in this way, through one-time or multiple, long-term phone sessions. In fact, many Employee Assistance Programs (EAPs) are using telecounseling as a means to deliver services (Rafter, 2004).

Internet: E-mail and Instant Messaging

E-mail is another means that human service professionals can use to deliver career services to their clients. E-mail can be used to respond to clients' career-related questions and to provide them with feedback on resumes, cover letters, or other application material. Live, online assistance can be provided through instant messaging

(IM). Instant messaging enables individuals to create private chat rooms with one another in order to communicate in real time (immediately) over the Internet. It is similar to a telephone conversation but uses text-based as opposed to voice-based communication.

Compressed Video

Compressed video is a method of delivering services to clients located at distant sites. This method is helpful when working with clients who are unable to travel to the location of the agency and/or live in a community where no comparable services are offered. Services and programs offered through compressed video are two-way, real-time audio and video, also referred to as interactive television.

The use of technology in delivering career-related services is not without controversy. Proponents claim that various forms of technology provide faster access to services, leading to higher usage and success rates, and ultimately increased productivity. Supporters say that it is especially beneficial to agencies with workers and clients in rural areas—areas that are often underserved. Opponents, on the other hand, claim that without face-to-face contact, problems can be missed or misdiagnosed. They are concerned with matters of confidentiality and point to a lack of empirical evidence to support the effectiveness of such techniques (Rafter, 2004). As you can see, technology has created a multitude of challenges as well as opportunities for the human service professional. With the appropriate ethical integration of technology, human service professionals can make career-related services more accessible to a wide range of client populations. See Chapter 19: Ethical Issues in Providing Career Interventions, for ethical guidelines in regards to technology.

Summary

Workplace issues for the 21st century are varied and complex. For the human service professional, these issues are often magnified as a result of the profession itself. For example, violence in the workplace is a greater problem for people in the helping professions than for individuals working in other professions. Burnout and **compassion fatigue** are more evident in professions where the workers are involved in emotionally demanding work such as work in the human service field. Diversity and the use of technology in the workplace offer additional challenges and opportunities for the human service professional. Along with these issues, human service professionals, like many workers, strive to maintain a healthy balance between their various roles. Corey and Corey (2003) summed it up perfectly when they stated, "the process of becoming a helper is intrinsically related to the process of becoming a person." This process involves maintaining your centeredness through personal reflection and by challenging yourself to continue and enhance your own professional journey.

Key Terms

Burnout
Compassion fatigue
DINK

Harassment
Sandwich generation
Sexual harassment

Web Sources

Note that website URLs may change over time.

Coping.org Tools for Coping with Life's Stressors
http://www.coping.org

Journal of Technology in Counseling
http://jtc.colstate.edu/Default.htm

Mind Tools: Essential Skills for an Excellent Career
http://www.mindtools.com

The Family Institute
http://www.family-institute.org/index.html

The Sandwich Generation
http://members.aol.com/sandwchgen

U.S. Equal Employment Opportunity Commission
http://www.eeoc.gov

References

Aaronson, D., & Housinger, K. (1999, Summer). The impact of technology on displacement and reemployment. *Economic Perspectives, 23*(2), 141–155.

Abramovitz, M. (1991, October). Social policy in disarray: The beleaguered family. *Families in Society: The Journal of Contemporary Human Services, 72*(8), 483–495.

Acs, G., Phillips, K. R., & McKenzie, D. (2000, October). *On the bottom rung: A profile of Americans in low-income working families.* (An Urban Institute Program to Assess Changing Social Policies, Series A, No. A-42). Washington, DC: The Urban Institute.

ACT, Inc. (1993). *WorkKeys assessments.* Iowa City, IO: ACT

ACT, Inc. (2002). *WorkKeys readiness.* Iowa City, IO: ACT.

ACT, Inc. (2004). *DISCOVER career guidance and information system.* Retrieved August 5, 2004, from http://www.act.org/discover/index.html

Adams, D. B., & Reynolds, L. E. (2002, August). *Bureau of justice statistics 2002: At a glance* (NCJ 194449). Washington, DC: U.S. Department of Justice. Retrieved July 2, 2005, from http://www.ojp.usdoj.gov/bjs/pub/pdf/ bjsg02.pdf

Adler, R. B., Proctor, R. F., II, & Towne, N. (2005). *Looking out/looking in.* Belmont, CA: Thomson Wadsworth.

Administration for Children and Families. (2004, May 8). *Temporary assistance for needy families (TANF): Fifth annual report to congress.* Retrieved May 10, 2004, from http://www. acf.dhhs.gov/programs/ofa/annualreport5

AFL–CIO (2005). Discrimination immigration status. *Discrimination on the Job.* Retrieved May 15, 2005, from http://www.aflcio.org/yourjobeconomy/rights/rightsatwork/disc_immigrants.cfm

Agarwal, N. C., & DeGroote, M. G. (1998, March). Retirement of older workers: Issues and policies. *Human Resource Planning, 21*(1), 42–53.

Age Discrimination in Employment Act of 1967, Pub. L. 90–202, 29 U.S. C. § 621 et seq. (1967).

Ahituv, A., & Lerman, R. (2004, November 4). *Job turnover, wage rates, and marital instability: How are they related?* (Report Pub ID# 411148)). Washington, DC: The Urban Institute. Retrieved May 24, 2005, from www.urban.org/url.cfm?ID= 411148

Altschuler, D. A., & Brash. R. (2004, January). Adolescent and teenage offenders confronting the challenges and opportunities of reentry. *Youth Violence and Juvenile Justice (2)1*, 72–87.

American Academy of Pediatrics. (1996, October). Health needs of homeless children and families. *Pediatrics, 98*(4), 789–792.

American Association of People with Disabilities (n.d.). About AAPD. Retrieved January 9, 2005, from http://www.aapd-dc.org/docs/info.html#background

American Educational Research Association (1999). *Standards for educational and psychological testing.* Washington, DC: author.

American Friends Service Committee (n.d.). *"Immigrant" or "refugee?"* Retrieved May 27, 2005, from http://www.afsc.org/immigrants-rights/learn/in-us.htm#legal

American Institute on Domestic Violence. (2001). *Domestic violence statistics. Crime statistics, Workplace violence statistics.* Retrieved January 16, 2005, from http://www.aidv-usa.com/Statistics.htm

American Psychiatric Association (2000). *Diagnostic and statistical manual of mental disorders* (4th ed., text revision). Washington, DC: Author.

Americans with Disabilities Act of 1990, Pub. L. No. 101–336, § 2, 104 Stat. 328 (1991).

Amundson, N. E., Harris-Bowlsbey, J., & Niles, S. G. (2005). *Essential elements of career counseling: Processes and techniques.* Columbus, OH: Upper Saddle River, NJ: Pearson Prentice Hall

Andersson, F., Lane, J., & McEntarfer, E. (2004). *Successful transitions out of low-wage work for temporary assistance for needy families (TANF) recipients: The role of employers, coworkers, and location.* Washington, DC: The Urban Institute.

Anderton, B., & Brenton, P. (1998, October). The dollar, trade, technology, and inequality in the USA. *National Institute Economic Review, 166,* 78–87.

Aron, L. Y., & Sharkey, P. T. (2002, March). *The 1996 national survey of homeless assistance providers and clients: A comparison of faith-based and secular non-profit programs* (Contract No. HHS-100-99-0003). Washington, DC: The Urban Institute. Retrieved September 14, 2004, from http://www.urban.org/ url.cfm?ID=410496.

Association for Counselor Education and Supervision (1993). Ethical guidelines for counseling supervisors. *Spectrum, 53*(4), 3–8.

Atkinson, R., & Rostad, K. A. (2003, May 19). *Can inmates become an integral part of the U.S. workforce?* (The Urban Institute Reentry Roundtable Discussion Paper). Washington, DC: Urban Institute. Retrieved May 24, 2005, from http://www.urban.org/UploadedPDF/410854_atkison_rostad.pdf

Austin, M. J., Cox, G., Gottlieb, N., Hawkins, J. D., Kruzich, J. M., & Rauch, R. (1982). *Evaluating your agency's programs.* Newbury Park, CA: Sage.

Bacharach, S. B., Bamberger, P. A., Sonnenstuhl, W. J., & Vashdi, D. (2004, July). Retirement, risky alcohol consumption and drinking problems among blue-collar workers. *Journal of Studies on Alcohol,* 65(4), 537–546.

Back, S. E., Sonne, S. C., Killeen, T., Dansky, B. S., & Brady, K. T. (2003). Comparative profiles of women with PTSD and comorbid cocaine or alcohol dependence. *The American Journal of Drug and Alcohol Abuse, 29*(1), 169–189.

Bankoff, E. A. (1983, November). Social support and adaptation to widowhood. *Journal of Marriage and the Family, 45*(4), 827–839.

Bardhan, A. D., & Kroll, C. (2003). *The new wave of outsourcing.* Fisher Center Research Reports, Paper 1103. Berkeley: University of California. Retrieved December 28, 2004, from http://repositories.cdlib.org/cgi/viewcontent.cgi?article=1025&context=iber/fcreue

Barko, N. (2000, June 19-July 23). The other gender gap. *The American Prospect,* 61–63.

Barnes, S. A. (2005). What is effective career guidance? Evidence from longitudinal case studies in England. *Warwick Institute for Employment Research Bulletin,* 78, 2–4.

Bartik, T. J. (2000a, April). Employment as a "solution" to welfare: Challenges over the next ten years. *Employment Research Newsletter.* Kalamazoo, MI: W. E. Upjohn Institute for Employment Research.

Bartik, T. J. (2000b, October). *Solving the many problems with inner city jobs. Bridging the divide conference.* W. E. Upjohn Institute for Employment Research.

Bartik, T. J. (2002, March). *Thinking about local living wage requirement.* (Upjohn Institute Staff Working Paper No. 02–76).

Bassuk, E. L., Mickelson, K. D., Bissell, H. D., & Perloff, J. N. (2002). Role of kin and non-kin support in the mental health of low-income women. *American Journal of Ortho-psychiatry, 72*(1), 39–49.

Bechtel International Center at Stanford University (2004). Glossary of immigration terms. Retrieved May 15, 2005, from http://www.stanford.edu/dept/icenter/InternationalScholars/portal/glossary.html#INS

Beck, A. J., & Maruschak, L. M. (2001, July). *Mental health treatment in state prisons: 2000* (NCJ 188215). Washington, DC: Bureau of Justice Statistics. Retrieved July 2, 2005, from http://www.ojp.usdoj.gov/bjs/pubalp2.htm

Becker, R. L. (2000) *Reading-free vocational interest inventory: 2.* Columbus, OH: Elburn.

Beckman, L., & Amaro, H. (1986). Personal and social difficulties faced by women and men entering alcoholism treatment. *Journal of Studies in Alcohol,* 47(2), 135–145.

Beebe, S. A., Beebe, S. J., & Redmond, M. V. (2005). *Interpersonal communication: Relating to others* (4th ed.). Boston, MA: Allyn & Bacon.

Benson, M. L., & Fox, G. L. (2004, September 4). *When violence hits home: How economics and neighborhood play a role* (NCJ 206004). Washington, DC: National Institute of Justice. Retrieved January 10, 2005, from http://www.ncjrs.org/pdf-files1/nij/205004.pdf

Berk, R. A., Lenihan, K. J., & Rossi, P. H. (1980, October). Crime and poverty: Some experimental evidence from ex-offenders. *American Sociological Review, 45*(5), 766–786.

Berkel, L. A., Vandiver, B. J., & Bahner, A. D. (2004, March/April). *Journal of College Student Development, 45*(2), 119–133.

Bernard, J. M., & Goodyear, R. K. (1992). *Fundamentals of clinical supervision.* Boston: Allyn & Bacon.

Bloch, D. (2003). *Salient beliefs review: Connecting spirit to work.* Indianapolis, IN: JIST Works.

Bloom, B., & McDiarmid, A. (2000). Gender responsive supervision and programming for women offenders in the community. In *Topics in community corrections annual issue 2000: Responding to women offenders in the community* (NIC Publication No. 180, pp. 11–18). Washington, DC: National

Institute of Corrections. Retrieved September 18, 2005, from http://www.nicic.org/Library/period180

Blow, F. C., & Barry, K. L. (2002). Use and misuse of alcohol among older women. *Alcohol Research & Health, 26*(4), 308–315.

Booth-Kewley, S., Rosenfield, P., & Edwards, J. E. (1993, December). Turnover among Hispanic and non-Hispanic blue-collar workers in the navy's civilian work force. *The Journal of Social Psychology, 133*(6), 761–769.

Bowles, R. N. (2002). *What color is your parachute?* Berkeley, CA: Ten Speed Press.

Bowlus, A. J., & Seitz, S. N. (2002, June 18). *Domestic violence, employment, and divorce.* Paper presented at the American Economic Association's Annual Meeting. Retrieved January 9, 2005, from www.aeaweb.org/annual_mtg_papers/ 2005/0107_0800_1202.pdf

Bradley, L. J. (1990). *Counseling midlife career changers.* Garrett Park, MD: Garrett Park Press.

Brady, R. P. (2002). *Work orientation and values survey.* Indianapolis, IN: JIST Works.

Brewer, J. M. (1918). *The vocational guidance movement.* New York: Macmillan.

Brewer, J. M. (1942). *History of vocational guidance: Origins and early development.* New York: Harper.

Bridges Transitions Inc. (2004a). *Bridges profile.* Retrieved August 13, 2004, from http://www.bridges.com/usa/about/index.htm

Bridges Transitions Inc. (2004b). *Our product family.* Retrieved August 13, 2004, from http://www.bridges.com/usa/product/index.htm

Broman, C. L., Hamilton, V. L., Hoffman, W. S., & Mavaddat, R. (1995, December). Race, gender, and the response to stress: Autoworkers vulnerability to long-term unemployment. *American Journal of Community Psychology, 23*(6), 813–843.

Bronfenbrenner, K., & Luce, S. (2004, October 14). *The changing nature of corporate global restructuring: The impact of production shifts on jobs in the U.S., China, and around the globe.* Report submitted to the US-China Economic and Security Review Commission.

Brown, D. (1996). A holistic, values-based model of career and life-role choice and satisfaction. In D. Brown, L. Brooks, & Associates, *Career choice and development* (3rd ed.). San Francisco: Jossey-Bass.

Brown, D. (2002). The role of work and cultural values in occupational choice, satisfaction, and success: A theoretical statement. *Journal of Counseling and Development, 80*, 48–57.

Brown, D., & McIntosh, S. (2003, July 10). Job satisfaction in the low-wage service sector. *Applied Economics, 35*(10), 1241–1253.

Brown, G. (2004). *Traumatic paralysis: An affirmative defense for battered women who cannot defend themselves or others.* Paper presented at the Association of American Law School's 2004 Conference on Clinical Legal Education. Retrieved January 18, 2005, from http://Swww.aals.org/clinical2004/Brown.pdf

Bruin, M. J., & Cook, C. C. (1997, July). Understanding constraints and residential satisfaction among low-income single-parent families. *Environment & Behavior, 29*(4), 532–552.

Bryant, E. C., Trew, M. E., Bruce, A. M., Kuisma, R. M. E., & Smith, A. W. (2005, February). Effect of retirement and change in activity levels on lower limb muscle strength. *Journal of Sports Sciences, 23*(2), 221–223.

Bullough, V. L. (1998). Why there is no 'crisis of families': They're different, but better. *Free Inquiry, 19*(1), 19–21.

Burden, D. S. (1986, January). Single parents and the work setting: The impact of multiple job and homelife responsibilities. *Family Relations, 35*(1), 37–43.

Burgess, P. L., & Low, S. A. (1992, July). Preunemployment job search and advance job loss notice. *Journal of Labor Economics, 10*(3), 258–286.

Burgess, P. L., & Low, S. A. (1998, January). How do unemployment insurance and recall expectations affect on-the-job search among workers who receive advance notice of layoff? *Industrial and Labor Relations Review, 5*(2), 241–253.

Burman, L., & Kravitz, T. (2004, November 8). *Lower income households spend largest share of income.* Washington, DC: The Tax Policy Center, Urban Institute and Brookings Institution. Retrieved December 29, 2004, from http://www.urban.org/UploadedPDF/ 1000704_Tax_Fact_11–08–04.pdf

Burt, M. (1980). Cultural myths and supports for rape. *Journal of Personality and Social Psychology, 38*(2), 217—130.

Burt, M. R. (2001, October). *What will it take to end homelessness?* (Pub ID # 310305). Retrieved September 13, 2004, from http://www. urban.org/url.cfm?ID=310305.

Burt, M. R., & Aron, L. Y. (2001, February). *America's homeless II: Populations and services.* Washington, DC: Urban Institute. Retrieved September 10, 2004, from http://www. urban.org/UploadedPDF/900344_AmericasHomelessII.pdf

Burt, M., R., Aron, L. Y., Douglas, T., Valente, J., Lee, E., & Iwen, B. (1999, December 7). *Homelessness: Programs and the people they serve.* Washington, DC: Urban Institute. Retrieved September 14,

2004, from http://www.urban.org/url.cfm?ID= 310291.

Burt, M. R., Hedderson, J., Zweig, J., Ortiz, M. J., Aron-Turnham, L., & Johnson, S. M. (2004, January). *Strategies for reducing chronic street homelessness: Final report*. Washington, DC: Urban Institute.

Burt, M. R., Pollack, D., Sosland, A., Mikelson, K. S., Drapa E., Greenwalt, K., & Sharkey, P. (2002, May). *Evaluation of continuums of care for homeless people: Final report*. Washington, DC: Department of Housing and Urban Development.

Burt, M. R., Zweig, J. M., & Schlichter, K. (2000, June 30). *Strategies for addressing the needs of domestic violence victims within the TANF program: The experience of seven counties*. Washington, DC: The Urban Institute. Retrieved January 9, 2005, from http://www.urban.org/UploadedPDF/dv_ tanf. pdf

Bushway, S. (2003, May 19). *Reentry and prison work programs* (A Report of the Reentry Roundtable). Washington, DC: Urban Institute. Retrieved October 8, 2005, from http://www.urban.org/url. cfm?ID=410853

Butrica, B. A., Johnson, R. W., Smith, K. E., & Steuerle, U. (2004, December). *Does work pay at older ages?* Washington, DC: The Urban Institute.

Camarota, S. A. (2001). *The slowing progress of immigrants: An examination of income, home ownership, and citizenship, 1970–2000*. Center for Immigration Studies. Retrieved May 27, 2005, from http://www.cis.org/articles/2001/back401. html

Camarota, S. A. (2004). *Economy slowed, but immigration didn't: The foreign-born population, 2000–2004*. Center for Immigration Studies. Re-trieved May 15, 2005, from http://www. cis.org/articles/2004/ back1204.html

Career Action Center. (n. d.). *Values-driven work card sort*. Menlo Park, CA: Prodigy Press.

Career Development Center, University of Cincinnati (1997). *Career portfolio: Professional development strategies for your future* (3rd ed.). Cincinnati, OH: Educational Publishing Resources.

CareerOneStop (2004). *CareerOneStop about us*. Retrieved September 26, 2004, from http://www. careeronestop.org/aboutus.asp

Carels, R. A., Sherwood, A., Szczepanski, R., & Blumenthal, J. A. (2000, Summer). Ambulatory blood pressure and marital distress in employed women. *Behavioral Medicine 26*(2), 80–88.

Carl D. Perkins Vocational–Technical Education Act Amendments of 1998. Pub. L. No. 105–332, H. R. 1853, 105th Cong. (1998).

Catalano, R., Aldrete, E., Vega, W., Kolody, B., Aguilar-Gaxiola, S. (2000, March). Job loss and major depression among Mexican Americans. *Social Science Quarterly, 81*(1), 477–488.

Center for Credentialing and Education, Inc. (n.d.). Retrieved May 30, 2004, from http://www.cce-global.org/

Centers for Disease Control and Prevention (CDC) (1998). Health-related quality of life and activity limitation—Eight states, 1995. *Morbidity and Mortality Weekly Report, 47*, pp.134–140.

Centers for Disease Control and Prevention. (2004, January). *Research in brief: Injury prevention*. Atlanta, GA: Author. Retrieved January 16, 2005, from http://www.cdc.gov/programs/2004/injury. pdf

Chan, S., & Stevens, A. H. (1999). Job loss and employment patterns of older workers. *Journal of Labor Economics, 19*(2), 484–521.

Chandler, S., & Czerlinsky, T. (1999a). *Vocational decision-making interview administration manual*. Indianapolis, IN: JIST Works.

CHAMPUS. (n.d). MedTerms Medical Dictionary. Retrieved November, 4, 2005, from http://www. medterms.com/script/main/art.asp?articlekey= 2693

City of New York (2005). *Mayor's office of immigrant affairs: Public benefits*. Retrieved May 22, 2005, from http://www.nyc.gov/html/imm/html/forim-mandagencies/public_benefits. shtml

Cohen, E., & Stahler, G. J. (1998, Summer). Life histories of crack-using African American homeless men: Salient themes. *Contemporary Drug Problems, 25*(2), 373–397.

Coker, A. L., Smith, P. H., Bethea, L., King, M. R., & McKeown, W. E. (2000, May). Physical health consequences of physical and psychological intimate partner violence. *Arch Family Med, 9*(5), 451–457.

Cole, P. R. (2001, February). Impoverished women in violent partnerships: Designing services to fit their reality. *Violence Against Women, 7*(2), 223–233.

Committee for Economic Development. (1999). *New opportunities for older workers*. Washington, DC: Author.

Copeland, J. (1997). A qualitative study of barriers to formal treatment among women who self-managed care in addictive behaviours. *Journal of Substance Abuse Treatment, 14*(2), 183–190.

Corey, G., Corey, M., & Callanan, P. (2002). *Issues and ethics in the helping professions*. (6th ed.). Pacific Grove, CA: Brooks/Cole Publishing.

Corey, M. S., & Corey, G. (2003). *Becoming a helper* (4th ed.). Pacific Grove, CA: Brooks/Cole.

Couch, K. A. (1997, January). *Late life job displacement* (Aging Studies Program Paper No 6). Syracuse, NY: Maxwell Center for Demography and Economics of Aging.

Couturier, L., & Scurry, J. (2005, February). *Correcting course: How we can restore the ideals of public higher education in a market-driven era.* Providence, RI: The Futures Project: Policy for Higher Education in a Changing World. Retrieved May 26, 21005, from http://www. futuresproject.org/publications/Correcting_ Course.pdf

Crandall, M. L., Nathens, A. B., Kernic, M. A., Holt, V. L., & Rivara, F. P. (2004, April). Predicting future injury among women in abusive relationships. *The Journal of Trauma Injury, Infection, and Critical Care, 56*(4), 906–912.

Creamer, E., Duggan, M., & Kidd, R. (1999, Fall). STD 105: Process groups as an instructional medium for re-entry women at Paul D. Camp Community College. *Inquiry: The Journal of the Virginia Community Colleges, 4*(2), 19–25.

Crime Control Act of 1990, Pub L. No. 101–647 § 1702, U.S. C. C. A. N. (104 Stat.) 4789. (1990, November 29).

Currie, J. C. (2001). *Best practices treatment and rehabilitation for women with substance use problems.* Ottawa, Ontario: Health Canada Publications.

Czerlinsky, T., & Chandler, S. (1999b). *Vocational decision-making interview.* Indianapolis, IN: JIST Works.

Da Costa Nunez, R., & Collignon, K. (1997, October). Creating a community of learning for homeless children. *Educational Leadership, 55*(2), 56–60.

Daly, M., & Bound, J. (1996, March). Worker adaptation and employer accommodation following the onset of a health impairment. *The Journal of Gerontology: Social Sciences, 51B*(2), 553–560.

Dane, A. V, & Schneider, B. H. (1998). Program integrity in primary and early secondary prevention: Are implementation effects out of control? *Clinical Psychology Review, 18*, 23–45.

Danziger, S., Corcoran, M., Heflin, C., Kalil, A., Levine, J., Rosen, D., Seefeldt, K., Siefert, K., & Tolman, R. (1999, June). *Barriers to employment of welfare recipients.* Anne Arbor, MI: Institute for Research on Poverty.

Davis, E. E., & Weber, B. A. (1998). Linking policy and outcomes: A simulation model of poverty incidence. *Growth and Change, 29*(4), 423–432.

Davis, K. (1984). Wives and work: The sex role revolution and its consequences. *Population and Development Review, 10* (3), 397–417.

Day, J. C. (1996, February). *Population projections of the United States by age, sex, race, and Hispanic origin: 1995 to 2050* (U.S. Census Bureau, Current Population Reports, P25–1130). Washington, DC: U.S. Government Printing Office.

Dean-Gaitor, H. D., & Fleming, P. L. (1999). Epidemiology of AIDS in incarcerated persons in the United States, 1994–1996. *AIDS, 13*(17), 2429–2435.

DeNavas-Walt, C., Proctor, B. D., & Mills, R. J. (2004, August). *Income, poverty, and health insurance coverage in the United States: 2003* (P60226). Retrieved September 18, 2004, from http://www.census.gov/prod/2004pubs/p60–226.pdf

Department of Health and Human Services, Centers for Disease Control and Prevention, & National Institute for Occupational Safety and Health (2002). *Violence: Occupational hazards in hospitals.* Cincinnati, OH: NIOSH

DISCOVER (Computer software). (1994). Hunt Valley, Maryland: American College Testing Program.

Dooley, D. (2003). Unemployment, underemployment, and mental health: Conceptualizing employment status as a continuum. *American Journal of Community Psychology, 32*(_), 9–19.

Dooley, D., & Prause, J. A. (1997a). Mental health and welfare transitions: Depression and alcohol abuse in AFDC women. *American Journal of Community Psychology, 30*(6), 787–813.

Dooley, D. & Prause, J. (1997b, December). Effect of favorable employment change on alcohol abuse: One- and five-year follow-ups in the national longitudinal survey of youth. *American Journal of Community Psychology, 25*(6), 787–808.

Doress-Worters, P. B. (1994, November). Adding elder care to women's multiple roles: A critical review of caregiver stress and multiple role literatures. *Sex Roles: A Journal of Research, 31*(9), 597–617.

Doweiko, H. (2002). *Concepts of chemical dependency* (5th ed.). Pacific Grove, CA: Brooks/Cole.

Duggan, M. H., & Jurgens, J. C. (2005). Career counseling in women's groups: A relational approach. *Virginia Counselors Journal, 28*, 16–20.

Duncan, S. F., Dunnagan, T., Christopher, S., & Paul, L. (2003). Helping families toward the goal of self-support: Montana's EDUFAIM program. *Families in Society: The Journal of Contemporary Human Services, 84*(2), 213–222.

Earle, A., & Heymann, S. J. (2002). What causes job loss among former welfare recipients: The role of family health problems. *Journal of American Medical Women's Association, 57*(1), 5–10.

East, J. F. (1999). Hidden barriers to success for women in welfare reform. *Families in Society: The Journal of Contemporary Human Services, 80*(3), 295–304.

Economic Policy Institute (2004a). *Facts and figures: Income.* (State of Working America 2004/2005). Washington, DC: Author. Retrieved October 11, 2004, from http://www.epinet.org/content.cfm/books_swa2004

Economic Policy Institute (2004b). *Facts and figures: Jobs.* (State of Working America 2004/2005). Washington, DC: Author. Retrieved October 11, 2004, from http://www.epinet.org/content.cfm/books_swa2004

Economic Policy Institute (2004c). *Facts and figures: Poverty.* (State of Working America 2004/ 2005). Washington, DC: Author. Retrieved October 11, 2004, from http://www.epinet.org/ content.cfm/books_swa2004

Elksnin, N., & Elksnin, L. (1991). Facilitating the vocational success of students with mild handicaps: The need for job-related social skills training. *Journal for Vocational Special Needs Education, 13*(2), 5–11.

Eller, T. J. (1996, June). Dynamics of economic well-being: Poverty, 1992–1993. Who stays poor? Who doesn't? *Current Population Reports* (P70–55). Washington, DC: Bureau of the Census.

Employee Retirement Income Security Act of 1974, Pub. L. No. 93–406, 88 Stat. 829 (codified as amended at 29 U.S. C. §§ 1001–1461 (1997)).

Employers Group Research Services. (2002, April 12). *Employment of ex-offenders: A survey of employers' policies and practices.* San Francisco: SFWorks. Retrieved June 24, 2005, from http://www.sfworks.org/Publications/BySF-Works.htm

Employment and Training Administration (2005, June 30). *Workforce system results* (PY 04 #4). Washington, DC: United States Department of Labor. Retrieved November 6, 2005, from http://www.doleta.gov/performance/results/Reports.cfm

Employment Training Project (1996, May). *Employment training: Successful projects share common strategies* (GAO/HEHS-96–108). Washington, DC: General Accounting Office.

Encyclopedia Britannica, Inc. (2004). *Encyclopedia Britannica online.* Retrieved January 1, 2005, from http://www.britannica.com

Erikson, E. H. (1980). *Identity and the life cycle.* New York: W. W. Norton.

Etaugh, C., & Folger, S. (1998). Perceptions of parents whose work and parenting behaviors deviate from role expectations. *Sex Roles: A Journal of Research, 39*(3–4), 215–224.

ETS. (2004). *SIGI Plus® educational and career planning software.* Retrieved August 5, 2004, from http://www.ets.org/sigi/

Family Business Institute, Inc. (2004). *The 4 Ps of marketing.* Retrieved September 19, 2004, from http://www.family-business-experts. com/ 4-Ps-of-marketing.html

Family Violence Prevention Fund. (2002, December). *The business case for domestic violence programs in health care settings.* San Francisco, CA: Author.

Farr, M. (2002). *Guide for occupational exploration interest inventory* (2nd ed.). Indianapolis, IN: JIST Works.

Farr, M., Ludden, L. L., & Shatkin, L. (Eds.) (2001). *Guide for occupational exploration*, 3rd ed. Indianapolis, IN: JIST Works.

Federal Bureau of Investigation. (2003). *Crime in the United States 2003. Uniform crime reports.* Washington, DC: U.S. Department of Justice. Retrieved January 12, 2005, from http://www.fbi.gov/ucr/03cius.htm

Fields, J. (2003, June). *Children's living arrangements and characteristics: March 2002* (P20 547). Washington, DC: U.S. Department of Economics.

Fields, J., & Casper, L. M. (2001, June). *America's families and living arrangements: Population characteristics* (P20–537). Washington, DC: U.S. Department of Commerce.

Finley, N. J. (1989). Theories of family labor as applying to gender differences in caregiving for elderly parents. *Journal of Marriage and Family, 51*(1), 79–86.

First Nations and Inuit Health Branch (2000). *Community health needs assessment: A guide for first nations Inuit health authorities.* Retrieved September 10, 2004, from http://www.hc-sc.gc.ca/fnihb-dgspni/fnihb/bpm/hfatran-sfer_publications/community_needs_assessment.htm#Decide%20on%20data%20collection%20methods

Fishman, M. E., & Beebout, H. (2001, December). *Supports for working poor families: A new approach.* Falls Church, VA: Lewin Group. Retrieved December 30, 2004, from http://www.lewin.com/Lewin_Publications/Human_Services/Publication-11.htm

Fitzgerald, J. (1999, July 16). *Job instability and earnings and income consequences: Evidence from SIPP 1983–1995* (JCPR Working Paper 99). Paper prepared for the Joint Center Poverty Research sponsored conference for 1997–1998 ASPE/Census Bureau Small Grants, Washington, DC. Retrieved May 28, 2005, from http://www.jcpr.org/wp/WPprofile.cfm?ID= 99.0

Fouad, N. A. (1995). Career behavior of Hispanics: Assessment and intervention. In F. T. L. Leong

(Ed.), *Career development and vocational behavior of racial and ethnic minorities* (pp. 165–192). Mahwah, NJ: Erlbaum.

Friedman, L., Tucker, S., Neville, P., & Imperial, A. (1996). The impact of domestic violence on the workplace. In G. VandenBos & E. Bulatao (Eds.), *Violence on the job: Identifying risks and developing strategies* (pp. 153–161). Washington, DC: American Psychiatric Association.

Friesen, J. (1986). The role of the family in vocational development. *International Journal for the Advancement of Counseling, 9*(1), 5–10.

Fullerton, H. N. (1999, December). Labor force participation: 75 years of change, 1950–98 and 1998–2025. *Monthly Labor Review, 122,* 3–12.

Garimella, R., Plichta, S. B., Houseman, C., & Garzon, L. (2000). Physician beliefs about victims of spouse abuse and about the physician role. *Journal of Women's Health and Gender-Based Medicine, 9*(4), 405–411.

Gerdes, K. E. (1997). Long-term AFDC mothers and posttraumatic stress syndrome: Is there a connection? *Journal of Women and Social Work, 12*(3), 359–368.

Gibson, K. J., Zerbe, W. J., & Franken, R. E. (1993, May). The influence of rater and ratee age on judgments of work-related attributes. *The Journal of Psychology, 127*(3), 271–281.

Ginzberg, E. (1972). Restatement of the theory of occupational choice. *Vocational Guidance Quarterly, 10*(3), 169–176.

Ginzberg, E. (1984). Career development. In D. Brown & L. Brooks (Eds.), *Career choice and development, applying contemporary theories to practice.* San Francisco: Jossey-Bass.

Ginzberg, E., Ginsburg, S. W., Axelrad, S., & Herma, J. L. (1951). *Occupational choice: An approach to a general theory.* New York: Columbia University Press.

Giordani, P. (2005). *Overcoming obstacles to employment: Help jobs seekers surmount past mistakes.* Retrieved October 17, 2005, from http://www. jobweb.com/resources/library/TwoYear_Focus /Overcoming_Obstacles_ 247_01.htm

GI Rights Network. (n.d.). *Getting out: A guide to military discharges.* Oakland, CA: Central Committee for Conscientious Objectors. Retrieved November 8, from http://www.objector.org/girights/military-discharges. html

Glaze, L. E., & Palla, S. (2004, July). *Probation and parole in the United States, 2003* (NCJ 205336). Washington, DC: Bureau of Justice Statistics. Retrieved July 2, 2005, from http://www.ojp.usdoj. gov/bjs/pub/pdf/ppus03.pdf

Glutting, J. J., & Wilkinson, G. (2003). *Wide range interest and occupation test* (2nd ed.). Wilmington, DE: Wide Range.

Goldberg, H. (2002, January 22). *Improving TANF program outcomes for families with barriers to employment.* Washington, DC: Center for Budget and Policy Priorities. Retrieved January 9, 2005, from www.cbpp.org/1–22–02tanf3.pdf

Goldberg, J. E. (1999, March/April). A short-term approach to intervention with homeless mothers: A role for clinicians in homeless shelters. *Families in Society: The Journal of Contemporary Human Services, 80*(2), 161–169.

Goldstein, T., Chun, M., & Winkler, M. (1994). *Job seeking skills for people with disabilities: A guide for success.* Northridge, CA: The Career Center, California State University.

Goozner, M. (2004, January). Higher skills, fewer jobs. *The American Prospect, 15*(1), 42–45.

Grall, T. (2003, October). *Custodial mothers and fathers and their child support: 2001. Current population reports* (P60–225). Washington, DC: U.S. Department of Commerce.

Grantmakers Concerned with Immigrants and Refugees (GCIR) (2001a). *Directory of funders supporting immigrant and refugee issues.* Retrieved May 21, 2005, from http://www.gcir.org/resources/funding_directory/index.htm

Grantmakers Concerned with Immigrants and Refugees (GCIR) (2001b). *Newcomers in the American workforce: Improving employment outcomes for low-wage immigrants and refugees.* Retrieved May 31, 2005, from http://www. gcir.org/resources/gcir_publications/workplace/ summary.htm

Grayson, M. (1999). Kicking habits: Preparing welfare recipients for the work force. *Spectrum: The Journal of State Government, 72*(1), 5–8.

Greene, W. H., & Quester, K. O. (1982). Divorce risk and wives' labour supply behaviour. *Social Science Quarterly 63,* 192–196.

Greenfield, L. A., & Snell, T. L. (2000, October). *Women offenders* (Bureau of Justice Special Report NCJ 175688). Washington, DC: Bureau of Justice Statistics. Retrieved July 2, 2005, from http://www.ojp.usdoj.gov/bjs/pub/pdf/wo.pdf

Greenwood, G. L., Relf, M. V., Huang, B., Pollack, M., Canchola, J. A., & Cantina, J. A. (2002, December). Battering victimization among a probability-based sample of men who have sex with men. *American Journal of Public Health, 92*(12), 1964–1969.

Groves, B. M., Augustyn, M., Lee, D., & Sawires, P. (2004, August). *Identifying and responding to domestic* violence: *Consensus recommendations for child and adolescent health*. San Francisco, CA: Family Violence Prevention Fund. Retrieved January 2, 2005, from http://end-abuse.org/programs/healthcare/files/Pediatric.pdf

Gysbers, N. C., Heppner, M. J., & Johnson, J. A. (2003). *Career counseling: Process, issues, and techniques* (2nd ed.). Boston: Allyn & Bacon.

Hagner, D., Rogan, P., & Murphy, S. (1992). Facilitating natural supports in the workplace: Strategies for support consultants. *The Journal of Rehabilitation, 58*(1), 29–35.

Harkness, J. M., & Newman, S. J. (2004, April). *Housing problems of the working poor*. Washington, DC: Center for Housing Policy. Retrieved December 29, 2004, from http://www.nhc.org/ CHP_Housing_Problems_of_the_Working_Poor_ 2004.pdf

Harney, E. E., & Angel, D. L. (1999). *Overcoming barriers card sort game kit*. Hacienda Heights, CA: WorkNet Solutions.

Harrington, J. C., & Harrington, T. F. (1996). *Ability explorer*. Itasca, IL: Houghton Mifflin.

Harris, K. M. (1993, September). Work and welfare among single mothers in poverty. *American Journal of Sociology, 99*(2), 317–352.

Harris, K. M. (1996, June). Life after welfare: Women, work, and repeat dependency. *American Sociological Review, 61*(3), 407–426.

Harris, S. N., Mowbray, C. T., & Solarz, A. (1994, February). Physical health, mental health, and substance abuse problems of shelter users. *Health and Social Work, 19*(1), 37–46.

Hattendorf, J., & Tollerud, T. R., (1997). Domestic violence: Counseling strategies that minimize the impact of secondary victimization. *Perspectives in Psychiatric Care, 33*(1), 14–24.

Hawes-Cooper Act of 1929, Pub. L. No 669. 1084, 49 USC 60. (1929, January 19).

Hayward, B. J., & Schmidt-Davis, H. (2003). *Longitudinal study of the vocational rehabilitation services program. Final report 2: VR services and outcomes*. Retrieved February 2, 2005 from http://www.ed.gov/rschstat/eval/rehab/vr-final-report-2.doc

Healy, C. C. (1990). Reforming career appraisals to meet the needs of clients in the 1990s. *The Counseling Psychologist, 18,* 487–488.

Heilman, M. E. (2001). Description and prescription: How gender stereotypes prevent women's ascent up the organizational ladder. *Journal of Social Issues, 57*(4), 657–674.

Heinrich, S. (2000, September). *Reducing recidivism through work: Barriers and opportunities for employ-*ment of ex-offenders (Workforce Development Partnership Series). Chicago, Illinois: Great Cities Institute, University of Illinois. Retrieved May 8, 2005, from http://www.uic.edu/cuppa/gci/publications/workforce_development_partnership.htm

Henley, J. R. (2000). Mismatch in the low-wage labor market: Job search perspective. In K. Kaye & D. S. Nightingale (Eds.). *The low-wage labor market: Challenges and opportunities for economic self-sufficiency* (pp. 145–167). Washington, DC: U.S. Department of Health and Human Services. Retrieved December 30, 2004, from http://www.urban.org/url.cfm?ID= 309642

Heppner, M. J. (1991). *Career transitions inventory*. Columbia, MO: Author.

Heppner, M. J. (1998). The career transitions inventory measuring internal resources in adulthood. *Journal Of Career Assessment, 6,* 135–145.

Herr, E. L. (2003). The future of career counseling as an instrument of public policy: Career counseling in the next decade. *Career Development Quarterly, 52,* 8–17.

Herr, E. L., & Cramer, S. H. (1996). *Career guidance and counseling through the lifespan: Systematic approaches* (5th ed.). New York: Longman.

Herr, E. L., Cramer, S. H., & Niles, S. G. (2004). *Career guidance and counseling through the lifespan: Systematic approaches* (6th ed.). Boston: Pearson Education, Inc.

Herr, E. L., & Niles, S. G. (1988). The values of counseling: Three domains. *Counseling and Values, 33,* 4–17.

Hershey, A. M., and Pavetti, L. A. (1997, Spring). Turning job finders into job keepers: The challenge of sustaining employment. *The Future of Children: Welfare to Work, 7*(1), 74–86.

Herz, D. E. (1995, April). Work after early retirement: An increasing trend among men. *Monthly Labor Review, 118*(4), 13–20.

Hill, H. & Kauff, J. (2002, March). Living on little: The stories of families with very low incomes and lessons for TANF reauthorization. *Policy & Practice of Public Human Services, 60*(1), 14–20.

Hill, R. P., & Stamey, M. (1990, December). The homeless in America: An examination of possessions and consumption behaviors. *Journal of Consumer Research, 17*(3), 303–322.

Hilton, N. Z., Harris, G. T., Rice, M. E., Lang, C., Cormier, C. A., & Lines, K. J. (2004, April). A brief actuarial assessment for the prediction of wife assault recidivism: The Ontario domestic assault risk assessment. *Psychological Assessment, 16*(3), 267–275.

Hirsch, B. T., Macpherson, D. A., & Hardy, M. A. (2000, April). Occupational age structure and access for older workers. *Industrial and Labor Relations Review, 53*(3), 401–418.

Holcomb, P. A., Tumlin, K., Koralek, R., Capps, R., & Zuberi, A. (2003, January). *The application process for TANF, food stamps, Medicaid, and SCHIP: Issues for agencies and applicants, including immigrants and limited English speakers.* Washington, DC: U.S. Department of Health and Human Services Office of the Secretary Office of the Assistant Secretary for Planning and Evaluation.

Holland, J. L. (1980). *My vocational situation.* Lutz, FL: Psychological Assessment Resources.

Holland, J. L. (1985a). *Making vocational choices: A theory of personalities and work environments.* Lutz, FL: Psychological Assessment Resources.

Holland, J. L. (1985b). *Vocational preference inventory.* Lutz, FL: Psychological Assessment Resources.

Holland, J. L. (1990). *Self-directed search form CP: Career planning.* Lutz, FL: Psychological Assessment Resources.

Holland, J. L. (1994). *Self-directed search form R.* Lutz, FL: Psychological Assessment Resources.

Holland, J. L. (1996a). *Self-directed search form E* (4th ed.). Lutz, FL: Psychological Assessment Resources.

Holland, J. L. (1996b). *Self-directed search form E* (4th ed.). [Audiotape]. Lutz, FL: Psychological Assessment Resources.

Holland, J. L. (1997). *Making vocational choices: A theory of vocational personalities and work enrichments* (3rd ed.). Odessa, FL: Psychological Assessment Resources.

Holland, J. L., Birk J. M., Cooper, J. F., Dewey, C. R. Dolliver, H., Takai, R. T., & Tyler, L. (1980). *The vocational exploration and insight kit.* Mountain View, CA: CPP.

Holland, J. L., Daiger, D., & Power, P. G. (1980). *My vocational situation.* Mountain View, CA: CPP.

Holland, J. L., & Gottfredson, G. D. (1994). *Career attitudes and strategies inventory.* Lutz, FL: Psychological Assessment Resources.

Holleman, W. L., Bray, J. H., Davis, L., & Holleman, M. C. (2004). Innovative ways to address the mental health and medical needs of marginalized patients: Collaborations between family physicians, family therapists, and family psychologists. *American Journal of Orthopsychiatry, 74*(3), 242–252.

Holzer, H. (2000). Mismatch in the low-wage labor market: Job hiring perspective. In K. Kaye & D. S. Nightingale (Eds.). *The low-wage labor market: Challenges and opportunities for economic self-sufficiency* (pp. 127–143). Washington, DC: U.S. Department of Health and Human Services. Retrieved December 30, 2004, from http://www.urban.org/url.cfm?ID=309642

Holzer, H., & Danziger, S. (1998, March). *Are jobs available for disadvantaged workers in urban areas?* (Discussion paper no. 1158–98). University of Wisconsin: Institute for Research on Poverty.

Holzer, H. J. (1999, February). *Employer demand for welfare recipients and the business cycle: Evidence from recent employer surveys* (Discussion paper no. 1185–99). University of Wisconsin: Institute for Research on Poverty.

Holzer, H. J., & LaLonde, R. J. (1999, May). *Job change and job stability among less skilled young workers* (Discussion paper no. 1191–99). Institute for Research on Poverty.

Holzer, H. J., Raphael, S., & Stoll, M. A. (2003, May 19–20). *Employment barriers facing ex-offenders* (The Urban Institute Reentry Roundtable Discussion Paper). Washington, DC: Urban Institute. Retrieved October 7, 2005, from http://www.urban.org/url.cfm?ID= 410855

Holzer, H. J., & Stoll, M. A. (2003). Employer demand for welfare recipients by race. *Journal of Labor Economics, 21*(1), 210–241.

Hopper, K., & Baumohl, J. (1994, February). Held in abeyance: Rethinking homeless and advocacy. *American Behavioral Scientist, 37*(4), 522–553.

Horwitz, A. V., White, H. R., & Howell-White, S. (1996, November). Becoming married and mental health: A longitudinal study of a cohort of young adults. *Journal of Marriage and Family, 58*(4), 895–907.

Hou, F., & Omwanda, L. O. (1997). A multilevel analysis of the connection between female labour force participation and divorce in Canada, 1931–1991. *International Journal of Comparative Sociology, 38*(3–4), 271–289.

Housing Opportunity Program Extension Act of 1996, Pub. L. 104–120. 110 STAT. 834. 12 USC 1701. (1996, March 28).

Hout, M. (1997, December). Inequality at the margins: The effects of welfare, the minimum wage, and tax credits on low-wage labor. *Politics & Society, 25*(4), 13–25.

Hoyt, K. B. (1977). *A primer for career education.* Washington, DC: U.S. Department of Education.

Hughes, T., Wilson, D., & Beck, A. (2001, October). *Trends in state parole, 1990–2000* (NCJ 184735). Washington, DC: U.S. Department of Justice. Retrieved July 2, 2005, from http://www.ojp.usdoj.gov/bjs/pub/pdf/tsp00.pdf.

Human Resources Development Canada[HRDC]. (1999, December). *Older worker adjustment programs: Lessons learned* (SP-AH093–12–99E).

Gatineau, Quebec: Author. Retrieved April 6, 2005, from http://www11.hrdc-drhc.gc.ca/edd-pdf/owap.pdf

Iceland, J. (2003, August). Why poverty remains high: The role of income growth, economic inequality, and changes in family structure, 1949–1999. *Demography, 40*(3), 499–519.

Imhoff, T. (n.d.). *Alfred Binet.* Retrieved May 29, 2004, from http://fates.cns.muskingum.edu/~psych/psycweb/history/binet.htm

Immergluck, D. (1998, April). Neighborhood economic development and local working: The effect of nearby jobs on where residents work. *Economic Geography, 74*(2), 170–188.

Individuals with Disabilities Education Act Amendments of 1997, Pub. L 105–17, H. R. 5, 105th Cong. (1997).

Individuals with Disabilities Education Improvement Act of 2004, H. R. 1350, 108th Cong. 2004.

Industrial Revolution. (n.d.). Retrieved May 29, 2004, from http://www.puhsd.k12.ca.us/chana/staffpages/eichman/Adult_School/us/fall/industrialization/1/industrial_revolution.htm

Institute for Women's Policy Research. (2003, November). *The gender wage gap: Progress of the 1980s fails to carry through.* Retrieved September 5, 2004 from http://www.iwpr.org/pdf/ C353.pdf

Institute for Women's Policy Research. (2004, August 27). Women's earnings fall: U.S. Census Bureau finds rising gender wage gap. Retrieved September 5, 2004, from http://www. iwpr.org/pdf/Wage RatioPress_release 8–27–04.pdf

Intimate Partner Abuse and Relationship Violence Working Group. (n.d.). *Intimate partner abuse and relationship violence.* Washingotn, DC: American Psychiatric Association. Retrieved January 22, 2005, from http://www.apa.org/about/division/abuse.html

Isaacson, L. E., & Brown, D. (2000). *Career information, career counseling, and career development* (7th ed.). Boston: Allyn and Bacon.

Jablow, P. M. (2000). Victims of abuse and Discrimination: Protecting battered homosexuals under domestic violence legislation. *Hofstra Law Review, 28,* 1095–1145.

Jacobs, D. (1990, October). Getting the homeless back to work. *Management Review, 79*(10), 44–48.

Jayakody, R., & Stauffer, D. (2000). Mental health problems among single mothers: Implications for work and welfare reform. *Journal of Social Issues, 56*(4), 617–634.

Jencks, C. (2004, January). The low-wage puzzle: Why is America generating so many bad jobs—and how can we create more good jobs? *The American Prospect, 15*(1), 35–37.

Jepsen, D. A., & Dilley, J. S. (1974). Vocational decision-making models: A review and comparative analysis. *Review of Educational Research, 44*(3), 331–349.

JIST Works. (2002a). *O*NET career interests inventory.* Indianapolis, IN: Author.

JIST Works. (2002b). *O*NET career values inventory.* Indianapolis, IN: Author.

JIST Works. (2002c). *Voc-tech quick screener.* Indianapolis, IN: Author.

JIST Works. (2004). *Careerexplorer CD-ROM.* Indianapolis, IN: Author.

Job Protections and Accommodations for Disabilities Caused by Domestic Violence. (2001, January). NY: *Employment rights for survivors of abuse.* Retrieved January 10, 2005, from http://www. legalmomentum.org/issues/vio/Disabilitiespercent 20Accomodations. PDF

JobQuality.ca (2004). *Work-life balance by region in Canada.* Retrieved November 28, 2005, from http:// www.jobquality.ca/balance_e/balance.stm

Jobs for Veterans Act of 2002, Pub. L. No. 107–288. STAT. 2033 (2002, November 7).

Johnson, P. R., & Indvik, J. (1999, Fall). The organizational benefits of assisting domestically abused employees. *Public Personnel Management, 28*(3), 365–371.

Johnson, R. W. (2004, July). Trends in job demands among older workers, 1992–2002. *Monthly Labor Review, 127*(7), 48–56. Retrieved April 6, 2005, from http://www.urban.org/url.cfm?ID=1000679

Johnson, R. W., & Crystal, S. (1996, Spring). Health insurance coverage at midlife: Characteristics, costs, and dynamics. *Health Care Financing Review, 18*(3), 123–149.

Johnson, R. W., & Steuerle, E. (2003). *Promoting work at older ages: The role of hybrid pension plans in an aging population* (PRCWP-2003–26). Philadelphia, PA: Pension Research Council.

Jones, L. (1991). Unemployed fathers and their children: Implications for policy and practice. *Child and Adolescent Social Work Journal, 8*(2), 101–116.

Jones, L. K., & Jones, J. W. (2000). *Career key.* Raleigh, NC: Author.

Juhn, C. (1999, April). Wage inequality and demand for skill: Evidence from five decades. *Industrial and Labor Relations Review, 52*(3), 42–46.

Jung, C. G. (1933). *Psychological types.* New York: Harcourt.

Jurgens, J. C. (2000). The undecided student: Effects of combining levels of treatment parameters on career certainty, career indecision, and client satisfaction. *The Career Development Quarterly, 48*(3), 237–250.

Jurgens, J. C. (2002). The Career Navigator sails. *Journal of College Student Development, 43*(1), 137–142.

Justice Research and Statistics Association (JRSA). (2004). *Juvenile Justice Evaluation Center online.* Retrieved August 21, 2004, from http://www.jrsa.org/jjec/resources/ definitions. html

Justice System Improvement Act of 1979, Pub. L. 90–315. 42 U. S. C. 3701, et seq. (1979, December 27).

Kalil, A., Born, C. E., Kunz, J., & Caudill, P. J. (2001). Life stressors, social support, and depressive symptoms among first-time welfare recipients. *American Journal of Community Psychology, 29*(2), 355–369.

Kausch, O. (2004, March). Pathological gambling among elderly veterans. *Journal of Geriatric Psychiatry and Neurology, 17*(1), 13–19.

Keane, M. P., & Wolpin, K. I. (1997). Career decisions of young men. *Journal of Political Economy, 105*(3), 473–522.

Keirsey, D. (1998, May). *Please understand me II.* Del Mar, CA: Prometheus Nemesis Book.

Kelly, G. A. (1955). *A theory of personality: The psychology of personal constructs.* New York: Norton.

Kelly, L. (2003). Disabusing the definition of domestic violence: How women batter men and the role of the feminist state. *Florida State University Law Review, 30,* 791–855.

Kim, M. (1998, March). The working poor: Lousy jobs or lazy workers? *Journal of Economic Issues, 32*(1), 65–89.

Kim, M., & Mergoupis, T. (1997, September). The working poor and welfare recipiency: Participation, evidence, and policy directions. *Journal of Economic Issues, 31*(3), 707–729.

Kinglsey, G. T., & Pettit, K. L. (2003, May). *Concentrated poverty: A change in course.* (The Neighborhood Change in Urban America Series Paper No. 2). Washington, DC: The Urban Institute.

Kletzer, L. G. (1998, Winter). Job displacement. *Journal of Economic Perspectives, 12*(1), 115–136.

Knobloch-Fedders, L. & Gorvine, B. (2003). *The Family Institute, featured tips: Achieving a balance between work and personal life.* Retrieved November 28, 2005, from http://www.family-institute. org/therapy/tips/8worklifetips.htm

Knowdell, R. (1998a, June). *Career values card sort.* San Jose, CA: Career Research & Testing.

Knowdell, R. (1998b, June). *Retirement activities card sort kit.* San Jose, CA: Career Research & Testing.

Knowdell, R. (2002a, June). *Motivated skills card sort.* San Jose, CA: Career Research & Testing.

Knowdell, R. (2002b, June). *Occupational interests card sort.* San Jose, CA: Career Research & Testing.

Kodrzycki, Y. K. (1997, May/June). Training programs for displaced workers: What do they accomplish? *New England Economic Review,* 39–57.

Kodrzycki, Y. K. (1998, November-December). The effects of employer-provided severance benefits on reemployment outcomes. *New England Economic Review,* 41–61.

Koehler, E., & Hagigh, S. (2004, May 11). *Offshore outsourcing and America's competitive edge: Losing out in the high technology r & d and services sectors.* White paper for Office of Senator Joseph I. Lieberman. Retrieved December 28, 2004, from http://lieberman.senate.gov/newsroom/whitepapers/Offshoring.pdf

Krishnan, S. P., Hilbert, J. C., & VanLeeuwen, D. (2001, April). Domestic violence and help-seeking behaviors among rural women: results from a shelter-based study. *Family and Community Health, 24*(1), 24–33.

Krueger, R. A., & Casey, M. A. (2000). *Focus groups: A practical guide for applied research* (3rd ed.). Thousand Oaks, CA: Sage.

Krumboltz, J. D. (1991). *Career beliefs inventory.* Mountain View, CA: CPP.

Krumboltz, J. D. (1996). A learning theory of career counseling. In M. Savickas & B. Walsh (Eds.), *Integrating career theory and practice* (pp. 233–280). Mountain View, CA: CPP.

Kuhn, P., & Sweetman, A. (1999, October). Vulnerable seniors: Unions, tenure, and wages following permanent job loss. *Journal of Labor Economics, 17*(4), 671–691.

Kurz, D. (1998, Spring). Women, welfare, and domestic violence. *Social Justice, 25*(1), 105–119.

Labor Occupational Health Program: University of California at Berkeley (2005). *The working immigrant safety and health coalition (WISH).* Retrieved May 29, 2005, from http://istsocrates. berkeley.edu/~lohp/Projects/Immigrant_Workers/immigrant_workers.html

Lambert, T. E. (1998, December). The poor and transportation: A comment of Marlene Kim's 'The working poor: Lousy jobs or lousy workers?' *Journal of Economic Issues, 32*(4), 1140–1141.

La Vigne, N. (2004, November 1). Who is leaving prison? In K. Beckman, K. D. Johnson, A. L. Solomon, & J. Travis (Eds.), *Prisoner reentry and community policing: Strategies for enhancing public safety* (Meeting summary of the Reentry

Roundtable, May 13–14, 2004, pp. 3–8). Washington, DC: Urban Institute. Retrieved October 6, 2005, from http://www.urban.org/url.cfm?ID= 411107

Lawrence, S., Chau, M., & Lennon, M. C. (2004, June). *Depression, substance abuse, and domestic violence*. NY: National Center for Children in Poverty. Retrieved January 9, 2005, from http://www.nccp.org/media/dsd04-text.pdf

LeBlanc, M. (2002). *Career counseling East Asian immigrants*. NATCON Papers. Retrieved May 23, 2005, from http://www.contactpoint.ca/natconconat/2002/pdf/pdf-02–05.pdf

Lee, S., Oh, G. T., Hartmann, H., & Gault, B. (2004). *The impact of disabilities on mothers' work participation: Examining differences between single and married mothers*. Washington, DC: Institute for Women's Policy Research.

Legal Action Center. (2000a). *Employment laws affecting individuals with criminal convictions*. Washington, DC: U.S. Department of Justice. Retrieved October 6, 2005, from http://www.lac.org/ pubs/gratis. html

Legal Action Center. (2000b). *Housing laws affecting individuals with criminal convictions*. Washington, DC: U.S. Department of Justice. Retrieved October 6, 2005, from http://www. lac.org/pubs/ gratis.html

Lerman, R. I. (2000, November). *Are teens in low-income and welfare families working too much?* Assessing the New Federalism, Policy Brief B-25.Washington, DC: The Urban Institute.

Leung, S. A. (1995). Career counseling and development: A multicultural perspective. In J. G. Ponterotto, J. M. Casas, L. A. Suzuki, & C. M. Alexander (Eds.), *Handbook of multicultural counseling* (pp. 549–566). Thousand Oaks, CA: Sage.

Lewis, J. A., & Lewis, M. D. (1983). *Management of human service programs*. Monterey, CA: Brooks/ Cole.

Lick-Wilmerding History. Retrieved May 29, 2004, from http://www.lick.pvt.k12.ca.us/glance/history. html

Lim, Y. W., Andersen, R., Leake, B., Cunningham, W., & Gelberg, L. (2000). How accessible is medical care for homeless women? *Medical Care 40*(6), 510–520.

Lindsey, E. W. (1998, March-April). Service providers' perception of factors that help or hinder Homeless families. Families in Society: *The Journal of Contemporary Human Services*, 79(2), 160–171.

Liptak, J. J. (2002a). *Barriers to employment success inventory* (2nd ed.). Indianapolis, IN: JIST Works.

Liptak, J. J. (2002b). *The career exploration inventory: A guide for exploring work, leisure, and learning* (2nd ed.). Indianapolis, IN: JIST Works.

Liptak, J. J. (2002c). *Job search attitude inventory* (2nd ed.). Indianapolis, IN: JIST Works.

Liptak, J. J. (2004). *Transition-to-work inventory*. Indianapolis, IN: JIST Works.

Livermore, M., & Neustrom, A. (2003). Linking welfare clients to jobs: Discretionary use of worker social capital. *Journal of Sociology and Social Welfare, 30*(2), 87–103.

Liz Claiborne, Inc. (2002). *Corporate leaders on domestic violence*, 2002. Retrieved January 10, 2005, from http://www.loveisnotabuse.com/relationship/survey. asp

Lloyd, S., & Taluc, N. (1999, April). The effects of male violence on female employment. *Violence Against Women, 5*(4), 370–392.

Lock, R. D. (2000). *Taking charge of your career direction* (4th ed.). Belmont, CA: Wadsworth/ Thomson Learning.

Lock, R. D. (2005). *Taking charge of your career direction: Career planning guide, book 1* (5th ed.). Pacific Grove, CA: Brooks/Cole.

Loeber, R., Farrington, D., Stouthamer-Loeber, M., & Van Kammen, W. (1998). *Antisocial behavior and mental health problems: Explanatory factors in childhood and adolescence*. Mahwah, NJ: Erbaum.

Logan, T. K., Walker, R., Cole, J., & Leukefeld, C. (2002). Victimization and substance abuse among women: Contributing factors, interventions, and implications. *Review of General Psychology, 6*(4), 325–397.

Long, S. K. (2003, May). *Hardship among the uninsured: Choosing among food, housing, and health insurance*. Assessing the New Federalism, Policy Brief B-54.Washington, DC: The Urban Institute.

Loprest, P. (2002). *Who Returns to Welfare?* Assessing the New Federalism, Policy Brief B-49. Washington, DC: The Urban Institute.

Loprest, P. (2003). Disconnected welfare leavers face serious risks (Snapshots of America's Families III, No. 7). Washington, DC: The Urban Institute.

Loprest, P. J., & Acs, G. (1996, August 1). *Profile of disability among families on AFDC*. Washington, DC: The Urban Institute. Retrieved September 9, 2004, from http://www.urban.org/url. cfm?ID=406491

Luck, J., Andersen, R., Wenzel, S., Arangua, L., Wood, D., & Gelberg, L. (2002, April). Providers of primary care to homeless women in Los Angeles county. *Journal of Ambulatory Care Management, 19*(42), 53–67.

Ludden, L. L., & Maitlen, B. R. (2002). *Individual employment plan (IEP): With 84 item employability assessment.* Indianapolis, IN: JIST Works.

Lynch, J. P., & Sabol, W. J. (2001, September 18). *Prisoner reentry in perspective* (Urban Institute Justice Policy Center Crime Policy Report Vol. 3). Washington, DC: Urban Institute. Retrieved October 6, 2005, from http://www.urban.org/url.cfm?ID=410213

Mani, B. G. (2001, September). Women in the federal civil service: Career advancement, veterans' preference, and education. *American Review of Public Administration, 31*(3), 313–339.

Marcy, H. M., & Martinez, M. (2000). *Helping with domestic violence: Legal barriers to serving teens in Illinois.* Chicago, IL: Center for Impact Research. Retrieved January 20, 2005, from http://www. impactresearch.org/publication/publicationdate.html

Marks, N. F., & Lambert, J. D. (1998). Marital status continuity and change among young and midlife adults: Longitudinal effects on well-being. *Journal of Family Issues, 19*(6), 652–687.

Marshall, J., & Heffes, E. M. (2005, May). Retirement: Nearly half would work past 64. *Financial Executive, 21*(4), 12–13.

Maruschak, L., & Beck, A. (2001, January). *Medical problems of inmates: 1997* (NCJ 181644). Washington, DC: Bureau of Justice Statistics. Retrieved July 2, 2005, from http://www.ojp.usdoj.gov/bjs/pub-alp2.htm

Mazzerole, M. J., & Singh, G. (1999, Spring). Older workers' adjustment to plant closures. *Industrial Relations, 54*(2), 313–324.

McCall, B. P. (1997, October). The determinants of full-time versus part-time reemployment following job displacement. *Journal of Labor Economics, 15*(4), 714–735.

McCollum, S. G. (1999, October). The vital connection: A job. *Corrections Today, 61*(6), 120–126.

McDaniels, C., & Mullins, S. R. (1999). *The leisure to occupations connection search.* Indianapolis, IN: JIST Works.

McDonald, D. L. (2002). Career counseling strategies to facilitate the welfare-to-work transition: the case of Jeanetta. *Career Development Quarterly, 50,* 326–330.

McFarlane, J., Parker, B., & Soeken, K. (1996, January/February). Abuse during pregnancy: Associations with maternal health and infant birthweight. *Nursing Research, 45*(1), 37–42.

McGuire, F. (1994). Army alpha and beta tests of intelligence. In R. J. Sternberg (Ed.), *Encyclopedia of intelligence* (Vol. 1, pp. 125–129). New York: Macmillan.

McKean, L. (2004a, October). *Addressing domestic violence as a barrier to work: Building collaborations between domestic violence service providers and employment services agencies.* Chicago, IL: Center for Impact Research. Retrieved October 25, 2004, from http://www.impactresearch.org/publication/publicationdate.html

McKean, L. (2004b, October). *Self-sufficiency and safety: The case for onsite domestic violence services at employment services agencies.* Chicago, IL: Center for Impact Research. Retrieved January 17, 2005, from http://www.impactresearch.org/publication/publicationdate.html

McKernan, S. M., & Ratcliffe, C. (2002, December). *Events that trigger poverty entries and exits.* Washington, DC: The Urban Institute

McNamara, C. (1999). *All about using consultants.* Retrieved September 12, 2004, from The Management Assistance Program for Nonprofits website: http://www.managementhelp.org/misc/cnsltng.htm#anchor1890598

McNichol, L., & Springer, J. (2004, December). *State policies to assist working-poor families.* Washington, DC: Center on Budget and Policy Priorities. Retrieved on December 29, 2004, from http://www.cbpp.org/12–10–04 sfp.pdf

McQuaide, S. (1998, September). Discontent at midlife: Issues and considerations in working toward women's well-being. *Families in Society: Journal of Contemporary Human Services, 79*(5), 532–543.

Mears, D. P., & Aron, L. Y. (2003, November 1). *Addressing the needs of youth with disabilities in the juvenile justice system: The current state of knowledge* (Urban Institute Justice Policy Center Research Report). Washington, D.C: Urban Institute. Retrieved October 10, 2005, from http://www.urban.org/url.cfm? ID= 410885

Mears, D. P., & Travis, J. (2004, January). *The dimensions, pathways, and consequences of youth reentry* (Urban Institute Justice Policy Center Research Report). Washington, DC: Urban Institute. Retrieved September 19, 2004, from http://www.urban.org/urlprint. cfm?ID=8721

Medjuck, S., Keefe, J. M., & Fancey, P. J. (1998). Available but not accessible: An examination of the use of workplace policies for caregivers of elderly kin. *Journal of Family Issues, 19*(3), 274–300.

Meehan, R. (2004). National origin discrimination in rental housing in Vermont: A study funded by the U.S. Department of Housing and Urban Development. Retrieved May 29, 2005, from http:// www.cvoeo.org/2004RentalAuditReport-FHP_files/2004 RentalAuditReportFHP.htm

Meinhardt, K., Tom, S., Tse, P., & Yu, C. Y. (1986). Southeast Asian refugees in the "Silicon Valley": The Asian Health Assessment Project. *Amerasia Journal, 12,* 43–65.

Mentally Ill Offender Treatment and Crime Reduction Act of 2004, Pub. L. 108–414 S. 1194. (2004, October 30).

Merriam-Webster, Inc. (2004). *Merriam-Webster online.* Retrieved January 1, 2005, from http://www.m-w.com/

Merton, Robert King. (2004). *The Columbia encyclopedia* (6th ed.). New York: Columbia University Press.

Metraux, S., & Culhane, D. O. (2004). Homeless shelter use and reincarceration following prison release: Assessing the risk. *Criminology & Public Policy, 3,* 139–60.

Metsch, L. R., Pereyra, M., Miles, C. C., & McCoy, C. B. (2003, June). Welfare and work outcomes after substance abuse treatment. *Social Service Review, 77*(2), 237–327.

Mikelson, K. S., Pindus, N., Nightingale, D. S., Egner, M., Herwantoro, S., & Sears, A. (2004, September). *Strategies for implementing priority of service to veterans in department of labor programs.* Washington, DC: Urban Institute. Retrieved November 5, 2005, from http://www.urban.org/url.cfm?ID=411105

Miller, B. A., & Downs, W. R. (1993, Spring). The impact of family violence on the use of alcohol by women: Research indicates that women with alcohol problems have experienced high rates of violence during their childhoods and as adults. *Alcohol Health & Research World, 17*(2), 137–144.

Miller-Tiedeman, A. (1988). *LIFECAREER®: The quantum leap into a process theory of career.* Vista, CA: Lifecareer® Center.

Miller-Tiedeman, A. (1999). *Learning, practicing and living the new careering: A twenty-first century approach.* New York: Taylor & Francis.

Miller-Tiedeman, A. (2002). *Student presentations.* Retrieved June 25, 2004, from http://www.life-is-career.com/studentpresentations.html

Miller-Tiedeman, A. (n.d.). *Surfing the quantum: Notes of Lifecareer® developing.* Retrieved June 25, 2004, from http://www.life-is-career.com/history.html

Mind Tools Ltd. (2005a). *Stress management techniques from mind tools.* Retrieved October 31, 2005, from http://www.mindtools.com/stress/rt/CongitiveRestructuring.htm

Mind Tools Ltd. (2005b). *Job stress management resources: Burnout—an introduction.* Retrieved November 28, 2005, from http://www.mind-tools.com/stress/Brn/StressIntro.htm

Mitchell, L. K., Levin, A. S., & Krumboltz, J. D. (1999). Planned happenstance: Constructing unexpected career opportunities. *Journal of Counseling and Development, 77*(2), 115–124.

Moe, A. M., & Bell, M. P. (2004, January). Abject economics: The effects of battering and violence on women's work and employability. *Violence Against Women, 10*(1), 29–55.

Montoya, I. D., & Atkinson, J. S. (2002). A synthesis of welfare reform policy and its impact on substance users. *American Journal of Drug and Alcohol Abuse, 28*(1), 133–146.

Montoya, I. D., Bell, D.C., Atkinson, J. S., Nagy, C. W., & Whitsett, D. (2002). Mental health, drug use, and the transition from welfare to work. *Journal of Behavioral Health Sciences & Research, 29*(2), 144–156.

Moore, J. D. (1999). Immigrants' access to public benefits: Who remains eligible for what? *Popular Government, 65*(1), 22–37.

Moore, M. (1999, November/December). Special report: Reproductive health and intimate partner violence. *Family Planning Perspectives, 31*(6), 302–312. Retrieved January 17, 2005, from http://www.agi-usa.org/pubs/journals/3130299.pdf

Morgan, L. A. (1981, November). Economic change at mid-life widowhood: A longitudinal analysis. *Journal of Marriage and the Family, 43*(4), 899–907.

Morgenstern, J., McCrady, B. S., Blanchard, K. A., McVeigh, K. H., Riordan, A., & Irwin, T. W. (2002). Barriers to employability among substance dependent and nonsubstance-affected women on federal welfare: Implications for program design. *Journal of Studies on Alcohol, 64,* 239–246.

Moskowitz, S. A., & Rupert, P. A. (1983). Conflict resolution within the supervisory relationship. *Professional Psychology: Research and Practice, 14,* 632–641.

Moss, P., Salzman, H., & Tilly, C. (2005). When firms restructure: Understanding work-life outcomes. In E. Kossek & S. Lambert (Eds.), *Work and life integrations in organizations: New directions for theory and practice* (pp. 127–150). Mahwah, NJ: Lawrence Erlbaum Associates.

Mukamal, D. (2001, June). From hard time to full-time: *Strategies to help move ex-offenders from welfare to work.* Washington, DC: Legal Action Center. Retrieved October 8, from http://www.lac.org/pubs/gratis/crimjus.html

Mulia, N., & Schmidt, L. A. (2003, December). Conflicts and trade-offs due to alcohol and drugs: Clients' accounts of leaving welfare. *Social Service Review, 77*(4), 499–524.

Murphy, G. C., & Athanasou, J. A. (1999). The effect of unemployment on mental health. *Journal of Occupational and Organizational Psychology, 72*(1), 83–92.

Mutran, E. J., Reitzes, D.C., & Fernandez, M. E. (1997, September). Factors that influence attitudes toward retirement. *Research on Aging, 19*(3), 251–274.

Myers & Briggs Foundation, Inc. (2002). Retrieved June 12, 2004, from http://www.myersbriggs.org/Qual_Cert/qualification.cfm

Myers, I. B., & McCaulley, M. H. (1985). *Manual: A guide to the development and use of the Myers-Briggs Type Indicator.* Palo Alto, CA: CPP.

Nash, J. K., & Fraser, M. W. (1998, July/August). After-school care for children: A resilience-based approach. *Families in Society, 79*(4), 370–383.

National Career Development Association (1991). *Guidelines for the preparation and evaluation of career and occupational information literature.* Alexandria, VA: Author.

National Career Development Association (2003a). *Information about CDF workshops and trainers.* Retrieved May 30, 2004, from http://ncda.org

National Career Development Association (2003b). *Mission statement, history, and purpose.* Retrieved May 30, 2004, from http://www.ncda.org

National Career Development Association (2003c). *Software description.* Retrieved September 17, 2004, from http://www.ncda.org/about/soft-desc.htm

National Career Development Association (2003d*). Career software review guidelines.* Retrieved September 17, 2004, from http://www.ncda.org/about/polsrg.html

National Center for Post-Traumatic Stress Disorder. (2004, June). *Iraq war clinician guide* (2nd ed.). Washington, DC: Department of Veteran Affairs. Retrieved November 6, 2005, from http://www.ncptsd.va.gov/war/guide/

National Coalition of Anti-Violence Programs. (2004). *Lesbian, gay, bisexual, and transgender domestic violence: 2003 supplement.* NY: Author. Retrieved January 22, 2005, from http://www.avp.org/

National Coalition for the Homeless. (2003, July). *People need affordable housing.* Retrieved September 10, 2004, from http://www.national-homeless.org/facts/housing.html

National Coalition for Homeless Veterans. (2005). *Background and statistics.* Retrieved November 11, 2005, from http://www.nchv.org/back-ground.cfm#facts

National Commission on Correctional Health Care. (2002, March). *The health status of soon-to-be-released inmates: A report to congress* (Vol. 1). Chicago, IL: Retrieved October 8, 2005, from http://www.ncchc.org/pubs/ pubs_ stbr.vol1.html

National Conference of State Legislatures (2004). *Chart of immigrant eligibility for federal programs.* Retrieved May 28, 2005, from http://www.ncsl.org/programs/immig/eligibilitychart04.htm

National Defense Authorization Act of 1991, Pub. L. No. 101–510, 104 Stat. 1485 (1990, November 5).

National Hire Network (2005). *Completing employment applications.* Retrieved October 17, 2005, from http://hirenetwork.org/employment_apps.html

National Institute on Drug Abuse (2005a). *Cancer.* Retrieved September 15, 2005, from http://www.nida.nih.gov/consequences/cancer/

National Institute on Drug Abuse (2005b). *Cardiovascular effects.* Retrieved September 15, 2005, from http://www.nida.nih.gov/consequences/cardiovascular

National Institute on Drug Abuse (2005c). *Gastrointestinal effects.* Retrieved September 15, 2005, from http://www.nida.nih.gov/consequences/gastro-intenstinal/

National Institute on Drug Abuse (2005d). *HIV, hepatitis, and other infectious diseases.* Retrieved September 15, 2005, from http://www.nida.nih.gov/ consequences/hiv/

National Institute on Drug Abuse (2005e). *Hormonal effects.* Retrieved September 15, 2005, from http://www.nida.nih.gov/consequences/hormonal/

National Institute on Drug Abuse (2005f). *Kidney damage.* Retrieved September 15, 2005, from http://www.nida.nih.gov/consequences/kidney/

National Institute on Drug Abuse (2005g). *Liver damage.* Retrieved September 15, 2005, from http://www.nida.nih.gov/consequences/liver/

National Institute on Drug Abuse (2005h). *Mental health effects.* Retrieved September 15, 2005, from http://www.nida.nih.gov/consequences/psychiatric/

National Institute on Drug Abuse (2005i). *Mortality.* Retrieved September 15, 2005, from http://www.nida.nih.gov/consequences/mortality/

National Institute on Drug Abuse (2005j). *Musculoskeletal effects.* Retrieved September 15, 2005, from http://www.nida.nih.gov/consequences/musculo-skeletal/

National Institute on Drug Abuse (2005k). *Neurological effects.* Retrieved September 15, 2005, from http://www.nida.nih.gov/consequences/neurological/

National Institute on Drug Abuse (2005l). *Other health effects*. Retrieved September 15, 2005, from http://www.nida.nih.gov/consequences/other/

National Institute on Drug Abuse (2005m). *Prenatal effects*. Retrieved September 15, 2005, from http://www.nida.nih.gov/consequences/neurological/

National Institute on Drug Abuse (2005n). *Respiratory effects*. Retrieved September 15, 2005, from http://www.nida.nih.gov/consequences/respiratory/

National Institute for Occupational Safety and Health. (1999, January 7). *Stress at work* (DHHS-NIOSH Publication No. 99–101). Cincinnati, OH: Author. Retrieved June 20, 2005, from http://www.cdc.gov/niosh/ stresswk. html

National Network to End Domestic Violence. (2004, September 13). *Housing, homeless, and domestic violence*. Washington, DC: Author. Retrieved January 20, 2005, from http://www. nnedv.org/pdf/Homelessness.pdf

National Organization on Disability (2000). *The 2000 N. O. D./Harris survey on Americans with disabilities*. Washington, DC: National Organization on Disability.

National Organization for Human Services (NOHS) (2004). *Ethical standards of human service professionals*. Retrieved January 1, 2005, from http://www.nohse.org/ethics.html

National Science Board. (2000). *Science and engineering indicators-2000*. Retrieved May 25, 2005, from http://www.nsf.gov/sbe/srs/seind00/

Native American Circle, Ltd. (2001). *Domestic violence, sexual assault, and stalking: Prevention and intervention programs in Native American communities*. Elgin, OK: Author. Retrieved January 21, 2005, from http://www.nativeamericancircle.org/resources.asp

Nelson, S., Zedlewski, S., Edin, K., Koball, H., Pomper, K., & Roberts, T. (2003, March). *Qualitative interviews with families reporting no work or government cash assistance in the National Survey of America's Families* (Assessing the New Federalism Discussion Paper Series 03–01). Washington, DC: The Urban Institute.

Neukrug, E. (2003). *The world of the counselor*. Pacific Grove, CA: Brooks/Cole.

Neumark, D. (2002, September). *Living wages: Protection for or protection from low-wage workers?* (NBER Working Paper No. 8393). Cambridge, MA: National Bureau of Economic Research. Retrieved December 29, 2004, from http://www.people.virginia.edu/~sns5r/microwkshp/lwunion.pdf

Ng, A. T., & McQuistion, H. L. (2004, March). Outreach to the homeless: Craft, science, and future implications. *Journal of Psychiatric Practice, 10*(2), 95–105.

Niles, S. G., & Harris-Bowlsbey, J. (2002). *Career development interventions in the 21st century*. Upper Saddle River, NJ: Pearson Education, Inc.

Nolan, C., Magee, M., & Burt, M. R. (2004, May). *The family permanent supportive housing initiative: Preliminary findings report*. Washington, DC: Urban Institute.

Nordenmark, M., & Strandh, M. (1999). Towards a sociological understanding of mental well-being among the unemployed: The role of economic and psychosocial factors. *Sociology, 33*(3), 577–591.

Obiakor, F. E., & Schwenn, J. O. (1995). Enhancing self-concepts of culturally diverse students: The role of the counselor. In A. F. Rotatori, J. O. Schwenn, & F. W. Littan (Eds.), *Advances in special education: Counseling special populations: research and practice*. (vol. 8, pp. 191–206). Greenwich, CT: JAI Press.

O'Brien, K. M. (2001). The legacy of Parsons: Career counselors and vocational psychologists as agents of social change. *Career Development Quarterly, 50*, 66–76.

O'Brien, P. (2002, June). *Reducing barriers to employment for women ex-offenders: Mapping the road to reintegration* (Council of Advisors to Reduce Recidivism through Employment [C. A. R. R. E.] Policy Paper #2). Chicago, IL: Safer Foundation. Retrieved June 24, 2005, from http://www.saferfoundation.org/

Occupational outlook handbook. (n.d.) Retrieved June 1, 2005, from http://www.bls.gov/oco/

Occupational Safety and Health Administration (2004). *Guidelines for preventing workplace violence for health care and social service workers*. Washington, DC: U.S. Department of Labor.

O'Connor, T. (2004). *Understanding discrimination against immigrants*. Retrieved May 29, 2005, from http://faculty.ncwc.edu/toconnor/soc/ 355-lect08.htm

Office of Disease Prevention and Health Promotion (2000). *Healthy people 2010, Volume 1* (2nd ed.). Rockville, MD: U.S Department of Health and Human Services.

Office of National Drug Control Policy (2001). *The economic costs of drug abuse in the United States: 1992–1998*. Washington, DC: Executive Office of the President.

Office of National Drug Control Policy (2005). *Drugs in the workplace: A summary of research and survey findings*. Washington, DC: Executive Office of the President.

Office of Technology Assessment (1985, October). Displaced homemakers: Programs and policy—An interim report (OTA-ITE-292). Washington, DC: U.S. Government Printing Office.

Older Women's League. (n.d.). *Faces of caregiving: 2001 mother's day report*. Retrieved September 4, 2004, from http://www.owlnational.org/owlreports/mothersday2001.pdf

Older Workers Benefit Protection Act, Pub. L. No.101–433, § 101, 104 Stat. 978 (1990).

O'Leary, C. J., & Wandner, S. A. (2000, January). *Unemployment compensation and older workers*. Paper prepared for the National Academy of Social Insurance Conference on Health and Income Security for an Aging Workforce, Washington, DC.

Oliveira, N. L., & Goldberg, J. P. (2002, March/April). The nutrition status of women and children who are homeless. *Nutrition Today, 37*(2), 70–77.

Olson, K. K., & Pavetti, L. (1996). Personal and family challenges to the successful transition from welfare to work (Contract No. 100–95–0021 Task Order No. 6). Washington, DC: Office of the Assistant Secretary for Planning and Evaluation and the Administration for Children and Families.

O*NET Consortium. (2003a, April). *O*NET ability profiler*. Washington, DC: Author.

O*NET Consortium. (2003b, November). *O*NET Online*. [Available http://online. onetcenter. org/]

O*NET Consortium. (n.d.a). *O*NET Interest Profiler*. Washington, DC: Author.

O*NET Consortium. (n.d.b). *O*NET work importance locator and profiler*. Washington, DC: Author.

O*NET® Consortium (n.d.c). *O*Net® consortium*. Retrieved August 15, 2004, from http://www.onetcenter.org/whatsnew.html

Osipow, S. H., Carney, C. G., Winer, J. L., Yanico, B., & Koschier, M. (1976). *The career decision scale* (3rd revision). Odessa, FL: Psychological Assessment Resources.

Pager, D. (2003, March). The mark of a criminal. *The American Journal of Sociology, 108*(5), 937–975.

Parrott, B. (n.d.). *James McKeen Cattell*. Retrieved May 29, 2004, from http://fates.cns.muskin-gum.edu/~psych/psycweb/history/cattell.htm# Theory

Parry, S., & Wright, G. (2001, February). *Domestic violence in lesbian, gay, transgender, and bisexual communities: Trainers manual*. NY: NYS Office for the Prevention of Domestic Violence. Retrieved January 22, 2005, from http://www.vanet.org/DomesticViolence / PreventionAndEducation / Training/LGTBManual. php

Parsons, F. (1909). *Choosing a vocation*. Boston: Houghton Mifflin.

Partnership for Prevention. (2002). *Domestic violence and the workplace*. Washington, DC: Author. Retrieved January 13, 2005, from http://www.prevent.org/publications/Domestic_Violence_and_the_Workplace.pdf

Pascarella, E. T., & Terenzini, P. T. (1991). *How college affects students: Findings and insights from twenty years of research*. San Francisco: Jossey-Bass.

Paul, R. J., & Townsend, J. B. (1993). Managing the older worker—Don't just rinse away the gray. *The Academy of Management Executive, 7*(3), 67–75.

Pawlas, G. E. (1994, May). Homeless students at the school door. *Educational Leadership, 51*(8), 79–81.

Peavy, R. V. (1992). A constructivist model of training for career counselors. *Journal of Career Development, 18*, 215–228.

Peavy, R. V. (1994). A constructivist perspective for counselling. *Educational and Vocational Guidance, 55*, 31–37.

Peavy, R. V. (n.d.). Constructivist career counseling. ERIC Digest. Retrieved June 23, 2004, from http: // www.ericdigests.org/ 1997–3/counseling. html

Penner, R. G., Perun, P., & Steuerle, E. (2002, November 20). *Legal and institutional impediments to partial retirement and part-time work by older workers*. Washington, DC: The Urban Institute. Retrieved April 6, 2005, from http://www.urban.org/url.cfm?ID=410587

Penner, R. G., Perun, P., & Steuerle, E. (2003, July). *Letting older workers work* (The Retirement Project, Brief Series No 16). Washington, DC: The Urban Institute. Retrieved April 7, 2005, from http://www.urban.org/url. cfm? ID=310861

Petersen, J. S., & Zwerling, C. (1998, September). A comparison of health outcomes among older construction and blue-collar employees in the United States. *American Journal of Industrial Medicine, 34*(3), 280–87.

Peterson, A. C. (1998). Using psychological type to assist career clients with resume writing. *Journal of Psychological Type, 44*, 32–38.

Peterson, G. W., Sampson, J. P., Jr., Reardon, R. C., & Lenz, J. G. (1996). Becoming career problem solvers and decision makers: A cognitive information processing approach. In D. Brown & L. Brooks, & Associates (Eds.), *Career choice and development* (3rd ed., pp. 423–475). San Francisco: Jossey-Bass.

Phillips, K. R. (2004, August). *State policies that affect working families*. (Assessing the New Federalism

Discussion Paper Series 04–05). Washington, DC: The Urban Institute.

Popkin, S. J., Katz, B., Cunningham, M. K., Brown, K. D., Gustafson, J., & Turner, M. A. (2004, May). *A decade of hope VI: Research findings and policy changes*. Washington, DC: The Urban Institute.

Potoczniak, M. J., Mourot, J. E., Crosbie-Burnett, M., & Potoczniak, D. J. (2003). Legal and psychological perspectives on same-sex domestic violence: A multisystemic approach. *Journal of Family Psychology, 17*(2), 252–259.

Presser, H. B. (1999, June 11). Toward a 24-hour economy: The social effects of nonstandard work weeks. *Science, 284*(5421), 1778–1783).

Prince, J. P., Uemura, A. K., Chao, G. S., & Gonzales, G. M. (1991). Using career interest inven-tories with multicultural clients. Career *Planning and Adult Development Journal, 7*(1), 45–50.

Proctor, B. D., & Dalaker, J. (2003, September). *Poverty in the United States: 2002* (Current Population Reports P60–222). Washington, DC: U.S. Government Printing Office.

Public Agenda (2005). *Immigration: Red flags*. Retrieved May 15, 2005, from http://www.publicagenda.org/issues/red_flags.cfm?issue_type=immigration#legal_illegal

Rafter, M. V. (2004). Telecounseling find favor with EAPs. *Workforce Management*. Retrieved November 30, 2005, from http://www.work-force.com/section/02/feature/23/88/09/

Raphael, J. (1995, January). *Domestic violence: Telling the untold welfare-to-work story*. Chicago, IL: Center for Impact Research.

Raphael, J. (1996, April). *Prisoners of abuse*. Chicago, IL: Center for Impact Research.

Raschick, M. (1997, January/February). Low-interest loans. *Families in Society, 78*(1), 26–35.

Raver, C. C. (2003, December). Does work pay psychologically as well as economically? The role of employment in predicting depressive symptoms and parenting among low-income families. *Child Development, 74*(6), 1720–1736.

Reardon, R. C., Lenz, J. G., Sampson, J. P., & Peterson, G. W. (2000*). Career development and planning: A comprehensive approach*. Belmont, CA: Wadsworth/Thomson Learning.

Recidivism. (n.d.). Dictionary of Law. Retrieved July 05, 2005, from Answers.com Web site: http://www.answers.com/topic/recidivism

Reeves, T. C. (n.d.). *Evaluation tools*. Retrieved September 22, 2004, from Georgia Institute of Technology, Center for Education Integrating Science, Mathematics, and Computing website: http://mime1.marc.gatech.edu/MM_Tools/evaluation.html

Rehabilitation Act of 1973, Pub. L. No. 93–112, H. R. 8070, 93rd Cong. (1973).

Reingold, D. A., Van Ryzin, G. G., & Ronda, M. (2001). Does urban public housing diminish the social capital and labor force activity of its tenants? *Journal of Policy Analysis and Management, 20*(3), 485–504.

Rennison, C. M. (2001, October). *Bureau of justice statistics special report: intimate partner violence and age of victim, 1993–1999* (NCJ 187635). Washington, DC: U.S. Department of Justice. Retrieved January 22, 2005, from http://www.ojp.usdoj.gov/bjs/pub/pdf//ipva99.pdf

Research Triangle Institute (1998). *A longitudinal study of the vocational rehabilitation service program. Third interim report: Characteristics and outcomes of former VR consumers with an employment outcome*. Retrieved February 2, 2005 from http://www.ed.gov/rschstat/eval/rehab/2001ls- int3.pdf

Rhee, S., Chang, J., & Rhee, J. (2003, Winter). Acculturation, communication patterns, and self-esteem among Asian and Caucasian American adolescents. *Adolescence*. Retrieved May 29, 2005, from http://www.parentsurf.com/p/articles/mi_m2248/is_152_38/ai_n6005508? pi=psf

Rice, J. K. (2001, Summer). Poverty, welfare, and patriarchy: How macro-level changes in social policy can help low-income women. *Journal of Social Issues, 57*(2), 355–368.

Riggio, J. (2002). *How to make a successful transition from the military service back to the civilian world*. Retrieved November 5, 2005, from http://www.joeriggio.com

Robertson, E. B., & Donnermeyer, J., F. (1997, August). Illegal drug use among rural adults: Mental health consequences and treatment utilization. *American Journal of Drug & Alcohol Abuse, 23*(3), 467–485.

Rogers, C. R. (1951). *Client-centered therapy*. Boston: Houghton Mifflin.

Rogers, C. R. (1961). *On becoming a person*. Boston: Houghton Mifflin.

Rogers, C. R. (1989). A client-centered/person-centered approach to therapy. In H. Kirschenbaum & V. L. Henderson (Eds.), *The Carl Rogers reader* (pp. 135–152). Boston: Houghton Mifflin.

Rogowski, J., & Karoly, L. (2000). Health insurance and retirement behavior: Evidence from the health and retirement survey. *Journal of Health Economics, 19*(4), 529–539.

Rokeach, M. (1973). *The nature of human values*. New York: Free Press.

Rose, S. J., & Hartman, H. I. (2004, May). *Still a man's labor market: The long-term earning's gap* (IWPR:

C355). Washington, DC: Institute for Women's Policy Research. Retrieved September 5, 2004, from http://www.iwpr. org/ pdf/C355.pdf

Rosen, D., Spencer, M. S., Tolman, R. M., Williams, D. R., & Jackson, J. S. (2003). Psychiatric disorders and substance dependence upon unmarried low-income mothers. *Health & Social Work, 28*(2), 157–165.

Ross, C. C., & Stanley, J. C. (1954). *Measurement in today's schools* (2nd ed.). New York: Prentice-Hall.

Rossi, P. H. (1994, January). Troubling families: Family homelessness in America. *American Behavioral Scientist, 37*(3), 342–396.

Rouse, C. (1995). Tech Prep Career Passports™ for rewarding futures. *NASSP Bulletin, 79*, 39–45.

Rubin, D. H., Erickson, C. J., Agustin, M. S., Cleary, S. D., Allen, J. K., and Cohen, P. (1996, March). Cognitive and academic functioning of homeless children compared with housed children. *Pediatrics, 97*(3), 289–295.

Ruhm, C. J. (1995). Secular changes in the work and retirement patterns of older men. *The Journal of Human Resources, 30*(2), 362–385.

Rumbaut, R. G. (1989). Portraits, patterns, and predictors of the refugee adaptation process. In D. W. Haines (Ed.), *Refugees as immigrants: Cambodians, Laotians and Vietnamese in America* (pp. 138–182). Totowa, NG: Rowman and Littlefield.

Sable, M. R., Libbus, M. K., Huneke, D., & Anger, K. (1999, Summer). Domestic violence among AFDC victims: Implications for welfare-to-work programs. *Affilia, 14*(2), 199–216.

Salkow, K., & Fichter, M. (2003). Homelessness and mental illness. *Current Opinion in Psychiatry, 16*, 467–471.

Sampson, J. P., Jr., Lenz, J. G., Reardon, R. C., & Peterson, G. W. (1999). A cognitive information processing approach to employment problem solving and decision making. *Career Development Quarterly, 48*, 3–19.

Sampson, J. P., Jr., Palmer, M., & Watts, A. G. (n.d.). *Who needs guidance?* Retrieved September 17, 2004, from University of Derby, Centre for Guidance Studies website: http://www.derby.ac.uk/cegs/publications/guidance.PDF

Sampson, J. P., Peterson, G. W., Lenz, J. G., Reardon, R. C., & Saunders, D. E. (1996). *Career thoughts inventory.* Lutz, FL: Psychological Assessment Resources.

Samuels, P., & Mukamal, D. (2004). *After prison: Roadblocks to reentry. A report on state legal barriers facing people with criminal records.* Washington, DC: Legal Action Center. Retrieved October 8, 2005, from http://www. hirenetwork.org/publications. html

Sanderson, N. (1998). Radio days. *American School Board Journal, 185*, 37–39.

Savage, H. A. (1999, August). *Who could afford to buy a house in 1995?* (H121/99–1). Retrieved September 18, 2004, from http://www.census.gov/hhes/www/hsgaffrd.html

Schlosberg, C. (2000). *Immigrant access to health benefits: A resource manual.* Boston, MA: The Access Project.

Schoen, R., & Urton, W. L. (1979, May). A theoretical perspective on cohort marriage and divorce in twentieth century Sweden. *Journal of Marriage and Family 4*(2), 409–416.

Schweke, W. (2004, September). *Promising practices to assist dislocated workers.* Durham, NC: The North Carolina Rural Economic Development Center. Retrieved May 10, 2005, from http://www.ncruralcenter.org/rdwi/PromisingPractices.pdf

Scoon-Rogers, L., & Lester, G. H. (1995, August). Child support for custodial mothers and fathers: 2001 (Series P60–187). Washington, DC: U.S. Department of Commerce.

Scully, H. (2003, August). *Elevations manual card sort system.* Roseville, CA: Author.

Secret, M., & Green, R. G. (1998, Spring). Occupational status differences among three groups of married mothers. *Affilia Journal of Women and Social Work, 13*(1), 47–69.

Seguino, S., & Butler, S. S. (1998). To work or not to work: Is that the right question? *Review of Social Economy, 56*(2), 190–220.

Shane, B., & Ellsberg. M. (2002, September). Violence against women: Effects on reproductive health. *Outlook, 20*,(1). Retrieved January 17, 2005, from http://www.path.org/files/ EOL20_1.pdf

Sharf, R. S. (1997). *Applying career development theory to counseling* (2nd ed.). Pacific Grove, CA: Brooks/Cole.

Sharf, R. S. (2002). *Applying career development theory to counseling* (3rd ed.). Pacific Grove, CA: Brooks/Cole.

Shepard, M., & Pence, E. (1988). The effect of battering on the employment status of women. *Affilia, 3*, 55–66.

Shin, M., & Gillespie, C. (1994, February). The roles of housing and poverty in the origins of homelessness. *American Behavioral Scientist, 37*(4), 505–522.

Simpson, W. (1987). Workplace location, residential location and urban commuting. *Urban Studies, 24*, 119–28.

Singer, A., & Paulson, A. (2004, October). Financial access for immigrants: Learning from diverse perspectives. *The Brookings Institution Policy Brief: Conference Report #19*. Washington, CD: The Brookings Institution.

Small Business Job Protection Act of 1996, Pub. L. 104–188 110 Stat. 1755. (1996, August 20).

Smith, D. (2003, April). *The older population in the United States: March 2002* (P20–546). Retrieved September 4, 2004, from http://www.census.gov/prod/2003pubs/p20–546.pdf

Smith, J. P., & Edmonston, B. (Eds.). (1997). *The new Americans: Economic, demographic, and fiscal effects of immigration*. Washington, DC: The National Academies Press.

Smith, M. W., Schnurr, P. P., & Rosenheck, R. A. (2005, June). Employment outcomes and PTSD symptom severity. *Mental Health Services Research*, 7(2), 89–101.

Sneddon Little, J., & Triest, R. K. (2001). The impact of demographic change on U.S. labor markets. *Conference Series; [Proceedings]*. Boston, MA: Federal Reserve Bank of Boston.

Snyder, H. N. (2004). An empirical portrait of the youth reentry population. *Youth Violence and Juvenile Justice* 2, 39–55.

Solomon, A. L., Johnson, K. D., Travis, J., & McBride, E. C. (2004, October 1). *From prison to work: The employment dimensions of prisoner reentry* (Report of the Reentry Roundtable). Washington, DC: Urban Institute. Retrieved October 8, 2005, from http://www.urban. org/ url.cfm?ID=411097

Solomon, A. L., Kachnowski, V., & Bhati, A. (2005, March). *Does parole work? Analyzing the impact of post-prison supervision on rearrest outcomes*. Washington, DC: Urban Institute. Retrieved May 23, 2005, from http://www.urban.org/url.cfm?ID=311156

Solomon, A. L., Waul, M., Van Ness, A., & Travis, J. (2004, January). *Outside the walls: A national snapshot of community-based prisoner reentry programs*. Washington, DC: Urban Institute. Retrieved May 17, 2006, from http://www.urban.org/url.cfm?id=410911

Sowell, R. L., Bairan, A., Akers, T. A., & Holtz , C. (2004, March/April). Social service needs and case management implications for individuals accessing a faith-based suburban homeless shelter. *Lippincott's Case Management*, 9(2), 72–86.

Spitze, G. (1988, August). Women's employment and family relations: A review. *Journal of Marriage and the Family*, 50(3), 595–618.

Spokane, A. R. (1991). *Career intervention*. Englewood Cliffs, NJ: Prentice-Hall, Inc.

Stand Down 2005. (2005, October 31). Retrieved November 4, 2005, from http://www1.va.gov/homeless/page.cfm?pg=6

Stark, L. R. (1994, February). The shelter as "total institution": An organizational barrier to remedying homelessness. *American Behavioral Scientist*, 37(4), 553–563.

Steuerle, E., Spiro, C., & Johnson, R. W. (1999, August 15). *Can Americans work longer?* (No. 5). Washington, DC: Urban Institute. Retrieved April 6, 2005, from http://www. urban.org/retirement

Stevens, J., & Ibanez, B. (2002). *Reducing barriers to employment for people with significant disabilities: Best practice guide*. Sante Fe, NM: New Mexico Developmental Disabilities Planning Council.

Stewart B. McKinney-Vento Homeless Assistance Act of 1999, Public L. No. 100-77.

Stone, D. (1997). Work and the moral woman. *The American Prospect*, 35, 78–87.

Strauser, D. R., & Lustig, D. C. (2001). The implications of posttraumatic stress disorder on vocational behavior and rehabilitation planning. *Journal of Rehabilitation*, 67(4), 26–30.

Suárez-Orozco, C. (1998). The transitions of immigration: How are they different for women and men? *DRCLAS News*. Retrieved May 21, 2005, from http://www.fas.harvard.edu/~drclas/publications/revista/women/suarez.htm

Super, D. E. (1953). A theory of vocational development. *American Psychologist*, 8, 185–190.

Super, D. E. (1957). *The psychology of careers*. New York: HarperCollins.

Super, D. E. (1980). A life-span, life-space approach to career development. *Journal of Vocational Behavior*, 16(30), 282–298.

Super, D. E. (1984). Career and life development. In D. Brown, L. Brooks, and Associates (Eds.), *Career choice and development*. San Francisco: Jossey-Bass.

Super, D. E. (1990). A life-span, life-space approach to career development. In D. Brown, L. Brooks, and Associates (Eds.), *Career choice and development: Applying contemporary theories to practice* (2nd ed., 197–261). San Francisco: Jossey-Bass.

Super, D. E. & Sverko, B. (Eds.). (1995). *Life roles, values, and careers: International findings of the work importance study*. San Francisco: Jossey-Bass.

Surgeon General's Report (1999). Culture counts: The influence of culture and society on mental health. *Mental Health: A Report of the Surgeon General*. Washington, DC: U.S. Department of Health and Human Services, Office of the Surgeon General, SAMHSA.

Sweeney, E. P. (2000). *Recent studies indicate that many parents who are current or former welfare recipients have disabilities or other medical conditions.* Washington, DC: Center on Budget and Policy Priorities.

Tennessee Board of Regents (2000). *What is Tech Prep?* Retrieved September 11, 2004, from http://www. techpreptn.org/techprep.htm

Teplin, L., Abram, K., McClelland, G., Dulcan, M., & Mericle, A. (2002). Psychiatric disorders in youth in detention. *Archives of General Psychiatry, 59,* 1133–1143.

The Abilities Fund (2005). *Why we do what we do.* Retrieved January 10, 2005, from http://www. abilitiesfund.org/about_us/why_we_do_what_we _do.php

The Center for an Assessable Society (2000). Identity, definitions and demographics of disability. Retrieved January 9, 2005, from http://www. accessiblesociety.org/topics/demograpics-identity/

The Urban Institute (2005). *Immigration studies: A program of the urban institute.* Retrieved May 23, 2005, from http://www.urban.org/content/IssuesInFocus/immig rationstudies/immigration. htm#findings

Thrasher, S. P., & Mowbray, C. T. (1995, May). A strengths perspective: An ethnographic study of homeless women with children. *Health & Social Work, 20*(2), 93–102.

Tiedeman, D. V. (1970). Comprehending epigenesis in decision-making development. In D. E. Super (Ed.), *Computer-assisted counseling* (pp. 23–36). New York: Teachers College Press.

Tiedeman, D. V., & O'Hara, R. P. (1963). *Career development: Choice and adjustment.* New York: College Entrance Examination Board.

Tjaden, P. G., & Thoennes, N. (1998, November). *Prevalence, incidence, and consequences of violence against women: Findings from the national violence against women survey* (Research in Brief, Report NCJ 172837). Washington, DC: U.S. Department of Justice. Retrieved January 10, 2005, fromhttp://www.ncjrs.org/pdffiles/172837.pdf

Tjaden, P. G., & Thoennes, N. (2000a, July). *Extent, nature, and consequences of intimate partner violence: Findings from the national violence against women survey* (Report NCJ 181867). Washington, DC: U.S. Department of Justice. Retrieved January 1, 2005, from http://www.ncjrs.org/pdffiles1/nij/ 181867.pdf

Tjaden, P. G., & Thoennes, N. (2000b, November). *Full Report of prevalence, incidence and consequences of violence against women: Findings from the national violence against women survey* (Report NCJ 183781). Washington, DC: U.S. Department of Justice. Retrieved January 1, 2005, from http:// www.ncjrs.org/pdffiles1/ nij/183781.pdf

Tolman, R. M., & Raphael, J. (2000, Winter). A review of the research on welfare and domestic violence. *Journal of Social Issues, 56*(4), 655–682.

Trade Act Participant Report. (2004, April 6). Retrieved May 23, 2005, from http://www.doleta.gov/tradeact/ participant.cfm

Transition Assistance Program Facilitator's Manual (2002). Retrieved November 6, 2005, from http:// www.nvti.cudenver.edu/TapFacilitator/home/index. htm

Transition Assistance Program Participant's Manual. (2002). Retrieved November 6, 2005, from http://www.dol.gov/vets/programs/tap/main.htm

Travis, J., Solomon, A., & Waul, M. (2001). *From prison to home: The dimensions and consequences of prisoner reentry* (Urban Institute Justice Policy Center Research Report). Washington, DC: Urban Institute. Retrieved September 18, 2005, from http:// www.urban.org / UploadedPDF/from_prison_to_ home.pdf

Tumlin, K. C., & Zimmerman, W. (2003). *Immigrants and TANF: A look at immigrant welfare recipients in three cities.* Washington, DC: The Urban Institute.

Tumlin, K. C., & Zimmermann, W. (2003, October). *Immigrants and TANF: A look at immigrant welfare recipients in three cities* (Assessing the New Federalism Discussion Paper No. 69). Washington, DC: The Urban Institute.

UNICEF. (2000, January). Domestic violence against women and girls, *Innocenti Digest 6.* Florence, Italy: Author. Retrieved January 15, 2005, from http: //www.unicef-icdc.org/publications/pdf/digest 6e.pdf

Uniformed Services Employment and Reemployment Rights Act of 1994, Pub. L. 103–353. 38 U.S. C. 4301–4333, (1994, October).

University of Cincinnati, Career Development Center (1997). *Career portfolio: Professional development strategies for your future.* Cincinnati, OH: Educational Publishing Resources

University of Oregon (2003a). *intoCAREERS history.* Retrieved August 8, 2004, from http://cis.uoregon. edu/history.htm

University of Oregon (2003b). *intoCAREERS products.* Retrieved August 8, 2004, from http://cis.uoregon. edu/products.htm

University of Oregon (2003c). *intoCAREERS components.* Retrieved August 8, 2004, from http:// cis.uoregon.edu/cis_statecomponents.htm

U.S. Bureau of Justice Statistics. (2002). *Federal criminal case processing 2002, with trends 1980–2002: Reconciled data.* Retrieved July 11, 2005, from http: // www. ojp.usdoj.gov/bjs/glance/tables/fedi-pctab.htm

U.S. Bureau of Justice Statistics. (n.d.a.). *Bureau of justice statistics correctional surveys.* Retrieved July 11, 2005, from http://www.ojp.usdoj.gov/ bjs/glance/corr2.htm

U.S. Bureau of Justice Statistics. (n.d.b). *Key facts at a glance: Four measures of serious violent crime.* Retrieved May 9, 2005, from http://www.ojp.usdoj.gov/bjs/glance/tables/4meastab.htm

U.S. Bureau of Labor Statistics (2004a). *Occupational outlook handbook, 2004–2006 edition.* Retrieved August 16, 2004, from http://stats.bls.gov/oco/

U.S. Bureau of Labor Statistics (2004b). *Occupational outlook quarterly.* Retrieved August 16, 2004, from http://stats.bls.gov/opub/ ooq/ooqhome.htm

U.S. Bureau of Labor Statistics. (2004c, July 27). *Employment situation of veterans: August 2003* (USDL 04–1378). Washington, DC: Author. Retrieved May 25, 2005, from http://www.bls.gov/news.release/pdf/vet.pdf

U.S. Bureau of Labor Statistics. (2004d, July 30). *Worker displacement* (USDL 04–1381). Retrieved May 25, 2005, from http://www. bls.gov/news.release/pdf/disp.pdf

U.S. Bureau of Labor Statistics. (2004e, August 25). *Number of jobs held, labor market activity, and earnings growth among younger baby boomers: Recent results from a longitudinal survey summary* (USDL 04–1678). Retrieved May 28, 2005, from http://www.bls.gov/news.release/nlsoy.nr0.htm

U.S. Bureau of Labor Statistics. (2005, May 6). *Employment situation summary.* Retrieved May 23, 2005, from http://www.bls.gov/news.release/empsit.nr0.htm

U.S. Bureau of Labor Statistics. (n.d.a). Household data annual averages. Table 25. Unemployed persons by occupation and sex. Retrieved May 25, 2005, from http://www.bls.gov/cps/cpsaat25.pdf

U.S. Bureau of Labor Statistics. (n.d.b). Household data annual averages. Table 28. Unemployed persons by reason for unemployment, race, and Hispanic or Latino ethnicity. Retrieved May 25, 2005, from http://www.bls.gov/cps/ cpsaat28.pdf

U.S. Bureau of Labor Statistics. (n.d.c). Household data annual averages. Table 29. Unemployed persons by reason for unemployment, sex, age, and duration of unemployment. Retrieved May 25, 2005, from http://www. bls.gov/cps/cpsaat29.pdf

U.S. Bureau of Labor Statistics. (n.d.d). Household data annual averages. Table 33. Unemployed persons by occupation, industry, and length of unemployment. Retrieved May 25, 2005, from http://www.bls.gov/cps/cpsaat32.pdf

U.S. Bureau of Labor Statistics. (n.d.e). Household data annual averages. Table 34. Unemployed jobseekers by sex, reason for unemployment, and active job search methods used. Retrieved May 25, from http://www.bls.gov/cps/ cpsaat34.pdf

U.S. Bureau of Labor Statistics (n.d.f). *U.S. Department of Labor, Bureau of Labor Statistics.* Retrieved August 21, 2004, from http://www.bls.gov

U.S. Census Bureau. (1996, February). *Current population reports: Population projections of the United States by age, sex, race, and Hispanic origin: 1995 to 2050* (P25–1130). Retrieved September 4, 2004, from http: //www.census.gov/prod/1/pop/p25–1130/p251130.pdf

U.S. Census Bureau. (2000a). *Population profile of the United States: 2000* (Internet release). Retrieved September 3, 2004, from http://www.census.gov/population/pop-profile/2000/ profile2000.pdf

U.S. Census Bureau. (2000b). *Money matters: Money income, 2000* (The Population Profile of the United States: 2000 Internet Release). Retrieved August 23, 2004, from http://www. census.gov/population/www/pop-profile/pro-file2000.html

U.S. Census Bureau. (2001, July 27). *National survey of homeless assistance providers and clients.* Retrieved September 15, 2004, from http://www. census.gov/prod/www/nshapc/NSHAPC4. html

U.S. Census Bureau. (2001a). Table 1A. Presence of a computer and the internet for households, by selected characteristics: September 2001. *Computer and internet use in the United States: September 2001.* Retrieved June 19, 2005, from http://www.census.gov/population/www/soc-demo/computer/ppl-175.html

U.S. Census Bureau. (2001b). Table 7. Use of a computer and the internet at work for people working 18 years and over, by selected characteristics: September 2001. *Computer and internet use in the United States: September 2001.* Retrieved June 19, 2005, from http://www.census.gov/population/www/socdemo/computer/ppl-175.html

U.S. Census Bureau. (2001c). Table 8b. Purpose of computer use at home for people 18 years and over using a computer at home, by selected characteristics: September 2001. *Computer and internet use in the United States: September 2001.* Retrieved June 19, 2005, from http://www. census.gov/population/www/socdemo/computer/ppl-175.html

U.S. Census Bureau. (2001d). Table 10. Purpose of computer use at work for people 18 years and over using a computer at work, by selected characteristics: September 2001. *Computer and internet use in the United States: September 2001.* Retrieved

June 19, 2005, from http://www. census.gov/ population / www / socdemo / computer / ppl-175. html

U.S. Census Bureau. (2002a, March). Table FG5— One-parent family groups with own children under 18, by labor force status, and race with Hispanic origin of the reference person: March 2002. Retrieved August 23, 2004, from http://eee. census.gov/population/socdemo/hh-fam/cps2002/ tabFG5-all.pdf

U.S. Census Bureau. (2002b, March). Table FG6— One-parent family groups with own children under 18, by marital status, and race with Hispanic origin of the reference person: March 2002. Retrieved August 23, 2004, from http://www. census.gov/population/socdemo/hh-fam/cps2002/ tabFG6-all.pdf

U.S. Census Bureau (2002c). *Facts for features*. Retrieved January 9, 2005, from http://www. census.gov/Press-Release/www/2002/cb02ff11. html

U.S. Census Bureau. (2003, June 12). Table FM2—All parent/child situations, by type, race, and Hispanic origin oh householder or reference person: 1970 to present. Retrieved August 23, 2004, from http: // www. census . gov / population / socdemo / hh -fam / tabFM-2.pdf

U.S. Census Bureau. (2004a, August). *Current population survey 2004 annual social and economic supplement*. Retrieved September 18, 2004, from http://www. census.gov/hhes/poverty/threshld/thresh03.html

U.S. Census Bureau (2004b). *Disability data from March current population survey (CPS)*. Re-trieved January 9, 2005, from http://www. census.gov/hhes/ www/disable/disabcps.html

U.S. Census Bureau. (2005a, October). National defense and veterans affairs In *Statistical Abstract of the United States 2004–2005*. Washington, DC: Author. Retrieved November 5, 2005, from http:// www.census.gov/prod/www/statistical-abstract-04. html

U.S. Census Bureau. (2005b, November 3). *Facts for features: Veterans Day 2005: November 11* (CB05-FF.17–2). Washington, DC: Author. Retrieved November 5, 2005, from http://www.census. gov/Press-Release/www/2005/cb05-ff17–2.pdf

U.S. Census Bureau. (n.d.). Table RDP2—Poverty status of families, by type of family, presence of related children, race, and Hispanic origin: 1968 to 2001. Retrieved August 23, 2004, from http:// www.ensus.gov/hhes/poverty/histpov/rdp02. html

U.S. Census Bureau Public Information Office (2001). *U.S. Department of Commerce news*. Retrieved

January 9, 2005, from http://www. census.gov/ Press-Release/www/2001/cb01–46.html

U.S. Citizenship and Immigration Services (2004a). *Education and childcare*. Retrieved May 28, 2005, from http://uscis.gov/graphics/citizenship/education.htm#Learning%20English

U.S. Citizenship and Immigration Services (2004b). *Glossary and acronyms*. Retrieved May 13, 2005, from http://uscis.gov/graphics/glossary.htm

U.S. Citizenship and Immigration Services (2004c). *Immigration through the diversity lottery*. Retrieved May 15, 2005, from http://uscis.gov/graphics/ services/residency/divvisa.htm

U.S. Conference of Mayors (2002a, December). *A status report on hunger and homelessness in American's cities: 2002*. Retrieved September 13, 2004, from http: // www.usmayors . org / uscm /news/ press_releases/ documents/hunger_121101.asp

U.S. Conference of Mayors (2002b, December). *A status report on hunger and homelessness in American's cities: 2003*. Retrieved January 20, 2005, from http:// www.usmayors.org/uscm/hunger-survey/2003/online report/HungerAndHome-lessnessReport2003.pdf

U.S. Department of Defense. (n.d.). *Selected manpower statistics: Fiscal year 2004*. Washington, DC: Author. Retrieved November 18, 2005, from http://web1.whs.mil/mmid/pubs.htm#m01

U.S. Department of Education (n.d.). *Gaining early awareness and readiness for undergraduate programs (GEAR UP)*. Retrieved September 19, 2004, from http://www.ed.gov/programs/gearup/ index.html

U.S. Equal Employment Opportunity Commission (n.d.). *EEOC, U.S. Equal Employment Opportunity Commission*. Retrieved September 1, 2004, from http://www.eeoc.gov/index. html

U.S. Department of Health and Human Services. (2000, July). *Welfare reform: Work-site-based activities can play an important role in TANF programs* (GAO/HEHS-00-122). Washington, DC: United States General Accounting Office.

U.S. Department of Health and Human Services (2004). *Human services policy: Summary of immigrant eligibility restrictions under current law*. Re-trieved May 28, 2005, from http://aspe. hhs.gov/ hsp/immigration/restrictions-sum.htm# sec2

U.S. Department of Health and Human Services (2005). *Results from the 2004 national survey on drug use and health: National findings*. Retrieved September 13, 2005, from http://www.drug-abusestatistics.samhsa.gov/nsduh/2k4nsduh/2k4-Results/2k4Results.htm#8.1

U.S. Department of Health and Human Services, Substance Abuse and Mental Health Services

Administration (2005). SAMHSA FY 2006 funding opportunities at a glance. Retrieved October 28, 2005, from http://www.samhsa.gov/grants/2006/ataglance.aspx

U.S. Department of Health and Human Services, Substance Abuse and Mental Health Services Administration (n.d.). Disclosure. Retrieved January 17, 2006, from http://www.mental-health.samhsa.gov/publications/allpubs/CS00–0008/disclosure.aspn

U.S. Department of Labor. (1994). *A guide to well-developed services for dislocated workers* (Research and Evaluation Report Series 94-B). Retrieved May 23, 2005, from http://wdr.doleta.gov/opr/fulltext/94-dislocated.pdf

U.S. Department of Labor. (2000, July). Workforce Investment Act: Final rules. *Federal Register, 65*(156), 49293–49464.

U.S. Department of Labor. (2002, November). *VETS fact sheet 2: Program highlights–Transition assistance program.* Retrieved November 20, 2005, from http://www.dol.gov/vets/programs/tap/tap_fs.htm

U.S. Department of Labor. (2003a). *WARN Act: Employer's guide to advance notice of closings and layoffs.* Washington, DC: Author. Retrieved May 29, 2005, from http://www.doleta.gov/layoff/warn.cfm

U.S. Department of Labor. (2003b, June). *A profile of the working poor, 2001* (Report #968). Washington, DC: Author. Retrieved December 29, 2004, from http://www.bls. gov/cps/ cpswp 2001.pdf

U.S. Department of Labor. (2004, October). *Health coverage portability: Health insurance portability and protection act of 1996 (HIPPA).* Washington, DC: Department of Labor/Employment Benefits Security Administration. Retrieved May 25, 2005, from http://www.dol.gov/ebsa/pdf/consumerhip-aa.pdf

U.S. Department of Labor (2005a). *Industry specific materials.* Retrieved September 10, 2005, from http://www.dol.gov/asp/programs/drugs/workingpartners/stats/is.asp

U.S. Department of Labor (2005b). *Misconceptions vs. realities regarding people in recovery.* Retrieved, October 12, 2005, from http:www. dol.gov/asp/programs/drugs/workingpartners/dfworkfroce/dfwf_miscon.asp

U.S. Department of Labor (2005c). *The costs of parity for substance abuse treatment.* Retrieved September 10, 2005, from http://www.white-housedrugpolicy.gov/prevent/workplace/health. html

U.S. Department of Labor (2005d). *Who are workers in recovery?* Retrieved November 25, 2005, from http://www.dol.gov/asp/programs/drugs/working partners/ dfworkforce/ dfwf_who. asp

U.S. Department of Labor (2005e). *Working partners for an alcohol- and drug-free workplace: General workplace impact.* Retrieved September 9, 2005, from http://www.dol.gov/asp/programs/drugs/workingpartners/stats/wi.asp

U.S. Department of Labor (2005f). *Tomorrow's jobs.* Retrieved May 10, 2006, from http://www.bls.gov/oco/oco2003.htm

U.S. Department of Labor (2005g). *Labor force characteristics of foreign-born workers in 2004* (USDL Publication No. 05–834), Washington, DC: Author.

U.S. Department of Labor. (n.d.a). *Occupational Outlook Handbook, 2006–2007 edition.* Retrieved July 11, 2006, from http://www.bls.gov/oco/

U. S. Department of Labor. (n.d.b). *Work opportunity tax credit.* Retrieved May 17, 2006, from http://www.uses.doleta.gov/wptcdata/asp

U.S. Department of Labor, Office of Disability Employment Policy (2001). *Statistics about people with disabilities and employment.* Retrieved January 12, 2005, from http://www.dol.gov/ odep/pubs/ek01/stats.htm

U.S. Department of Labor, Office of Disability Employment Policy (2005). *Attitudinal barriers.* Retrieved January 10, 2005, from http://www.dol.gov/odep/pubs/ek99/barriers. htm

U.S. Department of Labor, Secretary's Commission on Achieving Necessary Skills. (1991). *What work requires of schools: A SCANS report for America 2000.* Washington DC: U.S. Department of Labor: Author.

U.S. Department of Veteran Affairs. (2002). *Federal benefits for veterans and dependents, 2002 edition.* Washington, DC: Office of Public Affairs.

U.S. Department of Veteran Affairs (2005a, May 5). *Homelessness among veterans: Overview of homelessness.* Retrieved November 11, 2005, from http://www1.va.gov/homeless/page.cfm?pg=1

U.S. Department of Veteran Affairs. (2005b, June). *Fact sheet: Facts about the department of veteran affairs.* Washington, DC: Office of Public Affairs. Retrieved November 5, 2005, from http://www1.va.gov/OPA/fact/

U.S. Department of Veteran Affairs. (2005c, January). *Fact sheet: HIV and AIDS treatment and research.* Washington, DC: Office of Public Affairs. Retrieved November 5, 2005, from http://www1.va.gov/OPA/fact/

U.S. Department of Veteran Affairs. (2005d, June). *Fact sheet: Transition assistance in the VA military services program.* Washington, DC: Office of Public Affairs. Retrieved November 5, 2005, from http://www1.va.gov/OPA/fact/

U.S. General Accounting Office. (1994, March 10). *Multiple employment programs: Conflicting requirements underscore need for change* (GAO/T-HEHS-94–120). Retrieved September 6, 2004, from http://www.gao.gov/docsearch/app_processform.php

U.S. General Accounting Office. (1998, November). *Domestic violence: Prevalence and implications for employment among welfare recipients* (GAO/HEHS-99–12). Washington, DC: Author. Retrieved October 25, 2004, from http://www.gao.gov/archive/1999/he99012. pdf

U.S. General Accounting Office. (1999, August). *Social security reform: Implications of raising the retirement age* (GAO/HEHS-99–112). Washington, DC: Author.

U.S. General Accounting Office. (2000, March). *Pesticides: Improvements needed to ensure the safety of farmworkers and their children* (GAO/RCED-00–40). Washington, DC: Author.

U.S. General Accounting Office. (2001a, October). *Welfare reform: More coordinated efforts could help states and localities move TANF recipients with impairments toward employment* (GAO-02–37). Washington, DC: Author.

U.S. General Accounting Office. (2001b, November). Older workers: *Demographic trends pose challenges for employers and workers* (GAO-02–85). Washington, DC: Author.

U.S. General Accounting Office. (2002, February). *Workforce investment act: Better guidance and revised funding formula would enhance dislocated worker program* (GAO-02–274). Washington, DC: Author.

U.S. General Accounting Office. (2003a, February). *Older workers: Policies of other nations to increase labor force participation* (GAO-03–307). Washington, DC: Author.

U.S. General Accounting Office. (2003b, June). *Workforce investment act: Exemplary one-stops devised strategies to strengthen services, but challenges remain for reauthorization* (GAO-03–884T). Washington, DC: Author.

U.S. General Accounting Office. (2003c, October). *Women's earnings: Work patterns partially explain difference between men and women's earnings* (GAO-04–35). Retrieved September 6, 2004, from http://www.gao.gov/docsearch/app_processform.php

U.S. General Accounting Office. (2004a, March). *Food stamp program: Steps have been taken to increase participation of working families, but better tracking of efforts is needed* (GAO-04–346). Washington, DC: Author.

U.S. General Accounting Office. (2004b, April). *National emergency grants: Labor is instituting changes to improve award process, but further actions are required to expedite grant awards and improve data* (GAO-04–496). Retrieved August 2, 2004, from http://www.gao.gov/docsearch/app_process-form.php

U.S. General Accounting Office. (2005, May). *Military and veterans' benefits: Enhanced services could improve transition assistance for reserves and national guard* (GAO-05–544). Washington, DC: Author. Retrieved November 5, 2005, from http://www.gao.gov/cgi-bin/getrpt?GAO-05-544

Vega, W. A., & Rumbaut, R. G. (1991). Ethnic minorities and mental health. *Annual Review of Sociology, 17,* 351–383.

Velasquez, M., Andre, C., Shanks, T., & Meyer, M. (1996). Thinking ethically: A framework for moral decision making. *Issues in Ethics, 7*(1). Retrieved January 4, 2005, from http://www.scu.edu/ethics/publications/iie/v7n1/thinking.html

Vet Center Homeless Veterans Working Group. (2005, August). Commitments earn rewards: Part II of a series on homeless veterans. *Vet Center Voice, 26*(3), 1–4. Retrieved November 13, 2005, from http://voice.i29.net

Veterans Employment Opportunities Act of 1998, Pub. L. No. 105–339, STAT 3182 (1998, October 31).

Veterans Employment and Training Service. (2002, April). Transition assistance program: Participant manual. Washington, DC: US Department of Labor. Retrieved November 3, 2005, from http://www.dol.gov/vets/programs/tap/

Veterans Preference Act of 1944, Pub. L. No. 85–857, STAT 1105 (1958).

VETS Employment Services (n.d.a). Fact sheet 1. Retrieved November 4, 2005, from http://www.dol.gov/vets/programs/empserv/employment_services_fs.htm

VETS Employment Services (n.d.b). Fact sheet 2. Retrieved November 4, 2005, from http://www.dol.gov/vets/programs/tap/tap_fs.htm

Vietnam Era Veterans' Readjustment Assistance Act of 1974, Pub. L. No. 93–508, (1974, November 26).

Violent Crime Control and Law Enforcement Act of 1994, Pub L. 103–322. 108 Stat. 1796. (1994, September 13).

Virginia Department of Education (2004). Retrieved August 5, 2004, from http://www.vaview.vt.edu/index.htm

Vosler, N. R., & Robertson, J. G. (1998). Nonmarital co-parenting: Knowledge building for practice. *Families in Society: The Journal of Contemporary Human Services, 79*(2), 149–160.

Waite, L. (1995). Does marriage matter? *Demography, 32,* 483–507.

Waldron, T., Roberts, B., & Reamer, A. (2004, October). *Working hard, falling short: America's working families and the pursuit of economic security.* Washington, DC: The Working Poor Families Project. Retrieved October 12, 2004, from http: // www.aecf. org / initiatives / jobsinitiative / workingpoor. htm

Walker, L. E. (1984). *The battered woman syndrome.* NY: Springer.

Walker, L. E. (1994). *Abused women and survivor therapy: A practical guide for the psychotherapist.* Washington, DC: American Psychiatric Association.

Walker, L. E., & Lurie, M. (1994). *The abused woman: A survivor therapy approach* [videotape]. NY: Newbridge Professional Programs.

Wall, S. M., Timberlake, E. M., Farber, M. Z., Sabatino, C. A., Liebow, H., Smith, N. M., & Taylor, N. E. (2000). Needs and aspirations of the working poor: Early head start program applicants. *Families in Society: The Journal of Contemporary Human Services, 81*(4), 412–421.

Walsh-Healy Act of 1936, Pub L. 99–591. 881, 49 Stat. 2036, 41 USC 35–45. (1936, June 30).

Walters, R., Stark, S., Dunne, M., Moreland-Young, C., Mullins, L., Scott, J., & Battle, S. (2001, October). *Racial and ethnic disparities in TANF-barriers to the viability of low income families* (Technical Paper DE3888 Item #125). Battle Creek, MI: W. K. Kellogg Foundation.

Wanberg, C. R., Bunce, L. W., & Gavin, M. B. (1999, Spring). Perceived fairness of layoffs among individuals who have been laid off: A longitudinal study. *Personnel Psychology, 52*(1), 59–71.

Ward, R. A., & Spitze, G. (1998, December). Sandwiched marriages: The implications of child and parent relations for marital quality in midlife. *Social Forces, 77*(2), 647–660.

Wasserman, G. A., MacReynolds, L. S., Lucas, C. P., Fisher, P., & Santos, L. (2002, March). The voice of DISC-IV with incarcerated male youths: Prevalence of disorder. *Journal of the American Academy of Child and Adolescent Psychiatry, 41*(3), 314–321.

Wasson, R. R., & Hill, R. P. (1998, Winter). The process of becoming homeless: An investigation of female-headed families living in poverty. *Journal of Consumer Affairs, 32*(2), 320–334.

Watts, A. G. (2002). The role of information and communication technologies in integrated career information and guidance systems: A policy perspective. *International Journal for Educational and Vocational Guidance, 2,* 139–155.

Wehmeyer, M. L. & Schwartz, M. (1997). Self-determination and positive adult outcomes: A follow-up study of youth with mental retardation or learning disabilities. *Exceptional Children, 63,* 245–255.

Wilkins, A. (2002). *Strategies for hard-to-serve TANF recipients* (The Welfare Reform Series 6900–0005). Denver, CO: National Conference of State Legislatures.

Williamson, E. G. (1939). *How to counsel students.* New York: McGraw-Hill.

Willamson, E. G. (1965). *Vocational counseling.* New York: McGraw-Hill.

Willis, C. E., Hallinan, M. N., & Melby, J. (1996, April). Effects of sex-role stereotyping among European American students on domestic violence culpability attributions. *Sex Roles: A Journal of Research, 34,* 475–491.

Wittenburg, D., & Favreault, M. (2003). *Safety net or tangled web? An overview of programs and services for adults with disabilities.* Washington, DC: The Urban Institute.

Wittenburg, D., & Favreault, M. (2003, November). *Safety net or tangled web?: An overview of programs and services for adults with disabilities* (Occasional Paper No. 68). Washington, DC: The Urban Institute.

Wonacott, M. E. (2001). *Secondary career development interventions in brief no. 13.* Columbus, OH: National Dissemination Center for Career and Technical Education.

Worker Adjustment and Retraining Notification (WARN) Act, Pub. L. No. 100–379. (1989, February 4).

Workforce Investment Act of 1998, Pub. L. No. 105–220, 112 STAT. 936 (1998).

Worksystems Inc. (2004, February 12). *Closing the metals industry skills gap: Final report.* Portland, OR: Worksystems Inc. Retrieved May 29, 2005, from http://www.worksystems.org/businessServices/industrySectorInitiatives/content/reports/final/FinalReport-Meals 2.12.04. html

Wright, G. (1984). *Behavioral decision theory.* Newbury Park, CA: Sage.

Yeandle, S. (2005). *Older workers and work-life balance.* York, England: Joseph Rowntree Foundation.

Zang, N., & Dixon, D. N. (2001). Muticulturally responsive counseling: Effect on Asian students' rating of counselors. *Journal of Multicultural Counseling and Development, 29,* 253–262.

Zedlewski, S. R. (1999, September). *Work activity and obstacles to work among TANF recipients* (Assessing the New Federalism Discussion Paper Series B, No. B-2). Washington, DC: The Urban Institute.

Zedlewski, S. R. (2000, October). *Family economic well-being: Findings from the national survey of American families* (Snapshots of America's Families II). Washington, DC: The Urban Institute.

Zedlewski, S. R. (2002, September). *Left behind or staying away? Eligible parents who remain off TANF* (Assessing the New Federalism Discussion Paper Series B No B-51). Washington, DC: The Urban Institute.

Zedlewski, S. R., & Alderson, D. W. (2001, April). *Before and after reform: How have families on welfare changed?* (Assessing the New Federalism Discussion Paper Series B, No. B-32). Washington, DC: The Urban Institute.

Zedlewski, S. R., Nelson, S., Edin, K., Koball, H., Pomper, K., & Roberts, T. (2003, February). *Families coping without earnings or cash assistance.* (Assessing the New Federalism Discussion Paper No. 64). Washington, DC: The Urban Institute.

Zedlewski, S. R., & Rader, K. (2004, May). *Recent trends in food stamp participation: Have new policies made a difference?* (An Urban Institute Program to Assist Changing Social Policies, Series B, No. B-58). Washington, DC: The Urban Institute.

Zunker, V. G. (2002). *Career counseling: Applied concepts of life planning* (6th ed.). Pacific Grove, CA: Brooks/Cole.

Zunker, V. G., & Osborn, D. S. (2000). *Using assessment results for career assessment* (6th ed.). Pacific Grove, CA: Brooks/Cole.

Zytowski, D. G. (2001). Frank Parsons and the progressive movement. *Career Development Quarterly, 50,* 57–65.

Author Index

Subject Index

NOTE: Page numbers followed by *f* and *t* indicate figures and tables, respectively. Items in bold are defined in the glossary available on the companion website: www.ablonman.com/ duggan1e

Ability tests, 47, 48–49. *See also* career-related assessments tor specific populations
Ability Explorer (AE), 48
Career Key, 48
Inventory for Work-Related Abilities, 69
Motivated Skills Card Sort, 48,
O*NET Ability Profiler, 49, 64
Work Keys, 49
Acculturation, 422
Acquired-citizenship, 414
Addiction, 372
Adjustment counseling, 352
Adjustment to immigrant status, 414
Adult, 308
Adult Basic Education (ABE), 167
Affidavit of support, 437
AFL-CIO, 418
Age Discrimination in Employment Act of 1967 (ADEA), 289
Aggravated assault, 308
Aid to Families with Dependent Children (AFDC), 154
Alcoholism, 365
Alien, 415
American Counseling Association (ACA), 14–15
American Educational Research Association, 47, 58
American Federation of Labor, 11

Americans with Disabilities Act of 1990 (ADA) 339, 345
America's Career InfoNet, 63, 75, 117
America's Job Bank, 75, 117
America's Service Locator, 75,117
Aptitudes, 81
Army Alpha and Beta Tests, 13
Assessment, 46–59.*See also* Inventory
combining results of, 57–58
ethical and professional issues of, 58–59
human subjects and, 58
informed consent in, 58
proper interpretation of, 58
qualification levels for, 47–48
use of test data in, 58
Assessments, 47
Assistive devices and technology, 336
Association of Computer-based Systems for Career Information (ACSCI), 16
Asylee, 415
Auxiliary aids and services, 354
Avocation, 46

Baby boomers, 285, 287
Barriers to Employment Success Inventory (BESI), 54
Battery of assessments, 57
Binet, Alfred., 12–13

Binet-Simon scale, 13 (*see also* Stanford-Binet)
Blue-collar occupations, 285
Bridge job, 287
Brown, Duane, 41
propositions of, 41–42
values-based model of career choice, 41–42
Burglary, 310
Burnout, 477

Card sort, 47
Career, 3
Career Attitudes and Strategies Inventory (CASI), 54
Career Beliefs Inventory (CBI), 54
Career changers, 287
Career counseling, 3
Career decision-making theories, 33–35, 42
Career Decision Scale , 54
Career development, 3
Career Development Facilitator (CDF), 15, 453
roles of, 15
Career development inventories, 53–56. *See also* career-related assessments for specific populations
Barriers to Employment Success Inventory (BESI), 54
Career Attitudes and Strategies Inventory, 54,